THE LOST GENERATION

THE LOST GENERATION

Children in the Holocaust

AZRIEL EISENBERG

The Pilgrim Press
NEW YORK

The Acknowledgments starting on p. 367 constitute an extension of the copyright page.

Library of Congress Cataloging in Publication Data
Main entry under title:

The Lost generation.

   Includes index.
   1. Holocaust, Jewish (1939– 1945) — Personal narratives.   2. Jewish children — Biography.
I. Eisenberg, Azriel Louis, 1903-   .
D810.J4L625   940.53'15'30924   82-296
ISBN 0-8298-0498-6   AACR2

The Pilgrim Press, 132 West 31 Street, New York, N.Y. 10001

33852

940.5405
L 899

To
the hallowed memory of 1,200,000 Jewish
children who lost their lives during the Holocaust
years at the hands of the Nazi murderers and their
collaborators.
May the souls of the children martyrs be bound up
in the bonds of eternal life and may we never forget
their tragic end.

I Never Saw Another Butterfly

The last, the very last,
So richly, brightly, dazzlingly yellow.
   Perhaps if the sun's tears would sing
   against a white stone . . .

Such, such a yellow
Is carried lightly way up high.
It went away, I'm sure, because it wished to
   kiss the world good-bye.

For seven weeks, I've lived in here,
Penned up inside this ghetto,
But I have found my people here.
The dandelions call to me
And the white chestnut candles in the court.
Only I never saw another butterfly.

That butterfly was the last one.
Butterflies don't live in here,
   In the ghetto.

                                  — PAVEL FRIEDMANN

Contents

EXCERPT FROM "THE LAMENT ON THE SLAUGHTERED JEWISH PEOPLE"

They, the children of Israel, were the first in doom and disaster;
most of them without father and mother
were consumed by frost, starvation and lice;
holy messiahs sanctified in pain . . . ,
Say, then, how have these lambs sinned?
Why in days of doom are they the first victims of wickedness,
the first in the trap of evil are they!

The first were they detained for death,
The first into the wagons of slaughter;
they were thrown into the wagons, the huge wagons,
like heaps of refuse, like the ashes of the earth —
and they transported them,
killed them,
exterminated them
without remnant or remembrance . . . ,
The best of my children were all wiped out!
O woe unto me —
Doom and Desolation!

YITZHAK KATZENELSON

From *The Massacre of European Jewry,* published by World Hashomer Hatzair, Kibbutz Merhaviah, p. 208.

Yitzhak Katzenelson was the most prolific ghetto poet and dramatist, as well as a versatile teacher. A descendant of a dynasty of Hebrew scholars and rabbis, he wrote in Yiddish and in Hebrew. He was an active member of the Jewish underground and established close ties with the Warsaw orphanages.

In one of the roundups of Warsaw Jews Katzenelson's wife and two younger sons were deported to Treblinka. Yitzhak and his older son, who had obtained papers certifying their foreign nationality, were transported to Vittel, in eastern France, near Nancy, and were interned there with twenty-five so-called South American nationals. The Germans provided such certificates of nationality in exchange for German prisoners of war. The overriding purpose of these documents was to lure Jews who had been hiding in Aryan shelters to disclose their addresses. During this period Katzenelson wrote his famous poems, *Lament of the Slaughtered Jewish People,* from which the selection above was excerpted.

During his internment in Vittel from May 1943 to September 1943, Katzenelson also wrote his moving *Vittel Diary,* which was later published in his memory by the Ghetto Fighters' House. In September 1943, father and son were transported to the furnaces of Auschwitz.

I have sworn an oath –
To remember everything,
To remember and to
Forget not a thing.
      — AVRAHAM SHLONSKY

"HOW THEIR LITTLE HEARTS MUST HAVE TREMBLED"

During the war, children had their vehement persecutors, but also their devoted defenders. One such faithful friend of the poorest children was Dr. Korczak of Warsaw. During the liquidation of the Warsaw Ghetto, tempted as he was by the possibility of escape, he voluntarily remained with the children, and he died with them. This prominent psychologist and physician had made an interesting experiment before the war. He took a child from an orphanage and, without saying a word, went with the child on a walk along the noisy streets of Warsaw. Then he led him into a darkened lecture-room filled with students and placed him in front of an X-ray apparatus. The tiny heart of the child, trembling with fear, appeared on the X-ray screen. And Dr. Korczak, turning to his students, said, "Do not ever forget this picture. Before you raise your hand against a child, before you punish him, recall how his frightened heart beats."

When, a few years later, the children of occupied Europe were deliberately exposed to all the horrors of war, how their little hearts must have trembled! I can only hope that this book will be something like Dr. Korczak's X-ray screen.

From *The Tragedy of Children Under Nazi Rule* by Kyril Sosnowsky. A sociologist and member of Polish scientific societies, Kyril Sosnowsky was active in the Polish underground movement. He wrote *The Tragedy of Children Under Nazi Rule,* which was published in 1962 and translated into English.

Preface

The Lost Generation is a companion volume to *Witness to the Holocaust,* which I also authored, published by The Pilgrim Press. The reader is advised to refer to the companion work for information that will complement and elaborate on the chapters included in this book. In the companion volume, you will also find a list of recommended readings for further study.

Many selections included in this volume were translated from Hebrew or Yiddish by the author. These are identified by the initials A. E. at the end of the selection.

I am indebted to *Yad Vashem,* the Martyrs and Heroes Remembrance Authority in Jerusalem, and the Ghetto Fighters' House, in memory of Itzhak Katzenelson; for their invaluable services, and for the courtesy they both extended to me in permitting the reprinting of selections from their publications.

As in the case of my earlier book, I leaned heavily on the resources of five Jewish libraries and their librarians in greater New York. They are: YIVO, the Yiddish Scientific Institute; the Jewish Theological Seminary library; the Zionist Library; the Jewish Division of the New York Public Library; and the Leo Baeck Institute. I am thankful to two librarians who were especially helpful: Ms. Dina Abramowitz of YIVO, and Orah Alkalay of *Yad Vashem.*

I am very grateful to Dr. Paul Sherry, Publisher of The Pilgrim Press, to Esther Cohen, Sam Lowe, and the members of the staff for their cooperation. They have been a source of encouragement to me. To Mrs. Susan Grossman, I am appreciative of her excellent typing of the manuscript. To Mr. Irving Kusminsky I am indebted for his editorial and proofreading services; and to a dear old friend, Mr. Max Nadel, for giving earnestly of himself and his time to edit my writings.

Finally, as always, I record my debt of sincere thanks and appreciation to my wife, Rose, for her unending support. Of her I can say wholeheartedly, "Exalt her for the fruit of all her toils, and let her labors bring her honor."

Introduction

In his opening address at the Eichmann trial in April 1961, Gideon Hausner, Israel's Attorney General, who was Chief Prosecutor, presented evidence of the crimes committed by Eichmann against the Jewish people. Summarizing his indictment of the atrocities perpetrated against the Jewish children of Europe, Hausner accused the prisoner, declaring:

"No part of all [the] bloody work is so shocking and terrible as that of the million Jewish children whose blood was spilt like water throughout Europe; how they were separated by force from their mothers who tried to hide them, murdered and thrown out of trucks in the camps, torn to pieces before their mothers' eyes, their little heads smashed on the ground — these are the most terrible passages of the tale of slaughter. You will hear evidence of actions which the mind of man does not want to believe.

"You will hear about little ones thrown out of hospital windows when they failed to respond to orders to report for parade.

"We shall present to you the instructions issued by Eichmann and his office about the transport of children. One of these said that the children were to be divided among the transports intended for Auschwitz. Children of fourteen were considered 'independent' for purposes of transport to the extermination camps.

"Nor can we say who suffered the more terrible fate: those who died, or those who concealed themselves in every conceivable hiding-place and crevice, who lived in perpetual terror of expulsion, who survived by grace of Christian neighbors who agreed to hide them. Children would come home from the schools and centers organized by the community to find their parents' home empty, for they had been sent by some *Aktion* or 'operation' to their deaths; and the apartment was already occupied by others.

"You will hear evidence of tender infants pressed by their mothers to their bodies in the gas chambers so that they were not immediately poisoned, until the executioners came and threw them alive into the furnaces or the ready graves.

"Those unhappy children who lived for years in fear of the beating of a rifle butt on their door; who had been sent by their parents to the woods in an attempt to save them, who had been taught to choke their tears and sighs because a weeping child would be shot on the spot; who had been ordered to deny their origins and pretend to be Christians; who saw their fathers being lashed with whips before their eyes; in front of whom 'discussions' would be carried on by the German executioners as to who should be killed first — the father or the son; who went to the open grave with 'Hear, O Israel!' on their lips — these children and youths, who despite all the desperate measures and concealments would finally fall into the hands of their hunters, they are the soul of this indictment. Those Anne Franks and Justine Draengers and a million others, those un- plumbed treasures of radiant youth and hope for life and achievement — they were the future of the Jewish people. He that destroyed them was seeking to destroy the Jewish people.

"We shall submit pictures of some of those children, swollen with hunger, frightened and crushed, with eyes frozen with terror. We shall show you the photographs of their starved bodies thrown into manure wagons, of the helpless little ones on the threshold of the extermination chambers. Perhaps we shall succeed in painting a pale and inadequate picture of the calamity, wide as the ocean, that beset the House of Israel. . . . "[1]

The Lost Generation is the first book of its kind to present this incomparable tragedy. It covers the period from the 1920s, when the Nazis began to brutalize schoolchildren, through the 1940s, after their defeat. It includes the aftermath of liberation, the gathering of the surviving remnants, and their rehabilitations, as well as the breaking of the British blockade to find refuge in the Promised Land, and the effects of the painful, traumatic events on the survivors. It consists of personal and eyewitness accounts written or told by children whose ages during the Nazi carnage ranged from four through fourteen years.

The children were the Nazis' first target in the total destruction of the Jews. Indeed, with the very rise of Nazi Germany, Hitler's aides devised and exe- cuted programs to root out the unborn by sterilization and castration. Who can estimate the numbers lost by the Jewish people? Poland alone now has only 18 surviving Jewish communities, compared to the 17,000 before World War II.

Highest priority was given to the extermination of Jewish children even at the expense of mounting German casualities. In 1944, when Germany faced certain defeat and its armies were in retreat, the Nazi machinery of death in Hungary was glutted by the vast number waiting to be deported to the gas chambers in Poland. To expedite the "Final Solution," the Nazis disposed of the young by throwing them alive on burning pyres.

The renowned Jewish historian Professor Salo W. Baron, who was the first to testify at the Eichmann trial, made the shocking assertion that the extermination of the children, the mothers, and the unborn has had a lasting, devastating effect on the future generations of world Jewry. He declared:

"The sharp decline [in the population of world Jewry] is doubly pronounced when compared even with the fate of nations defeated in the War. Germany

[1]*Six Million Accusers: The Opening of the Eichmann Trial,* edited and translated by Shabbatai Rosenne, published by *Jerusalem Post,* 1961, pp. 84-85.

herself had suffered much retribution. At the time of its surrender many of its cities lay in ruins, certain regions were depopulated, and most of the others suffered from hunger and want. Japan had her Hiroshima and Nagasaki. Nevertheless, today, sixteen years after the war, the population of divided Germany has increased substantially, and that of Japan is about a third larger than twenty years ago. By contrast, world Jewry still numbers only some 12,000,000, as against the 16,500,000 or more living in 1939.[2]

"The extent of the decline becomes manifest when one realizes that, in the 22 years since 1939, the Jewish people should have *increased* by more than 2,500,000, if we assume a continuation of the average growth in the 1930s, namely, 120,000 per annum. If the Jews had participated in the general population growth of the 1940s and 1950s, the average might well have exceeded even the annual growth of the 1920s, 140,000. If that had been so, the world Jewish population now would have reached or exceeded 20,000,000. What is more, the Jewish communities in formerly Nazi-occupied Europe still are crippled, qualitatively even more than quantitatively. That great reservoir of Jewish population and of cultural and religious leadership has dried up, leaving the rest of Jewry, particularly the segments residing in Israel, the New World, and the British Commonwealth, bereaved.

"One's imagination is staggered if one considers what might have happened, if during the Franco-German War of 1871, a Hitler, rather than a Bismarck, had guided Germany. If that Hitler of seven decades earlier had succeeded in overrunning the same countries that were overrun between 1939 and 1945, and if he had had the same program of murdering the Jews from the Atlantic to the Russian Pale of Settlement, the genocide of the Jewish people would have been almost total. There would have been no Israel today, and the other present-day largest concentrations of the Jewish people — in the New World, the Soviet Union, and the British Commonwealth — would have consisted, at best, of small, struggling communities."[3]

The accounts included in this book were chosen from books written by eyewitnesses, about half of which have been translated from Hebrew and Yiddish into English by the author:[4] Only authentic personal and eyewitness experiences were selected. They will enable the reader to share the agony, the physical, emotional and spiritual torment of the martyred children. Pithy, comprehensive introductions and prefatory notes, which supplement and complement the selections, provide the backgrounds of the memoirs. Cross-references to two anthologies in English on the Holocaust, which include two chapters on Children in the Holocaust, and selective bibliographical references to books in English will direct students and readers who desire to deepen their studies of the Tragedy, the like of which has no equal in recorded history.

[2]Before the war there were 3,250,000 Jews in Poland. In 1978, there were about 6,000 Jews, most of them old people.
[3]From *A Historian's Notebook: European Jewry Before and After Hitler,* by Salo W. Baron, published by the American Jewish Committee, March 1962, pp. 49-50.
[4]These selections are designated by A.E., the initials of the author.

THE LOST GENERATION

1.

PRELUDE TO DOOM

"Race" (Aryan, Nordic), "Blood" (Volk, Peoplehood), and "Soil" (Greater Germany) were the three foundations of Nazi ideology. All Germans were subject to Hitler's will and power. Germany became a totalitarian state, and the Nazi party was in absolute control. The Nazis devised projects and programs — festivals, parades, demonstrations, huge mass meetings, ceremonies, radio broadcasts (loudspeakers were hung up in the streets) — to heat the imagination of young and old and to infuse them with an unswerving faith in and obedience to the Führer and the new "trinity" mentioned above. National Socialism became a religion, a faith, supplanting Christianity. Hitler was the new "savior," and his adjutants were his "apostles." All authority flowed from above, with Hitler the supreme source.

A key to his success was Hitler's conversion of the new generation to the cause. The public school was the incubator of young Nazis. A biased version of German history, chauvinistic literature, "character-building," which in Nazi education meant unquestioned obedience and service to the Führer and Volk, long hours of physical training — these were the foundations of the new order. After school hours, weekends and holidays were devoted to the party and its activities. The Hitler Youth and its girls' branch, the BDM (German Girls' Organization), were, in a real sense, vital adjunct activities to the formal school program. Parents and home abdicated their roles in the raising of children. National Socialism dominated every moment of their waking hours.

In this life pattern, which permeated every phase of existence, Jews were outcasts, the enemy, the anti-Germans. They became subjects for research and careful examination — their gestures and movements, their occupations, their physiognomy, their character, their psyches. The Jews were victims of their

I

heredity. They were products of the non-Aryan race; their blood was contami-
nated. They lacked all the superior qualities and creative powers of the master
race. In fact, they were considered degenerates and had to be eliminated.
Biology and physiology and other life sciences served as handmaidens to the
Nazi ideology and its teachings.

To preserve the strength of the Aryan race, sterilization of the unfit was
advocated. Hereditary health law courts were set up, consisting of two doctors
and a judge, whose responsibility it was to decree who was to be sterilized.
Sterilization escalated to castration, to euthanasia ("mercy killings"), and
ultimately to the death camps.

RAISING A GENERATION OF JEW-HATERS

Der Stürmer, *a weekly published by Julius Streicher, was the most vicious and*
depraved publication in Germany. As early as the 1920s it was used as text
material in German elementary schools. It carried obscene pornographic
illustrations depicting the Jews as the devil in human form and ever-present
menace to Germany. It poisoned the minds of children and youth. Pupils were
trained to pass on what they learned to their families, neighbors, and friends.
Der Stürmer's *circulation grew to 600,000.*

Streicher's Stürmer *utilized every possible avenue to train a generation of*
Jew-haters. In addition, he published books for Christmas gifts and created a
whole library of anti-Semitic literature on a juvenile level.

Don't Trust the Fox in the Green Meadow Nor the Jew on His Oath

("A picture book for grown-ups and little ones" by Elvira Bauer, published by
the printing dept. of *Der Stürmer*, 1936.)

[Page 6]: Jesus Christ, says, "The Jew is a murderer through and through."
And when Christ had to die the Lord didn't know any other people who would
have tortured him to death, so he chose the Jews. That is why the Jews pride
themselves on being the chosen people.

[Page 18]: The Jewish butcher. He sells half refuse instead of meat. A piece
of meat lies on the floor, the cat claws another. This doesn't worry the Jewish
butcher since the meat increases in weight. Besides, one mustn't forget, he
won't have to eat it himself.

[Page 24]: What a poor specimen the Jew is. He doesn't like his own women
and thinks himself clever if he steals a German woman for himself. Yet look at
the Jew: He doesn't even fit her.

[Page 30: Shows Streicher as friend and educator of German boys and girls.]
We have a fighter in the German Gau[1] of Franconia whom we have to thank that
our country remains healthy and free of Jewish residue.

[Page 32: (Shows German children reading the *Stürmer*)] Read the *Stürmer!*
Dirty Jews!

[1]Canton, region.

[Page 36]: (Expulsion of Jewish children from the schools whilst German children jeer). Now it is going to be nice at school, for all Jewish children have to go, big ones and little ones. Crying, weeping, fury and anger doesn't help. Away with the Jewish brood!

> From *Conspiracy and Aggression:* International Military Tribunal of Nazi War Criminals, the United States Printing Office, 1946, Vol. VIII, p. 20; a partial translation of Document M-32.

The Stürmer knows and rejoices at the effects produced on the impressionable and uncritical minds of children by its incitement, its falsified history and its hatreds. Proudly its pages feature children's compositions sent in by fanatical teachers and eager children, which testify eloquently to the effect upon the latter of the teachings of *The Stürmer* and of National Socialism.

> I have cut out of your wonderful paper, *The Stürmer,* a number of heads of Jews, such as were formerly allowed to misrule our Germany and, as you will see from the photograph enclosed, I have mounted them for use. With the aid of this collection I give lectures on the Jewish question to all my senior forms. . . . How deeply rooted the lesson is already is emphasized by the following little experience which I had with a nine-year-old boy in my class.
> One day he came to school and said: "Please, Sir, yesterday I was out with mother. Just as we passed the stores (evidently Jewish owned) she remembered she wanted some reels of cotton. She tried to give me the money to slip into the stores to buy them. Whereupon I told my mother: 'You don't get me going in there, go yourself! But, let me tell you, if you do I'll tell teacher tomorrow. Then he'll send for you and it may not be so pleasant for you.' "
> If the enclosed photograph of our mounted pictures should please you, the children would be delighted for you to publish it in *The Stürmer*. Personally, I am convinced that such pictures will encourage other schools to follow suit. (signed) Max Bukert, Teacher, Cologne-Ehrenfeld, Overbeckstrasse School. (*Stürmer,* No. 35, 1935.)

> *Dear Stürmer,*
> District Leader Streicher has told us so much about the Jews that we really hate them awfully. We were set a composition in school on "The Jews Are Our Misfortune." I should like you to publish mine:
> "Unfortunately, many people still say nowadays: 'The Jews, too, are God's creatures. That's why you must hold them in respect.' But we say: 'Vermin are also creatures, yet we destroy them. The Jew is a mongrel. He has the traits of Aryans, Asiatics, Negroes and Mongols. In any mongrel the bad part is always uppermost. The only good thing the Jews have is their white skin.' The South Sea Islanders have a proverb: 'The White man comes from God and the Black man comes from God. But the mongrel is from the Devil.' Jesus once told them: 'Your father is not God, but the Devil.' The Jews hold to a wicked law. This is the Talmud. The Jews consider us as animals and treat us accordingly. They take our money and goods from us by cunning. Jews ruled already at the Court of Karl of Franconia. That's why Roman Law was introduced. This wasn't any good for German peasants; it wasn't really any good for the Roman

peasants either; it was a Law for Jew tradesmen. Undoubtedly the Jews were guilty of the murder of Karl of Franconia.

"The Jew Grüneberg in Gelsenkirchen sold us stinking meat. This he is allowed to do by his own Law. The Jews have begun revolts and provoked wars. They have brought Russia to misery. In Germany they gave money to the Communist Party and paid all the rogues to murder. We stood at the brink of the grave. Then came Adolf Hitler. Now the Jews are abroad spreading atrocity lies against us. But we don't listen to them and we follow our Leader. We don't buy from Jews. Every penny we give them kills one of our people."

Heil Hitler!

Erna Listing.
Gelsenkirchen, 8, Oswaldstrasse.
(*Stürmer*, No. 2, 1935.)

A teacher, Hilde Palmedo (of Breslau) is thanked by *The Stürmer* because the fact that "she knows how to teach her pupils in the spirit of the new times" is proved by the composition of her nine-year-old pupil, Helga Gerbling:

THE CUCKOO AND THE JEW

In school the other day we were talking about the Cuckoo. He is the Jew among birds; for in looks, deeds and behavior he resembles him very much. His curved beak reminds us of the Jew's hooked nose. His feet are small, that's why he can't run very well. This is very much like the Jew, who also can't walk gracefully. When we call "Cuckoo, Cuckoo" he also scrapes and bows like the Jew merchant who always tries to be polite so that we Germans should buy from him. Both Jews, the one among the birds and the one among the humans, are parasites, which means to say that they want to become rich and fat at the expense of others. The female Cuckoo lays her eggs in the nests of other birds such as hedgesparrows and robin redbreasts and she wants them to brood them and bring up the little ones. (It's funny that the Jew does not ask us to do that too.) As soon as the Cuckoo comes out of the egg he gets impudent. He snaps for the best morsels and always wants to have everything. He squeezes back the genuine little birds as soon as the parents come with dinner. He is envious and greedy. His motto is: self-interest before common weal! Just like the Jew, who too thinks only of himself and his pocket. Only for his purse to be filled and himself to have a good time! When there is no longer enough room in the bird's nest, then he tries to push the young birds out of their own home. He very often does throw a little one out. Just like the Jew wanted to do with us Germans. He came, an alien, into our "nest" and tried to drive us out. But we humans are not as stupid as the birds. We don't let him do that to us and we throw the cheeky "Cuckoo" out of our land. We children in Roth do our bit too. Some of our class often stand in front of Baer's shop and when people want to go in, we shout: "You ought to be ashamed, shopping at a Jew's; fie upon you!" Then the women blush crimson and go away. Well, *Stürmer*, you like that, don't you?

Heil Hitler!

In the name of the Girls' IVth Standard,
Helga Gerbling

" HEIL HITLER!" 50 to 150 TIMES A DAY

Through the Nazi streets walks the Nazi child. There is nothing to disturb him, nothing to attract his attention or criticism. The stands sell Nazi papers almost exclusively; all *German* papers *are* Nazi; foreign papers are forbidden, if they do not please the men at the top. The child won't be surprised at their huge headlines: "UNHEARD-OF ACTS OF VIOLENCE AGAINST GERMANY IN CZECHOS-LOVAKIA!" "JEWISH GANGSTERS RULE AMERICA!" "THE COMMUNIST TERROR IN SPAIN SUPPORTED BY THE POPE!" "150 MORE PRIESTS UNMASKED AS SEXUAL CRIMINALS!"

"That's how it is in the world," the child thinks. "What luck we're in, to have a Führer! He'll tell the whole bunch — Czechs, Jews, Americans, Communists and priests — where to get off!"

There are no doubts, no suspicion at the coarse and hysterical tone of the dispatches, no hint that they may be inexact or false. No, these things are part of the everyday world of the Nazis, like the *Blockwart,* [1] the swastika, the signs reading "No Jews allowed." They add up to an atmosphere that is torture, a fuming poison for a free-born human being.

The German child breathes this air. There is no other condition wherever Nazis are in power; and here in Germany they do rule everywhere, and their supremacy over the German child, as he learns and eats, marches, grows up, breathes, is complete.

But, past the general influence of Nazi atmosphere, three special influences in the Reich determine the life of the child: the intimate circle of the family, the school, and the Hitler youth organizations.

Every child says "Heil Hitler!" from 50 to 150 times a day, immeasurably more often than the old neutral greetings. The formula is required by law; if you meet a friend on the way to school, you say it; study periods are opened and closed with "Heil Hitler!"; "Heil Hitler!" says the postman, the street-car conductor, the girl who sells you notebooks at the stationery store; and if your parents' first words when you come home to lunch are not "Heil Hitler!" they have been guilty of a punishable offense, and can be denounced. "Heil Hitler!" they shout, in the *Jungvolk* and Hitler Youth. "Heil Hitler!" cry the girls in the League of German Girls. Your evening prayers must close with "Heil Hitler!" if you take your devotions seriously.

Officially — when you say hello to your superiors in school or in a groups — the words are accompanied by the act of throwing the right arm high; but an unofficial greeting among equals requires only a comparatively lax lifting of the forearm, with the fingers closed and pointing forward. This Hitler greeting, this "German" greeting, repeated countless times from morning to bedtime, stamps the whole day.

"Heil" really means salvation, and used to be applied to relations between man and his God; one would speak of *ewiges Heil* (eternal salvation), and the adjective "holy" derives from the noun. But now there is the new usage.

German children say their "Heil Hitler!" as carelessly as they greeted each

[1] Block warden.

other in the War days with "God scourge England!" They will swallow half the consonants sometimes, making a strange new word. Or they will make a crack out of the "German" greeting, and say "Drei Liter" (three liters) instead of "Heil Hitler." That's fun, and no one can hold it against them. But always, formally and outwardly, and inwardly besides, the German child lives in the echo of "Heil Hitler!"

You leave the house in the morning, "Heil Hitler" on your lips; and on the stairs of your apartment house you meet the *Blockwart*. A person of great importance and some danger, the *Blockwart* has been installed by the government as a Nazi guardian. He controls the block, reporting on it regularly, checking up on the behavior of its residents. It's worth it to face right about, military style, and to give him the "big" Hitler salute, with the right arm as high as it will go. All the way down the street, the flags are waving, every window colored with red banners, and the black swastika in the middle of each. You don't stop to ask why; it's bound to be some national event. Not a week passes without an occasion on which families are given one reason or another to hang out thehswastika. Only the Jews are excepted under the strict regulation. Jews are not Germans: they do not belong to the "Nation," they can have no "national events."

From *School for Barbarians* by Erika Mann, New York; Modern Age Books, 1938, pp. 21-23.

SKEPTICISM AND PARTICIPATION

After Hitler became Chancellor things began to change in Germany. Great provisions were being made for the working classes to ease their lot and improve their standard of living. New houses were being built everywhere and the old slums torn down. There was going to be work for everyone. Fewer and fewer unemployed men were hanging around the cigarette and beer kiosks down by the cinema, shouting, arguing, and drinking. People were wearing better clothes and could afford to buy sufficient food for their families.

Slowly the bait worked. Even those who had been rigidly against Hitler before now became ardent followers. The various youth clubs were closed down and the Hitler Youth organization took their place. Freemasonry was strictly forbidden. Old comrade and student organizations were taken over by the party.

As the years went by the pressure on everyone who had not joined the party increased steadily. Those who did not join felt they were outcasts. At last, with a heavy hdart and many doubts, Father let me join the Hitler Youth, and he became a member of the NSDAP himself. The fact that his nerves were bad and that he suffered from severe attacks of asthma protected him from any active service.

Things were quite different for me, though. I, and all the other girls of my age, had to attend evening classes twice weekly. We had to be present every public meeting and at youth rallies and sports. The weekends were crammed full with outings, campings, and marches when we carried heavy packs on our backs. It was all fun in a way and we certainly got plenty of exercise, but it had a bad effect on our school reports. There was hardly ever any time now for homework.

The evening classes were conducted by young girls, usually hardly older than we were ourselves. These young BDM leaders taught us songs and tried desperately to maintain a certain amount of discipline without ever really succeeding. In summer, instead of conducting the class, they would give us a few hours' drill in the yard. We were marched up and down as if we were soldiers on the barrack square, with a girl leader barking orders at us like a regimental sergeant-major.

We were of course lectured a lot on National Socialist ideology, and most of this went right over our heads. In most cases the young girl leader did not know herself what she was talking about. We were told from a very early age to prepare for motherhood, as the mother in the eyes of our beloved leader and the National Socialist Government was the most important person in the nation. We were Germany's hope in the future, and it was our duty to breed and rear the new generaion of sons and daughters who would carry on the tradition of the thousand-year-old Reich.

The boys' evening classes were run in exactly the same way and in the same building. Frequently we would all have to go to the auditorium, where some important personage would give a lecture on racial problems and the necessity of raising the birthrate. He too would remind us of our duties as future fathers and mothers of the nation, and somehow I never managed to suppress a giggle when I looked at those spidery-legged, pimply little cockerels who were supposed to become the fathers of our children.

These lessons soon bore fruit in the shape of quite a few illegitimate small sons and daughters for the Reich, brought forth by teen-age members of the BDM and conceived in the grounds of our Hitler Youth Home. The girls felt that they had done their duty and seemed remarkably unconcerned about the scandal. The possible fathers could be heard proudly debating as to who had done it, whenever there was a chance that the girls might be able to overhear.

I soon got tired of it all and frequently found some reason for excusing myself from the evening classes. My education took up more and more of my time now, and doing my homework was a far more satisfying occupation to my inquisitive mind. It also brought my school report up again to a decent level. That this attitude earned me the reputation of a shirker did not worry me much, as there were quite a number of other girls who did exactly the same. . . .

During my third year at the grammar school a great change in the whole educational system took place. The nine years required to obtain the school certificate were reduced to eight. Every subject was now presented from the National Socialist point of view. Most of the old lecture books were replaced by new ones which had been written, compiled, and censored by government officials. Adolf Hitler's *Mein Kampf* became the textbook for our history lessons. We read and discussed it with our master, chapter by chapter, and when we had finished we started again from the beginning. Even though we were supposed to know the contents of the book almost by heart nothing much ever stuck in my mind. I hated politics and distrusted politicians, but I thought, as most people did, that Hitler was far above intrigue and perfidy and would prove to be the savior that Germany needed. Even so I found his book dull and boring. Rosenberg's *The Myths of the Twentieth Century,* which the majority of thinking Germans regarded as a bad joke, was the next most important book to *Mein Kampf.* A new subject, the science of the races, was introduced, and religious instruction became optional.

Our school had always been run on very conservative lines, and I am sure the situation was difficult for our teachers. Most of them had been doubtful about Hitler, but unless they wanted to lose their jobs they had to make a violent turn in his direction. Even if they sympathized with my attitude towards politics, they could not afford to let me get away with it. Some of the children in each class would not hesitate to act as informers. The Government was probing into the past history of every teacher, exploring his political background. Many were dismissed, and it was dangerous to act as anything but a National Socialist.

Once I attended one of the big youth rallies. It was held at Weimar. As I should have to stay away from home for two or three days, my father was reluctant to let me go. I was only thirteen, too young in his opinion to go anywhere without the protection of at least one parent, and he had not much faith in our young girl leaders who were to look after us. I promised that I would be very careful in every respect, and he finally gave in.

We were taken to Weimar by coach. Rooms had been booked for us beforehand in private households. I was accommodated by a very nice elderly couple, who seemed delighted to have me and treated me like a daughter. Early the next morning the coach picked me up at my billet to take me, along with all the other girls, to the stadium.

This was such an immense place that most of it was out of our range of view and we could see what was happening only in our own section. Many bands made their ceremonial entry into the great arena and marched round, each one with its own special military appeal. But the one I shall never forget consisted of about twenty-four young boys whose performance was so awe-inspiring that every time they marched past there was a hush. This band was called ''The Drums.''

The actual drums were very long, reaching from the waist to the knee, and they made an uncanny sound, hollow and threatening, as the boys beat them to the rhythm of the quick march. There was something symbolic about them. The monotony of the low-pitched beat, following the same pattern of rhythm over and over again, made me involuntarily think of doom.

These drum bands were meant to remind us of the drummer boys of hundreds of years ago, who had marched into battle ignoring the wounds they received, drumming until they fell and died. Their unlimited courage was meant to be an example for us throughout our lives. . . .

While the bands played, the gymnasts marched in. The boys, who were dressed in black P.T. kit, formed themselves into the shape of a giant swastika on the arena floor; then the girls, in white P.T. kit, formed a circle around the swastika of boys. Next the gymnasts started to perform, accompanied by appropriate music blaring from the various loudspeakers, and all the while they kept their formation as a gigantic black swastika in a white circle.

Races followed later and, during a sixty-minute break, girls in white dancing dresses performed folk-dances round the maypoles. Then there were more races, followed by a P.T. demonstration given by the younger age group, of which I was a member. For this we wore black shorts and white sleeveless vests, and were rather cold. When it came to the prize-giving we were too far away to see anything and too worn out to bother to listen to the results, which were announced over the loudspeakers.

To conclude, the boys and girls once more formed the swastika. The area Hitler Youth leader gave a speech, and when he had finished we stood at attention at the salute and sang the Hitler Youth song.

Finally the leader stepped forward and shouted: "Adolf Hitler." We replied: "Sieg, Heil! Sieg, Heil! Sieg, Heil!" We yelled these words with all the strength our lungs could muster, and they sounded enormously powerful.

From Ilse McKee, *Tomorrow the World,* London: J. M. Dent & Sons, 1960, pp. 7-9, 11-15. Quoted in *Nazi Culture,* New York: Grosset & Dunlap, 1966, pp. 276-280.

NEIGHBORS

The author who was caught up in the Hitler Youth movement endeavors to lay bare her sense of guilt to her Jewish classmates. Her family and the Lewys were good neighbors, tolerant of and helpful to each other until Hitlerism took root. As indicated by the title of the book, she is burdened by a sense of culpability at having participated in the anti-Jewish activities of the Hitler Youth and having condoned the atrocities Germany committed against them.

The house in which my twin brother and I were born stood in a street off the Kurfürstendamm. As far as I can recall, the majority of the occupants were always Jews. My parents were only on friendly terms with our Gentile neighbours across the landing. This family consisted of a brother and sister and their elderly mother. The brother was a bank official, the sister a teacher. As children we liked all three of them very much. They were already National Socialists during the 'years of struggle' and the first expressions of anti-Semitism with political overtones which reached our ears came from them. They clearly objected to having to live in a house in which Gentiles were in the minority. From odd remarks of theirs I gathered that Jews were "foreigners": our neighbours pronounced the word with scorn.

On the floor below us lived the Lewys. They were the only Jews in the house with whom my parents had any kind of contact. We profited from them because we shared their telephone for many years. I remembered Herr Lewy as a friendly old man with a fine, full beard. When we were at the nursery window blowing soap bubbles, he would smile at us. We knew for religious reasons he would never let himself be seen without his black velvet skull cap and it was at his flat that we first marvelled to see a seven branched candlestick. The fact that the Lewys must not be disturbed on Saturdays because it was their holy day was something our mother never forgot to impress upon us. They were the only orthodox Jews in the house, and I seem to remember that this made them more acceptable to our parents, probably because they came from a "good old family" and did not belong to the *nouveaux riches,* let alone the "foreign" families who had only come from eastern Europe since the war.

Contact with the other Jewish inhabitants of the house was limited to an exchange of greetings if one met them on the stairs.

Whether I had any Jewish classmates at my primary school I no longer remember; but at the secondary school Jewish girls at times made up one-third of my class. My parents often complained about this situation. Why it was lamentable I did not understand, but then our parents also complained about the unemployment, although we did not suffer from it ourselves.

I ask myself now how my Jewish schoolfellows struck me. First, almost without exception, by their physical and mental precociousness. They were "ladies" already, while I felt I was still a child, and the ostentatious clothes many of them wore annoyed me. Not one of them came from a poor home. Most of them, indeed, were rich, and there were some who sought to impress with their fathers' cars, in which the chauffeurs sometimes came to fetch them. The fact that these airs particularly upset me may have been connected with my mother's frequent complaints about *nouveaux riches.* If this expression refers to the time a family's prosperity dates from — and not to a style of life — then my mother came from a *nouveau riche* family herself, anyway. Her father was a tradesman who had worked his way to the top.

As regards accomplishments, the Jewish girls were above average. True, the top girl in my class from the lowest form to the Upper First, was always the daughter of a Catholic railway guard with a large family, but after her in almost all subjects came Jewish girls. They never formed cliques, and one might well say that they were conspicuously well bred. Their good behavior was for a long time a source of irritation to me, for until the Upper Third Class I regarded school as a playground, a place where one could get up to all kinds of silly escapades which would be prevented at home by parental discipline.

The first "political conversations" I can remember having with other girls at school were provoked by a girl in my form whose father had been an officer in the First World War and belonged to the *Stahlhelm.*[1] These consisted of boasting about the "exploits" of one's brothers or cousins, which were directed against the new German Republic and also, even before 1933, against the Jews. Gerda's brothers went out at night and tore down the "black, red and mustard" flags from flagpoles with hooks fastened to long lines or daubed swastikas on walls. One day Gerda brought me a railway ticket which looked like an ordinary one. It was on closer examination that I realized this was a "political joke." It carried the imprint "To Jerusalem." Underneath was written in smaller print: "And no return." We gave this ticket to Rahel K. for her father. We chose

[1] "Steel Helmet": a right-wing paramilitary organization.

Rahel because she was a particularly good-natured girl, somewhat simple in her friendliness. . . .

I liked her very much. When our cruel joke threatened to have repercussions and before my parents were summoned to the school, I went to Rahel's mother and apologized. The kindliness with which she received me filled me with shame. From then on I refrained from tasteless jokes of that kind. I was then twelve years old.

I do not remember our having serious discussions about internal politics in class – not even at the time when I belonged to the Hitler Youth. One of our classmates, a girl whose company I found particularly agreeable, ran the school group of the Union for Germans Abroad *(Verein für das Deutschtum im Ausland)*. . . . Hilde Sch. was a pastor's daughter. I regarded her as my exact opposite, because the Union was joined by all those consciously bourgeois girls who had no desire to join the Hitler Youth. Despite this rivalry we got on well as individuals. My membership in the Hitler Youth played no part in the life of the classroom. It did not even alter my attitude to the Jewish girls in the class.

A trivial episode from that period which has recently occurred to me throws some light on the situation. I was having an argument with Rosel Cohn, whom I had long disliked for her intellectual arrogance. She had a much sharper brain than I, and I was losing the argument. I can no longer recall what the argument was about, but I remember that for a moment I was tempted to keep my end up by making a derisive reference to the fact that she was Jewish. I rejected the idea almost at once, not because I would have been ashamed to use such an unfair weapon, but because I thought: What an absurd idea! You would only make a laughing stock of yourself.

Rosel Cohn was a Jewish classmate of ours, but I did not really connect her with "the Jews." *Those* Jews were and remained something mysteriously menacing and anonymous. They were not the sum of all Jewish individuals, who included yourself or old Herr Lewy; they were an evil power, something with the attributes of a spook. One could not see it, but it was there, an active force for evil.

As children we had been told fairy stories which sought to make us believe in witches and wizards. Now we were too grown up to take this witchcraft seriously, but we still went on believing in the "wicked Jews." They had never appeared to us in bodily form, but it was our daily experience that adults believed in them. After all, we could not check to see if the earth was round rather than flat — or, to be more precise, it was not a proposition we thought it necessary to check. The grown-ups "knew" it, and one took over this knowledge without mistrust. They also "knew" that the Jews were wicked. This wickedness was directed against the prosperity, unity and prestige of the German nation, which we had learned to love from an early age. The anti-Semitism of my parents was a part of their outlook which was taken for granted. Our father came from the university-educated middle class. In his day there were still not many Jews at the universities. They were widely regarded as intruders, particularly because their keen intelligence offered an uncomfortable challenge. My mother had grown up in the family of a tradesman "by appointment to the Court," who had risen to prosperity through hard work. In such circles as these, fear of competition may well have led to the early development of a thoroughgoing anti-Semitism.

My parents certainly grumbled about the Jews, but this did not stop them having a genuine liking for the Lewys and having social relations with my father's Jewish colleagues.

For as long as we could remember, the adults had lived in this contradictory way with complete unconcern. One was friendly with individual Jews whom one liked, just as one was friendly as a Protestant with individual Catholics. But while it occurred to nobody to be ideologically hostile to *the* Catholics, one was, utterly, to the Jews. In all this no one seemed to worry about the fact that they had no clear idea of who "*the* Jews" were. They included the baptized and the orthodox, Yiddish-speaking second-hand dealers and professors of German literature, Communist agents and First World War officers decorated with high orders, enthusiasts for Zionism and chauvinistic German nationalists. . . .

When you came into my class at Easter 1933 from another Berlin school I made friends with you, although I knew you were Jewish and despite the fact that I had joined the Hitler Youth at almost the same time.

I had learned from my parents' example that one could have anti-Semitic opinions without this interfering in one's personal relations with individual Jews. There may appear to be a vestige of tolerance in this attitude, but it is really just this confusion which I blame for the fact that I later contrived to dedicate body and soul to an inhuman political system, without this giving me doubts about my own individual decency. In preaching that all the misery of the nations was due to the Jews or that the Jewish spirit was seditious and Jewish blood was corrupting, I was not compelled to think of you or old Herr Lewy or Rosel Cohn; I thought only of the bogeyman, "*the* Jew." And when I heard that the Jews were being driven from their professions and homes and imprisoned in ghettos, the points switched automatically in my mind to steer me round the thought that such a fate could also overtake you or old Lewy. It was only *the* Jew who was being persecuted and "made harmless."

Perhaps I should have been more ready to learn from the sum of my own observations if I had not had the example of this fatal schizophrenia before my eyes from an early age; there is much to suggest that I might. Your father — if you will allow me to cite him as an example — was a man who epitomized the complete opposite of what was then depicted to us as typically Jewish. He had been awarded both Iron Crosses during the war, and as a doctor he was much sought after by poor people because they knew that he would take the trouble to help them sympathetically even when they could not pay his fee. During my schooldays I never felt more at home with any of the families I knew than with yours. Here the two generations lived together in friendship, without this ever calling into question the authority of your parents. There was always an opportunity to join in conversations, whether about plays, books or current affairs, which had a real educational value for us children, not only because of their intellectual level but also because of the personal example expressed in your parents' attitude to every topic.

What bound me to you — apart from a spontaneous liking for you — was a shared interest in literature and philosophy. You thought more slowly and more deeply than I. With an intensity at which I marveled, you would burrow into a question, remaining long silent, and surprising me with solutions which went deeper, both intuitively and intellectually, than ones I could have found.

On the question of whether we ever discussed anti-Semitism together, my memory gives me no clear answer. Perhaps we avoided it. I was used to respecting your reluctance to talk about very personal matters, even though I did not share it.

But I certainly remember my telling you quite freely about my experiences in the Hitler Youth and your equally open descriptions of those of your brothers and sisters in their youth groups. They belonged to the illegal "Federated Youth," to which the National Socialists were ruthlessly opposed. The leader of this group was known by the nickname "Tusk." It was said then — and as far as I can remember, this corresponded to everything you told me about him — that he had Communist leanings. Out of all the "Federated Youth" he was the Hitler Youth's enemy number one. One day I learned from you that many of your brother's friends, when their group had been closed down, had joined the Hitler Youth. This confirmed something about which I had heard frequent complaints in the Hitler Youth — the infiltration of National Socialist youth by "Federated" and indeed Communist elements. It was probably this circumstance which led me to review my own unclear position. I gradually felt its ambiguity to be unclean and oppressive. I reached the conclusion that it was not possible to be both a National Socialist youth leader and the friend of a Jewish family whose sons belonged to an illegal Federated – Communist group.

I also gradually lost touch with you physically, because I spent every possible free moment in the service of the Hitler Youth. And inwardly I had less and less patience with things that were not connected with this service.

I do not know if my behaviour hurt you. I fear it did. You never readily showed your feelings, and I was doubtless blind to any modest indications that you were upset.

From *Account Rendered*, by Melita Meschmann, trans. by Geoffrey Strachan. New York: Abelard-Schuman, 1964, pp. 37-41.

BABI YAR

Babi Yar, *by Anatoly Kuznetsoi, is an awesome account of the two-year occupation of Kiev, 1941-1943. The book begins with an account of the inhuman massacre of 50,000 Jews at a ravine located in the outskirts of the city Kiev, known as Babi Yar.*

Anatoly was twelve years old when he recorded the sickening mass annihilation of the Jews of Kiev.

The book covers the annihilation of men, women and children, but does not dwell specifically on those within the age ranges of four to fourteen, which is the theme of this book. However, we have included young Anatoly's reflections as provided in the title below, in order to give an idea of the monstrosities committed by the Nazi regime.

How Many Times Should I Have Been Shot?

By the time I had lived fourteen years on this earth I had committed so many crimes, according to the fascists, that I should have been shot at least 12 times.

1. I had failed to betray a Jew (my pal Shurka).
2. I had helped a prisoner (Vasily).
3. I had hidden a red flag.
4. I had violated the curfew.
5. I had not returned everything I had taken from a store.
6. I had not delivered our fuel to the authorities.
7. I had not handed over our surplus food.
8. I owned a pair of felt boots.
9. I had pasted up a leaflet.
10. I had stolen (beets, wood and so on).
11. I had worked for a sausage-maker illegally, without a license.
12. I had run away from Germany (at Vyshgorod).

From *Babi Yar* by Anatoly Kuznetsoi, trans. by Jacob Gurolsky, New York: Dial Press, 1967, p. 341.

THE KRISTALLNACHT RIOTS AND POGROMS

Waves of riots, pogroms, fires, arrests, and deportations to concentration camps were carefully staged in German cities, ostensibly in reprisal against the assassination of a German Embassy secretary in Paris. The name "crystal night" was given because of the smashing of thousands of expensive windows of Jewish stores, whose contents were plundered. Jews were terrorized all over Germany. Nearly 200 synagogues were burned, 5500 stores and shops were destroyed, 30,000 Jews were arrested — one half of whom were sent to Buchenwald — and a collective fine of 1 billion marks was imposed on German Jewry.

The following describes an incident in a Jewish orphanage in Dinslaken, Rhineland, which occurred at this time.

Crystal Night, November 10, 1938

Not satisfied with burning down synagogues, plundering Jewish shops and homes, and terrorizing their occupants, the Nazis invaded Jewish hospitals, old people's homes, and children's homes. Dr, Herz, who later fled to Australia and was awarded a prize from Harvard University in 1940 for his book *Life in Germany,* described the days in November 1938 when he was temporarily director of a Rhineland orphanage at Dinslaken. At about 5:45 in the morning of November 10 he was awakened by a vigorous ringing of the doorbell. Throwing a coat over his shoulders, he went to answer. Two Gestapo officers and a policeman announced that they had come to search for arms, as they were searching all Jewish homes. They cut the telephone wires, rummaged through drawers and books, and searched for money. The orphanage ordinarily held its religious services at seven o'clock. While the three officers continued the search, the staff and the children, forty-six persons in all, of whom thirty-two were orphans between six and sixteen years old, recited their prayers with no inkling of what was happening. Then Dr. Herz called them to the refectory to tell them. "Be brave," he said, "have faith in God. We'll get over these difficult times."

After eating breakfast together, they went off to their separate tasks until 9:30, when the doorbell was violently rung. As soon as the door was unlatched, fifty men burst into the building. They stormed into the refectory, which luckily was empty, and began systematically wrecking the place. The children screamed with terror. Flouting a Gestapo order, Dr. Herz told them to follow him into the street. He thought that the troopers would not dare harm the children out in the open. Despite the cold and wet, the children scrambled into the street, bareheaded and without coats, running after the director down to the town hall to obtain the protection of the police.

There were about ten policemen and a crowd of onlookers eager for excitement.

"We do not give protection to Jews," the police sergeant said. "Get out with those children or I'll shoot."

"All right. Kill me and the children. That way the matter will be settled."

The policeman gave a cynical smile, aimed his gun at the gate that led to the orphanage garden, and fired, shattering the lock. He forced the group onto the wet grass in front of the orphanage building, ordering them not to leave for any reason.

Sirens began whining at 10:15. A thick cloud of smoke drifted up from the neighborhood of the synagogue. Smaller trails of smoke pinpointed houses on fire.

At 10:45 the Dinslaken police chief arrived to "study the situation" with Dr. Herz. "What do you intend doing?" he asked.

"I want permission from the authorities straight away to take these children to Belgium or Holland."

While two men strolled through the orphanage, picking their way among heaps of rubble that had been left, a young man in civilian clothes asked the police chief in a sharp voice, "What does this Jew want of you?"

The chief was probably frightened and shouted at Dr. Herz, "Hurry up and join the other Jews."

Policemen came and led him to the school near the synagogue, where forty Jews from the town had been assembled. The commanding officer ordered Dr. Herz to take charge of the others who had been arrested and act as their spokesman, making a list of their names. A former director of a business school, who had previously been a city councilor at Dinslaken, sat groaning and holding his head, which was streaming blood. From a nearby tap, Dr. Herz managed to collect some water for him in an envelope.

The local Nazi Party leader appeared, in civilian clothes. "Unknown persons are responsible for the destruction which occurred this morning," he announced. "Their reasons can easily be understood. A mother and father in Düsseldorf are mourning their son, who was murdered in the flower of his youth by a Jew. It is understandable. No one will lay a finger on you. You have nothing to be afraid of. After all, we are not in Russia. . . . The doctor will soon be here. If you are hungry, collect your money — you will certainly have enough — and one of you may go and buy some food.''

He paused and then added, "The cow which belonged to the orphanage has been given to a German peasant, who will feed it. Animals must not be made to suffer for what happens.''

At half-past six in the evening the party leader returned, this time in uniform. He told the group to assemble in a room at a hotel in the town center. The children were shuffled into a cart, and the adults followed on foot.

The cart crawled to the hotel through a mob of curious onlookers. The hotel ballroom had been strewn with straw, and pillows had been taken from the orphanage. A curtain had been draped over a portrait of Hitler on the stage before the Jews arrived. They were served stew, with the SA commander's assurance that it contained nothing harmful. At about eight o'clock men over sixteen years old trooped off to sleep in a stable. The curfew began at ten, but it was impossible to get the children to settle down in the normal way with forty uniformed SS and SA troopers standing by. Summoning up his courage, Dr. Herz decided to act with the children as though nothing were wrong. He began chanting evening prayers in a sharp, clear voice. The children recited with him. The speechless Nazis withdrew, leaving only a police officer and a single SA trooper to stand guard.

The following morning, an official from the town hall arrived to purchase food with the 132 marks found at the orphanage. The orphanage staff were allowed to prepare the meal. While they were alone with the prisoners, the policemen explained that they had had nothing to do with the events of the previous evening. ''They got us out of bed at four in the morning with orders to report to the town hall. The police were supposed not to intervene until four o'clock in the afternoon. We were to allow the party to do as it liked until then. Apart from the commander, we are all good Social Democrats or Democrats, but what can we do in times like these?''

That afternoon the police chief's assistant asked Dr. Herz to return to the orphanage with him to hand over all the keys to the regional commander of the party. Dr. Herz was led to the refectory before about forty SA troopers. The regional commander, a former teacher, snatched the keys from his hand and ordered him into the courtyard. From the window he shouted, ''Come here criminal; it seems you've been complaining about being maltreated.''

''There must be some mistake.''

''A policeman told me. Officers do not lie.''

''The officer was mistaken.''

''You wait here, you criminal, until I call you.''

Some young people in civilian clothes were carrying off the objects which had not been destroyed, mostly books from the library.

''What do you want, Jew?'' once of them shouted.

''I'm waiting for the regional commander.''

''Commander,'' one of them shouted to the regional commander, who was talking with the police chief, ''there's a Jew waiting for you here.''

''Tell him to get lost.''

That evening relatives of the children, anxious at having received no news from them, telephoned from Anvers, Brussels, and Amsterdam. On November 15 the police took the director and the children back to the remains of the orphanage because the hotel owners needed the ballroom for a boxing match. The party leader forbade local tradesmen to make any deliveries or render any services to the orphanage. The children were forced to load the few possessions still remaining to them onto a carriage, which took them to Cologne. Here the Jewish community — or the vestiges of it — took them into their care.

The NSDAP used the orphanage funds to build a new regional headquarters for the party. The story of the Dinslaken orphanage ends here. The children were allowed to go to Belgium and Holland in January 1939, but it is not known whether or not their persecutors finally caught up with them a few months later.

Crystal Night, by Rita Thalmann and Emmanuel Feinermann, Holocaust Library, 1973, pp. 84-88.

2.

JEWISH CHILDREN'S EXODUS

The Weimar Republic had guaranteed full equality to all pupils, irrespective of religious affiliation. In 1933 the process of segregating Jewish children and dismissing Jewish teachers from government schools began. Jewish pupils were separated, concentrated in special classes, and taught by Jewish retirees — teachers as well as other government officials. Parallel to the special classes a Jewish private school system grew up which was maintained by the parents and directed by a representative Jewish body known as the Reichsvertretung der Deutsches Juden[1] (1933 – 39). In addition to directing education, this body was also active in occupational training, rehabilitation, and organized emigration.

Following the Kristallnacht pogroms, in November 1938, Jewish pupils were shut out completely from all German schools. The responsibility of the school system was now in the hands of the Union of the Jews in Germany, which was established by a government decree in 1939. Impoverished and drained of resources, the Jewish community now faced ruin and doom. The flight of families and children from Germany intensified.

FLIGHT TO ENGLAND

On the twenty-fifth anniversary of the first German Jewish children's transport to England (which numbered about 10,000), Karen Gershon began to collect

---

[1] Representative Body of German Jews.

18

material depicting the children's experiences during those critical days. From the replies she received to her appeal in the British press, she selected 234 statements, from which she skillfully constructed a collective autobiography. Each paragraph marked with ¶ represents the experience of a different individual. She herself went to England and later went on Youth Aliyah to Israel, where she now resides.

¶In October 1938 Jews with Polish passports were rounded up by the Gestapo and deported to Poland. We were ditched at the frontier and, together with a large number of other people, we were taken to an old deserted army barracks in Zbonszyn, Poland, where we were given temporary accommodation under terrible conditions. From there we were sent to a hostel near Warsaw, where we spent some weeks before sailing for England. My brother was thirteen, and I was ten years old.

¶My parents took me to Prague, where after three days of concentrated sightseeing, shopping and packing, and saying good-bye to people I had not known before and have no recollection of now, I was put on a children's transport with lots of other children of all ages to go to England. I was eleven years old.

¶We left Vienna sometime during the night, for I remember Mamma getting us out of bed, having to dress us, as we were too bewildered and fuddled with sleep to do it properly and quickly. One of my sisters was with me, we were lucky to be able to go together. I was eight years old, and she was nine.

¶During the time my father was in the concentration camp, my mother, trying everything to have him released, was advised by the Jewish committee to send my sister and me to England with the first children's transport leaving Berlin. This terrible decision fell on her shoulders alone — but what else could she do, at least it would mean safety for her children. . . . She sent us, not knowing what would become of us or if she would ever see us again. My sister was eleven, and I was twelve years old.

¶My mother took me to Berlin; when I left home my father was lying in bed ill; the concentration camp had damaged his health. He held me close and bade me look after my mother when she got to England in case he did not make it. I was then just ten years old. We got to Berlin to learn that I was too late for the first transport, but would be able to go on the second. There was of course no money for me to go back home, so my mother took me to friends in Berlin, who kindly put me up for a fortnight or so. My mother had to leave me there, and the last I ever saw of her was in the Berlin street, outside the friends' house, walking backward along the pavement to get a last look at me, until she rounded the corner and we were parted.

¶We were allowed one suitcase each, containing only clothes. I remember my main worry being that I might not be allowed to take my love tokens — a collection of small cloth animals. My mother, with the insight of selfless love, knew that these objects must be packed in the suitcase at all cost, and reassured me. I was twelve years old.

¶I left home late in the evening, with the whole family to see me off. At the station we were ushered into an enormous waiting room which was packed with children and parents weeping, crying and shouting. It occurred to me there for the first time that our grief was no longer a personal one. We all belonged to a group, but not a group that was determined through social, economic or intellectual dividing lines; we were all refugees. We were ordered to take leave of our relatives quickly and go straight to the train, which had sealed windows, and once we were all inside it the doors were sealed as well. Shortly before the train was due to leave, our relatives appeared again on the platform. From behind the sealed windows I saw my parents again, rigid and unsmiling like two statues, for the last time ever.

¶I remember the station and everyone was crying and I did not know why. I was seven years old.

¶My parents followed us through Berlin from station to station, just to get a few last glimpses of our faces. I was fourteen, and my brother was seven years old.

¶All the children from the different towns met at the Hauptbahnhof in Berlin, each with a small suitcase, ten shillings in German money, and a label round our necks giving our names. I was put into a compartment with several other children of my own age — I was eleven — my sister into the adjoining one because she was older. I recall vividly our arrival at the German–Dutch frontier, when the Nazis boarded the train for a last inspection before it crossed into another country. One Nazi per compartment. . . . The one in our compartment pulled down the blind, made us stand in the gangway, pulled down all the suitcases from the racks, opening them and throwing everything on to the floor. He took one or two small items, really of no value except a sentimental one. He also asked us for our money, taking the equivalent of nine shillings from each child, and so we left the fatherland with a shilling in our pockets. . . . Fear was in all of us, until the moment the whistle blew, the Nazis left, and the train passed over the frontier. At this moment we opened the windows, shouting abuse and spitting at them. . . . It was terrible that we children should have learned such hatred. At the first stop in Holland, we were met by some wonderfully kind ladies, who stood waiting for us on the platform with big trolleys filled with hot drinks, chocolate, sandwiches, etc. . . .

¶The journey was uneventful as long as we were on German soil. The train was an ordinary passenger train, and we sat on the wooden seats, slept as best we could, played games and sang. There were only a few adults with us, so we quite enjoyed the journey. As we crossed the German border, every one of us, young as we were, felt a tremendous sense of relief. In Holland we got a wonderful reception at each station we stopped at; people crowded the platform and literally showered us with food through the carriage windows.

¶My sister was unwell with ulcers in her mouth and still convalescing after an appendix operation. I was told to look after her; she was eight years old, and I was nine. Of the actual journey I do not remember much, except the hard wooden seats and the long time we were traveling. I remember the train being searched (by the Customs or the Nazis, I didn't know, but I was afraid). My sister was in the corner seat by the window and she was asleep. Her head was resting on one of our little string bags, with food for our journey, and I would not let those men look in the bag and disturb her. On thinking of it now, I am surprised that these men ignored us and allowed her to sleep on — but perhaps they were fathers of little girls.

¶Children under seven years old were meant to go to Holland, Belgium, or France. But my brother, who was only two was allowed to come to England with me. When we were going from the train to the boat, he was far ahead of me, leading the long line of children. He looked like a drummer, with his chamber pot strapped onto his back. I was ten years old and had promised my mother to look after him. But as soon as we had said good-bye to our parents we were separated and we have never lived together again at all.

¶I left home two weeks after my sixteenth birthday. Two compartments were reserved for us — a small number of girls and boys, all of whom I knew well. As we had been told to limit our luggage to one piece, we each had one enormous suitcase, so heavy we could hardly lift it. Leave-taking was restrained and brief. My mother kissed me and the train moved out. It was a final good-bye; I was never to see her again. The trip to Cologne was uneventful. The railway officials were not merely courteous, they were even helpful. I cannot remember what we talked about or even what I felt. My only fear was that we might all be turned back at the frontier, but there was really little likelihood of that, since the Nazis were only too glad to be rid of us. Cologne station was the point where we joined other transports, and the station was full of many hundreds of children from all parts of Germany, from toddlers up to the age of seventeen. When we moved on we were all looking out of the windows for the first sign that we were in Holland. At the first Dutch station a large number of people were on the platform, and as our train drew in they waved and cheered — they actually cheered. We were momentarily stunned and then returned the cheers and waved frantically. We were not only free, we were welcomed back to humanity by humanity. There followed a distribution of milk, lemonade, fruit, chocolate, sweets and sandwiches. I doubt if any of us were really hungry; most of us were stuffed with whatever our parents had provided. But this first meal on foreign soil, on free soil, I ate with genuine feeling of gratitude and thanksgiving. This touching reception intoxicated us. The milk might as well have been brandy. Up to then we had been subdued children — understandable in view of our recent experiences and the even more recent separation from our parents. But from this point onwards we were a noisy, boisterous bunch of boys and girls; being our age, in fact. Whenever in subsequent years I dreamed about Germany, there was always a fog. In these dreams, when I was questioned, I was unable to answer in English when I was trying to deny my German origin.

¶Then came the journey by boat across the channel at night, and I remember one little boy in our cabin being violently ill. I was eleven years old.

¶We embarked at the Hook of Holland at night and arrived at Harwich in the morning. The English customs officer asked us if we had brought any jewelry or other valuables, a question which made us quite indignant. I was eleven years old. We managed to exchange our Germany money for English money, and I was amazed when I saw the size of the pennies.

¶On the boat, my sister and I were allowed to be together; she was eight, and I was nine years old. I remember how worried I was because as we filed aboard an elderly woman with white hair piled on her head was standing at the top of the steps and directed each child, one to the left, the next to the right — I was so afraid that we would be parted, but she waved us on together. We could not find a place to wash, and I ventured outside our cabin and asked some "big" girls where to wash, and one of them showed me how the basin came out of the wall. We were very much alone. I can't remember any grownups coming to see if we were all right (though perhaps someone did come). I felt very anxious and responsible.

¶I was ten years old, and my total possessions were one small rucksack containing one change of clothes, some socks, handkerchiefs, a mouth organ, and some medical supplies for my ear. Also I had 1 Mark 50 Pfennig in a little satchet hung round my neck. When the ship berthed at Harwich I wandered about it, leaving my rucksack for a while, and it was a bad loss to find it gone when I returned. People searched high and low, but it was not found, so now I had nothing at all except an insignificant amount of worthless German money. ¶Not only had I never been on a large ocean-going ship but I had never even seen the sea. Alas, it was a night crossing, and I saw very little. The ship had been specially chartered for us. The only adults on board were the crew and those in charge of us. While they were busy I explored the ship, top to bottom, bow to stern. I stumbled into the crew's quarters, engine room, and all kinds of places I had no business to be. The only place I was denied was the bridge. Everything I saw was new to me; it was fascinating. My cabin had been allocated to someone more in need of comfort, and I spent the night in one of the salons, which had been improvised into a dormitory. Not much sleeping was done there that night. There were about forty or fifty boys, all about fifteen or sixteen years old, in that room. We did not know each other yet. We were all a little overexcited and for the next hours we exchanged, in the dark, all the political jokes which we had picked up. They were mostly variations of "Hitler, Goebbels and Goering . . . " The jokes, as such, were not memorable, but the occasion was. We did not need to look over our shoulders or lower our voices, and the realization that we could say what we liked with impunity engendered an atmosphere of enormous gaiety.

From *We Came as Children* by Karen Gershon, London: Gollancz, pp. 25-30.

CASTLES OF REFUGE IN FRANCE

OSE or OZE is the acronym of three Russian words meaning Jewish Health Society. Founded, in 1912, in St. Petersburg (now Leningrad), the movement spread to various countries. In 1923 it became international in scope.

As the persecution intensified in Germany, refugees fled to whichever country would admit them. The plight of refugee children was especially tragic. In 1938, OSE wrote a moving chapter in their rescue and relief. It launched a campaign to acquire castles in southern France to shelter the refugee children, and enlisted an eminent American child psychologist, social worker, and teacher, Dr. Ernst Papanek, to serve as the spearhead of its noble program. He recorded his personal experiences in the book Out of the Fire, *which he wrote in collaboration with Edward Linn.*

No longer could we be content to wait for Jewish parents to bring their children to France. It was now up to us to go and get them. Minkovsky, the famous psychologist who was also a war hero, was placed in charge of that phase of the operation. And then, at last, the OSE people turned to me. We would now, quite obviously, have to accommodate more than the thirty-two children in the one Home we had to start with, No? No! We would now only be able to accommodate twenty-four, because I was going to take the largest room and convert it into an office for myself. And did they want to know why? "Because I don't want to make this only a shelter for terrorized children, I want to make it a great Children's Home. To make a GREAT Children's Home, you start with administration. Everything else will follow."

With the rescue operation already being organized, it was necessary to find a suitable shelter quickly. They found it only three miles away. The Villa Helvetia was a rambling vacation hotel which in better days had catered to a wealthy Swiss clientele, *Helvetia* being a poetic name for Switzerland. For our purposes, it was perfect. Big enough to take care of eighty to one hundred children once we had broken it down into smaller rooms, and with spacious grounds, covered with huge old trees, for the youngsters to roam in.

The Baroness Pierre de Gunzbourg, the French wife of a Russian-born aristocrat who had made a fortune as an armaments manufacturer in Strasbourg, gave us the forty thousand francs we needed to rent it for the duration. . . .

"Forty thousand," she warned us, "and you'll never get another penny out of me."

It was really very funny. The Baroness was an imposing woman, with hatchetlike features that she refused to make the slightest attempt to pretty over, and a warm, beautiful heart that she was always trying to hide. She had become interested in the OSE because of the work we had been doing with convalescent children. . . . We had introduced an educational program — working with both the children and their parents — that was progressive by any standards and completely new to France. What had impressed her more than anything else was the casework-oriented approach Lene had developed, whereby the parents were given a special diet for each individual child plus written advice on how to handle the child's medical and emotional problems.

Impressed or not, the Baroness wanted us to understand that she was a completely assimilated Frenchwoman who wasn't giving us the money because the children were Jewish but only because they were children who happened to be in danger. "If you can do what you say you can do, here is the money," she said. "But I will tell you right now, here is also where it will end."

Three weeks later, she gave us another forty thousand francs to buy a castle on the outskirts of Montmorency. Before the year was over, she had bought castles for us all over France at a cost of more than a million francs and was serving very actively as the chairman of our Board.

The Baron de Gunzbourg would always joke with me about it. "What am I going to do with all those castles you're getting my wife to buy?" he would ask. "When the war is over the children will all return to Germany and I will be stuck with them."

There would always be children in need of an institution, I would assure him.

"No, no," he would sigh. "I will be the Castle King of France. I am resigned to it. The taxes alone will make a poor man of me. Nothing can save me from my fate now except a return to the Age of Chivalry."

He was hitting too close to the truth there for comfort. The castles were such a godsend to us not only because they were so large but also because the aristocrats who owned them were only too happy to find someone who would take them off their hands. They were ancestral castles, out of another age. The last ornate reminder of a style of life that had disappeared.

The first group of children arrived from Germany and Austria early in February 1939, thirty-odd youngsters between the ages of five and twelve. Most of them had come across the border holding tightly to the hands of Frenchmen or Frenchwomen who had volunteered to bring them through customs on their family passports. Since none of the children spoke French that well, they had been instructed to smile if they were spoken to but to say nothing that might give them away. The poor little things were so terrified in the aftermath of the Night of the Broken Crystal* that few of their benefactors were able to coax a single word out of them even after they were safely in France.

For us, it had been a race against time to get the old wooden hotel ready. As far as the remodeling of the house was concerned, we had to partition off the old rooms, which also made it necessary to put in some new doors and windows, paint the outside, redecorate the inside, strengthen the foundation and patch up the roof. Since we were going to need new furniture anyway, we decided to build our own. Chairs and tables staggered in size to fit every age group. And because I was determined that we would be as self-sufficient as possible — for educational reasons that far outweighed the financial ones — we drew up plans to construct a complete tailor shop in the basement.

We had eight weeks to get it all done and no money to hire skilled workmen. I passed the word among the political refugees who were sitting all over Paris going crazy, that we had plenty of work for them and that while we wouldn't be able to pay very much, we would be serving good meals and they would be working for children.

We had a hundred positions to fill, counting the double shifts, and as soon as the unions agreed to waive their rights we filled every position and had a long waiting list. Except for the Jewish intellectuals from Poland, who had a tradition of learning a trade, few of our workers had ever held a tool in their hands before. But they worked day and night — literally, day and night — and if some of the work wasn't very good at first, it improved every day. They were working for the love of the children and they were happy for the chance to be working, and that meant they were working with enthusiasm. A medical doctor who was well over fifty prescribed "fresh air and exercise" for himself, as his way of volunteering to cart the rubbish away in a wheelbarrow. Another doctor became a mason, and a pretty darn good one. Lawyers became carpenters, professors became painters, former ministers of state became roofers, writers became laborers. One of the professors, who is at Carnegie University now,

*(See page 14.)

was one of our most — uh, exuberant painters. He comes to visit us once a year and never fails to say, as if for the first time: "Ho, did we cheat you! We could not all paint." To which I answer — the ritual is unfailing — "I knew it. Number one, the painting was so lousy; and number two, it took you clowns three times as long as any ordinary lousy painters."

Nobody thought we could have the Home ready in time. But we did. We did it by working like hell through the final night and by leaving the decorating of their rooms to the children themselves. When the guests of honor arrived from Paris the next morning to officiate at our grand opening, the representative from the Office of the Interior came upon an unshaven , unkempt workman sleeping soundly on a bench in the garden. It was the architect who had drawn up the blueprints for us, stayed on to oversee the work, and then pitched in himself through the final night to get the job done.

The children had spent a couple of busy days themselves. By the time they arrived at Helvetia, they had already been processed through OSE headquarters in Paris, brought to the Rothschild Hospital in Paris for a medical examination, and taken by train to the railroad station at Enghien, a little town five miles away, where they had been picked up by their group counselors and driven in by bus.

They filed into the large dining hall, took their seats quietly and dutifully, and waited to be told what to do next.

I have always felt that when it comes to creating a feeling of community spirit nothing can compare with group singing. The only question was what songs would a group of children who had grown up under Hitler know? Looking at them sitting there so stiff and silent, I knew the song I wanted to start with. The song of the *Kinderfreunde* (Friends of the Children), which is the youth organization of the labor movement. "We are young, the world is open," it begins. "Oh, you beautiful spacious world." The directress of Helvetia, Margot Cohn, was an excellent piano player and singer. We began to sing, Margot and I, hoping for the best, and some of the other adults picked it up. The children looked at us and looked at each other. And then, very timidly, one of the older children began singing. And then another. And another. This was four years after the labor movement had been crushed in Austria, you understand, and six years after it had been crushed in Germany, and still almost half these children knew the song. To me, this did more than simply break the ice. It told me that in the privacy of their own homes the old values and traditions had been passed on.

When the singing ended, I explained that they were now going to have a little snack to eat and then go outside with their counselors and play until lunch was ready.

A moment of silence. A somber-eyed, redheaded girl, about nine years old, raised her hand tentatively, and when I encouraged her to speak up she asked, in a sweet, tremulous little voice, "Are Jewish children also allowed to go into the park?"

We were annihilated. It was all we could do not to rush out and throw our arms around her. What made it even more annihilating was that every other eye was turned up toward me, waiting just as anxiously for the answer.

When we did go outside, they just stood around waiting to be told what to do. They didn't ask any questions. They didn't even wander around aimlessly. They just followed whatever instructions or suggestions came their way. And so, at least, we knew what our first task was going to be. We were going to have to show them how to play. We were going to have to teach them how to be children.

With all future transports, I always tried to be at the station so that I could greet them in a way that would show them they were already a part of the Home. But whether I was on the scene or not, we would always have some of the other children come along to help the newcomers load their belongings onto the bus and, in the course of the conversation during the ride back, to let them know what we were like and what, in general, they could expect at the Home. In that way, the kids who had met them at the station would also have a sort of vested interest in showing their new friends around, and each of the newcomers would have an immediate contact within the established group. Someone to play with, you might say, and to show them how to play.

Once the operation was under way, new transports arrived so frequently that we opened the next Home, La Chenaie (The Oaks), in Eaubonne three weeks later, and the fourth Home in the complex, Villa des Tourelles (The Little Towers) in Soisy, three months after that. The next month, we opened three different castles down in the Creuse, a Department (county) in the middle of France, and from there it became a matter of buying them as fast as we could find them and having new directors and staff people trained.

From *Out of the Fire* by Ernst Papanek with Edward Linn, New York: William Morrow, 1975, pp. 44-49.

FIRST YOUTH ALIYAH GROUP IN BERLIN

Youth Aliyah, the Jewish child-rescue movement begun in 1933, has been one of the great humanitarian enterprises of the twentieth century. Launched in 1933 to save German Jewish children by transporting them to Palestine, it grew to include the Jewish children of North Africa, the Balkans, Asia, and Islamic lands — over seventy countries in all — where Jews were persecuted. Tens of thousands of children have been absorbed in labor villages, agricultural settlements, and educational instituions in Eretz Yisrael. Its support has come notably from the American Hadassah organization, Zionist women's groups, and the Jewish Agency.

Following is the story of the departure of the first Youth Aliyah group. The movement was initiated by Mrs. Recha Freir of Berlin, who influenced Henrietta Szold, founder of American Hadassah, to undertake the leadership of the movement. Miss Szold's remarkable record in establishing Youth Aliyah as an ongoing vital institution has rightfully earned her the name "Mother of Youth Aliyah."

Whoever walked into one of our classrooms could recognize the character of German Jewry of that period merely from the outward appearance and behavior of the children in the class. Next to the hungry and ragged ghetto children sat the smartly dressed son of a banker from Grunewald. His trousers were creased, he had a silk handkerchief in his pocket and wore a gold tiepin. George, stout and phlegmatic, was sitting next to the village lad from Hessen who was as restless as quicksilver. The pale, thin boy wearing the uniform of a porter was always looking about him with his youthful, sparkling eyes. He worked every afternoon at the Aid Committee for Jewish Youth, and on Sabbath his voice — clear as a bell — was heard in the synagogue choir. Betty worked every afternoon, serving at her parents' shop near the Stettin railway station. Dora, whose eyes were tired from night work, helped her mother in her business by sewing corsets. Henry was busy thinking of the barrow with which he had to cart coal from the cellar to the customers — work which usually lasted until midnight. Yesterday we took Paul out of the furnished room he had rented after he was sent away from the orphanage. His father had died, and yesterday his mother married a Persian. And the couple intended to travel by Orient Express to Persia the next day.

Most difficult of all was the situation of the children of mixed marriages. Not only were family relations often strained — the parents were separated, the younger brother was at the orphanage at Pankow, the younger sister in the children's home "Ahava." But sometimes the children themselves did not know where they belonged. At first sight, they seemed to belong to the Hitler Youth, and I knew that they were attached to it and longing for it in their heart of hearts and were trembling feverishly when the Hitler Youth headed by the band passed by the windows. Obviously they knew nothing of Jewish patterns of life and sometimes rejected them emphatically. We helped by inviting them to our hostels, first perhaps for a meal or to help in the kitchen. Later they came to live there, and after they had passed through our training camp they were given immigration permits like all the others.

Good-bye! A bright, sunny morning in September 1936. The hands of the big clock in the hall of the Anhalter Station pointed to three minutes past ten. In seven minutes the journey would start: Berlin, Eisenach, Frankfurt-on-Main, Mannheim. From Mannheim, according to the timetable, the itinerary was via Strassburg and Lyon to Marseille. On the station platform were crowds of people round the last carriages. Most were pale; many women were dressed in black; here and there stood a schoolchild with his satchel on his back. Among them were the members of our school staff, the officials of the Aid Committee for Jewish Youth, and over there the leader of the group going on aliyah. Youthful faces were looking through the windows. Nearly all were pupils of our school. "Do a good job, Ursula!" cried Mrs. Richter. "Peter, write every week to the old address in Goethestrasse for the present," said Mr. Wurm. "It's going to be a lovely trip," said Jackie, who showed me his camera proudly. "Yesterday I bought another five films!" "Where is Nina?" "Who?" "The one in front of us? She does not want to look out." "Mummy, don't cry! You'll soon be coming too"; that was Kathie calling from another window. She was trying hard to look happy, but her eyes were miserable.

"Take your seats." Doors were slammed. One late traveler was dashing forward. I went from window to window, shaking hands. . . . "Stand clear";

the stationmaster raised his flag. The windows full of faces glided past. Handkerchiefs were waved. A trembling voice from afar — "Shalom, see you again soon." For a moment I close my eyes, and as soon as I open them again, I see only empty rails. On the bridge beyond, an elevated train with red carriages passes and brings me back to reality. "Hullo, boys! Where are you?" A group of fifty from our school returns from the end of the platform. "That was a super engine," Klaus declares, "built in 1934 by the Borsig Works. Of course we were singing when the train moved off!" "Oh, what did you sing?" *Anu olim artsah* [we are off to Palestine]," replied twenty of the lads in chorus. A question had been put to me. Would the hundred immigration certificates that had arrived suddenly ten days before be the *last* ones because of the unrest in Palestine? More than a hundred children were still left.

Then another voice: "Please, sir, what is the situation like in Palestine now?" Renate's mother asked. "Don't worry," I answered, "the children will be taken to safe places. If you feel a bit nervous, come and see us at school. We get many letters from Palestine. Perhaps you would like to come on Friday to our Oneg Shabbat?" "Yes, please, and many thanks." "Perhaps it would have been better if my daughter were still at school, sitting with the others, instead of traveling on the train?" . . .

Suddenly a loud, rough voice calls out: "Clear the platform at once!" Two SS men in black uniforms hustle us towards the exit.

"Franz, old Mrs. Frank has fainted!" Ariel whispers in my ear. "She is lying over there on a seat." I turn to the SS men. "Excuse me, can a stretcher be got here?" "What for?" I explain. "No, we have no stretchers for old Jewesses. Phone to the Jewish hospital, but hurry up!"

Two big lads from the Hebrew class overheard the conversation and quietly went over to the seat. One or two girls helped them, and they gently carried the sick woman from the platform.

Those of us who were left got back to school after a short walk in the autumn air. Only two hours of work are left. The departure is over. Let's get back to work.

Reported by Franz and Ruth Ollendorf in *Let the Children Come*, by Recha Freir, London: Weidenfeld and Nicolson, 1961, pp. 94-96.

HENRIETTA SZOLD WELCOMES FIRST YOUTH ALIYAH GROUP

On Monday, February 19, on the steamship *Martha Washington* of the Lloyd Triestine Line, the first group of boys and girls organized for settlement in Palestine by the *Juedische Jugendhilfe,* the Federation of German Jewish youth organizations, arrived at the recently opened port of Haifa. There were forty-three of them, eighteen girls and twenty-five boys. An older comrade, Hanoch Reinhold,[1] their trainer and leader, accompanied them. The group was destined for settlement in Ain Harod.

[1]Now known as Hanoch Rinot, prominent Hebrew educator living in Israel.

The arrangements at the dock were in the hands of the director of the Haifa Branch of the Immigration Department of the Jewish Agency. He was assisted by a group of volunteers, among them representatives of various public bodies, such as the Central Bureau of the Jewish Agency for the Settlement of German Jews in Palestine, the Social Service Bureau of the Haifa Kehillah, the Haifa Section of the *Hitachdut Olei Germania,* and, above all, representatives of the Kevrutzah Ain Harod, the future home of the young people. Everything from quarantine to customs and from customs to the first meal on Palestinian soil moved flawlessly — except the weather. The vessel came in under a heavily shrouded sky, driven by a gale, with the rain pelting down steadily. Good humor prevailed, nevertheless. The merciless wet could not dampen the enthusiasm of the young travelers nor the joy of their grandparents, brothers, sisters, aunts, and friends who were on hand to greet them. All of them, travelers and relatives, apparently forgot their discomfort and swiftly adopted the point of view of the Palestinian farmer, who was rejoicing in the blessed downpour, a welcome change from the devastating drought of the three years preceding this winter of 1933–1934.

The luggage heaped up on the dock was a formidable pile. Amid the suitcases of every conceivable shape, size, and material, there stuck up flagpoles and cellos and mandolins and, first and foremost, bicycles. In addition, some of the boys and girls had chunky rucksacks strapped to their backs. In spite of the careful preparations made beforehand and the numerous willing and expert helpers and the courtesy of the officials, the formalities stretched out over hours, from the early afternoon until long after seven in the evening. Finally, in the dark and through the rain, stimulated by the hope of the first square meal of the day, the troop trotted gaily across the wide expanse of the new wharf to the Workingmen's Kitchen facing the shore. Their ravenous appetites had been only partially stilled by the sandwiches brought to them while the customs requirements were being met. Seated at the long T-table, they burst spontaneously into Hebrew song, the gift they had brought with them from their youth organization training.

The plan had been to have the group spend the night at the Bet HaOlim (Immigration Station) of the Jewish Agency, situated in Bat Gallim, the seaside suburb of Haifa. The intention could not be carried out because the Station was filled to the last bed with immigrants who had arrived from Europe on several of the preceding days. At the last moment, emergency arrangements had to be made. Happily they turned out to be most acceptable. Eighteen of the young people were entertained as guests at one of the hotels on Mt. Carmel, the rest for a nominal fee at two of the new children's houses recently established, also on Mount Carmel, by their German compatriots. The crowded Immigration Station is to be thanked for the opportunity thus granted to the new Palestinians, in the first moments of their sojourn in the land, to view one of the most beautiful spots of their new home, the ravishing combination of sea and mountain of the Haifa headland. Fortunately, early on Tuesday morning the sun broke through the pall of clouds and allowed the beauty of the unique scene to emerge for a short space. The rest of the day, indeed the rest of the week, the rain, interrupted by spells of hail, came down in torrents. On account of the change in the lodging place, and the necessity of dividing up into three sections, the planned medical examination had to be postponed until after settlement in Ain Harod.

At the railroad station the intimate scenes of the dock repeated themselves — relatives more or less acclimated to Palestine mingled with the new recruits and, as at the dock, good cheer prevailed.

Through the foresight of the Ain Harod hosts, a special car had been secured for the transportation of the group and considerable part of its belongings. On the railway journey of about one hour and three-quarters, there was much craning of necks and darting from windows on the one side of the train to windows on the other side, to catch a glimpse of Yagur, Nahalal, Kfar Yehoshuah, Kfar Yecheskel, and finally, the twin K'vutzot of Tel Joseph and Ain Harod. All these were names not unknown to the boys and girls, also a gift of their youth organization training. They greeted them as acquaintances and when the crossroad sign of Ain Harod and Tel Joseph hove into sight, they sang out merrily, "Main Station of Ain Harod." Again they broke out into song, responding to the greetings of the older pupils of the Ain Harod and Tel Joseph school, who had descended to the railroad station to welcome their new companions. In the crowd were two lads belonging to the German group who had preceded it to Palestine. Boisterous greetings!

All the way up to the settlement, the troop was met by members of the Kevutzah streaming down to catch a first glimpse of the new contingent added to the six hundred, among them ninety recently come from Germany, which constitute the cooperative community of Ain Harod. At the top, in front of the dining room, the veranda of which was crowded with the rest of the residents, the ubiquitous photographer snapped the scene.

The travelers were hurried into the dining room for lunch and again, to the delight of the long-established Ain Harodians, they sang out lustily one Hebrew song after the other, their hosts joining in with a will. After the meal came the inevitable horah, which at once integrated the new arrivals into the company of the old residents.

From *Youth Aliyah Letters* by Henrietta Szold, Collected by Zena Harman, Bulletin No. 2, Feb. 25, 1934.

EXILED CHILDREN PART FROM THEIR DOOMED PARENTS AT CAMP GURS, FRANCE, 1941

Gurs, located in southern France, was a concentration camp built for Polish Jews who had lived in France, as well as stateless Jews, intellectuals, and all who were suspected of being followers of General de Gaulle. They were dumped in Gurs by the German conquerors and their Vichy (French) collaborators. The region was desolate, damp, muddy and riddled with malaria and disease.

An estimated twenty thousand people were interned in Gurs, where they lived under inhuman conditions.

It is evening. The long, straggling line of weary children passes through the darkened streets of Marseille at a snail's pace. Not a soul is on the streets. The only sound of life is the monotonous clatter of oversized wooden shoes. No laughter, no whispers. Not even a childish squabble. The children trudge on into the night, silently, painfully.

From time to time a cry is heard. A child cannot walk. The hard wooden shoes — the only kind available in Marseille — are torturing his blistered feet. Patiently, the others wait. Then the slow march on into the night begins again.

It is bitingly cold, and everyone is hungry. Supper was very meager — only what the ration card allowed. But this is not the time to worry about one's stomach. The children realize that fact and make no complaint. Orphans are familiar with hunger, and all of these children are orphans, even those whose parents are among the living dead entombed in concentration camps.

At last we reach the railroad station, but the train is late. In no time at all the benches on the platform are packed. Those for whom there is no room stretch themselves out over their tattered bundles on the bare stone floor. When the train finally does arrive, they board it in orderly fashion.

Morning brings us to the ancient French university town of Montpellier, where a number of refugees are being maintained by OSE. Our train stops for a few minutes, and the men and women hurry down to greet the more fortunate youngsters on their way out of the hell that is France. "Remember us to our friends," they cry, and in their voices there is a desperate urgency. "Tell them the hour is growing late. They must save us."

As the train begins to get under way, I consult my list of names and begin to acquaint myself with the boys and girls. On each child's white identification card are several descriptive phrases, words which tell a pitiful story. On one card, I read: "Father died in concentration camp at Buchenwald." Another declares: "Mother died in French internment camp at Gurs." A third adds: "Parents sent to Lublin." Only two words appear on a fourth: "Parents unknown." I suddenly find myself choking and gasping for air. Ashamed to let the children see my tears, I hurry out of the car.

My wife and I ration the supply of food — three thin slices of bread per day for each one. There is no more than that. The children, however, do not complain. They have long since become inured to the pangs of hunger. Only their eyes reveal their thoughts; their lips remain closed. The dignity — almost indifference — with which they meet each new twist of fate is heartrending.

A wan little girl, no more than ten years old, who has been peering through one of the car windows, suddenly bursts into tears.

"What is the matter?"

Her lips remain shut tight. The only indication she gives of having heard my question is a slight lowering of her head.

"Well, say something," I insist.

She turns toward the window, toward the fields of the country to which she escaped from Germany. I try a new approach.

"Your parents — where are they?"

"Father is dead . . . and . . . only mother . . ." the girl begins to reply falteringly.

"Lives in France?" I encourage her.

"Yes, in a concentration camp."

"Do you have any relatives in New York?" I ask.

"No." That is as far as I can get with her. Tears once again begin to roll from her blue eyes. "I have no one in America," she manages to add between sobs.

Our train takes us through a seemingly endless chain of towns and villages, drawing closer with each moment to the Spanish border. But our trip is not destined to be a cheerful one. Not far from the border, in the lower Pyrenees, there is a small railway station called Oloron. The train normally stops there for about three minutes. Gurs, the notorious French concentration camp where thousands of Jewish refugees are living under the most primitive conditions, is close by. The camp was originally built several years ago for refugee Spanish Loyalists, but a few months after the war their place was taken by thousands of interned French and German Jewish families.

Gurs is even worse than a Nazi concentration camp, although the French officials are not as inhuman as German wardens. Last winter, for instance, hundreds of old and young people were compelled to sleep on the cold, frozen ground. Hunger and disease are rampant. When several Swiss Red Cross doctors first visited this Gehenna, the aged Jews refused to accept any medical help. Instead, they begged to be allowed to die. And many did before long. Even official French figures admit that at least thirty men and women died each day.

The mere thought that our train must pass by Gurs sends chills up my back. Many of our children have previously been interned there, and still have parents and relatives in the camp. Through the intercession of OSE, these refugees will be brought to the station at Oloron to bid their little ones farewell. The children know this, and although it is only Saturday afternoon and we shall not arrive before Sunday, they are already beginning to show signs of impatience. Even those whose parents are long dead are inquisitive: "Will they come?" My wife and I, however, are as uncertain as the youngsters. On Sunday the officials may not wish to be disturbed.

Toward evening, the two of us distribute the apportioned supply of bread. It is barely enough to keep the body alive, but the youngsters do not complain. They never complain. Silently, they go to sleep.

At dawn, even before the sky begins to turn bluish-gray, the children are wide awake. An almost festive spirit seems to pervade the car. All around me there is a flourish of activity. Shoes are being rubbed; small, untidy hands are splashing about in the basins. Jacques, an undersized, thirteen-year-old orphan, takes me aside to inform me that it is his companion's birthday.

"Then we ought to give him a present."

"He already has one," he exclaims ecstatically, his face aglow. "He has the nicest present. He is going to see his mother today."

His childish simplicity overwhelms me and, taking the orphan in my arms, I press him to my bosom. When I release him, I notice that his deep, pale blue eyes are moist.

Another boy, Klaus, who comes from Germany, draws a photograph of his father from his unkempt jacket. Tall and stately, bedecked with many decorations, a German officer's stiff, military mien looks out from the photograph. Today this veteran of the World War, driven from the fatherland he once defended, is held in Gurs.

As if to vie with the German lad, another youngster timidly displays a photograph of a sweet, comely young woman. "Minna," he explains, "my sister. She took care of me." The snapshot was taken only a year ago. Today, she too is in Gurs.

The train is approaching the station at Oloron. All the children rush to the window in anticipation. "They are here!" they shout as they bend forward. With a screeching of brakes, the train comes to an abrupt halt.

A loud cry, more piercing than any mechanical noise, suddenly rends the air. From the train comes the answering call of over a hundred shrill voices. Mothers, fathers, and kin, with the last few ounces of strength in their frail bodies, suddenly tear through the cordon of gendarmes and dash to the doors of the train. Their scrawny hands, quivering with excitement, are raised to greet the young ones. As the children pour out of the train, their parents and relatives hug them tightly, forgetting for this moment that their own clothes are indescribably dirty and shabby. They haven't the time to take such matters into consideration. The train leaves in three minutes. These moments will never again return.

Klaus' father, formerly the embodiment of elegance and dignity, looks like a tramp. Bearded, unkempt, rags now replacing his once-immaculate uniform, he stands looking longingly at his son. The boy, who has not seen his father for nearly two years, stares at him as at a stranger and is afraid to draw near.

"Klaus, my son, don't you recognize me?" the father finally asks in embarrassment.

The boy recoils for a moment, then, as though he had suddenly come to life, he lunges forward blindly and buries his head in his father's tattered coat. "Papa, papa," he sobs as he lifts himself up to the unshaven face, kisses the pinched forehead, and throws his small hands about his father's neck. "Papa, papa, papa," he shouts.

Minna, comely Minna, is now a living corpse. Thin as a lath, sallow-faced, she has no strength for words. Instead, she immediately falls upon her little brother's neck and smothers him with kisses. Her long, bony fingers — withered branches of a dead tree — busy themselves fondling the orphan. Her eyes are aglow with a strange unearthly light.

As these and similar scenes are taking place, an extraordinary incident occurs. As if from nowhere, the children draw forth slices of bread and offer them to the internees. "Father, take this — take this, mama — please take." Bewildered, the parents look at the bread and then at the children. Their eyes seem to ask many questions. They also tell a tale of hunger. But they refuse to take the bread. "My child, you'll have nothing left," one mother after another declares. The children are persistent. Again and again they cry, "Please take . . . please take."

One little girl attempts to force a slice between her mother's teeth. It is evident that the mother can hardly control her hunger. But she dares not eat the bread.

My wife and I are confused. Where could the children have obtained the bread? Their portions are so pitifully small and inadequate. Slowly, the answer begins to dawn upon us. Without our knowledge, the youngsters must have hidden last night's ration. We can scarcely believe our eyes. Children of eight and ten, themselves terribly hungry, are giving their own precious bits of bread to strange fathers and mothers.

My wife and I join the children in pleading with the parents to take the bread. They stare at us, and almost automatically their hands grope for it. They tear off little pieces, bringing them swiftly to their quivering lips. But the bread will go no farther. It remains stuck in their teeth. As the realization of the children's sacrifice begins to dawn upon them, a heartrending wail bursts from their throats. The hardened gendarmes lose control of themselves and begin to weep. The cry of the internees is long and pitiful, a cry of mingled shame and despair.

The French officer commanding the gendarmes draws me aside questioningly. I explain briefly what the children have done, and before I am through the eyes of this hard-bitten soldier are moist. One touching phrase escapes his lips: *"Quelle misère — what misery!"* Taking advantage of his aroused sympathies, I beg him to grant the children a few more minutes with their parents. With unexpected courtesy, he leads me to the station agent and, to my great surprise, pleads my case. ". . . We are also fathers," he beseeches. The station agent yields. The train remains a few moments longer.

Five minutes, ten minutes. The train begins to move, the clatter of the wheels drowning out the cries of farewell. Through the doors and windows, the children wave their hands to the group of living dead. The shriveled faces slowly grow less distinct, become distant specks, and then are seen no more. Perhaps forever.

In the corridor of the train stands little Klaus, holding a letter. With German deliberateness, his father, fearful that three minutes would not be sufficient for him to bid his son farewell, had written this note beforehand and had given it to the boy upon parting. Klaus now reads: "My dear son, my beloved Klaus, do not forget your father."

A little girl is weeping. Her mother, also at Gurs, had not come to the station at Oloron to see her. Evidently, permission to release her had not come in time. The girl continues to weep. . . .

We draw closer to the Spanish border. The train pulls strongly, as though in sympathy with the desire of its passengers to get away. Inside, the children are growing more cheerful. Some are showing off the presents their parents gave them. This one proudly displays an old moth-eaten shawl; that one, a small coin. Only we, the grownups, are still depressed. Is it because of the scene we have just left behind, or the childish forgetfulness about us? Whatever it is, it has left a dreadful impression upon our souls. It will continue to darken our days and haunt our nights. . . .

From *Contemporary Jewish Record,* by Isaac Chomsky, New York: American Jewish Committee.

3

EXTIRPATING THE
UNBORN GENERATION

Among Reichsführer SS Heinrich Himmler's many titles was "Commissioner for Strengthening the German National Character." In effect, the aim of this office was to exterminate Jews, gypsies, and other "undesirable" elements of the population by euthanasia, sterilization, and castration.

The question of how to solve the "Jewish problem" always loomed uppermost in the minds of Hitler, Himmler, Goebbels, et al. With typical scientific precision, Nazi medical men set out to find a way to eliminate "undesirable elements" by sterilization. The experiments were judged by the following criteria: speed, simplicity, and feasibility of "mass production." It was also hoped that the method would be imperceptible to the victims and would not raise a hue and cry among the populace.

Medical, chemical, and biological specialists were mobilized. A leader in this effort was Dr. Horst Schumann, who had been active in the euthanasia program. He studied the effects of X-ray radiation on human generative glands. Subjects for experimentation were abundant, and there were laboratories aplenty. Dr. Schumann selected able-bodied Jews, aged twenty to twenty-four, and exposed their sex organs to X-ray machines for fifteen minutes. Those who survived were castrated and their testicles carefully examined under the microscope. Those who fell ill were gassed. Himmler was kept informed of the results. Experiments were carried on in Auschwitz and Ravensbruck.

One of the conclusions reached was that castration by X-ray was too expensive. Operations to remove the testicles were much cheaper and more efficacious.

In Ravensbruck sterilization experiments were conducted on women. The results were partially successful, but "mass production" was not achieved. In 1944, when the Nazi regime began to totter, the program came to a halt.

A CRUEL HOAX: MIXED MARRIAGES AND STERILIZATION

In a sense Westerbork, situated in a windy peat-bog region of Holland, was a so-called model transit camp for Dutch Jewry prior to their deportation to the death camps in the east. Its population grew from 750 to 100,000 Jewish inmates. When it was liberated in April, 1945, only 1,200 survivors remained. Just as in Theresienstadt, the Germans used every deceptive scheme to mislead and delude the inmates.

One of its inmates, journalist and author Philip Mechanicus, born in 1889, kept a lengthy diary of life at Westerbork. He was killed in Auschwitz on October 12, 1944.

The hoax perpetrated by the Nazis was to offer escape to life if the prisoners would submit to castration and sterilization. . . .

Saturday, June 12th, 1943: Once again the partners of mixed marriages with children were all summoned to the Registration Department this morning — about 300 at a rough estimate. Gemmeker addressed them. They could either be sterilized and be sent back to Amsterdam without a star and with a distinctive type of J, or face the possibility of being sent to Poland, where they would collapse under an inhuman labor system. Those summoned to attend had to make known their decision by Monday. The whole episode has an ironical flavor. When the Germans started to discriminate against the Jews in our country, many Jews who had contracted mixed marriages had their marriages dissolved temporarily in order to safeguard their families and save their possessions. Until last year the Germans recognized mixed marriages and even dissolved mixed marriages with children, in the sense that the persons involved were exempted from deportation and the marriages were not broken up. Too bad for those who had got a separation from their Aryan better halves. But what the Germans gave with one hand they took away again with the other. First of all, the *dissolved* mixed marriages were flung on the scrap heap, then mixed marriages without children (unless they could show church membership or baptism before January 1st, 1941) were broken up, and recently partners of mixed marriages with children who wanted to escape the Polish hell were forced to let themselves be sterilized. Those who had their marriages dissolved to save their families no longer needed to have any regrets about this unless, in order to escape the threat of Poland, they had preferred to be sterilized. For men who had already given up married life in the true sense owing to impotence, the choice given them by the Germans was not a particularly difficult one, but for young men in the full prime of life it was horrible. They have fallen into the clutches of Moloch, who will not let them go. . . .

Sunday, June 13th: The sterilization problem has entered a new phase; a member of the Jewish Council went along the beds this morning to bring a message from the Commandant to Jews married to Aryan wives and having no children, asking if they were prepared to let themselves be sterilized *voluntarily.* A kind way of putting it! The messenger forgot to mention that anyone who was not voluntarily prepared to do so exposed himself to the danger of deportation to Poland, like those from mixed marriages with children. But he did add that those who were prepared to submit to the operation had to sign a contract — the *voluntary* nature of this business had to be clearly laid down — for the benefit of history.

For many the problem is a hard one. Opposite me are two men who had contracted mixed marriages, one of them with and the other without children, the first an Austrian of about sixty and the other an Amsterdammer in his thirties. The first man made up his mind. "I'll let myself be sterilized. I have lived my life," he reasoned with himself, "and I can't give my wife any children now. So why not?" Later he reconsidered his decision. "Until now," he argued, "sterilization has only been carried out sporadically on mental defectives to prevent them from reproducing themselves, but it hasn't yet been done on healthy individuals. It's not known whether an operation of this kind will cause mental illness later on." So he refused and accepted the possible consequence of his refusal — Poland. The other argued: "I know that sterilization is contrary to nature and ethically wrong, but I'll get it done all the same and return to Mokum (Amsterdam). My wife mustn't do work that I could be doing. I must support her."

The problem varies according to the individual. In all the huts there are serious discussions about what ought to be done; the young men and women in particular are faced with a dilemma. They feel they are between the devil and the deep blue sea. One is just as bad as the other, whichever they choose. Opinions are even divided among the doctors. They naturally agree that sterilization may produce unpleasant psychological reactions, but I have heard the view stated that anyone who allows himself to be sterilized is not entirely finished. After the war medical science will certainly find a means of undoing sterilization. But about one thing there is complete agreement: this measure marks the very peak of barbarity. Hitler has declared more than once that God gives His blessing to what he does. Of course he does not know what blasphemy means.

Tuesday, June 15th: The partners of mixed marriages have been told that they can postpone their decision about sterilization until next Thursday. Before then two Jewish doctors will explain to them the significance and consequences of sterilization. Yesterday a typed notice to that effect was put up in the vestibule of the Registration Hall, where the symphony orchestra gave its third concert before a packed audience. [. . .]

Wednesday, June 16th: A storm of criticism and indignation descended this morning after breakfast upon the young man who had decided to let himself be sterilized. "You're a coward!" "You've no strength of character." "No proper man would do that." "You just wait till you're faced with it yourself! I'm doing it for my wife." "Your wife shouldn't want that. Perhaps she doesn't. What a joke — a sterilized man!" "Do you know for sure that you won't be sterilized as soon as you get to Poland? I don't. Better have it done right away here. And stay with my wife." "You should just wait and see what happens in Poland. And what does it matter if your wife does have to earn her own living? There are others doing the very same thing." "The fact of the matter is that you have no strength of character. And the awful thing is that Jews in general don't have a very strong character. It's a pity, but it's true." "You don't say so!" "Oh yes. Forty years ago the Zionists warned the Jews in Europe. But nobody would listen. They were too well off in western Europe." "You could go right back to Egypt." "The great mistake is that the Jews have not learnt to think historically." "Just you try and teach the masses to think historically. Have you ever found the masses wanting to think? First of all, they must want to think. You should take a look and see what the masses think about here. They certainly do have problems to think about, problems of their own. They think about salt meat sandwiches and loaves and *hallah kugel* with pears on Friday nights. But as for spiritual and moral problems — well, I ask you!" "Don't Christians eat salt meat sandwiches?" "Of course they do. But the Jews are beastly materialists. Instead of taking the situation as it is and accepting the fact that there are no tasty morsels for them to eat and that they should toughen themselves up in preparation for the future, they think of their stomachs and their strolls along the Kalverstraat and dates with the 'birds.' They ought to make sure they have something in their knapsacks and see that they train the young people for the work they have to do. The young people represent the future." "Exactly. And isn't that just what the Zionists do? Don't they try to reach the young people and prepare them for the future?" "That is the very best thing they could do. But as for the masses — they've had it so good and they've led such happy-go-lucky lives, with the cinema, the radio, motor bikes, all the gifts of technical knowhow. But all these things aren't exactly calculated to strengthen the character, which is what a people needs. The moral ingredient is lacking." "Gentlemen, please be a bit quieter. This is a hospital ward." "Just so — the moral ingredient is lacking. And, if you thought along moral lines, you wouldn't allow yourself to be sterilized, I'm telling you. You're a coward." "Well, so I'm a coward. But you'll pipe another tune one day." "Perhaps. But you're running away before you smell danger. You're acting as if you've lost the war. And I'd like to see *that* happen!" "Quiet!" bellowed the nurse. "The doctor is coming on his rounds." The discussion was broken off.

From *Year of Fear* by Philip Mechanicus, New York: Hawthorne Books, 1964, pp. 44-46, 48.

BABIES AND PREGNANT MOTHERS KILLED

The author was the wife of a surgeon and gynecologist who directed a hospital in Cluj (better known as Klausenburg), Rumania.

The most poignant problem that faced us in caring for our companions was that of the accouchements [childbirths]. As soon as a baby was delivered at the infirmary, mother and child were both sent to the gas chamber. That was the unrelenting decision of our masters. Only when the infant was not likely to survive or when it was stillborn was the mother ever spared and allowed to return to her barrack. The conclusion we drew from this was simple: the Germans did not want the newborn to live; if they did, the mothers, too, must die.

The five whose responsibility it was to bring these infants into the world — the world of Birkenau-Auschwitz — felt the burden of this monstrous conclusion, which defied all human and moral law. That it was also nonsensical from a medical point of view did not matter for the moment. How many sleepless nights we spent turning this tragic dilemma over in our minds. And in the morning the mothers and their babies both went to their deaths.

One day we decided we had been weak long enough. We must at least save the mothers. To carry out our plan, we would have to make the infants pass for stillborn. Even so, many precautions must be taken, for if the Germans were ever to suspect it, we, too, would be sent to the gas chambers — and probably to the torture chamber first.

Now, when we were notified that a woman's labor pains had started during the day, we did not take the patient to the infirmary. We stretched her out on a blanket in the barrack, in the presence of her neighbors.

When the pains began during the night we ventured to take the woman to the infirmary, for at least in the dark we might proceed comparatively unobserved. In the koia [bunk] we could hardly make a decent examination. In the infirmary we had our examination table. Still we lacked antisepsis, and the danger of infection was enormous, for this was the same room in which we treated purulent wounds!

Unfortunately, the fate of the baby always had to be the same. After taking every precaution, we pinched and closed the little tyke's nostrils and when it opened its mouth to breathe, we gave it a dose of a lethal product. An injection might have been quicker, but that would have left a trace and we dared not let the Germans suspect the truth.

We placed the dead infant in the same box which had brought it from the barrack, if the accouchement had taken place there. As far as the camp administration was concerned, this was a stillbirth.

And so, the Germans succeeded in making murderers of even us. To this day the picture of those murdered babies haunts me. Our own children had perished in the gas chambers and were cremated in the Birkenau ovens, and we dispatched the lives of others before their first voices had left their tiny lungs. Often I sit and think what kind of fate would these little creatures, snuffed out on the threshold of life, have had? Who knows? Perhaps we killed a Pasteur, a Mozart, an Einstein. Even had those infants been destined to uneventful lives, our crimes were no less terrible. The only meager consolation is that by these murders we saved the mothers. Without our intervention they would have endured worse sufferings, for they would have been thrown into the crematory ovens while still alive.

Yet I try in vain to make my conscience acquit me. I still see the infants issuing from their mothers. I can feel their warm little bodies as I held them. I marvel to what depths these Germans made us descend!

Our masters did not wait for births to take action against fertility in Auschwitz. Intermittently — for all their measures, without exception, were in-

termittent and subject to capricious change — they sent all pregnant women to
the gas chamber.

Generally, pregnant women who came in the Jewish transports were immediately ordered to the left when they arrived at the station. The women
usually wore several layers of clothing, one on top of the other, which they
hoped to keep. So even obvious cases of pregnancy were difficult to discover
before the deportees were made to shed their apparel. Besides, they could not
count on the preliminary control to catch the very early pregnancies.

Even inside the camp it was not easy to determine which women were in the
family way. For the word went around that it was extremely dangerous to be
found pregnant. Those who arrived in this condition, therefore, hid themselves
when they could and, to this end, had the active cooperation of their neighbors.

Incredible as it may seem, some succeeded in concealing their conditions to
the last moment, and the deliveries took place secretly in the barracks. I shall
never, as long as I live, forget the morning when, during roll call, in the midst of
the deathlike silence among the thousands of deportees, a piercing cry rose. A
woman had unexpectedly been seized with her first labor pains. It is not
necessary to describe what happened to this poor soul.

It was not long before the Germans noticed that in the successive trains of
deportees an extraordinarily low percentage of pregnancies was reported. They
decided to take more energetic measures; one could always depend upon them
for that.

The barrack doctors, whose duty it was to report pregnant women, received
rigorous orders. Nevertheless, I more than once saw the doctors defy every
danger and certify that a woman was not pregnant when they positively knew
that she was. Dr. G. stood up to the infamous Dr. Mengele, medical director of
the camp, and denied every case of pregnancy that could possibly be contested.
Later, the camp infirmary somehow secured a pharmaceutical product which,
through injection, brought about premature births. What could we do? Wherever possible, the doctors resorted to this procedure, which was certainly the
lesser horror for the mother.

Still, the number of pregnancies remained unbelievably low, and the Germans resorted to their usual trickery. They announced that pregnant women,
even such Jewesses as were still alive, would be treated with special regard.
They would be allowed to remain away from roll call, to receive a larger ration
of bread and soup, and be permitted to sleep in a special barrack. Finally, the
promise was made that they would be transferred to a hospital as soon as their
time came. "The camp is not a maternity ward," proclaimed Dr. Mengele.
This tragically true statement appeared to offer great hopes to many of the
unfortunate women.

Why should anyone here believe anything the Germans said? First, because
many never saw the final horrors until it was too late for them to communicate
the truth to their neighbors. Second, because no human being could fathom the
ends of which they were capable, which they plotted daily, and which were part
of their master plan for world conquest.

From *Five Chimneys – Story of Auschwitz,* by Olga Lengiel, Chicago: Ziff
Davis, 1947, pp. 99-102.

THE FATE OF JEANETTE'S TWINS

Foremost among the Nazi angels of death was Dr. Josef Mengele, who concentrated on murdering Jews en masse. It is estimated that between 1943 and 1945 he liquidated 380,000 Jews. He presumed himself to be a "racial biologist" and hoped to discover the genetic secrets to help breed Aryan supermen. He experimented with sets of twins in an effort to produce large numbers of children for the Vaterland through multiple births. The story below addresses one incident of this nature. (Mengele is still free after 36 years of concentrated, relentless pursuit.)

Jeanette lived in Block 20 of the concentration camp at Auschwitz. This block which was like a stable was the so-called "maternity block," where Polish, Ukranian, Greek and Yugoslav women prisoners delivered their babies. There, too, the few Jewish women, who miraculously were still alive at the time the Nazi chief doctor's order extended the privilege of birth to them, delivered their babies.

Jeanette was French and a Parisian but she was very ugly. The city steeped in coquettish and harmonious beauty had obviously left no effect on her; she remained ugly. Her features were hard and masculine, and her quarrelsome personality was emphasized by the harsh sandpaper quality of her voice. She seemed to forget that she was surrounded by the constantly burning furnaces where death raged day and night, and she was unaware of the grotesque game being enacted in Block 20 by the perverse Nazi doctor. She considered her pregnancy as something very important and acted as though she were waiting to give birth in some private, elegant clinic in Paris. Each day was marked by new demands and increasing dissatisfaction; promises could hardly keep her comforted. No one liked her, no one understood her language, and the more she tried to impress her fellow-prisoners with her own extraordinary importance and that of her pregnancy, the more the others despised her.

But soon it was necessary to give Jeanette all the attention she craved — her labor-pains had started. She was not young any more. The tenseness of her abdomen and the intensity of her pains were not normal. In Auschwitz, delivery had to proceed quietly. Here any degree of suffering did not count, any body condition did not matter. But Jeanette's screams pervaded the camp: "Mon Dieu! Mon Dieu!" she cried, unmindful of her incongruous surroundings.

It was an abnormal birth — she gave birth to twins. We had to report this to the chief Nazi doctor. Dr. Mengele was on the spot, in the cell ironically named "delivery-room." "Twins! Twins!" he shouted, and this magic word and all its implications reduced him to frantic, maniacal excitement. He paced back and forth in the narrow cell, and muttered repeatedly: "At last! The first twins are about to be born here!" And this sadist who seemed to have no other emotions at all, now completely lost his self-control.

Dr. Mengele was not only the chief of the crematory but also its scientist. His hobby was twins. Skillful doctors did research under his order and control, to explain this secret of Nature: twins. His ambition was to multiply the *Herrenvolk* and to give to the German people the greatest manpower through twins. He performed the most execrable research on adult twins, and now he had the source of the secret — the newborn twins. He acted like a scientist who, after much tiring and exhausting research, had at last reached his goal and had discovered the heretofore hidden approach to the secret.

Ugly Jeanette became really important in Block 20, and Dr. Mengele seemed to be very polite and thankful to the mother of the twins. He provided a basket for the twins; they received baby shirts; they were even given a blanket to cover their frail bodies. (In Auschwitz the newborn were clad only in dirty rags.) Jeanette lay alone on her stretcher, which even had a white sheet, and boasted of her achievement.

But the next day two sinister-looking S.S. men appeared in the block. "The twins, where are the twins?" they shouted, and took them away.

Jeanette fought like a lioness, talked incoherently and bemoaned her children. We tried to console her by saying that perhaps the twins were only to be examined, and that surely they would be returned. The entire maternity ward waited anxiously for the return of the twins. It was night when they were brought back. And thus from day to day, the French twins were taken away every morning and carried to a special laboratory where Dr. Mengele performed his satanic research on them. During these hours Jeanette cried as only a mother can cry when her children are in great danger.

For fourteen days this torture of the mother's heart continued. And then one morning we found one of the twins dead — it had died, unable to endure life as a laboratory animal for Dr. Mengele. A few days later, the other little Frenchman followed his brother — he couldn't endure the life of a guinea pig either. And Jeanette in vain filled the camp of Auschwitz with her cries: *"Mes enfants! Mes enfants!"*

Jeanette was no longer important. And when Dr. Mengele appeared again and found that the twins had died, he became furious, and laughingly threw Jeanette into the crematory.

From *I Was a Doctor in Auschwitz* by Giselle Perl, New York: International Universities Press, 1948, pp. 124-127.

LEO BAECK PREVENTS AN ABORTION

Theresienstadt (originally Terezin) was built as a fortress by an Austrian emperor over two centuries ago. It was situated 60 miles from Prague and was built to house at most 10,000 inhabitants. During the Holocaust years, 60,000 and more were crowded into it; 15,000 of them were children, of whom only 100 survived. It was frequently disguised as a model camp for exhibit to visitors from Red Cross committees and foreign observers.

One of its prisoners, Rabbi Leo Baeck, had been the spiritual leader of German Reform Jewry. He was an illustrious rabbi, theologian, teacher, author, and a distinguished community figure. During the Nazi period he was elected head of the Representative Body of German Jewry and remained at this post until its liquidation.

Deported to Theresienstadt, he was recognized by all the inmates as their heroic spokesman and fountainhead of their will to survive. Liberated in 1945, he settled in London and was acknowledged as the spiritual head of liberal Judaism in the world. In New York City, the Leo Baeck Institute is a repository of German Jewish cultural achievements and a source of transmission of the Jewish heritage. To perpetuate his name, the Institute publishes an Annual which includes collections of learned articles. His name lives on through his books and immortal deeds.

The Nazis decreed that childbirth in the ghetto must end — "You are reminded, with all forcefulness, that women who find themselves pregnant or believe themselves, due to existing conditions, to be pregnant, are obliged to report immediately to a gynecologist at the proper health center." An American government report about Theresienstadt after the war said that a "tragic fact" was that no children were born at Theresienstadt. That was inaccurate; a small number of babies were born in the ghetto, at least in its early years — according to one history, 207 children were born there. It is true, however, that the Nazis demanded that pregnant women have abortions; giving birth in the later years of the ghetto, if the Nazis found out about it, could be cause for deportation to the east.

Leo Baeck had some young friends, Willi Groag and his wife, who was pregnant and hoped to have her child. Frau Groag worked in a section dealing with agricultural products and turned for help to her supervisor there, a non-Jew, who had been friendly toward her and Willi. He refused to intercede with the German authorities, explaining that his position was not high enough for him to be influential, and suggested she go to a member of the Jewish Council of Elders.

"What can I do?" said this Jewish official. "I'm under pressure from the Germans."

When Frau Groag was seven months pregnant, she was called before a health division official. Her pregnancy was evident, and she was informed that she must have an abortion. She refused and heard nothing about it for another month. Suddenly she was directed to the health clinic, and her husband Willi was called before the same Jewish official of the Council of Elders who earlier had refused to help his wife.

"You should know," said the official, "at this moment your wife is in the clinic, and they will perform an abortion on her."

"I understand that you want to shock me, but I believe that I can call on your humanity to prevent this abortion in the eighth or ninth month. It would kill my wife."

"I cannot go with that to the Germans. It is an unfortunate thing. Briefly, you must give your consent to it."

Rather than give his consent to the killing of his wife, Willi Groag went to the clinic and brought her back to tpe barracks. They would face the consequences together of wanting their child and defying the Nazi restrictions.

Leo Baeck always had been fond of the young couple. He had assured Frau Groag that the child would be born on the Sabbath. "You will have a *Sabbath-*

kind," he told her. When he heard of their plight, he was not a member of the Council of Elders. He was a "prominent," however, and not afraid of placing his prestige and position on the line in a confrontation with the Nazis so that the child could be born without fear of retaliation.

The boy was born at approximately four o'clock on a Friday afternoon, shortly before the Sabbath was to begin at sundown. A few days later, when Frau Groag could walk, Willi took her to see Leo Baeck. "I checked when the Sabbath actually had arrived, and it was at five o'clock," said Groag. "So I said to Dr. Baeck: 'Everything is fine except that you have not proved yourself as a prophet.' " Leo Baeck turned to Frau Groag and replied, "I am truly sorry for that, I have underestimated your ability."

From *Days of Sorrow and Pain: Leo Baeck and the Berlin Jews* by Leonard Baker, New York: Macmillan, 1978, pp. 292-294.

4.

CHILDREN IN THE NAZI GHETTO

The first war bombs dropped by the Nazi warplanes on September 1, 1939, hit, among other targets, the children's institutions near Warsaw. On September 8, Warsaw, the greatest center of world Jewry, surrendered. Terror and panic ensued. Jews were ordered to wear an armband, the Star of David, for identification. As the days progressed, their persecution was intensified. The first victims, who were liquidated, were the Jewish intellectuals, professionals, and public figures. In November 1940, the ghetto walls were erected and the Jews were segregated and shut in the ghetto, where they lived under intolerable conditions. The situation of the children was bound up with the fate of the entire ghetto. A carefully planned policy for starving the Jewish population was instituted; they were allowed 180 grams of dry bread or about a quarter of a pound (a pound has 453.59 grams) per day, and 220 grams of sugar per month. As a result, the constant hunger and vitamin deficiency led to tuberculosis and scurvy. Death began taking a toll of 7000 per month. The number of orphans grew steadily.

The ghetto was but a respite, a temporary suspension in the annihilation program. As the months progressed, the noose became tighter. In fact, the reprieve from total destruction lasted but a little more than two years. Ultimately starvation took its toll. No one, including those favored by the Germans, escaped their predetermined plan – total extinction. In these indescribable circumstances the fate of the children is self-evident.

One of the ghetto inmates describes the children's condition during the early years of the ghetto existence: ''Their poor little bodies are frightfully thin, the bones stick out of a yellow skin that looks like parchment. They crawl on all

45

fours, groaning; they have nothing human about them; they are more like monkeys than children.'' [1]

The ghetto, like the concentration camp, was a preparatory step, an integral part of the overall plan to ''solve'' the ''Jewish problem.'' It was more autonomous and its life was more diversified than in the concentration camp, but its final intention was the same: the liquidation of the Jews. Indeed, as the end of the ghetto loomed near, it began to look and feel more like a typical concentration camp.

A MEMORIAL TO A THREE-YEAR-OLD

A man with an unflagging mission was Eliezer Yerushalmi of Shavli in Lithuania, who wrote the following tragic chronicle. He was the director of a clandestine Jewish school which was scattered in different hiding places and included as many as five hundred pupils. He collected documents for the archives relating to the ghetto. He kept a detailed diary, mostly in Yiddish, from June 27, 1941, to February 2, 1944. In it he recorded all that went on in the ghetto; it included diverse documents in German and Yiddish. (His diary was the first book of its kind to be published in the Yad Vashem series.) When seven hundred children of Shavli were deported to the extermination camps, he immortalized a number of them in a book entitled Children of the Holocaust. *It contains verbal portraits of Jewish children in Shavli. One of the most moving stories is about Meierl.*

The life of this child was short — only three years, five months, and five days. But this brief span was filled with suffering and agony.

When he was a year and a half his father, together with hundreds of other Jews, was thrown into prison, and never came home again. In the ghetto his mother left him by himself, because every morning, before sunrise, she had to hurry to work in the factory. He remained alone in the house, watched over by a bedridden neighbor who could not give him any help. From the first day, he had to stand on his own feet and learn to take care of himself. He adapted himself very easily to this existence. He quickly learned to wash and dress himself and keep his scanty possessions in order. He knew how to take the few morsels his mother left for him, and learned how to get food when she had nothing to leave him.

He knew the exact hour of the neighbors' mealtimes, and when hunger tormented him, he appeared at their tables and stood watching. He did not ask for food, he said very little; he did not stretch out his skinny arms for bread — but his huge, hungry eyes gazed at their plates and followed every spoonful they raised to their mouths. Naturally, the people took pity on him and shared with him their meager rations.

He performed tricks with knives and forks. He knew that everyone at the

[1]Mary Bert, *Warsaw Diary*, New York: L.B. Fischer, 1945.

table smiled when they watched him, and used this to get another morsel. He did his tricks with a serious face, and did not allow the laughter of his hosts to alter his expression.

When he wanted fresh vegetables, he simply went into the vegetable garden and took a radish from here, a carrot from there, or broke off a piece of cauliflower and ate it raw. But when the sun began to sink in the west and the hour approached when the Forced Labor Brigade returned to the ghetto, he went with the grownups to the ghetto gate to wait for his mother. She was a small, thin woman, and next to her Meierl felt masculine and protective. Proudly he put his small arm in hers and led her home. His entire being, and all his actions, radiated serenity. He talked very little. Many people in the ghetto had never even heard his voice; in fact there were some who thought he was a mute. Only his closest neighbors sometimes heard him speak and admired the clear, short, but logical sentences with which he came to an understanding with his environment.

On the day of the "Children's Action" he hid himself even more carefully than usual. He climbed into his sick neighbor's bed and kept quiet as a mouse, without moving a muscle. He did not even lose his control when the Ukrainians, assisting the SS, made a house search.

The Ukrainians found him, but the sick old woman ransomed him with a gold watch. As soon as the hoodlums were outside, they sent in a second group, who knew about Meierl. But she did not have another watch, so the boy was seized and taken to the children's collection point.

I saw him during these final moments. He skipped between the two soldiers, trying to keep up with their stride. From time to time he raised his large, questioning eyes to them, as though asking: "Why all this?" Although the soldiers were drunk, those innocent child's eyes sobered them and slowed their steps. In one of them a human emotion flickered and he said to his companion: "He's a Jew, but still he's a child." He looked at Meierl sympathetically, took his hand and lifted him into the wagon among the desperately sobbing sacrifices. Meierl seemed calm. He stood quietly among the crying children and looked around with his large, naive eyes, until the cart started to move.

From *An Anthology of Holocaust Literature,* edited by Jacob Glatstein, Israel Knox, and Samuel Margoshes. New York: Jewish Publication Society of America, 1969, pp.116f. Trans. from the Hebrew of Eliezer Yerushalmi by Adah Fogel.

FAMILIES IN BUNKERS

Born in Lithuania, Dr. Aharon Peretz, his wife and son were imprisoned in Vilna, where he had served as a gynecologist in the ghetto hospital.

Dr. Peretz recorded what he saw around him, as well as his exile and wanderings, in a number of books which he wrote. A very touching story is the reunion of the Peretz family in Israel. His son had been saved by the Lithuanian Communist army, his wife by the British, and Dr. Peretz by the Americans.

The scenes that occurred at the railroad station when the children were torn from their parents, the wailing of the mothers, and the atrocities that were committed have already been depicted in various writings about the Holocaust. The dangers that lurked in the ghetto were formidable. Incidents of stealing children out over the wall and handing them over to non-Jews were increasing. Mothers gathered at the ghetto gates to buy sleeping pills for their children before their transportation to the unknown. A child who had received an injection of Luminal[1] was found dead after he was taken out of the knapsack. Children, aged three or four, sensed what was happening and begged that they be handed over to their "new" parents without drugs, promising that they would not cry. Very often I was astounded at the precociousness of tots who were fully aware of the dangers that awaited them. Occasionally I overheard their conversations, which pierced my heart.

I often observed the children's games in the courtyards. They would enact an "action," dividing their roles as Jews and Germans. The "Germans" shrieked and bellowed, dissembling as brutes and abusing the "Jew." At times they selected one of them to play Hitler, whom they imprisoned in a pit and covered partially with earth. Occasionally they played "labor brigades." The unspeakable Jewish tragedy was reflected in the children's games.

My son is pondering over ways to hide in time of peril. He does not want to leave us and we are rather glad at his light-minded resolve. . . .

The ghetto dwellers began to dig hiding places in the cellars of their homes. Like worms they sought to burrow into the depths of the earth to find shelter. A new vocation came into being — digging bunkers, or "malines," as they were known. Stories circulated about bunkers that were outfitted with comforts, well disguised and stocked with a supply of food and water to last a long period of time. . . .

March 1944. Spring was near. The ghetto is stirred up by the reports circulating about the German defeats on the war fronts. . . . The denizens are enlivened; hopefully every passing day brings Hitler's end nearer. The "strategists" among us crowd around the maps, arguing and forecasting the day of salvation.

The food problem is lessening simply because people have adjusted to being hungry. Life pulsates strongly behind the barbed wire.

Ghetto denizens eke out a living from barter and trade. Their source of income is from the sale of clothing, which, at the risk of life and limb, is sold to the peasants over the wall or bartered for food. Another source is the cutting up of bedsheets into kerchiefs, which are sold to peasant women. Artists paint flowers on these cuttings and sell them. In addition there develops the craft of producing soap, candles, and other products. . . . And there are some who deal in precious stones and gold, which had been skillfully hidden for sale in time of need.

March 27, 1944. I am getting ready to go to the hospital as usual, when a neighbor rushes in, panic-stricken, shouting, "Doctor, the guards have closed off the ghetto. Trucks are drawn up at the gates. The children!!!"

---

[1] A sedative.

We peer through the lattice and see an armored car, from which a shrill loudspeaker pierces the air: "Attention! Attention! Anyone who goes outside will be shot!" The announcement is repeated monotonously without stop, filling the air with deathly terror. The voice still knifes through the air when a battalion of the SS fan out and break into the houses. . . .

In a matter of minutes they are at our door. Suddenly a voice is heard, "Hide the children."

From all the rooms mothers burst out in a flurry with children at their heels and in their arms. My wife, her eyes gaping in terror, grabs our son in her arms and runs downstairs to the cellar. A closet covered with planks conceals the door to the bunker. We pry it open and begin to crawl into the dark "malina." I creep in last, with a full syringe in my hand, and seal the entrance.

All the inmates are sprawled on the cold floor, their children cleaving to them. With bated breath we strain to hear every whisper outside.

A woman's voice cleaves the air, "My child." It is followed by the heart-rending cry of another woman imploring the Germans to leave her only child with her. Her sobbing breaks our hearts. Our son presses himself deeper into our bodies. From the depths of our cellar we are witness to the tragic frenzy outside.

The little ones begin to manifest disturbing reactions, and I begin to inject them with sedatives. . . . A four-year-old will not quiet down and when he begins to cry his parents press his face down into a pillow. A coarse person threatens to choke him. The woman crawls over to me and implores that I give him a second shot. "Better," she says, "that he die from an injection than at the hands of the murderers." The danger to the lives of the other children is grave. So I give him another injection and he falls asleep.

From the porch above we hear the echo of heavy boots pursuing someone. Then a shriek, "Mother," sends a shudder to our marrow like an electric shock. My son thrusts himself deeper into me, whispering, "Abba, we're lost." I feel his heart pounding and the throb of fear pulsating in him.

A deep silence follows the cry from above. In the cellar the cry is frozen, reverberating in our ears and gripping our hearts with clamps of steel.

The nightmarish hours are continuing. Our eyes cannot penetrate the darkness. . . . We are awaiting a sign from above that the danger is past. The sounds are growing weaker and draw further away. We begin whispering to each other and start feeding the children quietly. . . .

A neighbor who has remained above knocks noiselessly to inform us that we may emerge. The electric lights blind our eyes. The little ones recover from their sedatives, and stagger about like drunkards. Later we learned of the day's fearful happenings: 1,500 children and adults were carted away by the Germans. Mothers were forced to deliver their children to the trucks. Those who tarried or begged to join their little ones were lashed and beaten. Trained hounds were incited to attack the struggling mothers and tore away at their clothes. One of the mothers who gripped the side of the lorry and refused to budge was shot dead. Her child saw his mother killed and sobbed pitifully. Radios blared, drowning out the cries of the children. The trucks returned after they had unloaded the victims and took on new loads. Grandmothers joined their grandchildren. . . . My son's playmate was torn from his mother's arms. All this happened quickly, in a matter of minutes.

Special trucks loaded the sick from the hospital's children's ward and from the orphan asylums. Some plucky youngsters saved their lives, for the moment, by hiding in the beds of the adults, the hospital cellar, or nearby homes. . . .

Once out of the bunker, our son's spirits recovered quickly and he began to plan safer hiding places. He wiggled into a clothing cupboard storage box and asked that we lower the lid. He wanted to test whether he could breathe inside it. He repeated the same in a clothes closet. We were too weak to respond; our nerves were shattered. Fear of tomorrow was gnawing away at our vitals. We put him to sleep. . . .

March 28, 1944. We anticipate another ''action.'' The Gestapo knew the number of children imprisoned in the ghetto and were aware that several hundred had slipped through their fingers. With the aid of informers, they determined to liquidate the remnant.

The streets were crowded. No one reported for work. Every car that passed aroused waves of panic. Fathers and mothers who had lost their young sat listless and desolate. Suddenly the masses of people in the street scattered as if a bomb had exploded. Down the street came marching Ukrainian gendarmes.

This time I determined not to hide but remain above ground. Mothers brought me their children, one after another, to an opening in the bunker for injections of Luminal. I did not see the faces of the little ones, only their buttocks, which were bared through a tiny slit of the bunker.

A little while passes, and the Nazi officers, accompanied by armed Ukrainians, are marshaling victims to their doom. . . .

The scenes that I witnessed I shall never forget. . . . A mother walks with her three children. The murderers separate the children from her. She beseeches the German overseer to leave her one child. He consents. She climbs up the lorry, and her children clutch her arms and legs. She stands bewildered, half crazed. It is evident that she is experiencing excruciating agonies. Finally she walks down alone.

From a nearby house a number of people are led out. Suddenly a little boy, about four years old, rushes out, shouting, ''What about me?'' His mother suddenly turns, uttering a cry that pierces the heavens. She falls to the ground in a dead faint.

The lorries, packed with children, left under heavy guard, as if they were transporting dangerous criminals. For some fortuitous reason our building was overlooked. I signal the bunker that we are safe for the time being.

I make a quick visit to the hospital. Soon an automobile nears the hospital. Gestapo officers step out, and one asks to see the director. He tells the director that he has heard about children hiding in the hospital. He threatens that if we do not deliver the children in half an hour they will take captive all staff members. Panic seizes all personnel because many children lie hidden and if the Gestapo should institute a search they would find them.

We gathered in the operating rooms and began our deliberations. Many of us felt that our fate would be no better than the children's. How can we live with ourselves if we buy our lives at the expense of the children? But there were some who cried hysterically, ''We want to live.''

A number of hidden children emerged, some with their mothers, and surrendered. A number hid themselves in the contagious wards, from which the Germans steered clear. For these children we hastily drew predated documents stating that they were contagious cases. A German hospital orderly, whom we bribed, helped us. He reported to the SS officers that there were no more children in hiding.

I go to the window and focus my eyes on our house. I see a couple approaching, an SS man in shiny boots and a Ukrainian soldier whose eyes are ablaze as he holds a large ax in his hand. My body is convulsed in a violent fit. I am glued to the window and strain to get hold of myself. I hear the sharp blows of his ax on the walls and windows. A cold sweat covers me, and my hair stands on end. I bite my nails. Soon they will find my wife and son. What shall I do? Join them or swallow the poison capsule that I always carry with me?

Seconds seem like years. Soon the hacking stops. My heart is still pounding. I see two little brothers walking toward the car, followed by a soldier armed to the teeth. The younger child trips and falls; the older helps him get up, and they continue their walk. This sight breaks me up — it was a normal action in ordinary times, but what a noble and heroic gesture! I sob and tremble and tear through the empty wards, hurling myself from one bed to another. . . .

When I became calm I went down to the bunker to see what had happened. The bunker held tight. Fortunately the drugged children were not awakened. The adults held their breath and were motionless throughout the ordeal.

On the morrow, when the immediate danger had passed, the bereaved mothers began to tear their hair, beat their heads on the walls, sobbing and wailing, ''God grant the children were not tortured, that they have already found their eternal rest.''

In the days that followed, bereaved mothers of children whom I had brought into the world met me and with heartrending sighs talked about their children. ''How beautiful, wise and good he [she] was! How can I go on living? What's the point of our agonies?'' And as for the children who remained alive, they were simply nonexistent; they were in perpetual danger of discovery. They were not on the food-rationing list and subsisted on a minimum allowance from the piddling rations of others.

Parents who had refused to part from their children sought in every possible way to sneak their children to the Aryan side. . . .

My son sat imprisoned in his room, looking out stealthily through the window. When he saw a man in uniform he scurried to hide. . . . We had already decided to find shelter for him on the Aryan side. He was willing but implored us to go with him. He did not want to live without father and mother near him.

A woman who had been his governess learned of the atrocities that were happening in the ghetto and offered to take him to her village home. But how to smuggle him across the fence? Three-year-olds could be concealed in knapsacks; our son was eight. Day after day she would wait as the Jewish labor battalions marched to their appointed tasks outside. Alas, each time she returned empty-handed. Five times we woke our son at the break of dawn, dressed him in work clothes, and, with our eyes pouring tears, tried to smuggle him across without success. . . . One morning he and I crowded into the workers' lines. Instinctively he grasped my arm, but I urged him to walk alone. His cap was pushed down well over his forehead, and I assured him that I would be at his side. Mother remained in the ghetto, her heart in her mouth, waiting, waiting for news from the other side.

We passed the guard, hastened to the river, and jumped into the waiting rowboat. I tore off the yellow star from his coat. At the other end his governess awaited us. Without a good-bye kiss I parted from him hastily, urging him to remain a Jew and, if he did not find us when it was all over, to avenge our blood.

The memory of his face, bathed in tears, pursued me for two long years in the concentration camps. When I lay sleepless on the boards of my cot, I saw him as he was reeling away from me in a stupor. And his tearful image was etched deep in my mind.

When I returned from the river, I found my wife in the cemetery, praying over the graves of her forebears, her eyes swollen from weeping. At the silent graves our deep-felt suffering was somewhat lightened. In our hearts we felt as if heavy stones had been lifted. Come what may to us, it was good to know that our son was beyond the barbed wires of the ghetto prison.

A.E.

From *Bamachnot LoBachu* (In the Camps They Did Not Weep) by Dr. Aharon Peretz, Massada Press, Ramat Gan, Israel, 1960, pp. 49-63.

LIVE GAME

Moshe Prager, who translated this story from the Polish, was a native of Warsaw and scion of the Gerre Rebbe's illustrious family, a leading Hasidic dynasty of many generations. During the Holocaust, Prager risked his life to send out reports about the tragedy to the world Jewish press. After the war he rose to great heights as the portrayer of the spiritual resistance of religious Jewry. He settled in the Orthodox community of Bnai Brak in Israel, where he is a prominent leader. He is an author, publicist, and journalist on the Holocaust, the underground movement, the postwar period, and the exploits of the Haganah. One of his books, written about youth for youth, is a collection of stories known as Sparks of Glory *and has been translated and published in English.*

In 1929, lawyer Hans Frank (1900–1946) joined the Nazi Party. In 1934 he became Reich Minister and Law Leader, and five years later he was appointed Governor General of Poland. He kept a diary which comprised forty-two large volumes. It was introduced as evidence against him at the Nuremberg Trials. During these trials, he became penitent, a devout convert to Catholicism. Ridden with guilt, he confessed readily to having committed the crimes which were charged against him by the prosecution.

His diary revealed with devastating frankness the incredible reign of terror during his regime. One of his entries read: "My attitude toward the Jews will be based only on the expectation that they must disappear. They must be done away with." Frank was sentenced to be hanged.

An Italian Army captain, who had served as attaché to the German occupation army in Poland, published his memoirs in a bulletin issued by the Polish Army in Italy named *Bialy Orzel* (The White Eagle). One of his articles describes the shooting of a Jewish child by Hans Frank:

"I was present at the Hotel Belvedere in Warsaw, in the same room where Marshal Josef Pilsudski [dictator of Poland in the 1920s] died. Present were the champion boxer Max Schmeling, Governor General Frank, and his wife, Brigette.

"We left the Belvedere in two cars. I sat with Hans Frank, Mesdames Fisher and Werther. In the second car sat General Fisher, Max Schmeling, and Mrs. Frank. We passed through several streets [mentioned by name]. Near the entrance to the Jewish ghetto, which was surrounded by a high stone wall, we parked our cars and went for a walk.

'Look well at this wall,' Frank said to me. 'Does it look like the horrendous wall ringed with machine guns which the American and British journalists have described?' And he added, grinning, "The poor unfortunate Jews suffer from tuberculosis. This wall at least shields their sick lungs from the cold winds.'

"To my ears Frank's arrogant voice sounded cynical and brutal. I replied, 'As I see it, the absurdity of this wall barrier is not so much that it prevents Jews from leaving the ghetto as that it restricts them from entering it.'

"The Governor General replied with a chuckle, 'Despite the death penalty to anyone who is caught leaving or entering the ghetto, the Jews manage to go in and out.'

" 'How?' I retorted. 'Do they leap over the wall?'

" 'No,' he answered, 'they burrow their way through holes under the wall like mice. In the dark of the night they dig openings under the wall, and during the day they cover them with dirt and leaves. In the dark they pass through to the Aryan side and buy all they can in the black market. Most of the merchandise in the ghetto is brought in through the holes by these "rats." Every now and then we lay a trap to catch them. Most of them are eight-to-ten-year-old children. We play a game of hide-and-seek with them. It's a game much like cricket.'

" 'You call it cricket?' I asked in astonishment.

" 'Certainly. Every game has its own rules.'

"At this point Mrs. Werther chimed in. 'In Cracow my husband built a wall around the ghetto with towers and decorated it with ornaments, pretty ornaments. Indeed the Jews there have no reason to complain. The decorative style is distinctly a work of Jewish art.'

"All laughed boisterously as they pounded their cold feet on the frozen snow to warm up.

" 'Silence!' ordered a soldier on patrol, who walked ahead of us. He stuck his rifle into an opening under the wall and fired. Frank approached him and asked him why he had fired.

" 'I shot a "rat," ' the soldier replied laughingly.

" 'A rat? *Ach, so!'*

"We drew nearer to the hole. The women laughed hysterically, as women do when they are in the vicinity of rodents.

" 'Where? Where is the "rat"?' Brigette asked.

" '*Achtung!*' (Attention!), the soldier called out and fired again.

"Protruding from the hole we saw a forelock and two small hands groping tremblingly in the snow. Evidently it was a Jewish child smuggler.

" 'You missed the mark,' Frank said accusingly. 'You're a poor marksman. Here, let me have your gun.'

"He grabbed hold of the rifle and fired."[1]

A.E.

From *Bialy Orzel* ("The White Eagle"). Trans. into Hebrew by Moshe Prager.

"WE WILL NOT HAND OVER THE CHILDREN ALIVE"

Fredka Mazia was a member of the Zionist Youth Movement and during the war served in many capacities as hospital nurse, governess, underground courier, and partisan. Her extraordinary narration begins in the fall of 1939. She was active in the three neighboring cities of Kattowitz, Sosnowitz, and Bendin, in Upper Silesia, which were centers of Jewish population and culture. Her main base of operations was Sosnowitz. After the ghetto was liquidated, she managed to survive and finally settled in Eretz Yisrael in 1944.

The excerpt below deals with Fredka's occupation as governess in 1943, in an infants' home in the Sosnowitz ghetto. The Germans had generously furnished and outfitted the children's home – another ruse to deceive the Jews. But the staff was not deceived.

My new job was at the children's day-care home. We adjusted quickly to the new conditions. . . . We had to provide shelter and care for the babies and young children of hundreds of mothers, who were compelled to go to work and had no place to leave them. We acquired a two-story house consisting of six rooms and a kitchen. On the first floor we outfitted the rooms for the two-to-six-year olds, who were under the leadership of Zusha Gelbard, who, in the pre-war years, had studied early-childhood education in Warsaw. She gave of herself fully and selflessly from six in the morning, when the mothers brought their young, until six in the evening, when they took them home. She was teacher and mother; she washed them, dressed and fed them, played with them — always with a smile and cheerful song. . . .

She would sing while leading her group in a long line, their faces pale but their eyes alight and bright, tapping with their small feet and clapping hands.

[1]During the slaughter in the ghetto of Lvov (Lemberg), young Jewish children were handed over to the Hitler Youth, who used them for target practice — Reuter Dispatch, February 14, 1946.

Zusha succeeded in restoring to them a bit of their blighted childhood, and in changing their sad surroundings into a magic retreat of freedom and happiness.

In the evenings, when the house was quiet, we would sit and talk. Around us were the playthings which the children had used and the drawings which adorned the walls. We would ask ourselves, "Until when will *they* let us go on like this?" Once Zusha burst out in a trembling voice, "What will happen if *they* come and take them away?"

I gasped. It was as if she read my mind, for this very question gave me no rest.

My "dominion" was upstairs with the infants, where beds, covered in white, were arranged in two neat rooms that were painted in cheerful colors. The third room contained cupboards filled with infants' clothing and diapers. The second floor was equipped with a large table, a bath, a small kitchen filled with cereals, margarine, and powdered milk. How much effort, tears and cajoling were required to acquire all this "wealth."

The man who initiated and made the home possible was Dr. Lieberman. He would scurry from office to office, from shop to shop, his hat askew and his coattails flying. He would burst in like a blast of wind, demanding, pounding on the table — and finally get what he wanted for the children. His counterpart, Dr. Zufia, carried on her supervisory work with an inexorable determination. Her almost impossible duty was to provide nutritious menus, examine the children regularly, and take care of their physical well-being.

Through the long day, when the children were in the home, I had no time to think. The tasks were endless — cooking, bathing, feeding, toilet duties, changing from wet to dry underthings, and so on and on. The infants knew me and would smile when I came near their beds: they would stretch out their thin arms to be lifted and embraced and would gurgle and babble cheerfully. And when they pressed their heads to my breast, when I fed them, a deep warmth enveloped my whole body.

Only when the mothers returned after their day's work and took them home, when I rearranged the cribs and covered them with clean spreads in preparation for the next day, did the ever-recurring fearful question return to haunt me: What if the Germans come to take them away? What can I say to the mothers, when they return from work and find their children gone? Never had I expressed this fear to anyone — when suddenly Zusha put it to me in all its brutality.

We went to the garden surrounding the house and sought possible hiding places, should, God forbid, the need arise. But it was evident that we were deluding ourselves. Should this happen, we could, at the very most, hide a very small number. Nevertheless, we did not relent. We sought a way out. In the end we decided to confront the mothers with this problem. Theirs was the right and the responsibility to decide what to do.

When we put it to them, the reactions were varied. Some broke down, sobbing, and could not utter a word. One shrugged her shoulders, saying, "What can we do? We are all doomed to die — some earlier, some later."

"But what will happen when you do not find your child?" I retorted with great emotion.

"God will help," she responded.

Some tearfully implored, "We beg of you, don't give them up. You are so kind. Watch over them. Save them."

They reiterated these words despite our arguments and reproofs. However, there were a number of perceptive and courageous parents who responded, "If and when this happens, give them an injection to put them to 'sleep' so that they do not suffer. You know how to handle little ones. Take pity on them."

"Am I capable of murder out of a sense of pity?" This thought gave me no rest. It was always with me in everything I did and wherever I was. And since I felt unqualified to act on my own, I turned for advice and guidance to my superiors. Dr. Zufia blanched. She was silent for a long time and then answered in a whisper, "You know that I handed over my daughter to a Polish family on the Aryan side before we were imprisoned in the ghetto. They took her. But they refused to accept my little boy. They feared that he would be discovered because of his circumcision. When I was with him I could not repress my tears. Should I let him suffocate in the jammed trains until he arrived at the death camp? Should I look on while they smashed his head and threw his body on the death pile? These horrors were ever with me day and night. I would wake from my sleep and hurry to his bed, feel him, hear him breathe. The nightmare would pass, and I behaved as if he was still in my care. Finally I decided I would not give him away alive. I would arrange that he go to sleep quietly, that he not suffer pain." Her head dropped. Big tears rolled down her cheeks. I heard her whisper, "Time was when they called this act 'premeditated murder.' Is there any act more monstrous?"

"Don't say it," I comforted her, as I patted her head, whose hair had turned prematurely gray. "You did an act of great kindness and of self-sacrifice — a noble, merciful act of a mother who had given him life. But what shall I do with my little ones, whom I did not bear and whose fate I have not the right to determine?"

Finally I turned to Dr. Lieberman for advice. I knew how much he loved the children. I would see him change from a despondent broken-down shell to a new man as soon as he passed the threshold of the home. He loved the children and was their greatest protection. One day, as he went from crib to crib, amusing the children by removing his glasses and putting them on again, I stopped him. "Have you a moment?" With a nervous gesture he looked at his watch.

"I shall not take up your time. Just one question."

"All right. Has anything happened?"

"Not yet. But what if the Germans take away the children?"

He pushed his glasses up his forehead and directed his sharp blue eyes at me. "Why this sudden question?"

"I cannot free myself of this thought. I am in constant dread. Every car that passes, every sound of a boot step, upsets my equilibrium. I cannot bear this tension any longer. I cannot carry this responsibliity, to which I find no solution. Perhaps we should close up the home and not assemble the children conveniently for 'them,' ready for shipment to be murdered."

The tension and fatigue of the last few days overcame my self-control as I banged my fist on the table, shouting, "*I do not want to give them the children. I* cannot take that awesome responsibility. Let each mother act on her own.''

Dr. Lieberman was silent for a long time while walking up and down the room, peering out of the window at the empty street. Then he turned to me, speaking tersely. ''Prepare a sufficient number of sleeping pills and capsules. We cannot burden the mothers with the children. If they do not report for work, they will be the first to be deported. But we will not hand over the children alive. We will not let them be subjected to torture. They will be put to 'sleep' quietly. But remember: *only at the very last moment; only if there is no way out, when all is lost*.''

''With my own hands?'' I asked as a great fear overwhelmed me. I repeated, ''With my own hands?''

''Yes, Fredka. *Your loving hands*. Not the brutal hands of barbarians. Be of strong courage and keep cool.''

He stood for a moment, hesitating. Then he rushed down the stairs.

A.E.

From *Reieem Basa'ar* (''Comrades in the Storm''), by Fredka Mazia, published by Yad Vashem, 1964, pp. 125-129.

5.

SPIRITUAL RESISTANCE

Incredible though it may seem, in the dismal conditions of the walled-in ghetto many of the habitants intensively and systematically pursued educational, intellectual, and artistic activities. In the beginning, the Germans allowed publication of only one thin Jewish newspaper, but secretly the ghettos published news sheets which appeared frequently. Proof of the ghettos' vitality was the comparatively small number of suicides. Another index of vitality was the ardor to study English – evidence of the living hope for emigration after the war.

Not enough has been recorded about the various forms of Jewish resistance. Nor has the term "resistance" been adequately defined. The maintenance of synagogues, Jewish schools, and libraries, the observances of Jewish ways of life were manifestations of resistance no less than forest partisan warfare. Episodes of underground activities and deeds of Kiddush Ha-Shem – *the sanctification of God's Name – through self-sacrifice, described below, were no less revelations of resistance than rebellion and underground warfare.*

Very few are more qualified to evaluate Jewish resistance then Dr. Meir (Mark) Dworzecki, on-the-scene witness and historian of the Vilna ghetto and a survivor of many camps. He writes: "I went through all the various stages of the Holocaust from 1939 to 1945, so I permit myself to say this: In all the days before the Holocaust and in all the years since, never did I witness so many manifestations of moral grandeur as I saw among the prisoners of the ghettos and the camps in the very abyss of the Holocaust. I feel it my duty to say these things as an eyewitness. . . . I simply must make this public attestation in order to counter the false impression that may be left by the quasi-scientific studies and the quasi-artistic best-selling novels that have been

58

appearing about the Jews in the Holocaust. . . . Those who did not themselves experience the Holocaust, if they will study the memoirs and the community records and put together the incidental details about them, there will be revealed to them the full epic of the steadfastness of the destroyed Jewish People.'' [1]

SCHOOL LIFE IN THE VILNA GHETTO

A glorious chapter of the Vilna ghetto was its spiritual resistance against the enemy. Vilna, which had been distinguished for generations as the "Jerusalem of Lithuania," came to be known during the Holocaust as the "Jerusalem of the ghettos" and as a symbol of resistance against Nazi persecution.

Despite the ever-present danger of deportation and "actions," despite the torment of hunger and suffering, Vilna's cultural activities did not abate. In the underground shelters, poets composed poems; in the cellars, books were stored; in the wreckage of the ruins, children were taught. Amidst the barbarous surroundings, the creative spirit of the ghetto was not crushed.

On the third day after the rise of the ghetto, Moshe Ulitzky, who was the chairman of the Hebrew Teachers Association and founder of the Hebrew secondary-school movement, assembled a group of women teachers in a Bet Midrash [2] and projected the establishment of a unified educational program to be conducted jointly by all the ideological groups. All assembled drew up a joint memorandum, which was submitted to the *Judenrat,* urging the founding of a comprehensive education program which would keep the ghetto children occupied during the day, while their parents were at work. It was reported that the *Judenrat* chairman, Jacob Gens, who was overwhelmed by his multifarious duties, replied to the delegation: "Don't bother me. Find yourselves quarters and do what you want."

I had served as a school doctor in Vilna Jewish schools for many years and always admired the devotion, ability, and spirit of the teachers' corps. But even in the good pre-war years I had not experienced such enthusiasm as pervaded teachers and pupils for reconstructing the ruined buildings and converting them into schools. They threw themselves into the work like one united family. Together they cleared up the wild grass and weeds, gathered the rocks and stones, which they transported to the building sites, where they erected schools. Here and there teachers and pupils tore out doors, collected wooden boards and broken windows frames, out of which they rebuilt a school. Women teachers and their girl pupils washed floors. Together they went around gathering bits and pieces of kindling wood to provide warmth.

During the early days there were no school benches. The children sat

---

[1] Proceedings of the Conference on Manifestations of Jewish Resistance during the Holocaust, Yad Vashem, Jerusalem, 1971, p. 188.
[2] House of study and worship.

propping up each others' backs, which served as desks, until benches were crudely constructed.

When the school quarters were ready for occupancy, signs were put up in the ghetto, inviting parents to register their children. Registration was handled by the hospital nurses. At first parents hesitated to register their children because they suspected that this was a ruse to compile a children's census. But when they realized that the people heading this effort were prominent pedagogues who had raised generations of students, their fears were allayed and they brought their children to the designated schools.

In September 1941, more than 2,700 children, ages six to fourteen, were enrolled. However, a substantial number did not report, either because of parental negligence, because of fear, or because many older children who had been orphaned were compelled to go to work to find a livelihood.

During the first semester there was evident an anti-Zionist and pro-Yiddish bias in the curriculum, because the head of the ghetto cultural department was a Bundist (Socialist). However, the Zionist coalition, headed by the underground movement of the Labor Zionists, strongly opposed this trend. They succeeded in fixing an equality between Hebrew and Yiddish and an equitable synthesis of the ideological orientations: Zionist, Socialist, and Communist. [Here the author lists the school directors, outstanding teachers, and the core elements of each curriculum.]

Pupils who came from traditional homes could chose to study religious subjects as elective courses. Orthodox parents were allowed to establish special supplementary schools, where their children received an Orthodox Hebrew education. Two schools and a small *yeshivah* were organized — the former for boys up to the age of twelve, the latter for those from twelve to sixteen. The hours of study were so arranged as to enable them to attend the public ghetto schools. Some two hundred students in all attended these schools.

The experiences and the tragedies that befell members of the children's families were reflected in the themes that they chose for their compositions: "How I Saved Myself from Camp Ponar [Vilna death camp]," "They Led My Parents to Their Death," "I Hid in an Underground Bunker," and so on.

Only a few days after the Nazi establishment of the ghetto (September 10, 1941) a ghetto library began to function. It served as the center for spiritual recreation. The walls were decorated with synagogue objects, candelabra, Holy Ark curtains and artistic inscriptions, photographs of Bialik, Mendele, Peretz, Sholem Aleichem,[3] and a large map of Eretz Yisrael. It was the only building which was roomy and where silence reigned. The readers, young and old, did their school homework, engaged in research, and prepared papers on different subjects.

During the month of November 1942, the library celebrated an unusual event — the borrowing of its ten-thousandth book. And when the second year of its existence rolled around in 1943, a fourteen-year-old girl was awarded first prize for having read the most books. She didn't stop borrowing and reading library books until the days of the final "action."

On one occasion an "action" began on a day when a woman teacher failed to

[3]Famous Hebrew and Yiddish men of letters.

bring her identification card. She was in the midst of a lesson. She continued to describe in glowing words the bright future that was bound to come. Hardly had she finished when she was seized and sent directly to Ponar, Vilna's death camp.

Very often the children came to school about an hour early. They eagerly waited for their teacher, who would tell them stories about an imaginary world where there were no ghettos and no "actions," and which was populated by heroic Jews who were as brave as the Maccabees and the heroes of Masada.

During the recess hour the children danced in a circle and sang, "We are young, we will overcome." Outstanding big events in the lives of the children were the holiday celebrations. They prepared for them with great enthusiasm. Adults joined eagerly in the festivities. Everyone sought to spend an hour or two in the midst of the warm, childlike, inspiriting atmosphere created by the young.

Never shall I forget the first children's celebration. Pupils, teachers, and parents sat huddled together. On the stage was a sign reading, "Think *not* the world is a roadhouse, lawless and without a Master." Children who but yesterday were saved from death, and others who were doomed to die soon, declaimed, sang and joined in dance. . . .

A pause ensues — an almost mystic moment of expectancy. We hold our breath, and suddenly we hear the intoxicating melody of Strauss's "Blue Danube." The teacher plays, and the children synchronize. . . . Everyone's thoughts go back to the beautiful world that was. . . . Amidst the overwrought tension and hushed silence, someone bursts into tears, then another and another, and soon the whole audience is sobbing. . . . In the audience I saw people who had lived through the horrors of the ghetto and they had not shed a tear. I recognized one who had escaped from the grave he had dug for himself, and he had not cried. But here and now, at this celebration, they lost control of their emotions; a mass psychosis overcame the audience.

Parents who were reduced to slavery were stirred by these children's festivals as if they were at a spiritual communion. In the songs and declamations of their children, they found outlets for their deeply felt prayers, hopes, and longings. As if hypnotized, they repeated with the children the lines of Yitzhak Leib Peretz: "Tears a river make/Rivers oceans make/Oceans — a flood/From sparks — thunder/Think not the world is a lawless place, sans Master."

A tremor seized the audience when their young appeared in colorful costumes, dressed as butterflies and angels. In those moments no one dared to look at his neighbor lest he see in the other's eyes the fearful thought, the almost fiendish certainty of the doom awaiting their little ones — tomorrow, the next day, and perhaps even this very night.

[The author describes various festival celebrations, of which the following is one.] *Hamisha Asar B'Shvat* (fifteenth of Shvat, when spring begins in Palestine): The evening program opens with the slogan: "Hearty greetings from the children of the ghetto to the children in Eretz Yisrael." An exhibition has been arranged of drawings showing life in the ghetto and illustrations of children in Eretz Yisrael. Teacher Yisrael Dimenstein addresses the audience and ends with a prayerful note: "The time will yet come when you children gathered here will plant trees and sing songs together with the children of Eretz Yisrael, and the memory of the ghetto will be but a nightmare, gone and forgotten.''

On the platform a sign is displayed, reading,

We are in the ghetto —
You are in Eretz Yisrael.

There was even a music school in the ghetto, specializing in piano, violin, and choir singing. About a hundred students attended the school. Frequently they gave public concerts. Also connected with the school were two reading and recreation centers. They offered a wide variety of services: a library, reading room, study circles, dramatic groups which presented plays by distinguished writers. A number of teenagers were active in the underground. Hidden deep in the cellar was a cache of firearms.

Very touching were the graduation ceremonies, when the students received their diplomas. The graduates were qualified to enroll in the technical and trade schools and were granted the ''privilege'' of receiving working papers. They bade farewell to their younger colleagues, their teachers and principals. They read the memoirs which they had written and impressions of their schooldays. They gave presents to their teachers and accompanied each gift with a talk or a song and often even a live flower that had been smuggled into the ghetto. [The author describes a graduation ceremony in the spring of 1943, comprising all the schools, which was held in the ghetto theater and was attended by all the communal and political bodies. Then he lists the various types of schools — e.g., Orthodox, technical, music, art, recreational facilities, sport clubs — and summarizes their activities.]

Following is a description of the ghetto sport club.

Four hundred youths were enrolled in the club. On the bulletin board of the Jewish Council House were posted announcements listing the schedules of various types of sport and athletic contests. A training field was set aside for this purpose, bearing a big banner reading: ''A healthy body — a healthy spirit.'' This was the same field from which the Germans deported the old people to Ponar. During the last days of the ghetto, it was the central meeting place of the partisans.

One day the ghetto staged an Olympiad which highlighted a race. [Here follow the names of the starting and ending stations of the race.] The leading runners were awarded prizes. The sidewalks were jammed with Jews who gathered to watch the races and who wanted to forget themselves during the contest. In the air hovered the grim end, the certainty of deportation to the Estonian concentration camps — death.

Looking out of the windows were the Aryan neighbors, who stared at the ghetto Olympiad — ''festivity in the midst of certain death.''

A.E.

From *Yerushalayim Shel d'Lita Bamri Uvashoah* (''The Jerusalem of Lithuania: [Vilna] in Resistance and Destruction'') by Mark Dvorjecki, published by the Israel Labor Party, 1951, pp. 215-222 (with deletions).

AN UNDERGROUND YESHIVA IN WARSAW

Dr. Hillel Seidman's book Diary of the Warsaw Ghetto *is one of a very impressive series of Yiddish books, entitled* Polish Jewry, *which have been published in Argentina. He had been officially appointed by the Warsaw Kehillah to direct its department of archives and was therefore in close touch with the daily occurrences in the ghetto, which he noted carefully and conscientiously. Dr. Seidman now lives in New York, where he is active in the Orthodox and Yiddish journalistic world.*

Today I made a special visit to the underground — the only one of its kind. In the morning two youngsters, Yeshiva students, came to tell me, "At 5:00 P.M. today we meet at 35 Nalevki Street. Be there!"

Five minutes before the appointed hour I was at the gate of 35 Nalevki Street. A young lad wearing a Jewish cap awaited me there. When he saw me, he said, "Follow me." He preceded me and I followed him. We pass one courtyard, then another, then a third. Now we enter a cellar about two stories deep. We go further until we emerge onto another street. We go up the stairs of a house. On the top floor there is a small room in which stands a ladder leading to the roof. We climb up, pass through corridors, and force our way through narrow openings until we reach 37 Zamenhoff Street. We go in and come to a room which had housed a Bet Midrash (house of study and prayer) and from there into another room in which there is a large oven. My guide enters the oven and disappears. I remain outside. I hear, "Come in." I creep after him into the oven and there I find an opening that leads to a cellar. I climb down a rope ladder until I reach a solid floor. Before me is a wide room. It is clear and is lit by electricity. At the walls are long benches and in the center of the room stands a long rough-hewn table.

They led me into a small, dark room where they showed me a kitchen electrically operated and containing gas stoves as well. The cupboards were well stocked with food. "For how long a period have you provided food?" I asked. "All that will be required for the number of students. Our estimate is eight months for a hundred and twenty people."

As I surveyed the bunker, thoughts ran through my mind. Certain words have acquired new meanings and new content in the ghetto. To the Germans, "bunker" meant an offense position in which were set up machine guns and military instruments for attack. In the ghetto it meant a den deep down, several stories underground, whose entrance was very carefully concealed and whose quarters were carefully hidden. The bunker in which I found myself was built by competent Jewish engineers under a bombed-out house. From the outside all one could see was a ruin, a pile of bricks. The gate and the remnants of the walls were surrounded by barbed wire. No one would think that people might live here in the bowels of the earth.

From the distance I hear the singsong chant of a Gemara lesson. I listen with wonder. Instead of explaining to me what's going on, my companion brings me into a second room. The surroundings remind me of descriptions of the conditions under which our people lived in former times, when Marrano Jews during the Spanish Inquisition studied Torah in caves.

Around the table sit about twenty Yeshiva students before open books, studying Talmud with fervor and zeal. Their faces are pale; their eyes flash fire. They are transported to another world. I recognize many who have lost their parents and families. It is soon evident that they are subtenants of the engineers who constructed the bunker. I learn that at first the latter viewed negatively these zealots who refused to cut their forelocks and discard their distinctive Hasidic garb. However, after a while they looked upon them with growing curiosity. Soon they began to admire their determination, their unbending resolution, and now they regard them with respect and admiration.

A well-known assimilationist whom I knew related to me how the boys sit and study through the night; how they worship together as though they were in an open synagogue; how they sing Sabbath chants at the table. He even hummed for me some well-known Hasidic melodies that he learned from them. I felt he was speaking with reverence, and perhaps even with a note of envy. He even told me some Hasidic ideas that he had absorbed from the young people. "They," he concluded, "know the reason why they suffer." I responded with the oft-quoted rabbinic statement, "Happy are you, Rabbi Akiba, for having been caught studying Torah."[1]

A.E.

From Warsaw Ghetto Diary *by Hillel Seidman, published by Central Association of Polish Jews in Argentina in cooperation with Federation of Polish Jews in America, Buenos Aires, 1947, pp. 221-226.*

CLANDESTINE HIGH SCHOOL IN THE WARSAW GHETTO

In his introduction to the book Wanderers on the Roads of Death, *Dr. Nathan Eck (Eckron) lists his various experiences and activities in the Warsaw Ghetto, his intimate associations with Dr. Emmanuel Ringelblum, with the immortal poet Itzhak Katzenelson, with the Underground movement, and with the survivors. He gives the exact dates of his escapes from city to city during his fiery ordeal in Poland, his imprisonment in two camps, and his postwar wanderings and final settlement in Israel.*

His book is an important contribution to the chronicles of the tragedy.

As a general rule, all that the Jews did or tried to do in the ghettos was, of necessity, temporary in nature. Every thought and every action was directed toward momentary survival, for it was futile and illogical to attempt to create anything of lasting value in conditions that everyone believed would soon undergo basic and complete change. The purpose of all action in the ghetto was to keep resisting physically, spiritually, and culturally — thus counteracting the atrocity of the regime.

[1] Rabbi Akiba was burned at the stake by the Romans about the year 135 C.E.

However, there is no rule without exception. I saw an astonishing thing in the Warsaw Ghetto, which was completely directed toward the anticipated future — namely, the founding of the Hebrew high school in the ghetto.

It is well known that under Nazi rule higher education was forbidden to the Jews. However, unemployed high school teachers clandestinely gave private lessons. They organized the students in groups of four to five and taught them in private dwellings. Several such "high schools" were in operation. In this way the teachers were able to earn some of their livelihood and a number of the pupils were able to continue their studies. This constituted one of the important fulfilments to which the need of the hour gave rise. The founders of this high school, however, did not consider its aim to be either a means of employment for teachers or a possibility for continued studies for students.

They were concerned with the "Life of the Word." The writer of these lines had accepted the responsibility for directing this institution. The pupils were chosen primarily from the graduates of the *Tarbut*[1] elementary schools in Warsaw, but students from elsewhere were also accepted. The basic principle was not to divide the students into small groups but rather to maintain unsectioned classes; not to conduct lessons in private homes, but rather in a place specifically designated for that. The aim was to appear as much as possible as an organized school even under the conditions of the ghetto Underground. Since the Nazis set up elementary schools for Jewish children, we wanted an actual high school as well, and were not satisfied with any makeshift arrangement.

During the first few weeks classes were held at 29 Lashno Street, in a workroom put at our disposal by the *Hanoar Ha Tzioni*.[2] Conditions there were most difficult. The room was small and unfurnished and I, the principal, had no corner of my own. I used to run back and forth in the corridor, or sit in an alcove in the next room, where workers were doing their craft. In spite of this, administrative duties were carried on by me with constant diligence. Attendance was taken, lesson plans and résumés were submitted, and several weeks later, when we moved to 68 Novolepky Street, the former quarters of one of the *Tarbut* schools, I instituted a system of bells to ring at the start and finish of each lesson. Now that we had at our disposal, for the hours of the afternoon, classrooms, benches, blackboards, platforms, and a bell, we regarded ourselves as a full-fledged high school.

By that time the number of freshmen was about thirty, and it included some older students with considerably more background, and we were thus able to form a class of sophomores from this group. We were delighted by this bit of progress. We found reward from our efforts and had no doubt that if we outlived the enemy, the Hebrew high school, which was born in the ghetto, would stand strong and firm in the free capital.

Mr. Michael Brandstater of blessed memory (son of David Brandstater, the Hebrew writer in the days of the Haskalah), a well-known educator and experienced principal, whom I made a member of the staff of the high school,

[1] Zionist Youth Movement.
[2] Hebrew Cultural Movement.

even though he knew no Hebrew, spoke his mind to me on one occasion. "Mr. Eck," he said, "perhaps you do not realize what you did for me when you found a way to include me in this work — what these hours I spend here represent for me, how before the eyes of these children upon school benches . . ." I don't remember his exact words, but their context in effect was: It is an escape from the world of ugliness and evil. Here one is blessed with the ability to forget the horror, to be purified, to be inspired. He was expressing the feelings we all had.

We had practically no discipline problem. The children behaved like adults. They understood the situation perfectly. Without any explanations they realized that this high school was especially important in the ghetto and that it held high hopes for the future. They maintained constant vigil without any need for warning. Like the adults, they knew all that went on in the streets of the ghetto and within the shabby dwellings, the schemes of the enemy and the fear nibbling at their hearts. The nightmare hovering over all of us hovered over them as well (they were all between the ages of thirteen and fourteen). In spite of that, laughter and joking did not cease from between our walls.

Measures of secrecy were not too severe, especially after we moved to quarters in a school building, where elementary-school classes were held with permission. However, I felt I dared to take a bold step when I announced that the following Sunday a parents-teachers meeting would be held, at which progress reports on each student's work would be given. The meeting was successful; almost all the parents were present, and it was evident that they were pleased at this chance to meet and to enjoy the illusion of normal living.

Public assemblies were held during the school year, among which were a Chanukah celebration and a Purim festival. The Chanukah program was a simple affair, presented while we were still on Lashno Street. However, it attracted many parents and guests. They filled the workroom of the *Noar Ha Tzioni* to capacity, and several public figures, such as Menachem Kirshenbaum, L.L. Bloch, David Gozik, Dr. M. Stein, and Dr. Nusblatt, were also present.

The Purim festival was rather elaborate and centered about a presentation of a Hebrew play. The play was directed with great effort and devotion by Mr. Harman, who was at one time a member of *Habima*.[3] The performance, as well as the entire celebration, surpassed all expectations. The hall was crowded, and the entire audience — teachers, parents, students, and dignitaries — was filled with a sense of joy and pride. They expressed this feeling not only in words but in the special glimmer of light in their eyes, which registered the depth of emotion upon each face.

Two months prior to the end of the school year we held registration for the following year, and scores of students re-enrolled. After vacation we were able to reopen with three complete classes — freshmen, sophomores, and juniors. In other words, only one class was lacking to make it a complete high school.

We completed our studies at the end of June 1942, three weeks before the Jews of the ghetto were massacred! We conducted examinations, held confer-

[3]Hebrew Theater Company.

ences to ensure proper grading, and issued report cards. As I took leave of my students, I did not avoid speaking of the dangers facing us. I recall using, several times, expressions like "if we are fortunate enough to meet again," and "if we live." In spite of the news which was reaching us about Ponar, Chmelno, and Lublin, I did not believe that complete annihilation was in store for us.

> From *Wanderers on the Roads of Death: Thought and Reflection of the Days of Doom* published by Yad Vashem, Jerusalem. Quoted in *Flame and Fury,* Material for Yom-Hashoa, National Remembrance Day, compiled by Yaacov Shilhav, edited by Sara Feinstein, New York: Jewish Education Committee Press, 1962, pp. 28-30. Trans. by Sara Feinstein.

SELF-AID IN THE GHETTO

Chaim A. Kaplan, a Hebrew teacher and a respected leader of Warsaw, kept a Hebrew diary in which he recorded the Nazi occupation from the invasion on September 1, 1939, to August 1942. His notebooks were found intact twenty years later. They were translated and edited by a prominent Hebrew scholar, Dr. Abraham I. Katsh, who has made notable contributions to many fields of Jewish history and literature.

November 29, 1940. Polish Jewry has become a self-contained organism. It is forced to rely on its own powers. Despite all its poverty, it must support its own destitute. The American "Uncle" of the last war has gone to rest. Willing or not, the misers of Poland are forced to give. The Jewish Self-Aid, which no one believed would succeed at the time of its establishment, has become a far-reaching charitable organization which brings in more than 100,000 zlotys a month. Self-Aid is a kingdom in its own right, and from the administrative standpoint it has no connection with its sister, the Joint, which is still alive and functioning in spite of being pauperized, and which is still completely supporting its officials, especially the directors. Its support of the Self-Aid has not yet stopped entirely, but it is stopping discreetly, without publicity. In the eyes of the general public the Joint is bankrupt and no longer has any say. On the other side of the ledger, the Self-Aid has much publicity.

The lowest rung in its broad organization is the courtyard committee. This is a successful organizational invention, of a kind that was never attained in times of peace when a raucous press existed. At that time no public project percolated down to the masses. This time every Jewish home from great to small has been affected. At the head of the courtyard committees stand men of the people, who awaken the drowsy public to give.

Their words, which emanate from simple hearts, penetrate into simple hearts. They find expressions which their listeners can understand, and so are successful. Social action is thus diffused through all levels of the broad public, and there is no boy over ten who does not have some public duty in his courtyard. There is not a tenant who is not among the members of some committee, or in charge of some courtyard duty. Every courtyard is divided into reporting subcommittees (financial, sanitary, educational affairs, political affairs, apartments, dress, food supplies, etc.) and each of these is further divided and subdivided, and in this way everyone is kept busy. Self-Aid is a legal organization and it thus gives the legal right to all its branches to call meetings and conferences, and to put their decisions into practice. At every meeting there is a broad field for politics, rumors, and all manner of gossip and slander. Everyone says whatever enters his mind, without fear that his words will be carried to those in power. The hatred of the conquerors is so deep that everyone is sure no one will carry anything he says beyond the room.

The Self-Aid is supported by regular monthly payments which the courtyard committees impose upon their ''subjects'' by the income derived from special projects and drives. Nearly every month it raises a hue and cry about a different rescue project. Once it was a drive to save the children, and the ''children's month'' became a watchword; then came the ''holiday month''; third, there was the ''immigration month''; the fourth, which we are presently involved in carrying out, is the ''soul ransom'' project to raise money for ''social improvements.'' The organization of these projects is not always successful, because it is a time of crisis and everything must be done in haste, without the technical and organizational tools required. But even if they are not a hundred percent successful, the people are satisfied with a sixty percent success. Compulsory giving has served to educate us. The recognition of collective responsibility which was so lacking in our brethren has penetrated to everyone. Everyone has come to realize that he is an organic part of a whole body. Anything good for the whole body is good for him too, and the reverse. This concept was brought to us by the conquerors. That which is good must be accepted, from whatever source it may come.

The concept that ''all Jews are responsible for one another'' has stopped being merely a slogan or a metaphor. It is realized in us.

The courtyard committees operate on the principle that the affairs of their own courtyard come first. And so they impose a double monthly payment upon their ''subjects''; one for the benefit of the Self-Aid, which supports the soup kitchens in the ghetto, the other for courtyard needs. This payment need not necessarily be in cash. It may be made in footstuffs, prepared meals, or used clothing.

When the ghetto was about to be set up and people were concerned about the hoarding, the courtyard committees began taking care of all the residents of the courtyard without exception, including even the middle-class and wealthy ones. It was deemed entirely possible that a day would come when all the private hoards would be eaten up and it would be necessary to set up a common soup kitchen for all the residents of the courtyard. So the courtyard committees hastily created a ''permanent fund'' for the establishment of soup kitchens. At once the necessary (relatively speaking) sums were collected to enable them to buy in advance a certain quantity of foodstuffs, to be stored in a special cellar belonging to the courtyard committee. It will thus remain, ready for whatever trouble may come.

When historians come to write the history of the courtyard committees during the days of the Nazi war against the Jews, let them end their chapter with a blessing of consolation: "May the Lord remember them with favor!"

From *Scroll of Agony: The Warsaw Diary of Chaim A. Kaplan,* Translated and edited by Abraham I. Katsh, op. cit., pp. 227-229.

THIS IS JEWISH REVENGE

Sometimes our work is done by schoolchildren. The children of our poor, with whom the streets of Warsaw are filled at all hours of the day, are not afraid even of the despotic conquerors. They remain as always — lively and mischievous. Their poverty and oppression serve to shield them from robberies and confiscations. No one will harm them. Even the conquerors' eye overlooks them: Let the Jewish weeds pine away in their iniquity. But these weeds watch every act of the conquerors and imitate the Nazis' manner of speech and their cruelty most successfully. For them this is nothing but good material for games and amusements. Childhood does much.

Once there came into the ghetto a certain Nazi from a province where the Jews were required to greet every Nazi soldier they encountered, removing their hats as they do so. There was no such practice in Warsaw, but the "honored guest" wanted to be strict and force the rules of his place of origin on us. A great uproar arose suddenly in Jewish Karmelicka Street. Some psychopathic Nazi is demanding that every passerby take his hat off in his honor. Many fled, many hid, many were caught for their transgression and beaten, and many were bursting with laughter. The little "wise guys," the true lords of the street, noticed what was going on and found great amusement in actually obeying the Nazi, and showing him great respect in a manner calculated to make a laughingstock out of the "great lord" in the eyes of all the passersby. They ran up to greet him a hundred and one times, taking off their hats in his honor. They gathered in great numbers, with an artificial look of awe on their faces, and wouldn't stop taking off their hats. Some did this with straight faces, while their friends stood behind them and laughed. Then these would leave, and others would approach, bowing before the Nazi with bare heads. There was no end to the laughter. Every one of the mischievous youths so directed his path as to appear before the Nazi several times, bowing before him in deepest respect. That wasn't all. Riffraff gathered for the fun, and they all made a noisy demonstration in honor of the Nazi with a resounding cheer. This is Jewish revenge!

From *Scroll of Agony: The Warsaw Diary of Chaim A. Kaplan,* New York: Macmillan, 1965. Trans. and edited by Abraham I. Katsh, pp. 153 f.

A CONCERT IN KORCZAK'S ORPHANAGE

In March 1941, before Passover, the house committee of the orphan home decided to arrange a concert and a traditional Passover celebration. The event was a great success, financially and artistically. It was conducted in Polish, Hebrew, and Yiddish. After the performance Dr. Korczak read some verses which he had composed.

It was in March 1941 that it happened. The house committee at 33 Chlodna Street had made great efforts to arrange the concert at the orphanage of Dr. Janusz Korczak and to have it performed before Pesach. Poverty and want were increasing every day, and we hoped to acquire some much-needed money. Dr. Korczak wanted to have a traditional Passover celebration, to which he had already invited a number of distinguished people, including Adam Czerniakow[1] and his wife. The cost of such entertaining would obviously be high.

Two aims were paramount, then, for the concert committee — a high standard of performance and a substantial income. A number of professional actors and instrumentalists had been asked to perform, and all of them were willing to give their services free of charge. But Dr. Korczak had also invited two other performers: one was a man often seen playing a violin in the streets of the ghetto. He was young, fair-haired and blue-eyed, and always attracted large crowds because of his polished performance. He did not have a big repertoire — Block's *"Baal Shem Tov,"* Acharon's "Hebrew Melodies," and some pieces of Grieg. He had come from Palestine to visit relatives before the war, and had been unable to leave. Korczak, like the others, was deeply moved by him.

The other person invited by Dr. Korczak was one of the many Jews expelled from their own small towns and forced to live in Warsaw. He became well known as a singer of Jewish folk songs, particularly those by Mordechai Gebirtig, the Yiddish poet and composer from Cracow, who wrote the moving song *"Es Brent"* ("The Town Is Burning"). He was shot by the Germans in 1942.

We, the committee, were anxious to sell tickets, hoping that this would bring in a fair amount for the orphanage. Dr. Korczak stubbornly opposed this idea. He insisted on free entry, saying it was better to trust to the consciences of the audience. They would donate lavishly, that was certain — and he was proved right. It was a great success, artistically and financially.

The venue was the assembly hall of the orphanage. Three hundred invited guests were present, the majority of them wealthy and important. Korczak sat among the guests, and the children were ranged around the hall with the staff. It lasted two hours; there were items in Polish, Hebrew, and Yiddish, the latter being the most popular. Oddly enough, the most assimilated members of the audience, whose mother tongue was Polish, were the most appreciative of the Yiddish songs and poems. Korczak's reaction was also interesting: he was overcome by the contributions of the two nonprofessionals and wept unashamedly. In later conversations, he often dwelt on this part of the concert, regarding it as a source of joy and comfort at a time of stress.

But the evening did not end there. During the tumultuous applause, we suddenly noticed Dr. Korczak up on the platform. We all thought he merely wanted to thank the guests and the artists, which he did, but he then asked us to

[1]Chairman of the Ghetto Council.

bear with him while he read some brief poems he had very recently written. The concert seemed to be starting again. He drew a few sheets of paper from his pocket and started to read aloud. The poems were heavy with satire — they described a small black mustache, a large fat belly, a hunchback, and, finally, an elegant dandy. Amid the scorn and mockery was a pervading regret that these people should hold the fate of many millions in their hands. He mentioned no names, but everyone knew he was referring to Hitler, Göring, Goebbels, and our own hangman, Hans Frank, the boss of the ''New Order'' in Poland.

People listened and were horrified. Had Korczak gone mad? Some of them even slunk out of the hall and ran home in terror, but Korczak did not even notice. He went on calmly reading to the few who had stayed behind — the house tenants.

Afterwards, we asked Dr. Korczak how he could have done such a thing. Hadn't he noticed people leaving? Did he not realize that he was placing us all in terrible danger? He merely smiled and said, ''The people who left are fools. What is there to be afraid of? Surely Jews can say that they think amongst themselves. Are you afraid of spies, or that someone will give me away? I don't think Jews would repeat any of this — they are all enemies of the 'New Order.' '' Undoubtedly Korczak believed what he was saying. He could not imagine that there were Jews willing to tell the Germans anything that would incriminate their comrades. This was typical of his character; his standards and values were high and based on loyalty and trust. But during those first few months in the ghetto, he had been in some ways a different person; he could never have done what he did at the concert. His fear of people, of what might happen, caused him to brick up the main entrance to the orphanage, and he scolded the tenants whenever, after careful observation from the courtyard, he saw a pinpoint of light coming from one of the windows after curfew. When a German policeman came to the house, he was absolutely terrified. This happened only rarely, when the police found a wandering or lost child at night and brought him in. This pattern of behavior was the direct result of his prison experience.

But in time he changed completely, speaking frankly about ''the murderers and outcasts of society.'' The tenants' windows were forgotten, and he was not afraid to denounce his enemies in public.

From *Warsaw Diary*, by Michael Zylberberg, London: Vallentine Mitchel, pp. 36-38.

KIDDUSH HA-SHEM *BY SON AND FATHER*

Naftali Rabs, who during September 1943 had fled from Buchnia, Poland, to Hungary and from there to Rumania, was a slave laborer in the cleaning-up squad. After the extermination of the Jews in various cities, the Gestapo left a detail of Jews to empty the homes, clean up, and assort and list the remaining valuables. In Buchnia after the final deportation, about three hundred Jews had been assigned to perform this job. Among them were the baker Herschel Zimet and his son. They had been the officially appointed bakers when the ghetto was still in existence.

In addition to the three hundred, there were another hundred who hid in the bunkers. A number of bunkers were discovered by the Gestapo and the Polish police. Those who remained hidden suffered from hunger and thirst. In the dark of the night the baker and his son would smuggle in loaves of bread and pitchers of water, which barely kept alive the scores of people who hovered between life and death. Even though the Gestapo used bloodhounds to find the bunkers, they had not succeeded in uncovering them. However, one night two Gestapo men lay in ambush and detected the father and his son returning from the bunker. They arrested the pair and brought them to the police station. They separated the boy from the father and promised to let each one go free if he would inform them where the bunkers were located. The father, who feared that his son would not stand up to the torture, shouted out with all his might, ''I implore you in the name of God of Israel and His commandment to honor one's father, do not reveal anything to the murderers. If you do, they will kill all the Jews.''

The boy broke away from his captors, held on to his father, and shouted to the Nazis, who pointed their guns at both of them, ''Murderers, kill us! I won't tell you anything.'' Both were shot embracing each other closely as they sanctified the Lord's Name.

A.E.

From *Zakhor*, (''Remember''), by Eliezer Unger, published by Massada Press, Israel, 1946, p. 106.

THE CIRCUMCISION

On May 7, 1942, the Germans issued a decree prohibiting the birth of children in the Kovno ghetto. If discovered, mother and infant would be put to death.

It is impossible to describe the panic that seized the pregnant women and the entire community. How to hide the newborn infants? How to silence them from crying? The Germans were on the alert and constantly prying into the ghetto homes. Dr. Zacharin, the hospital superintendent, was forbidden to admit pregnant women to the hospital.

The Jews, however, defied the edict. The delivery of infants was arranged secretly at home. The cirumcisions of boys were also performed at home.

I shall not forget the secret circumcisions, which I attended, and, by the grace of God, many of the children are now grown. Indeed, they are living testimony to their saintly parents, who died sanctifying God's Name.

How can I forget the clandestine circumcision ceremony at the home of Rabbi Itzhak Bloch? For five years the mother's womb was closed. And then suddenly, after the death decree was issued, they were blessed with a son.

They lived in a four-story building in Block C, which housed many ghetto offices, including the Zionist organization, religious youth groups, a school, a bathhouse (named ''delousing center''), a kitchen, food storage bins, underground bunkers to hide in, and other facilities. It also contained munitions caches and provided a meeting place for partisan fighters; as well as a trade school, which was sanctioned by the Gestapo. The Bloch family chose the premises of the school to initiate their son into the House of Israel on the eighth day after his birth, because they hoped that the noise of the hammers in the school would drown out the infant's wails.

The memory of the ceremony is still fresh in my mind. It was on a Sunday afternoon. Just as the *mohel* [the man authorized to circumcise] took the circumcision knife, a Gestapo car stopped before the building. Fear struck all present, and the *mohel*'s hands began to tremble. What to do? How to save the mother and infant? Fear paralyzed all who were there. Suddenly the mother cried out, "Quick! Circumcise the child. Our lives are doomed. Let him die a Jew."

We obeyed her command. The boy was circumcised in the shadow of death. We waited for the murderers, but, thank God, we suffered only fright. They had come to inspect the trade school.

To the end of my life the memory of that experience will remain fresh. The words of the brave mother reverberate in my ears to this very day.

A.E.

From *Ani Maamin,* ("I Believe"), Jerusalem: Mosad HaRav Kook, 1969, pp. 93f. Quoted in *Hurban Litte* ("Destruction of Lithuania") by Rabbi Ephraim Oshry.

IN THE CEMETERY NEW LIFE IS BORN

On December 25, 1942, the Shavli Jews marked the first annual celebration since the establishment of the Jewish hospital. It was a modest fete but of great significance to the community. The hospital had been set up at a very trying moment. The year before, at this time, we received a sudden notice from the German officials that we were to remove all Jewish patients from the city hospitals. All our appeals to win time were rejected. We had to act in twenty-four hours, no longer. The Jewish community officials forthwith began to prepare a new home in which to house the hospital — a building in the cemetery.

The building had been neglected for many years and was ridden with filth. It consisted of two rooms, one for the gravediggers and the other for washing and cleaning the dead before burial. The builders worked through the twenty-four hours to prepare the rooms for admission of the sick. At the same time, Dr. Shlomowitz and Dr. Marcus gathered the necessary hospital equipment: beds, linens, utensils, and all other hospital necessities. Dr. Paschowitz (who later settled in Israel) secured all the essential medicines — a very difficult undertaking indeed. All the work was carried out voluntarily and with dispatch. In a short time the hospital attained a high medical rating that could compare with and indeed exceed that of existing city hospitals. As evidence, here is one statistic: In the city, many non-Jewish children died of diphtheria; in the Jewish hospital, seventy-six diphtheria patients recovered. In all the cases of spotted diphtheria, no marks were left on the body. Very few children died. There was not a single instant of neglect of the sick. Never did the patients feel more at home and tranquil than in the Jewish hospital. Ninety percent of the rare medicines and serums were prepared by the chief medical director, where health itself was in grave danger. His example was emulated by all members of the staff. Thus there developed a flourishing medical institution, in the very midst of the cemetery, in which the lives of hundreds were saved. Those ill were, in the main, victims of the ghetto, where plagues and infectious diseases were rampant. There were many children, as well as adults, who were starved and emaciated. And when destruction of the ghetto was imminent the most tragic cases of all were pregnant women who had to have abortions or face death.

Our record of achievement was modest but comforting. To quote a father of a recently born baby boy, "In the cemetery new lives are being created and formed."

A.E.

From *Pinkas Shavili*, ("Memorial Book of Shavli, a Diary"), by Eliezer Yerushalmi, published by Mosad Bialik and Yad Vashem, 1950, pp. 148-149.

6.

CHILDREN'S DIARIES

There are a score or more of Jewish children's diaries that have been written and published in various languages such as Dutch, Hebrew, Yiddish, Polish, Hungarian, etc. Some have been translated into English and have won worldwide acclaim. Outstanding among these are the diaries of Anne Frank, Moshe Flinker and Yitzhak Rudashevsky. There is even a diary in pictures painted by Charlotte Solomon. [1] She had been a talented student in a Berlin high school. Her parents sent her to France to live with her grandparents, but the war caught up with her. She found an outlet to her misery by painting some one thousand pictures in gouache (opaque water colors mixed with a preparation of gum), in which she recreated her happy childhood and tragic adolescence. The paintings, together with an autobiography and notes, were found several years after her death. They are now in the possession of a Dutch museum.

Because of the merits of certain selections below which are not available as yet in English translation, we present fuller excerpts of their contents. Shorter excerpts are included of those that have appeared in English.

ANNE FRANK LOOKS BACK AT HER PAST

Anne Frank's Diary of a Young Girl *is known universally and is the most widely dramatized work of its kind. Anne was born in Frankfurt-am-Main in 1929, and*

---

[1]*Charlotte, A Diary in Pictures,* by Charlotte Solomon, brought to press by Paula Solomon Lindberg, pub. by Harcourt Brace, © Albert Solomon, 1963.

when Hitler rose to power her family escaped to Amsterdam. When the Germans overran Holland, the family and four others hid in Mr. Frank's warehouse, which was situated on one of the city's canals. Together with them was another family whose son, Peter, became very friendly with Anne. They maintained contact with the outside world thanks to the help of former Christian employees of Mr. Frank. They were cooped up in this hiding place for a period of two years. Isolated in the annex where they hid, uncertain of her future, Anne poured out her thoughts and feelings in her diary, which she kept very secret. In it are reflected her integrity and goodness. "I believe in the goodness of people," she affirmed. On August 4, 1944, she, together with her family, was deported to the death camps in the east. A Nazi sergeant threw Anne's diary notebooks on the annex floor before she was taken away. They were found by friends and preserved by Otto Frank, her father, who was the only survivor.

The diary won worldwide fame and was translated and published in many languages. A deeply moving play, based on the diary, has been presented in various parts of the world.

Anne Frank's house in Amsterdam has become an international museum. An Anne Frank Foundation has been set up, with a ramified program of activities and publications that are disseminated worldwide.

In March 1945, Anne's life ended in Bergen-Belsen. She left behind her an immortal monument — her diary. It reveals depths of feeling, keen introspection, and a level of intelligence that are very uncommon in a young adolescent.

Tuesday, 7 March, 1944

Dear Kitty,

If I think now of my life in 1942, it all seems so unreal. It was quite a different Anne who enjoyed that heavenly existence from the Anne who has grown wise within these walls. Yes, it was a heavenly life. Boyfriends at every turn, about twenty friends and acquaintances of my own age, the darling of nearly all the teachers, spoiled from top to toe by Mummy and Daddy, lots of sweets, enough pocket money, what more could one want?

You will certainly wonder by what means I got around all these people. Peter's word "attractiveness" is not altogether true. All the teachers were entertained by my cute answers, my amusing remarks, my smiling face, and my questioning looks. That is all I was — a terrible flirt, coquettish and amusing. I had one or two advantages, which kept me rather in favor. I was industrious, honest, and frank. I would never have dreamed of cribbing from anyone else. I shared my sweets generously, and I wasn't conceited.

Wouldn't I have become rather forward with so much admiration? It was a good thing that in the midst of, at the height of, all this gaiety, I suddenly had to face reality, and it took me at least a year to get used to the fact that there was no more admiration forthcoming.

How did I appear at school? The one who thought of new jokes and pranks, always "king of the castle," never in a bad mood, never a crybaby. No wonder everyone liked to cycle with me, and I got their attentions.

Now I look back at that Anne as an amusing, but very superficial girl, who has nothing to do with the Anne of today. Peter said quite rightly about me: "If ever I saw you, you were always surrounded by two or more boys and a whole troupe of girls. You were always laughing and always the center of everything!"

What is left of this girl? Oh, don't worry, I haven't forgotten how to laugh or to answer back readily. I'm just as good, if not better, at criticizing people, and I can still flirt if . . . I wish. That's not it though, I'd like that sort of life again for an evening, a few days, or even a week; the life which seems so carefree and gay. But at the end of the week, I should be dead beat and would be only too thankful to listen to anyone who began to talk about something sensible. I don't want followers, but friends, admirers who fall not for a flattering smile but for what one does and for one's character.

I know quite well that the circle around me would be much smaller. But what does that matter, as long as one still keeps a few sincere friends?

Yet I wasn't entirely happy in 1942 in spite of everything; I often felt deserted, but because I was on the go the whole day long, I didn't think about it and enjoyed myself as much as I could. Consciously or unconsciously, I tried to drive away the emptiness I felt with jokes and pranks. Now I think seriously about life and what I have to do. One period of my life is over forever. The carefree schooldays are gone, never to return.

I don't even long for them any more; I have outgrown them, I can't just only enjoy myself as my serious side is always there.

I look upon my life up till the New Year, as it were, through a powerful magnifying glass. The sunny life at home, then coming here in 1942, the sudden change, the quarrels, the bickerings. I couldn't understand it, I was taken by surprise, and the only way I could keep up some bearing was by being impertinent.

The first half of 1943: my fits of crying, the loneliness, how I slowly began to see all my faults and shortcomings, which are so great and which seemed much greater then. During the day I deliberately talked about anything and everything that was farthest from my thoughts, tried to draw Pim to me; but couldn't. Alone I had to face the difficult task of changing myself, to stop the everlasting reproaches, which were so oppressive and which reduced me to such terrible despondency.

Things improved slightly in the second half of the year. I became a young woman and was treated more like a grown-up. I started to think, and write stories, and came to the conclusion that the others no longer had the right to throw me about like an india-rubber ball. I wanted to change in accordance with my own desires. But one thing that struck me even more was when I realized that even Daddy would never become my confidant over everything. I didn't want to trust anyone but myself any more.

At the beginning of the New Year: the second great change, my dream. . . . And with it I discovered my longing not for a girlfriend, but for a boyfriend. I also discovered my inward happiness and my defensive armor of superficiality and gaiety. In due time I quieted down and discovered my boundless desire for all that is beautiful and good.

And in the evening, when I lie in bed and end my prayers with the words, "I thank you, God, for all that is good and dear and beautiful,'' I am filled with joy. Then I think about "the good" of going into hiding, of my health and with my whole being of the "dearness" of Peter, of that which is still embryonic and impressionable and which we neither of us dare to name or touch, of that which will come sometime; love, the future, happiness and of "the beauty" which exists in the world; the world, nature, beauty and all, all that is exquisite and fine.

I don't think then of all the misery, but of the beauty that still remains. This is one of the things that Mummy and I are so entirely different about. Her counsel when one feels melancholy is: "Think of all the misery in the world and be thankful that you are not sharing in it!" My advice is: "Go outside, to the fields, enjoy nature and the sunshine, go out and try to recapture happiness in yourself and in God. Think of all the beauty that's still left in and around you and be happy!"

I don't see how Mummy's idea can be right, because then how are you supposed to behave if you go through the misery yourself? Then you are lost. On the contrary, I've found that there is always some beauty left — in nature, sunshine, freedom, in yourself; these can all help you. Look at these things, then you find yourself again, and God, and then you will regain your balance.

And whoever is happy will make others happy too. He who has courage and faith will never perish in misery!

> From *Anne Frank, The Diary of a Young Girl,* New York: Pocket Books, published by arrangement with Doubleday & Company, pp. 149-152, copyright by Otto H. Frank, 1952.

DIARY OF MOSHE FLINKER: THOUGHTS OF MY PEOPLE NEVER LEAVE MY MIND

Three notebooks were found by the survivors of the Flinker family when they returned to the cellar in Brussels, where they had lived. The notebooks contained diary entries which Moshe had made while he was hiding in his room. Moshe Flinker was born in Holland in 1926. His father was a Polish immigrant who prospered in Holland. He had hired private Hebrew teachers for his seven children; Moshe, in particular, was very diligent in his Hebrew studies. They spoke Dutch at home, but Moshe also knew Hebrew and Yiddish, and studied French, English, German, Latin, and Greek. He also tried to study Arabic in order to prepare himself to become a diplomat in the future Jewish State.

In his diary, which he wrote in classical Hebrew, he describes his experiences in Brussels. Most of it, however, is taken up with his reflections about his Jewishness, his troubled faith, his feelings of anguish and guilt at being safe while myriads of his brethren are dying. Despite it all, his faith in God and his people remained steadfast.

Of all diaries, Moshe's is the most Jewish in content and spirit. It is an inspiring document of national and religious sincerity, love of his people and faith in the ultimate victory of good over evil.

March, 9, 1943. What shall I do? The emptiness has spread within me and now fills me completely. For a few days now, no new thought or idea has come to me. I have tried various measures and nothing has helped. I tried going to bed very late, and went to bed at three, but nothing changed. For two week I have reduced my daily meals from three to one, but this, too, has been to no avail. Maybe these things will yet help, but so far I am completely in the grip of this nothingness, this lack of will and thought. I have tried to find a reason for all of this, but I have been unable to settle on anything for sure. Maybe it is due to the fact that I am living a life of peace and quiet while my brothers are in a situation so bad that God alone knows its full horror. Maybe this void will disappear soon; there are some signs of this, but I cannot be sure.

Lately I feel so lonely, so barren — a feeling I have never had before. I feel myself so far from all my brothers, from everything nationally Jewish. And all that I see that reminds me of Jewish things I embrace and clasp to my heart with a love that I never before felt. Thus I found in the Hebrew library a Palestine school almanac. I had already seen it there a few months ago and taken it home, but then I did not feel so barren as I feel now. A few days ago I again took it from the library and read it in a spirit entirely different from the first time. It now seemed like a letter to me, as a sign of life of the rest of my people. I love it so much that I can hardly bring myself to return it to the library. The name of the almanac is *My Homeland*. How many times have I not said this word to myself in the last week, and each time it comes into my mind I am filled with yearning for it, and my soul longs for my country that I have loved — and still love — so much. Even before the war my heart longed for my homeland, the Land of Israel, but now this love and yearning have greatly increased. For it is only now that I feel how much we need a country in which we could live in peace as every people lives in its country. Each time I stand to say the Eighteen Benedictions[1] I direct my whole soul to my lovely land, and I see it before my eyes; I see the coast, I see Tel Aviv, Jaffa, and Haifa. Then I see Jerusalem, with the Mount of Olives, and I see the Jordan as it flows from Lebanon to the Dead Sea. I also see the land across the Jordan — I visualize all of this when I stand to pray. And when I pray and do not see my beloved country before my eyes it is as if my prayer had been rejected and as if I had been praying to the wall. O, I love all of it so much! My people and my country do not leave my thoughts for even a moment; all day long they are in my mind. Several times already I have asked myself whether I will ever get the chance to stand on its holy earth, if the Lord will permit me to walk about in my land, Oh, how my soul yearns for you, my homeland, how my eyes crave for the sight of you, my country, the Land of Israel.

April, 7, 1943. All day long, thoughts of my people never leave my mind, not even for a minute. They are with me everywhere, whether I am standing or sitting, eating or talking, or whatever I am doing. I try so hard to deprive myself

[1]A prayer said morning, evening and night while standing.

of the numerous pleasures that are to be found all around. I walk in the street and the sun is burning hot and I am covered with perspiration, and then I think of going for a swim — immediately afterward I remember where my people are and then I cannot even dream of going swimming; or I pass a pastry shop and I see in the window some attractive, delicious-looking cream-cakes and I am just about to enter the shop — and then the situation of my brothers flashes across my mind and my desires are destroyed, and I am overcome with shame for having forgotten their plight. But there is yet another place where I am continually brought in mind of them for wholly different reasons than those which I have noted and which brings me completely different thoughts than those I have mentioned. That place is school.

Lately I have been going to school, on the suggestion of my father, to learn typing and shorthand. I have been attending this school for about two months. I get there at nine in the morning and sit and pound the typewriter; then some girls who also study there enter and they are full of laughter, joy, and gaiety. And already, this sight — I mean seeing these impudent girls, laughing and gay at a time when the girls of my people are wretched and have not known the happiness these girls enjoy — excites in me jealousy and hatred for them. But that is not all. When they sit down and I hear them tell each other where they were the night before, what movie they saw, who their boyfriends are, or what love letters they have received, then because of my great jealousy as I remember our people, I am on the verge of tears. At such times I don't think so much of the physical affliction of my people as of their spiritual anguish, which may well be greater than their physical pain. I know full well how bitter it is when children have nothing to eat and when their parents can give them nothing — but how much more bitter it is when the entire you9h of a nation is sad, when its young girls no longer laugh and its young men are melancholy. It is at such moments, that I feel a burning love for my poor people which, because of my not being involved physically, makes me more aware than ever of its troubles. At such moments I feel as if the Lord has maliciously separated me from my people so that after the redemption I would know just how much they had missed.

Lately I have not been studying much; I haven't been as constant as I had been in my Arabic. Inside me I am continually aware of how the time we are living in seems to be growing larger and larger. I see this era as becoming greater, stronger, and more terrible. I am already sure that this war will not end as all previous wars.[1]

From *Diary of Moshe Flinker*, published by Yad Vashem, pp. 82-84.

YITZHAK RUDASHEVSKY RECORDS ASPECTS OF LIFE IN THE VILNA GHETTO

Yitzhak Rudashevsky was barely fourteen years old when the German Army invaded Vilna, the "Jerusalem of Lithuania." He was an outstanding student

[1]Original text is incomplete here.

in the secondary school and very active in Jewish youth activities. His special interest was the history of the Jewish community of Vilna, and he did research on the subject. His first diary entry is June 1941, and the last is on April 6, 1943.

Unlike other child diarists, Yitzhak did not write from the confines of a hideout. His diary ranges far and wide on life in the ghetto. He wrote in Yiddish and did not disclose the contents of his diary to anyone. After the war it was found buried in the ground, by a friend who had escaped death at Camp Ponar near Vilna.

The tenants of the house go into a hideout. We go with them. Three floors of warehouses in the courtyard of Shavler 4. Stairs lead from one story to the other. The stairs from the first to the second story have been taken down and the opening has been closed up with boards. The hideout consists of two small warehouses. You enter the hideout through a hole in the wall of an apartment which borders on the uppermost story of the hideout. The hole is blocked ingeniously by a kitchen cupboard. One wall of the cupboard serves at the same time as a little gate for the hole. The hole is barricaded by stones. The flat through which you enter the hideout is located near our apartment. Little groups of people with bundles go in. Soon we also crawl through the hole of the hideout. Many people have gathered in the two stories of the hideout. They sneak along like shadows by candlelight around the cold, dank cellar walls. The whole hideout is filled with a restless murmuring. An imprisoned mass of people. Everyone begins to settle down in the corners, on the stairs. Pillows and bundles are spread out on the hard bricks and boards and people fall asleep. The candle lights begin to die out. Everything is covered in darkness. You hear only the snoring of the sleepers, a groaning, restless murmuring. It is stifling. An odor of a cellar and of people crowded together. From time to time someone lights a match. By the light I see people lying on the bricks like rags in the dirt. I think: into what kind of helpless, broken creature can man be transformed? I am at my wit's end. I begin to feel very nauseated. I barely live to see the dawn. The people are crawling out. The dawn brings a new piece of news. Persons with yellow certificates must leave the ghetto with their families. They will leave, and now the game will begin. I look at the mass of people with bundles that is streaming to the gate. They are headed for life. How I envy them! I too would like to leave the accursed ghetto, which is becoming a terrible snare. I wish like them, the people with the yellow certificates, to go away, to leave the storm behind me, to save my life.

I meet my friend Benkye Nayer. He is pale, has not had enough sleep. He too spent the night in a hideout. It was the last time that I saw him.

We are in the hideout again. We expect something any moment. While lying thus on bundles I fell asleep. A noise, the sound of people crowding each other woke me. I understood that the Lithuanians were already in the ghetto. The hideout is becoming fuller and fuller. We are finally so tightly crowded together that we cannot move. The hideout is being hammered up. My parents are somewhere upstairs. I am downstairs with my uncle. The hideout is full of a restless whispering. Candles are being lit. People reassure each other. Suddenly there is a sound of steps. People mass together. An old Jew has remained hanging in the narrow passage of the second story. His feet are dangling over the heads of people below. He is taken down. People call: "Bring water!" But gradually everything becomes still. Everything becomes completely enveloped in a black, dreadful silence, a silence from which there shouts forth the great tragedy of our helplessness, the destructive storm which is now pervading the ghetto. You hear a faint sound, as though a tempest were being rent with shouts, with shots. My heart beats as though with hammers to the cadence of the storm outside. Soon I feel that the storm is approaching us. My head is dizzy, a cold perspiration oozes forth, my heart stops beating entirely.

We are like animals surrounded by the hunter. The hunter on all sides: beneath us, above us, from the sides. Broken locks snap, doors creak, axes, saws. I feel the enemy under the boards on which I am standing. The light of an electric bulb seeps through the cracks. They pound, tear, break. Soon the attack is heard from another side. Suddenly, somewhere upstairs, a child bursts into tears. A desperate groan breaks forth from everyone's lips. We are lost. A desperate attempt to shove sugar into the child's mouth is of no avail. They stop up the child's mouth with pillows. The mother of the child is weeping. People shout in wild terror that the child should be strangled. The child is shouting more loudly, the Lithuanians are pounding more strongly against the walls. However, slowly everything calmed down of itself. We understand that they have left. Later we heard a voice from the other side of the hideout. You are liberated. My heart beats with such joy! I have remained alive!

To save one's own life at any price, even at the price of our brothers who are leaving us. To save one's own life and not attempt to defend it . . . the point of view of our dying passively like sheep, unconsciousness of our tragic fragmentation, our helplessness.

We creep out of the hideout after a six-hour imprisonment. It is eight o'clock in the evening. Everything resembles the aftermath of a catastrophe. The tenants' belongings are scattered over the courtyard. Smashed locks lie around under our feet, everything is turned upside down, topsy-turvy, broken. All doors are wide open. The house is unrecognizable. Everything is scattered far and wide, many things are broken. A bottle of spirits lies smashed in the middle of the room. The bundles are ripped with knives. I go out into the street. It is dark. The street is full of the tragedy which has just happened here. On the pavement lie bundles, a bloody reminder of the people who have just been dragged away to their deaths. I enter the courtyard where my cousins live. I notice two large bright windows. I look inside. A house in the wake of a pogrom. Electricity is burning and no person is to be seen. It is so terrible. I enter my uncle's house. It is dark. I step on things. It is quiet. A clock strikes forlornly. No one is here.

I go back home. Frightened people crawl out of the corners. They too have found deliverance.

Poking Fun at the Germans

In the house we had a little fun. The workers in our house belong to the famous *Schneiderstube*.[1] Mother works there too. The workers tell about the events of the whole week; how Jewish tailors come to an understanding with Germans, and receive a small amount of provisions from them. The workers tell about the life there. You toil yet at the same time you must chase after your bit of bread. Make a living, trade, make an exchange with a peasant, make a deal with a rag. All this so , only until a German appears. Then people scatter at once in all directions. However, people are not impressed by the German either. If they meet some fool of a German who wants a cap, the fellows make fun of him, they bring out a Jew and introduce him as the best "capmaker of Poland." The German believes it. Then they tell him that this diligent Jew can make beautiful caps only when he receives a little food. He is persuaded. He takes out material which can suffice for three hats and gives it to them. And they tell him that this is nothing. When the time comes for delivery, he is simply told: "Listen, do you have cigarettes? Give us cigarettes and you will have 'a delightful cap.' " Finally they make him a hat which looks like a blintz on him and he exclaims into the bargain, "Jews are a capable people!" They add the blessing, *"mitn rosh in adome,"* [2] and he answers, "Thank you very much," and they shout after him, "A name after you." And he is also delighted with his "cap." That is how our tailors work. It looks sometimes, the workers say, like a Jewish bazaar. They get along well with the Germans. "Yankl," shouts one tailor to the other, "measure this gentleman for shrouds," or "Please take him to the *Taare bret,* hurry up!" or "Make a fine little coat in the side for this German woman" (it is supposed to mean "to sew her a coat"). The Jewish embroiderers make monograms. The ornament consists of four Jewish letters: *"g"* — *"a gzeyre,"* *"ts"* — *"a tsore,"* *"s"* — *"a sreyfe,"* *"k"* — *"kapore."* The truth is that all these stories are merely wishful thinking. People are actually afraid of the German. However, if it is possible to curse him, to play a trick on him, they do so whenever they can.

A.E.

From *Diary of a Boy from Vilna,* by Yitzhak Rudashevsky, published by Hakibbutz Hameuchad and Ghetto Fighters' House, Israel, 1973, pp. 37-40, 51-52. Transl. by Percy Matenko.

EXCERPTS FROM THE DIARY OF DAVID RUBINOVICZ: THE RURAL SCENE

Unlike the other child diarists, young David grew up in rural surroundings. He was a simple lad, unsophisticated and limited in his learning. He wrote his rather sporadic diary in the Polish language. It was spread over five different paper pads, beginning with March 21, 1940, and ending abruptly on June 1, 1942. Like other diaries, it was found accidentally, fifteen years later, in the garret of a neighbor's house. By chance it became known to the world through a woman who was a member of a small group of enlightened Poles who fought against the reactionary anti-Semitic movement in Poland.

[1]A tailor shop.
[2]Equivalent of "drop dead."

David was barely thirteen years old when he began his diary. He had been expelled from the Polish school and continued his studies on his own.

Because of the very nature of David's diary, which reflects the simple lives of village Jews, it won wide acclaim and was translated into Spanish, Italian, German, Czech, Yiddish, and Hebrew.

August 12, 1940. Since the war began, I study at home by myself. When I remember my school days I am moved to cry. Nowadays I am confined to the house and do not go out anywhere. And when I think of the war, the people who die from bullets, gas, bombs, and other deadly weapons I lose all desire to go on living.

December 26, 1940. Father was dressing when a boy came to inform him that a German gendarme had ordered him to come to the store immediately. Father dressed quickly and left. . . . After a short interval he returned and asked me to summon five Jews, who were to meet him at the store, but he did not explain the reason. When I notified the Jews of the gendarme's order, they came to the store immediately. Father told them that the authorities had issued a command that all Jews must give up all furs in their possession, even the smallest pieces, and that we would be responsible for carrying out the order immediately. Anyone caught hiding a piece of fur would be executed. The gendarme set the time limit for giving up the furs at 4:00 P.M.

In a very short time Jews began to bring fur coats, scarves, collars, and miscellaneous pieces. At 4:00 P.M. the gendarme came, accompanied by a Polish soldier, who made a list of all the items. Mother gave up her furs, including the fur collars from all our winter coats. We put them in sacks and delivered them to the collection point. The Polish soldier made a list of all the items collected, and they transported the pieces to the police station at Bitini.

January 15, 1941. As I was looking through the window, I saw a wagon stop, and from it emerged gendarmes. They came into the house and ordered us all to join the snow cleaners. I, my brother and aunt slipped away from the group and sneaked into the village. The gendarmes were making a check of the Jewish stores in the marketplace. . . . Mother and Grandma were caught and forced to join the snow cleaners. The cold was severe. Mother and Grandma wore no gloves and had not eaten lunch.

[David removes the yellow badge from his clothes and flees to a nearby village.] I finally came to my destination. I thought I would have a heart attack. When I finally returned home, our neighbor told me that all Jews, including my parents, had been conscripted to clear the snow.

When the family returned home in the evening, I was told that the gendarmes put chains on a Jew and took him to the police station. Two others were imprisoned and ordered to pay 100 zloty if they wished to regain their freedom.

I put on my coat and ran out to find out what had happened to the prisoner in chains. I was told that he was chained to a sled and forced to run behind it. Perhaps he was shot.[1]

---

[1] The following day David noted in his diary that the victim collapsed and was shot after he had been dragged a long distance behind the sled.

All evening long we sat sunk in our thoughts. How many hunters lie in ambush to trap us like exposed, helpless rabbits!

May 6, 1942. Today was a dreadful day. At about three, in the early morning, I was awakened by a banging at the door, but I was not panicky because my father and my cousin were visiting in the nearby town of Kraino. Polish and Jewish policemen came in and began searching the house. They asked how old I was. When I answered fourteen years, they let me alone. They took along two Jews from Plotsk who had lodged with us. . . . I shook as if in a fever. When they left I finally fell asleep.

In the morning my girl cousin woke me. Father had just arrived. I dressed hurriedly and went out to greet him. But he was not in sight. He had learned about the hunt of the Jews by the Germans and their accomplices. We quickly unloaded the foodstuffs which Father had brought in the wagon. Just then I saw a policeman entering our yard. He was yelling, "Where are the potatoes? Give us all you have!" I thought that our end had come. They confiscated all that Father had brought and took it to the police station. We were left without a morsel of food.

My father and cousin were imprisoned. My yearnings to see Father grew with every passing hour. We forgot about the confiscation of our food — all we wanted was our father.

Mother went to the Jewish Council to plead for his release. He was a sick man and sorely dependent on his medication. He could not live long without taking his prescribed medicines. If he should be sent to work in a camp, his life would be in grave danger. The authorities assured us that they would free him after the investigation.

I could not go out of the house because of fear that I would be caught. Only my brother and Anshel brought Father some victuals. Anshel returned and told us that the Germans had put out a dragnet to arrest all Jews. Panic spread like wildfire, and everyone sought to hide. The wives and relatives of all who had been caught wept and wailed without surcease.

Soon two automobiles drew near the police station. When I spied them coming, I knew that they would take away my father and burst out sobbing. Father asked my brother to quickly bring him some underwear, food, and a small pot. I broke down, crying bitterly, when I saw him take his things with him as he left. All this time, my mother was at the Jewish Council, crying and pleading for them to get Father released. They assured her he would be freed. My brother returned to get a warm head covering for Father, but when he came back the automobile had already left.

I cried out, "Father, where are you? I want to see you." I caught a glimpse of him crying.

My moans and tears did not cease. At the moment of parting I realized how much I loved him and he me. I lamented that I had had doubts whether he loved me. . . .

Suddenly my sister rushed in with the news that a policeman had informed her that all our things which had been confiscated had been returned and that we could now pick them up at the railroad station. We went and brought back the merchandise and food to our house. But our joy was only for a moment. Our greatest loss was our father, whom they retained in their custody.

The man responsible for returning our merchandise was a German gendarme, a decent man. Were it not for him, we would not have recovered anything.

Mother is completely exhausted from the day's happenings. She looks as if Father had been imprisoned for several weeks. When I went to sleep I thought: Here I lie in a comfortable bed, and Father may not even have a straw pallet to lay his head on. My heart constricted from pain and I broke into tears.

June 1, 1942. Today is a day for rejoicing. We had hoped to receive a letter from Father but were disappointed as usual. A postcard was delivered, written by our cousin, which included regards from Father. We prepared a large package for Father. Tomorrow there will be a visitation from the Jewish Council to his prison camp, and they will take it. We packed his clothing, a few potatoes, bread, and other odds and ends.

Longingly I waited and hoped for the third of June, when we might receive a letter from him. Maybe it would contain some hope that he would come home. Before evening, I visited our neighbor to order a pair of wooden sandals. While he was working I heard the sound of an automobile and voices singing. I thought immediately that these must be the Jewish prisoners coming back from the prison camp. I rushed to the door and saw a truck filled with people.

From the distance I saw them frantically waving their hands and hats. Among them I spotted my father waving his hands. I threw everything down and ran after the automobile. I stopped when the truck stopped. Quickly I took the bundle from father's hands as he climbed down. Mother took the bundle from me, and I ran at once to the police station to take back the bundle which we had posted to be delivered. When I returned home there was such a joyous outpouring that I could not even get near Father to embrace and kiss him. Our joy was indescribable; only one who has lived through our experience can put it into words. No one could possibly have imagined that this would actually happen. It seemed as if we were watching a wondrous film unrolling before our eyes, showing unbelievable scenes and arousing indescribable sensations.

Almost instantly our house was filled with a crowd of people, each one asking questions, wanting to hear all that had happened. . . .

Father had returned with his hand wounded. It turned out that his wound was the cause of his release. At first I was thrown into a fright because I thought he was seriously wounded, but my apprehensions were soon eased.

I find it very difficult to narrate Father's experiences. The first week at camp was the worst, until he got used to the surroundings. The labor was not so arduous, but the discipline was very severe. Anyone who did not join in group singing or did not keep step would be whiplashed. At four each morning they were awakened, and at five in the afternoon they returned from work — thirteen hours of unrelenting toil during which they were not allowed to sit down even for a moment.

We sat listening to him until two in the morning. He did not look very bad because he had kept strict care of what he ate.

In all this excitement I have forgotten to record this tragic happening. This morning two Jewish women went to the village — a mother and daughter. To their misfortune, they were overtaken by a wagon full of Germans. They fled as fast as their feet would carry them, but they were caught. The Germans wanted to shoot them on the spot, but the sheriff of the town restrained them, so the Germans brought them into the forest and shot them there. The Jewish police arrived and transported their corpses for burial. The wagon was smeared with blood. Who. . . . [1]

A.E.

From *Diary of David Rubinovicz,* published by Ghetto Fighters House and Hakibbutz Hameuchad, 1964, pp. 9, 23f., 29f, 69f.

EVA HEYMAN'S DIARY: THE DISINTEGRATION OF HER FAMILY

Eva Heyman's diary was written in Hungarian by a thirteen-year-old girl of superior intelligence. In it she describes the liquidation of Novigrod, which had been fully assimilated into the Magyar (native Hungarian) culture. She vividly renders the pathos of her family when they realize that, despite having been fully assimilated, they had not escaped the fate that awaited their co-religionists. They, too, are ordered to wear the yellow badge and are subjected to restrictions, deprivations, tortures, deportations, and ultimate extermination. The diary was preserved by the family cook.

Eva came from a prominent family. Her mother, Ági (Agnes), had divorced Eva's father and married a distinguished journalist. Ági lived with Eva's paternal grandparents. Eva's resentment of her mother is clearly evident in her diary. She always refers to her as Ági.

In the end, Ági deserted her daughter in the ghetto and, together with her second husband, was among those who were saved by Rudolf Kastner[2] from death at the Bergen-Belsen death camp. Eva and her grandparents died in Auschwitz. When Eva's stepfather died, her mother lapsed into a deep depression. Conscience-stricken, utterly alone and desolate, Ági committed suicide.

Eva's diary began on February 13, 1944, when the Hungarian Fascists began persecuting her family.

May 5, 1944. Dear diary, now you aren't at 3 Istvan Gyöngyösi Street — that is, at home — any more, not even at Anikó's, nor at Tusnád, nor at Lake Balaton, nor in Budapest, places you've been with me too before, but in the ghetto. Three days we waited for them to come and get us. There we sat in the apartment and watched for the policemen. Ági and Grandpa went out into the street between nine and ten in the morning to hear the latest news. The city was

[1]Here David's diary ended abruptly. Had he continued? Were the pages lost? Or did death catch up with him and his family?

The Jews of his town and surrounding villages were deported in the latter half of September, 1942 — five thousand in all. On Yom Kippur Day, September 21, 1942, they were transported in the death trains to Treblinka. Very likely David and his family were among them.

[2]A member of the Hungarian Jewish Council who took part in the rescue of Jews at a price.

divided into sections, and a German truck would wait in front of the houses and two policemen would go into the apartments and bring the people out. The notices tell what we can take with us. Dear diary, I'm still too little a girl to write down what I felt while we waited to be taken into the ghetto. Between one order and the next, Ági would cry out that we deserve what we get because we are like animals, patiently waiting to be slaughtered in the slaughterhouse. But now and then, after Ági burst into such an outcry, Grandma Rácz would have an attack, and then Ági would calm down. . . . From time to time, when the bell rang, I would be almost happy. I knew that we were being taken to the ghetto, but felt that if this silence went on much longer we would all go crazy. Then everything happened like in a film.

The two policemen who came to us weren't unfriendly; they just took Grandma's and Ági's wedding rings away from them. Ági was shaking all over and couldn't get the wedding ring off her finger. In the end, Grandma took the ring off her finger. Then they checked our luggage and they didn't allow us to take Grandpa's valise because it is genuine pigskin. They didn't allow anything made out of leather to be taken along. They said: "There is a war going on and the soldiers need the leather." They also didn't allow me to take my red purse. We took washing kits and Grandma's thick cloth bag.

One of the policemen saw a little gold chain on my neck, the one I got for my birthday, the one holding your key, dear diary. "Don't you know yet," the policeman said, "that you aren't allowed to keep anything made of gold?! This isn't private Jewish property anymore but national property!" Whenever something was being taken from us, Ági would always pretend not to notice at all, because she had an obsession about not letting the policemen think that it bothered us that our things were being taken, but this time she begged the policeman to let me keep the little gold chain. She started sobbing and saying: "Mr. Inspector, please go and ask your colleagues, and they will tell you that I have never begged for anything, but please let the child keep just this little gold chain. You see, she keeps the key to her diary on it." "Please," the policeman said, "that is impossible; in the ghetto you will be checked again. I, so help me God, don't need this chain or any other object that is being taken from you. I don't need any of it, but I don't want any difficulties. I am a married man. My wife is going to have a baby." I gave him the chain. In Grandma's night table I found a velvet ribbon. I asked the policeman: "Mr. Inspector, may I take a velvet ribbon along to the ghetto?" He said I could. Now your key hangs on that velvet ribbon, dear diary.

It seems that Mariska sneaked out of the house somehow when the policemen came, and I didn't see her anywhere. Although it's true that in all the excitement I forgot all about Mariska. Mariska already took Mandi [the canary] away yesterday. I trust Mariska to take care of her. She also loves Mandi very much. We tied the bedding in bundles. Grandpa and Uncle Béla took the bundles on their backs and carried them out to the open truck that stood by the gate. The truck driver was a German soldier, an SS, I think, because he wore a black uniform. Dear diary, the most terrible thing happened when we got to the gate. Then I saw Grandpa cry for the first time in my life. . . . I will never forget how Grandpa stood there looking at the garden, shaking from his crying. There were also tears in Uncle Béla's eyes. And only now I noticed how Grandma had turned into such an old woman, just like Grandma Lujza, and Grandma Rácz is only fifty-four. She walked out of the gate as though she were drunk or sleepwalking. She didn't even look back, and there wasn't a tear in her eyes. Ági put her hands under the bundle on Grandpa's back so it shouldn't be so heavy for him.

I heard Ági say to the policemen, referring to Grandpa: "So, you've got what you wanted: 'Nathan the Jew marches in the van, with bundle on back wanders the man.' " We waited for them to put the seal on the gate; then Grandpa was the first to get on the truck. It was impossible to sit, so we stood. Standing, they drove us up to Várad's main street. When we got to the pharmacy, Grandma and Ági looked the other way. All the way Uncle Béla held Ági in his arms. I cuddled up alongside Grandma so as not to see the Aryans in the street. They were taking their afternoon strolls, as though it were the most natural thing in the world that from now on we should live in the ghetto. We crossed the bridge, and when we got to the synagogue we saw them putting up the ghetto fence. Where the fence was already up, there stood gendarmes with bayonets and chicken feathers. Ági saw the gendarmes and doubled over as if bitten by a snake and said to Uncle Béla: "In other words, gendarmes are taking us to our death!" I know that ever since Ági was in Vác, before Uncle Béla was taken away to the Ukraine, she was more afraid of the gendarmes than of wild animals. In the middle of the synagogue compound there was a long table, with a commission sitting around it. Grandpa whispered to Uncle Béla that he knew "those gentlemen from City Hall," but they acted as if they had never seen Grandpa before, even though they probably had spoken to him in the second-person familiar "you," when they used to buy in his pharmacy. They assigned us to 20 Szacsvay Street. There was no truck anymore, so we had to drag everything along to Szacsvay Street. Uncle Béla didn't want Ági to drag anything, because of her scar, but we couldn't manage without her. Interesting, but it occurred to me only when we got to Szacsvay Street that we weren't going to have an apartment, because the commission had said: "Your place to sleep will be at 20 Szacsvay Street." It makes a tremendous difference, dear diary, because a normal person has an apartment, while people talk about "place to sleep" only in connection with animals. I swear that Ági is right; as far as the Aryans are concerned, we've become like animals.

What do you think, dear diary, who stood in the gate as we were about to go into house number 20 in Szacsvay Street? Pista Vadas! You know how really truly I love Pista Vadas, but now I can't care less whether he is here or isn't here, although he immediately took the bundles from Ági and Grandma and took them into the house. We found Pista Vadas here because his big sister, Aunt Nusi, is the wife of Chief Rabbi Vajda, and they always lived here, because this is the Rabbinical Residence. We used to visit here a lot, when Dr. Lipót Kecskeméti was the Chief Rabbi of Várad, and he was my uncle, Marica's grandpa. He died a few years ago, and this Vajda took his place. We knew the whole house and the garden very well. My grandparents even said: "Well, what a fine reunion with the Rabbinical Residence!" When we got here, there was already a big crowd of people. All the furniture had been taken out into the courtyard, and we tried to get ourselves arranged. The policemen had allowed us to take food from the house and the commission in the synagogue compound had said that the women should cook, wash, and keep house, because they wouldn't have anything else to keep themselves busy. In the Vajda house, the basement was packed to the ceiling with logs of wood, and Ági said we would at least be able to heat water so that the children could wash. It is impossible to count how many of us there are in the house, because even in the halls and stairwells people sit on mattresses. Because of them it is impossible to move about, and we always trip over someone's leg.

Later it rained, and Aunt Nusi's beautiful furniture got wet in the garden outside. But she said she didn't care; everything could rot, because anyway it was all going to belong to somebody else! Pista Vadas let me sit on the windowsill, the only place where there was still some room. I looked at Ági, curious to know what she thought about the whole thing, but she wasn't paying attention to anything and worried only about where Grandpa and Grandma and Uncle Béla would sleep. At first, Chief Rabbi Vajda said that the women and children should be separated from the men. But then none of the women wanted to leave their husbands, and the women said that we could undress in the dark, and that every effort should be made for families to sleep together. We were put in a room that had been used as an office. The bookshelves were sunk into the walls so it was impossible to take them out to the yard. The shelves are packed full of books. Uncle Béla said: "I hope we shall manage to read them all by the end of the war." In the evening we wanted to turn on the lights, but it turned out that City Hall had cut off the electricity, because Jews aren't entitled to electricity. Still, everybody somehow found a place, only nobody ate supper, because, of course, nobody thought that we would be left in the dark. Ági and Uncle Béla, Marica and her parents, Grandpa and Grandma Rácz, Uncle Dr. Samu Meer, who is very old and a good friend of Grandpa, and his daughter Aunt Lili and her husband, Pista Márton, who is also a journalist, all sleep together in one room. Also Uncle Ernö Markovits, a journalist too, who is not so young any more. The poor man is all alone in the ghetto. His wife could stay home, because she is an Aryan, but Uncle Markovits is Jewish and he was brought here. Uncle Lusztig and his wife, an old couple, also sleep here. They don't have any children. According to the order, sixteen people are supposed to sleep in a room, but it's no use; the room is small, and it's impossible to budge in it, even though we're only fourteen. When it got dark we lay down on the mattresses. I cuddled up with Marica and the two of us — believe it or not, dear diary — were happy. Strange as it seems, everybody belonging to us was here together with us, everybody in the world whom we loved. Of course, I didn't have my father, but I thought I would go looking for him in the morning. We chose Marica's mother, Aunt Klári Kecskeméti, to be in charge of the inhabitants of our room. Everybody has to obey her. In the dark she gave a speech, and even though I was almost asleep, I understood that we all have to take care that everything is kept clean, because that is very important, and that we all have to think of one another, since all the people in the room are relatives and friends. Marica and I kissed and we both fell asleep. I dreamt that Pista Vadas was the driver of the truck, and I was awfully angry that Pista Vadas had become an SS man.

May 10, 1944. Dear diary, we're here five days, but, word of honor, it seems like five years. I don't even know where to begin writing, because so many awful things have happened since I last wrote in you. First, the fence was finished, and nobody can go out or come in. The Aryans who used to live in the area of the ghetto all left during these few days to make place for the Jews. From today on, dear diary, we're not in a ghetto but in a ghetto-camp, and on every house they've pasted a notice which tells exactly what we're not allowed to do, signed by the commander of the ghetto-camp himself. Actually, everything is forbidden, but the most awful thing of all is that the punishment for everything is death. There is no difference between things; no standing in the corner, no spankings, no taking away food, no writing down the declension of irregular verbs one hundred times the way it used to be in school. Not at all: the lightest and heaviest punishment — death. It doesn't actually say that this punishment also applies to children, but I think it does apply to us, too.

> From the *Diary of Eva Heyman,* published by Yad Vashem, 1974, pp. 68-75.
> Translated by Moshe M. Kohn.

EXTRACTS FROM TAMARAH LAZERSON'S DIARY: DISCOVERING ZIONISM AND JUDAISM

"When war broke out," Tamarah wrote in her diary, *"Father, who was a successful psychiatrist, said to Victor [her older brother] 'Begin writing a diary for we are living in historic times.'"* Tamarah and her brother wrote individual diaries and would often compare notes. She was thirteen when she began her diary.

The Lazerson family was assimilationist, and Tamarah was greatly influenced by the Lithuanian culture and the Catholic religion. Actually, Tamarah was inclined to undergo baptism and become a Catholic.

In August 1941, 30,000 Jews of Kovno, where the Lazersons lived, were crowded into the worst section of the town, which had housed a population of 7000. About 2000 intellectuals, who were always among the first to be doomed, were liquidated. Some 4000 men, women, and youths were mustered for slave labor and were engaged in building an airfield.

Tamarah's parents made no move to seek shelter in the homes of their Catholic friends. "How can I endanger the lives of others by hiding ourselves among them?" Dr. Lazerson argued.

Tamarah outlived the war and completed her studies in chemistry. She married a fellow student, Michael Ostrowsky. In 1971 she and her husband settled in Haifa, Israel, where she now lives with her family.

These extracts begin with her depiction of life in the ghetto, to which the family was transported in 1941. The excerpt that follows is the second entry in her diary. In it, we begin to see a complete metamorphosis in Tamarah's inner self.

September 14, 1942. By chance I was conscripted to join a Jewish labor battalion. To my amazement the conversations centered around smuggling "bundles" into the ghetto, despite the threat of severe punishments. Our people endanger their very lives to obtain food. They hide their purchases in their clothing and smuggle them in at the gate or above the ghetto fence. And even if they are searched, they somehow get through. We are a remarkable people, indestructible. No decrees or edicts will break us. I declare this people will never be destroyed, despite their unspeakable suffering; therefore it is an eternal people and ultimately it shall overcome its enemies.

September 21. My old wound has reopened. The school year has begun. I am deeply pained that another year will go to waste. But what can I do? . . .

November 24. A long time has passed since I have read a book. It's terribly hard to obtain them now. To add to our troubles, the electricity has been cut off. My room is dark and unheated. Nothing to do but to crawl into bed. At seven o'clock, and sometimes even earlier, I'm in bed. These are my worst hours. Memories overwhelm me and there's no way to shake them off. I remain sleepless and toss about half the night.

April 4, 1943. I am now working in a trade school and am very pleased. The lectures are interesting. We take notes diligently and then study them at home. I cannot recognize myself, for I am now preparing for life in Eretz Yisrael. Today I handed in quite a long essay for our wall newspaper. I ended it with the slogan: "Eretz Yisrael awaits us!" I am happy! [In connection with this entry, Tamarah composed a sixteen-line poem in Yiddish, expressing her joy of achievement in her gardening activities and Yiddish studies.]

May 20. I am very pleased with myself. It seems to me that I had strayed and have been wandering about aimlessly. And now at long last I have found an aim in life. I am no longer forlorn — an individual without a homeland and a people. No! I have found an aim: to struggle, to study, to devote my strength to advance the well-being of my people and my homeland. I am proud of it. I am no longer blind — God and fate have opened my eyes. I now see that my goals in life were false, and I have atoned. My heart tells me that I am now on the right road. I trust that I shall not be blinded again. Hurrah! Long live the Homeland, our hope and our faith. . . .

August 10. Yesterday a group of Hitler Youth hikers visited our Jewish workshops. For them it was an entertaining excursion — a lark.[1]

August 15. I am working in a tailor shop and am continuing my Hebrew studies. I am absorbed in the cultural life of the ghetto. A large number of our youth participate and are avid to learn. They deserve praise. I myself take part in three study circles and am pleased. As may be expected, there are two kinds of young people in the ghetto. Some are permeated with love and longing for Eretz Yisrael and all that the Zionist ideal implies. They are thirsty for knowledge and pursue idealistic, meaningful activities. The others are unbridled and com-

---

[1]Here Tamarah drew an illustration of a barbed-wire fence and entrance gate and above the gate drew a caption reading; "We are captive prisoners."

pletely given over to satisfying their lusts. This is utterly disgusting and painful for me to observe. They are degenerates.

September 8. I am busier than ever and have little time to write. I now belong to four study circles, two of which I lead. I am engaged in important work. Celia and I have become attached to the pitiful children of Zeznier.[2] We help them; they are so dependent on us. We comfort them, teach them Jewish values, and inspire them with goals for living. I am alive and dynamic. I feel that I am needed and useful.

[During this period the ghetto was being emptied, and many of its inhabitants were deported.] I am deeply distressed about the future of our generation. I'd like to write a poem, "The Mother and the Child," but I haven't the time or the inspiration. I have no books and am very bored — especially on Sundays.[3] No one visits me, and I am no longer occupied in cultural activity. The big tenement houses are becoming empty and dark. The weather is cold. It is raining; my feet are frozen; my spirits are very low.

November 14. SS commander Wilhelm Geke is "busy" in the ghetto. His aim is to convert it into a concentration camp. He has promised to build a new hospital. I am deeply suspicious of his promises.

The "affair"[4] is frozen. All who can do so escape from the city. Mothers place their children with Lithuanian friends because concentration camp means death to all. . . .

December 5. I am struggling with myself. Kazis[5] is in the sixth grade. Two more years and he graduates. This thought pierces through me like a knife in my heart. And what of me? What will I be? Again the wound in my heart opens. Three years lost. O God, I recall the past. I advanced from class to class, ever higher, and suddenly the ban — a fatal blow to my future.

Three years. It's hard to take. Be it as it may, if I'm alive I shall yet catch up. I know I can be a person of value to mankind. . . .

I am weighed down by my enslavement and have no time or strength to write, to think, or even to read. I am mired in a morass, into which I sink as I daily labor from early morning to night with the slave gang. Around me is darkness. I thirst for light. . . .

April 7, 1944. Five months have passed. The landscape has changed. The ghetto went up in flames and has left behind ruin and devastation that boggle the mind. Not a building in sight. Where once proud edifices stood erect, only blackened chimneys remain. The place is now a graveyard. The blackened skeletons stretch skyward, calling down revenge for the outrage committed against them and their former inhabitants.

We are now free. It is five months since I have thrown off the prison shackles. The rescuers came to save me, but woe is me! Only a handful escaped, smoldering embers from the great conflagration.

[2] A neighboring town whose Jews had been deported.
[3] The day of "rest."
[4] A code word meaning that the underground organization had ceased sending its members to join the forest partisans.
[5] A Lithuanian boyfriend of former days.

My life has now taken on a new direction. I am a lone orphan, a stray stone. My parents were uprooted during the golden summer days. They were put to death. Ah, my poor father, doomed mother. They could not escape. I am left with an agonizing pain and an aching heart. Only little Vitas, my beloved younger brother, is left alive! With him I do not feel quite so desolate. How fortunate am I that he succeeded in escaping! We are but two remaining limbs of a time-honored stock.

Before me pass scenes of our happy past. Why do I say a "happy past"? Even though my hands and legs were manacled, my heart was free. Now even my poor heart is chained. Alone in the thick forest, I seek the way to a sympathetic heart — my mother's. Physically I exist, but spiritually? . . . I learn; I live, I swallow bitter grub. I subsist.

"Daughter mine, what else do you need?"

"You, mother mine," I reply silently in a corner of my heart.

Today I saw a dead body. A human being, beautiful and blooming, suddenly cut off by death, lying in a casket. He was Dr. Stokes. His hands, white as snow, rested on his breast, and his bluish lips looked as if they were about to smile. He is smiling, but not at life. He has experienced death but he looks as if he were still alive. He *is* dead. Explain to me O World, can it be that a man is so helpless before his fated end? If so, why struggle and suffer? Man's destiny is to end in a coffin, legs stretched out, lifeless. Not a teardrop will accompany you on your last journey. But why tears? Is it easier to observe the unspeakable distress of a mother near the dead body of her offspring? No, a hundred times no!

The ground will welcome you, the tired, to her bosom. The heavens will let fall, at the very least, a tear — and thus your life will end. Why sink into despair? Why mourn? Why love and hate? No need! Manifestly we are but withered grass in the parched fields of life.

December 29. I note with a pained heart that I am beginning to forget Yiddish, which is dear to me. What's with you, Tamarah? Have you already forgotten the affliction that you have borne together with your people? Now that you live among gentiles, have you blotted out the oath you took on that black and sinister night? Remember! There is still time. Open your eyes and see the torment of your people. A voice calls out of the darkness: Right the wrong! I hear the voice, and my heart is torn. I awake. About me the night is thick with darkness. I see the horrible devastation of war and hear the weeping of children. O my people Israel! I can't forget you. An inner voice calls me to you. I am coming. I am ready to crawl on my knees and kiss your sacred soil. Only tell me that you hear my call. Say you will not spurn your daughter who yearns to return to you. I struggle with myself. I am all wrought up. I am consumed with fears. I await your answer.

January 14, 1945. Boredom and cold; it is bleak outside and in my heart. Vitas left for some place afar, and I do not know where. Uncle and aunt are somewhere in a desolate land, and I am here alone, a stranger. O God, what a burden it is to be solitary among aliens, fatherless and motherless. There is no one to whom you can run for solace, to embrace, to kiss. Around me are apathetic faces of people. How long can this continue? How can one stand up under it and endure? I want to die so that my sufferings will end. Not to live any longer, not to feel the oppression, the hate. What have I done to deserve all this? Why have I borne suffering all these years? When will it all end? When will the tears cease flowing? When will the sun rise? Never! Only when the soul rises heavenward will I find surcease. Why is life so cruel? Is there any happiness on this earth?

May 9. Yesterday Germany surrendered unconditionally. The war is over. Red flags fly triumphantly over Kovno. At long last the ugly Fascists have been decisively defeated. . . . Whatever may come, I am delighted that the dictator has been brought to his knees. The arrogant fiend who touted "Germany, Germany above all' now has to stoop to the barbarian of the East — the USSR.

You have lost; just as proud and mighty Rome did not rise out of its ashes, so Germany will not raise her head again above the nations of the world. She has fallen. Her strong might has been crushed forever. Long live peace! Honor to the heroes who raised the flag of victory over the contemptible towers of Berlin.

August 10. Yesterday I met Gershowitz. He was a battalion head in Camp Landsberg.[6] There my poor father toiled until he breathed his last. How much he suffered! He was not built for back-breaking labor; he was not suited for slavery. He was aged and weak. This tragic news was confirmed later. The last small spark of hope in me has flickered and died. His book of life is closed. There is no return. I must fortify myself with strength and patience and pave a new road for myself to the future.

A.E.

From *Tamarah's Diary* by Tamarah Lazerson, published by Ghetto Fighters House and Hakibbutz Hameuchad, 1966, pp. 37f., 39f., 58, 77, 79, 85, 87f., 97f, 101.

EXCERPTS FROM JANINA HESHELE'S DIARY OF LVOV

Janina was nearly twelve when she began writing her diary in Polish, on the very day that the Germans overran Lvov. She stands out among the diarists because of her literary talents, especially in the writing of free verse, in which she poured out her emotions in stirring lines. She drew the attention of a select group of highly cultured prisoners, who extricated her from the Janowska Camp and smuggled her into Cracow, where she found refuge and lived to see her secret diary published. The diary entries are undated. The translation that follows is from the Hebrew translation by Abraham Bartura.

On the second day of the invasion, Father and I went out to view Lvov after the enemy's bombing. The city was unrecognizable; the stores had been destroyed and plundered by the populace. The houses were decorated with

[6] A concentration camp.

blue-and-yellow flags. Automobiles and cycles ornamented with flowers rolled through the streets, their drivers and fellow travelers jubilant.

[Janina and her father visit a friend. They engage in a whispered conversation. A woman friend tells them about her escape from injury and urges them to exercise great caution.] Father, sensing he was in grave danger, kissed me and said, "Yanya, you are a grown person, ten years old, and from now on you have to be independent, fully on your own. Do not pay attention to what others say or do. Be strong and of good courage." He kissed me again and was about to part from me when I began to grasp what would happen and started to cry. But Father declared sternly, "If you love me, leave me. Be brave. Never cry. Crying is degrading. Return home immediately and leave me here." I gave Father a last kiss. At the street corner I looked back and I saw him returning a flying kiss to me.

[Janina's father is caught in the dragnet of the doomed and is never seen again. Janina goes underground and assumes a Polish name.]

One day a strange woman came to see me. I thought she had a message from Yadjah [a Christian friend], but she did not. She said to me, "I serve in the Gestapo. Your name is Janina Heshele but you pass as Lydia Wirischinska. If you don't bring me 5000 gulden by four o'clock, you will be sent to death at Camp Janowska." I ran to inform my uncle, and he transmitted the message to Mother. At four the woman showed up, and so did Mother. Mother knew intuitively that she was an extortionist. After a little haggling, the "lady" left with 100 gulden.[Janina and her mother go into hiding but are caught.]

We were brought to prison and pushed into a small, crowded cell where we found sixty people squatting on the floor, one on top of another. When we were thrust in, someone growled, "Oh, another herring!" Another replied, "Two in one." Mother did not let me lie on the floor, and we stood upright a full day and night.

In the morning, coffee and bread were brought in. Everyone had to pay for the food and drink. But Mother and I could not swallow our food. Even though it was the month of February, the cell was hot and stank. In the corner was a broken bucket where women and men attended to their physical needs. I had no strength to stand on my feet any longer, but Mother would not let me lie down for fear of my becoming infected with lice. I argued with her, asserting that I wished to catch typhus, for I couldn't bear to live any longer. I lay down on the floor. Mother did too, but since there was no room for both of us, she had me lie on top of her.

The day for deportation arrived. We knew our end was near. The anticipation was unbearable. We wished it were over. We knew we were doomed. I lost all control of myself and wept without stopping. I did not fear my own death so much, or even the shooting of the children, but the terror of seeing children buried alive was too great. Some prayed and chanted in Hebrew. A number of us prayed to be shot immediately. Mother calmed me down and promised that she would blindfold me when the shooting began. My panic subsided and I joined in chanting with the other victims.

About three in the morning a policeman came and asked Mother to come out with him. He inquired if there was a child with her. We both went out into the corridor and were taken to another cubicle. Here we were prohibited from loud talk and not allowed even to sneeze. On Saturday, at seven in the morning an automobile arrived to remove those condemned to die. . . . Periodically, five of us were taken to the basement, where we heard shots. We were saved. When they led us outside and I breathed the fresh air, I fell to the ground like one intoxicated.

[Janina falls ill with typhus and is taken to the hospital where her mother works.]

Mother, who was deathly pale, lay in bed. I lay down near her and asked her "Why are you so crushed? I am still alive." She replied, "I do not care what happens to me. I have a poison tablet which will bring instant death. But what will happen to you?" She broke out in loud sobs and implored me, "Anula, save me from further anguish. Go away. I don't want you near me. I don't want to see what will happen to you. If you love me, leave me. If you love me, go to her.[1] I take the humiliation upon myself and I command you to go to her — no matter what." But I refused, saying, "What have I to live for? Without documents I cannot exist on my own. Mother, do you want to prolong my agonies? Isn't it better to make an end to my life once and for all? Let us die together, with me in your arms. Why live on?" Mother implored me, "You must go on! You must live to vindicate Father's death and mine."

[The agonizing dispute between mother and daughter continues.] My struggle with Mother robbed me of my strength. I could not glance at Mother's face because overnight it had become a network of wrinkles. She looked like my grandmother. I could hear her loud heartbeats. I gave in on condition that she give me a pill of potassium cyanide, but she refused. She gave me 2700 gulden, accompanied me to the exit, kissed me, and whispered to me, "Bear up for Mother's sake."

Again I went to Aunt W. [Janina had been shut out from her aunt's home earlier.] This time the door was open. I entered without knocking. When my aunt saw me, she could not drive me away. I gave her part of the money Mother gave me. Aunt W. had a friend, an anti-Semite, who took active part in the pogroms against Jews. . . .

[A short time later the aunt ousts Janina by fabricating a threatening note which reads: "You are housing a filthy Jewess. If you will not deliver the stinking Jewess to me, you will all be deported to Piasky" — a death chamber at Camp Janowska. Certain that the note was written by her aunt's Jew-hating friend, Janina leaves and finds shelter in a forced-labor battalion housed in a knitting shop.] The shop and working conditions were unbearable. From their roofless living quarters they were able to see the fires of Piasky incinerating corpses. The stench was all-pervading. [In spite of these obscene sights and intense suffering — or perhaps because of them — Janina composes free verse describing her anguish and desolation. In the midst of these inhuman conditions, the High Holiday season is approaching.]

I am so deeply depressed and almost lifeless. I am not affected any more by the panic and fright about me. I begin to understand why my fellow victims go

[1] Aunt W., her mother's sister, who was non-Jewish and hostile to Janina and her family.

to their deaths without resistance. I have lost the desire to exist and feel a deep disgust for living. . . .

A day before the Jewish New Year all the sick patients were sent to the death chamber. Urland, the Jewish police officer, greeted us loudly, "I bless all of you with a New Year of Freedom." All of us, including Urland, wept. . . .

[Janina describes the desolation in Camp Janowska and the despondent feelings of its inmates. All shed tears as they exchange New Year greetings. She recalls Yom Kippur at home, where only her mother had fasted. No candles had been lit for the holiday, since her father was nonobservant. She visits the barrack, which houses the camp laundresses.]

At the table sat Mrs. Jacobowitz, who had lit two candles which stood before her. Around her women crowded, exchanging New Year's blessings with one another and crying loudly. With composure, Mrs. Jacobowitz returned the blessings to each one. I could not bear to witness the scene and walked out.

A day before the great fast [Day of Atonement], we arranged a party with singing and constrained dancing. Urland prepared for each of us a repast of soup, two slices of bread, and an apple.

When we returned to our dormitories, night had fallen. The women lit candles and ushered in Yom Kippur with the appropriate blessings, accompanied by copious tears. I looked closely at the candles, at the halos ringing the burning wicks, and suddenly I felt a deep intuition that, despite it all, God is still with us. He sees how we give Him thanks for living, in spite of the horrors around us. I believed that ultimately He would not let the few remnants of Israel be wiped out.

I lay down on my bunk and asked myself, "Shall I fast?" I was uncertain. Fasting was a Jewish religious ritual, and I *am* a Jewess. I did not want to ponder long and deep, because I felt that if I did so, I would reaffirm my disbelief in God. I was persuaded that faith in God bears with it the hope to live. I decided to fast. . . .

[In the morning the prisoners go to the shower, where the women, as usual, create turmoil. The male guards break in and bring about some order by whipping. Janina, too, is whipped, but she bears it stoically. She is more affected by the fact that a Jewish policeman whipped her than by the pain of the whipping.]

From the showers the prisoners go to eat. On the tables are pots of soup, but no one tastes a spoonful. Ten men [a religious quorum for prayer] enter. Urland locks the door, and the Jews begin the prayer service. A few women draw forth paper leaves — remnants of prayerbooks — and recite the Yizkor [Memorial Service for the Dead]. Others repeat after them, and all weep in unison. But as for me — my doubts reawake and reassail me. Why should I fast? Does God really exist? My former doubts return and shatter my erstwhile faith.

Winter is upon us, savage and murderous. I am cold as ice and can't sleep. My benefactors [see the introduction on p. 95] give me strength to persevere and console me that I will yet find safety on the Aryan side of Cracow. I cannot persuade myself to believe them. All mankind is egotistic. They think first of themselves and of their own welfare. I have no strength to hold up, to hope, to live. But in my ears there still echo the last words of my mother, "Carry on, do not despair, for your mother's sake!'' Only these words keep the spark of life aglow within me.

I was often seized by a fit of shakes. On one such day I asked a doctor acquaintance of mine to admit me to the hospital. One night at the hospital when I went to the bathroom Rena [a companion] took me aside and whispered in my ear, ''Borochowitz is taking us to Cracow. We leave tomorrow.''

I heard her clearly, but her words did not penetrate my consciousness. . . .

[Postscript: Maria Hochberg Marianska, who published Janina's diary in Polish, affirms that the group rescued Janina because they had been deeply moved by her free verse, which she had composed and read to her circle even while the bodies of victims were being cremated. The group rescued her because of her great promise as poet and writer. In August 1943, she was smuggled out of the Cracow ghetto to the Aryan side, where she survived the war.]

A.E.

From *Hayeled Vehonoar BaShoa Ugvurah* (Children and Youth in the Holocaust and Resistance), published by Kiryat Sefer, Israel, 1965, pp. 165-176 (with deletions).

7.

"WHAT HAPPENED TO ME"—CHILDREN'S STORIES

In 1946 Benjamin Tennenbaum (Teneh) came to Poland, which had been the greatest world Jewish center, and found it practically kinder rein – empty of Jewish children. Then, one by one, children began to emerge from hiding places —from the Aryan side, the forests, the monasteries and convents, and isolated and distant villages. They were but a tragic handful; their appalling experiences were etched deeply on their faces. They were tight-mouthed; their eyes reflected unspeakable suffering and evinced perpetual fear. They were orphaned, bereft of families and friends —all alone in a devastated and hostile world.

Like their ancestors of old, the surviving remnants, old and young, were impelled never to forget and to keep fresh the memories of the years of the Holocaust in all its Satanic phases. The Jewish Historical Commission of Polish Jews was set up to seek, find, record, and preserve every piece of evidence of the tragic period.

Benjamin Tennenbaum was one of the recorders. He collected a thousand concise autobiographies from children who, at the outbreak of the war, were from three to twelve years of age. They wrote out their experiences in Yiddish and Polish. They had lived after the war in orphanages, in European youth kibbutzim, in refugee camps in Germany, etc. From the thousand, he selected seventy representative accounts, translated them into Hebrew, and published them in Israel.

By and large, their stories are told simply, without embellishments. They recount happenings: the rise of the ghetto walls, the smuggling into the ghetto of food and other necessities from the other side of the wall, their separation from parents, the "actions," the Umschlagplatz, and so on and on. Even their

33852   100

heroic acts of resistance and sabotage are presented in a matter-of-fact narration. Occasionally they bewail their fate in statements like "Why were the Jewish people chosen to suffer?" "How are we different?" A four-year-old girl in flight from her home in the deep dark of the night broods about her plight: "Why do so many children sleep peacefully, and I, like a mad dog, am dodging the killers?" Or a three-year-old girl watches her peers skating and frolicking on the ice and asks herself, "And why not I? There must be only one reason: I am Jewish."*

We shall skip their outbursts, the atrocities that they witnessed, the crematoria where their dear ones were gassed and burned. Some there were who experienced the British blockade of the "illegal ships." Quite a number of the autobiographies include experiences on the ship Exodus 1947, *which was sent back by the British to Europe with all its passengers.*

Following is a sheaf of children's autobiographies which are illustrative of the collection.

A SURVIVOR OF THE DESTRUCTION OF THE WARSAW GHETTO

Haviva Dembinska, age thirteen (six when the war began):

I was born on November 22, 1933, in Warsaw. My father was Adam, and my mother, Natalia. Father worked in an office; mother looked after the house. When the war broke out and the Germans attacked Warsaw, I was six years old. We lived on Szwetoyarska Street then, together with our whole family. Grandfather got sick and could not go down to the shelter during the bombardments. At that time we lived with others on the first floor in a little hallway. There was a baby among us about one month old, and his mother did not have any milk to feed him. There was also hardly any water. Whenever we got a little water we warmed it for the baby over the flame of a small candle.

Then a bomb struck and wrecked our yard and damaged half of the house. It happened on Rosh Hashanah, when the Jews were at the synagogue praying with all their hearts. There were very many victims. People who only a minute before had been talking to us and looking for shelter together with us were buried under the ruins. Many people came running out of the other wrecked houses. Mothers and children wailed loudly, and old men cried in grief-stricken misery: "God Almighty, that's enough; enough already!" We lived that way, bombs falling on us, from the first to the seventeenth of September.

On September 17 the bombing stopped. We waited a few more days until everything quieted down. Then I went with Mother to see the destruction the bombs had wrought. The Saxon Gardens [a park] were completely demolished. Wherever we looked, there were splinters, disabled cannons, fragments of bombs, and human skulls. I found out that Polish soldiers had camped in the gardens.

The situation in Warsaw grew worse from day to day. When the Germans entered, everyone relaxed a little and people whispered to each other that it would not be too bad. The Germans gave soup to long lines of people, but seldom were the Jews among those who received it. That was how the victors behaved for a few weeks, until they had the whole city in their hands. Then they began looting. They took furniture and all kinds of valuables from the people. They would come in trucks, take all the furniture out of the apartments, and leave four empty walls. For the job of carrying the furniture they would seize Jewish passersby in the street; they mistreated them terribly. Once they caught my grandfather, who was sick, and they were unspeakably cruel to him. They dragged him into a store and ordered him to undress. Then they pushed him out into the street and forced him to perform all kinds of gymnastics that were impossible for him because of his age and his illness. They beat him savagely with a whip and threatened to come back again on the next day to cut off his beard. In our courtyard they carried out executions by firing squads. Afterward the brains of the victims could be seen splattered on the ground, along with bits of flesh, and the blood would run down into the sewer. And they always ordered the tenants on the ground floor to clean it all up.

In November 1940, the Warsaw Ghetto was established, and we moved to Karmelicka Street. Conditions became unbearable. Going to school was forbidden, but I studied in secret with a class of ten children. Every night the Germans would come and drag Jewish men out of their homes to be executed. Twice they had Father in their clutches, but each time he managed to escape. They shot at him but missed, and he was saved.

One day some Jewish policemen came and ordered Father and some neighbors of ours to report at a point of assembly on Zamenhof Street. Father changed his name and made his way to the home of friends. Later they discovered his hiding place and demanded a sum of money as ransom. To save his life, Father paid the ransom they demanded.

The Jewish policemen faithfully carried out all the orders the Germans gave them. The hunger and poverty were frightful. One could always see great numbers of starved women and children lying in the streets, bloated and swollen, and also many corpses covered with newspapers. Walking right by them, one saw elegantly dressed ladies who went into sweetshops, to parties, to dances, and to other entertainments. Shop windows displayed trays of white cookies and other baked goods, and in front of the shops lurked the so-called snatchers, who waited for a lady to emerge carrying her package. They pounced on her and snatched it from her hand. The snatcher would run off, biting and chewing hungrily as he ran. Now and then the shop windows were shattered and the contents pillaged.

Every house arranged its own hidden "corner," where the children came to learn to read and write. I went too. Our teacher was a seventeen-year-old girl named Sokolowska. She talked to us about Palestine and told us stories about the history of our people. There were also special kitchens for the children of the poor, as well as soup kitchens for the refugees from neighboring towns. My mother worked in such a soup kitchen.

I remember that my mother took me with her to homes of refugees on Mila Street. We brought them bread and potatoes we had solicited in our building. The dwellings were very crowded and dirty. Some of the refugees were sprawled on rough boards, while others sat on their "beds" of rough planks; among them were many who were suffering from typhus, dysentery, and other diseases. When we entered, all eyes immediately focused on us. Little tots came running, and Mother and another woman started to distribute the bread.

Two months passed in extreme poverty, filth, and disease. July brought the raid, followed by the most terrible annihilation for masses of Jews. The raid was carried out by Jewish policemen, and they were unbelievably cruel to their own people. At first they seized only the poor; it was horrible. I witnessed a dreadful scene with my own eyes. It was on Nowolipki Street. A horse-drawn streetcar approached; it was filled to overflowing with Jewish policemen. Before I could make a move, it stopped and the policemen scattered swiftly, some over Karmelicka Street and others on Nalewki Street. They began a most frightful hunt. The hunger-bloated paupers who lay in the street and on the sidewalk did not want to move. The policemen crushed their flesh with their sticks, kicked them, and dragged them into the tram. They also came over to my father and me, but Father showed them a piece of paper and they did not touch us. I don't know what happened after that; I heard weeping and the wails of infants.

Mother and Father used to go to work and leave me at home with my three-year-old brother and my grandmother. Grandma was feeding my brother, and I was walking around in the room, when suddenly we heard shouts: "All Jews are to come right down from their flats into the yard! Anyone who stays inside will be shot!"

Grandma went down, but first she gave us some pieces of paper and instructed us to stay where we were. I did not know what to do; my brother cried bitterly. I locked the door and bolted it, but when I heard a terrible banging I became frightened and opened the door. A policeman seized hold of me and pushed me so hard that I fell sprawling on the floor and twisted my ankle. Then he shoved my brother into my arms, sick as he was and with only a shirt on his back. I begged the policeman to let me take my brother's coat, but he kicked me hard and yelled for me to go down.

There were a great many people in the courtyard. The policemen lined us up by fives and ordered us to get moving. The streets were full of Germans and policemen and people carrying bundles. All were weeping and wailing, and the Germans were busy shooting and running after those who tried to escape. Our rows of marchers extended over the streets. Those who faltered because of physical weakness were shot to death on the spot, while the people who marched ahead of them continued to advance without turning their heads to see. A policeman marched close beside me. I noticed that he stopped every now and then. Taking advantage of one such opportunity, I tried to escape with my little brother, whom I clutched tightly in my arms. At once I felt a sharp blow on my head; it was from the stick wielded by a Jewish policeman. "I didn't make it," I thought, and continued marching. An old woman collapsed on the road. The moving mass did not even stop to look, but just stepped right over her.

When we reached the *Umschlagplatz*[1] it was already very late. Those who

---

[1] A square beside the hospital on Stawky Street in Warsaw, which served as a concentration point for masses of Jews during the raids. Special tracks were laid there for transportation by train to Treblinka (a death camp).

had been caught early in the raid had already been sent off in a transport. We were left in the terrifying square. It was raining, and a strong wind was blowing. Suddenly shots rang out, and the crowd began to push toward the rear. People trod on one another; many were killed or wounded. . . . In the morning I recognized one policeman. He was a neighbor who lived in our court. I ran over to him and began pleading with him and promising that Mother would reward him for his kindness. He assured me that if he found a way to save me, he would do so. He told me to sit on the steps and wait for him. A few minutes later he returned, lifted my brother, and took me by the hand. He bribed the guards and left with us.

The road was littered with corpses. On the way we met my parents. They were hurrying to the death square of their own free will. When they saw us, they could not believe their eyes. We went home. Grandmother was not there yet. Later some strangers found her lifeless body in the street. Our home was empty. All the apartments throughout the whole building were starkly empty.

I do not remember in what month the Germans divided the Brushmakers' Street in two: the Tebbens sector and the Schultz sector.[2] My parents continued to work in the Tebbens workshops. My little brother was with Mother, and I stayed with all the other children in the storage courtyard. The children's parents were all busy in the workshops, and none of them suspected the approaching tragedy. Suddenly two trucks arrived, and the children were seized and dragged into them. Many hid. My girlfriend and I crept into a truck that stood in the yard. We were saved. Most of the children were brought to the *Umschlagplatz* and sent to the death camp.

Similar scenes occurred repeatedly in our courtyard. For that reason some of the children were concealed by their parents every day in a large pile of rags that lay in the yard. At night we went home to sleep.

One night the Germans issued a new command. All the Jews were to present themselves at once on Mila, Gensha, and Zamenhof Streets. Whoever failed to obey would be shot. The children were to take with them a plate, a spoon, and one change of bedclothes.

There was great commotion. People carrying bundles streamed in the direction of those streets. My parents were undecided whether to go or stay. Finally, having no alternative, they went.

We reached Mila Street. Throngs of people and their bundles filled the whole street. It was dirty; feathers were flying about. We went into a flat that stood empty because its tenants had been taken away a little while before. Policemen surrounded the entire area to make sure no one would escape. Shots were fired frequently; the shooting kept up all night long. Whoever ventured outside the limited area was killed. The piles of corpses in the streets grew larger by the minute. The liquidation had begun. The young people were taken to the ghetto. All the rest were brought to the *Umschlagplatz*. My aunt was one of those who was killed. A murderous hand had snatched her little six-year-old son from her

[2]Names of German shop-owners.

hand and ordered her to walk on. She refused to go. The German flung the child down on the pavement and shot my aunt to death.

Father did not know what to do. He found out that a wagon was coming to take away the children of the directors and managers of the factory. We waited for it to arrive. As soon as it came, the director, his wife, and their child got in and sat down comfortably in the wagon. Quick as a flash my father tossed my brother and me inside. The director and his wife were furious and screamed their heads off, but we were already sitting there and they couldn't throw us out. So we got to the storage court and quickly ran home. It was empty. No one was home as yet. A few hours later Mother and Father came; they had passed the selection safely.

Days of terror and horrible experiences followed. One day an "action" was started in the storage rooms. Father put my little brother into one knapsack, which he strapped to my mother's back, and me into another, which he strapped to his back, and thus we went to the selection. I remember that, lying stuffed in that bag, I wanted to cough and tried not to and started to choke. I still don't understand why the Germans didn't hear me.

We went through a second selection, a third, and a fourth, and somehow we succeeded in escaping. One day the Germans ordered all the Jews to go to Poniatow and Trabniki streets. Our neighborhood was assigned to Poniatow. Father had decided to build a bunker for the whole family. It was an ordinary workday. Everyone was at work; only my mother, brother, and I were at home. Father and three laborers were working in the cellar, when suddenly steps were heard. German soldiers came and went straight into the cellar. They dragged my father and the other men out of there. One managed to escape; the others tried but failed and were shot. Father was left all alone. They took him to the Pawiak, the most feared prison in Warsaw. There they tortured him for ten days and then they killed him.

We remained alone. We suffered terribly. Then the uprising started. There was endless shooting. Mother did not want to go over to the Aryan side; we had no one to go to. A certain gentleman took me to the home of an Aryan woman. To get there, we crept stealthily along in the night and stole through the Leszno Street gate.

This Aryan lady did not know me at all but she was a very intelligent woman and noble character. She got used to me in no time. She saved my cousin too. I had no uncommon experiences on the Aryan side. When the Polish uprising started,[3] we were driven to Skirniwica, where this lady continued to treat us with affection, like a mother. When Warsaw was liberated we returned to the city. I found an aunt of mine there. Our kind benefactress went to Pomerania, and I stayed with my aunt. From there I came to the kibbutz.

A.E.

From *Echad M'eer Ushnayim Mimishpachah* ("One of a City and Two of a Family"), compiled by Benjamin Teneh and published by Sifriat Poalim ("Workers Book-Guild"), 1947, pp. 15-20.

[3] In August and September 1944.

"I MUST LIVE FOR MY MOM AND DAD"

Edmund Lubianker, age sixteen (age nine when the war started):

I was born on June 7, 1930, in Boryslaw, near Lvov. My parents were Leon and Anna.

When the Germans entered, in 1941, they immediately closed our schools and discharged from their jobs all Jews who had been permanently employed. My father, too, was fired; he was an electrician. A week later the Germans together with the Ukrainians staged savage disturbances in which my grandfather was killed. Then the German barbarians conducted a raid (an "action"). This took place in August. During the following month, in the course of the third raid, nine members of my family were murdered. A gentile woman, whom my mother knew, concealed me during the first two raids, and I heard and saw everything that went on outside. I saw the Germans kill pregnant women and little children. Now that the war is over, the world will refuse to believe that such crimes were really committed.

More raids followed, and in the sixth one I was caught as I was going to work. While the Germans were taking me to the police station I escaped. I ran past the house where my mother and sister were and shouted to them to hide themselves. Fortunately they heard me and hid. At that very moment an SS man overtook me and began to beat me with such frightful cruelty that I begged him to shoot me. But he answered, "No, first you will have to endure plenty of torture. Death will not come so easily." Then he brought me to the movie theater which they had chosen as the place of assembly for those they caught. They kept bringing more victims, and I watched in fear of discovering some member of my family among them, but not one was brought in.

Into that hall, which was not more than thirty-five feet long and twenty feet wide, they jammed a thousand people without any food or water. In the course of three days, four hundred died. The victims did not have the strength to find a way of saving themselves. But five of my friends and I managed to devise a plan. On the night prior to the execution that the Germans had scheduled, we cut through some bars with our knives and helped three boys through a window. It was a clear night, and the guards saw them at once. They opened fire, and two boys fell. The third, a mere youngster, survived. The shots frightened everyone, but the thought of the executions scheduled for the very next day aroused desperate courage and made people jump one after another through that window. Chaos followed. I was small and could not push myself over to the window because the mass of people pressing forward shoved the weak ones aside. Then the guards discovered the open window and directed their fire straight at that point.

There was a deathly stillness in the hall. It was about four in the morning. Some people began to weep because they had learned that at six o'clock the executions would begin. At this time the guards brought back into the hall all those who had tried to escape except three — the two boys who had been shot and the child who had gotten away.

I look at my watch; it is 5:15. How the minutes creep! Why don't they go faster? Why must we wait so terribly long for the moment we are to be put to death? Better to be finished with such a life! Run faster, faster, you slowly ticking watch! Oh, when will it be six o'clock at last? What good is life? What does it give you? Nothing. Only trouble and sorrow. Here is the sun; it is already filtering its first rays through the windows. Birds are beginning to chirp outside. It is such a beautiful world, but not for Jews. The Germans are walking around and laughing. They are laughing because it is already half past five, almost time for the executions to begin. I start to laugh; yes, I'm laughing, I'm happy. Now there'll be an end to it all, an end to this bitter life.

But oh, no! What of the pain my mom and sister will feel if they survive? I am so selfish. Once I am dead, I'll feel nothing more, whereas Mom and Dad will suffer. No! I must live! I must live for my Mom and Dad. For the revenge I have to take upon those German barbarians. . . .

Cries of "Everybody out!" roused me from my musing. One single thought dominated my being: to remain alive, no matter what! I looked around for a possible place to hide. Suddenly I saw that one man — his name was Wachtel — had loosened a board in the bridge. He helped me down, and then another boy and two little girls. May his soul rest in peace for his kindness!

After the executions we crept out of our hiding place. I returned to the ghetto, to my mother, father, and sister. Their joy knew no bounds. Later we hid in the home of a gentile woman who risked her life to save ours. But a friend of hers who saw what was going on began to blackmail us so that we were forced to leave and go into the forest. We lived in the forest for about half a year.

They hunted us down in the forest. We were trapped; our whole family was caught and sent to the Plaszuw concentration camp near Cracow. The camp director was the bloodthirsty Amon Gett, known far and wide for his cruelty. After three months they separated us. My mother and sister were sent off to Schtuthoff, while Dad and I, after a great deal of wandering in Nazi Europe, were finally brought to Dachau. My number was 148793. We were imprisoned there for about two months; then the American Army came. The Germans hastily abandoned Dachau, telling the prisoners that they were being taken to Switzerland, but intending to to kill us all in the Alps. Fortunately the American Army came in time and gave the Germans barbarians a real surprise. On May 13, 1945, I was set free.

Now, as I write these lines and recall all that I experienced in those days, I can hardly believe it. Did I actually live through all that?

"We are like newborn babes now," my father said to me then. "We must start all over again and see to our future."

We are here with Father in the Feldafing camp en route to Eretz Yisrael. All this will not be repeated ever again in the future. For it is different with Jews in Eretz Yisrael. There they can defend themselves and they know what and whom they are defending. On foreign soil one cannot really defend himself, for the Underground fighters have no villagers to supply them with food or hide them in case of need. In alien forests the animals are alien, and even the trees appear strange.

For that reason I want to go to Eretz Yisrael and live there.

A.E.

From *Echad M'eer Ushnayim Mimishpachah,* op. cit., pp. 89-91.

A BOY SURVIVES THE DESTRUCTION OF THE WARSAW GHETTO

This document was written in Polish by a nameless thirteen-year-old boy in April 1944.

On September 28, 1939, the Germans invaded Warsaw. The next morning the pillaging, as well as the capture of males for forced labor, began. Among those rounded up was my father. The Germans beat their captives like dogs. My father worked from six in the morning till nine at night, and when he returned all his bones ached and he could not sleep. . . .

We were seven, my parents and five children. My oldest brother fled to Russia, where his documents were taken away and he was forced to join a labor battalion. Ultimately he escaped to Bialystok, where the Russian military ruled. He was mobilized and sent to work in Minsk. After a year's hard labor he was given a respite and he went to visit my uncle in Tashkent in Soviet Central Asia. On December 3, 1940, the mail carrier brought us a letter and a food package from him. We were elated to hear from him and to receive the package, which my mother sold. She needed the money desperately for trading in the marketplace.

About a month before (November 15, 1940) the Germans had segregated the Jews in a ghetto, around which they built high walls. Food prices rose precipitously, and, to keep body and soul together, we had to steal over to the Aryan side to buy potatoes and bread, most of which we sold in the ghetto. Whatever was left we kept for ourselves. Stealing to the other side of the wall was very dangerous because the Germans shot those whom they caught. However, we had no choice. There wasn't a piece of bread in the house, and we couldn't earn a penny by any other means. The adults were forced to join labor battalions. We simply had to run the risk of being caught and shot or dying of starvation. Unfortunately my brother was caught and all his merchandise taken. We were compelled to steal over to the Aryan quarter, where we traded in saccharin. To our misfortune, we were caught while bartering on Marshalkowska Street, identified as Jews, and threatened with death. We were brought to the police station on Poznanska Street, where we were imprisoned for forty-eight hours and ordered to return to the ghetto under threat of severe punishment. . . .

A few days later I was again caught peddling in the city marketplace on Koshikowa Street and arrested by an SS officer. He beat me cruelly on the head and ordered a Polish policeman to take me to the police station. This meant sure death. Luckily, at the station I was handed over to a decent gendarme who gave me a few blows on the head and ordered me to make off to the ghetto.

When I returned home I learned that my brother had been imprisoned for three days in the police station because he had been caught stealing into the Aryan side. His feet were severely frozen. I proceeded to the prison and after ''negotiations'' brought him home on a rickshaw.[1] He was confined to bed for a few weeks, until his feet healed. We returned to our usual tasks until July 1942, when the Germans began their ''resettlement'' program to the east, which we discovered soon enough was the Treblinka death camp.

[1]A small two-wheeled vehicle pulled by one person.

On the very first day that the "resettlement" program was instituted, my mother, father, sister, and little brother were deported and killed at Treblinka. Destitute and starving, my brother and I remained the only living members of our family. Food prices soared sky-high. Passage to the Aryan quarter was impossible. Ukrainian and Latvian police, who were stationed on top of the ghetto walls, shot to kill all smugglers, young and old. Nevertheless, we managed to cross to the Aryan side, where relentless searches were held to ferret out Jews, and indeed many of our friends were caught in the dragnet and liquidated.

Deportations from the ghetto to Treblinka were carried on without surcease. My brother and I resolved to steal back to the ghetto to ransack the abandoned houses for clothing, shoes, and winter wear, since the weather had turned cold and we were without winter clothing. We found shelter in the home of a friend, Mr. Cohen, who lived in an apartment on Mila Street.

On January 15, 1943, another "action" began. All who could hid in bunkers. . . . Leon, my brother, and I were lucky to find a hiding place. During March 1943 we stole over the wall because there were rumors that the Germans would initiate a final "action." Many good people helped us. The bloodbath this time was the worst. Many houses were burned, together with their inmates. Our protector, Mr. Cohen, and his son were caught and deported. The son managed to jump from the train, and, although wounded in the leg, he returned to Warsaw, where he found us. We treated his wound on the Aryan side, since there wasn't a house left standing in the ghetto. We went begging from door to door and with the little money we collected we bought medicine, bandages, and food to keep us alive.

To our unspeakable grief, after eight days someone informed on us. The local police surrounded our hiding place in the Drashar Park near Odiniatz Street, brought us to the police station, and handed us over to the German police. I succeeded in breaking loose and fled. Because of my successful escape, the Germans tightened their hold on my brother and the Cohen boy, who was handicapped because of his wounded leg. I never saw them again. . . .

I remained alone, and my life was in constant peril. Once when I passed through Unya Lubalska Square I was grabbed by a *Volksdeutscher*[2] who shouted, "Jew boy, I'll hand you over to the Germans." He yelled for the police, but, luckily for me, no policeman was around. I bit his hand hard and fled. He pursued me but he soon lost me. . . .

Thus began my wanderings. I met many merciful people who helped save my life. When I lost my brother and stood weeping, Mrs. Eva D. consoled me, brought me to her home, served me breakfast, and gave me 30 zloty for pocket money. She also invited me to visit her often.

A few days later I met a Jewish boy, Hayim Burstein, who was a year younger. We decided to stick together and we arranged a hiding place for both of us. A few days later we met Mrs. Eva D, who invited us to come to her home often for lunch. She also gave us clothing and enough money to buy food for a

[2]Pole of German origin.

week. Thus the time passed. When we walked the streets we were very cautious not to be caught.

Relatively speaking, we were safer on Rakoviatzka Street because the inhabitants were kind to us. We were able to buy a velocipede, which we rode all day. However, one day a tenant on a neighboring street informed the police that we we rode a velocipede and disturbed his rest. The police seized us, confiscated our velocipede, and let us go.

Once three policemen surprised on us on Pilitzka Street in the dark. They flashed their light on us, and we began to run. Thanks to the dark, we escaped. Another time a group of Polish and German youths stopped me on Narbut Street and began to hit me. One ran to telephone the police. Luckily, a fruit vender came to my help, and I made off quickly through a courtyard to an adjoining street and hid in a house. In a few minutes the house was surrounded by the gendarmes, but they could not find me. Angry at their failure, they confiscated the fruit stand of my rescuer.

Thus the time passed. One day one of our kind friends told us that a lady named Marisha[3] was seeking homeless Jewish children whom she desired to bring together under her protective care. We breathed a deep sigh of relief because we were worn out from sleeping nights in various hiding holes or under the stairs of houses. Besides, we were always exposed to the danger of being caught. . . .

At long last we were provided with a clean, warm lodging, thanks to the efforts of the Jewish National Committee, which clandestinely maintained a sheltering program with the cooperation of friendly Poles.

A.E.

From *The Destruction and Rebellion of the Jews of Warsaw,* compiled and edited by Melech Neishtadt, Tel Aviv: the General Workers Party of Eretz Yisrael, 1947, pp. 211-214. Trans. from the Hebrew.

FIVE YEARS OF BITTER EXILE AND WANDERING THROUGH SIBERIA AND AFRICAN JUNGLES TO ERETZ YISRAEL

This is a story of a brother and sister named Simha and Hannah, eleven and ten years old respectively. When I interviewed them they were studying at the Ben Shemen youth colony. They were thin, light-complexioned, blond, and well mannered. As I interviewed them, each complemented the other's remarks. Both had been born near Cracow (in Poland). Their father was a leather manufacturer who also owned oil wells.

When war began, the family escaped to Stanislavov, where they stayed a year. At the end of the year they and others, who refused to accept Russian citizenship, were exiled to Siberia. For fourteen long, unendurable months they served as slave laborers in the cold forests of north Siberia. When a reprieve was

[3]Marisha was Bracha Feinmesser, who was the liaison between the Jewish Coordinating Committee and the Jewish Fighting Partisans on the Aryan side. It was she who provided the writer with a permanent place where he and Hayim found shelter until liberation day.

granted to Polish prisoners, the family moved to Bukhara, a city in the Far East Uzbek Soviet Republic. There their children joined a group that was sent to Iran. From then on the children were without their parents. Their long trek to Eretz Yisrael began.

The group was transported to Karachi via Basra, India. After a month the Poles were exiled by boat and train to an African jungle. After a long trip they reached Nairobi, Kenya. There they were loaded on rafts, which were floated up the Nile River. They disembarked somewhere in Uganda and were taken by bus to a primitive camp in the heart of the jungle and settled in the midst of a dense, lush growth of rapidly growing bushes and flourishing trees. The newcomers had to cut these down every two or three months.

The camp housed 3500 adult Poles, men and women, most of whom were too old for military service. In addition, there were 5 groups of 100 children each. Anti-Semitism was rampant and virulent and exceeded tolerable bounds. The leader in Jew-hatred was an old schoolteacher who incited young and old against the few Jewish children who felt forsaken and oppressed. They were taunted and abused with outcries, "Jews, go to Palestine!"

Simha and Hannah wrote to their brethren in Eretz Yisrael, pleading for immigration certificates, but received no answer. Then, suddenly, like a ray of light amidst the thick darkness, a woman appeared — an emissary from the Promised Land, who had come to rescue the exiles. With her aid they again appealed, this time to an uncle who, they knew, lived in Palestine. And lo and behold, the certificates finally came.

In January 1944, they left the jungle where for fifteen long, unbearable months they had endured hostility and spiritual suffering, searing heat and loneliness. They began their tortuous migration to the Homeland, accompanied by a Jewish woman guide who had been a resident of Nairobi. They traveled four long weeks by foot, wagon, and boat to the last port city of Uganda in East Central Africa. From there they continued by car to a port city in Sudan and by train to Khartoum, capital of Sudan, and from there by boat to a port on the Nile River. From this port they took a train to Eretz Yisrael via Cairo.

After five years of painful wandering, Simha and Hannah finally reached home. They were welcomed warmly and treated with tender care. At long last they realized that life was worthwhile and rewarding. They had almost given up hope that they would ever again live as human beings, that they would not suffer endless hunger, and above all that they would never again be targets of hatred nor hear the caustic taunt "Zhid" (Jew).

I asked them where they had suffered more, in Siberia or in the Ugandan jungle. Brother and sister hesitated before replying. In Siberia they had worked like slaves. They had gone hungry and had frozen. In Africa they had been fed and physically had been quite healthy, but they would never forget the humiliations which they experienced as Jews. Their existence had been unbearable. They weree very young and lacked the stamina to withstand the rabid Jew-hatred of the Poles. The experiences of their persecutions had strengthened their spirits and had fortified their Jewishness, even though, while growing up at home, they had felt estranged from their people and faith.

When I asked them to draw a map of their wanderings until they reached their longed-for journey's end, their eyes lit up. The map which they drew should serve as a precious memento of their Jewish experiences and migrations, and as a contribution to the tragedy and its aftermath. With a warm smile they parted from me and thanked me for my interest and encouragement.

A.E.

From *Yeladim Mutzalim ("Rescued Children")* by Bracha Habas, Am Oved, pub. 1948, pp. 185-187.

"HEAR, O ISRAEL . . ." [1]

This is the story of Rifka K., eight years of age, who came to Palestine from Sosnovice with her mother and sister in January 1943.

I don't remember the beginning of the war very well. When they began shouting, and the airplanes started dropping bombs, Mummie wanted to go back to Palestine (I was born in Tel Aviv). That summer I had gone with my mother to visit Grandpa in Poland. The sea journey was lovely. Both my grandfathers lived in the same town, Sosnovice, and I had a lot of uncles and aunts there too. It was fun to visit them. At first I didn't know any Polish at all, I didn't even know Yiddish. Later I learned to understand both languages, and I knew what the enemy meant when they shouted and what they wanted. We lived with Grandfather Mordechai Mendel. He was about seventy years old, perhaps more. When my mother was taken off to forced labor by the Germans, who made her work in the factory, I was left alone in the house with Grandpa. One week Mother used to get up at dawn and work from five in the morning until four in the afternoon, and the next week she would work from one in afternoon until midnight. My sister Salusha (Sarah) had a labor card too, and she used to go off to work every morning. When I was left alone in the house I used to sweep and wash the floor and cook the dinner as Mother told me. Grandpa lay in bed almost all day long. When Germans knocked at the door, I used to open it at once. It was best to open immediately before they began shooting through the door, or they might even do something worse than that. In the beginning the German soldiers didn't beat women and children. But afterwards they made no distinction and they used to hit everybody. They even hit Grandpa with a rubber-topped whip. I used to cry bitterly when a German came into the house. Later I stopped crying — what was the use? I was quiet, but my heart beat fast from fear. The Germans didn't beat children, they killed them at once, or else they took them away with them. When one German came into the house, it wasn't so bad. Because there were a few good Germans, but only when they were on their own, they wouldn't hurt the children. Once a German came to our house for inspection and there was some meat cooking in a pot in the kitchen. To eat meat was a dreadful sin. I went into the kitchen and hid the pot. The German followed me and he saw what I was doing. I thought: Well, this is the end, he is going to shoot me. But he didn't do a thing. Another time

[1]This prayer *(Deuteronomy 6:4-9)*, known in Hebrew as *Shma Yisrael,* is the most significant and most frequently recited. It affirms the unity and love of God.

some German soldiers were chasing two Jewish girls. These girls were neighbors of ours and in their fright they ran into our house and Mother hid them. The Germans burst into our house and asked us if the girls were hiding there. Mother said she had seen nothing. They searched the house and they found both of the girls. They wanted to take Mother away with them as well. But I lifted up my voice and cried bitterly, and so did my sister, we cried with all our might, until the Germans let Mother go.

In Grandpa's house the furniture was very beautiful. Grandpa was afraid the Germans would come and take it all away. My grandfather was a very wise man. He called the carpenter and asked him to cover the furniture with ugly stains and spoil it so that the Germans wouldn't want to take it away. When the Germans came to the house they used to go straight to the cupboards and take everything they found inside. I knew that I mustn't scream or cry, that I had to wait quietly until they finished their work and went away.

All this was nothing compared to what the Germans did later, in the days of the deportations. Once Mother came back from work and said that tomorrow she would take me and my sister to the factory for inspection. The order was that every worker in the factory should bring his family with him. The others had to present themselves in the sports ground to sign their certificates. Grandpa didn't want to go. He was wise, that grandfather of mine. He stayed at home, and, as it happened, the Germans didn't come to examine the houses. Mummie wasn't afraid at all. She was an excellent worker, and the German supervisor was satisfied with her.

It happened on Wednesday, the 12th of August. At four o'clock in the morning Mother woke us up, scrubbed our faces, and washed our hair cleaner even than she used to do on the eve of Passover before the Seder. We put on our best dresses because Mother wanted us to look neat and nice at the inspection so that the Germans should find nothing at all wrong with us. At Mother's factory there were 500 workers, and all of them brought along the members of their families, and the place was very crowded. We had to wait until ten or eleven o'clock for the inspection. Then some men of the Jewish militia came along and told us to go to the sports ground. But when we went out into the street we saw the Gestapo, and we knew that it was all over with us.

The road to the sports ground was long. The Gestapo people pushed and hustled us along and shot into the air to frighten us. The congestion at the sports ground was terrible. Mother held our hands tightly so that we shouldn't get lost. Suddenly it began to rain; it was like a cloudburst. Mother covered our heads with a towel which she took out of her bag, but it didn't do any good at all — we got wet through and through and our legs began to ache with standing. Then I sat down on the ground, which was covered with puddles of water. Oh, it was awful. I see it all before my eyes now. The rain didn't stop during the night. The Germans threw a cordon around us to stop anyone from running away. Shots were heard all night. The children crouched in the mud and didn't even dare to cry or scream aloud. They wept silently. Then someone said: "May God hear the weeping of the children!" I couldn't fall asleep. Then Mummie sat down beside me in the mire and took me in her arms. Every once in a while she woke me up to ask: "Rifkele, my darling, are you asleep?" She was afraid I might have fainted from hunger and thirst, because many of the children, and some grownups too, had fainted away. From time to time we heard a cry, "Nurse, save me!", and the nurse of the Sanitary Service of the Jews' Council would come and attend to the sufferers. Once we heard someone scream in the darkness: "Help, a woman is going to give birth!" Yes, there in the mud and the darkness a child was born.

I was terribly thirsty, so thirsty that I couldn't bear it. Then Mother tried to collect a few drops of rainwater in her palms, which I licked. But that only made me thirstier. And in the morning the Germans began to play a game with us. They threw pieces of bread into the mud and they watched with pleasure as the mothers picked up the dirty crumbs and washed them in rainwater and gave them to their hungry children to eat.

When the inspection began before the deportations, the Germans drove the people from place to place, using whips and guns freely. Many were trampled to death in the awful crowd. And the Jews never stopped shouting, "Hear, O Israel . . ."

And then I got separated from my mother. The press of the people cut me off from her. I began to pinch the legs of the people around me to stop them from treading on me, and I bit their hands. But nobody paid any attention to my pinches, for they saw death before them. At last I fell down, and many feet passed over me. I thought it was the end and that I would never get up again. But one man picked me up and held me in his arms. He cried, "Save the child," and this good man rescued me from death. But I did not know where my mother was. There were thousands and thousands of people all jostling one another, and it was impossible to find anyone. Those at the outer edge of the crowd were better off, but on the other hand the Germans could hit them more easily. The Jews in the center of the crowd arranged a *Minyan* and they prayed. They prayed without *talit* [prayer shawl] and without *tefillin* [phylacteries], because they had not had time to take anything with them. And my poor mother thought that she would never see me alive again and she looked for me among all the trampled and dead children whose bodies had been pushed aside. Suddenly I saw my aunt, my mother's sister, and she took me back to my mother. Oh, how happy Mummie was!

Then the inspection began. There were two tables. They said that the table to the right was the "good" table, while the table to the left was the "bad" one. We all stood in a row and we could not choose. We went where we were told by the Germans. My mother went up to the table on the left. "Where is your father?" one of the Germans asked me. "In Palestine," I answered at once. He shouted: "A woman from the factory, two children, the father in Palestine." "To group No. 3!" came a shout in reply. And they gave us the number three. That was a bad number. It meant further examination, but number four was even worse, for it meant death. Only number one was good, because it meant immediate release. And number two was given only to two young men who were taken to the *Arbeits-Einsatz* (forced labor)!

On Thursday evening we were all collected together with hundreds of people from group number three in a courtyard and kept there until the following Sunday. All the houses were vacant, so we went into one house and lay down to sleep. The Jews' Council sent us a tub full of soup and bits of bread. Of all the hundreds who were with us then, only a few escaped deportation. Every day the deportations increased, and by Sunday evening there were very few of us left. My mother no longer believed that we would remain alive.

Suddenly we heard a German shouting: "Ethel K. with two children, come here at once!" This German pulled us out of the yard. He said that my mother was a very good worker and a "useful Jewess." Afterwards Grandpa told us that our uncle, his son from Bendin, had really saved us. This uncle had a big leather business, and he had put a German into his business who was connected with the Gestapo. And if it were not for this man and his connections with the Gestapo, we should also have been sent to Oswiecim [Auschwitz].

From *Rescued Children* by Bracha Habas, pub. by Palestine Pioneer Library, n.d. pp. 15-20.

"WRITTEN DOWN FOR THE SAKE OF HISTORY"

Riva Z. was one of the older girls in the group, a short, plump girl of about seventeen. Her speech and gestures were quick and nervous. She began with a question in Yiddish: "Forgive me, Madam, but why do you want to hear my story?" I explained to her that I thought the stories of refugee children should be recorded so that they should not be forgotten. But she didn't agree with me. "Whoever has lived through these horrors will never forget them till the day he dies. And whoever has been lucky enough not to experience them will never believe them, just as we don't really believe the legends about our ancestors in Egypt . . . "

She consented, however, when I told her that I thought these things should be written down for the sake of history. She listened a moment, reflected, and then burst out laughing. Half seriously, half mockingly, she called out to the others: "What do you say to that, girls? I shall go down into history! It was worth while living through all that for the sake of history . . ." And all through that evening she kept on turning to her friends and urging them to sit patiently and to tell me all the details of their stories "for the sake of history."

"Well," said Riva, "I'll tell you how it happened. Just so as not to cheat history, of course!"

I advised her to think a little, to choose her words well. She looked at me in amazement.

"Why should I think? What have I got to think about? If someone woke me up in the middle of the night I should remember every detail, as if it had all happened only yesterday."

Nevertheless she paused reflectively for a few moments before she began her story.

"At the end of 1939, shortly after the war broke out, we ran away from Poland to Bukovina, my two sisters and myself, our four brothers, Mother, and an aunt of ours. Father was dead. He was a mechanic in Brisk, and he was killed at work just a few weeks before the war came. We traveled from Brisk to

Czernovitz, but we weren't allowed to stay there because there were so many refugees in the city already. We traveled in a car belonging to one of our brothers, and we succeeded in getting as far as the Ukrainian border. This brother was the owner of a workshop where he made brushes out of pigs' bristles. He took his young wife with him, and there were twelve of us altogether. In the Ukraine our family grew. One sister got married and so did one brother, and we all lived together. We lived in the little town of Bar, in Russian-occupied territory. There were many factories there, and plenty of work for everybody. My sister worked in an alcohol factory. I was the youngest, and I went to a Russian school. One of my brothers got work as a mechanic, and another as a clerk in an office. We had everything we needed. Even when Russia entered the war and one of my brothers joined the Red Army, our situation didn't change much. A short time later my brother-in-law joined up, too, and still things went quite well. But then the Germans came down like a horde, just a few weeks after Russia entered the war. We couldn't get away because one of my sisters was about to give birth, and my sister-in-law was also pregnant. My brother who remained at home received work as a translator from German to Russian. My oldest brother also knew French and English. What that boy didn't know! He was all there, that one! You could talk to him! He had a good business head, too, and he was only twenty-four years old. Well, we got along all right for a year. That's what the German is like: if he needs anyone, even if it's a Jew, he 'buys' him and gives him what he needs. At first my brother used to bring all sorts of good things home. But after a few months the killings began. They murdered everyone, and I was the only one left, with a brother three years older than myself. It happened very early one morning. They went from house to house, dragging people out of their beds, and ordering us to gather in the center of the town. We thought they were going to drive us to another place. But it was nothing like that. They separated the men from the women and they killed them. They killed them all, and they left no one alive except twenty children, me among them. Believe me, I don't know how it happened that I was saved, and why they chose me and not someone else. They dug three big holes and they threw the bodies into the holes. No, I don't remember what happened to me. I stood there and watched, and it seemed to me as if all the world had gone mad. Dreadful deafening cries filled the air. It was not only the people screaming, but dogs howled too, and birds shrieked, as if the world had returned to a savage wilderness.

Later there was silence. The streets were so quiet that you could hear the tread of the sentries' footsteps. The children who were left were about fourteen or fifteen years old. They put spades in our hands and ordered us to dig holes for ourselves. We made twenty small holes in a straight row in the loose soil. Believe me, I didn't feel anything then. I was not sorry and I was not afraid. I did what I was told to do, and that's all. When we finished digging the holes, one of the Germans ordered us to jump inside them. Then another German came up and said, "No, let them first cover up the big holes." We did that. We covered the holes with lime, which turned red from the blood, and over the lime we threw black earth. For three days and three nights the blood still came through the layers of lime and dust. And the town of Bar was nothing unusual, for the Germans murdered and butchered in Proskurov and in many other cities.

Then they took us away, the twenty who remained, to a camp in Yakushinitz. You may put down in your book that this camp was seventy-five kilometers from the place of the slaughter. I was there for a month. But you couldn't call it living. They gave us a hundred grams of bread a day and two plates of soup. And the work was back-breaking. We were put to road-repairing. Ten meters were marked off for each person, and anyone who stepped outside the border of his ten-meter strip was shot without warning. Thousands of us worked there, all of us between fifteen and eighteen years of age. Anyone who became ill and couldn't work was shot. I said to myself: "Better risk an escape than to die here." So one dark and rainy night we got up. I and my brother and two other boys and two girls, and we ran away. I suppose you wonder how we managed to get away. Well, at the edge of the camp there was a trench — the Germans called it *schanze*. You see? Well, we crawled out to this trench under cover of darkness, very cautiously, like cats; we sprang into it and we stayed there until morning. At four o'clock in the morning (it was in the autumn of 1941) we left the trench and slipped away like shadows. We walked and ran until we came to a village, and then we went up to one of the Russian houses and we asked them to give us shelter. The family took pity on us and they brought us back to the town of Bar, to one of the four ghettos that still remained after the big slaughter. About a month later the killings began again. It was the day after Yom Hakipurim [Day of Atonement]. Again they went from house to house, collecting the Jews and taking them out to be killed. I was in the house with my brother. We had learned something from experience. I said to my brother: 'I'm going to try my luck. I won't go.' I tried to persuade my brother to do as I did, but he said: 'I'll just go up to the roof to see where they are taking the people.' Well, what could I say to that? A minute later I peeped outside through the keyhole. Whom were they taking? My brother! I wanted to scream, but my voice failed. For three days after I couldn't get a word out. Suddenly I heard a knock at the window. With one leap I sprang behind the cupboard. From there I climbed up into the stove and in the excitement I hurt my nose, and I suffered from the wound for a long time afterwards. Then the door burst open and two Ukrainian policemen and two Germans stood at the entrance. They looked here and there, and they searched the place, but they didn't find me. Oh, how wretched I was. If you had seen me then I'm sure you would have thought I was a ghost and not a human being at all. And blood was flowing from my nose as if I had been butchered.

When at last they left, and it was quiet as the grave in the house, I slipped out and ran, barefoot and almost naked, to the factory where my brothers and sister had once worked. The factory was outside the ghetto and every step was a deadly danger. But what had I to lose? I ran. When the *goyim* at the factory saw me they were horrified. At once they hid me away, and for a day and a night I roved among the boxes and barrels. At last one of the women took me in hand, smuggled me across the little stream, and brought me over to the Old Rumanian territory. A lot of children were saved in this way, with the help of the *goyim* — if it weren't for them, not a Jewish soul would have been left alive. I came to a village, and the Jewish community took me in. I was placed with a well-to-do Jewish family, and I worked for them as a servant. I stayed there for a year and a half and I was well looked after. There was a dreadful famine in the village. Children wandered in the streets in the hundreds, fainting and dying before our eyes. But I didn't starve, though I suffered because I couldn't forget my family and dear ones who had been murdered before my eyes, while I could do nothing to save them. I shall never, never forget my mother and sisters and brothers, nor the terrible things that happened. And as long as I live I shall remember those good people who were kind to me. And I shall always be good to others, and shall try to do as much kindness to people as those few good people have shown to me and to other children by saving us from death and torture.''

From *Rescued Children*, op. cit., pp. 26-31.

HIDING IN A BUNKER, PASSING AS AN ARYAN: MANYA'S UNFORGETTABLE STORY

Manya was born in Cracow, and was fourteen years old when she told her story to Lena Kichler in 1945 at the orphanage in Zacopina. The following is a short extract.

I have interrupted my story about that Friday when I first saw policemen surrounding the walls of the ghetto. I did not know whether they were then carrying out the final liquidation of the ghetto or not. I had returned from Buchnia, and had traveled to Limanowska Street in order to re-enter the ghetto from there. It was easier from there because there was no wall, but only a barbed-wire fence.

When I arrived there I saw a horrible sight. In the ghetto, opposite Czarenski Street, stood the Jewish police building, and behind it was the prison. On the steps of the prison, a huge German was standing, and around him there was a crowd of children — thousands of them. They were speaking to him, asking for something; their words did not reach me, because I was standing far away on the other side of the barbed wire, together with the Poles, but we heard the terrible crying of all the children. They must have been entreating him, for they pressed close to him and extended their tiny arms. . . .

The swollen, awkward German suddenly moved and hurled himself in all directions like a madman. He waved his heavy fists and threatened the children who were approaching him with their arms stretched out. The screaming increased. Then it seemed that the German got exasperated at it all. He drew out his revolver and fired into the crowd of children. A still, strange silence descended on the square.

The German's bullet struck a dark child about ten, who stood near the wall. From where I was standing, I saw clearly how the child suddenly began to lean forward, then bent over, as though his body had been broken in two, and fell to the ground. I did not hear any cry, nor the sound of his body hitting the ground. The children were standing quite still. They no longer asked for mercy.

Suddenly one of the Jewish policemen sprang from the group of children and ran to the child who had been shot. He lifted him above the heads of the children and walked, with the dead child in his arms, in the direction of the German. I do not know what he said to him. Perhaps he reproached him for having killed the child. Perhaps he thought he would awaken some mercy for the other children. His words did not reach my ears. But he was a brave man.

All at once, a terrible panic began. The children ran in all directions. In the midst of the noise, the German's cries split the air. "Put the child down! I will shoot you! I will shoot you all!" A shot was fired. He probably shot the policeman. Afterwards other shots came.

I was terribly frightened and ran away while I was still alive.

I returned to the city. I had no desire to eat or to trade. I only wanted to cry and cry. Had I been able to, I would have sat all day and cried my heart out. But I could not — I had to search for my family. I found Helena, my younger sister, in the evening. She too was terribly frightened and shocked. She told me that she had slipped out of the ghetto via the sewers. When I told her I had tried to re-enter the ghetto, she began to tremble. She said it was utter madness. People were prepared to pay thousands for an opportunity to escape from the ghetto. She managed to get away through the sewers with a handful of people — but the Germans had noticed and had placed a guard at the exit.

Helena told me things that I am incapable of repeating. Just to remember them hurts me. When she went down into the sewer, many children crowded around her. They kissed her hands, pulled her coat, and begged her to take them with her. "I shall not cry! I shall behave well! I want to live too!" Even the tiniest ones promised to behave well and not to cry. The children were so clever. They felt they had been sentenced to death. . . .

She would not take any of them with her. They were too small and would have drowned in the sewer. Only the bigger ones managed to get through.

On Saturday, at ten in the morning, all those who still had valid work-cards left the ghetto. At eleven, the large work-groups, such as that which worked in the Optima factory, left the ghetto. The remainder of the ghetto's population was condemned to death. They all knew that, and looked frightenedly at those who were leaving.

The fate of the children was the worst of all. The mothers were forbidden to take their children with them to the camp. The Germans did them one favor: they could stay in the ghetto and be killed together with their children. The Germans even used to torment them. They would seize some child that was crying in the street, accost any woman they saw, and ask, "Is this child yours? Do you want to stay here with him?"

There were some mothers who denied their children. They did not want to die . . . but many more chose death. There were cases when both the father and the mother went to death with their children. In our building there was a family which included a lovely daughter, with blond hair in a plait. Even though the parents had good work-cards, they remained in the ghetto and were put to death together with their daughter.

The children were terribly frightened to die by themselves. Even the little ones cried not to be left alone at the last moments.

My parents and Lola went to the camp, since they had the right to work. Apart from them, and Halinka and myself, there were another three girls in the family — Hela, who was thirteen years old, Justa, fourteen, and Renia, sixteen — and my brother, Ignatz, fifteen. We did not know what had happened to them. It was the following day when I met Ignatz and Hela in a suburb of Cracow. They told me they had escaped via the sewers. Our father had placed Justa and Renia in hiding with Mrs. Drenger at No. 13 Market Street in the ghetto.

It was a marvelous bunker. The entrance was through the lavatory, which was almost impossible to enter because of the revolting stench. There was a well-concealed door, which opened on a dimly lit corridor, where there was a dirty old cupboard. By going through the cupboard, a small room was reached, which could not be detected from outside. Twelve people sat there and did not leave it. Only Victor Tennenbaum used to climb onto the roof, via the small skylight, and then crawl to the parapet, from which he would bring them food. He went through all kinds of dangers for them, kept their spirits high, and saved them. He was a wonderful boy! He did not know what fear was. He prepared bars of iron and announced that the Germans would not take him alive. Thanks to him, they were all saved except Mrs. Drenger. It was her own fault that she was killed. She had left the bunker, even though Victor had strictly forbidden her to do so. She was killed together with her children. The Germans came with a dog after that, but did not discover the bunker. The dog smelt something and barked incessantly, but they searched in vain.

On Sunday, shots were heard in the ghetto. The Germans entered the hospital and murdered all the patients, all the doctors and the nurses. The Ukrainians who had entered the ghetto on Saturday drank all day and afterwards took little children, cracked their heads open against the walls, and tore them apart alive. I did not see it with my own eyes, but I heard it. I only saw large black lorries behind the church. I counted twelve. They were all covered. Such lorries had never been seen there before. Afterwards I saw open lorries full of Jews in Limanowska Street. Some of them had only children in them, some had old people only, and a few were mixed. In one of them I recognized Greenberg the baker's wife, who had borne a son only two weeks earlier. She still looked weak and could hardly stand on her feet. There was a German sitting at the front of the lorry, with his rifle aimed at the Jews, and there was another at the back. The streets were full of police.

It was a pleasant, sunny Sunday. The Polish Christians were going peacefully to church. They did not hurry. They stood and watched the lorries going their way. They counted and said that forty had passed by. Others said that sixty had gone by. What surprised them was that the Jews traveled quietly — no screams or wails were heard.

After that I saw large carts pulled by horses. Great piles of bodies swayed upon them, covered with blankets dripping blood. Some of them were still quivering.

I was forced to disappear quickly. One of the boys in the crowd recognized me and called to a friend, "There is Manya the Jewess!" and even though he almost whispered it, everyone was surprised and began to say, "A Jew! A Jew!" I slipped away immediately.

I had thought I was brave and that I was not afraid of anyone, but when I saw what the Germans were doing to the Jews, my spirits fell — I did not want to die.

I bought a Catholic birth certificate for my sister Hela and placed her with a Pole in Bubov. I continued to live in Cracow and to trade. I used to go to the Optima workshops, where Jews worked, and I would buy food and other goods for them, which they later smuggled into the camp. I used to take letters for them as well. I earned good money. I used to buy food for that money and send it to my parents and my sisters in the camp. I supported the whole family like that. This lasted for six months, until Gett (the German commander) forbade the Jews to leave the camp and closed the Optima factory. They moved all the workshops to the camp. I remember it took place one year after the liquidation of the Tarnov Ghetto — after the third of September 1943.

I was left by myself on the Aryan side. There were no more familiar faces in the street. All the Jews had been taken to the camp. Only Helena and I myself were left in the city. Our hearts drew us to the camp. We longed for our family — for Jews. We were so lonely among strangers.

We often went to the fence. It was a double fence, and electrified. There were watchtowers everywhere, with Ukrainians, armed with machine guns, and searchlights. In addition to them, policemen continually made their rounds. We wanted to throw bread over the fence for our father. On the other side of the wire we could see Jews at work, and I felt it could not be so very bad. While we were calling to one of the Jews, who was carrying sandbags on his back, to catch a loaf of bread, a Ukrainian descended from one of the towers and stopped us.

The blood froze in our veins. "What are you doing here?" the Ukrainian asked. We became confused and answered that our parents were in the camp; that we wanted to bring them bread and also wanted to go to the camp as well. We told the truth, because we were more frightened of Ukrainians than of any one else. To us, they were evil itself. The Ukrainian took the bread and said we were fools if we wanted to enter the camp, because it was a very bad place for Jews. In the camp, Jews were shot and killed, and many of them died of hunger. He advised us not to approach the wire, since if we were caught we would be shot. He even advised us not to walk together in the city, because Helena was a brunette and they would immediately recognize that I was Jewish too, and both of us would be trapped. He promised to give the bread to our sister inside the camp and asked us what her name was.

We were very surprised. We had never heard that there were good Ukrainians. We had only heard of their evil deeds. This Ukrainian was really a good man. Afterwards, Lola told me that when the Ukrainian entered the workshop and called her name, she began to tremble, but he called her aside and secretly gave her the bread.

After that, we were careful for a long time. But we could not remain quiet. We longed for our family and for other Jews. We wanted terribly to help them or to suffer and go hungry with them. We were incapable of living alone. I was always sure that sooner or later I should be among Jews and that I should go to the camp. So I once more went to the fence. Helena, who brought the bread, came with me, and Yuzia, a Polish woman who wanted to sell butter to the people in the camp.

Near the wires, a small boy of eight saw us and ran to the Ukrainians to tell them about the two Jewesses and to receive his reward of 10 zloty. A Ukrainian approached us and demanded our papers. While he was examining Yuzia's documents, I tried to escape. I bent down to the ground, as though I was playing with stones, and tried to move away. But he noticed me and began to shout, "Halt, or I shoot!" I stopped. He took both of us (Helena as well) to the German police station. The German to whom we were taken refused to believe at first that we were Jewish, and the Ukrainian had to go to great trouble to convince him.

We were extremely afraid, because anyone caught with false Aryan documents was shot. Luckily, we were not shot, but sent to the camp. We were placed in Hut No. 13.

The worst thing in the camp was the hunger. People talked only about eating. At first I could not understand it, because I was not as starved as they. Afterwards I too used to talk for whole days about delicacies. It was our good luck that we were not yet put down for work and did not have to rise at five in the morning and stand for hours at a time in the parade. We were not "registered" at all, and we received no food either. I used to sleep till midday in order to still my hunger. Then I would go to "organize" potatoes from the potato peelers' hut. My mother used to work there, but she did not dare "organize" anything.

There was a large number of us children who were neither registered nor did any work, and we therefore had to "organize" and scrounge food as best we could, since we did not want to take anything from our mothers' starvation rations. We were well organized and spent most of the day near the potato-peeling hut; whenever there was a chance, we would "organize" potatoes. Afterwards we would build a fire and cook them. We always posted a lookout, so that we should not be caught. Whenever a stranger approached, we quickly put out the fire and dispersed.

We were especially frightened of the commander, Gett. Every morning he would appear on a white horse, with a pack of dogs yelping and gallivanting around him. Whenever we saw him, our hearts stopped, and we hid ourselves. He invariably shot a few people during his daily hour of inspection. That was his early-morning sport. Sometimes he entered the showers while the women were washing, and beat them cruelly till they died. He would tell the builders to put up a hut in one day. If they did not manage to complete it — he shot them. They worked feverishly all night, and yet did not manage.

My face changed completely then. I was no longer the same pretty girl I had been, with the long plaits. I was forced to cut them off, because of the lice. I went around filthy, with clothes like a beggar. There was neither soap nor water in the camp. I was hungry all the time.

There were many children in the camp. Some of them were there legally. They were the children of the Jewish Police *(Ordnungsdienst* — OD), who had helped to liquidate the ghetto and who had been promised that their children would not be harmed. Some children had got there through "pull," like Farber.

He was the nephew of Gett's Jewish deputy, Hielwicz, who held our fate in his hands. There were the two Rosners, children of the violinist who played for Gett and even composed songs.

There were others who had been smuggled into the camp by their mothers in knapsacks, in bags, or in suitcases. There were girls who had padded their breasts and were taken for adults. There were those who were brought to the camp when they were caught with false Aryan papers. (That was later, of course. At first they shot Jews who were found with Aryan papers.) They were not registered and had to hide all the time.

In the morning, at inspection, they used to hide them in the bedclothes and cover them over; afterwards, they would appear, one by one. Then Gett established a "children's home." They set a special hut aside for it on the hill. The matron of the "children's home" was Mrs. Mandelbaum, who had been a teacher. It was better in the "children's home," because the children received better food than the adults. Mothers were allowed to visit their children every day. Even so, they did not send their children there. They had no confidence in the Germans, and they wanted their children to be close to them. However, as soon as Aryan women were placed in charge of the huts, they could no longer keep their children. The Aryan women used to pry and search the huts thoroughly, and if they discovered a child, they cruelly beat the mother. That is how they forced all the parents to surrender their children.

From *Massacre of European Jewry,* story by Lena Kichler, published by World Hashomer Hatzair, pp. 166-174.

8.

CAMPS

Deportation and Detention

Deportation of the victims to the death camps required a corps of competent and skilled professionals. They had to attend to many important details, such as train schedules, equipment, and capacity of the cars. Transportation had to be planned in relation to the needs of military traffic as well as the moving of slave labor, armaments, and military hardware, and also the readiness of the gassing installations to admit victims. Rolling stock had to be available and serviceable. Fuel had to be at hand; the rate of consumption and points for refilling were determining factors. Distances from the point of departure to the point of death presented intricate calculations — e.g., the number of cars needed, their load capacity, consumption of fuel, and coordination of schedules. To economize on the long ride from Hungary to Auschwitz, trains carried 2500 to 3000 victims. (Generally speaking, economical fuel consumption dictated a limitation of 20 boxcars or approximately 1000 bodies to a train.) Short runs could allow up to 60 boxcars containing 6000 souls. Return schedules had also to be calculated carefully. In addition, the severe competition for space and delivery dates between the War Department and Eichmann's extermination department was frequent and taxing.

Lists, inventories, timetables, itemized details required careful study and constant attention, especially in 1944 and 1945, when the military desperately needed everything it could muster to halt the advance of the Allies. The conflicts between the military and Eichmann were unending; the latter, backed by Hitler and Himmler, usually had the upper hand.

For these and other reasons, such as deceiving the victims and avoiding partisan attacks, it became necessary to set up detention camps where the condemned could be "accommodated" for a period of time before the swift final disposition. Theresienstadt in Austria was one such center; so were Drancy in France, and Westerbork in Holland.

DEPORTATION OF JEWISH CHILDREN FROM PARIS TO DRANCY

In 1940, when France fell, the northern region and the Atlantic coastline were occupied by the German military command, whose authority was supreme. Marshal Henri Philippe Pétain, figurehead Chief of State, and Pierre Laval, actual dictator, governed in central and southern France (1940 – 1944) in the region known as Vichy, which was not occupied by the Germans. However, they were tools of the Germans and collaborated with them fully.

On July 16 and 17, 1942, the Germans rounded up for deportation to death those Jews who were not citizens of France. Laval insisted that Jews of French nationality be exempted from deportation but was not interested in the fate of the stateless Jews, including their children. The French police cooperated fully with the German military police in the rounding up and the deportation of 12,884 Jews, including 4,051 children who lived in Paris.

In the velodrome (stadium) where the children were imprisoned, pandemonium reigned. Separated from their parents, hungry, thirsty, bewildered, they filled the arena with their weeping and wailing. Sanitary facilities were almost nil. The stadium was emptied only after a horrendous seven-day imprisonment. Following are eyewitness accounts of children's convoys to Drancy.

(Postscript: In 1945 Laval went on trial for treason and was executed. Pétain was also sentenced to death, but his sentence was commuted to life imprisonment.)

It was beginning to get cold. The kids were half asleep, and it was quite a job to get them down from their dormitories. Most of them sat on the ground, each with his little bundle next to him: just a few clothes tied up in a napkin, sometimes with a doll's head or the wheel of a wooden truck sticking out, their only treasure and perhaps also a symbol of their lost home. The gendarmes tried to get through the roll call, but it was impossible. The children did not respond to the names. Surnames like Rosenthal, Biegelmann, Radekski, etc., meant nothing to them, and some even wandered off from the group. One tiny boy walked up to a gendarme and started to play with the whistle hanging from the man's belt; a little girl saw some flowers growing on a slope and went off to pick them and make a bouquet. The gendarmes did not know what to do. Finally they were ordered to take the children to the railroad station nearby and not bother with the roll call, as long as the required number of children were put on the train.

We were standing only two hundred yards from the station, but that is a long way for small children hampered by clumsy bundles. I noticed one gendarme take the bundle of a boy of about four or five to help him walk. But he was immediately reprimanded by an adjutant, who told him rudely that a French soldier did not carry the bags of a Jew. Sheepishly the soldier handed the little bundle back to the boy.

I followed the procession of children going to the station, my heart bursting. I could not bear to leave them, after having cared for them for so many weeks. I could hardly keep myself from weeping, and I must say, that many of the soldiers also found it difficult to mask their emotion. When we got to the platform, I noticed a German soldier standing on an overhead footbridge crossing the tracks, with his machine gun pointing at us. Once we were in the station, the children were loaded onto the trains in a sudden burst of speed. Many of the children were too small to climb into the freight cars without the help of a ladder, so the bigger boys would climb in first and help the younger ones pull themselves up. The gendarmes lifted the babies, who were hardly weaned, and handed them to the women, nursing mothers, or the children who were already on board.

It was at this point that the children felt frightened. They didn't want to go and started to cry. They would call to the social workers standing on the platform for help, and would sometimes even appeal to the soldiers. Jacquot, a little five-year-old of whom I was particularly fond, started shouting for me: ''I want to get down, I want to stay with Mademoiselle. . . .'' The door of the car was shut and bolted, but Jacquot pushed his hand through a gap between two planks and continued to call for me, moving his fingers. The adjutant mentioned above hit him on the hand.

As the children came off the buses, the bigger ones immediately took the smaller ones by the hand and did not let go of them until they reached their dormitories. On the staircases they would carry the younger ones, puffing and panting as they staggered up to the fifth floor. There they huddled together like a flock of frightened sheep, hesitating for a long time before sitting down on the repulsively dirty mattresses. Most of them had lost track of their bundles by now. The few who had remembered to bring them off the bus did not know what to do with their shapeless parcels. Meanwhile the rest of the luggage had been piled up in the prison yard so that, as soon as the unloading was finished, the children went down to find their belongings.

The tiny, anonymous bundles were difficult to distinguish one from another, and for a long time small children four, five, and six went through them, thinking they had found their own things. But after undoing a package and quickly examining its contents, they would find some pants or a small dress which belonged to somebody else and would feel puzzled and discouraged.

In spite of their great distress, however they would hopefully start all over again. They never quarreled or argued; on the contrary, they were helpful to each other in a thousand different ways, surprising to see in children. After several useless attempts to find their property, they gave up and remained in the courtyard, not knowing what to do. Those who wanted to go up into the bedrooms no longer remembered which dormitory they belonged to. Very politely they would ask somebody to help them: ''Sir, I don't know where my little sister is. I think she may be frightened by herself.'' So one would take the bigger ones by the hand, and carrying the younger ones on one's arm, would wander through the dormitories on the various staircases until the little sister or brother in question was located. They demonstrated such affection as only children in unhappy circumstances can show.

From *Betrayal at the Vel d'Hiv* by Claude Levy and Paul Tillard, New York: Hill and Wang, 1969, pp. 158-160. Trans. by Inea Bushnag.

WHAT HAPPENED TO FOUR THOUSAND FRENCH JEWISH CHILDREN

Eichmann trial witness Professor George Wellers, a lecturer at the Sorbonne University in Paris, in his book (in French) From Drancy to Auschwitz, *records the intense suffering during the liquidation of the Jews of France.*

He was eyewitness to forty deportations from Drancy to Auschwitz[1] in 1942. The most horrid chapter depicts the deportation of the children from the camp in Drancy to Auschwitz. Below is a transcript of his testimony at the Eichmann trial in 1961.

When the Red Army freed Auschwitz, fewer than 450 Jews were among the survivors; not a child was left alive.

Prosecutor: How many children were there?

W.: About 4000.

P.: Did you see these children?

W.: Yes, I saw them.

P.: When did you see them after their arrival in Drancy?

W.: During the latter part of August 1942. They came in four transports, each with 1000 children and with an additional 200 adults, who were not their parents. They came from two detention camps in France. The four transports arrived within a few days of each other.

P.: Describe to this court how they looked and how they were received at the camp.

W.: The children came in buses. All deportations were made in buses, which were guarded by Vichy police and commanded by Vichy officers. The buses came into the camp proper. In the middle of the camp there was an area fenced in by barbed wire. There the drivers and police unloaded the live cargo with great speed in order to make room for the other buses, which followed one another rapidly. The children, who were confused and frightened, were unloaded hurriedly. About sixty to eighty children were in each bus; they went down quietly. Except for those who had special permits, the adults were restricted from approaching the newcomers. I had such a permit and was permitted to be near them. They were brought up to a house, which was empty of furniture and which had no toilet facilities. All it had was straw mats which looked disgusting and riddled with bedbugs.

P.: Did all the children know their names?

---

[1] Involving roughly about 80,000 souls.

W.: No. Among them were two-, three- and four-year-olds, little ones, who did not know what their names were. It was impossible to identify them except for the chance aid of brothers, sisters, and other children. We improvised names for those who were nameless. We prepared wooden disks which we suspended with strings around their necks. Later we found girls wearing disks with boys' names and vice versa. Evidently they played with these disks and often exchanged them.

P.: What happened to their possessions?

W.: In the main they were rags, packed hastily and poorly. Because of the precipitant rush to empty the buses, many forgot to take their baggage along. After they descended from the bus, we emptied it of what remained and asked the children to identify their belongings.

P.: What was the children's physical appearance?

W.: Terrible. Childen who came to us from transit camps [witness gives their names] had already lived through weeks of neglect and destitution. They were dirty, their clothes torn and badly worn. They came to us in the worst condition possible. Their clothes were without buttons. Many wore one shoe only; others did not wear shoes that matched. Their bodies were covered with sores. They suffered from diarrhea. They could not go down to the courtyard to attend to their toilet needs as frequently as necessary, so the attendants provided night pots. But these were too large for the young children. Four groups of women, who themselves were marked for Auschwitz, helped the little ones. Women who had been deported were replaced by others. These women would rise at dawn and spread out to the various rooms to clean up the young ones. About 120 children were crowded into each room. The women did not have soap or clean cloths with which to wash them. They used cold water and improvised materials to wipe and dry them.

When the containers of soup were delivered, there were no spoons to eat with. The keepers ladled portions of soup into old tin preserve containers and handed them out. The metal was thin, and the soup was too hot to hold. Those who did not receive their portion were too timid to raise their voices. The women who served them discharged their humanitarian responsibilities nobly.

P.: Were adults permitted to be with the children at night?

W.: No. After 9:00 P.M. all adults were required to leave, except for three or four who were guards and permitted to stroll around the camp, including the children's quarters. I was one of those privileged. Except for one electric blue-painted bulb which shone dimly, there was no light. The children slept side by side. They did not sleep through the night but would awaken, cry, quarrel, call for their mothers. It often happened that they would wake one another and break out in loud crying and weeping. The whole building would then explode in a common outburst of wailing, which shattered the stillness of the entire camp.

P.: Do you remember Jacques Stern? Can you tell us briefly about him?

W.: Yes, also René Blum, brother of Léon Blum, who was the world-famous statesman.

Presiding Judge: Did the prosecutor ask about Jacques Stern or René Blum?

P.: Jacques Stern. The witness mentioned René Blum. Why?

W.: René Blum was the director of the Monte Carlo Ballet. He was a very sensitive human being. One day he asked me if he might accompany me to the children's rooms. One day after the lunch hour, when the supervision was not so stringent, I took him up. When we opened a door of one of the rooms, we saw a beautiful boy, seven or eight years, old, who looked clever and alert. His clothes showed that long ago they had been elegant, but now they looked like all the others. He wore only one shoe, his coat was torn, but the boy was jolly. René Blum, who was tall, bent down and asked the boy's age and his name. He asked what his parents did. The boy answered that his father worked in an office and his mother excelled in playing the piano. He then asked how soon he would leave the camp and join his parents. In the light of the circumstances and their coming to Drancy, their deportation to Auschwitz made us very apprehensive. René had to lie to him and replied, ''Do not worry. In another two or three days you will probably be freed from the camp and join your mother.'' Then the boy took out from his jacket pocket a half-eaten biscuit, the kind we rationed to the camp inmates, and said, ''I am keeping this for Mother.''

René Blum wanted to pat the boy on the head, when suddenly the boy began to cry. A moment ago he had been cheerful, and now . . . We left the room.

P.: What happened to the 4000 children?

W.: They were all deported at the end of August and the beginning of September.

Each deportation numbered 1000 children and 500 adults.

P.: All were sent away?

W.: Yes. All.

P.: Do you remember the Hauptsturmführer, Ratke?

W.: Very well.

P.: Was he present when the children were deported?

W.: Yes. At each deportation. Not only of the children but of the adults.

P.: Did the children leave camp quietly?

W.: No. Most of the time it was a horrible and shocking operation. They would wake them at 5:00 A.M. and give them coffee. The children were still half asleep. In France, even in August, it is dark at five in the morning. They would march them down to the courtyard. The children were disoriented. The volunteer women workers asked to be allowed to take the children down, after the adults had descended, but the police did not always accede to their pleas. The children cried, quarreled, fought back. The police would then bring them down forcefully.

P.: When you came to Auschwitz did you see any of the children alive?

W.: No! No! Of course not.

P.: I now digress to another chapter. Were there many suicides in Camp Drancy?

W.: In 1942 there were many suicide cases. I would estimate about a hundred a month or more. The camp inmates looked askance at those who wanted to commit suicide because the prevailing idea regarding suicide was that it had better be done after the transport to Auschwitz, because each suicide was replaced by a living prisoner so as to complete the quota of a thousand per shipment.

P.: Did you witness mothers deported after they gave birth?

W.: Yes. The rule was that pregnant women were to remain in camp until they gave birth and then to be deported with their infants.

A.E.

From *Testimony at the Eichmann Trial* by George Wellers, published by Yad Vashem, Israel Information Office, 1974, pp. 425-446.

JANUSZ KORCZAK MARCHES TO DEATH WITH HIS CHILDREN

Janusz Korczak, was the celebrated pen name of a Polish Jewish physician who will be remembered as a lover of children, educator, and author. He devoted his life to homeless Jewish children, whom he raised in a world-renowned orphanage which he founded and directed. When the children were deported to the Treblinka death camp in August 1942, he could have saved his own life, but he would not part from them.

To honor his martyrdom, two literary prizes have been established recently by the Anti-Defamation League of B'nai B'rith and the Polish-American Catholic Committee, with Pope John Paul II serving as honorary chairman. One is for books written for children and the other for books about children written for adults. To commemorate his contribution to child welfare, UNESCO designated 1979, the centenary year of his birth, as the Year of the Child.

First to be deported were the children. And among the earliest victims were the "children of the streets" — the homeless and the orphans. Despite their sprightliness and elusiveness, they were rounded up for deportation. Thousands of refugee children trudged to the *Umschlagplatz* and ultimately to their death.

The Centos staff, who provided shelter and aid to some 25,000 children, many of whom were housed in dormitories, were fully alert to the grave danger of concentrating children in specific places. To avoid imperiling the children's lives, they considered many proposals, such as scattering the children in the homes of relatives, friends, and families; registering the older children as "productive shopworkers"; providing temporary day-care homes attached to shops (which were recognized and protected by the German military); smuggling children to the Aryan side; and other stratagems.

They knew that these steps were temporary, that the children would be living on borrowed time. Ultimately their end would be like that of their parents — annihilation. . . .

The deportation of the children in orphanages began in August 1942. One of the first institutions whose children were rounded up was the Korczak Orphanage. The whole staff, including the director, Dr. Janusz Korczak, and his associate, Steffa Wilchinska, would not part from the children and led the procession. Ringelblum noted in his diary (October 15, 1942): "Korczak (and his staff) set the pattern that the teachers accompany the children to the *Umschlagplatz*. Well did they know what awaited them, but they were commit-

ted not to desert their children. The teachers accompanied them to their death."
Two months later Ringelblum noted in his diary: "We bow our heads in
reverence to our educators, even though their self-sacrifice did not help or make
any difference."

These sentiments were also expressed by Dr. Adolf Berman, head of the
Centos organization. "Many communal leaders were moved by the martyrdom
of the educational personnel. Janusz Korczak headed the list of those who went
to death with their pupils, even though they could have saved themselves. This
lofty, noble act was motivated by psychological and moral considerations.
They would not abandon their dependents on their last march. Their souls were
bound up with the lives of their students. . . . True, some communal leaders
questioned the wisdom of their self-sacrifice: 'Would it not have been preferable for men like Korczak to remain alive so that they might be of vital service to
help rehabilitate the Jewish community after Hitler's downfall? Were they not
sacrificing their lives in vain?' "

We are not in a position to pronounce judgment on their actions. Beyond all
doubt they performed an exalted, incomparable historic act. They viewed
themselves as the guardians of the precious lives that had been entrusted to
them. Their consciences dictated their decision to live or die. Korczak's
immortal act served as example to other directors of orphanages.

The reactions of the children during their final hours were mixed. The older
ones knew well what awaited them, and yet they walked quietly and boarded the
train with their teachers, fully aware that they were going to their death. The
younger children did not know what was happening but were affected by the
noise, the crowding, the crying of the parents and relatives. They clung to their
teachers and would not let go. Many wept and kept repeating, "Will they drown
us *there?*" Death by drowning seemed to frighten them more than anything
else.

Thus some 4000 children of orphanages were deported to death, a fraction of
the 100,000 Jewish children of Warsaw who were exterminated. The march,
led by Korczak, consisted of 192 children and 8 staff members and, as stated,
was headed by Dr. Korczak and Steffa. It was a warm day, and the road was
long. Witnesses reported that Korczak clasped the hand of a five-year-old.

Journalist Yehoshua Perla, a witness of the procession, noted in his memoirs:
"The scene was unforgettable. The children were silent; 200 innocent souls
knew they were marching to their death. No one tried to hide or escape. The
little ones hugged their teachers, like helpless birdlings, seeking to give them
shelter and protection. Bareheaded Korczak, a leather belt around his waist,
wearing boots, walked bent over, holding a little child by the hand. The
children were dressed in their finest — sacrificial offerings brought to the Nazi
Moloch. They were surrounded on all sides by German and Ukrainian guards
and even Jewish police. The guards impelled them on with their whips and with
their smoking revolvers. . . . The very stones weep at the sight of this procession. . . ."

Nahum Remba, secretary of the Warsaw Jewish Council, narrates how he
and others tried to rescue the children: "It was an unbearably hot day. I
arranged for the older students to find benches far away from the train. I

believed that I could save them by delaying their boarding the train until late in the afternoon. I suggested to Korczak that he go with me to urge the Jewish Community Council to intervene with the killers. He refused, because he did not want to leave his children alone even for a short while. The loading of the cars began. . . . The victims were beaten by knouts to hasten the packing of the overloaded railroad cars. . . .

"Korczak, head erect, his eyes raised heavenward, walked at the head. This was an unforgettable march. The children walked in groups of four, Korczak leading the first group, Steffa Wilchinska second, and so on. . . . When the Jewish police spied Korczak, they saluted as one. The Germans asked, 'Who is this man?' I could not restrain myself and hid the flood of tears that burst from my eyes. I was convulsed with sobs at our utter helplessness.''

Many were the stories circulating about Korczak. In the turmoil during the final procession, an SS officer made a beeline to Korczak and handed him a letter. It was rumored the letter stated that he was free to go home — but *not* the children.

Another rumor has it that when the children were already in the train a German officer approached him and inquired, ''Did you write *Young Jack?*'' Korczak replied in the affirmative. ''A good book. I read it as a child. You may leave the train.''

''And the children?''

''The children will continue their journey. But you may remain in town.''

''You are mistaken,'' Korczak replied. ''Not everyone is a villain.''

The mother of twelve-year-old Halinka Pinchonson, who worked at the First Aid Station, which was conducted by the above-mentioned Nahum Remba, was summoned to save her daughter from deportation. Halinka refused to leave. ''When things were bad, you asked Korczak to admit me to the orphanage, and now you want me to leave them to their fate, and I am to remain alive. No! My place is with them.''

Korczak's martyrdom was a shattering experience to those who witnessed it, but to him it was a voluntary act performed without hesitation. It was the crowning moment of his noble life.

Anthony Shimanksy, one of the Righteous Poles, a partisan of the Underground, noted in his memoirs: ''Cry aloud! Give honor to his valor, to his death which crowned his beautiful and multi-blessed life! Eternal shame to the executioners — the murderers of infants.''

A.E.

Based on accounts by Nahum Remba, Halina Pinchonson and Anthony Shimansky, and from the book *Mister Doctor: The Life of Janusz Korczak*, by Hanna Olczak-Mortkowicz, London: Peter Davies, 1967.

Concentration and Death

In an article published in the April 22, 1953 issues of Der Spiegel, *the German weekly newsmagazine, it was reported that Adolph Eichmann, standing before the International Military Tribunal, said that six million Jews were murdered by the Nazis. Four million of these perished, he said, in death camps. Later, the International Military Tribunal made its own careful, independent study, lasting almost a year. It confirmed the figure of six million. This figure comprised roughly seventy percent of the European Jewish population before World War II. Of this number, 1,200,000 were children. The age limit the Nazis set for immediate extermination was fourteen years.*

The trip by train to the death camps usually lasted several days. Many died en route. When these death trains arrived at their destinations, the decision as to who would live and who would die took place immediately, right on the station platform. A wave of the wand in the hand of the commanding SS officer determined life or death. Women with children under fourteen years of age, old people, and cripples were instructed to go left. They were destined to die immediately in gas ovens set up nearby. All others were waved to the right.

In 1943–44, fifty camps were in existence, and many more sprang up later. The most famous were located near large cities, including Dachau, Buchenwald, Treblinka, and Auschwitz, near Cracow. Auschwitz had four gas chambers in which six thousand victims were exterminated daily. From a small opening the Nazis dropped into these death chambers Zyklon B gas in the form of crystallized prussic acid. It took three to fifteen minutes to kill the inmates. The bodies were then removed and cremated.

RECEPTION AT AUSCHWITZ

In the summer of 1939, when the German invasion began, Kitty Hart had just completed her first year of grammar school in her home town which was located a few miles from the German border. She came from a middle-class Jewish assimilationist family. Athletically inclined, she was the youngest member of the Polish national swimming team and entertained ambitions to compete in the Olympics.

In September 1939, Poland was overrun and divided between Germany and Russia. We shall skip the account of the experiences of Kitty Hart and her family during the twenty-two months of the German-Russian alliance. Their torment began when Germany's armies suddenly swept over the territory of its erstwhile Russian "ally" on June 22, 1941. Then began an endless nightmare for Kitty and her family. Kitty and her mother were separated from her father and brother, whom they never saw again. She and her mother managed to stay together during their five-year ordeal. . . .

I was dozing, when the train suddenly halted. The doors of our cell swung open and we were driven out.

"*Austeigen, alles austeigen, schneller, los.*" ("All out, faster, quick!")

It was pitch dark, the middle of the night. We were ordered to stand in fives and be counted. I suddenly realized that there were hundreds of people. I could hear the sound of whips, a lot of shouting, and the barking of dogs. At last we were marched off. The ground felt muddy, and my feet stuck deep in the mire. Not far ahead were bright lights — a floodlit fence, and every few yards a guard was perched inside a small shelter up high on a pole. Then I saw an iron gate and written on it in large letters: ARBEIT MACHT FREI¿ (Work brings freedom). This was Auschwitz I. But we passed by and carried on for some distance, walking along the railways tracks. On either side were fences, and beyond — the unknown. At last we, the women only, passed through a gate. This was Auschwitz II — officially known as Birkenau, Lager BIIa.

It was still rather dark, but we could make out in the distance queer-looking figures streaming out of kind of huts. One could hear whistles and shouts of "Aufstehen" ("Get up"), "Alles aufstehen zum Zahlappell" ("All stand for the count"). I wondered if I was hearing right. Was this really getting-up time? It must have been about three or four o'clock in the morning!

We were led to a building known as the Sauna, apparently a Finnish word which meant "baths." Inside were showers and large drums where clothes were being deloused. I looked around. No German uniforms could be seen. Walking back and forth were some sort of creatures. Were they men or women? It was hard to tell. They had very short hair, some wore trousers, others kind of dresses. All had heavily painted red crosses on their backs. They did not talk but screamed, and their voices were hoarse and deep, obviously from continuous shouting. Each had a whip in her hand. I decided to have a closer look, and noticed on the left breast a number and a green triangle. As we were later to discover, a green triangle identified German prisoners, the criminal category. It was obvious what type of person ruled the camp and who held key positions there.

Someone dared ask, "When do we get something to eat?" for we had had nothing since leaving Dresden.

"Ha, so you are hungry already du verfluchtes Arschloch?" came the barking reply. "And what are you looking through the window for? Curious? Watching the Muselmanns? You will soon become a Muselmann yourself, don't you worry."

Muselmann? What on earth does that mean? I could not make it out. This place seemed to have its own vocabulary, a complete language of its own. But I realized that we would get acquainted with it before long. Soon we would know everything.

A Muselmann was a living skeleton, and those figures in the distance looked just like skeletons. They walked slowly, dragging their feet, some even crawled along.

Someone plucked up courage and asked, "Does one die here right away?"

"Du blöde Kuh," came the reply. "Look at me. I have been four years in here, do I look dead? Do you think you will be served with ham and eggs and have a nice warm bed waiting for you? You only die of a 'cold.' " She swung her whip over our heads, spat out, and then turned away, laughing to herself.

We were stripped and under showers for some time, and still there were no clothes. Next came the disinfection — a dip in a foul-smelling, bluish-green fluid. This over, the Fryzerki, the hairdressers, go to work. These were prisoners whose occupation was to shave our heads, under armpits, and between our legs. The command was, "Arms and legs out." It only took a few seconds. I touched my head. It felt queer and cold.

I was thrown a heap of rags — some clothing at last. There was a vest, a pair of khaki breeches, and a blouse which had been part of a Russian prisoner-of-war uniform. The breeches were sizes too wide and too long, and the blouse had two odd sleeves. I had two odd stockings and a pair of wooden clogs, again sizes too big. I turned to look for Mother. I could not see her anywhere, in fact, I could not recognize anyone at all. In these clothes and with our heads shaved, we all looked alike. When I finally did see her I just burst out laughing. Goodness, was that what I looked like too? We all looked like clowns out of a circus.

"*Anstellen, anstellen schneller, verfluchte Bande,*" cried a hoarse voice. It was time for the next procedure. At last it was my turn in the long line. It seemed at first as though our particulars were being taken, for I thought I could see pens and ink. The girls sitting at their desks looked respectable, and their hair seemed longer than any of the others' we had seen so far. They were known as the *Schreibstube* — in camp language a sort of office worker, the camp elite. Theirs was an office job all right, but of an unusual sort. They were taking particulars of newcomers known as *Zugänge* and at the same time tattooing numbers on their arms. Mother was first, 39933, then I, 39934, below a triangle on my left forearm. There was a sharp pain each time the needle dug into the skin. I had never seen a tattoo before, and it did not really worry me. I thought I could just wash it off when they had finished. I had not the faintest idea that it was a permanent mark.

The procedure took quite a few minutes, and as the girl tattooed Mother's arm she began to talk to her. Had we come straight from home? Home? We had forgotten what that meant a long time ago. She was amazed that Mother was allowed into the camp at all, for she informed us that all older people and small children were being segregated and taken over there — pointing through the window.

"And what is over there?" I asked.

"You will find that out soon enough," she answered.

We learned that this girl's home town, too, was not far away.

"Anyway, I will see what I can do for your mother," she promised. "You will not find anyone with a mother in here."

What luck, I thought. Someone had actually promised to help. I knew her name was Thea, but where and how was I to get hold of her again?

It was broad daylight, and I thought I could hear music. Music in this place? Was I dreaming or had I gone mad already? No, it was a fact, a band was playing. I could clearly hear the beating of a drum, very loud. Curious, everyone looked out to see columns of women marching in time to the beat of the drum, and occasionally one could hear, "*Links* [left] 2,3,4, *links* 2,3,4." These were the women going out to work.

We were told we were going to Lager A, to be quarantined, and that we belonged to Block 20 — the blocks were the huts, our sleeping quarters. On walking out of the sauna, we had the full view of this particular camp. Along the center of Lager A (Camp A) was a road known as the Lagerstrasse. On either side of the road were the blocks. These were long stone-built huts, each with two tiny windows. To get to them one had to wade ankle deep through mud which clung to our wooden clogs.

We were met at the door by a vicious-looking woman. She, too, looked well fed and well dressed. Her voice was very gruff, and it was obvious that she was the boss of the hut, known as the *Blockälteste* or *Blokowa*. Each block had its own block senior, as well as her assistants, the *Stubenältesten* or *Stubowe*. These were mostly Slovakian girls, who were brought here when the camp was first opened, and they had literally built it up with their own hands. There were many thousands of them to start with, and only very few had survived. These survivors held the best posts in the camp. They were directly responsible to the German authorities. In fact the whole place was almost entirely run by the *Häftlinge,* the prisoners themselves, and I think it was entirely self-supporting.

In charge of the camp was the *Lagerälteste,* a female German political prisoner, who had spent eight years in various camps. Although she was known to be decent, she was greatly feared and whenever she appeared, everyone hid. She, too, had her assistants, known as the *Lagerkapos,* and usually people to be avoided, for most of them carried whips and lashed out freely, even when no German uniforms were in sight.

The *Blockälteste* turned to us and, holding her hands on her hips, screamed out: "So you are my *Zugänge.*[1] Off to the *Weise* with you lot." This was our first greeting.

A *Weise?* I was puzzled. Was there a lawn? For this is what the word meant. No, it was just a muddy patch of ground at the back of our block. We were told that this was where we had to spend our day, for the block could be entered only at night.

It was now midmorning, and still there had been no food, and so it was at least twenty-four hours since we had had anything to eat or drink. It seemed we had missed our breakfast on this, our first morning. It was raining heavily, and soon we were completely drenched. Nevertheless, everyone settled down in the mud.

I looked round. There were *Häftlinge*[2] behind the other blocks, too, and soon some came over to talk to us. Someone spoke to me.

"You new? Want to buy a scarf?"

The girl standing in front of me was French, and she held out a rag to me. I could just have done with it to cover my bald head.

"What do you want for it?" I asked.

"It will cost you two portions of bread or one of sausage."

I told her that we had no rations as yet and asked her how she managed to get the scarf.

"I organized it, of course," came the reply.

I was later to know that "organize" was *the* most important word in the Auschwitz language. It meant: to steal, buy, exchange, get hold of. My very first lesson was that anything here could be used as currency. Even water. I

---

[1]Newcomers.
[2]Prisoners.

learned fast. Apparently you could get hold of practically anything, if you were prepared to risk your neck. I had made up my mind to save up some food rations, to buy clothes, if only to get out of khaki uniform. I had to get shoes for both my mother and myself, for it was quite impossible to walk in those clogs. We needed jumpers, and something to cover our heads.

It was nearly midday, and from this distance we could see big drums being carried out from the kitchens. I had seen these before in the prisons and knew that soup was coming. From nearby blocks girls rushed up. Some soup had been spilled, and the girls lay on the ground, licking it off the mud. Others were raiding the dustbins in the hope of finding potato peel.

At last our soup arrived, and everyone was issued a red enamel dish with one ladle of soup in it. It was horrible tasteless stuff. It had a few bits of potato peel and some turnips floating on top. I tried it, and felt sick, but I was much too hungry to leave it. We had no spoons, but these could be "organized" like everything else. That was our dinner.

I soon found out how very precious our dishes were. No dishes — no food. Therefore these had to be carried about everywhere, tucked well inside the piece of string that was one's belt. Neither did it take long to find out that the dishes had to serve a threefold purpose. One had to eat and drink from them, wash in them, and use them when necessary during the night, for when we first arrived there were no lavatories. There was only a hut with a row of some fifty holes, and it was almost impossible to approach it, for it was mainly for the use of the privileged class of prisoners. We were supposed to use the buckets, but it was again impossible to get near those.

Water was another problem. For although there was the sauna, again only the privileged could get inside. Ordinary prisoners were forbidden access to it and were beaten up on entering and thrown out. I could see that the most important thing of all was to have decent clothes. To be dressed well meant one was somebody, not just an ordinary *Häftling*. The next essential was one's weight. It was most unfashionable to be thin, and *Muselmanns* of course were despised.

It was afternoon, and more girls came to talk to us. They were of all nationalities, but we had no language difficulties, for one soon got acquainted with the camp slang, which was common to all. Suddenly there was a warning shout and I jumped to my feet. "Run!" someone whispered to me, and I crawled to hide behind the wall of the block. Peeping out, I could see a woman approaching, she had a black triangle over the number of her dress. She was a German prisoner, her whip lashing as she hunted workers. At last she went, having caught about ten girls.

Next I heard a whistle.

"Zählappell. Alles anstellen," resounded over the camp.

This was the evening roll call. We stood for over two hours before we saw a green uniform in the distance, approaching on a bicycle along the Lagerstrasse. This was one of the *Aufseherinen,* an SS woman. Our *Blockälteste* screamed out, *"Achtung,"* and we all stood to attention. The SS woman passed slowly along the front rank, counting each row of five with her stick; this finished, she made her way to the main gate. There, at a specially erected desk, stood *Rapportführer* Taube, the SS man dreaded throughout the camps. It was his day on duty and he checked the numbers that were brought to him by the *Aufseherin*. Very often numbers did not tally and there had to be a recount. The old prisoners informed us that this two-hour roll call was a very short one indeed, for it generally took three to four hours. The *Blockälteste* relaxed and breathed again. She was responsible for producing the correct number of *Häftlinge*, and this was no easy task, for although there was no escape from here, prisoners were often found standing outside the wrong blocks.

We hoped that perhaps now, with the *Zahlappell* over, we should be allowed inside our block. Everyone was curious to see what it would be like. There was a rush to get in, and at the door rations were handed out. We were given fifteen dekagrams (under four ounces) of bread and a small piece of margarine. This, we were informed was our supper, and our breakfast as well. Twice a week a *Zulage* (addition) of a small piece of cheese or sausage was given. I wondered whether one could really exist on this meager and monotonous diet. And how on earth could anyone possibly save as much as a crumb from these rations to buy clothes?

At last we were inside. On either side of the two gangways was a continuous line of three-tier bunks known as *koje*. Each had to hold about fifteen persons when the block was full to capacity. There were eight hundred of us in our block, and it was full when it held one thousand. (This was not the case in the privileged blocks.) At the side of the entrance was a little room, which belnged to the *Blockälteste* and her assistants.

We hurried to find a place to sleep. It was obvious that the best places were at the top, but these were of course already occupied. At the bottom it was hot and stuffy. Somehow and somewhere one had to squeeze in, and finally we succeeded. We were just like sardines in a tin, head to tail. I was on the outside and neither the one and only blanket nor the straw mattress reached to where I lay. And of course there were no pillows. I was warned not to take my clogs off, if I wanted to see them again, and to hide my rations inside my clothes. I was wet through, but nothing could be taken off. It was too risky, and much too cold anyway. My immediate neighbor was a gypsy who had been here just two weeks. I think I shall always remember her voice. She looked closely at me and said, ''I can see great strength in your eyes, child. Let me have your palm, and I will see what it says. Yes,'' she continued, ''I can see quite clearly you *will* come out of here. How, I don't know, but you will be one of the very few to see freedom again. Remember, you must never lose your will to live. Fight for your life, or you will be finished very quickly.''

My first day in Auschwitz was over.

From *I Am Alive (Auschwitz and Birkenau)*, by Kitty Hart, New York: Abelard-Schuman, 1961, pp. 49-59.

CHILD HELL IN AUSCHWITZ

In June 1944, 129 Jewish children between the ages of eight and fourteen were brought from Kovno to Oswiecim (Auschwitz), and taken straight to the gas chamber in open trucks. The children knew where they were going. Before they entered the death trucks, a boy of twelve made a short speech to the rest of the children. He urged them to be brave and endure their sufferings to the last moment. "We shall soon be united with our murdered parents," he said, and then, turning to the SS, he went on, "And we have one more consolation. We know that you, our murderers, will meet your just fate."

The children were not always liquidated by gas. Dr. Jacob Wollman of Lodz declares that the SS clubbed about five hundred children to death with their rifle butts.

At the peak of the murder campaign in Auschwitz, during the summer of 1944, large numbers of children were thrown alive on the fire. Sometimes a more merciful SS man shot the child dead to save it from the gas chamber or the fire.

This Was Oswiecim, The Story of a Murder Camp by Philip Friedman, transl. from the Yiddish by Joseph Leftwich, London: United Jewish Appeal, 1946.

THE GAS CHAMBER

From a Memorandum by Mr. Lieberman, September 27, 1945.

Arriving at our station, which was three kilometers away from the camp itself, and situated in a wood, we were thrown out of the wagons with an unheard of brutality. We were then in a state of exhaustion caused by this particularly painful journey and due to the fact that we had with us old people, sick people, women and children of all ages, down to the age of four and five months. I have personally seen children lying all along the embankment who had been kicked onto the slope by SS, whilst other SS men prevented the mothers taking care of the children. During two and a half months I was employed in this station unloading potatoes, and I had ample opportunity of witnessing similar scenes over and over again; often several times a day the children abandoned on the platform were subsequently collected by prisoners and SS men and taken to the gas chambers, which were fifty meters away from the station. The gas chambers were camouflaged as shower baths. On the right-hand side there was an entrance for men and on the left-hand side an entrance for women, but, once undressed, men, women, and children assembled again inside the gas chamber. When a transport arrived, a percentage of three to fifteen of the able-bodied men and women were separated and sent to the labor camps of Birkenau and Auschwitz. The remainder were taken to the gas chambers. Up to 1944 no child was retained for work at the camp. From 1944 onwards a small percentage of male children between the ages of eleven and thirteen escaped the gas chamber.

As already mentioned, I was one of a working party whose duty it was to unload potatoes at the station. We had at this time no contact with the prisoners of the big camp. We were separated in quarantine but housed together with another working party, which was serving the crematorium and the gas chamber. It is due to this fact that I know how things occurred.

The men and women entered the so-called bathroom and undressed separately to avoid panic. Once they were undressed they entered by separate doors in the central chamber. This chamber could take 3,000 people. The gas was released through sprays of the showers and from bombs which were thrown through apertures designed to allow for that procedure. Death occurred within five minutes. On certain days, when enormous transports arrived at the station of Birkenau, 42,000 people were gassed. Once the gassing process had been completed, the floor of the chamber opened automatically and the corpses fell into the subterranean chamber, where prisoners in charge of extracting the teeth or cutting hair of a certain length, took over. On several occasions I have myself seen in the evening, after a good day's work, the gold teeth or the hair which came from the corpses and which had been kept by the prisoners who lived with us in quarantine. Once the gold teeth had been recovered, the corpses were loaded on to a moving belt and transported to cremation ovens, through subterranean gangways. There were four ovens, a big one and three small ones, which were capable of burning 400 corpses in five minutes. Later on, when the number of corpses exceeded the capacity of the ovens, trenches were dug and the corpses thrown in saturated with petrol. I have personally seen these trenches and smelled the stench of the combustion. I have equally been able to visit the gas chamber and the crematorium, when I was detailed to clean up on a day when they were not in use.

It so happened that one of the prisoners who worked at the station recognized a member of his family amongst new arrivals. He threw himself on his father and told him that he was going to die. Both were immediately beaten to death by the SS.

On another occasion, a very beautiful woman who was perfectly well aware of what was going to happen to her succeeded, in the billet of the block leader where she had been conducted under the pretext of having to wait, in taking his revolver and killing him and herself. After this four hundred women were selected in the camp of Birkenau and executed as a reprisal. I have personally seen these women before they entered the gas chamber.

I have no photographs of the gas chamber or crematorium of Birkenau in my possession.

Due to my employment of unloading at the station, I knew of the gas, called Cyclon. This gas was kept in little bombs, which were themselves kept in metal cylinders. They were marked "Cyclon Gas I.G.V. from Hamburg to Auschwitz."

When corpses were burnt, they were put on a platform, five adults being placed longways, whereas corpses of children were put aside, as one could place double their number on the platform. This explains the SS use of the word *Abrechnung*, which means "accounting."

I have never seen the trolleys for the transport of corpses personally, nor have I seen the ovens operating; but as I have already mentioned, several of the working party, which was serving the gas chambers and ovens, lived with us and have given me all the details. This special working party was called *Sonderkommando* [special commando]. A certain Jacob Weinschein of Paris, who is a survivor of this commando, is personally known to me. He escaped death because he was in hospital when his companions were gassed. In point of fact, members of this commando were themselves put to death in the gas chambers after two or three months of employment. I know this fact, which was witnessed by the new commando which replaced them and whose first task it was to gas their predecessors. They were selected from the new arrivals, who were completely ignorant of the procedure in operation. They told us that they had to transport the corpses of their gassed comrades, who had been tattooed on the first day of work.

As soon as the Red Army approached in August 1944, the ashes from the cremation ovens were exhumed by the prisoners, by order of the SS. I have held a handful of these ashes myself. I have seen them carried to the edge of a river which crossed the camp. The work was not carried out by the *Sonderkommando* but by several hundreds of prisoners of the camp itself.

From *Nazi Conspiracy and Aggression,* Vol. VI, Office of United States Chief Counsel for Prosecution of Axis Criminality, U.S. Government Printing Office, 1946; Vol. XI pp. 1100-1103 (Document D 251).

A DEED OF SAVAGERY: SS DRIVES BOYS INTO THE GAS CHAMBERS

In 1962, in the area of the Birkenau crematorium no. 3, were found the writings of three martyrs, Leib Langfuss, Zalman Leventhal, and Zalman Gradovski. Up to the time of the publication of the diaries, eight manuscripts had been found, which noted that numbers of documents had been buried in the ground by prisoners. It is quite likely that they had been destroyed by the local ghoulish "fortune-hunters," who had dug in the expectation of finding treasures buried by the Jews who had been cremated.

The above-mentioned writers were members of the Sonderkommando *(special command) whose job it was to cremate the dead. Like many martyrs, they left records of their experiences so that the world would remember the catastrophe.*

Langfuss's manuscript was found in a glass jar. In it he explained why the revolt of the Sonderkommando *had failed.* [1]

It was winter, the end of 1944. A contingent of children were brought in. They were from Shavel, Lithuania, where German patrol cars had picked them up from their homes. In broad daylight six hundred Jewish boys, aged twelve to eighteen, were brought in wearing flimsy striped pajamas all in tatters and wearing down-at-heel shoes or wooden clogs. The children looked so handsome, so radiant, so well-built that they shone through their rags. It was the end of October 1944. They arrived in twenty-five trucks guarded by heavily armed SS men. They got out in the yard of the crematorium area. The *Kommando* leader gave an order: "Take your clothes off in the yard!" The children saw the

[1] For the inside story of the revolt, read *Witness to the Holocaust,* New York: Pilgrim Press, 1981, pp. 393-443.

smoke from the chimney and instantly realized that they were being led to their death. Crazed with fright, they started running around the yard, back and forth, clutching their heads. Many of them broke into frightful crying. Their wailing was terrible to hear. The *Kommando* leader and his aide hit out ferociously at the children. He whacked so hard that his wooden club broke in his hand. He got himself another club and flailed at the children's heads. Brute strength prevailed. The children, panic-stricken though they were, with death staring them in the face, undressed. Stark naked, they pressed against each other to shield themselves from the cold, but they would not go downstairs [into the gas chamber]. A bold little boy went up and begged the *Kommando* leader to spare him. He would do any kind of work, no matter how hard. The answer was a tremendous whack on the head with the club. Many of the boys darted off frantically to the Jews of the *Sonderkommando,* threw their arms around their necks, imploring: "Save me!" Others raced about the yard, naked, running from death. The *Kommando* leader called in the SS *Unterscharführer* with his rubber baton to help.

The boys' high-pitched voices grew louder and louder in a bitter lament. Their keening carried a great distance. One was completely deafened and overcome by this desperate weeping. With satisfied smirks, without a trace of compassion, the SS men triumphantly hailed savage blows on the children and drove them into the gas chamber. On the stairs stood the *Unterscharführer,* still wielding his club and giving a murderous crack at each child. A few lone children were, all the same, still running back and forth in search of a way out. The SS men chased after them, lashing out at them and forcing them at last into the chamber. The glee of the SS men was indescribable. Did they never have children of their own?

From *Aleph-Tav: Tel Aviv University Review,* Spring 1975.

DR. MENGELE'S INHUMAN EXPERIMENTS

Dr. Miklos Nyiszli was transported to Auschwitz with his fellow Hungarian Jews in 1944. Separated from his wife and daughter, he was assigned to assist the vicious Dr. Mengele in his unspeakable experiments, some of which are described below. His duties were to work closely with the Sonderkommando *which cremated the corpses. He was appointed chief physician of the crematoria. He lived through horrors beyond all imagining and credibility.*

In presenting the unbelievable record of his firsthand experiences, in the book Auschwitz, *in March 1946, he signed a sworn document which prefaces the book. It contains a bona fide detailed account of the most hellish crimes of Nazidom.*

When the convoys arrived, soldiers scouted the ranks lined up before the boxcars, hunting for twins and dwarfs. Mothers, hoping for special treatment for their twin children, readily gave them up to the scouts. Adult twins, knowing that they were of interest from a scientific point of view, voluntarily presented themselves, in the hope of better treatment. The same for dwarfs.

They were separated from the rest and herded to the right. They were allowed to keep their civilian clothes; guards accompanied them to specially designed barracks, where they were treated with certain regard. Their food was good, their bunks were comfortable, and possibilities for hygiene were provided.

They were housed in Barracks 14 of Camp F. From there they were taken by their guards to the experimentation barracks of the Gypsy Camp, and exposed to every medical examination that can be performed on human beings: blood tests, lumbar punctures, exchanges of blood between twin brothers, as well as numerous other examinations, all fatiguing and depressing. Dina, the painter from Prague, made the comparative studies of the structures of the twins' skulls, ears, noses, mouths, hands, and feet. Each drawing was classified in a file set up for that express purpose, complete with all individual characteristics; into this file would also go the final results of this research. The procedure was the same for the dwarfs.

The experiments, in medical language called *in vivo, i.e.,* experiments performed on live human beings, far from exhausted the research possibilities in the study of twins. Full of lacunae, they offered no better than partial results. The *in vivo* experiments were succeeded by the most important phase of twin-study: the comparative examination from the viewpoints of anatomy and pathology. Here it was a question of comparing the twins' healthy organs with those functioning abnormally, or of comparing their illnesses. For that study, as for all studies of a pathological nature, corpses were needed. Since it was necessary to perform a dissection for the simultaneous evaluation of anomalies, the twins had to die at the same time. So it was that they met their death in the B section of one of Auschwitz's KZ barracks, at the hand of Dr. Mengele.

This phenomenon was unique in world medical science history. Twin brothers died together, and it was possible to perform autopsies on both. Where, under normal circumstances, can one find twin brothers who die at the same place and at the same time? For twins, like everyone else, are separated by life's varying circumstances. They live far from each other and almost never die simultaneously. One may die at the age of ten, the other at fifty. Under such conditions comparative dissection is impossible. In the Auschwitz camp, however, there were several hundred sets of twins, and therefore as many possibilities of dissection. That was why, on the arrival platform, Dr. Mengele separated twins and dwarfs from the other prisoners. That was why both special groups were directed to the right-hand column, and thence to the barracks of the spared. That was why they had good food and hygienic living conditions, so that they didn't contaminate each other and die one before the other. They had to die together, and in good health.

The *Sonderkommando* chief came hunting for me and announced that an SS soldier was waiting for me at the door of the crematorium with a crew of corpse-transporting *Kommandos*. I went in search of them, for they were forbidden to enter the courtyard. I took the documents concerning the corpses from the hands of the SS. They contained files on two little twin brothers. The *Kommando* crew, made up entirely of women, set the covered coffin down in front of me. I lifted the lid. Inside lay a set of two-year-old twins. I ordered two of my men to take the corpses and place them on the dissecting table.

I opened the file and glanced through it. Very detailed clinical examinations, accompanied by X-rays, descriptions, and artists' drawings, indicating from the scientific viewpoint the different aspects of these two little beings' "twin-hood." Only the pathological report was missing. It was my job to supply it. The twins had died at the same time and were now lying beside each other on the big dissecting table. It was they who had to — or whose tiny bodies had to — resolve the secret of the reproduction of the race. To advance one step in the search to unlock the secret of multiplying the race of superior beings destined to rule was a "noble goal." If only it were possible, in the future, to have each German mother bear as many twins as possible! The project, conceived by the demented theorists of the Third Reich, was utterly mad. And it was to Dr. Mengele, chief physician of the Auschwitz KZ, the notorious "criminal doctor," that these experiments had been entrusted.

Among malefactors and criminals, the most dangerous type is the "criminal doctor," especially when he is armed with powers such as those granted to Dr. Mengele. He sent millions of people to death merely because, according to a racial theory, they were inferior beings and therefore detrimental to mankind. This same criminal doctor spent long hours beside me, either at his microscopes, his disinfecting ovens and his test tubes or standing with equal patience near the dissecting table, his smock befouled with blood, his bloody hands examining and experimenting like one possessed. The immediate objective was the increased reproduction of pure Germans in numbers sufficient to replace the Czechs, Hungarians, Poles, all of whom were condemned to be destroyed, but who for the moment were living on those territories declared vital to the Third Reich.

I finished the dissection of the little twins and wrote out a regulation report of the dissection. I did my job well, and my chief appeared to be satisfied with me. But he had some trouble reading my handwriting, for all my letters were capitals, a habit I had picked up in America.[1] And so I told him that if he wanted clear clean copy, he would have to supply me with a typewriter, since I was accustomed to work with one in my own practice.

"What make typewriter are you used to?" he asked.

"Olympian Elite," I said.

"Very well, I'll send you one. You'll have it tomorrow. I want clean copy, because these reports will be forwarded to the Institute of Biological, Racial and Evolutionary Research at Berlin-Dahlem."

Thus I learned that the experiments performed here were checked by the highest medical authorities at one of the most famous scientific institutes in the world.

The following day an SS soldier brought me an "Olympia" typewriter. Still more corpses of twins were sent to me. They delivered me four pairs from the Gypsy Camp; all four were under ten years old.

---

[1]Dr. Nyiszli came to the United States in the summer of 1939, and remained until February of 1940, as a member of the Rumanian delegation to the World's Fair. He had intended to bring his family over and settle in America. But during his stay war broke out and he returned to his family. Once back, it was impossible for him to leave the country again. As a result, Auschwitz. — *Tr*.

I began the dissection of one set of twins and recorded each phase of my work. I removed the brain pan. Together with the cerebellum I extracted the brain and examined them. Then followed the opening of the thorax and the removal of the sternum. Next I separated the tongue by means of an incision made beneath the chin. With the tongue came the esophagus, with the respiratory tracts came both lungs. I washed the organs in order to examine them more thoroughly. The tiniest spot or the slightest difference in color could furnish valuable information. I made a transverse incision across the pericardium and removed the fluid. Next I took out the heart and washed it. I turned it over and over in my hand to examine it.

In the exterior coat of the left ventricle was a small pale red spot caused by a hypodermic injection, which scarcely differed from the color of the tissue around it. There could be no mistake. The injection had been given with a very small needle. Without a doubt a hypodermic needle. For what purpose had he received the injection? Injections into the heart can be administered in extremely serious cases, when the heart begins to fail. I would soon know. I opened the heart, starting with the ventricle. Normally the blood contained in the left ventricle is taken out and weighed. This method could not be employed in the present case, because the blood was coagulated into a compact mass. I extracted the coagulum with the forceps and brought it to my nose. I was struck by the characteristc odor of chloroform. The victim had received an injection of chloroform in the heart, so that the blood of the ventricle, in coagulating, would deposit on the valves and cause instantaneous death by heart failure.

My discovery of the most monstrous secret of the Third Reich's medical science made my knees tremble. Not only did they kill with gas, but also with injections of chloroform into the heart. A cold sweat broke out on my forehead. Luckily I was alone. If others had been present it would have been difficult for me to conceal my excitement. I finished the dissection, noted the differences found, and recorded them. But the chloroform, the blood coagulated in the left ventricle, the puncture visible in the external coat of the heart, did not figure among my findings. It was a useful precaution on my part. Dr. Mengele's records on the subject of twins were in my hands. They contained the exact examinations, X-rays, the artist's sketches already mentioned, but neither the circumstances nor causes of death. Nor did I fill out that column of the dissection report. It was not a good idea to exceed the authorized bounds of knowledge or to relate all one had witnessed. And here still less than anywhere else. I was not timorous by nature and my nerves were good. During my medical practice I had often brought to light the causes of death. I had seen the bodies of people assassinated for motives of revenge, jealousy, or material gain, as well those of suicides and natural deaths. I was used to the study of well-hidden causes of death. On several occasions I had been shocked by my discoveries, but now a shudder of fear ran through me. If Dr. Mengele had any idea that I had discovered the secret of his injections he would send ten doctors, in the name of the political SS, to attest to my death.

In accordance with orders received, I returned the corpses to the prisoners whose duty it was to burn them. They performed their job without delay. I had to keep any organs of possible scientific interest, so that Dr. Mengele could examine them. Those which might interest the Anthropological Institute at Berlin-Dahlem were preserved in alcohol. These parts were specially packed to be sent through the mails. Stamped "War Material — Urgent," they were given top priority in transit. In the course of my work at the crematorium I dispatched an impressive number of such packages. I received, in reply, either precise scientific observations or instructions. In order to classify this correspondence I had to set up special files. The directors of the Berlin-Dahlem Institute always warmly thanked Dr. Mengele for this rare and precious material.

I finished dissecting the three other pairs of twins and duly recorded the anomalies found. In all three instances the cause of death was the same: an injection of chloroform into the heart.

Of the four sets of twins, three had ocular globes of different colors. One eye was brown, the other blue. This is a phenomenon found fairly frequently in non-twins. But in the present case I noticed that it had occurred in six out of the eight twins. An extremely interesting collection of anomalies. Medical science calls them heterochromes, which means, merely, different colored. I cut out the eyes and put them in a solution of formaldehyde, noting their characteristics exactly, in order not to mix them up. During my examination of the four sets of twins, I discovered still another curious phenomenon: while removing the skin from the neck I noticed just above the upper extremity of the sternum, a tumor about the size of a small nut. Pressing on it with my forceps I found it to be filled with a thick pus. This rare manifestation, well known to medical science, indicates the presence of hereditary syphilis and is called DuBois' tumor. Looking farther, I found that it existed in all eight twins. I cut out the tumor, leaving it surrounded by healthy tissue, and placed it in another jar of formaldehyde. In two sets of twins I also discovered evidence of active, cavernous tuberculosis. I recorded my findings on the dissection report, but left the heading "Cause of Death" blank.

During the afternoon Dr. Mengele paid me a visit. I gave him a detailed account of my morning's work and handed him my report. He sat down and began to read each case carefully. He was greatly interested by the heterochromatic condition of the eyes, but even more so by the discovery of DuBois' tumor. He gave me instructions to have the organs mailed and told me to include my report in the package. He also instructed me to fill out the "Cause of Death" column hitherto left blank. The choice of causes was left to my own judgment and discretion; the only stipulation was that each cause be different. Almost apologetically he remarked that, as I could see for myself, these children were syphilitic and tubercular, and consequently would not have lived in any case. . . . He said no more about it. With that he had said enough. He had explained the reason for these children's death. I had refrained from making any comment. But I had learned that here tuberculosis and syphilis were not treated with medicines and drugs, but with chloroform injections.

I shuddered to think of all I had learned during my short stay here, and of all I should yet have to witness without protesting, until my own appointed hour arrived. The minute I entered this place I had the feeling I was already one of the living dead. But now, in possession of all these fantastic secrets, I was certain I would never get out alive. Was it conceivable that Dr. Mengele, or the Berlin-Dahlem Institute, would ever allow me to leave this place alive?

From *Auschwitz, a Doctor's Eyewitness Account* by Dr. Miklos Nyiszli, New York: Fawcett Publication, © 1960, pp. 50-56. Trans, by Tibere Kremer and Richard Beaver.

AN INCOMPARABLE ATROCITY: STORY OF A PIEPEL

In Maidanek there were a number of boys twelve to fifteen years of age, most of them Jews, who were selected for survival. They were the "runners" — the messengers and errand boys of the SS command. As they ran through the camp, they would call out orders such as "Prisoner 18765 report immediately to gate #1" or "the *kapo* of block #7 to report at once to the commandant." They would notify the supervisors when to distribute the bread rations or at what hour to awaken the prisoners for work. They also served as the shoeshine boys of the officers and important personalities. They were a privileged group because they served as male lovers of their masters, who had been forced to abstain from heterosexual intercourse for many years. It is easy to imagine to what uses their masters subjected these boys, who were called *piepels*.[1] This is a repugnant subject to write about. It filled us all with feeling of deep pain and shame. But it was a reality of camp life not restricted to Maidanek.

These boys exercised great power in camp, and all of us feared them. Many of them sought to imitate their elders. Some would beat prisoners without reason and pity.

The camp command appointed their *piepels* to take charge of the slave labor gangs. On one occasion when I, together with other prisoners, pulled a heavy load of stones, our overseer was a boy of thirteen. In his hand he held a large club, and he beat us no less cruelly than the guards did. He flayed our flesh severely and derived inhuman pleasure from seeing his elders tremble at the swing of his club. Every now and then he singled out a prisoner and subjected him to merciless flogging. When Germans happened to pass by during one of these atrocious scenes, they would encourage him to do his best. He would listen to their incitements like a puppy dog, and doubled his efforts to please them. To the camp inmates, the *piepels'* cold-blooded lust to please their superiors by inflicting pain was insufferable.

The commandant of area three had a *piepel* who was about twelve years old. He was dark and tall, dressed in black velvet pants. He came to the camp with his parents. When the doomed were driven to the gas chamber, one of the SS officers motioned to the boy to come over. The officer patted his head and said, "Do you want to become a *kapo?* You'll be dressed nicely, you will be treated to chocolate bars, and you will go around giving orders like one of us."

At first the boy was confused. But his parents, who thought that he had found favor in the eyes of the officer, motioned to him that he should agree to the

[1]The origin of the word is unknown.

invitation. The parents were taken out of the line. The prisoners envied them; they assumed that their lives would be saved because of their son. But what followed boggled the mind.

The boy was taken to area three, where he was appointed an official *kapo*. His father was brought to the same area, and his mother was sent to the women's camp. On the third day she was brought to visit with her son. That evening the camp inmates were ordered to gather around the gallows. The boy's parents were directed to take a position at the trap. The son was ordered to tie the noose around their necks and spring the trap.

Those who were compelled to witness this atrocity had seen many heinous acts in the camp. But later, when they told us of this one, even the tough and hardened among them bit their lips until they bled.

As I write about this incident now, I do not want to amplify on this fiendish episode. I could not forgive myself were I, a writer, to permit my pen to describe what happened. I shall therefore without elaboration, record the testimony given to me by a witness.

"We all stood breathless. No one of us in our wildest imagination could believe the scene which unfolded before our very eyes. We thought this was a macabre joke. The parents stood on the scaffold, their backs to the gallows, an indescribable look on their faces. It seemed as if they, too, imagined that the commandant was playing a hoax. The boy stood frightened, his head bowed. The commandant then said to him, 'You are still young. We want you to have a good time here. Your end will be similar to those of all the others — death. But I want you to live. Therefore from now on you will be my son, a German like all Germans. All those who are gathered round you will have nothing in common with you. Because from now on you are one of us — they are Jews. You are now a *kapo,* and like all *kapos* you will not think twice about hanging two filthy Jews. It is not so? Now show us all that you are not a Jew.'

"The boy's hands trembled as he tied the noose around his parents' necks. The father stood rigid and pale. The mother sobbed quietly. As she exhaled her last breath, she motioned as if she were thrusting away someone, something, with her dying hands. To me it appeared as if she was trying to blot out the memory of the horror."

At Maidanek this boy was the chief degenerate. He would walk about with his wooden club in his hand and break heads capriciously. It seemed as if the halo of patricide and matricide, the murder of his father and mother, accompanied him. He looked older than his age. Often he would break in to examine the barracks. He would be present at the tortures of the inmates, some of which lasted a whole day. I do not know if he felt any remorse, but it was clear to me that subconsciously he was agitated when he witnessed his fellow humans tormented and tortured. He wanted to prove to himself that no evil was too great as long as his end would not be like ours. But I must hasten to admit that I could not fathom his nature and gave up trying to understand him.

However, not all *piepels* were as demonic as he. There were eleven- and twelve-year-old boys who had relatives in the camp. They matured before their age and developed resourcefulness like adults. They sought every means and opportunity to be of help. I came to know a father who found out, after a month at camp, that his son was alive and was serving as "runner," in the adjoining camp area. I remember how one day toward evening the boy slipped into our barrack. The men lay exhausted on the floor. In the dusk of twilight we could not distinguish one shadow from another. Suddenly the "runner" appeared at the door. Some of us jumped up in fright; others looked at him dumbly. The boy peered at each face. Suddenly he leaped toward one of us who lay in a corner sunk in thought. "Father, Father," he called out with great pathos. The father looked at his son and burst into bitter tears like a child. But the boy, his face serious and solicitious tenderly patted his father's shaven head and implored him, "Don't cry, Father. Stop crying." Their roles were changed. The little one took out something from under his jacket — a slice of bread and sausage. The voice of the child was pleading, and comforting. "You are hungry, Father, no?" Shamefacedly the father fondled the bread. His fingers explored the small face near him. From the lips of the child flowed words that had been dammed up within him. "I'll bring you food every day. I will talk to my commander about you. Tell me, do they beat you? Tell me, who beats you?'

At the last moment before the barrack was locked for the night, he slipped out and disappeared. From that day on, he visited his father daily and each time brought something with him. Always he talked to his father as a father would to a helpless little son.

There were also "runners" who hid from others that they had relatives in the camp. Generally speaking, however, relatives of *piepels* were treated a little better than others. . . .

A.E.

From *Nerot Meukolim* ("Burnt Out Lights") by Mordecai Shtrigler, published by *Am Oved*, 1946, pp. 103-110.

CHANGING "PIEPELS"

In the gruesome selection below, K. Zetnick[1] depicts the pitiable aspects of the piepel's *existence to which he was eyewitness. The author, now living in Israel, suffered through the most horrendous experiences in Auschwitz. He is one of the early writers who depicted the Holocaust tragedy.*

The incident below takes place in block 12. The dramatis personae are: *the* piepel *Moni; Zygmunt,* Kapo *of block 12; Rostek, the kitchen butcher; Franzl, the block chief; and Ludwig Tien, the camp senior.*

The book opens with the initiation of Moni as the Piepel *of Block 12.*

The electric lamp hanging from the ceiling was sheathed in pleated red crepe paper, casting both their heads with a dull glow. Franzl sat on a chair in the center of the block cubicle, the boy standing between his knees. Franzl's fingers gripped the boy's upper arms in a vise that forced his little shoulders up to his

---

[1] Concentration camp inmate, a pseudonym.

ears. Franzl's glance glittered at the boy's gaping eyes. "Now that's a present from the camp commandant," his lips murmured. "Even the name's a teaser: Mo-ni."

Rostek, Franzl's private cook, who in this early-morning darkness had stopped in to get some provisions, stood against the closed door through which he had just entered. His shoelaces were untied; sleep was still in them. Rostek stood there, not moving. It was improper for him to show indifference now, when the block chief was so lovingly introducing his new *piepel* to him, although as for himself, he could not scrape up the least bit of emotion towards that skinny creature standing there between Franzl's hands.

The boy was bony, but his terrified black-velvet eyes held out towards Franzl an unknown lure. Franzl's heated glance burrowed into the eyes. He wanted to penetrate the mystery they held for him, to possess it. Without tearing his glance away, Franzl drooled toward Rostek standing nearby.

"Man! Just look at those maidenhead eyes. No block chief in this camp has ever rated a *piepel* like this. That's what I call a present!"

Beside the table, near the half-covered window, stood two backs of block orderlies. No sound came from them; they scarcely moved. Only their hands mutely prepared the bread rations for the camplings, one running a nail across the backs of the oblong dark loaves, the other slicing.

Outside the shout carried: "All block chiefs to the camp senior! Pass the word!" The lookouts before the blocks passed the command along to each other, and the cry flashed past the block like a nonstop express train. Franzl must report to the camp senior immediately. His fingers moved lower and lower down the boy's back. Reaching the lean rump, they reflexively drew back, as though not wanting to feel the disappointment. Franzl abruptly stood up from the chair and thrust his cap on his head. By the door he paused beside Rostek, with his cane lifted Rostek's jowly, long pork-head by the chin, speaking into his face: "See that my *piepel* gets some meat on his bones! I'm not going to bed with any Mussulman.[1] Get me, Rostek? It'll be your ass!"

And he was gone.

Moni, the new *piepel,* stood opposite the empty chair in which Franzl had just been sitting. The cubicle was small, but in the red density of the light its corners tapered off to a dark blur. Rostek went over to the breadcutters' table and, bending his bulk, took from the pile on the ground the bread rations for which he had come. Fixing Moni with his narrow pork-eyes, he slogged past him to the door and without a word went out.

Outside, it was still dark. But the camplings had long since been driven out of the blocks to the backpath. As far as they are concerned, it is "clean-up time." But actually, the loaves are now being cut up for distribution, and it is better that no campling be in the block to witness the cutting of ten or even twelve rations to a loaf instead of the required four, or to see the "stash" where the surplus loaves are cached away.

Beside the bed stood Franzl's black boots with their gleaming tall uppers. In the narrow locker, everything was meticulously arrayed: on the upper shelf,

---

[1]*Mussulmen:* camplings whose bones were all that held them together.

shoe brushes, clothing brushes, shoe polish; on the second shelf, the block chief's underwear, clean, laundered, folded as though freshly ironed. In every corner here one could feel the touch of the former *piepel,* the way a new wife coming into her husband's household feels the hand of her predecessor. Moni took a shoe brush and polish. "A *piepel* must attend to all the block chief's comforts," he had been taught. He closed the locker. On the door, outside, Franzl's striped jacket hung on a hanger, freshly laundered and ironed. On the breast was sewn the green criminal triangle like a medal. Beneath the green triangle, on a strip of white cloth, was stitched his Auschwitz campling number. Just two digits. One of the first numbers in Auschwitz.

The door of the cubicle swung open. Zygmunt, the chief block orderly, stormed in. Noticing Moni, his face broke into an obsequious smile. He went to the table, thrust his head in between the two backs to see how the work was progressing. "Whoresons!" he shouted, flourishing his bludgeon at them. "I want twenty-five loaves left over today. Net. I don't give a shit how you cut the portions. In the latrine they're asking two loaves for a pack of smokes, and Franzl without a butt to his name."

The two shadows were silent. They did not dare breathe a word. How thin can you cut a loaf? Only their arms now worked faster and more nervously. Zygmunt turned away from them. Moni stood there, one hand holding the shoe brush, the other tucked deep inside Franzl's boot. The rim of the tall upper reached almost to his neck. Zygmunt went over to Moni, bending his head close to him. The pockmarks on Zygmunt's face looked as if they had been carefully stippled, one beside the other, by an exacting craftsman. The red light filled them like tiny bowls. Zygmunt spoke to Moni softly, in a tone of fatherly reprimand:

"What do you think you're doing, *piepel?*" he said, pointing at the boot. "That's no job for a *piepel.* Don't you know what Franzl is in this block? He's king! And if Franzl is king, that makes you queen! You, shining boots? For one spoon of soup a thousand camplings won't only shine his boot for you, but they'll lick it with their tongues all day. Being *piepel* is the highest *Funktion* in the block, if you know what I mean. And if a *piepel*'s got a head on his shoulders and not only an ass" — he pointed at his posterior — "he can get anything he wants out of his block chief. Know what I mean, *piepel?* In bed they're all like little lambs."

Zygmunt returned to the breadcutters, and, as though to demonstrate that the job of chief orderly is also nothing to sneeze at, he brought the truncheon heavily down on the shoulder of one of the orderlies. The mute shadow snatched at the shoulder with a throttled groan, but immediately pulled himself together. It isn't proper for an Auschwitz block orderly to let out groans like a common campling. "Whoresons!" Zygmunt thundered at them with his former voice. "I want twenty-five loaves today!" His hand on the doorknob, he turned another fawning smile on Moni. "You're all right in my book, *piepel.* I see we're going to get along fine." He batted a knowing eye at Moni, nodded, and left the cubicle.

Hardly had the door closed on him when the orderly at the table pulled the jacket off his shoulder. Both heads looked at the bruise where the truncheon had landed. Suddenly the eyes of the beaten man met Moni's. For a moment the orderly's profile assumed a sheepish smile, as though he had been caught at some indecent act. The two backs immediately returned to their work.

Moni sank down on the bed. Near his feet lay the block chief's boot. The red light sharpened the gleam of the tall upper. The crimson density of the cubicle stifled him. He did not know where to go here or to whom to turn. An agony of fear and loneliness stopped his throat. He stood up. He could not bear to go on sitting there.

From his eyes the empty block streamed dim, unending. On either side, up to the rafters, the three-tiered hutches rose vacant. He passed into the hollow darkness of the vast block. From the rafters hung an electric bulb which barely lit several hutches. In the vacant darkness he sought refuge from everything encircling him. He had not yet fully grasped just where he was. He could still feel his hand held tight in his father's palm. His eyes could still see the sealed wagon doors sliding open. The herds of people tumbling out onto the Auschwitz unloading platform. All being lined up in a long row. An SS man at the head of the row, only his hand ordering: Right! Left! Right! Left! Papa tightening his clasp. They are standing together. The row moving forward quickly. Huge lorries waiting on the left. Men in striped uniforms snatching people out of the masses pushed to the left, and shoving them onto the lorries. Just a handful of people on the right. Papa presses him to his side. Everything happening without a sound. So terribly fast. Left! Right! No one knows which side is good and which is bad. The row moves forward. Now they are both at the head of the row. The German's eyes pause on him for a moment, smile, and suddenly Papa is torn from him. Their clasped hands break apart. Papa is dragged off to the lorries but his glance does not let go of him. Papa calls to him: "I'll be waiting for you at the gate!" What did Papa mean by that? In the wagons, Papa promised that the war would soon be over. There will probably be an awful crush getting out of camp. People will trample each other the way they did at the collection points in the ghetto. In the sealed wagons, on the floor, people lay underfoot, trampled by those standing on them. If he hadn't been riding on Papa's shoulders, he would have been trampled too. Papa was tossed into one of the lorries among all those feet, hands, heads, his eyes still locked with his from afar. They kept tossing and shoving the people on to the lorries. Until Papa's glance was sucked up among them and gone.

The front gate of the block swung open. The red light streaming through the cubicle window illuminated Zygmunt's stormy entrance. Moni made for an aisle between two hutches. Zygmunt climbed to a top tier. The orderlies handed loaves up to him, and he stowed them away. The open cubicle door fed the red band light to the top tier, and back and forth in this redness the block orderlies passed, bringing the loaves from the cubicle. Zygmunt's hands dangled towards them from above.

He wanted to get away from between the hutches, but his feet would not obey. From the kitchen came the smell of frying sausage. The smell mingled with the terror of his loneliness and Franzl's stare and made him want to retch.

He walked to the front gate. No one was there. He pushed the gate open and walked to the main path.

Opposite his eyes, on the upper row of barbed wire, the night bulbs still glowed red, in warning that the wire wall was charged with electric death. Behind him, above the block gate, a yellow bulb illuminated the number 12 — his block. A chill bluish mist lay on the main path, and in his eyes the lamps over the wire wall merged into a long red streak whose tip impaled the vapors of the horizon like an embedded spear.

Only Prominents now walked the main path. They passed Moni by, paying him no attention: he was one of their own. There were shoes on his feet and the striped cap on his head. A common campling does not wear shoes and is forbidden to be seen on the main path now.

A stream of Prominents and Funktioners: block orderlies with outlines of the oblong camp bread inside their trousers against the belly — furtive glances, jittery steps, scurrying up, up the latrine-exchange; cooks from the camp kitchen, sleeves rolled up fleshy arms, round faces, little striped Auschwitz caps perched on clean-shaven heads — sturdy shoes, firm steps. On the main road, the pulse of Auschwitz life now throbbed.

A new day rose on Auschwitz, revealing only barbed wire to his eyes: barbed-wire walls of his camp ringed with barbed-wire walls on the camps encompassing his camp. The new day wrapped them in fetters around him. On the horizon, black spots of SS men climbed ladders up and down the watchtowers: the change of the guard. Their up-and-down crawl was like a dream suspended somewhere between alien skies and earth.

"*Piepel! Piepel!*" The call came from behind Moni like a faraway echo. He turned around. Close to the ground of the assembly area, behind the corner of the bloc, a boy's head jutted towards him, calling him with frightened eyes: "*Piepel! Piepel!*"

Moni approached him. The boy's teeth chattered with cold. His body trembled. "Let's go to the backpath so Franzl won't see us together." The boy's teeth clicked out the words.

They entered the assembly area between two blocks. They walked side by side. The boy shorter than he. All at once Moni wanted to put his arm around the boy's bony shoulders and embrace him. He had not yet had a full view of him. He did not even know what the boy wanted to tell him. But a hot surge of devotion welled up in him as to a brother newly found in loneliness. The boy kept jerking his head around, darting frightened glances in all directions to make certain that no one was spying on them from the main path. His hands were wrapped around his chest, fingers tucked deep in his armpits to keep them warm. They reached the backpath, where stood a compressed gray mass of myriad skeletons, skulls drawn down between shoulders: the block outcasts. The boy entered the skull stream of the backpath as though entering a place where he belonged.

They stood face to face. "I was Franzl's *piepel*," the boy said to Moni. "If you let me have a piece of bread, I'll teach you love tricks that Franzl likes, and you'll be good with him."

Moni did not understand. All around them, backs rubbed against backs to produce a bit of warmth. The boy's teeth chattered with cold. He kept raising one shoulder to one ear, then the other shoulder to the other ear, rubbing his ears against his shoulders to warm them, hopping all the while from foot to foot, as though to sever them from the cold earth. "I know what Franzl likes. You'll be good with him," he said, shaking all over with cold.

Moni felt tears warm in his eyes. He shuddered. The blurry skeleton mass around him focused in the boy's face. A face just like his own — both from Franzl's cubicle. Suddenly he felt he had done the boy a terrible wrong: because of him the boy is no longer *piepel*. "Why aren't you *piepel* anymore?" Moni asked.

"Franzl has had enough of me," he said. "He got fed up with me. I knew he'd bring himself a fresh *piepel* from the platform. I didn't wait for Franzl to cool me off one fine night. I got away first."

Moni ached to hug the boy. "I'll go get you bread," he said. "They've just finished slicing the rations."

"No! No!" the boy exclaimed. "Not the rations. They'll be spying on you. I know it. Then they'll get me when you come to me. You're all right. My name is Berele." The boy's body drew close to him. Moni felt as though Berele was embracing him, although his hands were tucked deep in his armpits. "Never the ration slice. Better from the stash. They won't notice there. There you're the boss. I'll wait for you in the latrine, behind the partition of the water pump. I knew you'd be all right."

From Berele's eyes Moni's own fate now stared at him, and he was afraid. "How could you tell the block chief didn't want you any more?" Moni asked.

"I could see it in Franzl's eyes. A *piepel* can tell. The heart of a *piepel* can tell right off. The block chiefs just wait until they bring themselves back a new *piepel* from the platform, and that night they take the old *piepel* into the cubicle, lay him on the floor, put a cane across his throat, plant themselves with their boots on both ends of the cane and do a seesaw — and that's the end of the old *piepel*. I saw what Franzl did to the *piepel* before me. I didn't wait. I got away first."

Moni felt he wanted to tear away from here and flee. Before his eyes Franzl's mouth once more shaped the words: "No one in this camp has ever rated a *piepel* like this." He blurted: "Did Franzl bring you from the unloading platform, too?"

"Franzl saw me during the march from the platform to camp, and right off he picked me for himself," Berele said. "At the platform, I wanted to run after my father to the lorries, but the SS man put me in the group going to camp. When they opened the wagon doors, my mother dropped out to the ground, dead. Or maybe she was alive — because her eyes kept looking at me."

Opposite them, the gates opened: the camplings may now come into the blocks. They all pushed in at once. Each wanted to be first. Berele did not budge. All around the day now bared to Moni's eyes the countless wired camps of Auschwitz. *Papa must be in one of them.*

"Your father is probably also in one of those camps," Moni suddenly said.

"That time at the Auschwitz platform I didn't know yet how glad I ought to be that my mother fell out of the wagon dead, and that my father was taken right off in the lorries," Berele said, his eyes staring at the myriad skeletons shoving in through the block entrances as though to freedom.

Through the window of Franzl's cubicle opposite, he saw the table set for supper. Everything was in place there. Cleaned up. Tidy. It was all his work. His hands had handled it all. He, the *piepel*. But now more than ever he knew with terrifying certainty that he did not belong there. None of that was his. The red stillness in there glowered at him with Auschwitz eyes of *kapos* and block chiefs, hustlers of skeletons to the crematorium.

He knew that he was still around only thanks to Franzl. But he also knew that Franzl was not satisfied with him. "I'm not having any Mussulman in bed!" Block chiefs like a good, fleshy *piepel* to make love to after a spell of hustling Mussulmen to the crematorium. What will happen to him when Franzl is through with him?

All alone he stood there in the dark of the kitchenette, sodden with the agony of those lying in the hutches. All at once he stood face to face with the unspeakable loneliness of Auschwitz. He was afraid to move a limb. The loneliness was everywhere. All around him and as far as only his thoughts could reach. He flattened himself against the wall. His eyes tore open with terror. The darkness projected at him the receding lorry into which Papa had been tossed. He cannot hear what Papa is crying out to him from there, but he knows that Papa is telling him just what he had managed to blurt to him when they had been torn apart. "Moni, wait at the camp gate when liberation comes. We'll meet there!" Oh, Pa, why did you leave me?

He spoke, weeping, into the dark: "If we were together, I would be able to give you bread now. I'm *piepel*. Every day I could bring you marmalade in your hutch, and whatever was left on Franzl's plate I would keep just for you. I could take care of you here. You mean it, Papa, you won't go away from your block naked in a *Selektion?* You're strong, Papa! Pa, take care of yourself there! I'm terribly lonely here all by myself. Please, Pa! Hold on to yourself, and then I'll be able to hold out, too. Franzl yells at me that I'm a skinny *piepel*. You're the only one who knows how strong I really am. Remember in school how they always used to say, "For his height, Moni could use another few pounds," and how you always told them, "We Preleshniks are that way. At Moni's age, I could touch fingers around my waist," He raised his jacket, wrapping his hands around his bare midriff. "Look, Papa. See how my fingertips touch? But I'm strong. You'll see, I'll hold out. Promise you'll hold out in your camp! Don't miss me the way I miss you, because that will make you weak. When you miss somebody the way I do, you have to cry. And I don't want you to cry. Don't worry about me, Pa. . . . Do you hear what I'm saying? You're not to worry. The war won't last long. I'll be waiting for you behind the bars of the open gate. It's going to be very crowded. Everybody will be pushing to get out to freedom at once. But I won't budge from there till you come for me. I know what — I'll climb up to the top of the iron post at the gate so you can see me. You know what a good climber I am — "

The gate swung open. Franzl strode into the block. "*Piepel!*" he roared.

The latrine was packed with camplings. It was altogether impossible to recognize it for a latrine. The long rows of holes down the center of the block were covered with camplings who were invisible for the waiting throngs surrounded by throngs waiting for them.

"I just couldn't get to you," Moni said. "I tried and tried for two days. You do believe me, Berele, don't you?"

They were standing in the corner near the water-pump partition. Berele gulped snatches of the bread Moni had brought him. He crumpled it to bits in his pocket, holding each scrap in his hand as in a bowl. His frame shook all over, and his hand shivered, too. He ate rapidly, lest a crumb drop to the ground. In this crush you could never get back such a crumb, and you could never find it under so many feet. And in this crush you're liable to get a shove in your open hand holding a whole scrap of bread. He ate feverishly, feeling that he was committing a crime against the bread by gulping it so. But he was also aware of the menace of all the eyes around. The latrine is crawling with merchants. The camp is full of them. All he needs is for an orderly from block 12 to catch him with a portion of bread after Moni has gone. Now where does a lowdown campling come off having a bread ration in the middle of the day? Better get it down fast.

He licked the palm which had cupped the scrap of bread, the way you lick a bowl which had contained a soup ration. In his pocket, his hand felt quite a bit of the ration. He knew that afterwards there would be a whole hoard of crumbs there. He looked up at Moni. "You don't have to make excuses to me," Berele said. "Last time, when you came to my block early in the morning to see whether I'd gone off with the *Selektion,* I was really worried about you afterwards. Zbichev saw you leave me, and then he saw me eating bread. Bread, right in the morning! You know that the chief orderlies are all in cahoots about things like that. Zbichev and Zygmunt are best buddies. I was afraid to go and meet you afterwards. I told you not to come to my block. They know you're *piepel.* You mean a lot to me, Moni."

"After that night with Franzl I just had to come to you. I'm terribly lonely here, Berele. I was afraid you'd gone off with the *Selektion.*" His eyes halted mutely on Berele. His friend's face looked no better than those crematorium-marchers. Berele could have been one of them then, just as he is fit for the next batch. Moni reached out his hand, cupping Berele's little hand in his. Both their hands shivered. "You mean even more to me, Berele. I really love you, Berele."

Behind them throbbed the motor of the water pump. Breast to breast the two boys stood, Moni's back to the latrine block, so none of the merchants should see his face. The crush around them was great. Mussulmen wiped with their hands the feces trickling down their off-drawn trousers, as camplings kept shoving them away and passing them on to each other. Moni's arm embraced Berele's shoulders. He let his head down on Berele's shoulder.

"I'm scared, Berele. Franzl hasn't used me in bed for two straight nights. I'm really scared, Berele."

"Sh-h-h! Don't talk so loud," Berele whispered. "Did you do everything I told you?"

"He won't let my body touch him. He kicked me out of bed. He says I've got the bones of a Mussulman."

"I told you not to undress. Just let your hands do the whole job. Franzl likes that. Get him hot in all the places I told you. Then he'll go right at you."

"I do, I do, Berele. But the minute he lays eyes on my body — "

"I told you to turn out the light."

"Franzl yells 'I want to see those eyes of yours, Mussulman!' Oh, Berele, why can't I be fat? Back home once, when Miss Emilie was feeding me, she called me skinnymerink. But just in the children's room, so nobody should hear. My pa liked me just the way I was. He said I was a Tarzan. All of them liked me the way I was. Help me, Berele. I don't want Franzl to do a seesaw on my neck with his cane."

Berele's body shivered as though from cold. He felt Moni's tears hot on his throat. In his pocket he still had the bread remains and a trove of crumbs. But just then his mind was not on that at all. The hunger which leeched him asleep and awake now suddenly seemed to have petrified in him. He knew what was in store for him if Moni lost his *Funktion*. Just as he knew the meaning of a *piepel*'s foreboding that his block chief was preparing to do a seesaw across his throat. He clung to the corner of Moni's jacket, as though by this clinging he would safeguard Moni's life. He now loved Moni with the rare love what would manifest itself only in Auschwitz. Opposite his eyes, the camplings dissolved to a hostile infinity, insatiably consuming human bodies without cease, without cease. Now he was ready to offer himself to it if only Moni should be spared.

His jaws chattered as he said "I meant to tell you, Golden Lolek has been making eyes at Franzl lately. Whenever Franzl leaves the block, Golden Lolek is there waiting for him. What does your heart tell you, Moni? What does your heart tell you?"

They regarded each other. They knew that both their fates now hinged on the answer. When a *piepel*'s heart tells him, even at the height of lovemaking, that his block chief is thinking of a seesaw across his throat, it is time for him to flee for his life. Not one more single night in such a cubicle. The ear merely has to be attuned to the heart's signal. "What does your heart tell you?" As tremblingly as Berele, Moni awaited his own reply.

"Franzl says my eyes have him hooked. He says that even after he's had a hundred *piepels* he'll never forget my eyes. But he wants me fat. Berele, why can't I be fat?"

Two Corpse *Kommando* men — the crematorium's corpse disposal crew — came barging into the water-pump compartment, followed by two merchants. One of the corpse collectors drew off his body an elegant woollen pullover he had "organized" at the crematorium, while the others counted cigarettes into each other's hands like banknotes. Berele mutely jabbed Moni to leave. With a last hug he whispered feverishly into his ear, "A good angel protect you!"

Moni moved off into the swarm of camplings. Berele remained standing there. Moni turned his head to him from afar. His velvety eyes glistening with tears, he sent a soft, sad smile to him, his lips again breathing the prayer with which his mother used to soothe him to sleep in the ghetto: "A good angel protect you, my sweet Moni. . . ."

From *They Called Him Piepel* by K. Zetnick 135633, London: Blond, 1961, pp. 13-29.

OBLITERATION OF THE CORPSES BY THE DEATH BRIGADE

When the Germans marched into Lvov, Poland, teenager Leon Welles (Weliczer) remembered his father's exhortation, "Trust in God," and his uncle's prophetic utterance, "Perhaps you will be the last survivor of our family, the one who is destined to preserve it." Young Leon was imprisoned in Camp Janowska, where he was assigned to the Death Brigade, whose task it was to obliterate the corpses by burning them and by crushing the bones into the dust.

He succeeded in several escapes and lived to give witness at the trial of the war criminals in Nuremberg and of Eichmann in Jerusalem.

He arrived in the United States in 1949 and settled in New Jersey. Today he is a well-known engineer and inventor. His book, Janowska Road, *is a remarkable narrative, gripping, matter-of-fact, penetrating. . . .*

Friday, June 26, 1943. The morning passes routinely. Today one group is ordered to reopen three more mass graves. These three pits are about sixty feet away from the wires of our yard, and contain over seven hundred bodies. This morning, when we left for work, our chief told us that, starting Monday, he wants to hear singing while we march to work.

The pits to be opened are grown over with grass like the surrounding area, but the SD knows exactly where they are located. They have a double-check on these locations, too, for there are some SDs in our groups who were present at the original execution. And, indeed, if one only knows the approximate location of the grave, it is easy to locate the boundaries of the spot because the earth around it is cracked and loose.

The disinterred bodies are still clothed. Most lie piled in a heap, covered with about four feet of dirt. But there are a few bodies lying above these others, only about eight inches down. It seems that they were buried after the others. The explanation: These were the prisoners who had buried all the others. So that there wouldn't be any witness left alive, they were shot after their task was done and in turn buried by the Germans.

We in this Death Brigade now have nothing to look forward to but the same fate.

We start a new fire. To do this we first level out a piece of ground about five hundred square feet. On this spot we lay the so-called foundation. This is made of heavy wooden logs in the form of a grate, so that air can get underneath for speedier burning. On either side of this "fireplace" we erect steps leading up to it.

During the day, all three graves are finally unearthed. Then preparations are made for taking the bodies out of the mass graves and bringing them over to the fireplace.

Stretchers and long hooks, the kind usually used for pulling large blocks of ice, are brought to the gravesites. These hooks will be used to pull out the bodies.

And so passes Friday.

Saturday, June 27th. Today, after reveille, which was at seven o'clock, Herches, at the command of the *Untersturmführer*, picks out additional men to go to the three pits with yesterday's group. The remaining inmates go to the ravine.

In the ravine, where all the bodies are already burned, the ground is turned over to see if anything is left. After completing this task, we have to report to the *Untersturmführer* who checks very carefully to see if the work was properly carried out. In case anything is not thoroughly reduced to ashes, if even a little hair is left over, each of the inmates in the group will get twenty-five lashes with a cat-o'-nine-tails, which is as painful as a hundred whips.

This is how the work at the three pits is done: three men, with a hook, go down into one of the mass graves, and two, with another hook, stand at the top. The three who are in the grave put the hook into the corpse and pull it out of its original position. Afterward, the two on the top pull hard, and this sinks the hook deeper into the body. Then they pull it up. One has to be very careful while sinking the hook because the corpse, already in an advanced stage of decay, might break in two. Another group, the carriers, now put two to four corpses (depending on their size) on the stretchers that were brought here yesterday. Two inmates work with each stretcher and carry it over to the nearby fireplace. Here a mass of corpses is accumulated.

The chief fireman now pours gasoline and oil on the wooden foundation, and starts the fire. The carriers, with their stretchers, climb the steps and toss the corpses into the fire. On one side one pair goes up and on the other side another pair goes down. It is worked this way so that one pair does not interfere with the other. The carriers continually rub their hands in sand, because their hands as well as the handles of the stretchers become slippery from the bodies.

The chief fire-tender is black from the soot, and singed, and he has a rod in his left hand with which he stirs the fire and directs the traffic. He also shows where the bodies should be placed, that is, on which side to ascend and toss the bodies into the fire without extinguishing it. God have mercy if one throws the corpse the wrong way! Then one has practically to get into the fire and pull the corpse out and throw it in again. It is a large fire, and the heat can be felt at a great distance. Standing near the fireman are his assistant and the tabulator.

The fireman's assistant shovels the ashes formed of burned bones, and continuously adds more wood.

When all the bodies are pulled out of the grave, a special group now searches the grave. With their hands they pick up each bone or hair, putting it into a pail, and afterward they throw it into the fire. After examining and collecting everything, they report to the *Unterstrumführer,* who inspects the pit. This group now sprays the walls of the pit, which are greenish from the bodies, with chlorine, to kill some of the odor.

Now the pit is covered and leveled. Afterward, we plow the ground, but instead of horses we pull the plows ourselves. The grounds are seeded, and after a few weeks one cannot tell where the pits were. This is the final effect the Germans want. No one must know what has gone on here.

Today, as on last Saturday, we work only until twelve o'clock. After lunch, taking turns, we go in groups of ten to bring water.

We wash our clothing, as well as ourselves.

From *The Death Brigade* by Leon Welles, published by Holocaust Library, 1980, pp. 167-169.

CHILDREN'S IDENTIFICATIONS OF NAMES WRITTEN IN BLOOD

Hungarian-born Dr. Giselle Perl, an obstetrician and gynecologist, served in the maternity ward in Auschwitz. She wrote her book as a "monument and commentary of the events from 1940 to 1945 of Nazi brutality, Nazi sadism, and Nazi inhumanity. . . ."

Those who ever believed that organized murder served only to satisfy Nazi perversion would have certainly changed their minds had they spent one day in the stockrooms attached to the crematories of Auschwitz. There was not one single item on the European market, be it foodstuffs, household goods, luxury articles, cosmetics, tools, or dress materials, that could not be found in large quantities in those stockrooms. No, Auschwitz was not only a playground for perverts; it was also a treasure-trove which supplied the German civilians with everything their hearts desired.

A detachment of two hundred prisoners was assigned to the crematory. It was their duty to separate the different kinds of articles and place them on the numerous shelves linking the walls of the huge buildings. Whoever was sent to work there knew that his days were numbered. After eight to ten weeks of this heartbreaking activity, they were shot and thrown into the flames.

There were shelves and shelves heavy with blankets of all kinds, beautiful silken ones, woolen ones, featherbeds, and lovely, colorful quilts. There were shelves full of canned meat, vegetables, fruit, and sweets; there were large metal boxes full of the most expensive medical instruments and indescribable riches of drugs which could have saved our lives if we had only been able to put our hands on them.

When the ghettos of the various European countries were evacuated, the inhabitants had no idea where they were being taken. As every member of the family was permitted to take about fifteen pounds of luggage with him, everyone took what he valued most or what he thought would be most needed. Doctors were told to bring their instruments, as they would be permitted to practice their profession among the Jews. This is how I happened to bring along my best instruments and most expensive drugs, which were taken away from me as I entered the gates of Auschwitz.

In addition to what we were permitted to take, each of us tried to smuggle in something hidden in our clothes, sewed into the lining of our coats, so as to have something to sell, something to give away should our life depend on our capacity to bribe.

While doing an errand near the crematory one day, I went into the stockroom reserved for children's clothes. Old prisoners were working here, separating the boys' clothes from girls' clothes, shoes from stockings, underwear from dresses, and the various types of toys from one another, to pack them all in Red Cross packages and send them to Germany to clothe and amuse the children of good Nazis. One of the prisoners working there, an eighteen-year old French girl, Jeanette, could stand this life no longer and with a piece of glass found on the ground she cut the veins on both arms. She collapsed, bleeding, and I hurried to bandage her arms so as to save her life, if possible, although she would probably have been better off dead. To ease her position I grabbed a small girl's coat lying nearby and put it under Jeanette's head. As I turned the coat inside out I saw a white label sewn into its lining: "I AM JULIKA FARKAS, AGE FIVE, MY FATHER IS DESIDER FARKAS FROM MARAMAROS SZIGET."

The white label of this fine, light-blue coat had a long story to tell. It told me of a blond, blue-eyed little girl, the pride and happiness of her parents, who was one day picked up by cruel Nazi hands and thrown into a cattle car together with her father and mother. During the long trip to Auschwitz little Julika was hungry and thirsty, she cried bitterly in her mother's arms, asking for her soft bed, for her warm milk, for a tender word of comfort and love. But mother had lost her power to comfort her child. She could do nothing but hold her close to her heart, stroke the soft blond hair, and kiss the tear-filled eyes. And even that not for long. . . .

After eight days, the journey came to an end at the gates of Auschwitz. Julika was torn from her mother's arms, undressed, and thrown into a ditch to be burned alive, together with hundreds and hundreds of little boys and girls. Her mother was spared the torture of remembering her child's fate. She went straight to the gas chambers and found forgetfulness at the merciful hands of death. . . . And now this little blue coat waited to be sent to Germany to clothe another blue-eyed child — perhaps the daughter of her Nazi murderer. . . .

The shelves holding boys' clothing had another story to tell. When we first arrived at Auschwitz, children under sixteen, whether boys or girls, were permitted to accompany their mothers to the women's camps. Then, as usual, there came a counter-order, and all children of fourteen, fifteen, and sixteen had to come forward because they were going to be put into a separate children's camp and receive double bread rations. Gymnastics teachers were told to come forward too. They would go with the children and teach them physical culture. We were happy. We thought that the children would be used for work and thus escape the unavoidable death by starvation, disease, or burning which awaited them in Auschwitz.

The boys left first. They were kept in a camp near ours and we were able to watch them exercise from morning till night, tired, weak, and thin — without the double bread rations they were promised. Then one night the most horrible screams woke our camp from its deathlike sleep. We ran to the entrance of the camp and witnessed a sight I shall never forget as long as I live.

Several black trucks were standing before the entrance of the boys' camp, and a detachment of SS men were throwing the naked, crying, screaming little boys on the trucks. Those who tried to escape were dragged back by the hair, beaten with truncheons, and whipped mercilessly. There was no help, no escape. Neither their mothers nor God could reach out a helping hand to save their lives. They were burned alive in those crematories which killed and smoked incessantly, day and night.

First they had to exercise to become stronger and "more beautiful," and then they were all murdered in one single night. Why? Can anyone answer? Why?

A few days later I had some work to do in the barracks where these children had lived. There, on the thin plank walls, they had written their names and the story of their lives — with their own blood — and a last good-bye. They knew they were to die. They knew they were to be burned, young, innocent, the victims of a world whose conscience shall never rest for having permitted these monstrous crimes. . . .

From *I Was a Doctor in Auschwitz* by Giselle Perl, published by International Universities Press, 1948, pp. 48-52.

GIVING BIRTH IN AUSCHWITZ

The poor young women who were brought to Auschwitz from the various ghettos of Hungary did not know that they would have to pay with their lives and the lives of their unborn children for that last tender night spent in the arms of their husbands.

A few days after the arrival of a new transport, one of the SS chiefs would address the women, encouraging the pregnant ones to step forward, because they would be taken to another camp where living conditions were better. He also promised them double bread rations so as to be strong and healthy when the hour of delivery came. Group after group of pregnant women left Camp C. Even I was naive enough, at that time, to believe the Germans, until one day I happened to have an errand near the crematories and saw with my own eyes what was done to these women.

They were surrounded by a group of SS men and women, who amused themselves by giving these helpless creatures a taste of hell, after which death was a welcome friend. They were beaten with clubs and whips, torn by dogs, dragged around by the hair, and when they collapsed, they were thrown into the crematory — alive.

I stood rooted to the ground, unable to move, to scream, to run away. But gradually the horror turned into revolt, and this revolt shook me out of my lethargy and gave me a new incentive to live. I had to remain alive. It was up to me to save all the pregnant women in Camp C from this infernal fate. It was up to me to save the lives of the mothers, if there was no other way, then by destroying the lives of their unborn children. I ran back to camp and, going from block to block, told the women what I had seen. Never again was anyone to betray her condition. It was to be denied to our last breath, hidden from the SS, the guards, and even the blockova, on whose good will our life depended.

On dark nights, when everyone else was sleeping — in dark corners of the camp, in the toilet, on the floor, without a drop of water — I delivered their babies. First I took the ninth-month pregnancies, I accelerated the birth by the rupture of membranes, and usually within one or two days spontaneous birth took place without further intervention. Or I produced dilatation with my fingers, inverted the embryo, and thus brought it to life. In the dark, always hurried, in the midst of filth and dirt. After the child had been delivered, I quickly bandaged the mother's abdomen and sent her back to work. When possible, I placed her in my hospital, which was in reality just a grim joke. She usually went there with the diagnosis of pneumonia, which was a safe diagnosis, not one that would send her to the crematory. I delivered women pregnant in the eighth, seventh, sixth, fifth month, always in a hurry, always with my five fingers, in the dark, under terrible conditions.

No one will ever know what it meant to me to destroy these babies. After years and years of medical practice, childbirth was still to me the most beautiful, the greatest miracle of nature. I loved those newborn babies not as a doctor but as a mother, and it was again and again my own child whom I killed to save the life of a woman. Every time when kneeling down in the mud, dirt, and human excrement which covered the floor of the barracks, to perform a delivery without instruments, without water, without the most elementary requirements of hygiene, I prayed to God to help me save the mother or I would never touch a pregnant woman again. And if I had not done it, both mother and child would have been cruelly murdered. God was good to me. By a miracle which to every doctor must sound like a fairytale, every one of these women recovered and was able to work, which, at least for a while, saved her life.

My first such case was the delivery of a young woman called Yolanda. Yolanda came from my home town. She was the child of an impoverished family and made a living by doing fine embroidery on expensive underwear, handkerchiefs — and baby clothes. To make beautiful baby clothes was the greatest pleasure in her life and, while working on them until late into the night, she would dream about the baby she herself would one day have. Then she got married. Month after month she waited and prayed, but Nature refused to grant her most ardent wish. This is when she began coming to me. I treated her for a long time, until finally my treatment showed results and Yolanda became pregnant. She was radiant. "I shall give you the most beautiful present in the world when my baby arrives," she would then tell me every time we met.

In the end it was I who gave her a present — the present of her life — by destroying her passionately desired little boy two days after his birth. Day after day I watched her condition develop, fearing the moment when it could be hidden no longer. I bandaged her abdomen, hid her with my body at roll call, and hoped for a miracle which would save her and her baby.

The miracle never came, but one horribly dark, stormy night Yolanda began having birth pains. I was beside her, waiting for the moment when I could take a hand in the delivery, when I saw, to my horror, that she was falling into convulsive seizures. For two days and nights the spasms shook her poor, emaciated little body, and I had to stand by, without drugs, without instruments to help her, listening to her moans, helpless. Around us, in the light of a few small candles, I could see the thirteen hundred women of her barracks look down upon us from their cages, thirteen hundred death-masks with still enough life left in them to feel pity for Yolanda and to breathe the silent but ever-present question: Why?

The third day, Yolanda's little boy was born. I put her into the hospital, saying that she had pneumonia — an illness not punishable by death — and hid her child for two days, unable to destroy him. Then I could hide him no longer. I knew that if he were discovered, it would mean death to Yolanda, to myself, and to all these pregnant women whom my skill could still save. I took the warm little body in my hands, kissed the smooth face, caressed the long hair — then strangled him and buried his body under a mountain of corpses waiting to be cremated.

Then, one day, Dr. Mengele came to the hospital and gave a new order.

From now on Jewish women could have their children. They were not going to be killed because of their pregnancy. The children, of course, had to be taken to the crematory by me, personally, but the women would be allowed to live. I was jubilant. Women who delivered in our so-called hospital, on its clean floor, with the help of a few primitive instruments that had been given to me, had a better chance to come out of this death-camp not only alive but in a condition to have other children — later.

I had 292 expectant mothers in my ward when Dr. Mengele changed his mind. He came roaring into the hospital, whip and revolver in hand, and had all the 292 women loaded on a single truck and tossed, alive, into the flames of the crematory.

In September 1944, Camp C was liquidated to make place for new arrivals. Out of thirty thousand women, only ten thousand remained alive to be put into other blocks or taken to Germany to work.

As soon as we were installed in Camps F, K, and L, a new order came from Berlin. From now on, not only could Jewish mothers have their children in the "maternity ward" of the hospital, but the children were to be permitted to live.

Eva Benedek was eighteen years old. She was a violinist from Budapest, a beautiful, talented young woman who was separated from her husband only a few days after her wedding. Eva Benedek believed with an unconquerable faith that her life and the life of her child would be saved. The child growing in her womb was her only comfort, her only pleasure, her only concern. When the SS organized an orchestra among the prisoners, Eva became the violinist of that orchestra. I bandaged her abdomen, and in her formless rags, amidst women whose stomachs were constantly bloated with undernourishment, her condition went unnoticed.

Then came the "liquidation" of Camp C, and Eva Benedek came with me to Camps F, K, and L. When the order for the conservation of Jewish children came, nobody was happier than she. Her delivery was only a day or two off, and we both believed that the miracle had happened, a miracle of God for the sake of Eva Benedek. She smiled all day, and in the evening, in our barracks, she whistled Mozart concertos and Chopin *valses* for us, to bring a little beauty into our terror-filled, hopeless lives.

Two days later she had her baby, a little boy, in the "maternity ward." But when the baby was born, she turned her back on it, wouldn't look at it, wouldn't hold it in her arms. Tears were streaming down her cheeks incessantly, terrible, silent tears, but she wouldn't speak to me. Finally I succeeded in making her tell what was on her mind.

"I dare not take my son in my arms, Doctor," she said. "I dare not look at him, I dare not kiss him, I dare not get attached to him. I feel it, I know it, that somehow they are going to take him away from me. . . . "

And she was right. Twenty-four hours after Eva Benedek had her son, a new order came, depriving Jewish mothers of the additional food, a thin, milky soup mixed with flour, which swelled their breasts and enabled them to feed their babies. For eight days Eva Benedek had to look on while her son starved slowly to death.

His fine, white skin turned yellow and blotched; his smooth face got wrinkled and shriveled; and on the eighth day I had to take him out and throw him on a heap of rotting corpses.

From *I Was a Doctor in Auschwitz,* by Giselle Perl, see p. 294, op. cit., pp. 80-86.

HALINA NEVER LOST HOPE

In 1940 Halina was an eleven-year-old prisoner behind the ghetto walls of Warsaw. During her adolescent and teenage years she experienced suffering in several hellish camps: Maidanek, Auschwitz, Ravensbruck, and Treblinka. But she never lost hope and survived them all – hence the title of her book.

When we came back to the block from night shift one morning, drunk with exhaustion, and lay down on the hard mattresses after placing our dirty, wet boots under our heads to the accompaniment of the inhuman yelling of the room orderlies, suddenly terrifying whistling arose on all sides of the camp: ''Get up for roll call! All Jewesses for roll call!''

The orderlies pulled blankets off sleeping women, belaboring them with their fists and cursing.

My teeth were chattering with cold; agitated, I pulled on my rags, and finally both of us — Hela and I — went out to where the ranks were being assembled in front of the huts. We had no doubt what this special roll call for Jewesses meant, especially for those staying in the barrack during the working day. In terror and nervous strain, we looked at one another. Which of us would pass through the ''selection'' and go back to the block? I was seized by the monstrous and desperate certainty that this time they would take Hela away to the gas chambers. I had long since ceased believing in miracles. Feverishly I began persuading my sister-in-law to run away; she could hide in the toilet or some other nook. . . . But Hela firmly opposed this, she remembered how they had beaten and ill-treated her when she collapsed while hanging out the washing. . . . She would rather die than go through anything like that again.

We proceeded in fives to the large empty space in front of the bathhouse. Stripped naked, we all stood in line as the Nazis ordered, singly, one behind the other. Hundreds of women from numerous countries and towns; speaking various languages; tall and short, fat and thin, healthy with smooth skin, or sick, with scabs, wounds, bruises all over . . .

An uncanny SS tribunal took its place opposite; the little finger on Dr. Mengele's hand passed final sentence — to the left meant death, to the right, more life in the Auschwitz torture chambers. The line of naked bodies moved towards the bathhouse; Dr. Mengele, accompanied by *Unterscharführer* Taube, was sorting out his victims with deliberation. The women whose life he spared went into the bathhouse and after a brief shower returned to the block. Those he condemned to death by burning assembled, herded by *Lagerkapos,* on the left side of the square; their numbers were written down, so they could be crossed off the list of the living.

The day happened to be fine and beautiful. The sun shone in a clear, bright sky. To the satisfaction of the "Master Race," the selection was proceeding smoothly and correctly, as usual. The doctor's finger, on a hand covered by an elegant glove, moved slightly: right . . . left . . . left . . . right. Jewish people, who threatened the "German new order and the purity of a superior race," must perish. Now or later, what was the difference? There was no problem. The Nazis had decided to murder them all, and were doing so accurately and systematically.

I walked immediately behind Hela, to keep her in my sight all the time. As we came closer to the judges and executioners, I moved nearer to my sister-in-law. The line moved on relentlessly. There was no way to stop it, to retreat, or to hide.

My heart was beating so hard that there was a darkness before my eyes. Mother, what was going to happen? A few steps more, one step . . .

We were standing face to face with the fresh green uniforms, round green caps with stiff peaks, cold eyes calculating our usefulness, our physical condition.

I pressed close to Hela, wanting to protect her from their eyes with my own body. At this very moment, the gaze of Dr. Mengele fell on us. Cool, calculating, ironical. His finger moved without haste and divided me from Hela. To the right — to the left. My heart stopped beating. I embraced Hela. I no longer saw or feared anything; all I knew was that I had to be with Hela, no matter what happened. Curiously enough, I suddenly felt young, healthy, strong. This feeling lasted only a few seconds, but already a tumult had broken out in the square. The progress of the selection had been interrupted, the iron discipline broken. Everyone was staring at us. The storm trooper Taube was dumbstruck, apparently with amazement. Meanwhile *kapos* were running up from all directions, trying to tear me away from Hela. I would not yield: I clenched my fists spasmodically, kicked, shrieked. Who knows how long they would have gone on scuffling with me, a naked little thirteen-year-old girl, clinging for dear life to a half-dead skeleton, had not Taube decided that, since I did not want to part from a woman condemned to death, I should share her fate? So the *kapos* wrote my name down on the list of those "selected."

Meanwhile, the group of SS officers in the center of the square, shading their eyes from the sun with their hands, had been watching the entire incident. The scene apparently amused rather than angered them, since not one reacted or was indignant at my act of insubordination. Such things rarely occurred in the camp; people were used to blind obedience. My childish resistance had a sort of attraction for the bandits. At least, this is the way I explain it to myself today. Especially as something happened immediately afterwards that none of us could even have imagined. Hössler, the deputy camp commandant, beckoned to me with one finger.

I clutched my dress and ran over, without thinking, to the group of storm troopers. I looked up into Hössler's face.

All of them were tall, straddling, and self-assured. Hössler seemed even more formidable and ruthless then the others. I grasped the meaning of his question at once. He wanted to know the identity of the woman for whom I was fighting so hard.

I began explaining in a rapid, unrestrained flood of Yiddish and German, as though I had been waiting a long time for the opportunity to give voice to everything that filled my heart.

"She is my mother, my sister, my family, I cannot live without her," I cried.

The officers listened in silence. Not one of them moved or altered his stiff attitude.

Then, in the tone of voice people use to scold a disobedient child, Hössler told me to be silent. "Otherwise," he said, "you will go in there with this *Schweigerin*[1] of yours, do you understand me?" And he pointed to the crematorium smoking beyond the wires.

Did I understand him? I shut my mouth instantly, though involuntarily a single, brief, incredulous, hopeful word emerged: "Me?"

The storm trooper burst into harsh laughter, imitating me with a kind of fiendish, cruel mirth: "Me? Me?" Hössler called the *Lagerkapo* and, in my presence, ordered her to cross our two numbers off the list. At this, I could not restrain my wild joy and — forgetful of everything — rushed towards Hössler to thank him. . . .

A hard slap blinded and stunned me. I lost my balance and fell. The pain of the blow was nothing in comparison with my feeling of shame. . . .

Animals will always be animals, even if they make a gesture that seems human. How could I, at such a moment, influenced by joy and gratitude, remember that? So I was punished; the brutal slap brought me back to reality. But this reality — Hela's and mine — had been miraculously spared! They had spared our lives. Our lives!

From *Hope Is the Last to Die,* by Halina Birenbaum, published by Twayne Publishers, 1967, pp. 136-141. Translated from the Polish by David Welsch.

BUDEE – THE CAMP THE WORLD FORGOT

"I shall always think of snow as red; red with the blood of the Jewish girls who died on those walks from Budee to the mountain where we worked so hard."

Budee is a name unknown to almost everyone except Bess Freilich, who lived and almost died there in the winter of 1942. She feels she may be the only person to have survived Budee.

Bess Freilich is now a settled Jewish matron who lives comfortably in Havertown with her husband, Samuel, son Mark and son Howard, an honor student at Temple University's Medical School [in Philadelphia].

At least, she appears to be a settled Jewish matron. But just below that surface calm, that smiling face, there is a tragedy that Bess Freilich cannot, and will not, let die.

"I feel guilty. I lived when so many died, and no one even knows of the place where they were tortured and killed," she mourns.

Budee is a name not found on the various lists made up by students of the Holocaust. Somehow it has been missed. But, according to Bess, it existed at a spot just a twenty-minute ride by truck from Auschwitz.

[1]Sister-in-law.

"It was a punishment camp, and only the young, strong Jewish girls were picked to go there. We were given a physical there, and when they were sure we could work, the guards handed us a piece of bread and sent us into our barracks.

"It started right away. As we walked into the barracks, there were women SS guards waiting. They took away our bread and then lined up in a double row. They forced each girl to run between the rows. All of them hit us as we went through. They used their rifles and sticks, anything, to hit us.

"Then they told us to go to bed so we would be ready to work the next morning. We were all bleeding, but we couldn't fall down because they would begin hitting and kicking us again."

There is little emotion in Bess Freilich's quiet voice. And as her recitation continues, you begin to realize that she cannot afford to let emotion in. The hurt is too big, the emotions too powerful.

"So many of my friends, all the pretty young girls from my town, Pruzany, all dead. Every day we were made to get up at three in the morning so we would be ready to go to work and could work long days.

"We were building an artificial mountain," Bess explained. "We were made to fill little carts with dirt. Six of us girls had to fill it in four minutes or we were shot. Then we would push the cart up the side of the mountain, empty it, and go back to the valley to start over again.

"It was hard to push the heavy carts up the mountain, and it was hard to hold them back when we brought them back empty. But either way, if the cart came off the rails and the guards saw it, the girls were shot."

Even getting through the terrible ordeal of working the full day was not enough to guarantee a girl another day of life. At the end of the workday, the female SS guards would call out numbers of some of the girls.

The girls called were made to undress and dance for the guards. This was called "the show." The girls would dance, and then, when they were finished dancing, the women guards would begin shooting.

"All the girls died," says Bess in the same quiet tone.

"One time I watched as a young-looking mother was picked to dance. Her daughter was in the camp, too. The daughter joined her mother in 'the show,' and after the dance they died together, holding hands."

Next to "the show," the favorite sport of the guards was to herd forty girls into an area surrounded by electrified wire. Then they would set forty dogs in with them and watch as the dogs killed the young girls.

"We worked in the freezing cold, and we had no coats. Some of the young girls became so crazy or so sick that they would throw themselves into a deep well there. When there were so many of them that they would clog up the top of the well, we would have to pull them out and load their bodies onto the wagon to be taken back to Auschwitz.

"One day I felt that I could not live anymore — that it would be better to die, to end all this. But I told a friend of mine that I wanted to die, and she said to me, 'Not today. Today is Purim. Maybe God will make us a miracle. Don't die today.' I don't know how she knew it was Purim. I don't know why I didn't die.

"But she died, and the next day I walked back to the camp with the wagon that carried her body."

The voice drones on, and the memories that come so relentlessly are so vivid to Mrs. Freilich that she begins them again with ''I remember as if it were now.''

She remembers when she got sick from carrying the cold earth that she dug for the mountain.

''I used to hold the earth against my chest so that I could move it more quickly. I guess it was too much, and I got very sick. I was so cold, so weak. But I couldn't miss a day at work. They would have sent me back to the fire to die.

''We had thin blankets on our beds, and to tear one meant we would be beaten twenty-five strokes. I knew it, but I had to take a chance. I had to wrap something around my chest to help the pain.

''I tore my blanket and wrapped it carefully so that no one could see. But I was so sick that I fell as I was walking the three kilometers to the mountain.

''The guards started beating me. I fell. I tried so hard to stand up. One grabbed me by the front of the dress to put me on my feet. She felt the material from the blanket, so they started again.

''I counted sixteen before I became unconscious. They left me in the puddle of mud and blood, and they thought I would die, I guess.''

Bess stops for a moment and makes a conscious effort to remember why she chose not to die.

''I don't really know why or when I decided I should live. I guess it was just that I was very young, and I thought that life must be better than this somewhere.

''Sometimes I still wanted to die, and when the bombers would fly over our camps at night we used to wonder why they didn't hit us. At least it would be over.''

But on this particular day, Bess Freilich decided to try to live. When she regained consciousness, she heard the guards calling her number.

''They were looking for me to take me back to Auschwitz to the fire.

''I hid.''

Bess stops again and looks for an inoffensive way to continue her story.

''I hid in the toilet. I hid under the clothes the girls had thrown away because they had been soiled. Everyone had dysentery, and sometimes the dresses were so terribly fouled that they were given others. . . . '' With all the terror, all the oppression she was relating, this gentle soul wished to soften the harsh words.

She sighed and continued. ''I was conscious and unconscious. I was trying to remain hidden until my work group returned. I thought I might mingle in with them and not be noticed.

''It didn't work. They found me and beat me again.''

So weakened that she couldn't crawl to the relative safety of the second level in the barracks, Bess tried to hide from the eyes of the guards. But they found her again, and chose her to empty the big vats the girls were forced to use for toilets.

''I could hardly stand, so the woman guard beat me. I begged her to stop, to give me a chance to stand. Maybe, if she would just stop for a second . . .

''She didn't speak to me. She just picked me off the floor anf stuck her rifle in my back as a prop. I got the buckets and staggered out into the cold night.

"There was a man guarding the towers, and the woman behind me started to show off for him by hitting me and kicking me. Finally I fell. The buckets fell too, and they spilled all over me. I was so humiliated."

Humiliated — the word seems inadequate to the event.

"I looked up and begged the guard to shoot me. He laughed and told me, 'You will die anyway. It would be a shame to waste a German bullet.'

"They beat me than until I looked like something not human. Then they dragged me to the morgue and shut me in. All through the night, I heard strange noises from the pile of bodies beneath me. And someone kept pinching me. By morning it was all quiet."

The room was quiet too.

"In the morning the wagon came, and I was loaded with the rest of the bodies to be taken back to burn.

"There is an old superstition that to lift your right leg brings good luck. So I tried. I wished that the ride would last forever. But it didn't. It lasted only twenty minutes, and I was back at Auschwitz where I started from."

Apparently, her luck was better than she'd hoped. She was allowed to live. A hospital of sorts had opened that day for Jewish women, and she was sent there. She had typhus. Although she received no treatment, she was allowed to lie there.

"I looked at the walls of the hospital and I saw them move. There was no spot that wasn't crawling with lice.

"And my body, filled with open sores, moved too, because the sores were also filled with lice."

But Bess was determined to live this time, and she concentrated on learning to stand erect and then to walk, even though she knew she would probably be returned to the punishment/work camp that had been her home for so many months.

"But I never went back. The work was finished, and so they liquidated the camp."

"Liquidated the camp? Closed it up? You mean they killed everyone in it?"

Yes. That is what Bess Freilich meant. Everyone still alive at Budee was "liquidated."

She picked up the tale. "And that is why I feel so burdened with guilt. All my friends. All my young girl friends from my little town. All dead. And no one but me knows about it.

"For so long I couldn't talk about it. I feared I would lose my mind if once I started to talk about it. Even my own children didn't know. When I told my daughter, she couldn't believe it. She said, 'But you were always so calm. How could you be so calm always?' But I had to keep calm so I wouldn't go crazy."

By no means is this the end of Bess Freilich's story. It is just a piece out of the middle. Before the saga ended, she had been a prisoner in four camps, had been freed and then imprisoned by the Russians, and finally she had escaped to the American lines.

"The Russians first liberated us. They gave us guns so we could kill our guards. But we could not. Oh, I heard that some Jews had helped kill guards, but most of us were too crazy with our freedom to kill.

"But later, the Russians decided that if we were still alive it must be because we collaborated with the Germans. So they put us back in prison. They tortured us, too."

A friend got word to Bess and the remaining prisoners that they were to be executed the next morning. So they took one final gamble. They plotted their escape, and this time they succeeded.

From "Budee — The Camp the World Forgot," by Bess Freilich, published by the Philadelphia *Jewish Exponent,* September 16, 1977.

9.

THE KILLER SQUADS

On Sunday morning, June 22, 1941, the German Army and Air Force poured over the Russian frontier in a Blitzkrieg — a "lightning" war. For the Jews this operation meant the last phase of the Final Solution.

Side by side with the swift advance of the German forces, four Einsatzgruppen, *or killer squads, each consisting of 500 to 600 men, fully equipped and operating independently of the Army, were unleashed. Highly trained professionals directed by university graduates, they divided their fields of operation into four areas. No longer was there any need for the Nazis to shroud the extermination program in secrecy. Was it not now open warfare? Mass murder was but a day's work. The killers combed the entire countryside, not overlooking the villages and the back country.*

Over a million Jews were put to death mercilessly and with dispatch. Those who could fled eastward before the killers. Children, old people, and women, who could not escape, were slaughtered.

Three selections which follow present this aspect of the Holocaust.

THE KILL

This is how we lived — or rather, how we survived. On October 16, a frosty morning, while the city still slept wrapped in fear, the Gestapo surrounded the city. Their helpers no longer lurked in corners but strutted triumphantly along the main streets, grinning contemptuously. They carried whips and went out to hunt with eager appetite. Grandpa went to pray, as usual. My two uncles had

172

gone to search for food two days before and had not returned. Grandma, my aunt, her four-year-old daughter Salka, and I remained alone in the house. We were awakened suddenly by screaming. We remained glued to our beds, as though seeking safety there — like hunted animals in their lair. The screams came closer. Exactly what had happened we had no idea, but clearly it was something terrible. A woman burst into the house with her last reserves of strength.

She could barely speak, and at last gasped out: "Run, run for your lives! The Germans started an 'action' on Monastyr Street, and it's spreading all over the city. They are grabbing Jews and dragging them to the square at the courthouse. Whoever tries to escape is shot." Where they were being taken to from the courthouse square no one knew. In an instant we were dressed. The storm was already on our street; it raged before our very eyes, sowing death and destruction all around. I could not have imagined so terrifying a sight. People raced around madly, tottering as they ran, stumbling and falling. . . . Mothers lost their children, and the Germans wrung their necks as though they were chicks. They ran after the fleeing mob, shouting, threatening, and cracking their whips. We saw how they dragged our neighbors out of the house. We could hear the loud cursing — "Damned Jews!" There was no time to consider what to do. In the midst of the horror and the fear we lost all control. We rushed through the back door and up the steps. Auntie fainted. The belladonna drops she always carried with her were lost in the confusion, and we had nothing to revive her with. Grandma, seventy-two years old, could not run very quickly, and little Salka whimpered bitterly. Below us lay the blood-drenched city. Moans, cries of pain, and shrieks mingled with the shouts and curses of the Germans. The mob of people grew, and was compressed into a mass awaiting its bitter fate. Suddenly our neighbor, Sakovski, came by.

"Please, tell us what is happening," we begged him. "What is going on?"

"I don't know exactly," he answered. "I hear they are taking people to camps, and whoever tries to run away is shot. And they're shooting the old and the weak, and the children, too."

And with that he too fled in panic. Auntie was unconscious, and Grandma helpless; with them, a little child. I was the strong one. Suddenly Grandma exclaimed, "Precious child, tear off the yellow badge, fix your hair — maybe God will have mercy and you won't be recognized — and run to Savitzkah. Beg her — plead with her — to hide us. If we survive this we will reward her — and if we are lost, God will punish her. Hurry, hurry — don't be afraid. We have nothing more to lose."

All the same I was terrified. But the words "we have nothing more to lose" — and the pleading way Grandma looked at me — gave me the strength to go. I wanted to live as I had never wanted anything in my life. I rushed to Savitzkah. When she saw me she was startled. Quickly she locked the door. I began to tell her what I wanted. I don't remember anymore just what words came pouring out of me.

"I can't, my dear, I can't risk my own life." I heard the answer, and I understood how she felt. I did not plead anymore. I was about to leave. Her daughter Yadziah suddenly came into the room.

"Mother," she said, "let them come. We can find a place to hide them."

I rushed back, thankful for our good fortune and silently blessing Yadziah. Who ever would have dreamed that her sweet words were a snare and a delusion! She hid us in a corner of the attic, behind a wooden partition. We did not utter a sound — even little Salka understood enough to keep absolutely quiet. After a while Yadziah brought the Morgenstern family to join us — they had hidden in the bathroom while the Germans searched their home. The shooting continued without let-up.

"We would be better off in a *Lager* [camp] than getting killed here," Morgenstern said.

"Do you really believe they are being taken to camps? I heard that in Kolomiya they got all the Jews together and took them out to the nearby forest and killed them," his wife commented.

We were living in a vacuum, with no idea of what to expect further. Grandpa's voice suddenly reached us. He had managed to get back from the synagogue and was caught just as he reached the house.

"Lassen Sie mich leben, lassen Sie mich leben!" ("Let me live, let me live") he begged the murderers. His hoarse voice throbbed with fear. He begged for pity, like an abandoned child. I cannot describe what it did to me. I only know the sound of his pleading penetrated to the depths of my soul and agitated my very being. My spirit melted, like snow in a hot sun. I sank my teeth into my clenched fist and didn't feel a thing — as though the fist were paralyzed. Alternating hot and cold sweat drenched my body. It was not a German who had caught my grandfather, but a nameless hoodlum with a stick. He could barely pronounce the German words, *"Los, verfluchte Juden* [Away, cursed Jews]."

"I beg you, let me live," Grandpa continued to plead. A heavy blow stopped him. *"Ich bitte Sie* [I beg you]" he managed to get out — and no more. We parted from him; a silent farewell.

In the afternoon Yadziah came storming up to our hiding place. She seemed transformed. "You will give me your keys," she shrieked at us. Without a moment's hesitation we gave her our house keys, and then, through the wall, we could hear her moving about in our home as though it were her own, taking whatever she pleased. But we were completely indifferent to material things; they seemed to have nothing to do with us.

Two days passed. The shooting went on day and night. On the third day, after she had completely emptied our house, Yadziah turned us out.

I left first and again turned to Sakovski for help. The door of their house was locked. I wandered about in the courtyard and saw Fidel Steiner, who motioned to me to run away. I turned to go back and had taken but a few steps when a fifteen-year-old hoodlum suddenly blocked my path. I got away from him with difficulty, and he began to chase me. I ran, with him after me. He caught me, and I struggled with him until his father — the local dogcatcher — came and grabbed me by the hair. He made me walk along ahead of him. Auntie was lying in the courtyard, covered with blood. A redheaded girl, the daughter of "Grace of God" (that's what everyone called him), was dragging Salka along behind her, with Salka screaming to high heaven, "Mamma, Mamma, I want to live."

Grandma walked along behind me. The city was abandoned, desolate. There wasn't a soul to be seen. Dead bodies were strewn about in the middle of the streets and on the doorsteps. The sidewalks were bathed in blood. There was clothing strewn all over the ground. Heaps of sacred books had been piled up by profane hands. Their pages riffling in the winds, the books themselves shrieked, "Hear, O Israel."

How was it possible that the very foundations of heaven did not collapse? Why didn't the earth quake? How could the sun shine on such a day? Where was the human conscience? Where were the people?

Vicious Satan had spread his wings over the universe and, laughing maliciously, moved in frenzy about the streets and through the empty houses. The silence of the grave surrounded us. Death looked out of every corner. The stray dogs had hidden themselves, and even the house cats were at a loss. We were brought to the courthouse, which had become a death house.

When we got there, a gang of Gestapo men came out. They were dressed in black uniforms with skulls on their caps. "The action is over," one of them said. "You will bring these to the next action." He turned to one of the hoodlums. "Understand, you old dog?" Death itself had mercy on us, while those who had caught us knew no pity.

From the courthouse they took us up the mountain. All around us was devastation. We were abandoned, with no one to save us. We went helplessly, resigned to our bitter fate, like those scattered all about. Vainly we appealed to their consciences. The wind carried our words, and no one heard us. They led us up the mountain that towers over the village, Mount Pistin. There, in the shade of the trees, people once enjoyed the pure air and the beauties of nature. Couples once whispered there of their love. Now it was one huge grave. Twenty-five hundred people had been slaughtered and buried here, some of them not even quite dead. It had all been done in two days — in an "action" that lasted forty-eight hours.

We stood near a river of blood. A silent groan rose up from under ground. There was another pile of corpses nearby with no one near them: corpses did not need guards; the dead would not come to life, they would not raise a finger. It was quiet all around, frighteningly quiet. We who stood near the graves felt that the souls of the dead still lived. They pierced our consciences and shrieked for vengeance. It is a picture I shall never forget — it has not faded from before my eyes, but still tortures and torments me.

Twenty-five hundred people were murdered here, and they lay before me in a mass grave. Just two days ago I had talked with these people. Two days ago they were full of hope. And now — only the murmuring wind and black ravens hovered above their grave.

The ground was strewn with torn banknotes, documents destroyed hurriedly by trembling hands before death stilled them. At night the dead did not let me sleep. I could not eat the bread in front of me. On my plate I saw slices of their flesh; I saw their red blood in my cup. Up on the mountain there was no one to make us part of that murdered mass. The "action" was over. The Nazi murderers were tired. The shooting, which had not ceased for two whole days, had worn them out, though it had not touched their souls. The Ukrainian

Haidamaks regretfully freed us, consoling themselves with the thought that our respite was only temporary, only until the next "action."

Our house stood empty and abandoned, everything in it destroyed. We brought my wounded aunt there, her blood still flowing. We sat in despair, trembling, fear searing our souls; the horrors we had seen tore us apart, body and soul — we were the living dead.

We wondered who was still alive. We sat huddled together, unable to think. Had we really managed to remain alive? A day or two later, individuals began to appear, haunted, terrified people, almost insane with what they had seen. They fell into each other's arms, weeping and laughing hysterically. After all we had seen, it was hard to believe that we had, indeed, remained alive. We began to breath once again. Each of us thanked God for his salvation, even though we still did not believe we had really been saved. Before the day was over, each was talking about his murdered wife or his children who had been killed. A few days later my uncles appeared. The older one, Mendel Figer, was almost insane. He held little Salka by the hand and yelled, "Give me my children!" Zipporkah Brecher came to us, from Kuty; her parents had been murdered in Kossov. When we went into their apartment, we saw breakfast ready on the table; they had never got to eat it. A few loaves of bread, not completely baked, remained in the cold oven. The orphaned children wandered about in the streets, lost, aimless. They wandered near their homes, where two or three days ago they had been children with parents. Now suddenly they had been orphaned, left to themselves like lost sheep. Some of them clutched pictures of their dear ones. Others collected the toys scattered about on the floor — tragic relics of the life that had throbbed here just a few days earlier. In vain children looked for their parents; in vain, they called out their names.

Grandpa's trembling voice, his last pleas — *"Lassen Sie mich leben"* [1] — echoed in my ears even louder than when he had uttered them. The impress of death did not leave us; the people murdered on Mount Pistin did not leave us; nor did the people burned in the synagogue and the corpses strewn about the street leave us. The joy of being still alive faded quickly. The ominous reality weighed upon us. We sat in destroyed nests with no hope for the future and recalled those who had fallen victim to the murderers. We talked of Dr. Gertner, who at the brink of the grave on Mount Pistin had turned to his murderers and screamed at them in German, "This is German culture!" We talked about Rachel Letich, who refused to give in to the murderers and did not obey their orders. She refused to strip off her clothing at the edge of the grave. "When I'm dead," she said to her executioners, "you can do to me anything you want. As long as I'm alive I refuse to undress."

The days became darker and the nights more ominous. Every movement, the slightest sound, aroused fears of another "action."

Some of the survivors built bunkers, others devised different hiding places. They slept in ditches, under bridges — anywhere but in their homes. We had begun to accept the idea of a bitter fate, and we were certain that new misfortunes would not be long in coming. Every day that passed, every night of sleep, was thought of as a gift from heaven. The German Military Police, the Gestapo, the Criminal Police, and the Ukrainian Militia added to the number of deaths every day and brought new destruction, new tragedies.

---

[1] "Let me live."

The *Judenrat* (Jewish Council) had been set up to serve as a kind of intermediary between us and the Germans; between life and death. If one of the Germans, feeling playful, demanded something impossible, the *Judenrat* carried out assignments and fulfilled the most difficult requests — even those which seemed completely impossible of realization. Those who remained alive turned in the remnants of their pitiful possessions under the illusion that by stuffing the gullet of the dragon they were saving their lives. One day the Gestapo demanded that a Hutzul-style villa be built for them, and threatened that if it were not completed within the time set it would cost all the Jews their lives. The villa — they called it "Valligura" — grew before our eyes, like a real horror. The District Governor, Volkmann, kept demanding further refinements for himself and for his wife. Military Police Sergeant Bayer would send new lists of these requirements. Rebke demanded something new every day for himself and for his mistresses. There were dozens of others who did the same, whose names I no longer remember. And when the Area Governor, Frank, appeared one day, we were compelled to dig out the hidden utensils and food supplies for a reception in his honor. And so the winter passed, with no two days the same, no two hours the same, with misfortune following misfortune.

From *The Forest, My Friend* by Donia Rosen, published by Bergen-Belsen Memorial Press, pp. 12-18. Translated by Mordecai S. Chertoff.

PORTRAIT OF A NAZI KILLER OF CHILDREN

Professor Otto Ohlendorf was the commander of Killer Squad D (1941 – 1942), with the rank of major general. He reported at his trial that his squad killed 90,000 men, women, and children. Ohlendorf had been graduated as a Doctor of Jurisprudence and was a prominent member of the German intellectual class. He was handsome, suave, and haughty.

Presented below is a portion of the record of Ohlendorf's trial, which took place before the U.S. Presiding Judge Michael A. Mussmano at Nuremberg in 1948. Altogether, twenty-three criminals stood trial, of whom fourteen (including Ohlendorf) received the death sentence.

Ohlendorf's victims were mainly Jews, but he killed gypsies also. "On what basis did you kill gypsies?" Heath[1] asked.

"It is the same as for the Jews," Ohlendorf replied.

Since the Nazis had proclaimed the theory of a master race, Heath now put the whole ironic projection of that theory into a one-word question: "Blood?"

Ohlendorf answered, "I think I can add up from my own knowledge of European history that the Jews actually during wars regularly carried on espionage service on both sides."

Heath looked up to me, as if to inquire whether the translating machinery was working properly, because he was asking about gypsies and Ohlendorf continued to talk about Jews. I directed Ohlendorf to the subject of Heath's questioning. With a disparaging gesture of his hand, Ohlendorf answered,

---

[1]Prosecutor James E. Heath.

"There was no difference between gypsies and Jews. At the time the same order existed for the Jews. I added the explanation that it is known from European history that the Jews actually during all wars carried out espionage service on both sides.

I reminded the defendant again: "Well, now, what we are trying to do is to find out what you are going to say about the gypsies, but you still insist on going back to the Jews, and Mr. Heath is questioning about gypsies. Is it also in European history that gypsies always participated in political strategy and campaigns?"

Ohlendorf was pleased to open up the history books. "The gypsies in particular. I want to draw your recollection to extensive descriptions of the Thirty-Year War by Ricardo, Huck and Schiller — "

Since the Thirty Years' War was fought in 1618 – 48, I could not help interrupting. "That is going back pretty far in order to justify the killing of gypsies in 1941, isn't it?"

This suggestion that he was giving a three-hundred-year motivation to his death-dealing enterprise did not ruffle the ex-SS major general. "I added that as an explanation, as such motive might have had a part in this, to get at this decision."

What was the real purpose behind the killing of Jews and gypsies? Ohlendorf was almost annoyed at questions of this character. Why, it was a matter of self-defense, he explained in the tone of one who is wasting time explaining that the earth is round. The Jews posed a continuous danger for the German occupation troops. Moreover, they could someday attack Germany proper, and self-preservation dictated their destruction before they began an aggressive march on Berlin.

Heath was not impressed with this argument. Assume that the Jews in Bessarabia, the Crimea, and the Ukraine could one day shoulder guns against the Germans, he said; assume that their wives could help them — but what about the Jewish children, the gypsy children? Heath thundered his question at Ohlendorf.

Ohlendorf imperturbably replied, "According to order, they were to be killed just like their parents."

Heath walked away from the witness stand to control his anger at the casualness with which Ohlendorf had made this shocking revelation. Then, turning swiftly on his heels, he fired again at the defendant: "Will you explain to the tribunal what conceivable threat to the security of the *Wehrmacht* [armed forces] a child constituted in your judgment?"

Ohlendorf answered in staccatoed accents, amazed that Heath should still linger on the subject. "I believe I cannot add anything to your previous question. I did not have to determine the danger, but the order contained that all Jews including the children were considered to constitute a danger for the security of this area."

But Heath did not let up. "Will you agree that there was absolutely no rational basis for killing children except genocide and the killing of races?"

The atmosphere of the courtroom filled with electric tension. Many spectators lifted their hands to their headsets, pressing on the earpads as if to increase the volume of sound so as not be lose a word of the reply, which they anticipated would be momentous. Their nervous expectations were fulfilled as Ohlendorf delivered the answer, which set off a murmur of horror. ''I believe that it is very simple to explain if one starts from the fact that this order did not only try to achieve a [temporary] security but also a permanent security because for that reason the children were people who would grow up and surely being the children of parents who had been killed they would constitute a danger no smaller than that of the parents.''[1]

Heath caught his breath and launched on another subject of cross-examination. However, the tautness of his features clearly told that he was still concerned about Ohlendorf's explanation. It was as perfect a piece of logic as could be found in Aristotle, but is was too perfect. There had to be a flaw somewhere, so Heath returned to the bewitchingly macabre subject.

''To come back to the question of murder and the children of the slaughtered in Russia. I think you have not yet answered my question. What conceivable threat to the *Wehrmacht* was offered by the children of gypsies and Jews, let's say under five years of age?''

Ohlendorf said he had already answered that query, and so for Heath's benefit I summed up Ohlendorf's explanation: ''The witness has stated that the reason these children under five, under four, under three, down to conception, I imagine, were killed is that they were a possible threat to Germany in the future years. That is his answer, and he stands on it.''

But Ohlendorf had not been entirely without heart. There was one feature about massacring the children which had grated on his tender sensibilities. Some of his men were married and had children. Ohlendorf had five of his own. As the executioners looked at the helpless tots framed within the sights of their rifles, they often thought of their little boys and girls at home and sometimes aimed badly. Then the *Kommando* or platoon leader had to go about with revolver or carbine, firing into the screaming and writhing creatures on the ground. This was all quite unmilitary. Then, also , many of the riflemen missed their targets when they had to kill women, because they thought of wives, daughters, sisters, and mothers far away.

Adolf Eichmann found a way out of the awkward situation. He provided for gas vans, which would save the sentimental assassins from too much suffering. These vehicles resembled family trailers. Painted windows adorned the sides, frescoed curtains seemed to flap in the breeze, the image of a flowerpot on the image of a windowsill added to the charming deception. The attractive-looking autocars rolled up to the groups of waiting mothers and children, who were told that they were to be taken to their husbands and fathers. Ohlendorf described the procedure: ''One could not see from the van what purpose it had, and the people were told that they were being moved, and therefore they entered without hesitation.''

Thus, joyfully, the women clambered aboard, holding by the hand or in their

---

[1]The defendant Erwin Schulz also stated: ''Jewish women and children were, if necessary, to be shot as well, in order to prevent acts of revenge.''

arms their babies, some laughing, some crying, but everyone excited over the trip which was to take them away from hardship and persecution, to begin life anew in another land by the side and under the protection of their strong menfolk, who had already gone ahead to prepare the happy way for them.

As soon as the unsuspecting pilgrims entered the vehicle, the doors slammed shut, automatically and hermetically. The driver tramped on the accelerator; monoxide gas streamed into the interior. The women screamed as their children toppled to the floor or succumbed in their arms, but before they could rescue them or breathe encouragement, the deadly vapor had entered their own lungs; and soon the moving van had become a traveling mortuary. By the time the van reached its destination — a long, deep ditch outside the town — all the occupants were dead. And here they joined the husbands and fathers who had already preceded them into the "new land" via the submachine guns and rifles of that astonishing organization known as the *Einsatzgruppen*.

Ohlendorf was asked how long it would take to execute persons by the use of these lethal gas vans after they were subjected to gas. The ex-general lifted his hand to his forehead as if trying to assist the machinery of recollection. It was a detail of which apparently he had never made a mental note. At last he lowered his hand and said, "As far as I remember, about ten minutes."

Sometimes there were more demands for the gas vans than Ohlendorf could supply, but he was equal to every emergency. Thus, "If there were three requisitions, we would send the two cars to the two *Kommandos* who had the largest number of prospects. But that was done in a very simple, businesslike manner."

To the *Einsatzgruppen,* everything was quite businesslike about these ghastly vehicles of death. Communications between Eichmann's headquarters and *Einsatzgruppen* commanders in the field spoke of gas wagons with the casualness of correspondence on coal trucks. Nor, in keeping with the German passion for maintaining records, was there documentation lacking on this awesome subject. In the innumerable filing cabinets found in the Gestapo headquarters appeared copies of letters, invoices, repair bills, etc., having to do with the gas vans. One letter from the Security Police and Security Service Ostland to Amt IV, B4, dated June 15, 1942, asked for the immediate shipment of one five-ton van and twenty gas hoses to take the place of some leaky ones in order that there might be no delay in the treatment of Jews "in a special way."

In a letter, dated May 16, 1942, SS-*Unstersturmführer* Becker made a practical recommendation with regard to the operation of the lethal device. He said that many of the drivers failed to apply the gas properly. "In order to come to an end as fast as possible, the driver presses the accelerator to the fullest extent. By doing that the persons to be executed suffer death from suffocation and not death by dozing off as planned. My directions have now proved that by correct adjustment of the levers death comes faster and the prisoners fall asleep peacefully."

Eichmann, who had taken a course in engineering at school in Linz, looked into the "levers" situation and found no mechanical defect. He decided that all that was necessary in order to obtain maximum results from the gas vans was for the drivers to be given special instructions. Accordingly he set up a school for that purpose.

The vans themselves were constructed in Berlin and driven under their own power to the fields of action. It would be interesting to speculate on the thoughts of the drivers as they rolled through half of Europe, traversing city and country, climbing mountains and penetrating plains, traveling over a thousand miles with their gaseous guillotines to kill women they had never seen and children they could never know.

While the gas van had its advantages in that it brought death to women and children without the executioners' having to look them in the eye, it still did not prove to its users to be a faultless engine for human destruction. When the execution was accomplished by shooting, the job was quickly finished, since the bodies fell into the already dug graves. But the gas vans presented the job of removing the corpses and then burying them. Traces of gas still remained, and the mass of tumbled bodies produced a problem of its own. The executioners complained of headaches. As Becker worded the complaint in an official report, the unloading process inflicted "immense psychological injuries and damage to the health" of the loaders.

Ohlendorf maintained a physician on his staff to treat the "psychological injuries" and to supervise the health of his men generally. Occasionally the physician was used as an expert to determine if the people in the gas vans were dead before burial, but this precaution was really unnecessary, Ohlendorf said, because he "had a look that the people died without any difficulties."

Ohlendorf insisted that throughout his entire Nazi career he was motivated only by the highest of ideals and ethics. This caused Heath to inquire whether he regarded Hitler's order against the Jews and others as justified in the realm of morals. "Was it morally right, or was it morally wrong?"

Ohlendorf replied that it was not for him to pass on Hitler's intentions.

"I do not ask you for a judgment of Hitler's morals; I ask you for an expression of your own moral conception. The question is not whether Hitler was moral; but what, in your moral judgment, was the character of this order: Was it a moral order, or an immoral order?"

Dauntless and as sure of himself as a Prussian field marshal on parade, Ohlendorf nevertheless perceived that a discussion on moral issues could make him appear something less than the Spartan, valorous executant of military orders which he said it was his duty to obey. Accordingly he repeated that it was not up to him to pass on the moral quality of Hitler's actions. Heath insisted that the question be answered and appealed to the tribunal. I turned to Ohlendorf: "When this order was given to you to go out to kill, you had to appraise it, instinctively. The soldier who goes into battle knows that he must kill, but he understands that it is a question of battle with an equally armed enemy. But you were going out to shoot down defenseless people. Now, didn't the question of the morality of that order enter your mind? Let us suppose that the order had been — and I don't mean any offense in this question — suppose the order had been that you kill your sister. Would you not have instinctively morally appraised that order as to whether it was right or wrong — morally, not politically or militarily, but as a matter of humanity, conscience, and justice?"

Ohlendorf moved slightly in the witness chair. His eyes roved about the courtroom; his hand opened and clenched convulsively. He was aware that a man who would kill his own sister made of himself something less than human.

On the contrary, if he replied that he would refuse to execute such an order he would contradict his assertion that he had no choice in obeying his superior's command. Accordingly, he answered obliquely, "I am not in a position, your Honor, to isolate this occurrence from the others."

He sought a parallelism so as not to manifest alarm at the dilemma the question posed. He related how he saw many civilian Germans killed in Allied air raids and then declared, "I am not prepared, or in a position to give today a moral judgment about that order."

But Heath was not content to leave the subject dangling unresolved in midair. He pressed the question as to how Ohlendorf would respond to a direct order involving an obviously difficult assignment. "If you had received an order from Adolf Hitler to kill your own flesh and blood, would you have executed the order, or not?"

Ohlendorf parried the thrust. "I consider the question frivolous." But the question was far from frivolous for him. He actually had a sister, and two brothers, in addition to his five children.

Heath relentlessly pursued the query. "Then I understand you to say that if one person be involved in a killing order, a moral question arises, but if thousands of human beings are involved, you can see no moral questions; it is a matter of numbers?"

Ohlendorf's pale features went parchment-white as he retorted angrily: "Mr. Prosecutor, I think you are the only one to understand my answer in this way, that it is not a matter of one single person, but from the point of departure events have happened in history which among other things have led to deeds committed in Russia, and such an historical process you want me to analyze in a moral way. I, however, refuse moral evaluation with good reasons as outlined, so far as my own conscience is concerned."

Heath continued and intensified the attack: "Suppose you found your sister in Soviet Russia, and your sister were included in that category of gypsies — not a Jewess but in a gypsy band — and she was brought before you for slaughter because of her presence in the gypsy band; what would have been your action? She is there in the process of history, which you have described."

Ohlendorf fought for time as with flashing eyes he signaled to his attorney to intervene. Dr. Aschenauer, tall, dark, and, in his long flowing black robe, looking something like a Shakespearean actor, rose dramatically and, echoing his client's defiance, declaimed, "I object to this question and I ask that it not be admitted. This is no question for cross-examination."

The prosecution insisted on a reply. Ohlendorf with his expressive countenance urged his attorney not to abandon his protest. Aschenauer lifted his berobed arm in challenge, and turned to the bench. "I ask for a ruling of the tribunal upon my objection."

I conferred with my colleagues, and we decided the defendant should be required to answer.

I explained to Ohlendorf that the question was of course an extraordinary one and would not be tolerated in a trial other than one of this character, where the defendant was confronted with the unprecedented charge of having murdered ninety thousand people. Under those circumstances the question was relevant because his answer would throw a light on his reaction to the Führer Order.

Ohlendorf was not convinced he should answer. I explained further that he admitted the Führer Order called for execution of defenseless people. "You will admit that in normal times such a proposition would be incredible and intolerable, but you claim that the circumstances were not normal, and, therefore, what might be accepted only with terrified judgment ordinarily, was accepted at that time as a normal discharge of duty." Under those circumstances I ruled that he should answer and I repeated Heath's question: "Suppose that in the discharge of this duty you had been confronted with the necessity of deciding whether to kill, among hundreds of unknown people, one whom you knew very well."

Ohlendorf reflected only for an instant and then, with a contemptuous glance at Heath, which seemed to say he was sweeping him aside, he announced to the world that under the circumstances described he would indeed shoot his sister: "If this demand would have been made to me under the same prerequisites, that is, within the framework of an order, which is absolutely necessary militarily, then I would have executed that order."

Although Ohlendorf would kill his sister if Hitler ordered him to do so, he explained that he had no different feeling with regard to shooting others. He bore animosity toward no one. "I never hated an opponent or any enemy, and I still do not do so today," he testified, as he lifted his eyes to the newspaper reporters in the press box, as if appealing to world opinion for confirmation of his moral scruples.

He killed Jews and gypsies because of their offenses in history, current and past, but he did not hate them. In fact, he even suggested that he felt some antipathy to Hitler's order which required him to kill unarmed civilians. This prompted the question, "Could you not have, after a certain period of time, tried to evade this order by sickness?"

He stiffened in the witness chair as if to emphasize the invisible epaulets on his shoulders. Was the presiding judge trying to insult him? "I would have betrayed my men if I had left this command," he remarked rather icily. Solicitous about the welfare of his men, he would have had no assurance that, if he left, his successor would have manifested a similar solicitude. And, with a rising voice full of pride and moral justification, he added: "Despite everything, I considered this my duty and I shall consider it today as much more valuable than the cheap applause which I could have won if I had at that time betrayed my men by simulating illness."

From *The Eichmann Kommandos* by Michael A. Mussmano, New York: Macrae Smith, 1961, pp. 112-121.

10.

PASSING AS ARYANS
AND HIDING OUT

Dr. G.M. Gilbert, the prison psychologist at the Nuremberg Trial of the Nazi War Criminals, quotes Julius Streicher's ecstatic comment: "Circumcision was the most amazing stroke of history." Jews could dye their hair, speak perfectly the language of their native country, and assume convincing Aryan ways of behavior, but they could not hide the mark of the Covenant — their having been circumcised. To efface the mark of circumcision — i.e., to restore the prepuce or foreskin — required plastic surgery, high expertise, and enormous costs, and, of course, it was very risky.

In Holland and Scandinavian countries, where blond hair and blue eyes predominated, dark-haired individuals had to skillfully dye their hair blond. This is what Margo Minca did.

PHIMOSIS IS NOT CIRCUMCISION

Jo Joffo was ten and his brother Maurice twelve when their mother sewed a yellow star on their jackets. Then their father, who was a barber in Paris, sent them away to join their older brother in Vichy, France, with the injunction never to admit that they were Jewish. With only a knapsack for the two of them and without any identification documents, they started out. They went through harrowing experiences and narrow escapes, but they held on to life. To keep body and soul together, they engaged in black-marketeering and devious machinations, and scrounged around for food. One day in Nice they fall into the hands of the Gestapo. . . .

184

Maurice looks at me. He speaks through teeth that he can hardly unclench.

"You going to be all right, Joseph?"

"I'll be all right."

The door in front of us opens. The two women come out. Both of them are crying. I know they haven't been beaten — that makes me feel better.

The women go back downstairs, and we go on waiting. It reminds me of the dentist's office on the *rue* Ramey, when Mama used to take me there after school.

The interpreter appears. This time it's our turn. All three of us go in.

It used to be a hotel room, but the bed isn't there anymore; instead there's a table with an SS man behind it. He's in his forties, with glasses; he seems tired and yawns several times.

He's holding Ferdinand's identity card and looking at it. He says nothing and motions to the interpreter.

"You're Jewish?"

"No."

The interpreter has a childish voice and a Provençal accent. He's certainly from Nice.

"If you aren't a Jew, why do you have a forged identity card?"

I don't look at Ferdinand; I know that if I look at him, I won't be brave when my time comes.

"But . . . that is my identity card."

There's a brief exchange in German. The SS man speaks, and the interpreter translates.

"We can easily find out if you're a Jew or not, so start talking and don't give us any trouble — otherwise you're going to annoy people around here and get yourself a beating. That would be stupid, so let's have the truth right away, and we'll forget the whole thing."

He gives the impression that we need only talk, and everything will be all right — we'll be set free.

"No," says Ferdinand. "I am not Jewish."

There's no need for translation. The SS man gets to his feet, removes his hornrimmed glasses, goes around to the front of his desk, and plants himself squarely before Ferdinand.

A ringing slap on Ferdinand's sickly cheek sets his head wobbling; a second crack sends him reeling back a couple of steps. Tears stream down his face.

"Stop," says Ferdinand.

The SS man waits. The interpreter encourages Ferdinand.

"Go ahead, talk. Where are you from?"

In a voice that can scarcely be heard, Ferdinand speaks.

"I left Poland in 1940. My parents were arrested. I went through Switzerland and — "

"Fine. We'll see about all that later. But you do admit that you're a Jew?"

"Yes."

The interpreter goes up to him and gives him a friendly pat on the shoulder.

"There, you see? Don't you think you should have talked sooner? All right, you can go downstairs. Show that to the clerk at the foot of the stairs."

He holds out a green ticket, which Ferdinand takes. I'm soon going to learn what the green ticket means.

"It's your turn now, you two. Are you brothers?"

"Yes, he's Joseph, and I'm Maurice."

"Joseph and Maurice what?"

"Joffo."

"And you're Jews."

This is no question; this guy is stating a fact. I want to help Maurice.

"Oh no, you've got it all wrong."

He's surprised by my vehemence. Maurice doesn't give him a chance to get a word in edgewise.

"No, we aren't Jewish. We're from Algiers. If you want, I can tell you all about it."

He knits up his brows and speaks to the SS man, who now has his glasses on and is looking us over. The German asks us a question. I understand him better and better; it's really very close to Yiddish, but I musn't show him that I understand.

"What were you doing on the *rue de Russie?*"

"We came from New Harvest, the camp of the *Compagnons de France*. We went along with Ferdinand and were waiting for him — that's all. He told us that he was going in to see a pal."

The SS man rolls a pencil between his fingers.

Maurice gains confidence. I can sense that he's in perfect control of himself. He begins to give him our story right away: Papa, a barber in Algiers; the school; the vacation; and then the landing in North Africa that kept us from going back. It all goes like clockwork until — the only thing we hadn't planned.

"And you're Catholic?"

"That's right."

"Then you've been baptized?"

"Yes, we've also made our communion."

"What church?"

Rotten luck! But Maurice's voice is loud and clear, even clearer than before. "La Buffa. In Nice."

The interpreter strokes his belly. "Why not in Algiers?"

"Mama wanted us to make our communion in France; she had a cousin in this part of the country."

He looks at us, writes a few lines in a notebook, and closes it.

"All right, we're going to check and see if everything you've said is true. First, you go for physicals. We're going to see if you've been circumcised."

Maurice doesn't flinch. I try to remain absolutely calm.

The interpreter looks at us. "You understand?"

"No. What does that mean — *circumcised?*"

Both men look at us. Maybe you've gone a little too far, Maurice, a little too far. In a few minutes they may make us pay for that confidence. In any case, our pretty house of cards is about to go tumbling down.

A soldier pushes us up the stairs. They'll find out everything. I don't give a damn — I'll jump from the train while it's moving. They won't take me to Germany.

Then I'm in another room; this one is empty. There isn't any desk — just three men in white smocks.

The oldest one stares when we come in. "Oh, no, we're not staying here all night. I went off duty half an hour ago."

The other two grumble and slip out of their smocks. One of them is German. "What are these two?"

The soldier accompanying us hands him a slip of paper. Meanwhile the two others put on their jackets. The old one reads. He has very black eyebrows that contrast with his iron-gray hair.

"Take off your shorts and drop your underpants."

The two other men are still gabbing; I hear words, street names, the first names of women. They shake hands with the doctor who's going to examine us, and they leave.

The doctor sits on a chair and motions us to come closer. The German who led us in is behind us, near the door. Our backs are to him.

With his right hand, the doctor lifts the shirttail covering Maurice's penis. He says nothing.

Then it's my turn. He looks.

"So you aren't Jewish, eh?"

I pull up my underpants. "No, we aren't Jewish."

He sighs and, without looking at the soldier, who's still waiting, he says, "Don't pay attention to him. He doesn't understand French. We're alone here — you can tell me the truth and it won't go out of this office. You're Jewish."

"No," says Maurice. "Our parents had us operated on when we were little — because we had adhesions; that's all."

He nods. "A phimosis, that's called. Do you know that every guy who comes in here say he had a phimosis in his childhood?"

"It wasn't a — what you said — it was an adhesion."

"Where was the operation performed?"

"In Algiers, in a hospital."

"What hospital?"

"I don't know — we were very small."

He turns to me.

"Yes, Mama came to see me. She brought me candy and a book."

"What book?"

"Robin Hood — it had pictures."

Silence. He leans back in his chair and studies each of us in turn. I don't know what he sees in our eyes, but there's something that makes him try a new tack. With a wave, he has the soldier leave the room.

He walks to the window, looks at the street that's all yellow from the setting sun. His hands toy with the curtains. Slowly he begins to speak.

"My name is Rosen," he says. "Do you know what it means when your name is Rosen?"

We look at each other. "No."

I add politely, "No, doctor."

He comes near and places both his hands on my shoulders.

"Well, it just means that I'm Jewish."

He gives us a chance to take in this fact and, after glancing at the door, adds, "It also means that you can talk with me."

I am still silent, but Maurice reacts quickly.

"All right," he says. "You're Jewish — but *we aren't!*"

The doctor doesn't answer. He walks to the coatrack, fishes around in his jacket pocket, takes out a cigarette, and lights it. He goes on studying us through the smoke.

It's impossible to guess what's going through the man's mind. All of a sudden as if he were talking to himself, he murmurs, "Well done!" The door opens, and there in the doorway stands the SS man with the glasses who interrogated us. He asks one brief question. I catch only a single word of the doctor's reply, but it's the one that counts; it has saved our lives. "*Das ist chirurgisch gemacht worden*" (This was a surgical operation).

From *A Bag Full of Marbles* by Joseph Joffo, Boston: Houghton Mifflin, 1974, pp. 194-300.

MARGO BLEACHES HER HAIR BLOND

Bitter Herbs is the appropriate title of a book written by a young Dutch Jewish girl who dyed her hair blond, as did her brother, in order to "pass" as Christian. Bitter herbs — usually horseradish — are eaten by Jews on the two Seder nights of Passover, the holiday of redemption from slavery in Egypt.

For the first few days I reproached myself for leaving my father and mother in the lurch. I felt that it would have been better if I had stayed with them. Without stopping to think, I had run out through the garden gate, and it never entered my head to consider turning back until I stood in front of the house where my brother had gone into hiding some days before. But at that moment the church clock struck the hour after which no one was allowed to be out of doors, so I rang the bell.

"You did right," said Dave. "You couldn't have done anything else."

"But they'll wonder where I've got to," I said. "They'll start worrying about me."

"They'll understand," said Dave. "And they'll be glad you bolted."

I thought of the Hollandsche Schouwburg, the former Jewish theater, to which all our people were taken to begin with. "If I go and stand near the Schouwburg, and wait till they come out, perhaps they'll see me and know I'm safe," I suggested.

But Dave said I wasn't to do it. He found it far too risky.

From neighbors in Sarphatistraat we heard that, since my flight, someone had been keeping an eye on our house the whole time. As they had my identity card, they knew what I looked like, and because all my clothes were still in the house, they thought I might very likely come to fetch them.

Before I ventured out into the street again I underwent a metamorphosis. Lottie bleached my hair.

I sat in front of the mirror with a sheet wrapped round me while she brushed a mixture of hydrogen peroxide and ammonia into my hair with a toothbrush. It bit into my scalp and made my eyes smart, so that I did nothing but blink, like a child that wants to keep back its tears. I tried to watch my hair changing color in the mirror. But all I saw was the white lather of the stinging, hissing peroxide. After washing and drying, I was a redhead. But Lottie assured me that it would only take a few more such bleachings to turn my hair quite blond. I depilated my eyebrows until all that was left of them were thin, hardly visible streaks. There was no longer anything dark about my appearance. As I have blue eyes, bleached hair suited me better than it did Lottie. She had dark brown, almost black eyes, with long, bluish-black lashes. Fair hair looked unnatural on her.

At first we thought that nothing could happen to us now. We had other identity cards, and it was just as if we were "ordinary" people. But all the same, we did not feel safe in the street. When we saw a policeman we expected him to make straight for us, and it seemed as though every passerby turned to look at us and knew what we were.

Finally, Mrs. K saw it too. She was the woman from whom my brother had rented a room, under his assumed name. "Do you people like bleached hair so much?" she asked, when she saw that mine was one color one day and a different color the next.

"We love it," I said. "And we've got such good stuff for doing it with. It's not in the least harmful."

Perhaps Mr. K would not have taken any further notice if Dave had not started to do it too. He emptied the entire bottle of peroxide over his head. It was not very wise of him because it is quite impossible for a man to keep it up, and after a few weeks he would have begun to look extremely odd.

"Are you starting as well?" Mrs. K observed, with feigned friendliness.

"My husband poured my peroxide on his hair in mistake for his own lotion," Lottie explained.

Mrs. K laughed heartily. "I thought so," she said.

That day she invited us to have a cup of tea with her in her sitting room. A friend of hers was coming, and it would make such a nice, pleasant evening if we were there as well. Later it appeared that her guest, a flabby fat man with cunning little eyes, had been called upon to give his verdict on us and confirm her suspicions.

When we were back in our room again, she put her head round the door. "I think it would be better if you left early tomorrow morning," she said. The man was putting his coat on in the hall. He went down the stairs, whistling.

"I know an address in Utrecht," said Dave. "They'll certainly put us up there."

"It's to be hoped they will," said Lottie, "for if they don't, where else can we go?"

"There are still enough doors open to us," Dave said thoughtfully.

I could not help thinking about those doors when I lay in bed that night and could not get to sleep. I thought of the door which I always had to open on the night of the Passover, to show the weary stranger that he was welcome and could sit down at table with us. Every year I hoped that someone would come in;

but no one ever did. And I thought of the question which I, as last-born, had to ask, " *Manishtanno, halailo, hazay.* Why is this night unlike all other nights, and why do we eat unleavened bread and bitter herbs . . .?''

Then my father would chant the story of the Exodus from Egypt, and we ate of the unleavened bread and the bitter herbs, in order that we should taste again of that Exodus — from year to year, forever and ever.

From *Bitter Herbs,* by Margo Minca, trans. from the Dutch by Roy Edwards, New York: Oxford University Press, 1960, pp. 78-82.

AN OLD CHRISTIAN WOMAN HIDES A FRIEND

Two old gentile women saved the life of the hunted Donia Rosen when her western Ukrainian village was overrun in April 1942 — Olina and Parashka. Both were simple, humane Ukrainian peasants. Donia dedicated her book to Olina, who endangered her life more than once to save her. It must be noted, however, that an important factor in Donia's survival was the friendly forest where she wandered about, finding occasional shelter.

I fell asleep and had a sweet repose full of dreams of a brighter future. Suddenly, I heard footsteps crunching the snow. There was a noise and a loud bang on the door. At first I thought it was the sound of the wind, and then there was another knock.

"Olina, we are lost!" I said.

"Be still and don't budge from your place," replied Olina and motioned me with her hand not to move. There was another knock.

"Who is banging there, and doesn't let us sleep?" said Olina in a loud voice.

"The police," a rough voice came from behind the door.

Olina opened the door. On the doorstep stood one German and two local Ukrainians. "A plague on you, you murderers, you mischief-makers. Why hasn't the earth swallowed you? Why were you not struck by a bolt of lightning?"

Outside the snow was falling softly, and the wind was howling. What was I to do? Where was I to run to? I sprinted and hid under the bed. I squeezed myself into a ball and I clung to the wall. I thought to myself: If I had stayed outside a bit longer, I would have avoided this calamity. Now, everything is lost. I was totally discouraged. I accepted my fate and helplessly awaited the bitter end. The murderers stood on the threshold, and Olina blocked their way. This Olina who was endangering herself because of me, stood before them like a heroine, confident and unafraid. I almost felt ashamed before her. Michoelo Shinkarok spoke to her in a tone that was almost gentle.

"As you know, Olina, there are rumors in our village that Jews are hiding out here. It is our duty to find them and hand them over to the authorities. It is a disgrace for us that in our midst there should still be those who harbor Jews. Your house is on the outskirts of the village and close to the forest. It is a convenient hiding place. We are, therefore, turning to you. If there is anyone hiding here, turn him over to us. I assure you that if you will do so of your own free will, you will come to no harm.''

''You may look all you like; I am not harboring anyone here,'' answered Olina. She spoke with such courage that all fear left me. I felt strong and able to continue the struggle. I tried to contract my limbs even more than before and clung more closely to the wall.

''Well, you say there are no Jews here?''

''We will check and find out.''

A flood of memories rushed into my head at this moment: Grandfather and his last plea, ''I beg of you, let me live''; Salka, screaming, ''Mother, I want to live!''; my aunt in her wounds and my grandmother with the expression of doom on her face. The entire town of Kossow drenched in its own blood stood before me. Not only Kossow but also Stanislawow, Lvov, Lublin, Lodz, Warsaw . . . millions perished. Millions fallen prey to evil and cruelty. I thought to myself: Why did I not go into the flowers with my grandmother? Werner's words were still ringing in my ears: ''My wife murdered, my children murdered, tomorrow I will be no more — none of us will live through this.''

''Turn on the light!'' one of them shouted to Olina.

''I am poor,'' she answered. ''I don't have a candle or an oil lamp in the house.''

''How do you live in the darkness?''

''As you see, this is how I live.'' They started to search. They went up to the attic and poked around, searching thoroughly. Then they moved into the small corridor and looked with the aid of a weak flashlight whose battery was almost gone. A small yellow spot of light moved through the house from one place to another. They looked into the stove, under the stove, on the bench, and beneath the bench. They were almost at the bed; I already saw them, the death devils. They must have been deaf not to have heard the pounding of my heart, the mute outcries of my agony. The light came closer to me. The murderer bent down to look under the bed. I clung to the wall fiercely. I wanted to flatten my body completely, to shrink, to become part of the wall. I clenched my fists. The little blotch of light was only centimeters away from me. I contracted my leg even more, but the light paused for a moment in that spot and then moved to the other side.

''It's true; there is no one here,'' one of them said. ''And I was certain we would find someone.''

They went away. I remained dazed for a long time. I cannot tell how long it took before I came to myself.

The snow continued to fall outside, and the wind continued to howl. I kissed the hands of Olina and cried and cried. I cried for joy and for sorrow at my lot. I cried without really knowing why. Olina pressed me to her breast and said: ''We will not surrender! Under no circumstances will we give in. My courage is braced in this fight. As long as I live, you will live. Only now do I feel that my life has value, only now have I become convinced that I am needed by someone, that I live for someone, that I fight for something. You have freed me from a terrible feeling of loneliness, from aimlessness, from melancholy. Don't fear for me. Let me be a sister and a friend in your need. I want to share your horrible plight to the end. I don't fear death in the struggle I have chosen. I fear death of shame and dishonor. I don't want to die behind the fence of strange people, as an undesirable vagrant of no use to anyone. Tough luck has bound us together, you and me, and I cannot visualize a life of my own without you.'' Olina burst into tears. I knew that such devotion is rare and cannot be measured in gold.

> From *The Forest, My Friend*, by Donia Rosen. Quoted in *Flame and Fury*, compiled by Yaacov Shilhav, edited by Sara Feinstein, published by Jewish Education Committee Press, 1962, pp. 58-62. Trans. by David Kuselewitz.

WINTER IN THE FOREST

We were about to entrust the children[1] to peasants, but the children would not leave their mother. It was January 1943, freezing cold, and the snow half a meter high. At midnight we decided to escape, and we set out, without a crumb of bread, for the village of Zaluzhe, five kilometers from our town of Lyubatchow[2] where a Pole we knew made his home. We hid in his loft without his knowledge. Here we parted. I remained there with the children, and my husband set out for the forest.

On the third day they swooped down on the Jews from Lyubatchow who had sought shelter here. The local peasants betrayed them. All those Jews were rounded up in the *Geminah,* and from there the SS troopers took them to a field where animal carcasses were usually buried, shot them, and buried them. I remember the names of some of the Ukrainians: Stephan Holub, the *Woyt* [village elder], Mosa . . .

After three days the proprietor turned me out of the house. With my small children, I set out in freezing weather for a village where my little girl, aged ten, served a peasant family as a shepherdess. We trudged along frozen rivers and forests, and on reaching our destination the peasant woman refused to admit us, for fear of her neighbors. That night we walked nine kilometers to the village of Dachnow. There, too, no one would admit us. The children were chilled to the bone and hungry, and their cries seemed to touch no one's heart. Then we went to the small forest four kilometers for Lyubatchow, and there I saw the bloody "action" against the Lyubatchow Jews. Four Ukrainians and Germans shot at the Jews, who were lined up in rows. Since only one bullet was allotted per person many [wounded] Jews lay in the graves for hours, or moved about in the field until they froze to death.

Then peasants came with axes and chopped off feet which wore high boots, or fingers with gold rings on them. The executions went on for ten weeks. Day after day the neighboring Ukrainians and Poles would search out bunkers, from which Jews would be dragged. We remained three days in the woods.

At night I ventured out to buy bread for the children. Later, we would hide in stables, granaries, haystacks and so on, without the knowledge of their propri-

[1]Three children, ages five, ten, and eleven.
[2]Forty kilometers from Rowa Ruska, not far from the Belsen death camp.

etors. But this could not go on, and we returned to the forest. We were seen by the Germans and Ukrainians who happened to be hunting rabbits. They started to shout, *"Jude! Jude!"* — but the Germans were more anxious to catch rabbits just then.

It was twelve days after the "action." My ten-year-old daughter said to me, "Mother, why do you suffer so much on our account? Just leave us here, and try to save yourself." She had heard the peasants remark occasionally that they would hide me alone, but feared to hide the children.

"Mother," my little girl would say, "pray to God that we may have an easy death, and let us go by ourselves."

At last, one woman took pity on us and let us stay for the night. Early in the morning she told us to leave. In the courtyard we sought shelter in a chicken coop, from which we had been removed because of the severe cold. As we lay there, huddled, my daughter insisted on visiting a friendly peasant woman, merely to ask her for an easy death. The peasant gave her food and let her warm up. A Ukrainian boy who happened to be in the house followed her out and tried to make her disclose our hideout. She would not, and he let her go. She proceeded along a devious, circuitous route, unaware that he trailed her at a distance. She got to the hideout. I had left a few minutes earlier in search of food, and I was admitted to a peasant home. While there, I saw through a window the Ukrainian boy beating my child, choking her, torturing her, and dragging her to headquarters for interrogation about my whereabouts.

Later on, the Ukrainian guards reiterated her words: "Four lives must not perish on account of one. My life is lost anyhow." She pleaded for mercy, since she had not harmed anyone. She was taken to the small forest (I observed it from a distance). I knew she was about to be executed. She pleaded with the Ukrainians, "My blood will not let you rest." But in vain. She had to wait for a transport of two hundred Jews from Lyubatchow. She then asked to be shot, and her request was granted.

I am a simple Jewish woman and cannot describe what I endured while my innocent child was being killed.

From January 13 until February 11, my little son and I wandered through the villages, sleeping in stables without the peasants' permission. Our feet were frostbitten. When I would ask my child, "Are you hungry, Yankele?" he would answer, "Why do you ask, Mother? Are you going to help me?" I was desperate. The children could not endure any more, and pleaded for death.

On a pitch-black night, I walked nine kilometers to a peasant, to whom I had entrusted my pitiful belongings. He chased me out. (He was eventually killed by the Germans.)

When I was about to surrender to the Germans, a kindly peasant woman let us stay in her granary, under the hay. She fed us soup. We did not remove our shoes for four weeks. My elder son was troubled by a frostbitten, swollen leg, and his high boot had to be cut down. In the process I cut off the heel of his foot. He did not cry, and I was too benumbed. I had neither medication nor bandages, so I used my only undershirt. There was considerable bleeding, but luckily no serious infection. Later, I wrapped his ailing foot with straw and hay, and, carrying the little one, we trudged from one village to another.

The youngest, a child of five years, was suffering from bruised, frostbitten toes that were wrapped in rags. After considerable pleading I found a peasant woman who agreed to take the child, for the few gold coins I had cached underground. The child was kept hidden in the granary.

From *Winter in the Forest* by Feiga Kammer, in *Anthology of the Holocaust,* op. cit., pp. 155-157. Trans. from the Yiddish by Moishe Spiegel.

"IF ONLY I COULD BE A LITTLE BUG!"

When the Nazi invasion began, nine-year-old Yankel Kuperblum of Lublin came home one day to find his entire family gone. He never saw them again. Determined to live, he passed as a Catholic, assumed a Polish name, and wandered about the villages and farms, filling odd jobs as shepherd, farmworker, and handyman. He forgot his native Yiddish tongue, his Jewish faith and observances. In 1948, when he was fifteen, he emigrated to Canada. At the time he wrote his book, he was engaged by the Canadian Broadcasting Corporation as scriptwriter for radio and television production.

The following day was sunny and warm; the sky was clear, and the sun covered the village and its surrounding fields with bright rays of light.

After breakfast I started to take the cows to pasture, but Mrs. Paizak stopped me. That morning a neighbor had brought news that the soldiers had spent the night in the village, searching and questioning. They had found many Russians in hiding. And they had killed many others in the fields who were trying to escape.

Maybe they'll return and search our farm again. Where will I hide this time? And Sasha, where is Sasha now? Is he still alive? Or perhaps . . . And the others? Will I ever hear their songs again?

As I sat at the table I couldn't hear the conversation around me, for my mind was far away. Weeks and months have passed, and Moishe has not shown up. What has become of him? And Sasha, my friend Sasha. Is it possible that he is . . . No! I'd better not think of it.

My father, God only knows of his destiny. And my mother, Josel and my Uncle Shepsel: they are lost. But why am I so sure? I should not write them off the face of the earth so easily. There's still hope. I've got to have hope.

I looked up at Ivan, and now I noticed how pale he was. He sat quietly on the couch, listening to consoling words from Genia. Does Ivan feel the same way I do? Perhaps he does. I caught Stashek's gaze and felt uneasy. His eyes were telling me that I was in the way.

Suddenly there was a knock on the door. We froze to out seats and looked at each other. There was nowhere to run and hide now. Ivan pulled a revolver out of his pocket and stationed himself behind the door.

How daring! Could I do that? I wish I could.

He motioned with his hand for Mrs. Paizak to open the door.

Stashek sat on the bed, trembling with fear, his eyes on the gun. Genia covered her mouth with her hands to prevent herself from screaming.

The scene reminded me of a cowboy tale told to me by my Uncle Shepsel, but somehow it wasn't the same. The sense of excitement and adventure was missing, and instead of being thrilled I was frightened.

The knock was repeated, now a little louder. Mrs. Paizak made her way to the door and with quivering hands opened it.

I expected to see a German soldier or a Brownshirt, a gun pointed in our direction, and his eyes suspicously looking at me, his finger pointing accusingly, his voice saying, "You're a Jew!"

"No!"

"We'll soon find out, pull your pants down," and at that moment Ivan would shoot him from behind. The soldier would fall, his blood gushing like water from a fountain. And then he would . . .

The door opened, and framed in the doorway stood a little man with a heavy mustache and frightened face with large bulging eyes. He carried a straw hat pressed to his chest. With a handkerchief, he wiped the sweat from his almost bald head and perspiring face, and in a stuttering voice he greeted Mrs. Paizak who stood in front of him, blocking his way.

"I've been sent by the sheriff." He stopped, cleared his throat, and asked for a glass of water. Genia handed him the water; he swallowed it in one gulp, and then he stuttered, "You'll all come to the center of the village today at noon, outside the sheriff's home."

"Why? What did we do?" asked Mrs. Paizak.

"The whole village has to come. There's going to be a big meeting or something. It's an order from *them*."

"All right, we'll be there," said Mrs. Paizak.

"Don't forget now, every one of you. After twelve they'll be searching all the farms, and whoever is found will be shot on the spot." He departed, running like a wild rabbit across the fields to the next farm.

Mrs. Paizak shut the door, Ivan hid his revolver, Stashek sighed with relief, Genia hugged Ivan, and I began to worry anew as to where I would fit into the day's proceedings.

It was immediately decided that Ivan would hide in the same place, and the rest of us would go to the meeting at the appointed time.

Ivan slid into his dugout, and again we piled the potatoes on top of the boards. Stashek washed and dressed for the occasion as if he was going to a wedding.

Solemnly, as if marching behind a coffin at a funeral, we left the courtyard. When we reached the main road of the village we could see other farmers leaving their homes, all walking in the same direction. Unexpectedly, Mrs. Paizak stopped and threw her arms around me.

"Kubush,[1] I don't think it would be safe for you there. Go and hide somewhere, my child."

"But where?" I asked, my heart beginning to pound again.

"I don't know, just hide anywhere you can. Save yourself. Now run

[1]Kuperblum's pet name.

quickly.'' She turned and walked away, Genia and Stashek following her.

I stood for a moment looking at their backs, feeling abandoned. I turned in the direction of the nearby forest and began to run towards it. I stopped. The forest would be the first place they would comb for partisans. I thought of the fields and wanted to run there, but again I decided against it. Where, then? I looked around, and there was not a soul to be seen now.

"I have to get off the open road," I said out loud, and started towards the farm.

In the courtyard chickens were cackling and picking grain from the earth. How I envied them; they didn't have to hide or run. Perhaps I could hide in the chicken house. I ran in there. The place was small and covered with chicken droppings, and it offered no concealment. I left and ran into the house.

I studied the room, thinking of hiding under the bed, but that was too obvious a place. I looked at the ceiling, and my eyes rested on the trapdoor leading to the attic. With the help of a ladder I made my way into it.

I have never been there before, and now I forgot my reason for venturing there, for so many things caught my eye and I examined them with some satisfaction. Then I remembered. Perhaps I should hide here, or perhaps there, under the pile of grain. Inside this trunk . . . Yes, that's a good idea, I'll climb inside it. I closed the lid on top of me. It was dark; a terrible moldy odor filled my lungs, but I was safe.

Then I remembered the ladder. How am I to get rid of it? It's no good, I'll have to abandon the trunk and the attic, and look somewhere else.

Quickly I climbed down, left the house, and entered the barn. Upon seeing me, the cows mooed as if reminding me that I had neglected to take them to pasture. Perhaps I could hide in the hay. That's an idea, I'll bury myself in the hay. But what if they search the barn or set it on fire?

I looked at the piled potatoes, and now I envied Ivan. He was safe under there, protected in that hole. No, the barn will not do, I'll have to find a place they'll never think of searching.

But I can't waste much more time; they may be on their way this very minute. Perhaps they've entered the courtyard now.

I left the barn, and as I shut the door behind me, I saw my hiding place staring at me. On the other side of the courtyard stood the cooler. It was a hole dug in the ground, covered by a straw roof, and it had a small opening in the front. From the outside, the cooler resembled a small house with only the roof showing, and its walls were deep in the ground. In the summer the cooler was used to keep milk, cheese, and butter fresh, but its main purpose was as a storage place for potatoes during the winter. Now it was empty.

I walked over to it, scanned the area around me to make sure I was alone, and then I slid through the opening and jumped in. I squatted down in a corner.

The ground was cold and damp and the air had a stagnant odor. I looked on the earth beneath my feet, gazed at the earthen walls around me, and saw hundreds of minute bugs and insects busily engaged in their own little world. I envied them, for they were free to do as they pleased and didn't have to hide.

If only I could be a little bug! A small ugly insect, in fact anything at all but a Jew. If only I could be a cow, a horse, a bird in the trees, or a frog in the pond. Anything at all. I'd have a better chance of surviving.

Why did God create Jews anyway? There seems to be no reason for our existence. My mind wandered from one thought to another as I squatted in the corner, not daring to move at all, not even to brush off a fly when it landed on my nose. I was glued to the earth.

From the outside I could hear the birds chirp and sing sweetly; the crows cawed in the fields; the cows mooed now and then; and the rooster gave out with a loud cock-a-doodle-doo. Periodically I heard the bark of a dog somewhere in the distance, but otherwise it was quiet.

Several hours later I heard footsteps approaching from the distance. Perhaps I'm only imagining them, or perhaps the Paizaks have returned.

I waited and listened, but didn't move. The footsteps came closer and closer, and then I heard voices, German voices. Two soldiers were conversing. Their every step now was like a shot, and I could visualize them, although I couldn't see them.

The barn door opened. Silence. Then I heard their voices again. The door to the house opened . . . a few moments of silence . . . footsteps running up the ladder . . . some other sound . . . then their voices, again coming from the courtyard. The door to the chicken house opened, more conversation . . . laughter . . . more footsteps . . . now far away . . . now closer . . . closer . . . closer . . . and now the shadow of a soldier fell into my hiding place and onto one of the walls as he bent down, looking in.

I could hear him breathing. Does he see me? He must see me, and even if he doesn't, he must hear my heart pounding. It sounded like a loud drum. The shadow stayed there, moving only slightly. What is he waiting for? Why doesn't he order me to come out? Perhaps he's afraid. Perhaps he doesn't hear my heart beating after all. Wait a minute, I know what he's up to: he won't order me out, he'll simply throw a grenade in and blow up the whole structure and me with it. If that's what he intends to do, then I'll show him. Once the grenade lands, I'll grab it and throw it right back at him and blow him up with his own weapon. I've got to keep my eyes open for the grenade. I'll have to work fast.

Oh, God, what will I do? I have to sneeze. Will I be able to repress it? I could feel it coming. Why doesn't he throw the grenade and be over with it?

I now heard the other voice. "Something there?"

"Just bugs. It's amazing how well organized they are!" came the reply.

"All right then, let's get to the next farm."

The shadow straightened itself and disappeared. I heard footsteps moving away, and then silence. I now swallowed my sneeze.

Why did he leave? He must have sensed someone was here. Perhaps he thought I was a Russian partisan and was as much frightened of me as I was of him. No, they haven't left; they're still there. They know there's someone in here. It's a trap. They want me to come out into the open. Someone is at the side of the entrance, waiting, waiting for me to stick my head out. I have to deceive them to the end. I was not going to move at all, though by now my knees were giving way and and felt as if they would break.

In time I couldn't feel them at all, as if they had been disconnected from the rest of my body. I was numb. My eyes were wide open, staring blankly at the earthen wall. Perhaps the German has thrown the grenade into the cooler and I am now dead, that's why I can't feel my legs. If so, then there isn't much reason to fear death; it's quite sudden and painless. Alive or dead, I continued to stay in the same postion and lost all sense of time and sound. I heard nothing, saw nothing, and eventually thought of nothing.

Hours later I realized I was being called. "Kubush! Kubush! Where are you?" came Genia's pleading voice. "Come out, everything is all right now." Then I heard Mrs. Paizak's voice calling me, but still I didn't answer, and then I heard Genia sobbing. "They found him, Mamma, they've found him! He's probably dead by now." And she cried hysterically.

"So they found him," Stashek said.

I tried to stand up, but couldn't. My legs wouldn't straighten. I crawled over to the opening, looked out, and saw that night had fallen.

"Here he is," cried Genia upon seeing me, and ran towards me and embraced me. "Holy Mother, Kubush is alive!"

Mrs. Paizak's eyes were wet, Ivan was drinking water by the well, and Stashek looked at me with angry eyes and said, "Afraid, eh? I bet you shit in your pants." And he laughed, but no one laughed with him.

At the supper table, Mrs. Paizak recounted what had taken place outside the sheriff's house. As she was telling the story, her eyes would fill with tears; she'd wipe them with her sleeve, continue the sad tale, and then she'd cry again. Genia begged her to stop, but she insisted on telling. what her eyes had witnessed that day.

When the villagers were gathered in the center of the village, A Ukrainian officer delivered a speech about the danger of hiding Russian escapees. The German authorities were lenient, he said, but if the inhabitants of the village continued to give refuge to these bandits, the whole village and its occupants would be bombed and obliterated from the face of the earth. He also added that in the two days of operation, they had found and killed dozens of Russians.

From *Child of the Holocaust* by Jack Kuper, pub. by the New American Library, 1980, pp. 50-57.

11.

PHYSICAL RESISTANCE
AND VITALITY

The resistance of children and youth to Nazi inhumanity was multifaceted. It was evinced on the spiritual plane during the first year of the Nazi occupation. In the larger cities children attended schools and were avid readers of books which they borrowed from the ghetto libraries. On the physical level it was manifested when children escaped to the Aryan side of the ghetto and set themselves up as peddlers and venders. They smuggled food and other necessities of life into the ghetto from the other side of the wall. When the fate of the ghetto dwellers was doomed, they played significant roles as forest partisans, as described later.

Teenagers were among the first to foresee the diabolical plans of the Germans to liquidate the ghetto and kill its inhabitants. The young people underwent mental and spiritual agonies as they tried to convince their near and dear ones to escape by whatever means possible. They spared no pains to dissuade the members of the Jewish Community Councils who had been beguiled by the Germans to cooperate, with the promise that if they did so, a remnant would survive but otherwise all would be annihilated.

Young people raised funds, by threats if necessary, in order to purchase arms and ammunition to resist and fight the enemy. They were the vanguard of the ghetto inmates who stole out of the ghetto walls to join the forest partisans. Once in the forests, they wrote a glorious chapter in maintaining and protecting their kith and kin. Their tenacity to live, their courage in partisan warfare have earned a number of them immortality in the annals of the Resistance movement.

In its wider implications, Resistance is alluded to in various chapters of this book. In the selections which follow we cover its salient manifestations.

A BOY GROWS UP IN AUSCHWITZ

During my childhood I heard much about the First World War and the experiences of different people during the war. A child's imagination could not grasp it all. But now that so much has happened to me, I can understand the acute suffering of the victims who went through the torment and inferno of those years.

I was born on May 15, 1927, in the city of Prujani, Poland. I attended the sixth grade of the Tarbut school (a Hebraic and nationalistic-oriented school system). After Poland fell, the Red Army moved in and I continued with my studies. When the Germans invaded Russia I was at a children's camp. I fled with the Red Army to Russia but soon we all fell into the hands of the invaders, altogether 10,000 men. We slept under the open sky in a field surrounded by barbed wire. We got nothing to eat. Rumor had it that the Germans were waiting for more prisoners of war before killing us. "We do not bother with only 10,000 prisoners," they said. We could not bear the hunger. By chance a corps of cavalry passed by and left a sick horse behind them. At night we dragged the animal into our camp, and everyone who had a knife cut a slice of raw meat from the still-living carcass and ate it right then and there. As I observed what was happening around me, I thought to myself: What have I to lose? — so I decided to escape.

On a rainy, dark night I slipped through the wire and fled. I had hardly any strength, but the thought that I was escaping inevitable death gave me will and the stamina. During the day I hid in the forest and only at night continued my journey. My home town was only about 150 kilometers away.

Prujani had been turned into a hemmed-in ghetto. I learned that the police had been looking for me. The *Judenrat* did not record my return to the ghetto. If they had, the Gestapo would have hanged me in the marketplace.

All that winter I hid in my house. When spring came, I stole out of the ghetto and joined the partisans. They at first refused to accept me because I had no weapons. Nevertheless I remained with them because I spoke German. Our battalion was few in numbers and did not have sufficient arms. However, in the course of time we grew in manpower and became better armed.

The Germans feared us, and when they were on the move they traveled in bands. This did not save them from us, for we planted land mines. We captured carloads of food which they had stolen from the peasants to transport to Germany. We kept a portion for our needs, and the rest we brought to the Jews in the ghetto. We splashed benzine on their trucks and burned them.

It happened after one of our raids that twelve automobiles carrying German military personnel ringed our part of the forest and opened fire. They were afraid to engage us within the forest. The battle lasted all afternoon, and in the evening they returned to their base.

During the battle I was wounded in my left leg. The wound healed, and I soon returned to take part in attacking the enemy.

The ghetto was surrounded by the police. We learned that other ghettos in the area were being liquidated one by one. Jews were taken to the nearby forests and killed or were transported to various camps. The majority of the Jews refused to believe us when we told them that they would be liquidated. They were inclined to believe the Germans, who told them that they would be transported to labor camps in Germany. Thus our people were being exterminated in the fire chambers of Auschwitz, Treblinka, Maidanek, and other death camps. Only a few heeded our forewarnings, and it was they who ultimately survived.

Our situation worsened daily. News reached us about the total liquidation of the ghettos of Bialystok, Grodno, and other neighboring Jewish settlements. It was clear to us that Prujani would be next. We tried to get out as many Jews as possible, but they would not listen to our pleas. They denounced us as bandits and insisted that we would bring down disaster on them. Their end came all too soon.

I was caught in the dragnet. It happened one night while I was in the ghetto, that I was caught by the Gestapo. They were going to shoot me, but as we say in Yiddish, "my good luck lasted longer than the years I was destined to live." The town Jews redeemed me, and I was put under arrest in the ghetto prison.

On January 25, 1943, I was packed like a herring in a barrel, together with 2500 Jews of Prujani, and transported to Auschwitz. In the ghetto there had been 12,000 Jews, who were transported in four shipments.

In every car there were 150 Jews, loaded down with baggage. Many still refused to believe that this was their last journey. They were envious of those who took larger bundles along with them. With me were my parents and four little brothers, the youngest one and a half years old. We were so pressed together that those standing could not sit down and those sitting could not stand up. No one gave thought to food — only to water. Old and young thirsted for a drop of water. But the cars were sealed airtight and the small window openings were screened with barbed wire.

I managed to thrust a little pan through a hole in the window to snatch a handful of snow. The German guard who sat on the roof of the car detected what I was doing and took a potshot through the hole in the window. Fortunately no one was hurt, although in other cars where this happened, many were killed.

Near Chestnechov I wanted to jump out through the window. I had already torn out the wires, but my mother held me back. She said I would face certain death. Many jumped and were killed. One fell on the track and the train cut off his legs, and the German guards shot him. Nevertheless there were hardy souls who chanced escape and preferred death by shooting to the fire chamber that awaited them.

Even though it was deep winter, the heat in the train was unbearable. There wasn't enough air to breathe. People fainted from lack of air and water. The infants suffered most of all. They wept and cried out without stopping, "Water, water." Some mothers gave them urine to drink, which intensified their thirst.

I could not bear the scenes around me. My overpowering desire was to jump out, but Mother held on to me with all her strength. "If we die, let us all die together," she cried. I did not argue with her. I knew that these were our final hours together. To shut out the screaming of the infants, I stuffed my ears.

As we drew near Cracow, I succeeded in getting a handful of snow. Never shall I forget what happened the moment I drew my hand in. I gave a few pinches of snow to my youngest brother. Near me stood my other three brothers, their eyes faint with longing for a lick. But I drew back. Near me stood a woman, half alive, with a ten-month-old infant in her arms. I gave her the remaining pinch of snow. Even though my heart was hard as stone, tears began to flow down my face. My younger brother looked at me, broke out in tears, hugged me, and in a sobbing voice said, "I don't want to drink." I kissed him, and both of us broke out in sobs. When I think of these moments now, I break into sobs again.

After traveling three days and nights, we came to Auschwitz. The air was thick with a smell of burning flesh and bones. All knew now what was in store for them. Suddenly the doors were flung open, and glaring searchlights blinded our eyes. We had been in the dark for seventy-two hours and were temporarily blinded. A hail of blows greeted us. Confusion reigned; children cried; old folks groaned painfully. Above the cries was heard the yell of the guards: "Cursed Jews, get down!" We began to jump down. I jumped first in order to take from my mother my infant brother, whom she had held in her arms during the long trip. She handed the child to me. I retreated one step, and a German threw my mother to the ground. I ran to raise her up, but I was struck by a club and started to bleed profusely. Those who had breathed their last or were in a dead faint were left in the cars.

Around us pandemonium reigned. People were beaten right and left. In the bedlam the voices of the German guards were heard: "Men to the right, women to the left, children and old folks to the side." The latter were thrown into trucks. SS guards stepped on them with their boots to make room for more victims.

All the trucks drove off in the direction of the tall chimneys, which spewed forth fire, smoke, and stench. Young mothers who refused to separate from their children were loaded on the trucks and led to death with their children.

I stood stunned and paralyzed. I had not eaten for three days and nights; blood spurted from my head. In one moment I lost all my dear ones, except my father, with whom I was taken to the camp. We had not been given a moment to part from our beloved ones, to kiss them good-bye. All this happened in the blink of an eye. . . .

After finishing with the children, the murderers turned to us. Each of us had to pass before the doctor (Mengele?) in whose hands rested our fate. Those who were sent to the right were to be spared to live for a while; to the left meant immediate death. . . . During those fearful moments things began to quiet down. Of the 2500 arrivals, only 150 males and 150 females were left standing. The rest went up in flames.

We were brought into the camp. I could not stop asking myself: "Who is better off? My father and I, who are still living, or my mother and four brothers, who are on their way to the fires?" All of us behaved like wild beasts, each one trying to save his skin, if only for a little while.

I don't know what happened to my mother and brothers. I am certain that Mother would not have left them and that they all went together to their death.

As I write these lines I live through the experiences over and over again. I hear the cries of the children and the aged. That night is etched deep in my mind.

We approached the gates of Birkenau. I could see immediately that escape was impossible. It was surrounded by an electrified double barbed-wire fence, with a stockade every fifty meters on which were posted two SS guards with machine guns. In addition, the camp was lit up through the night by powerful searchlights. We realized that escape was hopeless, and many of us prayed that we would not be subjected to torture before our inevitable death.

We were admitted to barrack 20. There we went through a careful examination, and everything we possessed was taken away. Indeed, there was nothing much they could take from us, for while we had been standing in the square we were told we would be robbed of all we possessed; so we had thrown away our watches, torn up our paper money and trampled on our valuables, which we threw in the snow. Nevertheless there were some who had still tried to save their silver and gold possessions and now were relieved of their valuables.

On the morning of the next day, they led us to the camp's bathing quarters, where we were ordered to shower. The water was ice-cold. They forced us to stay under the shower for fifteen minutes. Then they drove us out, wet and nude, onto the snow outside. They did not give us back our clothing. In exchange they threw at us tattered shirts, pants, an outer garment, and wooden clogs. Then they took us to another part of the camp, where they tatooed our forearms. My number was 98728.

On the very first day at camp many of my acquaintances died from hunger, thirst, and the severe cold. We had not eaten a morsel of food or drunk a drop of water for a long time. Next morning, at the roll call, many were already missing. One *kapo* had already killed five of us with his bare hands.

Our *kapo* had been a Polish sailor and a prizefighter. No one could stand up to his blows. And when his victim fell to the ground he would crush him by pressing one foot on his neck and the other on his belly. And when blood began to flow from the mouth of his prey he would beat him on the kidneys and lungs until the victim died. This he repeated often before breakfast.

That first morning we remained standing in the bitter cold until evening — our bodies exposed, our heads shaven, and some of us barefoot. No wonder that only one-third of us survived after the first week.

The meals were very meager. In the morning a liter of coffee was apportioned among fifteen or twenty prisoners. Many a morning when we were punished, the coffee was spilled to the ground and we were compelled to sit on our haunches the whole day. For lunch we got a portion of rotten unpeeled potatoes immersed in a ''soup'' which contained rotten beets. At first I could not, I would not touch it. But I got used to it soon enough. For supper we got a small piece of bread covered with a thin smear of margarine or jelly, or a sausage filled with horsemeat. Usually the orderlies kept back half of our portions, which they later divided among their personal friends.

In the first month we were quartered in the quarantine block, which was located in the gypsy camp. I did not bathe even once. In the morning we used to dip our fingers in the coffee and wipe our eyes. Then we would drink the coffee.

On March 17, 1943, we were moved to nearby Auschwitz, where we went through the same initiation as in Birkenau — shower, change of clothes, beatings. There we were assigned to various jobs. I became a carpenter, and my father, who was an experienced locksmith, became a slave laborer.

I proved to my overseer that I was good at my job, and my diligence saved me from the usual punishment — blows. I was even assigned to work indoors, which benefited my health. I worked there two years, and the superintendent was kind to me. In time he transferred me to do office work. There I contrived to obtain extra food rations. Occasionally I helped my father, uncle, and others to get a little extra food. More than once I was caught perpetrating a "crime" by giving a slice of bread to a girl. The usual punishment was twenty-five lashes, but it was worth the punishment.

I became acquainted with the Underground leaders, to whom I transmitted news and occasionally even German newspapers. Our first meeting took place on November 7, 1943, the day celebrating the Russian revolution. We celebrated by singing the "Internationale" quietly.

Early in 1944 we underwent disinfection for lice on an icy night. We stood naked in the snow until morning. Many dropped dead. One of my close friends died. It happened that he had been in a bunk whose inmates had typhoid fever. The Germans set fire to the bunk, and all were burned.

As a result of that terrible night of disinfection, I fell ill with pneumonia. I did not report to the camp hospital, for that would have meant certain death. I reported to work regularly, despite a high fever. Luckily I recuperated in a fortnight. But as a result of my standing in the cold, the old wound in my leg reopened and discharged pus. I was unprepared for this affliction.

Every so often the SS would make selections and send the sick to the ovens. I was in grave danger. If caught, I would be sent to the crematorium. On the other hand, if I was caught trying to evade the selection, the punishment was also death. Nevertheless I chose the latter course and lived through some twenty-five selections. My foot swelled, and I had to keep my condition secret. I disclosed the secret to Dr. Gordon, who worked in the hospital, and in the dead of the night he would bring me ointments and bandages for my leg. Thus a year passed, until I recovered.

The Allied front drew nearer. Often I heard encouraging radio announcements, which I would transmit to my friends. The Germans continued with their liquidation of transports of Jews which arrived from Poland, France, Hungary, and Greece. The fire chambers were burning day and night.

At that time occurred the rebellion of the *Sonderkommando* (the special corps which was engaged in the burning of the bodies after gassing). They dynamited crematorium #3, broke through the barbed-wire fence, and scattered. They were all caught and killed, but they died heroic deaths. To our great sorrow, there were few heroes like them, and that explains our failure to resist.

On January 12, 1945, our director did not report. I took advantage of his absence and turned on the radio to hear the news from Moscow. Suddenly I learned the good news that the Russian Army was advancing. The news spread like wildfire, but there was no evidence of panic on the part of the SS. On January 14, I had to go into the hospital. On January 16, I was awakened by a loud command, "Get up. Burn all documents!" I was occupied all night in destroying the documents.

In the morning I slipped out of the hospital to visit my father. Camp was in a turmoil, and all were preparing to leave. We all knew that the exodus from camp meant certain death. But to remain in camp also meant death, because the commander had ordered that everything should be blown up.

Hour by hour, the number of those who dared to remain became fewer and fewer. We, the hospital patients, were scheduled to leave with the last transport at ten in the evening. Half an hour before departure my father came to part from me. We embraced and kissed — our last kiss. We were lined up five in a row next to our barrack. My father reported to his barrack. We never saw each other again.

I asked myself: What shall I do? The snow was deep. My leg was swollen. I decided to hide and not join the march. Near me was an iron lid covering the camp sewer. I cleared away the snow and let myself down into the sewer. There I stood all night long, immersed in the stench of the hole. When morning broke, I felt I could not stand any longer on my swollen legs. Calling on my last reserve of strength, I crawled out, crept to my barrack door, and fell into a faint.

When I awoke, I found myself in a bed. Around me were others like me, sick, frozen, half alive. They had come from a sister camp of Auschwitz and had been dumped into our sick ward for final liquidation with the rest of us.

Despite my swollen and frozen leg, I got out of bed and set out in search of food. On the road I met several acquaintances who had found arms. We joined forces and marched to the SS storehouse. We killed the guard and returned laden with food.

Our numbers grew, and so did our arsenal of weapons. We decided to proceed to Birkenau to save the women and children who were still living. On the way we commandeered horses and wagons and transported the survivors to our barracks. We took good care of them until the day of freedom.

Among the women were young Jewish and Ukrainian girls. We set guards to watch over them. At night a number of young Poles tried to break into the barracks where the girls were lodged. There was an exchange of fire resulting in casualties on both sides. But we stood our ground and permitted no one to go into the girls' ward.

The front drew nearer. One evening an SS battalion suddenly appeared. They commanded us to leave the barracks and ringed us around with machine guns. However, suddenly they received orders and scattered in a great hurry, leaving behind some of their machine guns. We stood guard all night — including me, with my swollen leg. . . .

On January 22, 1945, the Red Army entered camp. A number of us captured a few Germans, and that night we shot them on the spot, without obtaining permission from the Russians. It was our revenge for their shedding the blood of our near and dear.

I was brought to a military hospital but refused to lie convalescing in bed. I kept busy serving as an interpreter.

When I returned to Poland, I became a patient at the hospital in Bielsko. On my birthday my left leg was amputated. Now I am working in the children's home in Bielsko. I am an orphan, crippled and lonely. I have an uncle living in Munich and an aunt in Eretz Yisrael. My life's ambition is to emigrate to Eretz Yisrael and help build our homeland. If we want to avoid a recurrence of our incomparable tragedy, we must have a land of our own. I am confident that I shall realize my aim in life, to help build Eretz Yisrael, and in this way fulfill the last wishes of my family and of all who were murdered and burned and whose graves are scattered all over Europe.

A.E.

From *Anoshim v'Eifer* ("Men and Ashes — Auschwitz and Birkenau"), by Yisrael Gutman. Story by Leon Shlofsky, who was twelve when the war began.

DETERMINED TO LIVE

The author, Zvi Goldberg, now living in Israel, is the only survivor of a family of seven. The Goldbergs had moved from Lodz, Poland, to the port city of Gdynia (near Danzig) on the Baltic Sea, where Zvi was born. Gdynia had a large German population and, with the rise of Hitler, experienced a rapid growth of Jew-hatred. As a result, the family moved back to Lodz.

Zvi's story begins on September 1, 1939, when the Germans invaded Poland. At Auschwitz he joined the labor force, where his beautiful singing voice attracted the attention of the kapos (camp police) and the SS. He was frequently invited to entertain the kapos and the SS with songs in Yiddish and German.

SS Captain Dr. Josef Mengele was the chief medical officer at Auschwitz. He was obsessed by a craze to research into the origins of dwarfs, cripples, and twins. He was ruthless and cynical in his treatment of prisoners and in selecting the new arrivals — children, women, and men — to be sent to the gas chambers for immediate death or to the labor battalions, which few survived.

The following is Zvi's story.

When we arrived in Auschwitz we were 30,000 Jewish children. The "actions" (selections of children sent to death) were always on Saturdays, and the number picked was 1500 children weekly. We lived from selection to selection. When I looked at the emptying barracks, I knew my doom was near.

In 1944 new transports began to arrive from Hungary. Among them were men of learning, university professors and artists. When the newcomers saw the scenes around them, they looked despondent. One early morning, at lineup, we saw a number of charred, electrocuted dead bodies hanging on the barbed-wire fence. The Germans left them hanging through the day to serve as a lesson. I shuddered when I looked at them. I thought to myself that this was one way to part from the hell around us.

In order to receive extra rations of bread, I took on additional chores like pulling wagons loaded with refuse, stones, and rocks. Usually older people were chosen for the laborious work, but occasionally I succeeded in joining them and was rewarded with a portion of extra food.

One Saturday morning, as I wandered about lost in thought, I heard an ear-piercing SS command ordering the children to assemble immediately in the square. The SS announced that they would select volunteers who would be sent to German farms to help pick potatoes.

The children all ran to the square, eager for the opportunity to get out of Auschwitz, if only for a short period.

When I came to the square, I found nearly all my fellow inmates standing at attention. I pushed my way to the middle of the line and saw an SS man nailing a bar to an overhanging barrack beam. When the job was completed, he ordered each child to pass under it. Those who did not reach the bar were sent off to one side, where guards were stationed to receive them. The others were ordered to the other side.

At this spectacle, my suspicions were aroused, and I saw through the Nazi hoax. It was a ruse to eliminate the younger children for immediate extermination. As my line drew nearer to the bar, I let others go ahead of me. My instinct told me to remain unnoticed. But how and where to hide? SS men were all around me, guarding us carefully.

As the lines moved forward, I found myself near the latrine. I fell to the ground and crawled on all fours to reach it. In the commotion around me I gained entrance to the latrine unnoticed. But once in, the question arose of where to hide. Everything was exposed.

Suddenly an idea struck me. I crawled into one of the holes which had been dug deep in the ground to contain the excrement. I felt sure that no one would search for me in these nauseating holes. When I jumped into the hole I recoiled from the noxious stench and felt sick, but my will to live sustained me. I sank into the loathsome, slimy mess up to my neck and began my long vigil.

During the noon hour I heard loud shouting and the resounding steps of the booted SS and the shuffling of the children marching to their death. My heart constricted when I thought that only a short time earlier they had hoped to be sent to dig potatoes. I decided, come what may, I would remain where I was.

I heard the roll call and the bread rations being distributed, and a little later heard the *kapos* counting off loudly over and over again. I knew they were looking for one who was missing. They could not determine who it was, because we were listed by our tattooed numbers, not by our names.

Soon a *kapo* came into the toilet and made a hasty search to find me. He could not possibly imagine that anyone would hide in the depths of the underground excrement hole. He left; I was safe.

When I finally emerged, it was pitch dark. A horrible stench exuded from my body and clothing. I rushed to the showers and soaked myself with my clothes on. Quietly I crawled to my bunk and lay down on the floor, but I could not sleep. My empty stomach grumbled; it reminded me I had not eaten a morsel for over twenty-four hours.

Suddenly the stillness of the night was shattered by the heartrending cries of the victims being forced into the death chambers. I forgot my suffering, my hunger, the foul stench, and the cold. I was sustained by the knowledge that I had again foiled the designs of the murderers.

As the days passed, the camp was becoming more and more empty of children. I knew my end was very near. I racked my brains for new ways of escape but could not find any. I was becoming inured to the idea that my end was inescapable, and I sank deeper and deeper into a mood of melancholy, lethargy, and apathy.

The slave labor went on nevertheless. It happened that while I was pushing my wheelbarrow filled with rocks, I found myself in the women's camp. There I heard that my mother and sister had been killed. The news crushed me completely. I did not want to live any longer.

A new Saturday selection was imminent. I could not close my eyes all night. I prayed that the sun would never rise again. Dawn broke, and the sun began to rise. The remaining victims lined up for roll call and a piece of bread. At noon we were doled out a plate of soup. I sat down on the ground and drained every drop of it. Suddenly a band of drunken SS men swooped down on us and marched us out of the camp. It all happened with such dizzying speed that I could hardly comprehend what was going on. My knees buckled as I realized we were being driven to the gas chambers. I was hastening to my death, despite former successful efforts to escape the enemy's deadly clutches. I had been sustained by the hope that someday, in some way, I would overcome the fate of the myriads who had been exterminated. Now we were approaching the death ovens.

This was the first time I had stood near the iron doors behind which a hideous death awaited all of us. As they were opened I saw a large empty room with shower heads jutting out from the ceiling. We knew that the showers contained deadly zyklon gas, not water. The Germans went through their usual deceptive routine. They ordered each of us to take a piece of soap and a towel, undress, leave our clothing outside so that we might identify it when we came out, and walk into the "bath" room.

We stood petrified, refusing to move. Our captors flew into a rage and began to force us into the gas chamber. We responded with hair-raising cries.

The delay and tumult helped save some of us. Dr. Mengele heard the noise and came out to see what was happening. (Later we learned that a group of SS men had gotten drunk and had decided to have some "sport" with us.) Another moment, and we would have been breathing the death fumes. Mengele's appearance occurred at the final critical moment. He ordered an immediate halt to the "action."

After sternly reproving the SS, he began to make his own selection. When he reached me, there were only a few on the survivors' line.

"How old are you?" he asked.

"I am seventeen," I replied, knowing that by adding a couple of years to my age I stood a better chance of remaining in the labor battalion.

"Why do you lie to me?"

"I am not lying," I answered in fluent German. "I am seventeen and am physically fit to do all kinds of hard labor."

"Your German is very good. Where did you learn to speak it so well?"

"I was born in Danzig and studied in German schools."

He looked me over from head to toe and said, "Well, you may get on the other line."

From a group of about three hundred, Dr. Mengele chose fifty-two, and ordered the SS patrol to take us back to camp. As I returned to the camp, it looked to me like a veritable Garden of Eden.

A.E.

Yaldut B'tzel Ha'arubah ("Childhood in the Shadow of the Auschwitz Chimney"), by Zvi Goldberg, pp. 42-46, Special Edition, 1975.

SONDERKOMMANDO *IN BIRKENAU*

At first we were evacuated from Lodz to Konske. It was very bad there. Though I was not quite fourteen, I was very independent, and I was permitted to travel to my uncle in Skorzhisk. I spent five weeks there, but I became rather restless when I received no news from my parents, two sisters, and a brother. I returned to Konske, and at that time Jews were also coming back to Lodz, because the "evacuation" order had been revoked; others smuggled themselves back. It was more agreeable to be in one's own town than be wretched far away from home. A *Judenrat* came into being in Lodz, headed by Rumkowski. He drove through the city like a count, always accompanied by militiamen. One of the public kitchens of the "Approvisation Sczenshlivi" still functioned. All those connected with it regarded themselves as big shots and assumed the Germans would leave them alone.

Autumn 1940 — a time when they began to fence in the ghetto with barbed wire. Jews were being kidnapped in the streets, and I was one of them. Seven hundred men were rounded up and sent to Czarnecki Prison. After being jailed only two days, I was transferred to Posen, where I worked with Poles in the local workcamp. Things were not too bad, but, being only fourteen, how could I carry on among total strangers without my parents? I brooded and continually racked my brains to plan a way to return home.

Once, marching with my work detail early on a dark autumn morning, I managed to slip down into a ravine. I lay there quietly until everyone had passed on, then shuffled off toward Lodz.

There I found the ghetto already closed, its entrance guarded by Jewish militia. Quickly, I noticed a trolley car passing along Znierska Street in the ghetto. I rode to and fro on the trolley, to become familiar with the situation. All I had to do was jump off as the car passed Popzhechna Street, where the ghetto gate was, then wait until a wagon entered or left the ghetto, and jump through the gate.

I kept on riding for a long time, waiting for an opportunity. But a Jewish militiaman, a real blockhead, seized me and took me to a German. I ended up in Gestapo headquarters on Anstaat Street.

I told my interrogator everything, for I still believed the Germans would be compassionate toward a youngster. I said I could not be without my mother. "You wish to join your mother? Very well, you will go to her!" my interrogator told me. And soon I was on my way to the SK [Punitive Commando] in Dachau. I never saw my parents again; and most likely they did not know I was so anxious to be reunited with them.

I traveled with a transport of 120 Jews and Poles, mostly picked up for various "crimes," just like myself. In the SK I was the youngest, and no one harmed me, not even the SS men. We worked in pairs, carrying limestone to a ditch where it was burned, fifteen hours a day. Toilers fell from exhaustion and hunger. SK prisoners were starving. When someone collapsed the SS men threw him into the lime pit, where he was consumed in the flames. At least two or three men died that way every day.

I suffered many privations for four months, hoping things would get better. But the only prospect seemed to be landing in the lime pit. Then I teamed up with four other Jews, and we began to "organize" food.

There was a food storehouse not far from our barracks. At night I would crawl through a casement window and hand out bread, sugar, marmalade and sausage. For a long time no one suspected anything, until I stepped one night into a keg of marmalade that was near a window, and left tracks all over the camp. A search was initiated. A Czech who had seen me eat my fill denounced me. Adults would have been punished by hanging; all I got was twenty-five lashes.

Later, whenever possible, I "organized" again. I was whipped every once in a while, so that my buttocks became tough as leather, and I didn't mind the beatings so much. Word reached the block foreman that I seemed to make light of my punishment, and I was warned that my next offense would be punished by hanging. I was well aware the threat would be carried out, and since I could not go on in the SK, I decided to escape again.

Barbed wire arrived at the station, and we were ordered to unload it. I watched for my chance, slipped under a lorry, and got to Posen. I was prepared for a journey; I carried 14,000 marks. It was fairly easy to obtain money in the camp; some inmates had considerable sums and didn't know what to do with their money. I knew no one in Posen. Although I had had some experience in Dachau, I was still childishly foolish. I stayed the night with a Pole, who turned out to be a *Volksdeutsche*. He took my money while I slept and turned me over to the Gestapo in the morning.

After being interrogated by the SS, I was taken to Birkenau and assigned to the *Sonderkommando* Field D, barracks 32. There were four hundred men, mostly Jews, some Poles, and a few Germans. Some wore red emblems [political prisoners]; others the usual green [criminals].

During the first few days I didn't go to the ovens, but did housekeeping chores. But then the squad leader Müller appeared and said, "Such a sturdy lad ought to be assigned to a shift." And I started to work on the ovens. The first days were very hard, and I began to wonder how to extricate myself. Our *Kommando* had just plunged into the task. Everyone knew that within three months all of us would be dispensed with and replaced by others.

Our unit consisted of four hundred men, working in two shifts. One oven belonged to us. We were accompanied by orchestral music on our way to work. The SS leader, Dr. Mengele, was our supervisor. He delivered the inmates to the gas chambers. He was followed in rank by Müller, then the Jewish *kapos*, Poles, and Germans. We were generally guarded by five SS men. When new transports of human cargo arrived, people were unaware of just what was in store for them. Before entering the building carrying the sign "Baths," the people had to disrobe completely and received a number for their belongings, presumably to be reclaimed later. They got soap and towels for their shower. Then the *kapos* would dash in to beat the unfortunates, to create confusion. During the ensuing commotion, when people trampled over one another, the door of the gas chamber would be thrown open, the prisoners pushed in, and then the door would bang shut after a cylinder of poison gas was flung into the mass.

I worked ten weeks in the *Sonderkommando*. I never entered the gas chamber itself; only *kapos* were admitted there. After the gassing a door in the other side of the chamber would open; there the *kapos* would enter to throw out the corpses. All of us wore rubber gloves and wads of cotton in our mouths. The corpses exuded a pungent odor that could asphyxiate one. Small cars, loaded with forty corpses apiece, would ride along rails that extended from the gas chamber to the oven. The cars disgorged their cargo into the oven, where the bodies were reduced to ashes by electric current in ten minutes. A weak current left the bones intact; a strong current left small heaps. There was an apparatus, known as an exhaust, that blew the ashes into an adjoining pit, where they were piled into barrels by workers, then hoisted by an elevator and ultimately dumped into the Sala River.

The corpses I loaded onto the carts were yellow from the gas. Some of the cadavers had open, glazed eyes, hands holding their mouths, or clutching stomachs. None of us in this work could tolerate it. We often spoke of escape. The S camp bordered on ours, and we occasionally exchanged words with friends, whom we urged to make an attempt to avoid our lot — or even to be gassed.

What could they do? Many resorted to the only alternative: get near the electrically charged wires and die quickly. I felt this death was preferable to being gassed. On my way to work in the early morning, I would occasionally catch sight of the suicides clinging in an upright position to the wires instead of lying prostrate. They looked as though alive.

I had it fairly good then. Each day I got a loaf of bread, a piece of butter, two eggs, a pint of milk, and a special soup. But how could anyone enjoy food under those circumstances? Many inmates destined for the gas chamber carried considerable provisions, frequently fine clothes, especially in the case of foreign transports; and anyone could help himself to these things. We were also allowed to wear civilian clothes. Twice a week we got extra bread rations. But who cared for all that?

From the intimate daily conversation there evolved an organization. We began to assemble weapons obtained from fellow inmates engaged in the warehouse of plundered belongings. Later, in January, a group of Poles arrived, presumably from an uprising, and we got hand grenades from them. We hid these weapons in crates and buckets and straw sacks. A Polish officer, whose name I don't recall, was our leader. He taught us, with permission, calisthenics. He instructed us in all the motions an escape would require — crawling, dropping to the ground, and so on. The Germans watched us and asked, a bit baffled, "Do you intend to make soldiers out of them?" He replied that, as an officer, he could not proceed in any other way. We discussed our plans in the barracks at night. The *kapos* had also been drawn into the conspiracy, for they too could not stand the work and wanted to escape.

The escape occurred in January 1944 — perhaps the eighteenth day. The day before, we learned a great human cargo was due to be gassed, and all 400 of us would be called to work simultaneously. This seemed a good time for an escape. Dr. Mengele appeared; he singled out 73 "Mussulmen," i.e., the frail and sick, and told them to remain in the barracks. The remaining 327 men proceeded to the work detail.

During the preceding night the leaders of our group dug a subterranean passage beneath the electrically charged barbed wire, leading beyond the crematorium to the open fields and woods. To avoid the shock of strong electric current, an open barrel was placed under the wires, and we crawled through it without mishap. The Polish officer taught us to go in single file and hold on to one another.

When we got to work that morning, we changed into civilian clothes because some of us wore the camp uniform. We told the German squad leader our uniforms were getting soiled and we wished to change. He consented. The second leader of our group we nicknamed Franz von Mannheim, a German from the city of Mannheim.

Everything was in order. It was resolved to shoot anyone disobeying the commands. At a signal from the Polish officer, we killed one SS man and threw the German squad leader into the lime pit. Then we began to throw grenades into the oven. Those on the other side of the gas chamber with the other three SS men, who guarded the new arrivals, shouted that it was an air attack alarm. Hearing the explosions, the SS men believed it and ran for cover. The inmates, standing in front of the gas chamber, were at a loss what to do. Meanwhile we fled individually. . . .

An hour and a half went by before the Germans really got their bearings. Then they opened fire in all directions and began to reconnoiter the surrounding area. I learned later from witnesses that about two hundred men were killed in the wake of that event. The rest escaped; it is hard to determine the number killed among the latter.

I was trudging together with a group of twenty-seven men in the direction of Germany. We were led by a Jew from Berlin familiar with the land. We had plenty of money, so we bought shovels and marched along, singing German songs in the manner of German workers. We had already penetrated deep into Germany when we were taken by the German authorities in some town. We declared that we had escaped from a transport in Dachau; they believed us and sent us to Dachau.

I was back in Dachau in March 1944. I said my name was Casiemierz Dudzinski (though they knew I was Jewish).

At that time there was a munitions factory 100 meters underground at Dachau, producing the weapon *"Fau* 1." There were huge chambers linked by electric trolley cars. We not only produced bombs but manufactured the entire apparatus, including five bombs and a bombing vessel. The Germans boasted before us that this weapon would wipe England off the face of the earth. They would point to newspaper reports telling of the daily devastation by those bombs in England. We were aware of their lies and did not believe everything told us. But it was no comfort to realize we contributed to the production of such deadly weapons.

Former Soviet officers working with us taught us the art of sabotage. They told us to drop a few straws into receptacles filled with gasoline. When the mechanism was heated, the straws would ignite and create havoc. We also mixed sand with the powder. The sabotage was not carried out carefully, and one day all the apparatus was destroyed in the same manner. A military commission investigating the explosion found sand and straw. A roll call of those employed in the tunnel followed, separating the Jews, the Poles, and the Russians. Every tenth man was condemned to death — 160 deaths all told. Thereafter the supervisor was most rigorous. At the least suspicion, 30 to 50 workers would be hanged. Later we resumed the sabotage, so that two or three parts of the apparatus would be defective.

We lacked proper food. Though the bread ration was increased, the soup was rotten, as usual. I learned locksmithing on this project. On May 15 we were loaded into railroad cars, but in the absence of a locomotive we soon were sent back to camp.

The SS armed the German *kapos* so they could guard us properly. It was an unforgettable moment when those *kapos* started target practice and an American tank appeared in the distance. The *kapos* turned away and discarded their rifles.

The next day the Americans came to our camp. The first American soldier I met was a Jew from Lemberg. We spent four weeks with the Americans. Of the 28,000 inmates, 4,000 were Jewish. There was not enough bread, but plenty of chocolate.

I returned to Lodz but found not a single survivor of my family. I am all alone, and there is no reason for my staying here. In the environs of Lodz, bandits shot at my companion and robbed us. I wish to leave this place.

By Shaye Gertner, from *Anthology of Holocaust Literature,* published by Jewish Publication Society, 1969 pp. 141-147. Translated from the Yiddish by Moshe Spiegel.

BLOWING THE SHOFAR *AT AUSCHWITZ*

On Rosh Hashanah I went from one prison house to another, with the *shofar* in my hand, to sound the call for prayer. This was a very perilous act, risking my very life. Blessed be He and blessed be His Name that I was privileged to perform this self-imposed mission, which revived the depressed spirits of the camp inmates and eased their conscience in the knowledge that they were granted the privilege of hearing the sounds of the *shofar* even in Auschwitz.

When my daring act became known to the 1400 children who were locked up in the dungeon where they were doomed to be cremated, they began to weep and scream. They pleaded that I visit them also so that they too might take part in the observance of this commandment during their last moments on this earth.

I did not know what to do, because if I were caught by the SS it would mean sure death and I would join them on their last walk to the crematorium. But the children's bitter cries, imploring me not to fail them, gave me no rest. And so I decided not to refuse their plea.

I began to negotiate with the *kapos* and Jewish camp police, and after much haggling I arranged to collect a sizable bribe for their hush money. They consented, but warned me that if I heard a bell ringing it was a sign that the SS were coming, and that if I were caught I would join the children on their death march.

I accepted these conditions and effected an entrance into the children's prison block. I had instructed my son to stand guard, and as soon as he caught a glimpse of the SS he was to run and inform me.

Actually I was aware of the *Halakha* (Jewish Law) that one need not sound the *shofar* if life is endangered. But seeing the gassing, the dying, and the slaughter of thousands of my people, I considered my own life of very little importance. This motivated me in performing the *mitzvah* (commandment) of blowing the *shofar*.

No pen and no writer can describe my feelings when I entered the doomed area. As I began chanting the introductory prayer, "Out of the depths I call unto Thee, O Lord," they all let out a cry for me to say a few words before blowing the *shofar*. Suddenly my power of speech was lost. My tongue stuck to my palate. Also the fear that every passing minute imperiled my life made me gasp for breath. But I could not allow myself to ignore their cries. I spoke to them briefly on the theme of suffering. I developed the idea that what is happening to us is a great mystery. All is covered and secret. Who knows our destiny? What will happen to our families and dear ones? We are all in God's hands.

I then proceeded to blow the prescribed one hundred sounds of the *shofar*. As I was about to leave them, a boy stood up and cried out tearfully, "Dear comrades, the Rabbi's inspired words and *shofar* sounds have strenghened our resolve. All I can say to you is we may hope that our lives are saved, but we must be prepared for the worst. God willing, let us not forget to recite the Shma Yisrael at the last moment." And they all responded in a loud chorus the words of the Shma: "Hear, O Israel, the Lord is our God, the Lord is One."

Before I left, another boy arose and said, "Let us give thanks to the Rabbi for his readiness to risk sacrificing his life to enable us observe our last *mitzvah*. Let us all bless him that with God's help he will survive and continue to serve our people."

As I departed, a number of boys asked me if I could find them some crusts of bread so that they might observe the *mitzvah* of feasting on Rosh Hashanah. With a broken heart I replied that I could not possibly help them. . . .

I learned later that shortly after my visit they were led to their death. May God revenge their death soon, in our time. Amen.

A.E.

From *Tekiat Shofar B'Auschwitz*, ("Blowing the Shofar in Auschwitz") in *Ani Maamin* ("I Believe") by Rabbi Zvi Hirsch Meislish, published by Mossad HaRav Kook (Jerusalem), pp. 93f. Quoted from *Responsa on Sanctification of God's Name*, in the book *Shaar Machmadim*, 1964.

A SEQUENCE OF HORRORS

J.A., a young girl, was born in Cracow in 1931 and lived there. She describes the war's outbreak in Cracow, the Cracow Ghetto during the first and second deportation actions of 1942; then she continues. . . .

But since my parents had work, I wasn't taken out of the ghetto when they deported the other children. My parents worked at this time in the *Nachrichten Geräte Lager*, where cables, telephones, wires, and things like that were made and sent to the German front lines.

The second *aktsye* [1] in the Cracow Ghetto was started in the summer of 1942. Even the masses of Jews who were working and carried offical work permits were led away, supposedly because all economic productivity was being suspended. Some permits were extended with attached blue slips, *Ausweisen*, meaning these people could stay on in the ghetto. Half of all the people in the ghetto were deported during this *aktsye*, along with almost all the children. My parents got these blue-slip extensions so they could keep working, but my problem was critical — they were deporting all the children of the parents still allowed to work in the ghetto. I remember that the people were then led off to Maidanek.

I was able to hide out while this *aktsye* was going on. This is how it happened:

The wives of both the *Yidnrat* [2] members and the Jewish police lived in one building in the center of the ghetto, which also served as the headquarters for these groups. During the second *aktsye*, the heads of the *Yidnrat* and the Jewish police took their wives, children, and close relations back inside the building — they were exempted from this deportation. While the children of the ghetto were being lined up in rows, I hid out in a garbage can which stood in the courtyard of the *Yidnrat* building. I crouched inside it in the most horrifying moments — when they went from house to house searching for Jewish children. When it was all over, I ran into the *Yidnrat* building, where the wives and children of the men and Jewish police were, and I rushed in among a group of children. Outside, in the ghetto, they were leading away the children and the adults with them. My father also stood on line with those being taken away, even though he had a blue-slip permit, an *Ausweis*. But he paid out 500 zloty, and the *Yidnratler* got him taken out of the line.

As night fell, the people — most of the children, the old, and the sick — were gone, and I ran back home. I came in to find my family and the other family staying with us still there. My mother was sure they had taken me with the other children. When she saw me walk into the room, she burst out in tears of joy — as if I'd come back from beyond the grave.

My mother paid the *Yidnrat* a specified sum of money, and they wrote me out a false birth certificate making me older than I really was. The document said I was sixteen, but I was really only eleven years old. Now the Germans would no longer consider me a child, and there was less danger of being deported with the

[1] Action.
[2] Jewish Ghetto Council.

other children. Soon after, my parents gave the factory overseer some jewelry to take me on as a worker. I was eleven, looked like I was going on five, and was passing for a sixteen-year-old. . . .

The Cracow Ghetto was liquidated at the start of 1943. Most of the people still left inside the ghetto were taken to the death camps. Those who could still work were interned in the Plaszów concentration camp. The entire Cracow *Yidnrat* was lined up against a wall and executed inside the ghetto. The hundred Jews who worked at the factory — including my parents and me — were taken to Plaszów. There, my mother and I were put in the women's camp and my father was separated from us along with the men. The hundred of us were taken to work at the factory from Plaszów just as we'd been taken from the Cracow Ghetto. After two months in Plaszów, I was no longer allowed to work at the factory because the Germans said my strength was failing and I could no longer do the work right. They had me work at the brush factory in Plaszów for the time. I could no longer see my parents, either, because the hundred Jews who worked at the factory were locked up inside and never let out — they were no longer part of Plaszów as they had been till now. I heard that this happened because the Poles and Germans of Plaszów protested against the Jews appearing on "their" streets.

Selektsyes[3] took place all the time now, and the people were sent either to other labor camps or to Auschwitz. The most tragic *selektsye* was the one in August 1943. Children, sick people, and the aged were hunted down, herded together, and packed off to Auschwitz.

There was a children's home in Plaszów where the workers left their children for the day. The children of the *Jüdischer Ordnungsdienst* were also kept here. I was put inside this home with many other children while the big *selektsye* I just mentioned was going on.

The head of the Jewish police in Plaszów had been a suspected informer, but said he'd only been a milkman in Cracow. His name was Chilewicz. He knew I was going by a false birth certificate, that I was still a child. His wife was the head inmate of the women's camp. Soon, during an *Appel,* Chilewicz's wife took me out of line and sent me to the children's home, where all the other children were being gathered for deportation. She said I was also a child and belonged with them.

There were about five hundred to six hundred of us inside the children's home. The building was sealed behind barbed wire and guarded by Gestapo agents and not the sentries of the *Ordnungsdienst*. I spent only one night inside this children's home. The following morning, they started loading the children into trucks headed for Auschwitz. I felt sure they were leading us away to die, and I decided to escape. As they were pushing me toward a truck with the other children, a German guard stopped a moment to light his cigarette. He stood spread-eagled. In a second, I and three other children — a boy and two girls — dropped out of line and, running low on the ground, we shot through the German's spread long legs. We broke for the latrine. The German whirled around and fired, but he didn't hit anyone because we dropped to the ground as

[3]Selections for liquidation.

soon as we heard the first of his many shots. He couldn't come after us because he was afraid if he left the other children, they'd break away too.

The camp latrine in which the three children and I hid was exposed. As we stood there, we could be seen from all sides and we were afraid they'd spot us. So I quickly ripped out one of the boards covering the pit and jumped right into the hole, into all the excrement. The children jumped down after me. The last child dragged down the board I had ripped out with him, and this saved us. The latrine ditch was very deep because they dug the waste out every few days. We edged the board in between two walls of the pit and sat over the feces on it for six long hours, not knowing what to do or how to get out.

When the *aktsye* had finished, after the children and the old people were gone, the Jewish women started coming into the latrine to relieve themselves in the ditch we were in. The excrement was dropping all over us. We screamed and yelled to them for help, but no one could hear us because we were down so deep. So we dug our feet into the pit wall, and, holding each other up, we used the board to bang on the floor above our heads. The Jewish women finally heard our screams and knocking; they yanked the boards out of the floor and pulled us up. Two children were half faint from the stench they'd breathed in during the long hours at the bottom of the pit, and collapsed. There were now no other children left in the camp — we were the last four Jewish children of Plaszów.

The women brought us inside their barracks and hid us in the top bunks. We were separated — each one of us to a different barrack. The women got one of the Jewish doctors in the camp to come see us, and he gave us shots against cholera — this was all done secretly, of course. We were hidden inside the four separate barracks for a week. The women took very good care of us and brought us food. Finally, the head of the women's camp — Chilewicz's wife — found out about us and informed the camp commandant, Goeth. This German said to her that if we four children had the guts to jump into the waste to save ourselves, then we should be spared and not deported like the other children. This is how we were able to remain in camp legally. We were the only children there and were really well taken care of — this was because the thousands of Jewish women who lost their children to the death camps treated us like their own.

My mother no longer believed I was alive — she again thought I'd been taken away with the other children when they cleared out the children's home. Someone who took food to the factory where my mother was locked up let her know I was alive and that I was still inside the camp. When my mother heard I'd survived, she went straight to the factory supervisor and begged him to let me come to her, to let me work by her side. The supervisor was a German, Captain Fischer — a decent man. This German gave in to my mother's pleas and went to the Plaszów Gestapo chief himself to take out a permit that would let me work in the factory with my mother. Captain Fischer then sent his adjutant, Hilbig — also a German — to bring me to my mother by auto. My mother had no idea this would happen — she didn't even believe they had really listened to her at all. But Captain Fischer and his aide were kind — it's because of them I'm alive. From then on, I stayed at the plant with my mother and the others — we worked together past the summer of 1943.

In the beginning of 1944, all the men were taken out of the plant and marched back to Plaszów. My father was among those taken away, and I saw him that day for the last time. When my father came back to Plaszów, he met a friend from Cracow there who was assigned to making out the work schedule in camp. Many Jewish youths from Hungary, aged fifteen to sixteen, were being brought into the camp then. My father's friend made him supervisor for the over two hundred Hungarian Jewish youths who were used for slave labor, and this was how he got out of doing the work which would have killed him shortly.

My father was a quiet and kind person. Having a child himself, he never goaded these Hungarian Jewish youths to work. The youths became undisciplined and rebellious. Once, the camp commandant, Goeth, rode his white horse up to where my father's *Kommando* was working. He ordered the youths to line up for an *Appel* — he wanted to take a head count. After he finished counting, it turned out that two youths were missing. During the *Appel* that same night, my father got twenty-five lashes across the face with a riding crop. Goeth, the camp commandant himself, was the one to administer the whipping. The strokes completely lacerated my father's face, and Goeth forbade anyone at the hospital to treat my father. But, being a pharmacist, my father had many acquaintances who worked at the hospital — they pilfered the medicaments from there and treated my father secretly. A few months later — it was in July or August of 1944 — my father was sent to Mauthausen in a transport of many Jews, and he was killed there.

In September of 1944, they liquidated the Media Equipment Plant, and everyone was taken back to Plaszów. My mother and I were also returned to the women's camp. The group of hundred women from the plant was held in Plaszów for six more weeks; then we were transported to Auschwitz. They crammed us into two lorries, and the traveling took all day.

When our group of one hundred women were led into Auschwitz, there was an orchestra playing at the camp entrance. We were taken into zone C, where the transit camp was. As we passed through the zone, they shaved the hair off our heads and bodies. Jewish women cut our hair — *Kapos* — but SS men stood guard. After they shaved us, we were lined up naked outside. We had to pass in front of a team of SS, and they were the ones who decided which of us was healthy, able to work. Most of us were still strong enough, because in the camp where we worked before, there were food rations given out. Then each of the women in the group was given a dress, a pair of shoes, but no undergarments. We were passed into a barrack, where we just milled around — there was no work here. This was zone C, the quarantine camp. We were there for six weeks.

We found out that they were planning to send us away to Germany for labor, but this didn't happen, because a typhus epidemic broke out at that time in the Auschwitz camp. This was in summer, 1944. It was November 1944 before they could take us out and bring us to the camp at Gundelsdorf, in Germany. We were shipped in freight cars used for cattle. This voyage lasted a full three weeks. When we finally came into Gundelsdorf, we were immediately dragged off to do the same kind of labor we did at the *Nachrichten Geräte Lager*. Later, about a hundred Jewish men were also transferred to us from the camp at Flossenburg to do the labor. Three women came along with this group, German SS, who were put in charge of guarding our women's *Kommando*. We worked in the camp six days a week, ten hours a day. The same German guards who were in control of us in the last camp by Plaszów, were now also stationed in the factory to watch over us. Besides them, there were now these three female SS supervisors from Flossenburg, and together, they oversaw everything. They didn't beat us — they saved all the torture and beatings for the men. We were also given larger cuts from their rations.

We were in the camp at Gundelsdorf till January or February 1945. One night, they cornered a group of one hundred women and led away seventy, leaving the thirty others behind. The men had all been taken out of the camp before. My mother and I were among the thirty women who were left behind in camp. After this, we were made to work for another four weeks. When the Americans started bombarding the village, our group of thirty women were rushed off to a truck and taken away to Helmbrechts. There was a big concentration camp there for about three thousand women. Most of the women were from Poland — there were also Jewish women there from Hungary and Greece. No one did work here.

The American Army kept advancing, and the Germans gathered up the whole camp and took us all out on foot — without any of us knowing what our destination would be. The SS men who were pushing us on didn't know either — they were just running with us away from the American artillery barrages. They could only take us along the roads during the daytime — the nights we spent in village stables that we passed on the way. Food was thrown to us once a day. The German guards used to collect burnt potatoes in the villages, and this is what was left for us. This forced march lasted two long months.

On May 2, 1945, we came into a forest near Husinec, which is in Czechoslovakia by the German border. Of the over three thousand women who had started this march, only 120 women were still left standing on their feet. Most of the women had died along the way from hunger and exhaustion. Many were just shot by the SS men because they couldn't drag their feet another step.

As we walked into the forest near Husinec on the second of May, the SS men ordered all of us to lie face-down on the ground. We were sure they would just shoot us all now. We lay like this with our faces on the ground for long hours into the night. In the darkness, a few women started lifting their heads a little and saw none of the SS who'd been guarding us around. They had run away somewhere while we were all lying facing the ground. It was the middle of the night, and we huddled together in the forest.

In the morning, May 3, 1945, we walked out of the forest toward the village of Husinec. The women of our group split up and started going from house to house where the Czechs lived. The Germans had all abandoned the village. The Czechs told us the Americans were coming near. The Czechs brought together all of our women who were wandering around in different places, and we were all taken inside a large theater hall. The Czechs started bringing in some food, and we all stretched out on the floor to sleep. Doctors started coming in to treat the sick and emaciated women. Of the 120 women who had survived the forced march of 3000, another 40 women died right there that day in Husinec. . . .

[The witness was brought by the Labor Zionist Alliance to America, where she became active in Jewish affairs for the first time. Her social life was spent almost exclusively with other Jewish youth who had survived the war. She was completing a degree in physics when this interview was conducted.]

From *Jewish Responses to Nazi Persecution* by Isaiah Trunk, New York: Stein and Day, 1978, p. 117-122.

GRETEL'S INSCRIPTION

On the wall of a house in which twelve-year-old Gretel had hidden before she was captured and killed, her parents found the following inscription:

"I believe in the sun even though the sun does not shine for me. I believe in love which I still have not experienced. I believe in God even though He has not saved us."

From *Hiyuniyut Yehudit Bashoah* ("Jewish Vitality During the Holocaust") edited by Carmon A. and Oron I., Israel Office of Education and Culture, Dept. of Pedagogics, 1975, p. 28.

THE GOD MOMENT

Twelve-year-old Yanka, an inmate of the Janowska death camp near Lvov, Poland, wrote this memoir in her diary.

It is the eve of Yom Kippur the holiest day of the year. Mrs. Jacobowitz lights two holiday candles and recites the blessings. The eyes of the women about her overflow with tears. I stare at the candle lights. Until this moment I have not believed in God. Suddenly I feel that He sees us and will be merciful to us. He is bound to feel that, despite our intense suffering, we look to Him and see His mercy and loving kindness. Up to this moment I was undecided whether I would fast. Now I am persuaded that faith in God will lead me to hope. I join the group that is fasting.

On Yom Kippur day the cynical German murderers try hard to break us down and induce us to eat despite the fast. During the noon hours they place at the doorsteps of each of our block houses two buckets of warm, savory soup. But no one touches it. One of the prisoners recites the *Yizkor* [Memorial Services for the Dead]. Women take out pieces of paper from their pockets, on which they have written verses of the memorial prayers. I look on, listen attentively, and join in the devotional prayers.

A.E.

From *Hiyuniyut Yehudit Bashoah*, op. cit., p. 29f

THE BREAD CRUST

Hayim, a boy in the concentration camp at Rawa-Ruska told this story.

The Nazis rounded up thirty boys and ordered them to dig their own graves. I do not know why we were privileged to dig individual graves for burial instead of a common grave. I dug my grave and lay down facing the sky and the floating clouds. I heard individual shots and I waited for mine.

Suddenly I reminded myself that I still had a hard crust of bread left over from the day before yesterday. To die and to leave such treasure! To whom can I leave this gift? Not finding an answer, I took it out of my pocket and began to chew it hungrily. Suddenly a Nazi killer looked in, saw me eating, and burst out laughing. ''You miserable little Jew! You glutton! About to die, and you still won't stop eating. I kind of like you for this. Get up and go back to camp.''

As long as you breathe, affirm life. Even at the very last moment!

A.E.

From *Hiyuniyut Yehudit Bashoah*, op. cit., p. 28.

AN IMAGINARY TUNE THAT SAVED A LIFE

Thirteen-year-old Uri was a native of Kovno. His father was caught in an ''action'' and was not seen again. His mother died of hunger. Desolate and forsaken, Uri sought to commit suicide. He found an abandoned, isolated corner, a rope, and, after an intensive search, even a few nails. He went down to the cellar, where he began to hammer them into the wall. As he pounded them into the wall rhythmically, one by one, they aroused in his mind words accompanied by a melody, which said: ''To live, to live, not to die!''

He successfully hid in the cellar until the Russians overcame the German garrison and freed the few Jews in the town who remained alive. Today Uri is a member of the Israeli Philharmonic Orchestra.

From *Hiyuniyut Yehudit Bashoah*, op. cit., p. 28.

12.

JEWISH FAMILY CAMPS IN THE FORESTS

From the spring of 1942 through the first half of 1943, Jews in western White Russia and western Ukraine were exterminated, except for some survivors in labor camps. Yitzhak Arad, now director of Yad Vashem, estimates that about ten thousand Jews found refuge and survival in Jewish family camps which were located in the forests of eastern Poland and western USSR. Varying in number of occupants, they consisted of Jewish partisans: men, women, and children. The men were armed and were ever on guard against the Germans and the unfriendly villagers. They were constrained to obtain food for the camps by force when necessary.

The family camps were hidden in the thick forests of those regions. Their members came from nearby settlements; many of them had burned their ghettos before fleeing to the forest. Only remnants succeeded in reaching their forest hideouts. In a small number of cases they fled to the forest prior to the destruction of the ghetto. In order to make it easier to obtain food, camps were set up near villages. But in doing so they exposed themselves to attacks by the Germans. As time progressed, they moved deeper into the woods.

Differences of opinion arose in camps when new members sought to join them. Security accommodations and ease of mobility were vital factors which dictated the need to keep the group small. However, many felt that every Jew who managed to escape should be provided with shelter.

For obvious reasons, family camps were also affected adversely by the presence of women and children. Life in the camps was primitive and harsh. Generally speaking, with the exception of a few peasants, the local population was unfriendly or downright hostile. Polish partisans and Ukrainian nationalists were also ill-disposed toward the Jews. Although there were frictions between the Jews in the camps and Soviet partisans, the latter were less hostile and more cooperative. In time, the Jews became part of the Soviet partisan movement.

In the following selections we read of Jewish children's heroic participation against the enemy.

MOTELE, AN EXEMPLAR OF THE CHILD PARTISAN MOVEMENT

Misha Gildenman,[1] *who achieved fame under the name of Diadia (Uncle) Misha in the partisan high command, was one of the best-known commanders of the forest partisans. His field of operations was in the Ukraine, and his command consisted mostly of Jews. One of them was Motele (the* le *is a dimunitive denoting endearment). The story of Motele's blowing up the soldier's home in August 1943, is part of a book describing Diadia Misha's experiences as partisan commander.*

Information had reached Diadia that a number of well-armed Ukrainian police were ready to surrender to the partisans. Diadia took advantage of a church holiday during which worshipers were allowed to enter and leave the town without examination. He sent a group of partisans to reconnoiter the lay of the land . . .

Together with the band of partisans I sent along Motele. The least suspicious-looking of the group, the boy was to get in touch with the partisans, observe them from a distance, and inform me at once if anything happened to any of them.

Motele took along his violin in the wooden violin case, and he was supposed to pose as a little beggar playing in front of the church and collecting alms. As an added precaution I gave him a document made out in the name of Dimitri Rubina, son of Ivan Rubina, from the village Listvin, in the Velednik region. If questioned, his excuse was to be that he was on his way to Zhitomir in search of his father, who, presumably, was in a Russian prisoner-of-war camp. The document was properly stamped with forged stamps made by one of our partisans, a former stampmaker.

The big church, surrounded by a high white wall, looked like a medieval fortress. A whole gallery of beggars and cripples, some standing, others squatting, at the entrance of the church, tried to evoke sympathy from the holiday crowd in a variety of voices and gestures. Motele was the last in the row. He sat down, took out his violin, and placed between his legs a clay saucer he had bought in the market.

Motele knew many Ukrainian songs. He had learned them in his village, where he used to stand for hours in front of the church, listening to the beggars'

---

[1]He was a *Landsmann* of the author's — that is, they were both born in the same town. The author left there for the United States in 1914.

singing and playing. Now he tuned up his violin and in his pleasant voice began to sing the song of the ''Ant.'' His young voice and violin-playing set him apart from the rest of the beggars' chorus. A crowd began to gather around him, and when he had finished the song, peasants threw lead coins into his clay saucer and peasant women put *pirogy* into the linen sack he carried on his back.

Suddenly a commotion arose in the crowd and people began to push back and make way for a German officer who appeared, accompanied by a German nurse. The officer walked up to the place where Motele sat and stood there, listening to his singing and playing. Motele did not notice him. When the German touched Motele's shoulder with his riding crop, the boy raised his head and, seeing the officer, rose to his feet and bowed.

''Come with me,'' the German commanded.

Motele put his hand in his pocket to make sure he still had the document. Then he put the violin back in the case, gathered up the coins in the saucer, and followed the officer. After passing several blocks, they came to a one-story building in front of which were parked many limousines and motorcycles. A German guard stood at the entrance. They went up one flight to a large, bright hall where officers sat around tables, eating, drinking, and talking loudly. In one corner of the hall stood a brown piano, at which sat an elderly gray-haired man, wearing a black dress coat. The officer led Motele over to the man and said something to him.

''Do you read notes?'' the man asked Motele in Russian.

''Yes,'' the boy replied.

The pianist selected a sheet of music and placed it before Motele, who tuned up his violin and began to play, with the man accompanying him at the piano. It was Paderewski's ''Minuet'' — when they had finished, there was a burst of applause.

Motele was offered the job of playing in the Soldiers' Home for two hours at lunchtime and from seven to eleven in the evening. For this he would receive two marks per day, lunch, and dinner.

He could not decide what to do. First, he said, he must go to Zhitomir and find his father. He also told the German that he had left a sick mother with three children at home, whose sole provider he was. The officer promised him to write to the regional commandant of Zhitomir about his father, and if he was really there, in the prisoner-of-war camp, he would have him transferred to Ovrutch. Motele had to agree to this proposal and remained in the Soldiers' Home.

When he had finished playing, he went to see our contact, Keril, and asked him to inform me about the situation he was in. I ordered him to remain there, observe everything carefully, and keep me posted through Keril.

The Soldiers' Home was one of the many restaurants which the Germans had set up for their military forces, where they received the best food and the finest French wine for the cheapest prices, and they were served in more ways than one by young and pretty Ukrainian waitresses. All this was to raise the spirits of the soldiers on the way to the terrible Eastern Front, from which few returned alive and unwounded.

Motele played at the restaurant and memorized the numbers of units and the types of uniforms the Germans wore on the way to the front. He eavesdropped on conversations of those who had returned from the front. Between lunch and dinner he wandered around town, read the signs on government institutions, noted the streets he was on, and later relayed all this information to me through Keril. The director of the Soldiers' Home was satisfied with the talented and modest young musician. The elderly pianist, a *Volksdeutsche* whose home was not far from Karastien, became very friendly with Motele and was delighted with his musical skills.

Thus, two weeks passed. One day the regional commandant, who used to spend every evening at the restaurant, ordered Motele to appear the next morning at nine in his office. When Motele arrived, somewhat frightened, the commandant gave him a friendly reception, called in the military tailor, and ordered a German uniform and cap for the boy. A few days later Motele came into the Soldiers' Home dressed as a little soldier. The pianist and the other employees seemed highly pleased.

Motele ate lunch and dinner in the kitchen, which was located in the basement. On the way down from the first floor one had to pass a dimly lit corridor. On its right were the kitchen and laundry; on its left some storage rooms. The fat cook served Motele the tastiest dishes, in return for which the boy played for him his favorite song, "Rose Marie."

One afternoon when Motele came out of the kitchen, he noticed that the door to one of the storage rooms was open. Out of curiosity he peered in and, by the dim light from a small grated window, he saw a large cellar filled with empty wine cases, herring barrels, and other useless things scattered about in disorder. He noticed that the wall opposite the entrance was cracked, apparently by a bomb explosion nearby, during a bombardment. It was a crooked crack, veering leftward.

Remembering the stories he had heard the partisans tell about their various sabotage acts, an idea flashed through his mind: If a mine could be stuck in the crack of the wall, the explosion would destroy the Soldiers' Home, together with the hated German officers. The idea gave him no rest, and every time he passed the corridor he peered into the basement and thought of such a sabotage act.

He wasted no time and passed on his plan to me through Keril. I, too, liked the idea, and so I delegated Popov — our mine manufacturer, as we called him — to meet with Motele and find out the precise details.

It was harvest time. Peasants went back and forth between Ovrutch and the fields. The guards at the town's exit were not as strict as usual. Keril piled up a wagonload of straw sheafs for binding hay and rode out into the field. The German guard who allowed Keril to pass over the bridge did not, of course, suspect that underneath the heap of straw twists lay a Jewish boy who planned to blow up the Soldiers' Home.

At the appointed place, five kilometers out of town, Popov was already waiting for them. Motele presented his plan. Popov inquired thoroughly about the thickness of the walls, whether they were brick or stone, the distance Motele would have to run after igniting the wick, and many other details. Popov figured out that it would take eighteen kilograms of the expolosive available to me at that time.

A few days later Popov brought a bag full of the explosive to the same place.

Keril again came with Motele, and Popov began to teach him how to assemble the little blocks of *tal* and how to make a mine, how to insert the capsule detonator, etc. All this was not entirely unfamiliar to Motele. He used to watch Popov teach the partisans how to do it. After the lesson, Keril took Motele and the explosive to his house.

Now came the difficult task of transporting the explosive material to the cellar of the Soldiers' Home. But Motele found a way. In the evening, after dinner, when he said good-bye to the cook, he took his violin with him. He passed through the cellar door and hurried inside. Then he took the violin out of its case and put it inside an empty barrel and left the Soldiers' Home with the empty violin case. On the second day, when he came to the Home at lunchtime to play, he had in his violin case three kilograms of the explosive. Before he went up to the hall to play, he went, as always, first to the kitchen for his lunch. He looked about him cautiously, then entered the cellar, took the *tal* out of the violin case, and put the violin back in. In several days he had thus transported all the eighteen kilograms of the explosive into the cellar.

Later he used every opportunity to go down to the basement and remove some stones from the wall to enlarge the opening in which to place the bomb. He followed Popov's instructions, then inserted the capsule with the long Bickford wick, and camouflaged it. All that was left to do was ignite the end of the wick and realize the act of revenge which was his dream.

Whenever he had free time, Motele worked out with Keril the details connected with the plan. They would go daily to the lake, ostensibly to catch fish or to bathe. Actually they were looking for a shallow spot that would make it possible for Motele to cross when he escaped after the explosion. They took careful note of the streets and orchards through which Motele would have to run to the lake, on the other side of which the partisans were to wait for him and take him to the woods. Everything was ready. Motele was merely awaiting the proper moment.

There was much excitement in the Soldiers' Home. High-ranking guests were expected. A division of SS was on the way to the Eastern Front to rescue the situation and to encourage the disorganized German armies after the severe blows they had received in the area of Kursk. Because of the insecurity of the railway lines — according to statistics, every fifth train was blown up by partisans — the SS division was transferred at Karastien from railway cars to trucks, and now it was on the way to Chernigov via Ovrutch-Mazir.

Around three in the afternoon, automobiles and motorcycles began to arrive in front of the Soldiers' Home. The rooms were filled with elegantly uniformed SS officers. They ate and drank. Above the din of clanking dishes, clinking glasses, and loud laughter, Motele's violin was heard to the piano's accompaniment. The officers amused themselves and sang. From time to time they ordered Motele and the pianist to play tangos and waltzes, to which they danced. With few interruptions, Motele played throughout the afternoon and evening.

At eleven o'clock the accompanist finally induced the director to put an end to the playing. There were some officers who could play the piano, so they took over and continued with the entertainment. As usual, Motele went down to the kitchen to have his dinner. He was too exhausted to eat and explained to the cook that because he had played for eight hours without a stop he had no appetite. Soon afterward he said good night to the cook and left the kitchen. The corridor was dark. His hand groped for the cellar door and found it. He went inside and closed the door behind him. In the dark he found the end of the bomb wick and ignited it. He slipped out of the cellar and ran through the corridor. When he came to the exit he slowed down and approached the German guard and allowed himself a joke. He held up his right arm and called out, *"Heil Hitler!"*

"Ach, you little Ukrainian swine!" the German said, laughing.

Motele left the Soldiers' Home and quickly disappeared in the darkness. After running about two hundred yards, he heard a powerful explosion. The earth trembled, and windowpanes shattered. Moments later he heard police whistles and sirens. Red rockets lighted up the sky over the town. Both frightened and elated, Motele hugged the walls of buildings as he ran toward the lake. He entered the cold water, which in some places reached his neck, and held his violin above his head with both hands. He glanced back to the city and saw a big fire shooting up into the sky.

On the other side of the shore, at the foot of a small hill, a wagon waited for Motele. On it were five well-armed partisans. Ten hands reached out to hoist the boy into the wagon. With lightning speed the horses — the best in our detachment — galloped away and disappeared into the nearest woods.

For the first few minutes Motele was speechless. Gradually he calmed down and, raising his clenched fists to the red sky, said in a trembling voice, "This is for my parents and little Bashiale, my sister."

[EDITOR'S POSTSCRIPT: In his account of Jewish children who displayed heroism as partisans, Kaganovich brings some additional information about twelve-year-old Motele, based on Diadia Misha's memoir. When Diadia Misha's partisans discovered a boy sleeping in the woods, he gave his name as Mitka, and they thought he was a Ukrainian. Later they learned that he was Jewish, the son of a miller, and that he was born in Krasnuvka, a village in Volhynia.

"By coincidence," writes Kaganovich, "Motele was not at home when Germans and Ukrainians killed his father, mother, and little sister. That same night he escaped to the woods and hired himself out to peasants as shepherd, for his room and board. In Diadia Misha's detachment the clever, daring, and alert boy was utilized for intelligence and espionage work." In addition to blowing up the German Soldiers' Home, Motele is credited with, among other things, saving the lives of two Jewish children and a Russian partisan, and with shooting a German to death with his revolver. Motele fell in battle shortly before liberation. He was crawling over to a new position to warn the Soviet officers of an impending danger when he was struck by a German bullet.]

From *They Fought Back,* edited and translated by Yuri Suhl, New York: Crown, 1966, pp. 262-267.

DAVID, A PARTISAN FROM THE EDITOR'S HOME TOWN

David Mudrik was about fourteen when I met him as a ward in the children's home in Otwotzk. He was eight when the war began. He lived in Dombrowitz, the town where the editor of this book was born and raised. At the turn of the century Dombrowitz, in the province of Volhynia, Russia, had a total population of about 25,000, including 6000 Jews. David's family consisted of his parents and a brother and sister. In 1942 the Germans overran Dombrowitz and rounded up all the menfolk in the marketplace. David told the following story.

My father, who was a resourceful man, escaped with my mother, brother, and me, and hid in the fields. The Germans imprisoned a number of Jews; some gained temporary release by bribe, and some hid. The "actions," however, kept on, recurring several times until the final liquidation, which took place in the neighboring town of Sarne. I saw its streets covered with corpses.

I do not know exactly how it happened. Somehow we found hiding places in the hills nearby, in which we lived through the winter. . . . My father, disguised as a gentile, dropped in to visit the huts of the Ukrainians and to make inquiries whether the Germans were preparing for further raids. My sister became the cook of the group.

The enemy confiscated the harvests. Our partisan group waged sudden attacks on them, seized the cows, grain, and potatoes which they had taken away, and returned them to their owners. Occasionally we attacked with knives and spears and seized quantities of firearms and ammunition.

During the days we slept, and in the night we went out to reconnoiter. It happened once that the forest warden lost his way and blundered into our camp. We wanted to kill him, but he pleaded so hard that we let him live. In gratitude he became our friend and thereafter passed on to us valuable information about the Germans.

Our partisans made contact with the Soviet Army. Every month a Russian plane brought us needed material. We would signal the landing place by lighting five fires.

In the spring of 1944, Father and Mother went out to pick berries in the forest and did not return. I waited a full day, then began vainly to look for them. Later on, young shepherds found their dead bodies. They had been killed by Ukrainian bandits from nearby.

Our partisan group moved to the swamps near Pinsk, where we stayed half a year. The Germans feared us so much that they did not dare impound the grain harvested by the peasants. And we were not fearful of sleeping over in the peasants' huts.

One night the partisans left the swampland to join the Soviet Army, which was drawing closer. I and another partisan remained where we were, and later struck out for the woods by ourselves. It was wintertime; heaps of snow covered us. . . . The peasants guided us through the swamps, and we found ourselves at the front lines, where the opposing armies were locked in a fierce battle. We suffered from severe hunger and existed by eating raw beans. Fortunately for us, there was a Baptist colony nearby whose inhabitants believed in God and kept us from being discovered.

[As the victorious Soviet Army advanced closer, David left the partisans and went to Rowno, the nearest large town. From there he moved on to Warsaw and later found refuge in the Otwotzk children's home, where he narrated this story.]

A.E.

From *Kiddush HaShem*, by Sk. Niger, New York: Cyco Bicher Ferlag, 1948, pp. 646-648. Translated from the Yiddish. Quoted from a story by Jacob Pat in *The Jewish Daily Forward*, June 19, 1946.

A TEN-YEAR-OLD PARTISAN

My name is Hananiah Kuton. I was born in 1930 in the town of Bitan, near Baranowicze. When I reached school age I studied in a Polish public school. When the war broke out, in 1939, the school closed down. The Soviet Army marched into the town, and I continued my studies in a Russian school, but that too, came to an end when the Germans bombed the town and set it afire. With the invasion of the Germans, Jews were rounded up and forced to engage in slave labor. Every day five to ten Jews died from exhaustion. Soon we were ordered to wear a yellow patch on our backs and forbidden to walk on the sidewalks. Then we were required to sew a yellow Star of David on our breasts.

In the street, the Germans set fire to the Torah scrolls, which they had removed from the synagogue. Five days later they drove the Jews to the forest and commanded them to build a ghetto surrounded by a wooden fence covered over with barbed wire. The job had to be completed in one day.

[The writer describes how the Germans tormented the Jews by starvation, inhuman crowding, and frequent "actions."]

The Jews built bunkers and hid in them to save their lives. In the bunkers children fainted for lack of air. Infants cried, and a few mothers choked them to death for fear of discovery. In the evening I felt I would suffocate unless I got out of the bunker. On one occasion when I emerged, I learned of my father's death. I fled to join the partisans.

After great exertion and mental stress, a number of us finally reached the forest. Suddenly we saw a horse-drawn wagon and bicyclists. We were surrounded and taken prisoners. Great was our joy when we learned that our captors were partisans. They received us warmly. The commander emptied the wagon of its occupants and asked us to get in. We told him of "life" in the ghetto, which moved him deeply.

After a long ride we saw bonfires, around which sat partisans cleaning their rifles. They fed us and provided tents for us to sleep in.

New families joined us daily. Soon we were about five hundred souls in all.

In 1942 the Germans laid siege to the forests and routed the partisans. They maneuvered us into a pocket. Our situation was desperate. Many died of starvation. Mothers smothered their young. Once I saw three women sitting together, among them a young nursing mother. Her neighbor suddenly fainted;

the nursing mother fed her sick comrade by squeezing milk from her breast into her neighbor's mouth.

We had no food or drink for nine days. On the tenth day, after much searching, we discovered a hollow watery pit. We dug deep with our fingers until we reached muddy water. We continued laboring like busy ants until we found drinkable water. . . .

A company of Russian partisans in our group set out from our midst to counterattack. When the Germans found out that we were left without the Russian fighters, they attacked us in force. It was deep winter with the snow piled a meter [39.37 inches] high. We were surrounded and could not retreat. They killed fifty of our people — men, women and children. Our family escaped alive.

In 1943, parachutists began to arrive from Moscow, and they took charge. In the middle of 1943 the enemy laid siege to the forest. They surrounded the area where we were and opened fire from all side. I fled across the nearby river and continued to run as fast as I could without looking back. I chanced to find my sister. She told me that Mother was in flight with our little brother.

In the morning we returned to the camp, which was aflame. Scattered about were dead bodies — a horrible sight. In the river I found my little brother, who had been killed. I pulled his body out and laid it on the shore. When I reached our tent I saw two dead women; one had been burned and the other murdered. I was told that my mother was lying dead somewhere in the vicinity. I decided to find her even if it took all night. Finally I found her at five o'clock in the morning.

When I saw her body from the distance, I was terribly shaken up. Her hair was matted; her eyes were wide open and bloodshot. Her breast had been pierced by a bayonet, and as I came closer I saw that there were three bullet holes in her head. Nearby were two other corpses. I was horrified at the scene. I dug a grave, gathered the dead, and buried them — my mother, brother, two friends, and two strangers. All day I worked, preparing their final resting place. I covered it with earth and built a fence around the grave to prevent the wolves from getting to them. And then I inscribed what I knew of the slain, their names, ages, and the date of their death.

Then and there I determined to dedicate my life to seeking revenge for the death of my mother, brother, and friends.

The next day, at two in the morning, I went out with a squadron of partisans and attacked the nearest enemy village. We opened up with a barrage of incendiary bullets. The whole town went up in flames. To save their lives, Germans who were stark naked jumped out of windows and ran. We took many of them prisoner and brought them to the forest, where we avenged the deaths of our dear ones. We were so bloodthirsty that we actually pushed each other to be the first to get at the murderers. Similar incidents recurred frequently.

It was now 1944. One early morning two partisans and I returned from the village, all worn out, and lay down to sleep. Suddenly the enemies' planes began bombing us. I was so dead-tired that I did not hear them. At eight o'clock in the morning a platoon of Germans attacked us. All in the partisan camp fled; only I was left. Suddenly I awoke, rushed out of my tent, and escaped miraculously. The next day our men recaptured the camp, and we carried on as before.

At the end of 1944 the Russian troops left us, and we partisans were on our own. Almost immediately the Germans began firing mortar shells at our position. The commander sent me on horseback to reconnoiter. From a distance I saw one of our patrols waving his hands and heard him shouting, "They are coming in tanks."

Straight as an arrow I made for my horse. I was then only thirteen. Quickly I clambered onto my horse. A tank was about a hundred meters from me. I galloped away as fast as the horse could go, while the tank fired missiles at us.

I came to a spot where I had to cross to the other side of the road. I tied my horse to a tree and began crawling away from it. The men in the tank saw what I had done. A number of infantrymen began to pursue me. I ran, divesting myself of all I could except my rifle, and looked for protection. At long last I met up with the partisans and found safety. It was deep winter. I collapsed on the snow and fell asleep. When I rose in the morning the clothing was frozen to my body.

In 1945 the Red Army began to counterattack the Germans. The Germans surrendered to our partisan army. With each position they relinquished, we, the Jewish partisans, remembered our vow to avenge the blood of our dear ones.

When the war ended I traveled to Stettin, a major seaport on the Baltic Sea and industrial center. I soon realized that there was no future for Jews in the new Poland. For some time I had been dreaming of settling in Eretz Yisrael. I joined a Hashomer Hatzair *kibbutz* in Europe, where I prepared myself to live in Eretz Yisrael. It did not take long, and here I am.

A.E.

From *One from a City and Two from a Family,* op. cit., pp. 224-228.

DR. ATLAS'S FOREST PARTISANS

The writer, Shmuel Bornstein, was a member of Dr. Yehezkel Atlas's partisans. Atlas was a young Jewish physician who, in 1939, had fled with his family from Lodz to Russia. When the Germans attacked Russia the family was murdered, but Dr. Atlas was spared because of his profession.

At the time there was no organized partisan movement. Dr. Atlas devoted himself to create a fighting group of forest partisans. From the very beginning he proved to be an exceptional leader and an undaunted fighter.

Dr. Atlas's partisans quickly achieved fame in the neighborhood as a fearless fighting force. They were among the first to ambush the enemy battalions, derail German military trains, burn bridges, and save Jewish lives. He was highly regarded by his partisans, both as a commander and as a father figure. He lost his life while courageously leading his men against a concentrated attack by Germans who were superior in numbers and armaments.

Our travels through the forests were like travels during the nineteenth century in horse-drawn vehicles. A peasant would drive us in his wagon from one point to another. Then we would pay him and engage another to take us to another destination. These changes were necessary to insure security and safety.

Late one night we came to a village, and suddenly we heard a boy's voice appealing to us: "Partisans, please wait."

We stopped. A boy about ten years old, in tattered clothes, stood in the road in the drenching rain. He was shivering, wet and cold.

"What do you want, my boy?" I asked.

"I want to go with you," he answered.

This happened to be one of the points where we made our regular exchange of drivers. Wet and frozen, we knocked on the door of a peasant's shack and soon found ourselves in a warm, dry room. The boy stood, frightened and trembling, near the door. I called him to join us to eat.

He scrutinized us closely; his large dark eyes suddenly widened and lit up in astonishment and wonder. He blurted out, "You are Jews! I am Jewish too."

His words shook us up. We looked him over closely; there was no doubt that he was Jewish.

His name was David. He told us that he had been saved miraculously from the slaughter of his family and townfolk by the Germans. He fled to a village where he was known and worked as a shepherd. He matured very quickly and got along reasonably well. But his luck soon ran out. The Germans extended their invasion, and the peasants feared to hide him because in doing so they risked death. By chance he heard about the forest partisans, so he decided to drop everything and join them in their war against the Germans. He truly believed that all Jews had been destroyed, and was wondrously glad to learn from us that Jews were alive and fighting.

While eating, one of our leaders, Bogdush, listened intently to the boy's story. Suddenly he got up and went over to the peasant's bed, under which lay children's shoes. He lifted a pair and began to fit them onto David's feet. The peasant and his wife objected strongly and complained that their son would be left barefoot, but Bogdush was not deterred. He told David to put on the shoes, and off we went to our next station. . . .

"Pss, Shmuel." I heard a whisper from the roadside. I was sure that my ears deceived me. My nerves are going to pieces, I thought. The sibilant sound was repeated. I looked around and spied young Itzhak crouching near a tree, with his rifle cocked, motioning noiselessly.

Itzhak was only thirteen when he, his mother, and two brothers fled from the Germans to Russia, where they found shelter for three years. In July 1942, when Germany invaded Russia, they escaped death miraculously and joined a Soviet partisan battalion. He became the sole provider for his family and soon acquired fame as an expert scout and rifle shot. His rifle was bigger than he, but no one dared jest about it. His fame as a valiant fighter spread far and wide. He took part in all the raids, shoulder to shoulder with his elders.

Because of his short stature, Itzhak could get places unseen. His fellow partisans took advantage of his diminutive size and depended on him in their raids.

I understood that he was standing watch at this post because his family was hiding nearby. And indeed, nearby, under an uprooted tree, his family had found cover in a hole in the ground. . . .

Nearly all those who volunteered to fight with the Red Army fell in our battles with the enemy. Of those who survived, I want to devote a few comments to Itzhak, the boy partisan. In the last battle, his mother and one of his brothers were killed. He took personal care of his little brother, and when the enemy was routed he registered his brother in an orphanage in Slonim. He himself enlisted in the Red Army and participated in all the battles, including the conquest of Berlin. I met him in Lodz, dressed punctiliously in his military uniform. On his breast were pinned medals and decorations testifying to his valor in battle.

A.E.

From *Plugat Hadoctor Atlas* ("Dr. Atlas's Battalion,") by Shmuel Bernstein, published by Ghetto Fighters' House and Hakibbutz Hameuchad, 1972, pp. 99f., 165f.

AN ELEVEN-YEAR-OLD FIGHTER

Shimon lived in Baranowicze. He was fourteen when he narrated his adventures as a partisan. We shall skip the earlier part of his story, which is quite similar to the preceding ones. He too had to hide in the swamps around Pinsk. Many days and nights his group hid deep in the mud, without food and drink. When the Germans finally retreated, the partisans were fed potatoes, which they considered sweetmeats.

We pick up his story as a fighting partisan when he was about twelve years old.

We lay concealed in an ambush near a railroad track. We had planted three explosive mines equidistant from one another. The fear that gripped me when we spied the approaching train will remain with me for life. I held the string to pull the trigger that would set off the explosion. I knew that I held in my hand the fate of thousands. I shook all over before and during the explosion, as if in an ague. I went through serious inner conflicts until I became more used to the awesome execution of my responsibility. . . .

The partisan group had assigned me to take revenge on a German who had murdered my mother. I was then only eleven years old. They ordered me to burn out his eyes. "They do it to us," the partisans said. I could not do it. I can still see the anger of my outraged comrades. "Unworthy son" they shouted at me. I had to do it against my will. I felt that my own eyes were being burned — not that I was burning his eyes. I tried to find some solace in recalling the victim's vicious murder of my mother, but I failed. Every act of vengeance I committed pierced my sides like a sharp knife. I avenged my mother's death, but I was left limp and dejected.

Three years I served with the partisans. I recall my wanderings through the swamps and tremulous marshes covered with moss. With every step the squishy path quaked and shook under my feet. . . . The forests were full of noise and life, but I was depressed, my heart pounding a rhythm of despair. . . .

I was daring and bold. I looked like a young gentile teenager, barefoot and threadbare. I volunteered to help the German outposts, water their horses, supply drinking water to the military. When I returned to the partisan camp I furnished valuable information.

I got used to this way of life — a life full of risks. Almost every night we rode out to "do a job." I avenged myself threefold for the death of my brother, mother, and father. . . .

Now, as I look back everything that happened was a nightmare — a succession of nightmares.

[When the Soviet Army was victorious, Shimon and his sister began wandering through Poland until they found shelter in the children's home at Otwotck.]

A.E.

From *Kiddush HaShem*, op. cit., pp. 650-653.

CHILDREN COURIERS IN THE GHETTO OF MINSK

Yuri Suhl is an American Jewish poet, novelist, and biographer. In his book on Jewish resistance in Nazi Europe he presents impressive evidence that a widespread Jewish Underground existed, which was active in sabotage and forest warfare and carried on successful armed revolts in the ghettos and concentration camps.

Among the couriers who led people out of the ghetto, three children distinguished themselves. They were Sima, Banko, and David. Three times a week they took groups of Jews to the forests of Staroje-Sielo, covering a distance of fifty kilometers both ways. Despite their age, they were fully aware of the nature of their mission and of the dangers involved.

The three children were our main contact with the forest. They came to the ghetto armed, their pistols always loaded, determined not to fall into the hands of the Germans alive. They were at ease and showed no signs of fear, though they were constantly exposed to death. They carried out the orders of our general staff with strict discipline.

Sima was a twelve-year-old girl with blond hair, blue eyes, and dimples that showed when she talked. Her parents perished in the first German pogrom. In the beginning Sima lived outside the ghetto and carried out important assignments for the Underground party committee. Later, when we began to lead Jews out of the ghetto, Smolar brought the little girl to the ghetto, and she became our contact with the forest.

No assignment was too difficult for Sima. Before going out on a mission, she listened carefully to the given instructions, then she would repeat what she was told, trying hard not to miss a single word. Her small pistol was always in the special pocket sewn into her coat. Before starting out, she would always point to it and say, "Don't worry, the Fritzes will not take me alive."

On cold winter nights Sima would sneak out of the ghetto through an opening beneath the barbed-wire fence. She returned to the ghetto through the cemetery. There were times when she did not succeed in getting into the ghetto at night. When this happened she would spend the night, hungry and cold, in some bombed-out building, and remain there throughout the next day. At dusk, when the Jews returned from work, she would stealthily join their column and together with them enter the ghetto. After the liquidation of the Minsk Ghetto, Sima participated in the combat operations of the partisan detachment.

In the summer of 1944, when the Germans were driven out, Sima marched in the front lines together with other decorated partisans in the large partisans' parade in Minsk. From her youthful chest shone a silver medal — first-rank Partisan of the Fatherland award.

Banko and David were two thirteen-year-old boys who had been schoolmates and had lived on the same street. Their fathers were also friends. The boys went together to Pioneer camps. Together they hid out during the German pogroms and worked at loading coal into the freight cars at Tovarne station, and together they escaped to the forest.

They wandered for weeks through the forest and villages until they came upon a group of partisans called the "Stalincy." There they found Smolar, Feldman, Zorin, and other Jews of Minsk.

When Feldman called Banko into staff headquarters and ordered him to get ready to go to the Minsk Ghetto and bring out some Jews, Banko said, "I am ready to carry out your every command on one condition — that David go with me." His request was granted.

Banko's mother was still in the ghetto. All the other members of his family had perished in the German pogroms. His mother knew of Banko's activities and the dangers he was facing. But she was proud of him. Whenever Banko came for more people, he visited his mother. She would put him to bed and sit near him for hours, watching him as he slept. When he awoke he would relate to her in whispers how the partisans were fighting the enemy; how they were blowing up troop trains and killing Germans.

"And when will you take me along to the forest?" his mother asked.

"I spoke to the commander, and he said the next time I'm in the ghetto I'll be able to take you along. I'd like you to be in my detachment and not in a family camp. Ours is a combat detachment; you'll have to stand guard and hold a rifle, but we'll be together. In a detachment, in a dugout, it is good to have a mother."

Banko was a small, skinny boy, who looked ten years old. The ghetto experiences had left deep marks on his elongated, youthful face. David was taller and also older-looking than Banko. But it was Banko who was in charge of their activities, and David was his companion.

David was an orphan; his entire family had been killed. He was the sole survivor. His only friend was Banko. David carried out his work quietly and scrupulously, not overlooking a single detail. But he had one weakness — he did not like to remain long in the ghetto. He would become nervous and hurry Banko on by saying, "We've already been too long in the ghetto. So many Jews are waiting for us to take them out. Time is short."

Their mission was to bring combat-fit young men and women and weapons from the ghetto to the partisan detachment Parchomenko.

When Banko had gathered the people and supplies, the Underground set the departure hour and selected the lookouts to guard the exits. Then Banko gave the final instructions. He addressed the people like a commander speaking to soldiers:

"In two hours we will be leaving the ghetto. From that moment on you are partisans. Until I deliver you into the hands of the partisan chief of staff, you must obey my every command. The order of the journey is as follows: I go first, and you follow behind me in single file, according to the numbers I gave you. If we should run into a German patrol, there is no way back, because it would endanger the Jews in the ghetto. If the situation becomes critical, we resist. Those who received grenades will throw them at the Germans, and those who have pistols will open fire on them. Retreat is possible only in the direction of Staroje-Sielo. The Germans will not pursue us very far because they are afraid of the night. Under no conditions must you abandon the knapsacks which you carry on your backs. Anyone who creates a panic or refuses to obey my command will be shot without warning! I hope that all will go well and that in a few hours from now you will be free people without yellow badges."

At the precise moment past midnight the two boys led the Jews out of the ghetto. As always, Banko was at the head of the line, his loaded pistol in his pocket. The others followed after him. David was last. All along the way to the wide fence our people were standing guard, including some members of the Jewish ghetto police who were cooperating with the underground. The people moved quietly, holding their breath, thinking of the instructions Banko had given them.

For months these children engaged in such operations, leading out hundreds of Jews — among them practically all the doctors — and covering hundreds of kilometers. Later they participated in actual combat operations together with the others.

Here, in the natural surroundings of the forest, the children caught up on their physical growth, which the ghetto had stunted. Banko grew tall and manly-looking, and David surpassed him by growing a head taller. They had many friends in the Parchomenko and Budiony detachments, which they regarded as their own; and hundreds in the Zorin's family detachment, where Banko's mother was. He could not persuade the commander to let his mother be with him. A combat detachment had to be combat-ready at all times, and Banko's mother had suffered too much hunger and illness in the ghetto to be able to keep up with the young partisans.

On August 15, 1943, the Germans surrounded our forest, with the aim of annihilating the partisans. The Germans threw two divisions of the regular military into this operation. A few days before the blockade, they burned down the farms in the forest area. Because the peasants of these farms had maintained friendly relations with the partisans, the Germans had herded them all into one house and burned them alive.

The German attack lasted fifteen days; it was prepared and carried out like a full-scale front-line operation. There were bombardments from the air; heavy and light artillery were fired without letup; mine sappers cleared the way where the military had to pass; and the Germans went into attack in three waves. Every bush, every tree, was shot at.

During the first days of the attack we offered resistance. We mined the roads, dug trenches, and engaged the Germans in minor battles. The Parchomenko detachment had mined the main Ivenic-Bakszt highway, and the first truck, carrying more than thirty Germans, was blown up as soon as it entered the forest. They were all blown to pieces, together with their vehicle.

After several days our resistance collapsed. We could not hold out against a regular army. From headquarters came the command that we scatter in small groups and wait out the blockade. On September 15 the Germans abandoned the forest. At the time of the German attack several hundred partisans perished, among them between fifty and sixty Jews.

The Parchomenko detachment suffered the heaviest losses. Twenty-two men, twelve of whom were Jews, were hiding out in a cave close to the base. They were discovered because of a child in their midst, and all suffered martyrs' deaths. We found them burned, some only in part, their arms pulled back and tied with barbed wire. According to all evidence, they had been burned alive. We found no bullet holes on their bodies. Among the burned was Banko. His body was half-burned, his eyes open as though petrified. I untied his arms but could not straighten them out.

With clenched fists and anguished hearts we swore to take revenge on their murderers. David stood at Banko's open grave and cried bitterly. The entire detachment cried with him.

From *They Fought Back*, op. cit., pp. 241-245.

SMUGGLING OUT ARMS

For thirty years the author, Dr. Yitzhak Arad, was an active participant in the war against the Nazis and later in the wars of Israel: the Sinai Campaign (1956), the Six Day War (1967), and the Yom Kippur War (1973). He retired from the Israeli Army with the rank of brigadier general and is now serving as head of Yad Vashem in Jerusalem.

He had been a young teenager when the Germans invaded Poland in 1939. Ultimately his family fled to a small town, Yitzhak's birthplace, which was located near Vilna in Lithuania. He and his family underwent great torment under the Soviets (1939 – 1941), and suffering during the German occupation from 1941 to the end of the war, and under Soviet rule after the war.

In his early teens, the Germans assigned Yitzhak to work in a large arsenal which contained a variety of weapons and ammunition. He saw an opportunity

*to smuggle out armaments for the youth Resistance movement, of which he was
a leader. . . .*

I sat down next to my two friends and proceeded to clean rifles. A German
sergeant came in to inspect our work. Apparently he was satisfied, because he
marched directly up to the three of us and ordered us to follow him into another
building exactly like the one we had just left. As we entered I noticed boxes
filled with ammunition for Russian rifles. The sergeant led us to a corner where
there was a big pile of all types of weapons and ordered us to clean and sort
them, making a separate pile of each type. A German soldier came in; the
sergeant ordered him to guard us and left.

We decided to do the sorting first and the cleaning up afterward. We found
Russian, Polish, Czechoslovakian, and Lithuanian guns, all types of machine
guns, a number of revolvers, most of them damaged beyond hope of repair. My
attention was drawn to a type of weapon used by no other army in the world; the
sawed-off rifle the peasants call *otrezanka*. This is a gun with a shortened barrel
and butt. A full-length rifle was cumbersome for the peasant because of its
length. He needed a weapon that could be carried hidden beneath his jacket to
the village dance and other festivities. Following the retreat of the Polish Army
in September 1939, and that of the Red Army in June and July 1941, peasants
found abandoned rifles and turned them into *otrezankas* by sawing off the butts
and part of the barrels. When the Germans came, they ordered the civilian
population to turn in all weapons, including the sawed-off rifles, which we now
found in the pile before us.

The German guard watched our every move. I stealthily indicated the
otrezankas to Moshe and Gershon. We continued sorting, and, finding a few
more of these in the pile we put them all together. We arranged the batches in
such a way that the German standing some distance from us could not count the
pieces of each pile — above all, the number of *otrezankas*. We had significantly
replaced the original pile, when suddenly the sergeant entered. He stood beside
us for a moment, watched us work, said a few words to the guard, and then went
out to the yard, the guard following him. I heard their voices outside the door
and looked all around to make sure that, except for my friends, there was no one
in the arsenal. This was our chance. I grabbed a sawed-off gun that looked
slightly less used than the others, thrust it into the belt under my shirt, and
quickly put on my jacket. It all took less than a minute, and when the guard
returned I was working quietly, sitting between my two comrades.

The German gave us a long, searching look but said nothing. Nor did he
notice that whereas I had been working without a jacket, I was now wearing
one. My problem was to continue working normally and moving freely without
arousing suspicion. I was also afraid that after we finished work we would be
searched; in that case all of us might be killed because of my transgression.
Nevertheless, I was convinced that we had to grasp any opportunity to acquire
arms. Who could tell whether such an opportunity would ever come again? The
rifle beneath my belt prevented me from bending properly; and in general I had
to be very careful to keep it from slipping out of place. My friends tried to raise
objects for me, but I bent over from time to time anyhow, to keep the

conscientious German from growing suspicious. Several more hours passed, and evening finally came. The sergeant entered and ordered us out to the yard. The rest of the workers were already there. The corporal lined us up in two rows. I was sure that they would search us. I felt the blood drain from my face, but with great effort I overcame my agitation and stood still like everyone else. The sergeant moved down the two rows, inspecting us, and then made a speech. He said he was satisfied with us and wanted us to come again the next morning, since there was a full month's work to be done. That very evening, he said, he would go to the *Judenrat* to ask that we be assigned to him for the entire period. After he had finished, the corporal announced that he and a few more soldiers would come to take us out of the ghetto every morning and bring us back in the evening.

I stood there as if on burning coals, waiting for the order to march. Finally it came. We went out to the road, escorted by the corporal, and two other soldiers. The way seemed endless. Ordinarily, when I returned to the ghetto from outside, I felt as if I were returning to a prison, but this time I actually looked forward to the ghetto as an island of safety. I was afraid the gun would fall from my belt on the way and from time to time had to hitch it up, making sure that neither the Jews nor the Germans noticed what I was doing. When we arrived at the ghetto, a Lithuanian policeman was at the gate, but when he saw the Germans escorting us, he let us pass without searching us.

Once past the gate, I felt as though I had won a great battle. I was the first person in the ghetto to possess a weapon. My two friends could hardly wait to have a look at my treasure, so we went into the public toilet, locked the door, and I displayed the *otrezanka*. Eyes shining, they gazed at my acquisition as if it held a promise of deliverance; it was our instrument of revenge. Promising each other to keep the gun a secret, we agreed to meet after supper and decide what to do next.

From *The Partisans: From the Valley of Death to Mount Zion*, by Yitzhak Arad, published by Holocaust Library, 1979, pp. 56-58.

THE VOW AND THE CHARGE

It happened long ago, when I was only nine years old. No one of my family had remained alive except for my father. He was a skilled worker and was needed by the Germans for the manufacture of war matériel, and so they let him live. To safeguard my life, he took me along with him wherever he went.

Most of the Jews in our town had been killed. The Germans slaughtered 1200 of our community on the very first day of their invasion in 1941. Those who had been left alive were murdered later, in the days that followed.

One day as I returned home with my father, suddenly a drunken SS man burst forth from a side street. He swept down on my father and began to hit him full force, shouting, "Cursed Jew, lie down on the ground when you see your master.'' Father prostrated himself on the ground, and the SS man began kicking him with his heavy boots and beat him on the head with the butt of his rifle. I looked at my father and lowered my eyes in shame. I couldn't look at his face. He was my father, my strong and courageous *abba* who guarded and guided me all through my life. And now I saw him abject, debased and bloody. I loved him very dearly and could not bear seeing him, who had been my proud father, so degraded.

It seemed to me Father detected what was going on in my mind. He rose up suddenly and looked defiantly at his assailant. The German yelled, ''Down on the ground.'' But my *abba* refused. He stood erect, looking straight at me, his eyes flashing a message to me, vowing his defiance and courage.

The German stormed, railed, and ranted like a mad hound. He struck my father to the ground, hitting him again and again with the butt of his rifle, beating him with his fists and stomping on his body with his heavy boots, screaming, ''Cursed dog that you are, Jewish pig. I will teach you to obey my orders.'' My father lay limp and lifeless. I stood helpless. To my dying day I shall not forget that scene.

Fellow Jews surrounded the crushed body of my father and questioned one another. ''Why didn't he obey the order of the murderer?'' They shook their heads in grief. They could not apprehend what had happened. But I understood. I knew that *Abba* had showed me how to die with honor and not to bow before the German murderers. His death was a covenant which he sealed between him and me, a vow we pledged to one another before he breathed his last breath.

I fled from the ghetto to the forest. At first I joined the family camps. Our suffering was beyond endurance. The frost was so intense that children lost their hands and legs from the cold. All of us were swollen from hunger. Fortunately my father's friend recognized me and took me under his care. He taught me to shoot, and I soon became an active partisan.

I shall never forget the parting words of my father's brave friend. He must have felt that his death was near as he spoke to the surviving fighters:

''Fellow partisans, these are my last words to you. Remember them! You well know how much we have suffered together. How our parents, our wives, and our children were put to death. No one mourned our losses. Many scoffed at us. Here in the forest we were always sent to the front lines. We were most exposed in our battles with the enemy, and we fell like flies. No one acknowledged or appreciated our sacrifices. Now they are dividing us up again. They are scattering our forces. Why? To obliterate all recognition that Jews have fought the enemy bravely and courageously — no less, indeed more, than our so-called allies.

''I say *enough!* Our sufferings have been beyond measure. I command you: an end to our absurd stupidity, our imbecility. Do you hear me? Enough of our sacrifices, our deaths for the sake of wretched strangers. We are not beholden to them. The time has come to join the fighters of our own people, of our own wars. I command you to get away, to scatter, to live to fight for our own land, our own future.''

Those were his last words. Three days later he fell in battle. But his stirring call to us has been etched deep in our minds and hearts. His charge blended with the vow between my father, of blessed memory, and me. It showed me the way. . . .

A.E.

From *The Hundred Who Returned to Their Homeland,* by Lena Kichler-Zilberman, New York: Schocken, 1968. Quoted in the *Guideline to the Memorial Day of the Holocaust and Valor* (April 11, 1972), published by the Office of Information and Education of the Israeli Defense Forces.

13.

RESCUERS, SAVIORS, AND RIGHTEOUS GENTILES

This is a heartening chapter dealing with rescuers, saviors, and righteous gentiles, some of whom sacrificed their lives to save Jews. The latter were self-motivated Christian nationals of various European countries who were active in hiding, smuggling, and keeping alive the hunted who had been marked to die.

Outstanding were the Danes, who practically snatched all of their Jewish fellow citizens – about eight thousand – from death; the Dutch, who saved about one-fifth; the Bulgarians, who protected their Jewish citizens but did not lift a finger to help Jewish noncitizens. Even in Berlin, some five thousand Jews survived to the end with the help of friends who arranged for them one hiding place after another.

The saviors came from different walks of life – from Raoul Wallenberg, scion of a Swedish aristocratic family, to the Ukrainian peasant woman Olina, who rescued Donia (see pp. 190-92). Dr. Aristides de Sousa, the Portuguese Consul at Bordeaux, France, in defiance of his government, issued visas to all Jews who applied. Working for three days, fifteen hours per day, he stamped Portuguese passports for nine thousand fugitives from France. He also sheltered and fed those who were in need and provided them with transportation to the railroad station.

Truss Wijsmuller, a Dutch social worker, endangered her life to gather Jewish children in her country for entry into Great Britian. When Holland surrendered on May 14, 1940, Mrs. Wijsmuller miraculously rescued some two hundred Jews, many of them orphan children, for shipment to England. She even interceded successfully with Adolf Eichmann to permit hundreds of Jewish children to be transported to England. She arranged to provide food, escorts, and immigration clearance for the first transport to England of six hundred Jewish children, who were later followed by others.

Yad Vashem, the impressive Heroes and Martyrs Memorial in Jerusalem, has commemorated these noble lives by immortalizing names and deeds in publications, and by planting trees in the Avenue of the Righteous Gentiles in order to preserve their memories and a record of their deeds.

ON RESCUING CHILDREN

In certain circles a plan is now under discussion to rescue a certain number (several hundred) of Jewish children by placing them in monasteries in various parts of the country. Three factors have motivated the men of the cloth to propose this: first, soul-snatching. The Catholic religious leaders have always exploited such difficult moments in Jewish life as pogroms, deportations, etc., to convert adults and children. This is perhaps the most important factor motivating the proposal, although the clergy assure us they will not attempt to convert the Jewish children entrusted to the care of their institutions.

There is a second, *economic* factor. Every Jewish child will have to pay 600 zloty a month, and for a year in advance, too. This is a very good stroke of business for the monastic orders. Since they have their own fields and gardens, their food costs are very low. For the Jewish children who are unable to meet this fee, costs are to be covered by the children of the rich, who will be taxed double.

The third factor is that of prestige. Until now, the Polish Christian spiritual leaders have done very little to save Jews from massacre and "resettlement," to use their euphemism. In view of the worldwide protest against the mass murder of Polish Jews, rescuing several hundred Jewish children may be offered as evidence that the Polish clergy did not sit with hands folded in these difficult times, that they did everything they could to help the Jews, particularly their children.

I was present at a discussion of this question by several Jewish intellectuals. One of them categorically opposed the operation. He argued that though it was agreed that [only] children between ten and fourteen years of age were to be put in the convents (as desired by the Jewish negotiators), the children — though supposedly old enough to resist indoctrination — would fall under the priests' influence and would be converted sooner or later. The priests' promise not to convert the children would be of no avail; time and education would take their toll. He maintained that we must follow the example of our fathers and accept martyrdom in His name. We have no right to give our blessing to the conversion of our children. Jewish society has no right to engage in such an enterprise. Let it be left to every individual to decide and act on an individual basis.

When, he concluded, 300,000 Jews have been exterminated in Warsaw, what avail is it to rescue several hundred children? Let them perish or survive together with the rest of their people.

However, others argued: We must look after the future. In time of massacre such as this, with all of European Jewry being slaughtered, the soul of each and every Jew is precious, and we must take pains to try to preserve it. After the war, the clergy will have no influence. Who knows whether they will even exist? This being so, there is no need to fear lest the children fall under the influence of the monastic orders. When one studies the pages of Jewish history closely, one discovers that martyrdom in His name was not the principle of our history. On the contrary, marranism was pseudo-Christianity.[1] Jews have always adapted themselves to the hardest conditons, have always known how to survive the hardest times. Sending a handful of Jewish children into monasteries will enable us to rescue those who will be the creators of a new generation of Jews. We have no right to take away the coming generation's right to live.

Those who took this position argued that one must strongly underline the difference between conversion and pseudo-Christianity. The priests themselves state that the children will not be converted, but will have to conduct themselves outwardly like Christians. True, there is some danger that if this persists for a long time some of the children will fall under the influence of the clergy — but there is a second, worse danger. If we do not carry out this child-rescue operation with the aid of the clergy, in a short time none will remain, the handful whom we are now in a position to rescue will perish as well. Numbers, some of the intellectuals said, are the most important consideration at this time. At any cost, we must rescue the largest possible number of Jews; so we must agree to the proposal to place some of our children in convents.

Still others argued that the thing had to be done, but not with the sanction of the representatives of Jewish society. Individuals were rescuing themselves in various ways — let the convent operation be a matter of individual choice.

From *Notes from the Warsaw Ghetto: The Journal of Emmanuel Ringelblum*, edited and translated by Jacob Sloan, published by Schocken, 1974, pp. 336-338.

RESCUING CHILDREN IN SOUP POTS

Witness to the Truth, *by Nathan Shapell, is an unusual book in Holocaust literature. It is a stirring success story of an Auschwitz survivor who valiantly and sagaciously led the pitifully bewildered Jewish D.P.'s (displaced persons) in the wasteland of postwar Europe through the jungle of bureaucratic obstructions and insufferable red tape and aided them in rebuilding their lives.*

Bold, resourceful, and enterprising, Shapell has carved out for himself a successful career as realtor and builder in the United States. His name appears on developments of homes built by his company in California and elsewhere. Latterly he and his brother have established a Chair teaching the Holocaust at Tel Aviv University, in memory of their parents, who perished.

[1] At the time of the Spanish Inquisition, many Jews accepted baptism in preference to death. But they continued to observe Jewish religious practices in secret. They were always suspect to their Christian neighbors, who called them *marranos*, or "pigs."

Every evening after work my four friends and I met to make our plans for the next day. We were not permitted to enter the *punkt* at night, or we would have gone in then, too.

Each time I entered and left I tried to think of some plan for saving women and children. We had discarded the idea of hiding children in the rubbish carts for fear they would suffocate. And no other ideas came to us.

On the evening of the fourth or fifth day, my four friends and I sat talking. As we decided on the crew for our next trips, I suddenly had a mental picture of the soup kettles I had seen left empty.

"Listen," I said, "I think I know how to bring out some children along with the men."

"How?" they chorused.

I reminded them of the size of the soup pots. "We can put three children in three pots, and each of us can carry out a pot while the other three men wheel out the carts. We'll have to alert the militiamen. If they let slip to the Germans what we're doing, we're dead."

Thus began our rescue of the children. However, instead of taking only three carts into the *punkt,* I decided to increase our crew to five. Time was running out.

No one, not Smoloz, Schmidt, or the Kultusgemeinde, knew when the Germans would make their next move, but we knew it had to be soon. And so the very next trip all five of us entered, each with a cart.

I had only to mention that we would try to take out children, and their mothers thrust them at me.

"Take my son," one said. Then more voices joined in. "Take mine, take mine." They knew the danger, but in their mothers' hearts they also knew it was preferable to whatever horror lay ahead for them.

When we left, that trip, Gold and I carried out our first two soup kettles with a little child in each one. Four men from the *punkt* brought out our two carts, and three more from the *punkt,* together with our three colleagues, brought out the other three carts. Neither Gold nor I knew the children we carried, nor did they know us. As in the case of the men, we rescued whoever was at hand. On that first trip and the ones that followed, we took whom we could as fast as we could.

The children we brought out in those few days left an indelible mark on my life. Although they were strangers to me, their faces live forever in my memory. I have never forgotten, nor can I ever forget, their suffering.

Especially one child, a little girl of five or six years who had suffered unknown tragedy. Like the rest, she dumbly accepted being placed in the greasy pot and made no sound as I carried her past the guards and into the street. When I set her down at the nearest safe corner, the child turned her face up to me and asked, "Where shall I go?"

I had to tell her, "Child, I don't know. Run, run."

I no longer knew one Jewish household still intact that could possibly take her in. We had no way of planning for the safety of the children once they were outside the *punkt.* I could only hope that they would find a place, not with a Jewish family but with a Christian family still courageous enough to shelter them and pass them off as one of their own.

In the moment I looked down at her tiny, pinched face and heard my voice telling her, an infant still, that she was on her own, the insanity and depravity of the monsters who had made this moment happen engraved her small face indelibly on my heart, and to me hers will always be the face of all the children who suffered.

From *Witness to Truth* by Nathan Shapell, New York: David McKay, 1974, pp. 71 – 76.

HOW THE FRENCH SAVED JEWISH CHILDREN

If the full story of France under the German occupation is ever told, if some historian succeeds in piecing together the whole epic of French resistance, one of the most dramatic epsiodes will be the battle waged by a few hundred courageous people to prevent the Gestapo and its Vichy aides from sending the thirty thousand Jewish children in France to their death in the lethal chambers of Poland.

They succeeded only in part, for some fifteen thousand children, it is estimated, were killed or deported during the four years of Nazi rule in France. But many of the surviving children were saved by those men and women, Jews and Gentiles, who organized their escape, found refuges for them, and maintained unceasing watch over them.

Some 1400 children, interned in three concentration camps awaiting deportation with their parents, owe their lives and liberty to demonstrations of public opinion voiced through outstanding leaders of the Catholic and Protestant Churches, which led directly to their release.

The work of protecting the children from the Gestapo was done by various groups and organizations. It was more successful in "Vichy France" — south of the armistice line of demarcation — than in the German-occupied zone, because there was a year and a half more to prepare underground activity. Thus, about thirteen thousand of the fifteen thousand children deported were captured in the northern zone.

The rescue activities required a considerable amount of organization. First, the children had to be supplied with false identity papers and ration cards. Then homes had to be found for them where the Gestapo and its Vichy henchmen would not easily ferret them out. A system of contact had to be set up for the children, dispersed as they were in private homes and institutions. They had to be watched, moved speedily if danger threatened, and given new identities from time to time. And their board had to be paid monthly.

The work was done mainly by women and girls, for they could circulate more freely without arousing suspicion and were less subject to detention and interrogation. Many Catholic and Protestant women associated themselves with Jewish defense organizations for this work. And many priests and pastors risked arrest to aid and shelter threatened children.

There was, for instance, Pauline Gaudefroic. A Catholic, twenty-two years old and active in the Resistance movement, Mlle. Gaudefroic offered her services to the *Oeuvre de Secours aux Enfants* (OSE), the Jewish child welfare organization which ''went underground'' during the Nazi occupation and continued its prohibited functions. She was given a group of children scattered in homes about the countryside as her special charges.

In February 1944 the Gestapo caught her at Limoges with a list of the names of her charges. They weren't so much concerned about catching one Resistance worker as in forcing from her information about the organization to which she belonged so that it could be destroyed.

She was tortured by the Gestapo. She was branded with a red-hot iron. But she wouldn't talk. A Frenchman employed by the Gestapo helped her to escape. The last the OSE heard of her was that she had gone underground in the Resistance movement in the vicinity of Grenoble. They would like to meet her again and thank her publicly for what she did.

Then there was the case of some forty children in Lyon who were to be arrested for deportation with their parents. Jewish relief workers saw Cardinal Gerlier, Archbishop of Lyon, and told him of the situation.

''Give me the children,'' the cardinal told them. ''When the police come looking for them, say that they are in my house.''

The committee did as instructed. Father Chaillet, who had been instrumental in the rescue of many Jews, concealed the fugitive children in Catholic institutions and homes. When the police came for the children, they were received by Father Chaillet, who refused to surrender them. He was arrested but subsequently released on Cardinal Gerlier's energetic intervention.

The OSE cared for six thousand children throughout the occupation period. Five thousand of them were in the southern zone and one thousand in the north. The work in Paris was directed by Dr. Eugen Minkowsky, a worker in the organization for many years. The whole underground machinery for the southern zone was set up by a young Jewish engineer of Lyon known under the *nom de guerre* of Georges Gorel. So effective was this machinery that the OSE lost only eighty of its charges to the Gestapo during four years.

Thirty-eight children, properly ''camouflaged,'' were placed in a home at Izien, in the Ain, with child refugees from the French war areas. The local prefect knew they were Jewish and aided in protecting them. But in March 1944 a resident of the town denounced the children to the German authorities.

''The Gestapo came with trucks at eight o'clock in the morning,'' Jacques Ratner of the OSE relates. ''They rounded up all the children, who were still having breakfast, and loaded them into trucks without letting them finish their meal. The children began to sing. They were beaten to silence them.

''They were brought to Lyon for examination. The non-Jewish children were sent back to the home. The thirty-eight Jewish children simply disappeared. The French police said they had been murdered by the Gestapo. They had heard that a group of children had been murdered by injections of poison. But their bodies were never found. They never arrived at the Drancy camp. There is simply no trace of them.

''Those were the only children the OSE lost in southern France.''

Most of the deported children were seized with their parents. It is only natural that parents should want to keep their children close to them when danger impends; but in France this was fatal.

In Paris 7000 children were trapped with their parents in the wholesale raids during July 1942, which resulted in the deportation of 50,000 men, women, and children. In southern France many children were seized with their parents in the great raids by the Vichy authorities during August and September 1942, which resulted in a total of 14,000 men, women, and children being turned over to the Germans for deportation.

Many families were trapped in April 1944 in the departments of La Corèze and Dordogne when the Nazis began taking reprisals against the villages where they were sheltering for having aided the Maquis. Some of the families fled to the forests and caves of Dordogne, where they existed like hunted animals, in a state of near-starvation. Devoted OSE workders penetrated even there to bring aid and relief, Ratner reports.

One of the most tragic incidents, because it came so shortly before liberation, was the seizure of 220 children in Paris last June. These children had been placed in a home in the Rue Lamarck operated by the UGIF — the *Union Générale des Israelites de France,* a Vichy-organized and controlled body. All these children were deported.

One aspect of the situation that will not easily be forgiven nor forgotten was the attitude of the Vichy authorities. They prosecuted the search for Jewish children with a relentless vigor. Their agents were more feared than the Gestapo, because it was more difficult to escape them.

Under the pretext of "reuniting families" the Vichy police tried to track down the the children of all arrested Jews so that entire families could be deported together.

A few instances where French officials refused to obey orders to arrest children have been recorded. OSE workers tell of one French police officer who, when he discovered that the person he had come to arrest was a fifteen-year-old girl, refused to take her into custody. But, in general, the police raided the children's homes, loaded their victims into police vans with gendarme escorts, and drove them through the streets.

In La Cruse, OSE officials say, public feeling ran so high at one time that the police, carrying out a roundup of fifty children, put placards, "Vacation Camps," on their vans.

The OSE organization suffered a heavy toll in its battle with the Gestapo. Twenty-eight men and women of its organization were captured; they were shot or deported. Others were arrested but managed to escape.

There was Jacques Salon, thirty, and his wife Nicolle, twenty-five. Nicolle was one of the four OSE workers rushed to Nice in September 1943, to try to save the children during the Gestapo roundup which netted five thousand victims for the deportation trains. Nicolle and her comrades were all arrested, and it has been ascertained that she was deported.

Jacques Salon continued his work with the OSE. Last spring he was organizing convoys of children to Switzerland — the OSE smuggled some 1500 children past the Gestapo and Vichy guards to safety there — when he was caught in Lyon with the names of the children to be included in one convoy and with a quantity of money.

Taken to the Gestapo headquarters in the Avenue Berthilot, he underwent tortures for two weeks, steadfastly refusing to reveal the nature of the list. At

Montluc prison he was given the same treatment. Then he was put in a train for the infamous Drancy camp — way-station for deportees to Poland. Jumping out of the train, he escaped. Retaken in a Paris hospital where he was receiving treatment for his injuries, he escaped again. Today he is working in the OSE bureau in Paris.

Julian Samuel, head of the OSE medical services, also arrested by the Gestapo, escaped by jumping out of the train taking him to Drancy. René Borel, a non-Jew, treasurer of the OSE since 1935, was arrested but subsequently released.

From *Menorah Journal* by Victor E. Bienstock, Spring 1945, pp. 93-97.

THE LITTLE DANE: BLESSED "MOTHER" OF FORTY CHILDREN

The name of a lively, intrepid girl, Anna Christensen, has been intimately bound up with the rescue of forty children during the tragedy. Until the outbreak of World War II the ties between the Danes and the Jews were taken for granted. The German invasion of Denmark was a turning point, and the relationship intensified. As Hitler rose to power, Jewish fugitives from Germany and Austria began to arrive in Denmark. They were received with open arms and were warmly welcomed by Danish families. With the outbreak of the war in 1939, their numbers grew. Among them were members of Youth Aliyah groups who were sent to Denmark and were accompanied by their leaders. One of these groups came to Niborg, where Anna Christensen's family lived. Anna's mother had been active in the International League for Peace and Freedom. She regarded the German invaders as enemies not only of the Danes but also of humanity and liberty.

The first concern of the Danes was to provide schooling for the newcomers. But when the Germans overran their country, the Danes feared what might happen to them and the Jews. Anna set up a secret school for forty Jewish children in the basement of her home. She herself taught the general subjects, and the Youth Aliyah leaders taught the Jewish subjects. Anna viewed herself as the mother of the group. Over and over again she insisted, "As long as an individual breathes, he must keep on learning." When the Germans instituted searches to round up hidden Jews, Anna scattered the children and found billets for them among her friends.

One of the rescued children, I.R., who now lives in Haifa, described her activities: "First she inspected carefully the homes in which she placed the children. And if she was not absolutely certain that they were safe, she did not rest until she found homes which met her standards of security. The children were housed among peasant families so that they could continue their *hakhshara*, agricultural training, before making *aliyah*. She notified the Danish Underground of the various hiding places of her wards so that in case of danger they could transfer the children to a safe place.

"Anna arranged weekly get-togethers at her own home, despite the near presence of Germans in the area. These meetings were vital to the morale and spiritual well-being of the children, who felt deeply their loneliness and isolation. Anna knew each child personally and was aware of their feelings and fears. She buoyed up and strengthened their spirits. And even though the children knew well the dangers they faced during their weekly meetings at Anna's home, they would not give them up.''

When, in November 1940, letters from their parents ceased coming, they knew that their dear ones had been transported to the concentration camps. Anna made special efforts to comfort and console them. She was a constant source of solace and encouragement to her new adopted family.

A.H., who now lives in Haifa, described the reaction of the homeless children during this period: ''I was one of the children who met weekly in Anna's home for a period of for a year and a half. Parentless and homeless, we all felt that she filled a void in our lives. We have remained attached to her by ties of love to this very day. Without any doubt, she helped restore and keep alive our faith in mankind and encouraged us to prepare for life in our homeland. Many of us took part in the war of liberation, and several lost their lives on the battlefield.

''Anna's children well remember the holiday talks which we prepared for our festival programs. She and we ended each celebration with fervent prayer that we might live to rejoice together in the observance of the holidays in Eretz Yisrael. At the end of the fast on Yom Kippur she would prepare a repast for us to break the fast. And for other festivals she cooked special dishes appropriate to the holiday. She was concerned not only with our physical but also with our spiritual needs. She made sure, insofar as she could, that her 'children,' whose lives she preserved, would not grow up ignorant and uncultured. Each week before we left she provided us with books and reading material in our hiding places until we should meet again.''

Anna's great test occurred in September 1943, when Germany began to transport the Jews of Denmark to the death camps. Anna hastened to find secure hiding places for her ''children'' and instructed them not to move until they received instructions. With the help of her family, friends, and the Danish Underground, she succeeded in delivering most of her ''children'' to the coast, where they embarked in small craft for the Swedish shore.

One of those who was rescued recalls: ''I well remember how I was saved. One terror-filled night I had undergone an operation in the hospital. I was certain that in my condition there was no power on earth that could prevent the Germans from capturing me. But one day after the operation Anna visited me and told me not to worry, that I would be taken out of the hospital. I could not believe that this would be possible. But after a few days a strange man whom I had never seen appeared at my bedside. I learned later that he was Pastor Jeppensen, an Underground worker. He gave me all the necessary instructions about what to do when I was removed from the hospital. I was provided with necessary documents testifying that I was mentally ill and was transferred to an asylum for the mentally ill. From there, after a few weeks, I was taken by a Dane, whose name was Jurgen Sabor, to Sweden.''

To this day Anna Christensen has kept in touch with her children. She remembers not only their birthdays but also the birthdays of their spouses and their children. She sends them greetings for the Jewish holidays. She subscribes to an Israeli newspaper, through which she has kept in constant touch with events in Israel.

Her dream of visiting Israel was realized when in 1966 she was invited by Yad Vashem to receive the medal of honor awarded to the Righteous Gentiles and be present at the planting of a tree bearing a plaque with her name, in the Avenue of the Righteous Gentiles, which fronts the memorial buildings. During her visit she met with all her "children" and "grandchildren" and returned to her homeland exalted in the knowledge that she had indeed been like an eagle that flutters over its young, spreading out its wings, catching them, and bearing them on its pinions (Deuteronomy 32:11). She has immortalized her noble name not only in the hearts of those she rescued but in the annals of Jewish history.

A.E.

From *Righteous Gentiles* by Aryah Bauminger, published by Israel Office of Education and Culture, 1967, pp. 33-36.

THE AFFAIR OF THE FINALY CHILDREN

Not since the Dreyfus case had France been so deeply stirred as it was over the affair of the Finaly children. Nicolas Baudy, the writer of this piece, was editor of Evidences, *a publication of the American Jewish Committee in France. He ends his report before the Finaly children were finally found and returned to France. The postscripts that end this selection contain the final developments. The translation from the French is by Maurice J. Goldbloom.*

Between seven and eight o'clock on the morning of February 3, 1953, Robert Finaly, aged eleven, and his brother Gerald, aged ten, were carried out by unknown persons from the College of Saint Louis de Gonzague at Bayonne in southern France. Forty-eight hours earlier, the district attorney of Bayonne had been informed of their secret presence at the college, and Father Silhouette, the director, had been told to hold the children for the authorities. But when Mr. M. Keller, who represented Mrs. Rosner, aunt and legal guardian of the two boys, presented himself at the college at 8 A.M. on February 3, Robert and Gerald had disappeared.

The next day, the news reaching the French public, the "Finaly Case" was born. The kidnapping of the two children, as a common-law crime, was a matter for the Court of Assizes, but the unusual implications of this particular case of kidnapping rapidly began to overshadow the crime itself. The French term *"affaire"* — one not employed indiscriminately in common newspaper usage — in a few days replaced the specific term "kidnapping" in the newspapers, in private conversations, and in public debate.

Who were these two children who became the stakes in a strange struggle that has pitted a sadly tried Jewish family against a woman some regard as a saint and others as a lunatic; princes of the Church against the Grand Rabbi of France; Jesuit fathers, nuns, and members of the lower clergy against politicians; and French Catholicism in general against that section of the nation which invokes the Rights of Man and the laws of the Republic?

Fleeing Austria in 1939, Dr. Fritz Finaly and his wife Annie *(née* Schwartz) had found refuge in Grenoble in southeastern France. He was at that time thirty-three years old; his wife twenty-nine. Though he had been the head of a clinic in Vienna, Dr. Finaly, as a foreigner, was not allowed to practice in France. The couple lived modestly in La Tronche, a suburb of Grenoble, where two children were born to them during the war: Robert Michael on April 14, 1941, and Gerald Pierre on July 3, 1942. Dr. Finaly had both babies circumcised.

As we know, the Germans occupied the whole of France in November 1942. Until that time the Free Zone, in which Grenoble was located, had, in spite of Vichy's racial laws, provided a relatively safe refuge for Jews. Now raids and arrests began. Jewish men, women, and children were deported to camps in Poland. In January 1944 German police action was intensified, particularly in the southeast of France, where every suspect person was arrested. The Jews were the first to be rounded up, and had little chance of escape. The plight of the children was tragic. Those who fell into the hands of the Germans met the same terrible fate as the adults — in some cases even sooner, being poisoned or given fatal injections by Nazi orderlies.

As a precaution, the Finalys placed their two babies in the Catholic nursery of Saint Vincent de Paul, in a village near Grenoble. Some time later, on February 14, 1944, both adult Finalys were arrested, he in the streets of Grenoble, she at home. Both were sent to the notorious Drancy camp, and thence deported to the East, after which nothing more was ever heard from them.

Immediately after their arrest, some friends, learning that the Gestapo was continuing its investigations and fearing that the children would be discovered, took Robert and Gerald out of the nursery of Saint Vincent de Paul and asked the nuns of Notre Dame de Sion in Grenoble to hide them in their convent, where several other Jewish children were being sheltered. The Ladies of Zion took the Finaly boys, but since their institution was an educational one, they were afraid that the presence of two children under school age would attract notice. So they entrusted the little boys to the directress of the municipal nursery of Grenoble, Mlle. Antoinette Brun.

Mlle. Brun's decision to harbor the children was certainly not taken lightly. The racial laws enforced in occupied France included ferocious penalities for helping Jews. Antoinette Brun was later to repeat many times that she had accepted the Finaly children "at her peril," and nobody would dream of denying it. What she did was more than charitable: it was heroic.

The months passed, and brought with them death for some and suspense for others. The Gestapo did not bother about the municipal nursery of Grenoble. Some Jewish friends of the Finalys were able to escape the police and stay alive in France. Robert and Gerald grew older. At the beginning of August 1944 the German troops withdrew in disorder from Grenoble. The Finaly children were saved. On March 12, 1945, a letter from New Zealand was received by the mayor of La Tronche. It had been written on February 9 by Mrs. Margaret Fischel, oldest sister of Dr. Finaly and now married to a veterinarian. Dr. Finaly's original family had been dispersed by Hitler's annexation of Austria: two of his sisters, Mrs. Fischel and Mrs. Rothbaum, had settled in New Zealand; the third, Mrs. Rosner, in Palestine.

As soon as the intercontinental mails began running again, Mrs. Fischel had tried to get news of her brother and his wife. She had not, she says, heard about them since September 7, 1942, the date of a letter — the last anyone received from him — that Dr. Finaly got through to a friend in the United States. The mayor of La Tronche wrote to Mrs. Fischel that the Finalys had been deported but that their two children were safe. The mayor had known Dr. Finaly personally, and wrote: "Your brother's dearest wish was that you should take the children in case of any mishap."

As it happened, Mrs. Fischel's letter to the mayor of La Tronche was crossed by a letter from a friend of the Finalys who had survived in France, a Mr. Ettinger. He told Mrs. Fischel of the arrest of the Finalys, and of their last wishes. Dr. Finaly had felt that Mr. Ettinger's fate as a Jew was as uncertain as his own, so had given over his power of attorney to a non-Jewish French-woman, a Mme. Poupaert. She was the one who had taken the actual responsibility of placing the two children in the municipal nursery run by Mlle. Brun, and thus had the authority to get the children back and send them to Mrs. Fischel. Mr. Ettinger wrote: "Dr. Finaly and his wife, in the course of numerous conversations, clearly expressed the desire that the children be entrusted to you if anything should happen to themselves."

The evidence provided by Mr. Ettinger and the mayor of La Tronche is definite as to the desires of Dr. Finaly: Mrs. Fischel was to get the children. Moreover, she herself expressed the wish to take them.

As soon as she got Mme. Poupaert's address from Mr. Ettinger, Mrs. Fischel wrote to her. The mails were still slow at this time. On July 5 Mme. Poupaert replied. She had seen the chldren in the municipal nursery the day before. "They are," she wrote, "in excellent health, and the person who is taking care of them begged me to ask you to leave them with her. She is a very good woman who has already adopted five children. . . . The idea of parting with the children is very painful to her, since for eighteen months she has cared for them and is genuinely attached to them. As for myself, I do not want to advise you one way or the other. The doctor asked me to hide them and afterwards to get in touch with you. . . . I hope that my letter will not make you unhappy; for I speak with complete frankness and no mental reservations; you alone shall decide what you ought to do." Antoinette Brun had poured out her heart to Mme. Poupaert. She had adopted five children, one of them Jewish. One of these five, a boy of eighteen, had been accidentally killed some weeks before. Her sorrow and the care she had given the Finaly babies deserved consideration.

Mme. Poupaert had received very precise instructions from Dr. Finaly, but from now on she remained prudently silent, confining herself to thanking Mrs. Fischel when the latter sent her a food package. Mrs. Fischel now wrote to Mlle. Brun, but had to wait until November 1945 for an answer. This answer was to become one of the crucial items in the *dossier* of the Finaly case. In it

Antoinette Brun sang her own praises and called attention to her nobility in taking charge of the children. She made much of their health; according to her, they were still too young to travel all the way to New Zealand. She also suggested that certain objects of value entrusted to friends by the Finalys be sold "in order to pay the expenses of the trip."

She ended her letter: "No one had the courage to take them then. I took them, without knowing them, without knowing their relatives, their family; I took them without anything, almost anything. These are bonds of affection which one has no right to break just like that. Their money is nothing to me. But they are in a way my own little ones, and I am disgusted to see that people, so-called friends of the family, want to take them away from me in order to share their inheritance.

"I am French and Catholic; along with these two children I have adopted or received seven children whom I have raised as well as I could, with the fruits of my labor and my own money. The affection of my children is my recompense, I ask no other. Your nephews are Jews, that is to say, they have remained in their religion."

Six months before, on May 25, 1945, the Fischels had already got permission for the children to enter New Zealand. They undertook to pay the entire cost of the trip and offered to reimburse Mlle. Brun for all her expenses in caring for the boys. On that same May 25, M. de la Tribouille, Free France's agent in Wellington, mailed a request to the Foreign Ministry in Paris that the children be sent from France. Strangely, this letter remained unanswered for some months — as is shown by a follow-up letter for the French legate in Wellington, Mr. Gazel, dated December 28, 1945. What had happened? Official communications between Paris and French overseas offices were still undependable, and the functioning of the administration itself was still erratic. These factors were not propitious to the Fischels. As we shall see, Mlle. Brun took advantage of the delays.

In August 1945 Margaret Fischel wrote to the district attorney of Grenoble, asking him to facilitate the departure of the children. He did not reply. In October she sent another note to the district attorney, asking that the children be entrusted to her care. Again no response. Antoinette Brun was a power in Grenoble. On the local level she was able to block the steps taken by the distant Fischels, who were themselves immobilized by the slowness of the replies to their inquiries.

Finally, they got in touch with the French Red Cross through the British Red Cross, and a report by the Red Cross social worker in Grenoble, dated October 5, 1946, was sent to them. She wrote: "Mademoiselle Brun categorically refuses to hand over the children. She was named their guardian on November 12, 1945, in accordance with Article 142 of the Civil Code, which authorizes the establishment of a provisional council of guardianship when the parents of children are deceased. This article makes no provision for the case of other members of the family presenting themselves subsequently."

Thus, back in November 1945, at the very time when Mlle. Brun was at last writing her answer to Mrs. Fischel, she was also assembling a family council before a justice of the peace in Grenoble. Mlle. Brun was by that time perfectly well aware of the existence of Dr. Finaly's sisters, and in particular of Mrs. Fischel, since she was friendly with Mme. Poupaert. The family council that Mlle. Brun gathered together consisted of four Jews who had been more or less closely connected with Dr. Finaly but were completely ignorant of Mrs. Fischel's desire to have the children and the steps she had taken to get them. By concealing this fact from the court, Antoinette Brun was able to put the law of the Republic on her side.

More months passed. On March 16, 1946, and then on August 9, Foreign Minister Georges Bidault sent notes to the Veterans Ministry, under whose jurisdiction the case of the children came. These two memoranda, based on information from the French minister in Wellington, gave a completely accurate and detailed account of the situation. The British Red Cross, which was to care for the children on their voyage, had multiplied its communications to the French Red Cross.

The Fischels did not know where to turn. For two years they wrote everywhere. The attorney of the French Red Cross advised them to appeal the guardianship judgment as formally defective.

In July 1948 Mrs. Fischell decided to give up her rights in favor of her sister, Mrs. Rosner, who was living in Gederah, Israel, and, being nearer to France, could intervene more effectively. The Rosners gave their power of attorney in the matter of the children to a trusted friend, an engineer in Grenoble named Mr. Keller.

But who was Antoinette Brun? She was a native of Grenoble and, after a somewhat checkered youth, a lady of good works. She lacked neither courage nor enterprise. She was a Catholic, yet enjoyed the favor of the Socialist mayor of her city, as well as having numerous other intimates in the magistracy and the municipal administration. A fat, loud, expansive busybody, with an inordinate taste for quarrelling.

People were somehow a little afraid of her. Behind the respectable façade of small-town life, many scandals lie dormant. Antoinette Brun had seen her share of them. With the approach of age she had become devout, yet remained bossy, gossipy, and jolly. Only her charitable work gave her from now on an almost sacred halo.

She terrorized some people, fascinated others. Some people would do anything for her. Grenoble was her personal kingdom, her home. Later on she was able to act the role, superbly, of a woman in revolt against the powers that be. A short while ago she, the fervent Catholic, declared to *Figaro* that she didn't give a fig for the Pope. But before assuming the role of rebel, she made use of her influence with the powers that be with astonishing skill.

When she learned that Mr. Keller was preparing to recover, step by step, the ground she had conquered, she had the Finaly children baptized — as Mr. Keller learned from her own mouth in July 1948. The exact reason why she took this step has remained obscure. Nor was the act of baptism made public. Did she take advantage of the good faith of a priest, or did she find an accomplice?

Next, she called a new family council on January 24, 1949, pretending that the alternate guardian named by the first family council, Mr. Imerglick, had disappeared without leaving an address. Again, she was lying. Mr. Imerglick, who had sent Christmas presents to the children in 1948, subsequently showed the judges a letter of thanks from Mlle. Brun that showed she knew his address perfectly well. But for Antoinette these were mere venial sins, and the end justified the means. She invited a new set of people to the new family council, choosing them from among her own friends: a watchmaker in Grenoble, her deputy directress in the municipal nursery, her lawyer's clerk. They all took orders from her. Maitre Maurice Garçon, when he took over the case for the Finaly family, declared in court with regard to this episode: "Never has anyone seen the provisions of the law for the protection of minors made mock of with such effrontery."

On September 27, by virtue of the rights vested in him, Mr. Keller called a different family council, which assigned the guardianship of the children to their aunt, Mrs. Rosner, and authorized Mr. Keller to recover them. But Mlle. Brun refused to hand them over, and got the courts to annul Mr. Keller's family council.

Mr. Keller, who showed an endurance equal to every trial, assembled a new family council on November 14, 1949, in which the three aunts — Mrs. Fischel, Mrs. Rosner, and Mrs. Rothbaum — were represented. After taking three weeks to consider the question, the judge named Mrs. Rosner guardian, and ordered Mlle. Brun to hand over the children.

Later, after the kidnapping of the children, the big newspapers all reported as a fact the main claim of Mlle. Brun and her supporters that the relatives had not bothered themselves about the children until five years after the liberation of France. Borne up on a flood of articles written to order, Antoinette Brun became a Lady of Seven Sorrows from whom an ungrateful family, moved solely by religious and national fanaticism, was snatching the beloved children who had grown up in her bosom. It took the persistence of lawyers Maurice Garçon and David Lambert, the patience of Mr. Keller, and the day-by-day work of some honest reporters to acquaint the public with the true background of the Finaly case. The facts had been systematically and tendentiously twisted, and some of them omitted in the rightist and Catholic press. Even today [1953] a section of French public opinion is still badly informed, and continues to be misled about the Finaly case by the propaganda working to convert it into a solely religious issue — this in complete disregard of the moral questions involved and the natural rights of the family.

Again, Antoinette Brun refused to hand over the children. Instead, she once more started proceedings to annul the legitimate family council. Though her arguments were entirely specious, the local court complied by decreeing another annulment on November 15, 1951, on the pretext that the council assembled by Mr. Keller had not included the late Mme. Finaly's brother, Otto Schwartz, who was living in Gmünd, Austria, after his return from exile in Shanghai. But Mr. Schwartz had already given his consent to the appointment of Mrs. Rosner as guardian.

The local court was now overruled by the Court of Appeals on June 11, 1952, and Mrs. Rosner was confirmed as guardian. On this occasion the boys appeared in court, but on July 15, 1952, when the bailiff went to the Brun home to take them, they and Mlle. Brun had disappeared. Mr. Keller filed a complaint, and the magistrate summoned Mlle. Brun. She appeared but refused categorically to hand over the boys, then left without being disturbed. Where were the children? No one knew. Mlle. Brun kept her silence, and the court did nothing.

On August 12, 1952, the boys' uncle, Otto Schwartz, was visited in Gmünd by a Franciscan father from Vienna, Eugen Berthold, who brought him a letter from Mlle. Brun dated August 8. On the pretext of needing an authorization to enter the children in a state school, Mlle. Brun asked Mr. Schwartz to "designate her officially as guardian." Also, she proposed a meeting with Mr. Schwartz so that he would have a chance to see his nephews.

One detail, however, had escaped Mlle. Brun. Scattered though it was, the Finaly-Schwartz family had preserved firm ties. Otto Schwartz was not unaware of the troubles his sisters-in-law were having in their efforts to get hold of their nephews. He saw the trap and refused to sign.

On September 12 Father Berthold himself wrote to Mr. Schwartz on behalf of Mlle. Brun. She was going to take Robert and Gerald to the Franciscan monastery in Strasbourg, and she offered to pay for a ticket from Vienna to Strasbourg for Mr. Schwartz, who was poor. Mr. Schwartz wanted to see his nephews, and to get a clear view of the situation, so he went to Grenoble and from there to Strasbourg, where Mlle. Brun had made a rendezvous for October 3. He called at the Franciscan monastery. Antoinette was there, but not the children. The tenor of his conversation with the woman took him so much aback that Mr. Schwartz went to a bailiff and drew up an affidavit, part of which read: "Having indicated in the first place, in a letter to Mlle. Brun, that I would not come unless I could see my two nephews, Robert and Gerald Finaly, and having twice gone in vain to the monastery of the Franciscan Fathers in Strasbourg, where I had been asked to come, I found Mlle. Brun there without the children but in the company of two gentlemen unknown to me. Our conversation was interpreted by a father of the Franciscan order. Mlle. Brun declared that she had lost a trial and that they wanted to rob her of the children. Then she proposed to take me in an auto, with herself and the two gentlemen, to Grenoble. When, after a long discussion, I accepted her proposal, she suddenly declared that the children were in a college at Chambéry, although she had at first pretended that they were in a convent at Grenoble. In addition, she declared that she would not agree to my going there. In the course of the conversation Mlle. Brun offered me money and asked me to declare that I had visited her at Christmas or Easter, and that I had at that time reached a decision on the subject of the children. I refused. I was very disappointed, after a thirty-hour train trip, to meet Mlle. Brun and two gentlemen whom I did not know, but not my nephews. She also mentioned a bank account in Switzerland in the name of my brother-in-law, F. Finaly; she suggested that if I came to an agreement with her, she would send me the papers and I would be able to take it over.

"Having been deeply disappointed after having made the acquaintance of Mlle. Brun, and having been displeased by her behavior towards me, I have come to the firm conclusion that Mr. Keller of Grenoble should proceed as rapidly as possible in the execution of the judgment, and that the children should be taken to their guardian, Mrs. Rosner, in Gederah [Israel]."

As we see, a religious order had now entered the picture. After the kidnapping of the children, the Franciscans protested their good faith, and since Mlle. Brun made a habit of lying by omission, it is quite possible that the fathers had been left in complete ignorance of the real situation.

On November 18, 1952, Mlle. Brun was brought up before a criminal court. She claimed that until 1950 the children's relatives had given no sign of life. The court's decision was set for December 2, and on November 28 the attorneys for the family submitted a voluminous supplementary *dossier,* every detail of which was irrefutable. On that very same day, however — four days before the date set for the decision — the court handed down a verdict, without examining the *dossier,* in which it censured the Court of Appeals for confirming Mrs. Rosner as guardian and accepted the allegations of Mlle. Brun: "noted . . . the accused affirms that the Finaly family did not claim the minors after the liberation of the territory." The decision also questioned the validity of Mr. Keller's authority, and mentioned as a weighty factor the baptism of the children. However, because she had not produced the children, Mlle. Brun still fell under article 357 of the Penal Code and was liable to a year in prison. Yet the court ruled that she was not guilty because the care of the children had not been *expressly* entrusted to Mrs. Rosner! This time a question of mere syntax and form saved Mlle. Brun.

On January 8, 1953, Maitre Maurice Garçon pleaded for the Finaly family before the Court of Appeals in Grenoble, and went into the question of the precise nature of the exclusive and jealous maternal passion Mlle. Brun was protesting. Actually, while Robert and Gerald were at the municipal nursery, from 1944 to 1946, they were taken care of by Mlle. Brun's old maidservant. In its order issued on June 11, 1952, the Grenoble court had demanded that the children be produced; when this was not done, it was discovered that they had left the Grenoble municipal nursery in 1946 for a religious boarding school, and then for a religious day school in Voiron (Isère). While there, they had boarded with a lady in town under the names of Robert and Gerald Brun. In 1949 they had left the school of Saint Joseph of Voiron for a religious *pension* in Lugano, Switzerland, where they remained for a year. From September to December of 1950 they had been with the Dominicans of Coublecie (Isère) under the names of Louis and Marc Quadri. During the school year 1951 – 52 they were again at Saint Joseph of Voiron under the names of Louis and Marc Brun.

After their kidnapping, evidence was produced showing that in September 1952 they had been placed with the Ancelles (the lay branch of the order of Notre Dame de Sion) in Paris, but that at the beginning of October 1952, at the time when Antoinette Brun was summoning their uncle Otto Schwartz to Strasbourg and telling him that they were at Chambéry, they were in a school of the order of Notre Dame de Sion in Marseille under the name of Quadri. In January 1953 they were placed in another school of Notre Dame de Sion in Marseille under the names of Martella and Oliveri.

When they had appeared in the Court of Appeals in June 1952, the boys politely told the court, as if it were the most natural thing on earth, that they usually saw Mlle. Brun only once a year. The presiding judge was so startled that he repeated the question and got the same answer from the children.

Obviously, Mlle. Brun's maternal passion was not excessive. At this time, in 1952, the Finaly case was still nothing but the Brun case. Partly out of religious fanaticism, partly out of a sheer taste for squabbling and intrigue, Mlle. Brun was obstructing justice. People were talking about her, and she liked it. Her letters reveal her penchant for florid histrionics. In one, she assumes that everybody knows about her warm heart. In another, she complains of being misunderstood, persecuted. She writes, "The Jews are ungrateful," and again, "I am Catholic and I have rescued large numbers of Jews and I have received nothing but hate in return."

On January 29, 1953, the Court of Appeals reversed the criminal court's decisions, confirming the rights of Mrs. Rosner and issuing a final order against Antoinette Brun.

She had lost. The only resort which remained to her was an appeal to the Court of Cassation, the highest court of appeal in France, but before she could go there she would have to give up the children.

As was later discovered, at midnight, January 29, Abbé Mollard, pastor of the Marseille church of Saint Michel, appeared in the St. Charles railroad station in Marseille and handed Robert and Gerald Finaly over to a certain Mme. Bleuze. She was the sister of Mother Antonine, Superior of Notre Dame de Sion in Grenoble. At three in the afternoon of January 30, Mme. Bleuze and the children arrived in Bayonne, in the foothills of the Pyrenees, only thirty miles from Spain. She went to the boarding school of Saint Louis de Gonzague, saw its Superior, Father Sihouette, and requested him to accept as students Francois and Antoine Martela — otherwise Robert and Gerald Finaly.

But Mme. Bleuze talked too much, never doubting the "discretion" of Father Silhouette. In the course of the conversation she told of how bored the boys had been on their journey from Grenoble. Father Sihouette had a lively intelligence; he had read in the newspapers of the decision of the Court of Appeals, and knew about the Finaly children. He became suspicious: no, he would not accept the children. Mme. Bleuze bit her tongue, a little late. But she showed him the boys' school identity cards — forged ones in the name of Martela that she had received from Mother Antonine — and Father Silhouette yielded. Mme. Bleuze took the train for Grenoble, where she arrived the following day and reported to Mother Antonine. After Mme. Bleuze had left, Father Silhouette reflected. The whole business was suspicious. He informed the Bayonne district attorney, who alerted the district attorney of Grenoble. The latter asked Bayonne to make sure of the identity of the children, and to hand them over to the Director of Population, a functionary of the Ministry of Public Health. But the Bayonne prosecutor contented himself with an order to Father Silhouette to keep the children under his supervision.

On February 1 Mother Antonine, worried by her sister's clumsiness, left Grenoble for Biarritz. There she went to the Mother Superior of Notre Dame de Sion of Biarritz, who told her of Father Silhouette's action. Mother Antonine went immediately to the palace of Bishop Terrier of Bayonne, who saw her at nine in the evening. She told him that Mlle. Brun had asked her help in placing the children in a religious school out of reach of "court quarrels."

Bishop Terrier had one of his canons telephone Guy Petit, mayor of Bayonne (who a few days later became Minister of Commerce in René Mayer's cabinet). Mr. Petit was at a meeting of the Municipal Council and could not come to the phone. A half-hour later he called the Bishop's palace and told Canon Narbaitz that he would get in touch with the district attorney of Bayonne, and when he went to Paris the following day, would ask the Keeper of the Seals for "additional information."

On February 3 Mr. Keller, armed with the proper papers, arrived at eight in the morning at the Saint Louis de Gonzague school to take the children. But, again, they had disappeared. Accompanied by the district attorney, he went to the Bishop, who declared he knew nothing at all. About what happened to the boys during the next few days, little is likely ever to be learned. (When Mother Antonine, Antoinette Brun, and the Basque priests were arrested, later, they refused to answer many questions, and admitted only what was common knowledge.)

The police searched for the children in vain. Subsequent investigation disclosed, at a time when the boys were already out of reach of French authority, that on February 12 a professor at the Catholic seminary in Bayonne, Abbé Laxague, had entrusted them to an Abbé Aristiart, who had carried them off to St. Jean de Luz. A businessman in the city, Mr. Fagalde, took them by auto to Guétary, and there handed them over to another Basque businessman, Mr. Etchesaharetta, who took them during the night to the pastor of Biriatou, Abbé Ibarburu. On February 13, Abbé Ibarburu, with a ferryman named Susterreguy, took Robert and Gerald to the Spanish border, which was not far from Biriatou. The weather was bad. Abbé Ibarburu went back to his parish, while Susterreguy crossed the frontier with the boys, making them do a five-hour forced march through deep snow. This would have been a grueling ordeal for an adult, let alone for two small children raised in convents, and, on top of that, certainly weakened by the wandering existence they had been made to lead for two weeks.

Once over the border, they were on the way to Vera in Spain, but Abbé Ibarburu followed them in Etchesaharetta's car, caught up with them, and brought them to St. Sebastian, where he asked the organist of the church of St. Ignatius, Abbé Ahlister, to put them up. When the latter refused, Abbé Ibarburu went to the Abbey of Lascarro. From then on all trace of the children vanishes.

The law had been violated. Arrests began. Mother Antonine cursed the police who came for her, in language not usually associated with a Reverend Mother. The Basque priests gave themselves up without a word. But Antoinette Brun's arrest caused a commotion in print. Pierre Scize, writing in *Figaro,* gave "the good lady of Grenoble" a place in the lives of the Saints. For some weeks the French press was divided into two camps, her partisans and her adversaries.

The most fantastic stories were put in circulation. Writers lost themselves in hypotheses as to the place where the children were hidden but, with rare exception, nobody except the boys' relatives really worried about their physical fate. It took almost two months to bring home to the public the fact that these relatives had been claiming the children since 1945. On February 6, 1953, Gérard Bauer of the Académie Goncourt wrote in *Figaro* under the pen name

"Guermantes": "At least there is nothing base in this case; the affair is one of a conflict between the passion of faith and the rights of the family and the heart."

These "rights of the heart," about which a great deal was heard in the days following the kidnapping, were immediately taken for a proven fact by the Catholic press and used as an argument in the Brun woman's favor. On March 30, a provincial newspaper, *Le Lorrain,* reporting a judgment of a court in Nice giving a foster mother the guardianship of a boy born of an unknown father and abandoned at birth by his mother, did not hesitate to write that the same issue was involved in the Finaly case, and that the Nice judgment "was a model for the one which the Court of Cassation should give in the Finaly *affaire.*"

But very soon the debate left these "rights of the heart" to dwell on "the fanatical passion of faith." On February 11, 1953, Francois Mauriac, the Catholic novelist and editorial writer of *Figaro,* entered the arena. He tossed forth a formula, "the children's point of view," and wrote: "The faith of the two children is involved. I can testify that at their age my religious life became conscious and took on a certain tone and coloration which it has never since lost; that it became fixed, less perhaps in a dogmatic and moral sense, than in a personal relation established with someone invisible yet present. . . . Which of their two allegiances will win out in these children's hearts? The allegiance to their fathers, to the ashes of martyrs, or the allegiance to that Son of David who was crucified for them, too, who has marked them with his sign, and who, since their baptism, knows them by their first names? Perhaps they themselves will know how to affect a synthesis between these two allegiances. Is not Christianity, for a baptized Jew, the fulfillment of the word given to Abraham our father?"

The novelist of Thérèse Desqueyroux, of the delights of sin and of efficacious grace, now set the tone. Baptism supplanted Antoinette Brun in the leading role. From then on it was not a mother or a pretended foster mother who claimed the children, but a church. Mauriac, as a Christian "of the world," returned to the notion of the sovereign Church's right to decide. On February 10, only a week after the kidnapping, the Reverend Father Gabel, in *Le Croix,* the official organ of the French Church, distinguished between the juridical and moral aspects of the Finaly case: "Juridically, it can be said, a decision of the courts was disregarded and the police were deceived. In every society, respect for law and justice is a condition of peace and order. Morally, it is much more complex — two orphan children who have been baptized, have known affection, have been educated, are uprooted, were to be snatched away from her whom they called 'mama' and entrusted to an aunt whom they did not know, transplanted to Israel against the will of their lost father, and thrown into a society whose language they did not know."

It will be noted that after a formal salute to "the rights of the heart," Father Gabel introduces a new idea — that of the children's nationality. Dr. Finaly had in fact got French naturalization for his elder son, Robert, and would have done the same for Gerald if the racial laws in force by that time had not prevented it. It is certain that Dr. Finaly considered France his adopted country, and that the children, raised in France and speaking French, could be regarded as French. Now Israel was brought into the case, as it was to be increasingly. But if Mrs.

Fischel had been able to get the children in 1945, there would have been no question of Israel, since the Fischels had become subjects of New Zealand. It was only by chance that Mrs. Rosner, living in Israel, became their legal guardian. And the laws of Israel and France, both, allow children to postpone their choice of nationality until they have grown up. Until then Robert and Gerald would have remained French in the eyes of French law.

Father Gabel wrote further: "The Church is a perfect society that has authority over those men who have become its members by baptism." He emphasized that there were nevertheless certain cases in which a complex of problems "suggests that the Church should not press the exercise of that right." And in conclusion: "These children are now eleven and twelve years old. One must take account above all of what they are; one must take account also of the love which has saved them at the risk of liberty and of life."

What did this mean but that the authority of the Church over anyone baptized into it having been proclaimed, it was still necessary for ecclesiastical authority to take protection behind the appeal to such secondary considerations as "rights of the heart," nationality, and culture? A week after the kidnapping, the ecclesiastics involved were anxious to keep the gates neither open — "the children are baptized, hence ours" — nor closed: the turn of events might bring about their forced return at any moment. On the one hand, the official press of French Catholicism does not disavow a Catholic, Antoinette Brun, or the priests and nuns who caused the children's disappearance. But neither does it openly take the side of these disturbers of public order who have broken the laws of the Republic.

Each succeeding day through February and March the discussion of the Finaly affair took an increasingly theological turn. But the approach was often oblique, hiding behind sociological, juridical, or psychological considerations, if only in order to appear more amiable. The question of baptism, and of the irrevocable character in general of the Catholic sacraments, dominated everything. Even the columns of big, respectable nonconfessional newspapers like Le Monde were suddenly drenched with religiosity; writing in Le Monde February 25, the Reverend Father Riquet invoked Canon 1351, according to which "no person may be forced to embrace the Catholic faith," and was disputed by a certain Abbé Deroo, who answered, March 10: "In similar circumstances, the Church respects the rights of the family, but it cannot avoid its own duties; baptism makes the child a Christian, and the child comes under the jurisdiction of the Church. The latter had the duty of assuring its members the riches and blessings of the life eternal which are superior in dignity and worth to the bare demands of the natural order."

Meanwhile negotiations for a compromise solution were being set in motion. It is clear that they were bound to fail, although promoted by persons of good will. At the date of writing nothing has been accomplished. The negotiations have a semisecret character, and, although mentioned in the press, are categorically denied by the person involved.

A week after the disappearance of the boys the attorney for the relatives, Maitre Garçon, received certain proposals from the other side through a magistrate in close touch with, and speaking for, the Bishop of Lyon. At the same time Grand Rabbi Kaplan received a sort of plan for the restitution of the children from a well-known Jesuit who had behaved with especial heroism under the German occupation and saved many Jewish children from the Gestapo. This Jesuit father declared that he was ready to go to the Basque country and thought that, backed by the authority of Cardinal Gerlier, he would be able to find the children and restore them to their family. It seemed that there was a chance for agreement, and that a desire for a settlement existed on the part of certain members of the French clergy, particularly among the bishops. Had not Bishop Gaillot of Grenoble issued an appeal that anybody with information about the whereabouts of the boys should give it to the proper authorities immediately?

All these proposals on the part of the clergy contained controversial points, but an agreement should not have been hard to reach nevertheless. The children were to remain in France at least until the decision of the Court of Cassation, which would definitively determine Mrs. Rosner's rights; they were to receive a French education; and they were to make their own choice of religion. Mr. Keller, spokesman for the family, made a statement that was headlined in the newspapers: "The children shall go to Mass if they want to."

But the days passed and the Jesuit father, returned from Spain, was unable to restore the children because he had not found them. Certain newspapers, while publishing urgent appeals in the name of "Judeo-Christian friendship" for a compromise, circulated strange rumors: the Spanish Church, with its historical inability to compromise, was blocking the search; the children had left Spain for Austria, Brazil, Chile. *Figaro* even went so far as to say that nothing could be done without the benevolent cooperation of the Spanish police, and that General Franco was asking in exchange for the children the surrender to him of a score of Spanish Republicans in asylum in France. Only a *quid pro quo* of this kind, *Figaro* claimed, would make it possible really to look for the Finaly children in Spain.

Meanwhile, a campaign for the release of the jailed kidnappers and their accomplices was under way. Antoinette Brun was described as lying sick on a damp and lumpy straw mattress in her prison cell, and the Basque priests as playing pelota in the courtyard of their jail. A committee for the defense of "Basque liberties" put up a poster signed by Jean Ybarnegaray, notorious for his collaboration with the Germans during the war, that read: "Are we going to let the Jews and their bought press insult and persecute with their hatred the priests and nuns who, in the hour when they were being hunted down, saved them from the Gestapo at the risk of their own lives?" At the same time special reporters from the great evening papers were camping on the Spanish frontier. Every day announcements came that the children were to be returned on the following day. The negotiations continued. The French cabinet deliberated. In the name of the independent and peasant ministers in the cabinet . . . [spokesmen] insisted on the urgency of freeing the Basque priests, whose imprisonment, according to them, was stirring up certain "regionalist disturbances." A weekly repeated Premier Mayer's phrase: "My name does not permit me to keep priests in prison." Until March 11, when the full facts were publicly stated by Maitre Garçon, the newspapers were filled with rumors that the release of the secular and regular clergy arrested at Bayonne and Grenoble had become an indispensable condition for the success of the negotiations. At last the priests, the nuns, and Mlle. Brun were freed. March did not bring the children. Nor did April.

Today the point of the negotiations initiated by the clergy seems clear. By approaching Jewish community leaders, the Catholic representatives aimed to shift to a religious plane a case that came exclusively under the criminal law of the Republic, and should not have required the intervention of either Jew or Catholic *as* Jew or Catholic. The Church wanted discussions with Jews as *the Jews* in order to set up a *religious* adversary against whom it could be proved that it, the Church, had acquired the souls of the children, and *therefore* had authority over their baptized bodies. If the issues in the Finaly *affaire* could be staked out along such lines, questions of law and legality could be disregarded. The rights of the Family, which the Catholics never cease proclaiming when it suits their purposes (in the name of which, for instance, they got the Baranger Law passed, giving state subsidies to religious schools in a country where the tradition of lay schools is so old as to be an essential feature of the Republican order) — these rights of the family, being subject to legal, not theological, determination, were never even mentioned in the hubbub raised in asserting the supreme validity of the sacraments.

On March 2 a university professor, Paul Benichou, sent *Le Monde* an open letter in which he clearly set forth the dimensions of the problem: "What can be the meaning of this doctrinal complaisance, of which we see so many signs, in the presence of flagrant attack on the laws? Of these allusions to the rights of the Church over baptized children, these higher considerations that are set up as against the legal code, these mysteries of faith and conscience that are bound up with the violation of the law, this pretense at reaching a compromise between the law and something else whose name is not mentioned? Is it not time for us to recall that the law is the sole authority in France, that no church has legal powers, that no sacraments of any religion have any civil validity? This has been the case for over a hundred and fifty years. One would think that there could no longer be any question about it. The Finaly case proves that the contrary is true, and this is why it is a serious affair."

The children have disappeared. The protests of organizations of all sorts, from the League of the Rights of Man to the Alliance Israélite, can multiply. But by now it is apparent that nothing less than a Papal command can unbind tongues and open the doors of convents in Spain. No such order has come. The Court of Cassation will soon give its verdict for or against Mrs. Rosner. But will that verdict be able to do anything that the verdict of the Court of Appeals could not? Today as yesterday, all roads lead to Rome. And Rome is silent.

But in the Vatican time is measured in terms of eternity. France, oldest daughter of the Church, has become a land of little faith. Few Frenchmen live without baptism and die without extreme unction; but for most of them the sacraments are just custom and mundane convention. It is only for the moment that theology has become a favorite newspaper subject, morning and evening, in France. Tomorrow the latest news from the Kremlin, the floods, or the horse races will have consigned it back to the seminaries. But, if the Finaly children are not returned, every Frenchman will know in the future that there is a difference between his act of baptism and his certificate of vaccination. They will also know that once a child is baptized, sole authority over it lies in the hands of the Church.

But, in 1953, is this the last word?

From *Commentary*, June 1953; by Nicolas Baudy, translated by Maurice J. Goldbloom.

A powerful movement in which Jews and non-Jews took part grew up in the country. Finally, on June 23, 1953, all of Mlle. Brun's claims on the children were legally invalidated.

On June 26, 1953, the children finally returned to France. Early in July, Mrs. Rosner and the boys flew to Israel with false passports and settled in Gederah. The Finaly children adjusted rapidly to the Israeli environment and Israeli youth.

In August 1960, they joined Zahal (the Israeli Army) and rose in rank. Today they, like all other citizens, are making their contributions to the building and defense of Israel.

Several Frenchmen were put in jail, including six Roman Catholic priests and two nuns. Also arrested were a number of guides who smuggled the children over the mountains into Spain.

The case also stimulated the publication of books based on the scandal, in French and English. The two most prominent are: L'Affaire Finaly, *by Moise Keller, Paris; Libraire Fishbacher, 1960, 594 pp. (French); and* Michel, Michel, *a novel by Robert Lewis, New York: Simon and Schuster, 1967, 735 pp. (English).*

Based on *"Yaldei Finali"* ("The Finaly Children") by Moshe Katan, in *Mishpatim v'allilot Dam,* "Public Trials and Blood Accusations Against Jews," published by the Office of Security and Defense, Tel Aviv, 1967, and *News,* a bulletin of the AAmerican Jewish Committee, Paris and New York City, prepared by David Lambert in Paris, translated into English by Ted Hudes.

A GIFT OF LIFE FROM GERMAN MOTHERS

Paula, a sister of one of the survivors of Buchenwald, who herself had been saved from Camp Bergen-Belsen, attested to the following happening.

We were ten girls, survivors of Bergen-Belsen, who had been assigned the very risky task of clearing out the unexploded bombs that were strewn in the streets of Hamburg. We each faced the danger of accidentally detonating the bombs and being blown to pieces. The German guards kept a safe distance from us. A few buildings had been left intact among the devastated ruins. We did not know that some of the tenants watched us from their windows.

One day I discovered a paper bag on the ground. I picked it up gingerly and opened it with trembling fingers. It contained about a dozen slices of bread spread with a thin layer of fat, and also included a letter: "Here is a gift from a small group of German mothers whose sons are fighting at the front. We see you from our windows and think about *your* mothers, and we feel pity for you. We'll try to provide you with another package tomorrow. Take good care of yourselves and be sure to destroy this letter."

This present of life-giving food which the German mothers risked imprisonment to give to us awakened in me the will to survive. I distributed the bread slices to my companions and said to them, "Someday we too will be mothers."

They looked at me as if I were crazy, but one remarked, "You're either a fool or a prophetess."

From *Children of Innocence*, op. cit., p.31.

14.

THE TEHERAN CHILDREN

Some twenty-two months after the Nazi-Soviet pact had been signed (August 23, 1939), which led to the dismemberment of Poland, the "honeymoon" between the two nations suddenly ended. On June 22, 1941, at 3:30 A.M., the hitherto invincible Nazi war machine began to roll over the soil of "Mother Russia." It seemed that in a few weeks the USSR would be overrun, like all of Europe. Hard pressed, Stalin now turned to the Polish government-in-exile to unite with the USSR against the German invaders. He desperately sought an alliance with Britain and the United States in the common cause of defeating Nazi Germany. The Polish government responded with alacrity and began to recruit soldiers and civilians who had fled to the eastern Soviet Russia, to fight the common enemy. The Jews who had fled to the wilderness of Siberia, where they existed under inhuman conditions, began to migrate to the USSR south central republics of Kazakhstan, Turkmenistan, and Uzbekistan, where the climate was milder. They flocked to join the Polish Army which was headed by General Anders. But for most of them there was no surcease from suffering. Short of open violence, Polish anti-Semitism was no less vicious than during the prewar days.

In the spring of 1942, General Anders' army began its long journey to Iran. The Polish soldiers were accompanied by their families and war orphans. With rare exceptions, Jews were not allowed to join up. To save their children from hunger and disease, Jewish parents handed them over to Christian orphanages, but before doing so they had their children swear that if and when they found a safe asylum they would return to their faith.

When parents encountered difficulties in finding safety for their children, they would hang crosses on their necks and leave them at the doors of Polish

Catholic orphanages. The separation from weeping parents left an unforgetta-
ble trauma in the children's consciousness — a shock that had a lasting effect
on their lives.

A little girl writes of her experience:

"Days without end I wandered about in the streets of Samarkand [capital of
Uzbekistan], a cross suspended over my breast. Always my father trailed
behind me, not far off. Vainly did I implore Polish officials to admit me to an
orphan asylum. At long last a nun responded to my pleas. From then on I never
saw my father again. Only once did he smuggle a note to me in the orphanage,
appealing to me never, never to forget that I had been born a Jewess and to
remain loyal to my faith."

Another child writes: "The morning we arrived in Samarkand, Mother
gathered us together and said that there was only one way for us to be saved,
and that was to be admitted to a Polish orphan asylum. When we objected to
being separated from her, she carried on as if she were going insane. We
refused to part from her and burst out into bitter cries. But mother was
adamant. 'If we do not do it now,' she insisted, 'we shall all die from hunger
and cold. In the orphanage you will have a chance to be saved.' Toward
evening she herself brought us to the gates of the orphan asylum, left us there
helplessly alone, and fled. We waited at the gate for many hours, until a sister
was moved to bring us inside, where we were given lodging and safety. We
concealed our being Jewish, but since we wore no cross, all were suspicious of
us.

"In the orphan home the rooms were overcrowded. Images of the Holy
Mother hung everywhere. Morning and evening we would kneel before the
image, whisper our prayers, and cross ourselves."

Life was very rigorous. The code of discipline was strictly observed. Re-
veille, wash-up, meals, curfew were conducted as severely as in military
barracks. The piercing eyes of the nuns probed the children as they knelt before
the image of the Virgin to intone the "Ave Maria." Jewish boys underwent
untold ordeals when they undressed or bathed, in order to hide their circumci-
sions.

Those who had not found refuge, especially boys, joined the ragged army of
hundreds of vagrants who roamed the streets begging for alms and for a bite of
food. Only those families whose fathers had been accepted in the Polish fighting
forces were accommodated by the Poles.

Meir Ohad succeeded in organizing the only independent asylum for 150
Jewish orphans in Samarkand and later brought them to Pahlevi in Iran. Tzvi
Netzer, Ohad's aide, writes about this momentous event and its aftermath.

In the latter half of August 1942, the children arrived in various transports at
Polish camp #2 in Pahlevi. There I met them for the first time. Our meeting
took place under harsh circumstances. On the hot desert sands, under tattered
straw mats, the children lay, ill, feverish, and scantily dressed. Nearby lived the
Christian children in tents, healthy-looking, sun-tanned, and quite content.
And why not? They were with their parents and teachers, and well cared for.
They frequently abused the Jewish children. Ever so often a sick child broke out

crying when he was hit by an object thrown at him by his Polish neighbors. Every half-hour a sullen security officer would make his rounds and bellow gruffly, "Quiet, Zhids."

We arrived towards evening and settled in the tents of the "dirty Jews." Soon a whistle blew, and all the refugees, young and old, emerged and arranged themselves for the roll call and recital of the inescapable evening prayers in Polish and Latin. Shouting abuses and curses, the officers dragged out the sick children, who were required to participate in the evening prayers to the Holy Mother together with all the others.

Daily new ships carrying thousands of Poles landed, bringing new orphans. Among them we found young Jews, some of whom had already been converted or were near conversion. We determined to help take care of them, and indeed we did all in our power to welcome them. But we ourselves were half naked and barefoot, and we too needed no less care, protection, and encouragement than those we cared for.

The situation seemed hopeless when suddenly the happy news came from the Polish legation that we might establish a Jewish orphanage. Was this a partial atonement for the wrongs and maltreatment they had committed against us? Did the British, who actually were the rulers in Pahlevi, repent because of the deprivations afflicted on us?

In September 1942, the immigration of the children to Iran began in larger numbers. With them came the *halutzim* from Russia and Poland who were on their way to the Promised Land. They were instructed to set up educational programs for the children in camp #2. Our work was strenuous. Though we were empowered by the Polish legation to gather together all the Jewish orphans, even those who had been admitted into Christian asylums, the priests and nuns did not easily give up their "redeemed or redeemable souls." In many cases we had no difficulties, especially with the older children, who were considered by the clergy as "lost souls." But we had to wage a vigorous fight to save the little ones. There were cases when we had to "abduct" them stealthily and hide them. Often we lodged sharp complaints in writing, to which we received favorable replies, but in the meantime the children concerned disappeared. We even took the officials to court to prove that the children whom they held in custody had been born Jewish and should be released to us.

The struggle of the Catholic clergy to keep the Jewish children took on various guises. They inveigled their wards by promising that they would find their parents. They intimidated the children by telling them that their food rations would be diminished. They frightened the children by maligning us, by telling them that we were Russian agents who had come to bring them back to Russia. It took us a long time and much effort to repudiate their deceitfulness and monstrous lies. Often they denied to the authorities that Jewish children were housed in their monasteries or convents. However, the young non-Jewish inmates knew no wiles and with contempt pointed out the *zhids* to us. Indeed, owing to their help, I was privileged to remove many crosses from the necks of children who had already undergone conversion.

Alas, sometimes we were too late. We knew of eight young children who were dispatched to India or Africa before we got wind of them . . . It is quite likely that tens of children were permanently lost to us without our knowing their names, their parents, or their whereabouts.

Once I was riding in a carriage with a six-year-old boy on my lap. On each side sat older children. I had removed them just in time from a railroad car bound for Africa. They had already experienced what it meant to be a Jew — the deprivations, scorn, and physical suffering. When I finally won them over and took them home with me, they broke out in torrents of tears. One of them, a boy, told me of the beatings he had received, the constant gnawing hunger and spiritual pain he had experienced during the last few weeks. He wept as he told me, "Once they beat me because of my Jewish nose, another time because the smell of onions was on my breath, and a third time because I did not know the prayer to the Holy Mother." The children inquired, "In the children's home where you are taking us, are the teachers Jewish? Do they speak Yiddish? They don't hit and don't steal bread from the children? And will we go to Eretz Yisrael? When? And what of our parents? Will you also bring them there?" I had to wage constant, valiant struggles to obtain their release. Most of the children came to us ill and sore and often bloated from hunger.

In the morning, many would awaken and complain, crying, "I can't open my eyes. My lids are stuck together." The nurses were so beset that they did not know whom to treat first. All asked for eyedrops. The camp was short of absorbent cotton and essential medicines.

Many suffered from scabies, a nasty skin disease. In the isolation room, which normally contained eight beds, eighty children slept on the floor. Hospital attendants were unavailable. The only ones who took care of the sick were the *halutzim* and *halutzot* (male and female pioneers on their way to Palestine). Never shall I forget the morning when I came into the isolation ward and found the children sobbing from pain and the two helpless girl attendants weeping with them.

Until they finally came to Eretz Yisrael, the children went without wearable shoes and adequate clothing. They were the very last in line at the commissary to receive any apparel or any kind of footgear. Sometimes it happened that the counselor who came to the commissary to obtain desperately needed items for the children received a beating instead.

The local Jews, who at times brought gifts of clothing to the children, did so stealthily lest, God forfend, the Poles might catch sight of them and stir up trouble. Never did we experience the joy of hearing from the children, "We are satisfied."

Despite it all, the children's physical condition improved steadily. Their fears and insecurities waned, and their spiritual depression decreased.

"The Sands of Pahlevi" in *Red and White and the Aroma of Oranges: The Children of Teheran,* arranged, edited and translated into Hebrew by Ben Zion Tomer, Jerusalem: the World Zionist Organization, 1972, pp. 84-92.

Meir Ohad continues with the narrative: "When we came to Teheran we were eyewitnesses to the care and love of Jews for one another. The Jews of Teheran, led by Aziz al-Kanin, mobilized the Jewish community for our support. Daily transports of food, clothing, linens, and other necessities were delivered. They were gifts from the Jewish inhabitants. Who knows what our lot would have been, physically and spiritually, had it not been for their concern and care?''

In Meir Ohad's narration about the Teheran children, he quotes from David Umansky, director of Youth Aliyah at the time, who describes the beginnings of the children's home.

To conduct the orphanage adequately, an experienced staff of youth leaders was essential. Fortunately, the children had been accompanied by a small group of guides and nursemaids. As the numbers of children increased, it was necessary to add to the staff and to find suitable substitutes for those who were incompetent. Regrettably, none could be found in Iran. The Jewish Agency and Hadassah's Youth Aliyah attempted to find a group of youth leaders in Palestine but could not obtain immigration visas for them. The only one who was given a visa was Mrs. Tziporah Sharett, wife of Moshe Sharett, who at the time headed the political department of the Jewish Agency. Arriving in Teheran on October 28, 1942, she undertook to supervise the entire operation for the duration of the children's stay. Among the refugees there were a few *halutzim,* who had served as leaders of diverse European Zionist youth groups. They assumed various responsibilities.

Highest priority was given to instituting a disciplined daily regimen, to keep the children occupied in meaningful activities and to provide hygienic and medical care. Mrs. Sharett succeeded in enlisting the financial aid of Iranian Jewry to provide food and clothing, medical and hygienic supplies and facilities. An educational program modeled after the Israeli orphanages was established. Hebrew courses, lectures, popular discussions, choirs, and dance groups were organized.

However, lack of textbooks and reading materials made it impossible to institute a school program. Moreover, the staff worked under impossible conditions. They were in a hostile environment and a difficult climate, and were under perpetual strain. Nevertheless, the children began to thrive in an atmosphere of warmth and friendship created for them by their own people.

As life in camp settled down, we decided to habituate the children to the patterns of life in the Israeli *kibbutzim,* to which they were preparing to immigrate. When they rose in the morning, they lined up according to age and were trained to stride in rhythm, accompanied by marching songs. An original hymn entitled ''We Are Ascending and Singing'' was sung every morning and on special occasions. News of world events and camp happenings was announced at the morning lineup. The day's agenda was proclaimed.

To celebrate the occasion of Tziporah Sharett's arrival, we arranged a festive program which impressed her very much. Her three-month stay at camp, until our departure to the Promised Land, was of inestimable value in preparing us for *aliyah.* The camp expanded to accommodate seven hundred children, and we waited impatiently for the day of our departure.

Life at camp is described by Shlomo F., a youth leader.

Red brick abodes are scattered over a large plot of ground, and in their midst are pitched rows of tents. Boys and girls are separated from one another. The boys are in the majority. Most of them are unruly, snatching anything they can lay their hands on. When mealtime approaches, they become especially greedy and grasping. Gradually, however, the children learn to be orderly and more conscious of the fact that their counselors are like father and mother to them and are truly concerned for their welfare.

Progressively they begin to learn about Eretz Yisrael, to sing Hebrew songs, even though they do not understand most of the words, and to dance the *hora*. They begin to raise questions: Do Jews really live in Eretz Yisrael in large numbers? Do they have enough to eat? When will we get there? Will they accept us? The older ones begin to recall the Hebrew prayers of their childhood and fragments of the Bible they had learned long ago. Little by little a craving begins to stir in their hearts to settle in Eretz Yisrael.

Meir Ohad describes the difficulties in arranging to transport the children to the Promised Land: "The Jewish Agency strove in every way possible to prevail upon the Iraqi government to permit the children to cross its borders on their way to Palestine. But Iraq was unyielding because of its anti-Zionist policy. Efforts to transport the children via Turkey also failed. The American and British governments rejected the Agency's requests for air transportation on the basis that they could not spare the planes, which were needed for the war effort. The only route that was open to the children was the sea."

Moshe Sharett, in his letter to Ohad dated March 7, 1965, summarized his efforts to obtain transportation. He wrote: "When I was in London, in 1942– 43, I gave up the idea of transporting the children via Iraq, but I did make strenuous efforts to obtain a ship to take them by sea. As you know, in the fall of 1942 this effort was crowned with success."

At the beginning of January 1943 the children and counselor staff left Iraq on the S.S. Dunera for Karachi in what is now West Pakistan, on the Arabian Sea, and from there changed boats for Suez. The ocean lanes between Karachi and Yemen were strewn with mines. Sea battles were frequently fought in the Indian Ocean. Veritable miracles saved the ship from the underwater mines and the German submarines that lurked everywhere.

When the time for the children's exodus approached, the Polish military requested that the camp administration mobilize a number of Jewish counselors for service in the Polish Army, on the pretext that they had been "loaned" to the children's asylum. Hastily, and in utter secrecy, Saul Avigor[1] smuggled out the six counselors to Bagdad. Their railroad journey was fraught with dangers, because Polish and Iraqui secret-service men were ever on the lookout for army deserters.

When they reached Bagdad, they were met by a porter who took charge of them and motioned them to follow him. After a perilous trip through the city, they came to a cellar, where they were hidden. The porter turned out to be Enzo Sereni.[2]

[1]Prominent leader of Aliyah Bet, the so-called illegal immigration to Palestine.
[2]Heroic partisan who later lost his life trying to save the remnants of European Jewry.

After six weeks of underground activities in Bagdad, the men were disguised in British uniforms and passed as laborers of the Solel Boneh[3] who had worked in Abadan, the largest oil-producing center in Iran. They were supposed to be returning "home" on an extended leave, via the desert and Jordan. At long last they crossed the Allenby Bridge to Palestine.

About the same time (February 17, 1943) the Teheran children reached Suez and were received with unbounded joy by the Jewish Brigade, who served in the engineering corps of the British Army.

This emotional meeting was later described by Meir Bar-Rav-Hai, who years later addressed the children and their overseers on behalf of the citizens of Haifa in an impressive ceremony which took place on March 19, 1977, on the occasion of the naming of the street Yaldei Teheran (Children of Teheran).

I recall standing among ten or fifteen soldiers on the Suez dock when you arrived by ship and we waited to transfer you to the train which would bring you to our Homeland. Those were the days when the news of the Holocaust first began to reach us. Then and only then did we begin to grasp the enormity of the tragedy of European Jewry. Only then did we, who had originally volunteered for war against Hitler, begin to grasp and appreciate our rendezvous with destiny — to help rehabilitate the survivors of the destruction. This meeting at Suez was the first of a series of meetings by the soldiers of Eretz Yisrael with the Spared Remnant, whose welfare became *the* life mission of my colleagues.

One day before your arrival, Hans Beit, the devoted assistant of Henrietta Szold in the work of Youth Aliyah, informed us of your coming. We emptied all the stock in our army canteens. All night long we were engaged in filling packages, on which we inscribed: "And the children will return to their homeland" (Jeremiah 31:17). In the morning, when you stepped ashore, our pent-up emotions veritably exploded in outbursts of rapturous joy. And when you sang, "We are all children of Mother, of Mother," we were stirred to the quick, knowing that it was we who represented Mother, we who were privileged to welcome you with open arms in place of Mother, who is no more or is still a prisoner in Russia. The following morning, after the raising of the blue-white flag and the singing of *"Hatikvah,"* you took off by train.

When, on February 18, 1943, the train arrived at Rehovot, thousands of representatives welcomed the children with overwhelming enthusiasm and expressions of joy and happiness. Among them were school pupils and delegates of organizations led by the chief rabbis Herzog and Uziel. Above the station a big banner bore the slogan "And the children will return to their homeland." Young Shlomo F. describes his first meeting with the Homeland:

On February 17, 1943, an assembly was held at Port Suez, marking the first meeting of the Teheran Children with the soldiers of His Majesty, the Jews of Eretz Yisrael. We were regaled with a good meal, gifts, and abounding love.

[3]The largest public works contractor and industrialist cooperative involved in building in the Near East, founded in 1923.

The train left at night and in the morning arrived at the outskirts of Gaza. Our impressions of the scenery were very moving. The orchards were laden down with oranges; the heady aroma of the fruit expanded our breasts and shed luster on our surroundings. At every station we were greeted with profound joy and treated to showers of gifts — chocolate, cookies, and, above all, oranges. Everywhere we were asked the same question: Did we, by chance, know about this or that family? Did anyone from town X or Y come with us? and the like.

The outpouring of emotions was so powerful that we could not quite comprehend and appreciate their intensity. Most arousing was the reception at Rehovot, where we were not only greeted with goodies and gifts but also welcomed with speeches, posters, the singing of *"Hatikvah."* Weighed down with gifts and expressions of love, we reached Camp Atlit at twilight, where we went through a similar experience. In the midst of Camp Atlit a veritable hill of oranges was piled high for our consumption.

At Atlit the children finally met Henrietta Szold and the staff that had been selected to live with them. After several days, the children were distributed to absorption centers throughout the land: 298 children to the Labor Zionist Kibbutzim; 288 to the orthodox religious colonies and institutions; 38 to the Agudat Yisrael (ultrareligious) settlements, and 36 to traditional settlements, i.e., those that were middle-of-the-road religiously.

This is the story of the first transport of the Teheran children.

The second transport, of 120 Russian Jewish children, came to Eretz Yisrael on August 28, 1943, also via Teheran. This time they were transported by buses through the desert and across the Yarmuk River bridge directly to Camp Atlit.

The full list of names, birth dates, and birthplaces of the first transport of the Teheran children is appended at the end of the book.

From *Yizkor Leyaldei Teheran* ("In Memoriam to the Children of Teheran"), published by the Public Commission to Commemorate the Teheran Children, by Meir Ohad, 1977, pp. 220-224.

THE BABIES WHO WOULDN'T CRY

As the sun began to set, our fears grew. God forbid, something might have happened; there might have been a mishap at the very last minute, which delayed the train. This was a special train, and it carried a very precious cargo — two hundred little children, all of them less than four years of age.

At long last, the train came to its last stop in Jerusalem. The little ones who were the passengers had traveled a long distance to get here — much more than most adults have covered in a lifetime. And the hardships they had endured were more crushing than those their forebears had ever experienced.

Those who were assigned to take care of them had to have nerves of steel to look after them, to bandage their wounds and ease their aches and pains. Have you ever seen a three-year-old who does not utter a whimper when he or she is injected against infection? Have you ever seen little ones who do not burst out crying when they see fierce-looking strangers dressed in uniforms and armed with rifles? Have you ever seen tots who accept food rations without batting an eyelash and then rapidly swallow what is given, without a murmur? Did you ever in your life meet a group of very young children who do not quarrel or squabble with each other?

Such were the little ones who arrived in Jerusalem that Friday as the sun was setting. Yael, Dr. Chaim Weizmann's niece, who was dressed in a white apron, circulated among the children and greeted them warmly. Her aunt, Dr. Helena Weizmann, welcomed them group by group. A pediatrician was busy giving out cups of milk, wiping the children's moist chins. To a little girl whose eyes were filled with tears as she tried very hard to refrain from weeping, the doctor offered a clean white handkerchief to wipe her eyes. "Cry if you want to," she said. "Don't hold your tears back." The child did not listen to her. The pediatrician exclaimed, "What kind of children are you? There's not one among you who will shed a tear. What is the matter with you?"

Many of these children had been born in Nazi concentration camps in Poland, Czechoslovakia, Russia, Rumania, Holland, and other parts of Europe. Some had first seen the light of day in the world of the DP camps, which had very recently been liberated by the Allied forces. What higher power had disciplined them not to cry or let out a whimper because it would endanger their lives?

Indeed, no one had warned the little ones of what might happen. They understood by and of themselves. They had seen the man in uniform shoot balls of fire into the bodies of their brothers and sisters when Mother tried to silence their crying. Did they need more warning? They had been well disciplined to shut their mouths and not utter a sound. They knew that if they showed any sign of weakness they would be doomed. The older ones among them learned this harsh lesson with their own eyes. They had seen weeping children silenced by the firing of little round, shining balls. Some had seen members of their families felled by these balls of fire. They had learned quickly that only total silence could save them from what had befallen their companions.

True, a change had come in the uniforms worn by the men who now guarded them. But the new guards continued to speak a strange language, like those who preceded them. They did not harm the children, but still they kept them apart from their parents. The children were still herded together in wards. (These were childrens' wards, but to the little ones they were prison wards like those before them.)

With a deafening noise the train pulled into the station. All who could walk came to see the newcomers, eager to see and meet the children who had gone through the seventy-seven way stations of Gehenna (hell). Housewives and matrons competed among themselves for the privilege of carrying a tiny one in their arms. Dr. Helena Weizmann, who observed all that was going on, exclaimed, "How adult-like the newcomers are! If only *we* could learn self-discipline from them!"

The buses to which the newcomers were transferred were decorated with large blue-and-white flags. The drivers, who as a matter of principle always spoke Hebrew, conversed with them in Yiddish so that the children would hear the language which their parents had used. The drivers thought maybe it would help bring them closer and gain their confidence. A Yemenite driver who lived in Meah Shearim[1] surpassed his colleagues in trying to communicate. He spoke Yiddish, Polish, even Hungarian and Rumanian. But to no avail — the newcomers remained silent. They did not let out a sound; they behaved like little adults and did not utter a complaint or a groan.

The WIZO[2] children's home had been completely vacated to admit the guests. The children who had lived there were transferred to other homes. Each bed was prepared lovingly with fresh clean linen, bedsheets, pillows, and colorful blankets. The bedroom walls were decorated with pictures, flags, and paper lanterns. A holiday atmosphere pervaded everywhere.

The wide dining room was set up with round tables and small chairs. It was arranged only for the children. At Dr. Helena Weizmann's request, the children were to be left alone, in the hope that when they were by themselves they would communicate with each other. But this did not help. They continued to behave like frightened little animals. They sat still, and their eyes continued to reflect deep fear.

A corps of doctors and nurses initiated a program of medical care. The law required that each child should be inoculated against the diseases that had been rampant in the DP camps and the countries which they passed through on their way to Jerusalem. The nurses calmed the children as they inoculated them: "This will hurt you only a moment. The pain will disappear quickly." But their fears were groundless, and their efforts were really unnecessary. The children rolled up their tattered sleeves, stretched out their skinny little arms to the doctors and nurses who stabbed their needles into them. The children did not cry out. Under no circumstance would they display painful reactions, which in the past had meant death.

The inoculations lasted quite a while. Someone remembered that it was almost candle-lighting time. The Yemenite driver borrowed two shining copper candle holders and two tall white candles. Although it was already a little too late to light them, the nurses nevertheless proceeded to go through with the ceremony. One of them came forward to light the candles and to recite the blessings, but someone in charge called out, "One of the girls will light them and make the blessing."

I did not know the girl's name; like all the others, she was skin and bones and looked like a four- or five-year-old. Her eyes were large and brown; her hair was uncombed. She was dressed in a garment that was too large for her — as were her shoes.

"May I light the candles?" she asked in Yiddish. "I know the blessing," she added shyly.

She was given the candles and matches. On the matchbox were printed Hebrew words, which must have reminded her of a *siddur*.[3] With trembling hands she lit a match and kindled a candle. The burning match slipped out of her fingers and fell on the carpet. She extinguished it with her fingers. We were sure

---

[1]The orthodox section of Jerusalem.
[2]Women's International Zionist Organization.
[3]Prayerbook.

that in doing so she burned her fingers, and expected her to cry out, but she was silent. Only her eyes and face showed a flash of intense pain. After a few seconds, however, she recovered, removed another match, and struck it on the box. With trembling fingers she lit the second candle and recited the blessing: "Blessed art Thou, O Lord our God, King of the Universe, who has sanctified us by His commandments and has commanded us to light the Sabbath candles." Her voice sounded as if it came from a Jewish woman who had suffered great affliction and pain.

"Amen," the children and the audience answered with a devout fervor. Among those who responded, I recognized many adults who had rejected the Jewish traditional rituals and ceased to light candles in their homes.

Tears shone in the eyes of the little girl-woman, who probably for the first time in her life had lit candles before an audience. She covered her eyes with her little palms and whispered a silent personal prayer, which is said after the lighting of the candles.

When she finished, she uttered loudly a *"Gut Shabbas"* greeting and then continued, "Children, I have lit the *Shabbas* candles *on Shabbas. Oy Ribbono shel Olam* [God of the Universe], I did not want to desecrate the Sabbath, but we all would have had the feeling that we are still fugitives and not among our own people, because we would not have seen the light of the *Shabbas* candles. But now we are all assured that we *are* at last among our own people, that we *are* Jews, even though we ushered in the *Shabbas* a little later than usual. I feel that God understands and forgives."

This was the first Sabbath of freedom of the children who some years later became famous as the Teheran children.

A.E.

From an unpublished manuscript by Asher Lazar.

15.

PALESTINE

After the Nazi defeat in 1945, tens of thousands of Jewish refugees, including thousands of families, fled from Eastern Europe to settle in Eretz Yisrael. They were known as the She'erit Hapletah, *the "spared remnant" or "saving remnant." The Hebrew name of this mass movement,* Bricha, *meaning "flight" or "escape," was also adopted to designate the underground network that was organized to thwart the British blockade designed to prevent the Nazi victims from settling in Palestine.*

The heroism of the spared remnant aroused the sympathy of the world community and the support of World Jewry. This movement finally led to the establishment of the State of Israel in 1948.

Ephraim Dekel was the European chief of Operation Bricha. In its heyday, about a thousand people, who were scattered in various countries of Europe and Asia, were involved as members of the staff.

Haj Amin el Husseini, a rabid Arab nationalist, had been appointed in 1922 as head of the Supreme Moslem Council as well as the Mufti (chief Islamic religious functionary) of Jerusalem. He was a fierce opponent of the Balfour Declaration, the British Mandate to establish a Jewish state, and the Yishuv (Jewish settlement). At the outbreak of the war he fled from Palestine, joined the Nazi Axis, and fomented rebellion and terrorism among the Arabs of Palestine against the Jews.

MEMORANDUM TO THE ITALIAN FOREIGN MINISTER
FROM THE JERUSALEM MUFTI

Rome, June 10, 1943

His Excellency, the Italian Foreign Minister, Rome:

On May 13, 1943, I submitted to your excellency a memorandum regarding the emigration of Jews from Bulgaria, Rumania, and Hungary, to Palestine. In it I laid stress on the intensive efforts being made by the British Jews, in response to the declaration of the Colonial Minister advocating the transportation of 4500 Jews from Bulgaria to Palestine. I requested of you that you use your influence to prevent their emigration and avert a great calamity that would befall the Arab lands and the Axis powers [Germany and her allies].

Since then the following important events have come to my attention:

1. A group of 75 Jews left Bucharest on March 10 and arrived, via Bulgaria, in Palestine.[1]

2. The British Colonial Minister stated to the Parliament that serious difficulties have arisen concerning the emigration of 4500 Jews from Bulgaria to Palestine. But the Minister added, ''I am happy to report that there is hope that we can overcome the difficulties soon.''

3. The Jewish Agency published in its bulletin information about the Jews who are on their way to Palestine via Turkey. The bulletin includes the following information:

a. 270 young Jews from Rumania and Hungary have already arrived in Palestine, and a fourth group, numbering 75, is still in Bucharest, ready to leave.

b. 700 women and children from Poland, who have relatives living in Palestine, are on the way.

c. 5000 refugees from Bulgaria, Rumania, and Slovakia have already received immigration certificates.

d. In the aforementioned bulletin, there appears an announcement that the British have agreed to grant to the Jewish Agency an additional 12,500 certificates.

In view of the strenuous and ongoing efforts that our enemies, the Jews and British, are making to transport thousands of Jews to Palestine, I find it necessary to bring to the attention of Your Excellency that the Arabs, who are faithful friends of the Axis powers, view with deep regret the fact that their friends and allies make it easy to implement the Anglo-Jewish objectives of promoting the immigration of Jews, who are British and Communist agents and enemies of the Arabs, to Arabic Palestine.

The granting of immigration permits to thousands of Jews is not to be viewed as a humanitarian act. Rather, it will lead to grave results for all concerned. If the motive is to relieve the Jews from imperilment in European lands, we must not forget for a moment, that their presence in Palestine will lead to greater

---

[1] The Mufti indicated the sources of his information.

dangers, both in the immediate present and in the future. They will be free to ally themselves with our enemies in the Near East and make available helpful information as well as their intellectual abilities and knowledge in general. These hazards can be avoided only if they are constrained to remain in Europe.

For the above reasons, I request your excellency to give your immediate attention to this important matter and use all efforts at your disposal with the above governments to prohibit the emigration of these Jews and to frustrate the designs of their allies.

The Arabs will be deeply grateful to your excellency for your endeavors in their behalf.

(Signed) Amin El Husseini

A.E.

From an article by Daniel Karpi in *Yalkut Moreshet*, Tel Aviv, Israel.

A NEAR CATASTROPHE

One day in February 1946, a transport of eighty orphans from Lvov arrived at our emigration center. I immediately made special arrangements to smuggle them across the border to Italy. They were dispatched on a large Diesel truck covered with tarpaulin. We left at 8:00 P.M., and in two hours we reached the town of Landek. The cold was intense and the snow deep. We took a breather at a café where we usually stopped with our transports for a warm drink. I asked the guides to remain in the truck and watch the children, while I went to the café to order hot tea for all. While the owner took care of my request, I telephoned our office with instructions, because of the heavy snow and icy conditions, not to send any children in the other two trucks, which had been scheduled to leave at 11:00 P.M. I feared for their safety.

While waiting, the children in the trucks chatted with each other in Polish. They were overheard by one of the border patrols. He immediately communicated with his superiors, informing them that a group of Russians (he confused the languages) was about to steal across the border to Italy.

After a stopover of some twenty minutes, we resumed our trip. Soon we caught sight of a number of border patrol men running toward us. The strong wind and the sound of our motor drowned out the cries of the patrol telling us to halt. We continued on our way, unperturbed. When we arrived at the barrier, we suddenly heard the shattering of glass at the front of the truck. The glass chips sprayed the face of the driver. Luckily I was not struck, even though I sat next to him. The driver managed to apply the brakes, and we stopped about a hundred meters before reaching the barrier. I opened the door and jumped out. Facing us were a number of armed men with flashlights. They recognized me and inquired if all was well with us. I directed their attention to the shattered glass and the bleeding driver. They ran to the truck, helped the driver to get out, and led him to the guardroom. When they learned that they had shot at our vehicle, which was transporting Jewish orphans, they were beside themselves with grief and could hardly speak. The officer who had given the order to shoot burst into tears. The telephone wires hummed as the officer tried to explain his mistake. He invited the children into the station, apologized profusely, and explained what had happened. He offered them hot tea and goodies. On the Italian side of the border they treated us to glasses of wine and oranges, and again apologized and asked our forgiveness. We were all happy that, despite the scratches on the face of the driver, there were no more serious wounds.

This is what they told us. "We received instructions to stop a truck carrying Russians who were trying to cross the border illegally. They ordered the patrol to shoot if necessary. Thereupon the patrol stationed two machine guns at opposite sides of the road, ready to fire. Luckily the commanding officer instructed the patrols not to shoot before you reached the border. Only he fired a number of shots with his revolver. One of them struck the glass, and when the truck stopped he gave the order to search the occupants."

The border guards took tender care of the driver, and bandaged his face, and we continued our journey into Italy. I gave Ephraim, the guide in charge, the amount of money needed to purchase railroad tickets at the next station for the train leaving at 5:00 A.M., as well as the cost of a substantial breakfast for each child. We returned to Innsbruck, happy and thankful that we had miraculously avoided a serious accident and bloodshed.

A.E.

From *Heres U'Tkumah* ("Destruction and Revival") by Moshe Weiszand, Tel Aviv: Hamenorah, 1970, pp. 191 ff.

RESCUED AT HAIFA PORT

Bracha Habas is a veteran Hebrew publicist and author. She is especially notable for her chronicles on halutzim, *the Youth Aliyah, and the* She'erit Hapletah, *as well as stories and plays for children. Her book,* The Gatebreakers, *which has been translated from her original Hebrew work, has won wide renown.*

This is the story of Tovah B., age thirteen, who came to Eretz Yisrael from Berlin and was saved from sinking with the S.S. Patria, *which was blown up at the port of Haifa on November 2, 1940. About eighteen hundred passengers were on board.*

I came to Eretz Yisrael with my father. I do not remember Mother at all. My parents separated when I was a little child. Abba [Father] was a tailor in Berlin, he was a Polish citizen and was referred to as an *Ostjude*.[1] Hitler put him in prison and later into a concentration camp. I stayed with Grandma. When they freed Abba from camp, we wanted to go to Eretz Yisrael, but Grandma was very old, bedridden. It was impossible to travel with her, and we could not leave her. When she died, Abba wept and remarked, "Now we can travel," but we had no Palestine immigration visa.

[1] East European Jew.

One day a man came to us and said, "It's possible for you to travel, but as illegal immigrants." Abba sent a telegram to inquire about travel arrangements and received word, "You can arrange to go to Vienna." We sold everything we had except for three or four suitcases packed with necessities, and we started out. It was forbidden to take along gold or silver — only ten marks each. My father's friend advised us to hide silver and gold coins in the heels of our shoes. This we did, and we succeeded in smuggling out a little money.

We lived three months in Vienna, the first days at an immigrants' shelter. We slept on the floor, which was riddled with bugs. Later, room was made for me in an orphanage, where I stayed three weeks. But I was unhappy.

From Vienna we traveled to Budapest, where we met many fugitives from Czechoslovakia and Austria. One day we boarded three riverboats and floated down the Danube. The ships anchored at the mouth of the river where it empties into the Black Sea. Of the two ships besides ours, one transported coal and another mail; all three were old and decrepit. At first we had enough food on board, and as we anchored at various ports on the way we added to our provisions. But when we entered the Black Sea we ran out of food. We were rationed moldy biscuits and tea prepared from boiled seawater.

The boats were named *Atlantic* and *Pacific,* and the mailboat was named *Melk.* The latter delivered mail to the region of the Danube River. Abba and I were on the *Pacific.*

Once we had a frightening experience. The passengers gathered to attend a general meeting. They went up to the top deck and assembled in a corner. The concentration of weight in one corner created an imbalance. The waves tossed the boat, and it began to lurch. As the passengers were listening to the speaker describing Palestine, suitcases and bundles suddenly began falling into the sea. Women and children began crying, and the captain rushed around shouting frantically, "Get below deck! All of you go down!"

When we arrived near Crete, sailors from nearby boats threw pomegranates at us. A wild melee ensued. Quarrels and fights arose as the passengers reached to catch the fruit.

When we neared Eretz Yisrael, we ran short of fuel oil. We were at a loss how to run the engines. We removed the wooden boards from our berths and fed the furnaces. We were terribly overcrowded. We took turns sleeping; one half sat up part of the night while the other half slept, and vice versa. Even the children's sleep was rationed. The wooden boards we threw into the furnace were old, twisted, and full of splinters. Soon even this miserable supply was burned up, so we distributed our weight on the deck and dozed through the night. There just wasn't enough room for all of us.

Our boat, the *Pacific,* was the first to draw near to the longed-for shores of our dream land. When we saw the peak of Mount Carmel, we embraced and danced for joy. To our dismay, we learned that we would not be permitted to land. "The British forbid us to land," we were told. You can well imagine our panic. A pall settled over us. One long week we lay tied up at the docks of Haifa, and then they began to transfer us to a large ship named *Patria,* which had been moored at Haifa, empty and ready for us.

The second ship, S.S. *Melk,* followed and anchored soon after our arrival, and by the end of three weeks we were joined by the S.S. *Atlantic*. Rumors spread that after all of us on the ships were transferred to S.S. *Patria*, we would be free to go ashore.

But we learned soon enough the bitter news that we would be sent to Mauritius, a distant island in the Indian Ocean. We began to scream and wail. There were many among us who had close relatives in Eretz Yisrael. They cried, "Better death than exile to a far-off island prison." At night, when stillness descended on the port, they would scream at the top of their voices. In Haifa the Jews demonstrated and called general strikes — but the British were not moved.

Came the day when S.S. *Patria* was to leave, at 4:30 P.M. In the early morning the passengers on the S.S. *Atlantic* began to be transferred to the *Patria*. They were brought under guard for hot showers so as to avoid the spread of illness. Next morning at 10:00 A.M., the engines were under steam and the ship was ready for departure, even though the last of the newcomers were standing naked under the hot showers. Suddenly there was a loud explosion, and the ship began to list, as if it were about to turn over on its side. Pandemonium broke out. Abba was on deck, wrapped in a blanket and sleeping in the sun. I was downstairs looking through the porthole. Panic-stricken, my cabinmate, a woman, began to shout, "Grab lifebelts! We're sinking!" Through the porthole I saw young people jumping into the water. I rushed up to the deck to look for Father but couldn't find him. An English soldier who was to accompany us to Africa thought that we were being attacked from the air and called me, "Get down below deck." But I paid no attention to him. I kept screaming, "Where's Abba? Where's my Abba?"

The bedlam on deck was indescribable. From all sides people ran, crying, weeping, pushing. They jammed the stairs. It was impossible to ascend. Below, torrents of water poured into the boat, covering the lower floors and rising rapidly. People were drowning and dying. . . .

When a sailor told me to go down, I entered a cabin. Since the ship was listing badly I found myself standing on the cabin's wall. Eight souls were crowded into the cabin — a man, three women, and children. One was a little girl of eight who had become separated from her family. Her parents, brother, and grandma had crowded the stairs to get to the upper deck but had been trampled underfoot. From our cabin salvation could come only via the round, large-sized porthole. The sole man in our cabin commanded one of us to climb on his shoulders and call for help through the opening. One of the women followed instructions. Soon a lifeboat approached and pulled her out into the boat. An older woman followed. I turned around and saw a large flow of water entering through the door. The water level rose, and I found myself partly submerged. In great fright and trembling I scrambled to the porthole, yelling, "I want to get out. I must get out." I didn't think of Abba, of anyone, only of myself. I shoved those who were in my way and strained to climb onto the man's shoulder. But a woman beat me to it. I pinched her leg hard, but she persisted. I jumped up and held onto the porthole with all my might. Someone pulled me down, and I found myself at the bottom again. We fought with one another. Everyone wanted to save his own life.

At last I got onto the man's shoulders. He was wet through and through, and exhausted. I did not see any rescue boat around. I yelled and cried until someone took notice of me. I don't know who my rescuer was. He snatched me and later put me down on the deck of a ship anchored opposite the shore near the port. I was alone amidst a load of wet lumber. I did not stop crying and yelling, but no one responded. I crawled to the end of the boat and was about to jump into the water to try to swim to the shore when a man in a lifeboat appeared out of nowhere, stretched out his hand, and pulled me into his boat.

I found myself at the boat's edge, surrounded by an overload of people. Men in the boat were in danger of being overpowered by people in the water who fought desperately to climb into the boat. Around us we saw a sea full of heads, arms, and legs thrashing about. I sat at the edge of the boat, my feet dangling in the water. Every so often someone grabbed them to hoist himself or herself into the boat, and several times I was nearly pulled into the water.

When I finally reached shore, wet and barefoot and shivering, I bethought myself of Abba and also of the man whose shoulders had saved my life. To this day, I do not know whether he was drowned or saved. I only saw his shoulders; his face remained a blur.

I met Abba at the customs. He had wounded his leg badly. When the ship listed, he had fallen to the floor and had struck a piece of underwater timber which was covered with sharp seashells and infested with underwater crustacean marine life and jutting barnacles. The appearances of the rescued were awful; they were disheveled, naked, and disoriented. They milled about, weeping and crying and seeking their loved ones. Everyone knew that the ship was sinking rapidly and that the fate of those who had remained aboard was sealed.

I was among the last of the rescued. Someone wrapped me in a long, wide dress and encased my feet in large high-heeled shoes. There I stood like an apparition in the midst of the noisy melee. I had to restrain myself from laughing. . . .

The *Atlantic* passengers were shipped to Mauritius, but we, the passengers from the *Pacific* and *Melk,* were transported to the detention camp Atlit, where we were confined seven months. We were housed twenty in a shack. Because of lack of space and facilities, we all ate our meals in bed. The food was edible.

A.E.

From *Yeladim Mutzalim* ("Rescued Children"), op. cit. pp. 63-73.

TEL AVIV CHILDREN BATTLE THE BRITISH

Chicago-born Meyer Levin was a distinguished writer and dramatist, who wrote novels about American life, like Citizens, The Old Bunch, *and* Compulsion, *and others that dealt with the pioneers who built Israel, like* Yehuda, The Settlers, The Harvest. *During World War II he covered the front in Europe as a correspondent for news agencies. He wrote this report in November 1945.*

It took a full week for even the Jerusalem population to realize that wounding fifty-one people by shooting into a crowd and by subsequent sniping without a single serious case of injury to police or soldiers during four days of high-powered military occupation hardly added up to "terroristic mob rule in Tel Aviv."

I was in Tel Aviv during those eventful days.

I went about among the police and troops for two days and encountered not a single human remark, while murderous conversations about the Jews were endless. Since I was in a correspondent's uniform, they never bothered to ascertain my sympathies and embarked directly on vilification of Jews. The special riot squads of Palestine police who were first called into action are known for their anti-Jewish attitude. Troops who immediately followed the police and thereafter occupied the town were veterans embittered because they had to face what to them was just another campaign after they had managed to survive Italy and Germany. For this new danger they naturally blamed the Jews. They had apparently been indoctrinated with the idea that every Jew in Palestine carried a knife, revolver, and garrote-rope, and they were determined that they would shoot at the slightest shadow rather than run any further risk. They were jumpy and mean. Never in all Germany did I see so tight and wary an occupation as they established in Tel Aviv.

On the fourth night, when the fever presumably had passed, I went out in a press car with local newspapermen, each of whom had a special pass. The car was halted for examination three times in four blocks, though the guards could see that the car had been halted and passed at the previous block. . . .

It began on Wednesday the fourteenth. I attended a mass meeting of fifty thousand people in the outskirts of Tel Aviv. I joined the crowds streaming homeward through the streets. (I understand some newspapers later described them as fifty thousand rioters in the streets of Tel Aviv.) About an hour later a local newspaperman phoned to say that Government House had been set afire. I walked up the length of Allenby Street. For half a mile the street presented its usual aspect, with evening strollers casually window-shopping. Then the crowd thinned out and I saw some fifty people down a side street, watching something. I saw a bonfire further along the street, found no police or soldiers, but a few hundred civilians lining the sidewalks while two firemen solemnly hosed the bonfire.

Meanwhile, from the second floor of the building housing the government Light Industries Control Office, a score of teenagers where hurling documents and pieces of furniture onto the fire. The culprits were mostly Yemenite kids and they were obviously having a great time. At one point something scared them and they came trooping out of the smoldering hallway, but presently others went in and resumed the job.

Now these kids could have been arrested or stopped by a dozen policemen. On the corner of Rothschild Boulevard the fire in the Income Tax offices had already been put out. I walked over to Allenby Road and found a roadblock. Soldiers in full jungle-fighting regalia let me through. The street was thick with stones and a few shop windows were broken, though none of the display merchandise had been touched. The post office door and window were broken. I went inside and found a few counter glasses broken, but the post office was open for business next day. At the circle on the upper end of Allenby Road, I found paratroopers set up with a few radio-equipped armored cars. The men standing around the armored cars said to me: "This ain't like a proper war where you know what to do. When I arrived I heard a shot, so we started shooting and they scattered quick enough."

An officer told me there had been just a few volleys fired and the crowd had vanished. "Some heavy stoning, that's all. No shooting from them." I went over a block to where the government building was still burning and found a group of Palestine police squatting on a corner, lamenting their lack of guns. "How they scattered as soon as we showed up, but I'd like to shoot some of them," said one of the police. "Maybe tomorrow they'll give us guns and let us fire. I hope so."

As far as I could gather, the three fires must have been set up by members of a secret organization. They were definite protest targets and were timed carefully to follow the organizational pattern of attacking places only when there is limited danger of destruction of life. As there was a protest strike all day, the building was unoccupied when set afire. Once the fires started, youngsters on the street were attracted and they formed the nuclei of the "unruly mobs." One story had it there was a street fight between young workers coming from the meeting carrying a red banner and a gang of Revisionists.

In any case, it was no great affair and was easily dispersed by the reinforcements of police who quickly arrived. When soldiers came, some stoning was still going on from the retreating kids. Most of the crowd were onlookers. Then troops fired directly into a crowd on Allenby Road; many of the wounded whom I later talked to in Rothschild Hospital were simply bystanders.

I walked around the streets for hours and found the curfew being well obeyed except for some gangs of kids who had formed in the Yemenite district at the lower end of Allenby Road. Excitable and angry, these kids, six years old and up, darted out from around Rabbi Akiba Street and, in plain sight of the soldiers, hurled stones. Some of them got around to Bialik Street and joined groups of European and Palestinian Jewish kids who took up the war.

This engagement was the strangest battle manifestation I have ever watched. For here was war reduced to its primitive form — a circling of hostile little groups calling out names at each other while individuals darted toward the enemy, hurling stones. The paratroopers, highly trained representatives of the final art of civilized warfare were forced by the challenge of childhood to fight kids with their own weapons — stones.

While the scene had ironically comic undertones, it was played in dead seriousness by the children and the soldiers saw little humor in it. The children were plainly pure, if violent, little souls attacking the enemy who had come to drive their people from their homeland. They had heard enough talk at home and over the radio to reduce the situation to its simplest equation — even four-year-olds asked their mothers how soon soldiers would come into the house to shoot them.

So boys gathered in the street to do battle. They dragged out bits of broken furniture and built their own barricade half a block from the soldiers' barbed-wire blockade, and from these they hurled stones. The soldiers would rush out from cover and point their tommyguns at the kids, who would reply by pointing their wooden guns at the soldiers. Stones would fly, paratroopers would dodge and return them.

Finally several trucks arrived with police and more tommygun troopers. They lined up in rows across the street, with the police in front, and marched after the kids. The kids backed up, still hurling stones, and then vanished into passageways, vacant lots, and around corners.

I walked with the soldiers and heard many of them muttering, ''Why don't they give us the order to fire?'' I asked, wouldn't they mind firing on children, and they shrugged, saying, ''Why not, they're mean little devils.'' The street was cleared; the men stood around feeling foolish, especially as kids darted from passageways behind them, again throwing stones. Several men picked out the kids they would shoot as soon as the order to fire was given. ''See that one in the red jersey just behind the fence. . . . '' During this entire scene, every window and porch on both sides of Bialik Street was crowded with spectators.

After some minutes the situation became unbearably silly and the officers ordered the men to retire, so they backed up the street again, and within a few minutes the kids had recaptured their territory. A few soldiers took after the kids, chasing them into passageways. Most of the men mounted the trucks.

I heard an officer who was peering into a side street. ''Try to pick off the ringleaders, the adults who egg them on.'' So any adult seen talking to the kids got a slug in him. I don't know how the officer could tell from that distance whether the adult was egging the kids on or telling them to go home, but later I spoke to a wounded man in Hadassah Hospital. He lived at 11 Bezalel Street, next street to where I had witnessed the engagement. He had been taking some injured kids off the street into the house for first aid when he was shot.

I suppose the soldiers unconsciously felt themselves stripped and somehow insulted. They couldn't conceive that the attack was plainly natural, but decided this was a combination of Jewish cowardice and diabolism — ''pushing in the children.'' The officers, perched on the armored cars, neatly pointed out targets to their men. ''See that fellow just beyond the barbershop — he comes out of that doorway and starts them up and takes cover again. You, Jenkins, pot him next time he sticks his nose out.'' So the designated sharpshooter does his job. I heard yells from the Yemenite crowd a block away as a shot rang out, and I went over and saw the man who had just been potted being carried to a waiting ambulance. There were three other wounded already in the ambulance. One had been shot in the back.

Sporadic fire of this sort went on all day and during the evening curfew. In the hospital were twenty children under sixteen, all with bullets in them. Although I witnessed no shooting of children during the Bialik Street engagement, there had been other ones in which troops had not exercised such ''superb restraint.'' Shalom Bahaloni, a nine-year-old lad, was shot on Thursday while he stood near his house watching other boys throw stones. Eight-year-old Moshe Beckermat was shot just after curfew while standing on a second-floor balcony. A fourteen-year-old Yemenite kid told me he was shot at seven-thirty in the morning while going to work. Several youngsters said they had been in what they thought were non-curfew areas bordering Jaffa when yelled at and shot.

Among older people, the most scandalous case was that of a fifty-year-old milkman who had a son in the Palestine Brigade and was shot in the back while bicycling to his job. And all this time Jewish officials were apologizing for Tel Aviv's lack of restraint.

A week later I talked in Haifa to a Palestine policeman who agreed that from a strictly professional view of maintaining order, the Tel Aviv events seemed, from the record of casualties, to have been a bad show. Clubbing and hosing, he thought, would have taken care of whatever disorderly elements there were in the street.

From *Commentary*, December 1945.

THE MUTE

I must admit that I do not know the name of the boy to this day — a serious oversight. Yet I doubt if he would have told me had I asked him, for he was mute for a long time.

The story is as follows: Toward the end of 1942 news reached Jerusalem about the Holocaust. However, those horror stories were not confirmed, and, God is my witness, no one suspected that they would be confirmed. Those who had succeeded in escaping alive were either ignorant of what was happening or, for whatever reason, were silent. When I asked a fugitive from the Nazi Hell what had happened, he would mutter, "Please understand. It was dreadful . . . unspeakable. I left members of my family there and anything I say may reach the enemy and bring down on them death and destruction." I understood, of course, and did not pursue the matter any further.

Early in 1943, more and more gruesome stories reached us, many of which were confirmed by English, American, and French correspondents whose newspaper assignments brought them to Jerusalem. . . . I became friendly with officers who after the British defeat at El Alamein came to Jerusalem. I often invited them for a drink at the bar of the Government News Agency, or at the Hotel King David. In February 1942, one of them revealed to me that a group of Jewish youths had succeeded in escaping from the Warsaw Ghetto to Budapest, and would soon arrive in Palestine. The information was top secret, and he warned me that if it was leaked, he would face grave consequences. . . . A week or two later we met again, and he informed me that the group, numbering 72, had finally succeeded in stealing across the border into Yugo-slavia and were, at long last, on the way to Eretz Yisrael.

Would the British give them immigration certificates? Would they allow them to enter the land? These thorny questions struck me immediately. My friend did not know the answer, except that the British Mandate Government had issued instructions to arrest them on arrival in Palestine. He also told me that British intelligence officers had been dispatched to Yugoslavia to keep guard over their movements.

It so happened that an Australian journalist who was a close friend of mine had been assigned to report on the operation. One day he disclosed to me that the group was scheduled to arrive in a day or two, and that it would be interned (at Camp Atlit). I found out the exact date of disembarkation at a Lebanon port and learned that, after a thorough investigation, the government would permit the Jewish Agency to set aside immigration certificates from its monthly allotment of 1500 allowed by the British Immigration Office for settlement in the land. It was small comfort, but a solace nevertheless. As soon as I learned about these plans, I received permission to go to Lebanon, where the group would be detained on landing. I wanted to see them and find answers to my many questions. After much effort and wire-pulling, I got a permit to meet them after their landing.

Early Sunday morning, in the midst of an unparalleled storm, I reached the Lebanon border at 5:30 A.M. The British officer in charge could not believe his eyes when he read the permit that was granted me. He informed me that the group would be delayed because there was not a sufficient number of buses to transport them. . . . Ultimately, I decided to stay overnight at Nahariah, nearby, to await the newcomers. Early the next morning I again reported at the immigration station. The officer agreed to take me along in his car to the port of Tyre. He armed himself with a machine gun, two revolvers, and hand grenades for protection against the bandits who roamed the neighborhood.

After an hour's travel, we met the young immigrants, who were traveling toward us in two buses driven by Arabs and accompanied by a British security patrol. I introduced myself to the group as a Palestinian Jewish journalist from Jerusalem who had come to welcome the newcomers to the Promised Land. I had begun speaking to them in Hungarian, but they did not respond. I tried Yiddish. With stern faces and cold glances, the older ones among them responded in their native Polish and Russian languages. They answered politely but in a restrained tone, about their experiences, how they crossed the borders, which had been under tight Nazi vigilance, and their long trek through Europe and Asia.

During my many journeys I have carried a pocket-sized book of Psalms in addition to my reporter's notebook. When I asked the group leader some questions, I took out my notebook to record the answers, and suddenly the Psalm book fell to the ground. One of the group picked it up. His eyes flashing, he opened it and with trembling hands raised it to his lips, kissed it lingeringly, and returned it to me. I thanked him and asked his name, but he did not answer.

"He is mute," the leader said. "We know he is Jewish, but that's all we know about him."

"How sure are you he is Jewish, since he doesn't talk?"

With a broad smile the young man replied, "Come closer and you will see for yourself." As we approached, the leader unbuttoned the lad's torn shirt and said, "See for yourself." I saw the *tephillin*[1] thongs of the arm and head pieces wrapped tightly around the boy's torso.

Deeply moved by what I saw, I offered the book of Psalms to the boy, as if suggesting that he open it for worship. At first he seemed reluctant to accept it; then he again raised it to his lips and kissed it reverently, his eyes filling with tears. Diffidently and silently he returned it.

[1] Phylacteries which are worn at weekday morning services.

I do not know what promoted me to think that the lad was pretending muteness. I tenderly put my hand on his shoulder and said in Yiddish, "Do not fear. You are in Eretz Yisrael, among brothers." I requested the officer in charge to permit me to travel in the bus with the youth, in return for which he would use my car. The officer consented, and I got into the bus where the "dumb" boy sat.

As soon as I was left alone with the group, their reticence disappeared and they opened up to me. "Where are they taking us?" They inquired. This question was also evident in the dumb one's brown eyes. I told them that they would be interned for a limited period at the Atlit detention camp and after that they would be free to go where they wanted in Eretz. I sat near the mute, who read the Psalms without uttering a sound and from time to time wiped a tear from his eyes.

We were met at the border by Mr. Eliyahu Dobkin, a director of the Jewish Agency's Immigration Department, and his entourage. They brought refreshments with them. My "ward" drank thirstily the cup of warm tea but pushed aside the sandwich. "You may eat it," I said. "It's kosher." He took it and ate ravenously. I was overjoyed, for at last I knew that I had won his confidence.

When the British officer ordered the convoy to proceed to Camp Atlit, I interceded for the group, saying, "May I respectfully suggest that you take the long route, via Haifa. Please consider their feelings at being taken directly from the concentration camps to another camp surrounded by barbed wire, watchtowers, and armed guards ready to shoot. It will have a traumatic effect on them. They have risked their lives to escape from such places.

He saw my point and assented to my request. When the convoy entered Haifa, the eyes of the young people lit up as they read signs in Hebrew: KOSHER MEAT, BET KNESSET (Synagogue), HANUT SEFARIM (Bookstore), and saw Hebrew newspapers and periodicals displayed at the kiosks and heard the newsboys shouting the names of the Hebrew papers. The newcomers looked wonderingly, and in their eyes I could read, "Have we at long last reached the end of our wanderings? Are our miseries over?"

My young mute friend began to squirm and show great nervousness. He could not sit still; he rose up and sat down several times; he drew near the door, then opened the window. . . . I feared that he would try to escape. Impulsively I asked him if he had heard of Jerusalem. Did he have relatives there?

"Is the Gerre Rabbe still living?" he burst out. Now his companions were speechless. For months they had been certain that he was mute. Suddenly they heard him speak clearly in a Polish-Yiddish dialect.

I was deeply affected and answered him tenderly. "The Rebbe is living. Only recently I met with him. He is old and weak. But he dwells in Jerusalem in the neighborhood of Mahneh Yehudah in the Yeshivah Sfat Emet.

Words began to pour out of the mute's mouth as if the floodgates had been opened. His life story was shocking. With his own eyes he had seen the Nazis murder his father, mother, brothers, and sisters, his grandmother tortured and killed. He saw the murderers throw all their bodies onto a truck piled high with dead bodies. He, too, was thrown with them. At the first chance, he jumped off the truck. A Christian who had known his parents hid him.

All this happened a week after his Bar Mitzvah. When the Nazis burst into the house, the lad, thinking that the family was being dispossessed, impulsively snatched his *tephillin* bag. That's all he took with him. "The man who saved me," he continued, "cut my hair, including my side locks. He warned me not to tell anyone I was a Jew. If I did, he and I would be killed. I replied that as a believing Jew I was forbidden to lie. If I was destined to die, I would die as a Jew. He lashed out at me and raved about my obstinacy. He promised to provide me with kosher food and endeavor to find a Hebrew prayer book for my daily worship. He did not find a prayerbook but once he brought me a fowl, which, although he assured me it was kosher, I did not touch. All through my stay with him I ate bread, raw vegetables, and fruits.

"My protector and his family were kind to me. On Sunday, for safety's sake, he implored me to attend church with his family, but I pleaded illness every Sunday. Once he brought a doctor to examine me. The doctor asked me my name. My protector answered, 'Stephan.' This was the moment I vowed I would not utter a word until the All-Merciful saved me. The doctor declared I was ill and I was to be taken to the hospital. I went wild, held tight to my savior, and refused to budge. The doctor left me in his care. I feigned loss of speech, and they believed me.

"One day the master of the house came home deeply distressed. He locked himself up with his family. Suspecting that he was upset over my presence, I eavesdropped and learned that the Nazis were making a minute house-to-house search for hidden Jews. The master knew that I had my *tephillin* and was terrified that they would be discovered. He had implored me time and again to burn them, but I refused. In dumb language I made it clear that I'd rather die. We struggled. When they forcefully removed the *tephillin* from the bag, I grabbed them and before their eyes I wrapped them tightly around my body and covered them with my clothes. They calmed down.

"When the Nazis made the search of the house they asked me questions, but I was mute. The owner stated that I was his nephew and that I had lost my speech as a child, because of cerebral fever. He produced a birth certificate to confirm my relationship to him, and I was not touched.

"When the master died, his son took over. One day he returned home with the news that the Nazis had built a death camp at Maidanek, where they had erected a factory to make soap. He brought back a few samples of soap, which he said was kosher because it was made of Jew-fat. I have a sample of it." He took out a piece of soap, on which was stamped the letters R.J.S.

Fatigued from his prolonged outburst, my young friend became silent. He took my *tehillim* book and in a mournful tone began to recite Psalm 107, beginning with verse 10: "Sons of men who dwell in darkness and in gloom, prisoners in chains and misery . . . " I stayed with the group until the evening.

When I reached Jerusalem the next day, I wrote out all that the boy had told me and transmitted it to my newspaper in Tel Aviv. The next day I went to the Gerre Rebbe and told the lad's story to Rabbi Itze Meier Levine, the Rebbe's son-in-law. When I completed my tale, he proceeded immediately to Atlit and brought the lad to the Yeshiva Sfat Emet.

A.E.

From an unpublished manuscript by Asher Lazar.

16.

LIBERATION

About 715,000 Jewish men and women who survived in the camps were liberated by the Allied forces — but only a bare 4000 orphaned Jewish children. Many were on the verge of dying. Another few weeks, and they too, would have died. A number had gone through the hell of several concentration camps. All had lost hope of finding living members of their families. They were entirely on their own, lone survivors in a chaotic world, surrounded by ruin and desolation and hordes of liberated prisoners who filled the roads as they trudged back to their homes. These people were too preoccupied to give any attention to others in need. Many Jewish children had nowhere to go and no one who would help them. They were living skeletons, Mussulmen, who were near death and needed careful medical care and relief. Their lives depended entirely on the help of humanity.

Some response to the surviving remnants came from countries like Sweden, which had been spared the ravages of war. Relief and aid came from the Jews of Palestine, the United States, Canada, Latin America, and Australia, who organized to rescue the surviving orphans and provide homes for them. The Palestinian Jewish Brigade and Jewish angels of mercy, whom we shall meet later, wrote a glorious chapter in reviving the spirit and will to live.

"MAMA, MAY I CRY NOW?"

The narrator of this moving incident is Abba Kovner, an intrepid partisan in the Vilna region and chronicler of the Holocaust. In 1945 he settled in Eretz

292

Yisrael, where he has achieved a reputation as Hebrew novelist, poet, and writer for children. He is a prominent spokesman for the She'erit Hapletah, *the survivors of the tragedy, and active in preserving the remembrance of the Holocaust. Latterly he became notable as one of the prime movers in the erection on the campus of the University of Tel Aviv the* Bet HaTefutzot, *the unique, world-renowned Museum of the Diaspora.*

When we broke into the ghetto, suddenly a woman ran toward us. She held a little girl in her arms. She froze in her steps, burst out into loud crying, and tried to run back to hide. Some of us were dressed in German uniforms, which we had taken from German prisoners. Evidently she thought that we were the enemy, who had come back.

We spoke to her in Yiddish and calmed her fears. When she ascertained that we were Jews, she broke out sobbing hysterically and told us what had happened to her. I gathered that she and her little girl, who was probably four but who looked three years old, had hidden in a pit for more than eleven months. She poured forth her tale of agony in a torrent of words. I could not quite understand what she was saying, but I could not stop her. At the end she wept bitterly and without stop.

At that moment the little girl in her arms, looked and behaved as if she were a mute, opened her mouth and said, "Mama, may I cry now?"

Later we learned that the mother had drilled into the child that she should not cry out under any circumstances because she would be heard and endanger their lives.

From *Testimony at the Eichmann Trial,* testimony by Abba Kovner, published by Yad Vashem, 1974, Vol. 1, pp. 336.

THE MARCH

It was the spring of 1945, and there was no more work to be done at the ammunition factory in Sommerda, Thuringia. Sommerda was only thirty kilometers away from the notorious death camp of Buchenwald; and it was partly fear of being sent there that kept us hard at work in spite of hunger and exhaustion. Since no more ammunition was being produced, it seemed that the war was drawing to a close. But when there was no work, we went hungry. Food was scarce in wartime, and the Nazis would not waste it on unproductive Jews.

So, hungry and weak as we were, the Germans forced us to begin marching away from the advancing Russian and American troops, who might have liberated us. Our unit of laborers marched in rows of five each. My younger sisters Frieda and Judy, my close friend Martha, another girl from our home town, and I were always together. Our long march took us through farm country, and friendly peasants would give us a potato or two each day. This was our only food. When night fell, we were assigned to sleep in a huge barn piled high with straw.

Our guards were handicapped young men who were not considered fit for battle. But with weapons in their hands and uniforms on their backs, they became cruel and powerful. They kept us continually on the march.

For two months we marched; each day was like the one before it: endless walking and little food. Our feet ached with the pain of the long march, and we were weary. Hunger was our constant companion. We all lost a great deal of weight.

After two days without any food — not even a single potato — I felt that I could not go on without eating something. To continue marching like this could only mean death. So that night, when we lay on our beds of straw and the others were asleep, I told my two sisters that we should stay in the barn and not join the marchers in the morning. When the sun rose, we discovered that others had the same idea. About ten of us had hidden in the barn and stayed back from the march. But even if we did not march, without food we could not last long.

In that moment of utter despair, a miracle happened. The villagers found out about us and came to our hideout with a huge pot of hot soup, which in my starved state seemed the best I had ever eaten. With each spoonful, I felt that I was regaining my strength and would surely make it. After we had eaten our fill, the villagers told us to leave as quickly as possible because we could not hide there.

We knew that if we did not rejoin the others, the villagers would report on us. We were forced to catch up with the marchers, guarded by the dread SS men. As we approached the camp, the SS officers came forward. Pointing a gun at us, one of them said, "If you ever try a stunt like this again, you will be shot." It was no idle threat.

I will never forget the sunny afternoon that we were all lined up in front of a barn to witness the shooting of one young woman, whose only "crime" was that she had broken away from the line of marchers to beg for bread from the villagers. How terribly frightened and horrified we were. Each one of us thought: It could have been me.

One beautiful morning, not long after we returned to the line of marchers, we awoke and found that our guards had disappeared. Immediately we had a premonition that something good was happening. Just a few moments later, another miracle occurred: We heard the welcome roar of Russian tanks rolling by. Hungry and worn out, we rejoiced. We were finally liberated. It was May 8, 1945 — VE Day, Victory in Europe.

From *World Over Magazine,* published by Board of Jewish Education of Greater New York, April 7, 1976. Written by Helen Lazaros.

FIRST FREE BABY BORN AT BELSEN

While in Auschwitz, I believed that it was the site of ultimate horror, a place which made Dante's Inferno appear a musical comedy, and Hell, as described by the Catholic Church, a sinecure. When I arrived in Belsen-Bergen, I discovered that Auschwitz was no more than a Purgatory. Hell was enclosed between the barbed-wire fences of Belsen-Bergen.

In Auschwitz we still had the strength to keep our past alive and find comfort in reliving our memories. Here, as if our very brains had dried out, no thought came to our minds, our imagination refused to function; for had it dwelled on the sight which opened before our eyes, we would all have gone stark, raving mad. Our conversation was restricted to the essential topics: food — pain — death. . . .

Surrounded by mountainous heaps of rotting corpses and by ditches full of bodies, some of which still retained a breath of life but not the strength to climb out from under their dead companions, stood Block III, the "maternity block" of Belsen-Bergen. From concentration camps all over Germany, pregnant women were sent here to bear their children in this torture chamber of Hell. There were German, Hungarian, Dutch, French, Gypsy, Russian, Polish, Czechoslovak women lying in the cages along the walls, two in each. Their tremendous stomachs, swollen to a bursting point with child and hunger, did not permit them to move, and their moans, their screams, their helpless cursing filled the building with a constant deafening cacophony. Lice covered their bodies in thick layers — hungry, persistent, insufferable lice, sparing nobody, not even the faces and hands of the doctors.

Block III was my responsibility, but what can two empty hands do to relieve the indescribable suffering of hundreds?

Everybody in the block had typhus, and, as if the disease were bent upon faithfully serving the Nazis, it came to Belsen-Bergen in its most violent, most painful, deadliest, form. The diarrhea caused by it became uncontrollable. It flooded the bottom of the cages, dripped through the cracks into the faces of the women dying in the cages below, and, mixed with blood, pus, and urine, formed a slimy, fetid mud on the floor of the barracks. Without water, without medicine, without help, every attempt at life-saving seemed futile. And yet, the doctor in me never gave up, even when the human being reached the limits of its endurance. I fought on with bare hands, cut my shirt into rags to wipe the hot, moist, soiled faces of my patients, tried to smile at them through the layer of filth that covered my own face, and whispered hoarse, unconvincing words of comfort.

The air was so thick and humid that one could hardly breathe; the horrible smell of human excrement, blood, pus, and sweat invaded our nostrils in nauseating waves, until the desire for fresh air became just as torturing, just as unbearable as the desire for a mouthful of water, a bite of food. Our eyes hurt from the sight we couldn't escape; our eardrums hurt with the sounds we couldn't shut out. Burning compassion, helpless pity filled our souls until they, too, hurt like an open wound. . . .

I had been working in Block III for several weeks, when, around April 12, 1945, a whirlwind of excitement changed the atmosphere of the camp. Our SS guards left their posts, and Hungarian soldiers with white armbands took over the policing of the camp. Something was happening beyond the barbed-wire fences, something of great importance, of which we were not told. And yet, rumors began to travel from mouth to mouth, wonderful, encouraging rumors, which for the moment seemed louder than the screams of those writhing in birth-pains. "The Allies are coming! The liberators are coming!"

Those who had the strength to get up came out of the barracks and went from group to group to listen to the news. "We are going to be free! We are going home! We can be human being again! We can eat — drink — eat — drink. . . ." Only the incorrigible pessimists did not believe in life. "They are going to blow up the camp before they go. They are going to kill us first," they moaned. Could the Nazis permit this proof of their bestiality to survive?

The camp was seething with joy, fear, uncertainty, hope, expectancy. . . .

April 15, 1945. Young Marusa from Warsaw is about to bring her child into the world. In her superhuman pains she tears the filthy rags from her body, her dirty hair sticks wet to her pale forehead, and she holds on feverishly to my dirty hands. "Help me, Doctor! Help me. . . ."

Before having been brought to Belsen-Bergen, Marusa was a member of the Underground movement, the partisans in Warsaw. She had done everything a human being could do to fight the Nazis, and then, eight months ago, she was caught and condemmed to rot alive in Belsen-Bergen. The child she carried under her heart grew on the hatred Marusa felt for the Nazis. It grew until April 15, 1945, when it was ready to leave the typhus-infected, lice-ridden, feverish body of its mother.

I did not leave her side even for a moment, although the confused sounds coming from the outside came nearer and nearer. Suddenly I heard trumpets, and immediately afterwards a tremendous shout of joy coming from thousands of throats shook the entire camp. "The British have come! The liberators have come! We are free . . . free."

Marusa's last scream of pain sounded almost jubilant. . . . And a moment later there was between her legs the first free child born in Belsen-Bergen. Pale and exhausted, the young mother could hardly smile, but the words leaving her bloodless lips were like a prayer: "Freedom . . . freedom . . . ."

The first free child of Belsen-Bergen was safe. But her mother's blood wouldn't stop flowing. She grew paler, weaker, and wide streams of blood came gushing out of her womb. My heart beat wildly. I had to save this partisan mother! I had to save her! What did I care about freedom, about the British, about anything in the world if I couldn't save this heroic, tortured young mother? I ran out of the barrack and stopped the first British soldier I saw. "Water! Get me water and a disinfectant!" He didn't understand. I ran on and came face to face with a tall, impressive-looking soldier. With my bloody, dirty hands I grasped his sleeve. "Do you understand French?" He nodded. "Get me water, please, and some disinfectant. . . . I have to perform an operation. . . . Hurry . . . hurry. . . ."

He looked down on me from his tremendous height, uncomprehending but moved to the core. He must be an officer, I thought, a soldier who is used to the sight of blood. . . . And already I was pulling him by the sleeve, pulling him toward Block III. Half an hour later I had the water, the disinfectant, and could wash my hands and perform the operation, not as a helpless prisoner, but as a doctor. . . .

Here in the first hour of liberty, I saved the lives of the partisan woman Marusa and of little Marusa, her daughter.

The tall, hardened soldier looked on, with tears rolling down his cheeks. He could understand war, yes, and he was not afraid of death. But what he saw in Belsen-Bergen was beyond the limit of his understanding, of his imagination. For weeks he fought, day and night, against sickness, against death, against lice, against starvation. He did much, but in most cases he was too late. Yet he was a real liberator. All the inmates of Belsen-Bergen who survived will forever bless his name. He was Brigadier General Glyn Hughes, Chief Medical Officer of the Second British Army.

From *I Was a Doctor in Auschwitz* by Giselle Perl, op. cit. pp. 170-175.

THE CHILDREN OF BELSEN

Hadassah Bimko-Rosensaft and her late husband, Josef, were indefatigable, devoted leaders of the central committee of the DPs in the British Zone and later of the World Federation of Bergen-Belsen. This federation has achieved universal fame and esteem for its ramified program of mutual help, its publications, and its leadership in the relief and assistance of camp survivors throughout the world. Their son, Menachem Z. Rosensaft, a child of Bergen-Belsen camp, is a poet whose poems on the Holocaust have been published in magazines and books.

At 3 A.M. on a bitterly cold December day in 1944, our block at Belsen was suddenly awakened by the noise of an automobile and the crying of children. Soon we heard the shouting of the SS, so familiar to us in those days. We were ordered outside, and there we saw a huge lorry full of children of various ages. The SS told the children to get out. There were forty-nine of them, from eight months to fifteen years.

We took the children inside. Ours was supposed to be an ambulance and treatment unit. We learned a little later that these were children of Dutch Jews who had been removed the same day from one of the internment camps at Belsen, allegedly to teach the Germans the art of diamond polishing.

It should not be difficult to imagine our feeling at being given the opportunity to care for these abandoned Jewish children. We gave them all our love and whatever strength was left to us.

Some weeks later, more children arrived, from Buchenwald and Theresienstadt. These were children of Polish and Czech Jews, who survived and reached us by some inexplicable "miracle."

Our girls and women took care of the children. Weak and ailing as they were themselves, they attended to the children day and night, fed them, washed them, and played with them.

When our men who worked in the SS stores and chemist shops learned that we had children in our block, they risked their own lives and stole food and other commodities, which hey passed on to us for our charges.

Without these splendid Jewish men and women, the children would not have survived. Thanks to their efforts, none of the children succumbed to the raging spotted typhus and other epidemics, although they all went through it.

I vividly remember a long and terrible night, when we were sitting by the feverish children, who tossed and turned and cried, and were telling them that soon everything would be different, although we did not believe it ourselves at the time.

And then April 15, 1945, came — the day of liberation by the British forces. The first job of the British medical team, headed by Brigadier Glyn Hughes and Colonel J. Johnston, was to save the sick and care for the children. They were helped by liberated doctors and a number of liberated women, some trained nurses and some not. All our women who could still walk volunteered to help the medical team.

The British medical personnel and the liberated doctors and nurses performed superhuman tasks. The children were soon transferred to proper buildings, the well-known R.B. 5, 6, and 7 — bright, spotlessly clean, and white sheets on the beds, good food, and constant medical attention. There were toys for the children. English doctors brought the toys into the camp. They went round the neighborhood, confiscated toys from German families, and told the German mothers to call their children, and explain to them that the toys were being given to Jewish children who were wronged by Germans.

We, on our part, did everything in our power to teach the children to laugh and play again. Gradually they returned to normal. Some children's parents turned up; some children found one parent; and some at least a relative. The Dutch and Czech Red Cross took those children home who had a home to go to. The rest stayed with us, and were educated in our own schools, where they received an excellent Jewish and general education, thanks to the sacrifice of our teachers and heads of the children's institutes in Belsen, as well as at Blankenese and Luneburg, where some of the children lived.

One of the brightest days in this period for all of us and — if I may be personal — for me in particular, was the day when the first children's transport left for Israel, on April 9, 1946. I was privileged to accompany this transport. The certificates — the first batch we ever had — were brought to us by the representative of the Jewish Agency in Paris, Ruth Kluger. I remember with gratitude her help and understanding in organizing the transport.

Now, just a few highlights of a remarkable journey.

Our transport had a thousand children, who were assembled from all over Germany, and twenty expectant mothers, whose husbands were already on the high seas with Aliyah Bet. We went by train to Marseille and thence with the good ship *Champollion*. At the railway station in Lyon, we witnessed a moving episode — a couple of local Jews, who had learned about our arrival with the children, appeared on the platform and offered us bread; they were still hungry themselves at the time. They cried unashamedly, looking at the surviving children.

We celebrated the Seder in Marseille, and it was a festive and joyous affair, held in the open; and then we embarked on our journey to Haifa. On the first day at sea, we received an additional passenger: a child was born, and still another child was born aboard ship just before we entered Haifa harbor.

The children were happy and in high spirits, full of expectations about Eretz

Yisrael. When our ship docked at Bizerte harbor, a delegation of local Jews, headed by their rabbi, came to pay us a call. The rabbi appeared in his festive robes — a white *abaya* and a red fez. He gave us wine and his blessings. The Jewish children of Bizerte brought us fruit. They marched on board carrying baskets of oranges on their heads in Oriental fashion. Needless to say, we were deeply moved.

In Haifa, we were received like long lost brothers and sisters, which we in fact were. Alas, the joy was not complete. The children had to go to [Camp] Atlit for eight days, and I insisted on going with them and staying with them until they were all released.

All the children were distributed among *kibbutzim* and schools. Our Belsen group of 105 children were divided between Dorot, Kiryat Anavim, and Ben Schemen.

I paid the children a visit at Kiryat Anavim, and I saw with what love and affection they were treated. On that Friday night, as we were sitting at the *Shabbat* meal, I knew that our children had at last come home.

There was no problem of absorption. For our children had been prepared for Eretz Yisrael in our Belsen schools. They were immediately and easily absorbed into the *Yishuv,* where they are today free and proud citizens of the Jewish State.

Care of the Sick at Belsen

The hell of Belsen was at its worst about three weeks before liberation. Typhus was raging in the camp, and about one thousand people, succumbed to it daily. The small crematorium could not cope with all the corpses, even though it burned day and night. There were unburied corpses all over the place.

The SS, who felt that their end was near, tried to exterminate us all. They cut off the water and gave us bread only three times a week. For the rest, we received about a half a pint of so-called soup a day. On top of it all, the SS kept us in mortal fear by informing us that the camp was mined and we would all be blown up before the day of liberation came.

Such was our position on the eve of liberation: disease, starvation, despair, fear of being killed by an explosion — and no ray of hope.

The camp was liberated on April 15, and next day there appeared in our midst Brigadier H. L. Glyn Hughes, the Chief Medical Officer of the Second Army. At the sight of the huts, with their dead and half-dead, the brigadier, a medical officer hardened to human suffering cried unashamedly. He decided on the spot to try and save as many of the sick as possible, in spite of the conflicting call of military casualties.

From *Belsen* by Hadassah Bimko-Rosensaft, published by Irgun Sherrit Hapletah Mehaozor Habriti, Israel, 1957, pp. 98-105.

LIBERATED!

The author, Dr. Moshe Avital, was born in Czechoslovakia and as a young boy was deported and went through nine concentration camps, beginning with

Auschwitz. On April 11, 1945, he was liberated by the American Army in Buchenwald. He is now the Director of the American section of the Department of Education and Culture of the World Zionist Organization, and lives in New York City.

My last concentration camp, Buchenwald, was located deep in a forest near the city of Weimar, site of the founding of the German Republic (1919), which is today in East Germany. This camp was among the largest and became well known throughout the world. The inmates included not only Jews but many other nationalities, even prisoners of war. In this tremendous prison there were also some of the famous statesmen of Europe, as well as German prisoners who had resisted the Nazi regime. These Germans were mostly Communists and Socialists or other people with a conscience, who were opposed to the Nazi ideology. These prisoners suffered a great deal; however, they were still much better off than the other inmates. . . . They received food packages and enjoyed other privileges. Later on, when Buchenwald was converted into an international concentration camp, the conditons became unbearable to all.

The camp itself was subdivided into smaller units. Once I was taken, together with a group of boys, to work in the kitchen. We passed by the barrack of the important people. In this barrack there were political leaders who had refused to cooperate with the Nazis. Among them were Léon Blum of France, Admiral Miklos Horthy of Hungary, and others. We were always anxious to look at these personalties, and it was known that they were treated better than the rest of the inmates.

The children's barracks was an institution in itself, thanks to a gentile Czech educator. In them were crammed two thousand youths from various European countries, most of whom were Jewish. The Czech supervisor was one of the "righteous gentiles." The Germans had arrested him in Czechoslovakia for his resistance to the Nazi ideology and deported him to Buchenwald. Since he was an educator, he requested that he be appointed to supervise the children's barracks. Many times he endangered his own life in order to protect the young boys. The children did not work outside the camp but were utilized for all kinds of tasks within the camp grounds, such as working in the kitchen, cleaning the officers' quarters, and other chores.

When I was transported to Buchenwald, in January of 1945, I found it an inhuman habitat. The cruel treatment of the prisoners also extended to the children, in spite of the efforts of our Czech supervisor. Especially the last few months before the liberation, the camp was like hell on earth. Trains full of victims arrived daily from other East European camps which had been evacuated. Most of the arrivals were on the verge of death. The hunger in Buchenwald became more severe day by day. These inhuman conditions caused thousands of deaths daily.

Each morning the corpses of those who had died overnight were piled up in front of the latrines. Some of these victims died from slave labor, which they had endured over the years, others from torture or from malnutrition. The corpses lay around until other inmates were ordered to take them in wheelbarrows or wagons to the crematorium, which was in full operation day and night.

Buchenwald did not have enough ovens to cremate all who died, and therefore many bodies remained lying around. When the forces of General Patton entered Buchenwald, they found piles and piles of corpses which the Germans had not been able to cremate.

Rumors were spread in Buchenwald that the Allies were making inroads deep into Germany and that the end of the war was near. In the meantime, I was getting weaker and weaker; my legs were swollen from hunger and frost. My whole body shrank, and my bones were sticking out. A few days before the liberation, the Germans started to evacuate the camp. This time they did not make selections but took barrack after barrack en masse. We heard constant shooting around the camp but did not know who was doing it. The evacuation continued for four days, until the SS men reached the children's quarters.

Suddenly SS men surrounded our barracks and started to push and pull us out, screaming, hitting, kicking, and clubbing. Our Czech supervisor marched in front of us; he did not want to abandon his children at this critical moment. The SS guards lined the path from the doors of the children's barracks all the way to the gate of the camp. We had to march between these lines so that we could not escape. Each Nazi guard held a gun in one hand and a club in the other. When we passed these devils, we felt that this was the end. I was very weak, and each step required a tremendous effort. I prayed silently and wondered whence help might come. In my mind and heart I was asking, "Father in Heaven, why do we young children deserve such a horrible fate?"

As we came closer to the camp gates, we heard the shooting louder and clearer; one could discern that these were machine guns. Just as we were about to go past the gate, the alarm system went off, and the German guards began to run for cover. We were left standing inside the fence near the closed gates.

Out of the blue sky there appeared bombers, which strafed the Nazi military barracks. A number of bombs also fell inside the camp. At that moment we started to run back into the barracks. The bombing continued all day and through the night. With the help of friends, I made my way back and lay on the ground throughout the bombing.

When morning arrived, there was complete silence — a deadly silence. No more shooting, no guards around — not a living soul was seen outside. Suddenly we saw some prisoners running with guns in their hands. The SS guards were abandoning their posts, jumping off the towers and disappearing into the forest. A few minutes later some inmates raised a white flag. This happened so fast that we could not believe our eyes. It was evident that the super-race was defeated and was now on the run.

A few hours later, General George Patton with his Third Army Tank Corps entered and liberated Buchenwald. Those of us who could walk went out to greet the liberators. Almost all were hysterical with joy. I was in bad shape; I could not stand on my feet and had no strength to celebrate. I prayed in my heart that God would give me strength to overcome my weak condition, especially at this moment of liberation. I reminded myself of Samson's prayer, and I whispered it: "O Lord God, remember me, I pray Thee, and strengthen me only this once."

As the American soldiers entered the barracks, you could see on their faces the shock at the sight of the prisoners. They found skeletons of human beings who were dying. During the entire war they had not witnessed such a ghastly scene. Although they had experienced the death of their comrades and of the enemy, they had never seen atrocities of such magnitude.

Suddenly an order was given for the American troops to retreat from Buchenwald, since the Germans had begun a counterattack. They retreated, while we in Buchenwald remained in no man's land — on one side the Germans, and on the other the Americans. The Germans shelled and bombarded the camp. We were pinned to the ground all the time. Those of us who could run ran for cover into the trenches. The battle lasted a few hours. The Americans retook the camp and the entire area.

The final liberation of Buchenwald took place on April 12, 1945, the day President Roosevelt died. We were informed by the American soldiers that in the forest thousands of camp prisoners lay dead; they had been shot during the last few days before liberation day. These were the victims of the last evacuation. Only twenty thousand inmates survived.

We were also informed by the Americans that on the way to Buchenwald they had captured a train with thousands of Hitler Youth. The Hitlerites had instructions to take over the camp in order to relieve the SS men for duties at the front, and annihilate the rest of the prisoners.

After the liberation, a number of military doctors and nurses arrived to look after the living. We looked upon these people as if they had come from another planet. We were given food, clothing, cigarettes, candy, and many other "goodies." The American soldiers did not know how to do enough for us.

However, they made a terrible mistake by giving rich food to very sick people who had not tasted a morsel of food for a long time. Instead of feeding us bland food at first, they unintentionally caused many deaths by the rich diet which they provided. Our stomachs were not accustomed to it. As a result, thousands died.

During the first days after liberation, the inmates who were able to walk broke into the storehouses and took whatever they found, and there was plenty. These prisoners also tried to take revenge for their dear ones who had been annihilated. On the first day after liberation, the Americans did not prevent the inmates from taking revenge, but after that they protected the Germans from being attacked.

I was not able to be among those who tried to take revenge, since I could hardly move and breathe. Nonetheless, many thoughts crossed my mind of the innocent victims in my family, of all the Jewish victims and the decent human beings who had been murdered. A voice was calling in me: "Take retribution for the blood of thy family, for the babes and the children, the pure and innocent who were destroyed before they had a chance to live." More than once it seemed to me that I heard the voices of my family ringing in my ears, which brought me to a breaking point.

Another thought which occurred to me at that moment was that there are moral values in Judaism which emphasize that a Jew should have pity and compassion even for the enemy. It is not fitting to a Jew to learn the ways of the wicked and turn murderer.

There was a tug of war in my mind about this problem, which continues to this day. At some moments I have a great urge to take revenge, and moments later the Jewish moral obligation comes to mind and overpowers this desire. I can imagine that this struggle, this unrest, and the terrible memories of those horrible years plague most of the survivors.

Since the Jewish moral fabric which does not permit us "to do unto them that which they did unto us" is deeply woven into our souls, we will probably never find peace and tranquillity. These two opposite forces will continue to struggle within us.

I saw, at the liberation of Buchenwald, the Russian prisoners of war grab military vehicles and speed into the city of Weimar, where I was told they attempted to take retribution. Do you know what the Jewish inmates did? They gathered together to pray, to cry, and to say *Kaddish* for their dear ones. Despite it all, they somehow found strength to overcome their grief and anger and rise above the impulse to take revenge. If the Jewish survivors had decided to set entire cities on fire, one could have found justification for them, because in everyone's heart there was a tremendous accumulation of anger, grief, and deep despair.

A chapter in itself was the blessed activities of the American Jewish chaplains immediately after the liberation of Buchenwald. In the military code there were no specific orders about how to handle the survivors. However, the Jewish chaplains had a wonderful guide — the Bible. I well remember Rabbi Marcus and Rabbi Herschel Schechter and their tremendous efforts to help us, their wonderful, comforting words and deeds.

There were a number of mines around Buchenwald where the Germans had employed the prisoners. After the liberation, the Allies found these mines full of Jewish silver ornaments which the Germans had stolen, such as Torah crowns, Torah breastplates and pointers, *Kiddush* cups, spice boxes, *menorahs,* candlesticks, *esrogim* boxes, Chanukah candlelabra, Sabbath knives, Eternal Light lamps, and many other sacred objects. For days and days their military trucks carried this loot away to an unknown destination.

Those of us who did not die shortly after the liberation gathered strength little by little, but our tragedy did not come to an end. It deepened, because only then did we realize how great our losses were. We also suffered a tremendous feeling of guilt. How is it that I am the one who survived? Am I more worthy to live than our dear ones who were annihilated?

From an unpublished manuscript by Moshe Avital.

"WE SHALL NOT SET FOOT ON GERMANY'S CURSED SOIL"

The day of departure finally came. The children were very thrilled at the news. The girls jumped with joy; they embraced and kissed each other. The boys assured us that ten minutes was all the time they needed to pack. After that they would be ready to help pack the infants' things, and they volunteered to carry the *bubbeles*[1] on their backs.

I thanked them and sketched out what lay ahead of us. "We will travel in three buses, which are chartered from Thomas Cook Tours, until we reach the Czechoslovak and German border. From there on we shall pass through southern Germany until we arrive at Strasbourg, France."

"How many kilometers?"[2] one asked.

"A lot — about fifteen hundred. It's a long, weary journey, especially for the very young and those who are not physically in condition to undergo such a long trip. But there will be seats for everyone. We shall travel only during the day and rest at night. The rest stops in Germany will not be pleasant, but — "

I had not finished talking when Saul[3] jumped up as if he had been stung. "What? We'll sleep and eat in Germany? In the houses of those who murdered our parents and families? Never! If I see anyone engage in a conversation with a German, I'll break his teeth. No! We will not set foot on Germany's cursed soil."

His one eye flashed fiercely. The scars on his face turned blood-red. The veins on his neck swelled. His outburst was followed by a dead silence.

My assistant, Mr. Menlich, tried to interject an objection — the problems posed by the need to go to the toilet. Saul cut him off sharply. "I would not be repelled from emptying chamber pots on the clean German soil, which has absorbed the blood and sweat of millions of innocent people."

"Saul is right," the children cried out unanimously. "We will be uncomfortable, but at least we will not see the repulsive faces of the murderers."

A girl who had escaped Dr. Mengele's selection at Auschwitz declared her opposition.

"And I say," added her sister, who after Auschwitz had lived through twelve other camps, "we would be justified in beating them up for once, as they did us."

"They did not hit me even once," Saul said, "but every time they assailed a Jew, I felt as if they were hurting me."

"I too agree with Saul," added Meier, a tubercular boy who was the only one left alive from his town. "We dare never forget what this Amalek[4] did to us."

"I also agree with Saul," said Victor, who had participated in the Warsaw Ghetto rebellions by the Jews and Poles. "His proposal will be more effective than physical revenge."

"Children," I proclaimed, "I accept your decision. It will be difficult, but we have overcome many difficulties and we shall prevail over this one too. But we shall need to organize ourselves to carry it through. Shall we now set up a roster of duties?"

"There's no need for arranging a rotation of services," Saul insisted. "The

[1] An affectionate term in Yiddish for little children.
[2] A kilometer is 0.62 mile.
[3] For the life story of Saul see *Witness to the Holocaust*, p. 447.
[4] See Deuteronomy 25:17-19.

responsibilities will be shared by all. Each of us vows not to set foot on German soil.''

The next day we watched the traffic on the highways. The roads were clean and smooth — not at all like the muddy, unpassable Polish roads. We traveled like free men carrying authentic passports and certified documents. This was the first time in their lives that the children had traveled in freedom, without armed guards. They sat on comfortable seats in open buses. The morning was alight with the golden sun. At long last the youngsters began to experience the joy of living.

The Czech drivers, with their broad shoulders, white hats, and gloved hands, fascinated them. Seated on their high chairs, hard by the powerful, humming motors, these drivers appeared like gods from Olympus. Every child wanted to be near them. The little ones presented them with candies; the "juniors" called for quiet when the tired drivers took naps; the "seniors" asked them questions related to mechanics and driving. . . .

As we neared the German border the children began to grow tense; their conversations became agitated. Victor, who had been deported to Auschwitz, spoke up. "Do you know, Saul, here is the border where the "iron curtain" was rung down between the East and West. After we leave this border we will be in the German-American zone.''

"What's the 'iron curtain'?'' asked Reuben, who had overheard the conversation. "Is it really a shutter made of iron?''

"Of course it's a real curtain,'' Milek replied in jest. "It is made of lightning absorbers and death rays.''

Witold joined in. "It reaches deep down to the center of the earth and divides the globe in two halves.''

"Is this true?'' The younger ones turned to me.

"They are joking,'' I assured them. "Soon you will see with your own eyes how we shall pass through the iron curtain.''

We kept going until we came to a shack at the side of the highway, where border guards were stationed. Our drivers stopped and showed them our passports. The guards examined them and motioned us to go ahead. This was at the Czechoslovakian border. After a few minutes we approached a barrier extending across the road, behind which was another shack. Two American soldiers, one white and one black, came to meet us. They stood at the door of the bus, chewing gum, and counted the number of children. Then they saluted us, said "O.K.'' and the inspection was over.

The children were disappointed. Was this really the fabled iron curtain? They saw nothing sensational. But they were compensated by having seen a living black person for the first time.

When we reached German territory their faces took a serious mien. Saul was in a dark mood. He clenched his fists and did not look out of the window. Victor explained to the Czech driver why the children had decided not to set foot on German soil.

The driver nodded his head in sympathy. "All of you are orphans?'' he asked softly.

"Yes," Victor replied. "In my family there were seventy-two souls. Only my sister and I are alive today."

"Did you take part in any rebellions against the enemy?"

"Yes. But long before we began rebelling, our families had been slaughtered because we were Jewish."

The driver nodded his head in understanding. When the drivers stopped for a rest, the children asked them please to help them fulfill their vow by drawing the buses close together, so that they might skip from one to the other without touching German soil. The drivers assented willingly.

It was hot, and the drivers brought us bottles of water, but the older children, despite their thirst, refused to drink.

All the children suffered from the choking heat and thirst. Their backs hurt from sitting so long. Their legs swelled. They could not move about. At night they lay without changing position. I tried not to look at their faces, because they reminded me of the nightmares I had suffered in the camps.

For three days and three nights we drove on without a stop. We were all exhausted. The children did not show any interest in the landscape. They told me that they dreamt of a bed, a bath, a plate of warm soup. Their faces were lined with dust, and I was very apprehensive about the long road still ahead. When will we reach the end of this cursed land? I thought.

The sun set. Night descended. Far off on the horizon I discerned rows of lights and tall lit-up buildings.

"What is the name of the city in the distance?" I asked the driver.

"That's Strasbourg," he answered. "In another hour we will be on French soil."

I heaved a deep sigh of relief. "Children," I proclaimed, "children, we will be in France very soon, in a land of liberty, equality, and brotherhood."

A.E.

From *Hameah Ligvulam* ("The Hundred Come Home"), by Lena Kichler-Zilberman, New York: Schocken Books, 1969, pp. 31-35.

THANK YOU FOR OUR TEARS

Four hundred and fifty youngsters sit on the grass lawn, silent, dumb, hard-hearted.

Usually when you tell children that guests are coming with hands full of gifts, their eyes light up with gladness and joy. Not so here; the guests are greeted with a resounding silence.

"Who are these people anyway? Why did they come here? Who needs them? Are they not like all the others we knew? — Sly foxes that are harboring a plot of some kind? Those we knew in th camps were at least open and frank. They at least did not cover up their impending cruelty.

"Once long age we knew different people — father, mother, brother, a little sister with a blue ribbon in her hair, grandma whose hands were gnarled and wrinkled from age and hard work. But they are long dead. . . .''

These were the thoughts of the Buchenwald ''spared remnant.'' Only yesterday they were the slaves of the Third Reich, ready fodder for the fires of the furnaces. Now they sit dumb and repressed — volcanoes about to burst. Soon will be heard their thunderous eruptions, as from a crater that spews lava, drowning everything and everyone in its way.

The guests arrive. One is a representative of the Republic of France and another is a delegate of French Jews, those saved from the Holocaust; a third, a man with a gray beard, was sent by American Jews to welcome them. Not a child rises to greet them. This time the guests greet the hosts.

The French representative begins, ''Dear friends, victims of the most horrendous crime that the world has perpetrated we welcome you wholeheartedly. We extend to you a hearty invitation to become full French citizens with all the rights and privileges of citizenship in our country.''

From the rows of children are heard derisive cries and biting comments. ''To be diggers in your mines?''

''Black laborers? Is that what you need?''

Suddenly, in a split second, everyone is taken aback as the graybeard arises. He is a Polish Jewish refugee. He looks hard at the children before him. Not a word passes his lips, but a moan which rises into a crescendo of sobs.

An astonishing thing happens. The volcano stirs; a river of lava gushes forth and spreads — not a flood of anger, disbelief, or despair, but waves of compassion that purify the atmosphere.

From the ranks of the youth, Aaron, who is sixteen, arises and speaks in a trembling voice. ''Thanks from all of us for our tears. We did not know we could still shed tears. We thought that a heavy stone was lodging permanently in our hearts. When they led our parents to slaughter, we did not weep. When they sent us to remove the unexploded bombs from the rubble of destroyed cities and we were in constant danger of being torn to shreds, we did not cry. When we marched day and night on icy snow-covered roads, our eyes were dry. We had one all-consuming thought, *to stay alive*. We did not have hearts. Only now have we suddenly become human beings again.''

Aaron stopped speaking, but his companions beseeched him with their eyes and intense faces to continue.

''Our house in Warsaw was near the Vistula River. There my grandfather long ago read with me the vision of the prophet Ezekiel about the revival of the dry bones. It was a long, long time ago. I didn't know that the words would still live in my memory after what he lived through. But now they came back to me.

'''O dry bones, listen to the word of God. I will make the breath of life enter you, and you shall live again.' (Ezekiel 37:4-5). We are those dry bones, who have been restored to life by your tears. We felt that we had lost faith in man; now we have been brought back to life.''

Sweat covered Aaron's forehead as he sat down. The rays of the setting sun shone on the children's heads.

A.E.

From *Children of Innocence*, op. cit., pp. 20-22.

A REVERSAL OF ROLES

April 1945. The United States military force breaks into Buchenwald, located near Goethe's Weimar in Germany. From one of the barracks that is distinguished by the name "Youth Barracks" painted on it, a number of children sally forth. Only yesterday they had been commanded by the SS to leave camp. Those who obeyed were killed on the road. Those who obstinately held on to "their" shacks, to "their" walls, to "their" barbed-wire fences felt that they would escape death and live. Precisely these revolting holes which they despised and where they frequently preferred to die rather than live — these vile, pest-ridden dumps had preserved their lives. Twelve hundred children and youths from Poland, Hungary, Rumania, and Czechoslovakia remained alive.

From a pile of bodies emerges a boy — a skeleton of bones. A soldier, overcome with pity, draws near to him. The boy looks at him, astonished at seeing tears rolling down his face.

This nine-year-old boy, Lulik, told me later about the incident. "The American soldier lifted me, embraced me in his arms. He wanted to cheer me up, so he began to dance, and hugged me in his arms. He danced, laughed, and wept, holding me close. I said to myself, 'He can still laugh and can still cry. *He* is the child, and *I* am the old man — his grandfather.' "

A.E.

From *Children of Innocence* op. cit., p. 15.

SWEDEN WELCOMES THE CHILDREN

On liberation day visitors streamed to witness the horrors of the Nazis. Chava and her sister seemed to draw more attention that others because they were child mussulmen (breathing cadavers), gasping their last breath, as it were. They had not seen themselves in a mirror for a very long time, and they could not grasp why they were the center of attention. They sat on the floor, wrapped in a black blanket, and trembled when they saw a man in uniform or heard a noise. They refused to go to the hospital because they knew that going to the hospital had meant death. Aware of their condition, the Red Cross officials fed them carefully, preparing special meals for them containing rich vitamins. Gradually their strength returned, and they began to re-enter the living world.

Chava now lives in Toronto, Canada, close to her and her husband's families. She is a registered nurse and in her spare time is engaged in teaching Jewish children their heritage and the tragic chapter of the Holocaust. The following is her story.

The negotiations regarding our leaving Germany were fruitful. We were told that anyone interested could sign up to go to Sweden. The offer was being extended first to the sick and to the young people up to the age of eighteen; they were to be accompanied by any of their relatives. Sweden had volunteered to give us all the help we needed, to bring us back to health, to offer us security and faith in ourselves. They wanted to show us that another world still existed, where people behaved humanely, to provide us with the economic and spiritual aid we now required, and with education. In brief, they were eager to start us on a new, normal, productive life.

Sweden! I knew nothing about this country, its geographic location, its history, people, or culture. But I did not doubt that we would be among the first to sign up. We wanted to leave the horrid past behind us, the biggest graveyard in the whole world. And indeed we were among the first to board the train for Lübeck, the famous harbor.

When we reached Lübeck, we were brought into a large bathhouse, then into a Turkish bath, and finally disinfected thoroughly. New clothes were given us, and then we were put up comfortably for the night in yet another building. From the window in our room we could see the port, ships arriving and departing. I watched them, fascinated, wondering. Were we actually going to sail one of these ships to a country none of us knew? I could hardly wait to get acquainted with the Swedish people, to see how they would receive us. Would they be able to understand us? How would we communicate, since we did not know a word of their language? They would probably find us strange, and we would need to explain our experiences. But how? My worries and apprehensions subsided once we were on board ship, for the warmly devoted attention of the nurses and the entire staff put us at our ease. I enjoyed the voyage immensely except at night, when nightmares brought the past back vividly and I would wake up too terrified to breathe, until I realized where I was. I decided not to go to bed anymore, to stay up until dawn. Why should I spoil this wonderful trip with those nightmares?

I stepped from the cabin up to the deck and looked at the moon and the stars and the deep blue sea all around me. I could see nothing but sky and water. It was like something I had never seen, or could only vaguely remember feeling, the beauty of this quiet, romantic night. I walked along the deck for a very long time until a nurse found out I was missing and caught up with me. She asked me what the matter was, and I tried to tell her, but she did not understand German. Instead she took me to my bunk and made sure I undressed and went to bed.

In the morning she reported my behavior to her superior because it worried her. The doctor called me to him and asked me kindly, ''Why were you walking on deck when you were supposed to be sleeping? Were you hungry? Would you like a drink of milk before going to sleep?''

''No,'' I said. ''I feel very well and I don't want anything.''

''Are the nurses nice?'' he probed further.

''Yes, they are very nice,'' I said.

''So, what is the reason?''

''I am very grateful to all of you, but since my liberation I dream every night about my past. I see myself running and running; the SS chase me and I run in terror, they catch me and shove me into a cattle car jammed with people, they beat me and threaten to kill me. So I prefer not to go to bed. I am in a beautiful boat, and the blue sea and the stars make me feel better just looking at them. Why should I struggle with SS men all night?''

He sat listening, very quiet, very sad. ''Now I understand,'' he said, ''but, you know, everybody needs eight hours' sleep a night. Tell me, when you fall asleep at dawn, don't you dream then?''

''Yes, I do, but they wake me up in three hours, and it cuts the dreams off.''
Then I begged him for some medicine that would stop the nightmares.

"I wish I knew of any such medicine to help you, my dear," he replied. "You will have to try and help yourself to get over this. There is no medicine for it."

"How long will it take?"

"I cannot tell. Try to direct your thoughts to the good things that await you in my country. The Swedes are truly wonderful people. I'm sure that living among us will drive the bad dreams away."

I soon found that he was right.

A few days later we reached Malmö. The nurses called to us, "Come quick, look at our country!" This city, they explained, was their third largest and an important port. We began to disembark and were received by a big WELCOME TO SWEDEN sign. Greeted by everyone with warm cries of "Welcome!" we entered Sweden in a happy mood and lifted spirits.

Again we were led to a bathhouse. It was clean and shining, but what puzzled us was the sight of men walking about in the shower rooms. Every time we started to undress, a man or a boy would walk in or pass by. Blushing, we would stop and wait for him to leave. We were puzzled, too, by the sight of women walking at will through the men's shower rooms. We were all girls with firm Orthodox upbringing behind us, and this was, to us, an extraordinary situation. Men coming into the shower room to wash your back! The next man who came in we tried to tell, in sign language, to leave, but he only stared uncomprehendingly. Finally a young man approached and asked in German whether he could help us. "No," I replied, "we don't need help, but you are in the wrong place. This is a women's shower." He still did not understand, for he only laughed and said jokingly, "I know. I work here. If you drive me away I'll be unemployed."

We appealed to some women who worked there and asked them to tell the boys that unless they left us, we would not undress and wash. The women looked mystified. "Why? They work here just as we do." But the boys, noting our insistence, left of their own accord. We chattered and wondered amongst ourselves. What kind of country is this? we thought. What strange habits! Men who work in showers intended for women! We were indeed curious, and wanted to get to know these people as soon as possible.

When we finished, each of us was given a little bag containing soap, toothbrush, and toothpaste, a comb, a mirror, and a packaged hot meal. Buses were waiting for us. We now boarded them and rode for half an hour to a quarantine camp. Here everything had been prepared for us: there was a big, beautiful building surrounded by a lovely garden, with large rooms equipped with beds, cupboards, a table and chairs. It was all spanking clean. A large sign at the gate read WELCOME! We were assigned to our rooms, rested a while after our trip, and then were called to dinner in the living room. The staff were uniformed. They served us a hot meal. I looked about me in wonder — was it real or a dream?

That night, for the first time, I slept as soundly and sweetly as a baby and awoke fresh and rested. The pleasant atmosphere, the pure air, the fragrance of the flowers in the garden, and the clean bed had the calming effect of a narcotic. The entire staff tried very hard to create a homelike setting for us, and each one remembered to say a kind work to every single girl, remarking on the best trait she had: "How pretty you are," "You have lovely eyes," "Your hair is so thick and beautiful." Everybody had something beautiful to say to each one of us. And how we needed it! So utterly opposite from the abuses we had encountered for years, these Swedish people were a healing and timely revelation to us and worked wonders for our rehabilitation. I shall never forget them and will always be grateful to the Swedish crown and people for the marvelous way they restored us to our humanity as well as our health.

After we had been in quarantine for several days, a team of doctors and nurses arrived and began a series of examinations and X-rays. All the ailing were sent to the hospital or sanatorium for specific treatment, while the healthy were granted permission to go out and mix with the Swedish people. I was lucky to be among the latter. Blithely we set out in groups to see what we could see and gather our first impressions of Sweden. On our first expedition we noticed that all the Swedes seemed to be tall and slim, blue-eyed and good-looking. We walked the entire length of a street without seeing anyone with brown eyes and hair. The streets were immaculate and free of beggars. We went into a store. Upon entering, everyone took a number and stood quietly in line. Quiet was a characteristic everywhere, and this same quiet — or serenity — marked their faces, reflecting calm natures and a respect for others. We were excited, constantly pointing out to one another new discoveries. In the evening whole families came out to meet and chat with us, and many invited us to their homes for visits. A good many families also offered to adopt us, not formally but informally, to give us a feeling of belonging, of being wanted and cared for. They sent us packages of candy, took an interest in our problems, and invited us for meals. They sent us holiday greetings, cards, and gifts. They employed every means they could think of to make us happy. . . .

We visited cinemas where, because of our dark hair and eyes, we were the center of attraction, especially for the boys. They turned their heads to gaze at us and said what evidently were complimentary things about us. We relished their attention.

Toward the end of the week a small group of boys and girls were invited to visit the Eriksen family for Sunday tea. I was among those chosen. We dressed in our best clothes on Sunday afternoon, and the Eriksens came and took us by tram to their home. We entered a tasteful flat, furnished in Scandinavian style, and met two other couples, friends of the Eriksens. Cakes and sweets were laid out on a small table. Some folk music was playing, and the atmosphere was serenely quiet and warm. The Eriksens asked us questions and after each reply they would shake their heads, exclaiming in Swedish, "Incredible! Impossible!" I too had questions I soon asked. First, about the strange presence of males in the ladies' shower — I hadn't forgotten that. "Is this customary here," I inquired, "or did they think we were not women with self-respect?" Our hostess laughed and then assured me this was customary in their public baths. No one had dreamed of offending us. "I'm awfully sorry," she said, "that you were so hurt, but when you get to know us better you will understand that we Swedes are very free and open in all aspects of our lives. It's quite different from what one sees elsewhere, to be sure, but I've no doubt you will be proud to be part of our people."

My second question was related to a bus we had ridden by mistake. "Why did the driver toss the letters and newspapers and magazines out into the road, where no one was waiting to receive them?''

''Why,'' Mrs. Eriksen replied, ''they are for the village. After a while the postman cames along to pick them up and distributes them.''

''But might not passers-by meanwhile pick up something, and no would even know?''

''Oh, no! This has never happened. Who would take a letter or something that did not belong to him? That would be stealing! I don't think it would enter anyone's mind to do such a thing. We're brought up from earliest childhood to believe in honesty and dignity, and this training has not disappointed us. Was it different where you came from?''

Neither she nor her guests could understand why we burst into hysterics at this. ''Yes,'' we said, ''it was quite different. . . . ''

When we quieted down, Mrs. Eriksen, a truly lovely woman, asked whether we had any more questions. So I asked her about something that had become quite puzzling to me. I had noticed, I told her, and that while many people who passed the quarantine camp stopped to talk with us, there were some who merely looked at us for a long while in silence. Why was this? I wanted to know. We felt as if we were inmates of a zoo.

''Well,'' she said, ''first of all, many people are unable to talk to you because of the language barrier. But I have an idea there is another reason too. Let me just show you something. My husband collects all kinds of unusual things, so we have these clippings at home.'' She left the room for a moment and returned. ''Look at this . . . and this . . . and this.'' She handed me ugly, horribly repulsive caricatures of Jews, deformed, with huge hooked noses, that made me recoil in disgust, with captions under them which read, ''These are the Jews from Eastern Europe.'' ''These were circulated by the Nazis as part of their anti-Jewish propaganda, to quiet any opposition people might have to their treatment of the Jews, to convince them they were killing monsters, not people,'' Mrs. Eriksen explained. ''People who were informed and kept abreast of the news knew better than to believe such things. But some people, basically decent people, but ones who had been brought up to believe without question all that they read and heard, and who were absorbed in their own daily worries, tended to accept this propaganda as the truth. They simply didn't know any better. But when they heard of your coming, they went to look at you — and they were probably amazed how unlike these cruel caricatures you are, how good-looking and gentle you are. You can imagine how they must have felt for believing such lies. You understand, many did not want to believe, but the Nazis had a powerful propaganda machine and they used it very cleverly.'' We nodded our heads. . . . Yes, we had known it well.

From *I'm Still Living* by Chava Kwinta, Toronto: Simon and Pierre Publishing. Co., 1974, pp. 260-267.

THE POSTCARD THAT SAVED A LIFE

Lawyer, diplomat, and Palestinian Jewish emissary, Moshe Ishai went on two important missions for the Yishuv *to Persia and to Poland (1945 – 1946). He wrote up these missions in two separate books. The latter, from which this selection is taken, incorporates valuable documentary information reflecting the physical and spiritual conditions of the survivors during the period immediately following liberation.*

My first visit was with the survivors at the Hehalutz center in Warsaw. At the gate I met three young people who attached themselves to me. The youngest wore a long winter coat with deep pockets. He was silent, but when he heard my name he joined in the conversation.

"Did you say your name was Yishai?" he asked.

"Yes, that's my name."

"Were you perhaps in Teheran?"

"Yes, I was there."

"And you directed the Jewish Agency in Teheran?"

"Yes, I was the director."

With trembling hands he took from his pocket a printed postcard. On one side was his address in Russian and on the other side a printed statement reading that we had sent him a food package on a specific date and requesting him to notify us when he received it. Below were my name and address, printed in full.

In 1943 and 1944 we had sent out thousands of these cards. First, we wanted to be sure that the addresses were correct. Second, we found the cards an effective means of stimulating the survivors in the USSR to establish contact with us without arousing suspicion and opposition from the Russian authorities. As we exchanged correspondence, we sought information about other survivors. The program was efficacious in igniting sparks of hope and in generating a desire among survivors to emigrate to Eretz Yisrael.

The boy persisted in questioning me. "So it was really you who signed the postcard?"

"Yes, I personally signed it," I assured him.

He seized my hand, squeezed and shook it with great warmth, then with a faltering voice declared, "I thank you for saving my life."

"How could I have saved your life? I was in Teheran, and you were far away."

"Indeed, you saved me from suicide. At the time I was contemplating ending my life. I was starving, ridden with lice, homeless, hopeless. I slept in the railroad station, lived in the mud and dirt in the depths of the slums. I saw no prospect for relief, so I resolved to end it all. Why continue to suffer? For whom? For what? I decided to drown myself. On the way to the river I passed the post office, and just by chance I inquired if there was any mail for me. The postmaster handed me the card. It was like a flash of light amidst the thick darkness. Someone was thinking about me — maybe even trying to save me. It was like being reborn. Every day I stopped at the post office and made inquiries whether a package had come for me. At last it arrived, and my life changed completely. Since I received your card two years ago, I have wandered across the width of Soviet Russia until I finally reached Teheran. I held on to your postcard as if it were a life-preserving drug. It was my lucky amulet, my warranty to live. Yes! I have you to thank for being alive today.''

A.E.

From *Bitzel Hashoah* (''In the Shadow of the Holocaust'') by Moshe Ishai, Ghetto Fighters House, 1973, pp. 166f.

A MOTHER AND HER DAUGHTERS ARE REUNITED

On the twentieth anniversary of the liberation of Bergen-Belsen, Berta Ferderber-Salz's Hebrew book, And the Sun Shone, *appeared. It is a unique document describing life in a Galician community which became a Gehenna after the Nazi conquest and the ''actions,'' atrocities, deportations, and liquidation of the Jews. Above all, it vividly conveys the living faith and determination of a mother who did not give up hope of ultimately finding her children, whom she had hidden away with a Christian family, and her final success. It is a triumphant story of Jewish motherhood.*

Despite our having been liberated we were still isolated from the outside world. No one bothered to get in touch with relatives of the survivors who lived in America or in liberated European countries. As soon as we were able to get on our feet we felt an impelling urge to go alone from camp to search, to scour around. Who knew? Perhaps . . . ? But our movements were hindered and impeded.

One day a military vehicle came to the camp office. It was loaded with food stuff. The driver and a few British soldiers descended from the car and announced through the loudspeaker that the inmates should line up to receive their rations. I did not join the queue. I was seated on the grass nearby and read a book I had checked out from the camp library.

While distributing the food two soldiers noticed me and wondered why I did not join the lineup. They probably thought I was not Jewish and that I did not want to mix with Jews. They came over and glanced at my book. When they saw it was in Yiddish they asked me why I didn't want to receive my share of the food. I answered that I was not interested in receiving physical assistance, but that I did need spiritual support.

''Why? What's the matter?'' they asked. I replied, ''You do not relate to us as human beings who have human feeling and human needs.'' One of them introduced himself by his Jewish name and asked me to explain what I meant. I told him that three months had passed since our liberation, that throughout this period I had turned to scores of soldiers and civilian officials for help in a small matter (to forward a letter to my brother in the United States) and no one had responded favorably. Further, I needed help to find my children in Poland, but all the people I had spoken to had been evasive.

The British-Jewish soldier told me to prepare the letter and he would come the next day and dispatch it. With a bitter laugh I replied, ''I don't believe you.

You're no better than the rest.'' I saw that he was deeply hurt. He persisted and swore to me that he would fulfill his promise. ''What have I to lose?'' I thought to myself, so I wrote the letter. The next day the soldier came, brought me a food package and took the letter. Within a week I received a reply. The news spread throughout the camp. This was the first letter that had broken the barrier around our isolated little world. . . .

In August 1945 I determined to begin a search for my children. Both my brother and my soldier benefactor implored me to desist for awhile because of the chaotic situation on the roads, the dangers lurking everywhere, and my debilitated physical condition and lack of nervous stamina. But I remained firm in my resolve. I refused to believe that I would not be able to find my daughters. ''They are living and waiting for me,'' I repeated to myself over and over again. ''I must find knapsacks to bring them food and gifts.'' That was how I dissipated my doubts and fears.

I got a piece of canvas from a military tent and sewed two knapsacks. My niece, Sabina, who had also left a child in someone's keeping, joined me. Together we traveled to Hanover, the headquarters of the central committee for aid to the uprooted and displaced. They gave us the necessary travel documents. They provided us with official papers which requested that the border police facilitate our journey. We also received fifty German marks for expenses.

When we returned to Belsen we began to gather information for reliable sources about the problems in getting across the Soviet border. We were warned that the Soviets made travel very difficult. Trains did not run. Even if we were to steal onto military transport trains which did run, they were more often stationary than mobile. The roads were strewn with dead bodies and other ravages of war.

But the writer and her niece were not deterred. Their journey, mostly on foot, was long and arduous. They were helped occasionally by fellow Jewish DPs and by the American military. For obvious reasons, they did not disclose that they were Jewish. After a wearisome and hazardous trek lasting four weeks, they finally reached Krakow.

We got on a streetcar leading to the Christian home where our children had been sheltered. I remembered the address. My heart hammered away as if it were trying to break through my ribs. Would I have the strength to stand the momentous reunion? Another few minutes and I would know the answer to the question that tormented me for days. Did the hands of the murderers get to my dear children?

I got off the tram. My feet seemed not to want to move. My head was spinning. I forced myself to shuffle up the street. I reached the house. I said to myself, ''I must plod forward. The moment of discovery is near.'' I dragged myself foot by foot. I stopped, rested, and pressed on. My feet were like lead pillars. The Polish woman with whom I had left my children lived on the ground floor. Before venturing in I looked through the window. The apartment was empty!

I pulled myself together and asked one of the neighbors what had happened.

Where had my family moved? I knocked on the door of the next door neighbor, introduced myself as a relative of the woman who had lived in the empty apartment, and asked where she might be found. "Oh, she's become rich and now lives in the center of town in a building with an elevator." With waning breath I continued, "Are they well? And her brother's daughters who had lived with her, are they still alive and in good health?" I received a positive reply and got directions to the new address at 86 Deluga Street.

Pushing onward with trembling feet I walked up Deluga Street. Suddenly I stopped dead. In the distance I made out a form — an image that had recurred a thousandfold in my dreams. On the street corner stood my little girl. Two golden tresses drooped on her lean back. In her hands she held single cigarettes which she peddled to the passersby. My older daughter was nearby, also selling cigarettes and making change. Suddenly she turned her head. I was standing a few paces away, dressed in worn, old clothes which were covered with the dust of many roads. "Mother!" Her voice sent echoes from one end of the street to the other, and she fell in a faint in my outstretched arms.

Other children gathered the cigarettes from the stool and brought them along behind us. Embracing each other, we ascended the stairs of the apartment. The door was open. At the threshold stood my younger daughter. Her mouth was halfway open, and I saw that she had already lost her baby teeth. She was now seven years old. With a penetrating eye she looked me up and down wondering who was this beggar woman.

Suddenly the lady of the house appeared. She embraced and kissed us. The little one disappeared into a room. "What happened to the rest of the children?" I asked breathlessly. "They're all alive, whole and well." My older daughter asked about Father. In a choked voice I replied, "He is gone, and the same has happened to all the rest of our family."

We ate supper and after washing myself I lay down with my two dear daughters at my side. Suddenly I *saw* the little one go down from the bed, kneel on the floor, and whisper a prayer before the icon hanging on the wall.

At the door stood their guardian on her face a smile of self-satisfaction. "You see," she said to my little one, "thanks to the Holy Mother, whom you prayed to every night, your mother was saved and has at least returned." I learned later that my older daughter had rejected the rituals which had been imposed on her.

That night I did not close an eye. I was afraid that I might waken to find that I was dreaming those recurring dreams of the horrible years. I closed my eyes halfway and pretended to sleep. I saw my younger one sitting up in bed scrutinizing me carefully. Suddenly I opened my eyes wide and returned her gaze lovingly. Up to now she hadn't uttered a word.

Without addressing me as mother, she began to speak. "You said that we have no father any longer, that he is dead. Maybe you can do something to bring him back to life at least once. I want so much to see how he looks. I don't know him at all."

After becoming reacquainted with Cracow, I decided to seek out my brother's two children — one an eight-year-old and the other seven. They had been saved by their Polish governess who was very much attached to them. When war broke out she had volunteered to shelter them; indeed, she had been like a mother to them. She guarded and protected them. She had prepared adoption papers and in fact had determined to adopt them as her own. Through the years, the thought that their parents might have survived bothered her, and when she learned that they had been liquidated she had felt relieved. No wonder when she received me she was at first hostile. Though ruffled and annoyed, she finally relented and permitted me to see the children.

I deliberately did not talk to her about the future but visited the children daily. I told them about their parents; I introduced them to my daughters, and I assured them that I would take them home with me as soon as I could. I brought them gifts and tried hard to win them over in every way I could. The children were not enthusiastic over my plans. However, when a Jewish school was founded by the local Jewish community I enrolled them for study together with my daughters. This continued for several months.

One day I met the sister of the governess and learned that she, too, had rescued a little Jewish boy, aged five. I determined to extricate him also. I recorded on the roster of the Jewish community the names of eight children (including my two) for whom I took responsibility, and I became known as the *Mother Burdened with Children.*

I was financially distressed. The rescuers of the children began to complain that they had expended large sums of money for their upkeep and demanded compensation, even though a few did not want to give them up. Poverty stricken, I turned to the Jewish community council and was granted a monthly stipend. I distributed most of my monthly allowance to the rescuers of the children and promised them increases. It was evident that before I completed final negotiations to get the children back I would have to obtain more money. To accomplish this I began the rounds of the Polish homes where members of my family had left their valuables for safekeeping. With pleas and threats I finally succeeded in recovering a number of valuable items which I sold. I distributed the money to the children's guardians. But the more I paid them the more they demanded.

It was time to take the children out of Poland. I promised the children's guardians that I would not leave the country until I had met my financial obligations. But I also reminded them that the children's parents had left substantial wealth with their children. ''It was not sufficient,'' they retorted immediately. ''For security reasons we could not leave the house to earn a livelihood, so we managed to make ends meet by selling these valuables.''

I assured them that I could make no demands on them. ''All the wealth of the world is not sufficient to repay you for your sacrifice, but please understand that I cannot compensate you for your goodness. However, I pledge to pay back the expenses incurred in keeping the children; I will recompense you until the end of my life. But please give me time to organize myself.''

The High Holy Days were approaching. How orphaned the Cracow Jewish quarters looked! Only a few years ago at this season, worshipers were heard in every courtyard. With difficulty I found a private house where services were conducted. I gathered all my children and brought them there for worship on Rosh Hashanah and Yom Kippur.

After the holidays I began to plan our departure from Poland. Sabina returned to Belsen and married her fiance.

While I waited, I gathered the addresses of my relatives and good friends who had escaped the *gehenna* at the last moment. A few days before the outbreak of war they had hired a plane which flew them to Eretz Yisrael. I wrote to them about my situation and my efforts to get the children out of Poland.

In a few weeks Sabina returned. We decided that she would take my daughters to Belsen and that I should remain to carry on the struggle to resuce the rest of the children from their guardians. My relations with the guardians became very strained. They incited the children against me, and soon the youngsters refused to leave their homes to meet me.

[*The writer narrates about her receiving a substantial loan from one of her friends to help pay some of her obligations to the rescuers. She arranges through an intermediary to bribe the Polish border guards to look the other way when Sabina and the children "steal" across the border. She finally returns to Cracow to complete her mission.*]

When I arrived in Cracow a surprise awaited me: two British soldiers had been looking for me and were waiting for my return.

Not losing a moment, I went to meet them at the address they left. It turned out that they were Palestinian Jews who had served in the British army. They had come to Krakow in response to the letters I had sent to my friends in Eretz Yisrael. When I saw them I broke down, weeping and sobbing. I could not restrain myself. After years of terror and bondage I was finally privileged to embrace emissaries from Eretz Yisrael. I reported to them that five of my list had already left Poland and that I was having trouble getting the other three out. The "guardians" would not separate from them and I expressed my fervent hope that, with their help, I would now succeed in my efforts.

I went with them to visit the children. The soldiers, who had been born in Poland, remembered enough to converse with the children in Polish. The youngsters regarded them with open admiration. Out of respect for their uniforms the "guardians" did not dare object to their frequent visits. The soldiers took the children for long walks. Little by little the ice was broken and the children looked forward keenly to each visit of their new friends.

While the soldiers were making friends with the children I was busy making arrangements to get them out. I obtained official documents designating me as their legal guardian. It so happened that the third child (for whom I had papers) had already departed with his aunt, so in addition I substituted a Jewish orphan from the city orphanage.

When all was ready we came to the children's home and told the guardian that we were taking the children for a stroll. The woman sensed that we were hiding a secret so she said she would join us.

Parked at the street corner was a military lorry. We told the children that it was waiting for us. They sprinted to the car and jumped into it, the soldiers following them. I remained standing on the sidewalk and I said to the woman, "May they go in peace. Let us hope that they will be happy."

She understood what had happened, and began to weep and pull her hair.

"Woe unto me," she cried. "I raised them, took care of them, guarded them, endangered my life for them — and now they are taken from me." I felt a deep sorrow for her. Her pain was genuine. I begged her to forgive me.

"The children have to be raised amidst their own people, in the bosom of their family. I could not relinquish them to you. It is best that we execute this in the quickest way possible. Both of us wish and pray for their happiness. Please forgive me. We shall never forget what you did for them."

The Palestinians left an address in Frankfurt where I would find them on my return to Germany.

A.E.

From *Vehashemesh Zarchah ("And the Sun Shone")* by Berta Federber Saltz, pub. *Neie Leben*, Tel Aviv, 1968, pp. 157-160; 164-170; 176-78.

STRANGER THAN FICTION

In a Polish train a boy was caught without a railroad ticket. His belly was bloated from hunger, his clothing was tattered. The boy pleaded for mercy and protection. He told his captor that he was all alone. By chance he had heard that his aunt lived not far away, and he was trying to reach her; she could perhaps help him find his parents.

The Polish ticket collector replied that despite all his sympathy and pity for the boy, his duty, was clear; he must report him at the next station. There the stationmaster would decide what to do with him.

A Jewish woman who was sitting nearby paid the fare, and a Polish military man began to persuade the boy not to stay with his aunt even if he found her, but to find a children's home or an orphanage where he could live a more normal life with children his age.

The boy was irritated by the advice of the stranger and told him not to mix into a matter that did not concern him. He broke down and sobbed out the story that his father, too, was in the Polish army, but he hadn't heard from him and did not know how to find him. His mother had been killed by the Nazis, and he was left alone, wandering from city, seeking his relatives. As he talked he took a photograph from his pocket. He held it in both hands and commented, "This is all that I have left from my family."

The officer took a look at the photograph and fainted. When he recovered, he fell on the boy, hugging and kissing him and crying, "You're my son. Thank God I have found my son."

A.E.

From *Sridei Herev* ("Those Spared from the Sword") by Ephraim Dekel, pp. 107-108, published. by Israel Government Security Office, 1963.

17.

REHABILITATION

World Jewry, especially American Jewry, through the Joint Distribution Committee, Hadassah, women's Zionist organizations, the Palestinian Jewish Brigade, the Bricha *or the Underground movement to bring the DPs to Palestine despite the British blockade, mobilized to aid, rehabilitate, and transport the surviving remnant to the Promised Land or to overseas Jewish communities. To prepare the orphan refugees, a number of extraordinary individual saviors organized and conducted schools. A widespread movement known as Mosad Aliyah Bet, or the illegal immigration movement, sought out refugees in Poland and the USSR and led them on the long secret roads to the Promised Land. Youth Aliyah, which had its start in the thirties, was now in full swing, including later not only the surviving remnant from devastated Europe but also the fugitives from hostile Arab countries.*

Finding the children was the first step in redeeming them. It was necessary to seek out and win over the children who had found shelter and refuge in Christian homes, monasteries, and convents. Many Jewish children who had been hidden in Christian environments at a young age had easily been taught to accept Christianity. Many had actually undergone conversion. Certain Christian families had developed attachments to their "adopted" children. Some tried to extract from the redeemers as much money and/or valuables as possible, in exchange for the release of the child. In short, the redemption of the children was a gigantic, seemingly endless task — not to mention the unrelenting anti-Semitism of the Polish military and government, with whom the redeemers were most involved.

A very impressive chapter, which in a sense typifies the difficulties and ultimate triumph, is the story of the Teheran Children (see Chapter 14).

A MODERN-DAY ELIJAH

The remarkable story that follows is included in the biography of a Hebrew teacher, Tziviah Wildstein, who lived through the war in Soviet Russia.

We decided to open a school for Jewish children and submitted a formal request for permission to the local government authorities. They refused and countered with an array of arguments: "Why open anew a Jewish ghetto? Why should you not be like all others and enroll the children in Lithuanian orphanages, where they will be with other children of their age and where their needs will be met by the government?"

We had no confidence in their pious statements. We well remembered how they had treated us during the Nazi ghetto period — how they led us to slaughter.

At one of our meetings I was informed that Professor Rebelsky was interested in our project. He was a Jew and a world-famous psychiatrist, who served as the general director of all hospitals for the mentally ill. He enjoyed high military rank and worked closely with the top authorities of the Kremlin. Word had reached him that a woman teacher, a survivor of the Holocaust and the war, was interested in helping the surviving Jewish children to rebuild their lives anew. He invited me to meet him at his hospital.

Professor Rebelsky, dressed in a colonel's uniform, welcomed me warmly, saying, "I have heard about you and your concern for the welfare of our children. It's a great and noble idea." Suddenly he added in Yiddish, "You want to become mother of our unfortunate children; I want to be their father."

He asked me to tell him of my experiences, how I had managed to remain alive. I told him about what had happened in the Vilna ghetto, the slaughter at the Ponar death camp, my escape, and the orphanage that I helped establish. He listened attentively and evidently was deeply moved.

Despite his high rank and the imposing rows of medals on his chest, I was drawn most by his deepset eyes — sympathetic, warm, Jewish. Suddenly he rose, grasped my two hands, shook them warmly and said with great pathos, "We'll work together. You are a historic personality, and we shall create a historic institution."

He told me that during the war he had gathered stray Jewish children and provided them with asylum in military hospitals. They were embers saved from the burning ghettos. He offered me his full cooperation and assured me of his wholehearted dedication to helping Jewish children and providing for their safety and well-being. After strenuous efforts and overcoming numerous obstacles, I was granted permission to open a Jewish school. However, the authorities failed to provide support. I was appointed director of both school and orphanage, but we had no home, no teachers, and no staff. Nor had we rounded up any children. Without the active assistance of the authorities in providing a house, adequate provisions, and domestic necessities, the idea remained hanging in the air — a daydream.

The High Holy Days were drawing near. The pitiful remnants of Jews in the region gathered for worship. The prayers were steeped in sorrow. To the few survivors, these were solemn days in the full sense of the word, awesome and disquieting.

On "Kol Nidre" night a handful of Jews gathered in the old synagogue. Also in attendance were high-ranking officers of the Soviet military — among them Professor Rebelsky. Before the "Kol Nidre" chant I went over to the rabbi and asked him to permit me to address the worshipers. Despite the fact that this was an unheard-of occurrence in the synagogue on Yom Kippur, the rabbi granted my wish.

I ascended to the pulpit and broke out in a tearful appeal for help for the orphaned, destitute children who were victims of the Nazis. I stressed the need for immediate action to find and gather together the homeless, beaten remnants and enable them to rebuild their lives. I ended with a plea: "We must not only revive them physically but also spiritually. We must give them a Jewish education so that they may not be lost to our people and assimilate among the gentiles."

My audience dissolved in tears and wept with me.

I was fully aware that I was soliciting them to muster their strength for this effort. I impressed them with the warning that they would meet both unconcealed and veiled opposition. I told them that as I began my campaign I had found out that children had been taken into Christian homes and that it would be difficult to extricate them. Many had been sheltered in monasteries and convents. The priests and nuns refused to give them up. It was necessary to organize an intensive search-and-rescue campaign — a long-drawn-out cooperative effort. It was an arduous task and called for great courage and stamina. Most of our people were themselves broken shells. One all-embracing worry dominated their lives: to find jobs and recreate their lives anew. I was adding to their burden by asking them to discover where the children might be found and all that they could learn about their situation. Then I myself would undertake to redeem them and have them rejoin our people and faith.

Professor Rebelsky accompanied me home. He was deeply stirred by my plea and wept like a child. He told me he had witnessed the mass destruction of our people by the Germans and that he had gathered the pitiable remnants of our youth, sheltered and fed them, healed their wounds, and left them in safe hands. "I swear to you that I shall dedicate my life to achieving the high ideal you have set before us, and that I shall help you in every way that I can."

The day after Yom Kippur I began to receive information on the whereabouts of Jewish children. On Succoth we sat down with Professor Rebelsky and Dr. Blutz (who was in charge of the military sick fund) and sorted the various addresses. I now began to put my plan into action, to pluck out and to free the Jewish children from the Christian families and restore them to their people and heritage.

It was a hard and sorrow-laden task. Many peasants and householders did not want to give up the children because they were efficient and cheap workers. I recall arriving at a peasant's home and seeing an emaciated and undersized boy pasturing the cattle. He looked very melancholy and would not talk. Evidently he had been forbidden to speak to a stranger. A well-fed, bellicose peasant came out and asked what I wanted. I explained my mission. "I do not have Jew boys in my house," he replied sullenly and bade me leave his property. I did not budge and persisted in my request. The farmer roused his dogs to attack me. They jumped on me and tore my dress. Dogs in the neighboring yards responded, and some joined in the attack. I fled from the premises as fast as I could. I had similar experiences many times. In some homes the peasants chased me away, waving sticks and shouting curses at me. "We thought that we had seen the last of you Jews, and here you are again."

Their young Jewish serfs served them well and inexpensively as shepherds, peddlers, and venders of cigarettes, matches, and saccharine on the black market. The youngsters had forgotten their origins. They were depressed and neglected. No one showed them sympathy or kindness. They were constantly beaten if they did not meet the expectations of their "adopted parents." They were no better off than during the Nazi reign.

However, some householders were happy to get rid of them. They brought their wards to us and said, "Here, take them. Times are hard. We haven't enough to feed our own. Why should they die with the rest of us?" Conditions were bad. Under the Soviet rule, peasants were forbidden to produce vodka, and this edict affected their income adversely.

There were some who in reality wanted to dispose of the children but, when they realized how much we wanted to have them, demanded payment for the period of their custody. We, of course, could not meet their demands. In such cases Professor Rebelsky sent soldiers along with me, and we took the children by force and brought them to Vilna. There was a case where a priest refused to hand over a boy to us, claiming that he had embraced Catholicism and was no longer a Jew. I begged him to ask the boy what his wishes were. But the priest declined and asked me to leave. Convinced that I would not succeed in extricating the boy from the monastery, I turned to Professor Rebelsky, and the military removed him by force.

Many children came of their own accord. Among them were thirteen- and fourteen-year-olds, independent spirits and self-reliant, who had fought with the partisans in the forests. Having left the partisans, they felt lonely and desperately in need of rest, shelter, and companionship. They needed attention, friendship, a bed to sleep in, and they had a desire for schooling; in short, they wanted to become human beings again — and, above all, to be with Jews.

Establishment of the Orphan Home

Most of the Jewish teachers had been liquidated. There remained only a few; they were dispirited and were not fit psychologically to return to teaching. They were obsessed by their personal problems of rehabilitation, building new homes and families. I turned to a select few and urged them to help me in setting up a home for the orphans. Some of the more qualified had abandoned hope in a Jewish future. The Soviet authorities had offered them attractive positions and would not release them. Often as I pleaded with them I would burst into tears.

Once more I listed my troubles and difficulties to Professor Rebelsky, and again his collaboration brought results. He succeeded in obtaining the release of Eliezer Yerushalmi (see p. 46), who became the head teacher. [Here follow the names of teachers who joined the staff, all of whom ultimately settled in

Israel.] [To our good fortune] we also succeeded in securing a competent, devoted, and loving housemother to take care of the orphans, whose lot in life had been degradation, constant abuse, hunger, and cold.

We needed desperately a dwelling that would house our growing numbers. The war was still on, and the region was under military rule. Professor Rebelsky and I asked to meet with the military commissar. As in the past, the professor's reputation stood him in good stead.

I found myself in a Soviet military office, where we were received with respect. Professor Rebelsky described the sad fate of the stricken Jewish children, who had gone through one hell after another and were now destitute, without parents and family. The commissar and his staff listened sympathetically but were perplexed as to why we wanted to set up a separate orphanage. "Why don't you register the children in existing institutions? Have they not suffered enough as ghettoized Jews? Why should they again be kept apart?"

Smilingly the professor replied, "You do not understand the unique problems of the bereaved Jewish children." Then, as an expert psychiatrist, he proceeded to explain that the young victims had seen their parents slaughtered by the Lithuanians. They felt a deep need to be with their own kind as one family. If we handed them over to strangers, they would suffer deep traumas. He finally succeeded in persuading the commissariat to confiscate a house to serve our purpose.

[After a number of unhappy experiences, the children were finally assigned to a vacant Hebrew school building. They slept on the floor until bedding was provided.]

The place was small, but all of us pitched in with enthusiasm to clean it up and outfit it. We had hardly moved in when we received notice from the central education office to get out because the building was to be occupied by a vocational school. Professor Rebelsky was shocked. He could not imagine that his colleagues would engage in such vile plots to dispossess us, but he did not give up. He quickly made a study of available quarters and came up with the address of a four-story house which, although windowless, doorless, and with a partially wrecked roof, could nevertheless be restored to use. But where to find the skilled workers to do all the necessary repairs?

On the next day I visited him at his hospital. He gathered a number of inmates who were in solitary confinement and who had worked as carpenters, as glaziers, and in other building trades. He spoke to them and then distributed various materials — boards, windowpanes, cleaning utensils — and he warned them to heed the instructions of their supervisors, to do their job well, or else . . .

Wide-eyed in amazement, I asked, "Professor, how can you expect these people to carry out such important professional tasks?"

Smiling, he replied, "They are not insane; they are passing as insane so as not to be sent to the front. I told them that I have seen through their game, and that if they did not discharge their duties faithfully I would send them back to their homes — which ultimately meant the front."

The "insane" performed well, and the building looked habitable. But what about the furnishings? Professor Rebelsky requisitioned beds, tables, and chairs from various hospitals and dispensaries under his supervision. To supplement the supply, all of us, teachers and children, ransacked the neighborhood, which was deserted, and found tables, benches, and even blackboards in the rubble and garbage heaps. We dragged them into the house. It did not take long, and the house was ready to accommodate its juvenile inhabitants.

Now our real struggles began. The attitude of the authorities and neighborhood was inimical. The higher echelons were Lithuanian, and they, like their peers, were of the opinion that the "final solution" had been consummated. And here they were confronted again by recurring Jewish problems.

Everyone threw questions at us. "A ghetto again? Shouldn't you adjust to the life of the general society? Why build barriers all over again?" They suspected that we were small in numbers, that we were exaggerating our population in order to "rob" them of their rations. They refused to sell us staple foods, and I was compelled to buy on the black market at higher prices.

Again Professor Rebelsky came to our aid. He spread far and wide the story about us and that we were the only Jewish orphan asylum in the USSR. Many doctors and people from all walks of life visited us, Jewish and non-Jewish. Those who had lost their families were particularly moved to see our large family arising from the lowest depths and being rebuilt over the ruins. Soldiers sent us their ration cards, candy, chocolate. The professor sent medicines, vitamins, kindling wood, bedclothes. He made automobile transportation available to us. Thanks to him, Jews prominent in the theater and literary world visited us, talked with our children, and came away highly impressed and inspired.

Our benefactor's name spread far and wide. In time, Jews in distress came to him for help and advice. He became known as a modern Elijah. He was always gracious and full of humor. His conversations in Russian were always spiced with popular Yiddish and Hebrew expressions. He had been born near Odessa and had been brought up in a traditional home which was saturated with Jewish folkways. He loved to tell about his family. His mother had given birth to seven sons. Once one fell ill. It was necessary to take him to the doctor by train, so she seized one of the seven, and off she went. The doctor examined him and found him healthy. He was astonished that she had brought him for a physical examination. She scrutinized the boy and shouted, *"Oy vey,* instead of Yankele I brought Meishele." Each time he told this story, he roared with laughter.

He never applied for membership in the Communist Party. However, when he was fifty he was invited to join, as were all high-ranking military officers. The associate commissar of the Office of Education was Lithuanian, a party member, and a rabid anti-Semite. Once the professor and I met her on the street. He confronted her and, pointing at me, said, "Comrade Mashkauskania, you are not obliged to love her, but she deserves your respect. She has given her life to revive the survivors of the Holocaust. As a true party member, you should suppress your anti-Semitic feelings."

When we left her, I remarked, "That's a Communist for you, full of hatred of mankind." And, turning to him, I said, "What made you join? You see how they suppress us, how eager they are to root us out."

Sadly he turned to me and replied, "Do you think I joined the party of my own free will? Had I wanted to, I would have become a member long before I reached the age of fifty. Could I have refused? Could I have otherwise accomplished all I have done?''

He was one of our family, happy to observe the growth of the institution; overjoyed to hear the children recite, sing, declaim in Yiddish; delighted at the praise heaped on the student body and staff by the most prominent visitors. The renowned Yiddish writer Kushnerow wrote a report about us in the Yiddish paper *Unity* which reached the entire USSR and made our institution known far and wide as the most unusual of its kind in the world. All its residents, staff, faculty, and student body had been saved from sure death, beginning with Minna Stein, age four to the directress, Tziviah Wildstein.

A.E.

From *Mitofet el Tofet* (''From Inferno to Inferno: The Story of Tziviah Wildstein'') by Leah Tzari and Tziviah Wildstein, published by Tarbut V'Hinuch, 1971, pp. 166-180.

DITTA COHEN: A STORY WITH A DRAMATIC HAPPY ENDING

During one of my surveys of Jewish educational institutions in Rome which housed Jewish fugitives, I found myself with a Youth Aliyah group. The director, a member of the Jewish Brigade, used every possible opportunity at his disposal to promote the welfare of the children. He built up the institution into an active, lively ''children's kingdom.''

When I met with him, he told me that he had recently enrolled a new child referred to him by UNRRA, whose name identified her as being of Jewish origin. He complained that she had been giving them a hard time because, having been raised in a convent, she was meticulously observant of all Catholic rites. She would not part day or night from the cross on the chain around her neck. Normally he wouldn't have minded her overzealousness, but most of the children were Jewish survivors of the ghettos and forests. The cross and the ritual of crossing oneself reawakened painful memories and aroused their anger.

I looked about his apartment and remarked, ''You should accommodate her here. I am sure your daughter, Dalya, will easily make friends with her.''

His eyes opened wide in amazement, and, as if speaking to himself, he murmured, ''How can my Dalya, a *sabra*, [1] become attached to a child who has been raised in a convent?''

''If you can't do it, then send her back to the nuns.''

He looked at me with even greater astonishment and said, ''What are you saying? Are there so many survivors left that we can bear giving up even one?''

''If you feel that way, you must invite her to live with you, for the cross she wears takes the place of father and mother. You and your wife must assume the

[1] A native Israeli.

role of parents, and your daughter that of a sister. You will see that she will change. Moreover, instead of Catholic prayers and observances, teach her Jewish rituals and prayers, such as *Modeh Ani, Shma,* and others. Teach her the traditional chants for the blessings and prayers. Sing them with her, for she loves to sing the liturgical chants which accompany the prayers in the convent. And exchange the *Magen David* for the cross."

To ease his mind I added, "If you do not succeed, I'll take her off your hands. In the near future I shall open a children's health camp which will be conducted along religious lines. I am sure that she will adjust readily to the group."

His wife approved the suggestion and persuaded her husband to go along.

It did not take long for Ditta Cohen — this was the name on her birth certificate, which had been issued in Budapest — to learn the Jewish blessings and prayers. At first she chanted them kneeling; later she gave up kneeling and was content just folding her hands and rolling her eyes heavenward. She willingly accepted the *Magen David* as a substitute for the cross. And when she had mastered the Jewish rituals, she worshiped with the same fervor she had exhibited when she recited the Catholic prayers.

But even more than that, she learned from the adults and absorbed knowledge from her intimate circle. Surprisingly, she learned to speak Hebrew quickly. Above all, she developed a joy in living. Simultaneously, as Dalya became attached to Ditta, she became more serious and responsible and obedient, joining Ditta frequently in reciting and chanting certain Hebrew prayers which she had not heard at home.

Meanwhile, the preparations for opening the rest camp were completed. Located near Rome, it was set amidst beautiful forests and fruit orchards. Nearby was situated the Morpurgo family villa, which was surrounded by tall pines and cypress trees. The Morpurgo family was distinguished in Jewish history. Rachel Morpurgo (1790– 1871) was the first Hebrew poetess. The family was notable for its generations of eminent Jewish scholars and rabbis. When the Nazis invaded Italy, one of its prominent sons converted. He was now the proprietor of the estate. And since the spark of Judaism still glowed within him, he welcomed the refugees.

The children came from Europe, North Africa, and Asia. It was a modern Babel of languages, cultures, and ways of life. In order to prepare this polyglot multitude for Eretz Yisrael, we conducted an intensive, all-embracing program, consisting of the study of the Hebrew language; formal and informal activities, such as singing, dramatics, campfires, games; and, of course, Hebrew studies.

I invited Ditta and Dalya to join the camp. When Ditta came, I hardly recognized her. Her pale face was rosy, and in her deepset eyes I detected a gleam of sophistication and mischief characteristic of children her age. She was alert and vivacious. She adapted to her new circle immediately. In a short period of time, she evinced many talents as a singer, dancer, and actress. Above all, she was fluent in Hebrew. She soon became the oustanding participant in all our public functions.

Ditta was an outstanding figure at our graduation ceremonies, to which were invited parents of the children, and leading figures of the JDC and UNRRA, as well as of the local Jewish community. She was self-confident and spirited. The climax occurred at the enactment of a Jewish wedding. Ditta wore a costume, and her face was made up. Suddenly an extraordinary thing happened.

In the audience sat a couple whom nobody knew and whom no one had seen before. They sat apart from each other, riveted to their seats, their eyes fixed on the stage. They did not move when Ditta, whose name had not been announced, sang a solo. But after the tumultuous applause, as the master of ceremonies called out her name, both strangers catapulted from their seats, speared through the crowd, and enveloped Ditta with hugs and kisses, crying, "Ditta mine, Ditta mine." They shook with deep sobs. The audience too broke into tears. All sensed that these were her parents.

It came out later that Ditta's parents had fled from Hungary to Italy. The Gestapo and the Italian Fascists caught them and sent them to the death camps. Ditta was saved by hiding in the convent. Both parents survived and returned to Italy separately, to seek their daughter.

By chance they learned about our camp celebration. They had not abandoned hope of finding her, nor did they overlook any possibilty of discovering her whereabouts. They had not recognized her at first, for she had grown and matured. Only when they heard her name did they identify her.

A.E.

From *Yaldei Hashoah* ("Children of the Holocaust"), op. cit., pp. 81-86.

THE CROSS

The writer, Nusiah Orlowitz Reznick, was a teacher of orphaned Lithuanian children, most of whom were Jewish, who had found refuge in Soviet central Asia. The school authorities prohibited Yiddish and any mention of Zionism and Palestine.

Her fascinating book, Mama, May I Cry Now?, *narrates the story and the long journey of the children from central Asia to Eastern Europe. The Jewish children, who had gone through the inferno of the Holocaust, the horrors of the war, and the harrowing experiences of the postwar period in Soviet Russia, remind us of Abba Kovner's experience, which is narrated on p. 292. The author very appropriately chose to name her book after the heart-piercing question asked by the little girl of her mother.*

Henka, whom we meet in this story, was a member of the kibbutz in Cracow whose job was threefold: to seek and find Jewish children who had been hidden in monasteries, convents, and Christian homes; to endeavor to bring them back to the Jewish fold; and to smuggle them across the borders on their way to the Promised Land.

Tall, blond, and blue-eyed Henka sat near a skinny young girl with sad black eyes and two long black braids. When I came into the room, Henka embraced the haggard-looking girl and said, "Meet Leah Mandelstam. I do hope that she will feel at home here with us. Do you agree with me, Leah?"

Leah was silent, her eyes fixed on the table, her lips tightly shut. She was very tense and almost on the verge of tears. "You promised to take me back to the convent," she retorted in a colorless voice, as if she had been repeating this statement many times.

"Of course I promised, and I will keep my promise. But you have to rest awhile. Look around. Think it over. You are very tired now. I'll come back to see you in a week or so, and if you still insist, I will take you back."

Henka spoke soothingly, without releasing Leah's hand. She looked straight into her eyes. Leah kept silent but emitted deep, sorrowful sighs. She followed Henka to the shower room as if she were being led to a prison cell. Henka and I waited in the foyer for her return.

Henka told me that she had been confronted with a difficult task. When she came to the convent, the girls were still in class. She inquired about Maria Mishnevska and said that Maria was her niece and that she had come to visit her. When the girls returned from school, Henka went to meet them and spotted Maria immediately.

The nun said to her, "Marisha, someone has come to see you."

Henka introduced herself as Maria's aunt, who had come to meet her niece. Henka took hold of her hand and kissed her warmly. The girl stood confused and murmured that she did not recognize her. However, she accepted Henka as her aunt and sat down for a chat.

Henka asked Maria to tell her about herself, whether she remembered anything about her family and home.

The girl was taciturn and refused to talk.

"Do you remember your father? He was a baker. I have searched for you everywhere, and at last I have found you. Now I would like to take you for a visit to my home. Maybe you will want to stay with us awhile."

Henka continued to talk to her soothingly and nonchalantly, and then she let a question drop. "Do you remember that you were born Jewish?"

"Me? Jewish?" Maria jumped up as if bitten by a snake. "I am Polish," she cried. She tore herself away from Henka and was about to flee.

"Calm down," Henka soothed her. "Sit here awhile, Leah Mandelstam. You must have forgotten your real name, but I remember." The girl burst into tears and ceased to protest.

"I wondered how I should approach the Mother Superior for permission to take Maria with me for a chat," Henka went on. "I entered the office of the Mother Superior, crossed myself like a pious Catholic, and extended greetings according to the accepted religious salutations. She received me politely but would not hear of Maria's leaving the convent. 'We are presenting a performance tomorrow, and the child is playing a major role. I cannot possibly let her go today.'

"I persuaded the Mother Superior to permit me to take Maria out for a cup of tea and a snack. In the café I revealed to Maria that I was Jewish and told her the story of my life. She sat listening quietly. I induced her to spend the night with me. She grudgingly consented, and now here we are.

"Leah will have a hard time adjusting to the change," Henka declared. "I will come to visit her as often as I can, and between visits I shall write to her." Henka departed, and Leah remained with me.

During the first few days, Leah's behavior was fair. She went about attending to her needs without uttering a word. In the mornings, when the girls reported to their various activities, she would retire into a corner, kneel, and pray at length. A heavy silver-plated cross hung from her neck, which she fondled. At meals she would chew her food lackadaisically and then report to class, to sit silently with her hands clasped tight. Again and again she refused the invitations offered by her fellow students to join them in various games and activities. She always excused herself by saying that she had a severe headache, or that she was very tired, or that she felt sleepy. The books in Polish which her roommates lent her to read remained unopened. Whenever I peeped into her bedroom I would find her lying on her bed with her eyes glazed and wide open.

I urged her to go to the infirmary for a medical examination, but she refused. When I finally succeeded in bringing her to the doctor's examining room, she would not undress. The doctor examined her fully clothed and prescribed a medicine, but she declined to take it.

Leah would report to me daily for her Hebrew lesson and would go through the motions of studying, writing in her notebook, and reading the text. Suddenly she would complain of a splitting headache and request permission to leave.

One day I said to her, "Look here, Leah, I don't want to force you to study. If you don't want to stay here, tell me, and we will take you back to the convent."

She burst into tears, crying, "You have already spoiled everything for me. Even before this happened, the girls at the convent would whisper to one another that I was Jewish. How can I go back now? What can I say to them? I was given the most important part in the play and then suddenly disappeared. You spoiled it all. How can I face them now?"

"If you want my advice, stay here. In the convent you lived in constant fear that the others would find out that you are Jewish. The war is over now. It is time to forget your apprehensions. Why don't you let yourself be what you are, a Jewess with the name of Leah Mandelstam? Why do you reject the name your parents gave you? We will not remain here long. Soon we shall depart for our homeland, Eretz Yisrael. We shall all be with our own. And you will be a Jew among Jews."

Suddenly she interrupted my exhortation. "I am no longer Leah. *They* shot Leah — not once, but twice. Why should I be Leah? Why?"

I was silent. She continued, "I lied when I told you I don't remember. I remember *every* incident, *every* moment. Oh, God! I wish I could forget! I just cannot obliterate the memories. I remember the attic where we hid." Her voice turned into a whisper as she turned away from me and continued, "I remember how we were discovered. They lowered us to the ground and led us through the streets. There was a pump in the marketplace where they lined us up and shot us. I fell. I don't know how long I lay on the ground. I was sure that I was dead. Suddenly my eyes opened and I saw our neighbor, the tailor's wife, standing on her feet and groping about her. Blood flowed down her face and from her wounds. Night fell, and darkness surrounded us. A thought came to my mind: Maybe I too am still alive.

"I stood up, and the neighbor ran to me, embraced me, and pressed me to her heart. Both of us walked to the ghetto without uttering a word. Even though I was bewildered, I remembered that my mother had hidden my two younger sisters and brother in the attic. I found them. It was night. I ransacked the empty houses nearby and found food. The tailor's wife helped me prepare the food for all of us. While I was doing all this, I kept on imagining that I was not alive but dead."

Leah's face changed as if it were covered with a transparent veil. She continued her whispering. "The second time I was shot, things were different. I was alone. I fled from Camp Stutcha when the extermination began. Alone, all alone, I wandered in the forest. Suddenly I met a group of partisans who befriended me. But the Germans soon discovered our tracks. They captured us and ordered us to dig our own graves. I dug mine. They shot us. I fell into the pit. They poured lime over us. I felt hot and suffocated. I was all wet but I remained alive. This time I felt my being alive and waited until everything was quiet. I tried to get up and out of my grave, but couldn't move. A very heavy weight pressed down on me. Suddenly I felt a hand stretched out toward me. At first I was frightened, but then I grasped the outstretched hand and came out. Before me was a grown man, wounded and silent. He took my hand and accompanied me a short distance to the edge of the forest, where he left me. I ran and soon reached the home of friendly gentiles, who gave me shelter."

Suddenly she looked up at me, her eyes wide open and her lips tightly pressed together in a straight line. "You see, Leah was shot twice. I do not want to be Leah any longer. I want to be Marisha."

She continued, but now spoke in the third person. "Many more horrible things happened to Leah. I haven't divulged them to anyone. Many times she was about to tell them to the priest at the convent during confessional, but she was afraid. One event she could not get out of her mind. When she returned home from the 'action,' she fed the children and went to sleep. In the morning she dressed her six-year-old sister, Dinah, who was light blond and looked non-Jewish. She put on her short blue apron and gave her a knapsack. She accompanied her to the street and parted from her, saying, 'Go to the gentiles and hide in their houses.' My sister left me silently, without shedding a tear. Leah remained standing and saw her little sister turning back to look at her. Her eyes, her look, Leah will never, never forget. But that is not all."

A deep silence followed. I was motionless, afraid to utter a sound. A few minutes passed, and I heard Leah's voice speaking again in the first person.

"During one of the 'actions' I hid my other sister and brother in bed under the covers. I was then eleven. The Germans came, accompanied by a Jewish policeman. The tailor's wife and I stood trembling at the wall. 'There must be more children here!' the *Jew* said. The soldiers searched and found my brother and sister. As the Germans marched out with us, an idea suddenly occurred to me. I turned to the Gestapo officer and said, 'I'll show you where there are more Jews.'

" 'If you are lying to us, I'll shoot you,' he warned me.

"I led the line and brought them down to the cellar. The stairway curved, and it was dark. In one of the corners I suddenly spun around and got away. As I ran, I heard the cries of my sister and brother. Their cries echo in my ears to this day.

I ran with all my might, and broke into a house where I found two Jews hiding. 'Leah, Leah,' I heard them cry louder and louder. I couldn't bear it, and I turned round to get back to them. The two Jews caught me and wouldn't let me move. No! I do not want to be Leah any longer. I can't bear to hear the name.''

We continued to meet daily for her Hebrew lessons. Invariably the book would be set aside after a brief period, and we would return to Leah's story. We tried to assure each other that Dinah, the first sister she sent away, must have been adopted by a Christian family, because she could pass as a Christian. We explored whether Leah could have saved her brother and sister had she returned to them. I always ended our discussion by stating emphatically, "No, Leah, you had no choice. The Gestapo officer would certainly have carried out his threat to shoot you. Only five steps more down the stairs, and he would have seen that you had fooled him.''

When I analyzed the situation to her she looked at me with wide, pleading eyes. She devoured every word that I uttered and in a whisper repeated after me, "No, there was no other way.''

On one occasion, as she recounted her experiences, she recalled her mother's words: "You, Leah, will outlive the enemy. You will be saved even amidst flames of fire.'' These words Leah quoted in Yiddish and imitated the intonation of her mother.

Leah's physical condition began to improve. She was given vitamins and medicines to restore her health. She was fed well. Occasionally she even smiled. After much persuasion, her friends succeeded in bringing her to group meetings, and it began to look as if she was on the mend. But suddenly one morning in class she reverted to her old self and refused to open her books. She repeated her laments, bemoaning her miserable lot in life. During this period she narrated to me another one of her horrible experiences.

"I found shelter in the home of a kindhearted Polish woman named Babiash. But I have always been unlucky. One day the Gestapo suddenly surprised us and found me. The neighbors gathered around the house. I opened the window and jumped out. The Gestapo's dogs ran after me. A Pole intercepted me and yelled, 'Zhidowska' [a derogatory word for Jewess]. Somehow I wriggled out of his grasp and ran as never before. I came to an open field and fell breathless to the ground in a bed of nettles. I lay there until midnight and returned to Babiash's house. From that day on I hid in her cellar.

"One day I went upstairs and drew the curtain just a little. Whom did I see? My father, holding a little boy whom I did not recognize! We looked at each other silently without saying a word. Since then I have not seen my father.''

Again she repeated her lament in a pathetic tirade. "I never had luck. I was always hunted. I was always exposed as a Jewess, even after Babiash had dyed my hair blond with peroxide. A gang of hoodlums recognized me. Again I ran away, but they caught me. 'Pay us, or we'll take you to the Gestapo,' they threatened. I still had my mother's watch, so I yielded to their demand. I had to leave my protector, Babiash. That's how it has always been.''

[Leah sank deeper into her melancholy mood. The writer sought advice and guidance from Leah's friends.]

One day I was told the following by her roommate, "Leah and some of us happened to stand together at the gate and look outside. Two nuns walked by slowly. Leah broke away from us and rushed to the nuns, shouting, 'Sisters, sisters.' I understood immediately what was happening. I ran after her and pulled her back. The nuns looked at us. They probably thought that we were mocking them."

On hearing this, the girls became upset. But I remained calm. "Perhaps she had wanted to have a chat with them, or they might have been old acquaintances."

"No, we are sure that she wanted to go back to the convent," they insisted.

That day, when Leah was to report for her lesson with me, she complained of a severe headache and remained lying in bed. Every time she heard my steps she pulled the bedsheet over her head and pretended to sleep.

Days passed. Leah's mood remained unchanged. However, she continued narrating her experiences to me.

"In the convent, my classmates suspected that I was a Jewess, and I avoided them as much as possible. I became popular because of my singing voice. When I was compelled to sing anti-Jewish songs, I would pray in my heart, " 'God of the Jews, do not punish me.' "

[Leah began to attend the meetings of the *Ken* social club. The girls were extremely kind to her and bore her sullenness patiently. Once Leah burst into song, and her friends applauded her. They treated her as if they were older sisters.]

Then one day one of the boys brought me a letter, written in Polish, which he had intercepted. It was addressed to the Catholic convent. It read: "Dear Father, I write to inform you that I, Maria Mishnevska, have been kidnapped by Jews. I beg you to come at your earliest convenience to take me back. I can't bear being in a Jewish atmosphere. Please come soon."

[The boy explained how and where he found the letter. The teacher confronted Leah with it.]

"Tell me, when do you want to go back to the convent? We will ask Henka to take you back. Just tell me *when*." I could not contain myself and did not wait for her answer. My bitter disappointment, helplessness, and pain intermingled as I poured out my feelings in a torrent of despair. "You *are* Jewish. You cannot escape it. You may perhaps convince one or two, but the third one will hurl *zhidowska* at you. If you want to go, leave us! No one will stand in your way. You don't need to trouble the priest to come to fetch you. You're free. But what of your mother? Have you thought of her? What would she say to you?"

Out of the haze of my anger loomed up the blurred face of a pathetic little girl with big black, frightened eyes, who stood utterly helpless. A wave of pity engulfed me. "Tell me," I implored in a restrained voice, "how can we convince you that we are concerned only with your welfare? Tell me. Why don't you believe in us?"

Her eyes streaming tears, Leah gathered the books from the table, about to leave. "It's not too late yet for you to decide," I called after her.

She stopped, turned to me, her lips pressed together; then she left without saying a word.

[During the three-day interlude that followed, twenty-seven members of the

Kibbutz Gordonia were ambushed while trying to steal across the border. Fourteen were killed by the Polish home army, six were wounded, and the rest escaped. A meeting of the members was held at the *Ker,* and the tragic events were reported to them.]

On the third day I came back from the meeting and reported for the lesson with Leah. She was waiting for me. I opened the book and without comment began teaching the new lesson. I felt that she was not listening to me. Nevertheless, I continued. I had no desire to start a conversation. Suddenly a shining object was placed on the book. It was the silver-plated cross which she had worn around her neck all the time. I raised my eyes. Leah sat, her face white as chalk.

"Take it." She pointed to the cross. "When we get to Palestine you may return it to me."

"I can't take care of it for you. Avraham, the watchman, takes care of all valuables. Give it to Avraham." I tore out a page from my notebook and wrapped the cross in it. My heart beat like a hammer. I felt I had to say something — something that would substitute for the cross which she held dear — but my mind was blank. All I could say was, *"I* will give it to Avraham, but listen well to our lesson today, because tomorrow you will have to go over it with me — all of it."

Leah drew close to me. Her black Jewish eyes, looking pacified and serene, caressed me.

A.E.

From *Imma, Hamutar Kvar Livkot* ("Mama, May I Cry Now?") by Nusiah Orlowitz-Reznik, published by Moreshet-Sifriat Poalim, n.d., pp. 258-276.

THE MIRACLE: EDUCATION IN BELSEN

The Eternal and Relentless struggle between the destructive power of war and the animating, life-giving vigor of culture — so vividly phrased in the Talmudic saying about the sword and the book — was never more visibly manifested than in the years 1939–1945.

As long as the sword was hovering over our heads, Jewish culture was in abeyance.

As soon as the sword was sheathed, the book was opened again.

After the 15th of April, 1945, when a pale and weak spring sun, consumed by years of darkness and nightmare, had glimpsed down into the valley of death in Belsen, a handful of young Jewish women, who had been connected with Jewish educational life, became aware of a disastrous spiritual void.

While gazing at the wasteland around them, they dreamt a rosy dream, a dream which brightened the gloomy horizon: there may have remained some Jewish children among survivors! . . .

Fascinated by this thought, they decided to search the vast area of the camp. It was still dangerous to go out. Disguised Nazi mobsters were continuing their sadistic work, shooting from ambushes, poisoning food. The Moloch was evidently not yet sated, demanding more victims.

A couple of dozen Jewish children miraculously survived. A number of them were housed in a separate compound — a puzzle which has never been solved.

Educational work began immediately. After school the children were taken for walks outside the rotten and filthy camp. They responded to the motherly approach for which they had been craving so long.

Jewish children among the ruins of the Thousand-Year Reich, singing Hebrew songs!

"G'di vaseh, seh u-g'di yatz'u vachdav lassadeh." [1]

This little group constituted the nucleus of the famous Belsen Hebrew School, which bore the name of Dr. Jacob Edelstein.

Their number grew rapidly. They came out of bunkers and basements and monasteries.

Only six weeks after liberation a large educational institution was established, with regular classes and teachers; even with janitors and bells. . . .

The uniformed boys of the Jewish Brigade, who arrived a few months later, soon became our beloved heroes. They helped the pioneering men and women of the Jewish Committee to shape a new life and a new Jewish generation in the camps of the British Zone of Germany.

A regular teaching staff was recruited, mainly experienced teachers among the members of the Brigade, and a full school program, with Hebrew as the language of instruction, was drawn up. There were no textbooks in the beginning, but the youngsters mastered with ease all the subjects taught orally, absorbing quickly the "flying letters."

It didn't take long before supplies of books, stationery, and sports gear poured in from the World Jewish Congress, the Central British Fund, the American Joint Distribution Committee, and the Jewish Agency.

The school's reputation grew steadily. Its Hebrew plays and shows, imaginatively produced by the children, were attended by excited crowds as well as by distinguished personalities from all over the world.

The grave problem of orphan pupils was quickly and successfully solved. All the orphans were transferred to the magnificent estate of the Warburgs, the well-known philanthropists, located at Blankenese (near Hamburg). To them was added a staff of teachers and supervisors.

For the first time after years of want and torture, the children were able to enjoy a restful and comfortable existence in large and convenient rooms, and to continue their education in a Jewish atmosphere and in high spirits.

You can well imagine how happy and proud these homeless children were when they could play host or hostess to visitors (especially their schoolmates from Belsen) on weekends. These children eventually found homes in Israel, where they went with the Youth Aliyah

In the meantime the camp of Belsen, with its varied Jewish activities and its drive for Aliyah Bet, became a veritable Jewish metropolis, and a great attraction for residents of other DP camps, survivors from the different countries of Europe, and returnees from Soviet Russia.

Since many of the newcomers, especially those from Russia, brought with them youngsters who had already completed their elementary schooling, the need for a secondary school became increasingly pressing.

[1]Hebrew nursery rhyme.

The establishment of a secondary school was not an easy task, rendered all the harder by the fact that the Jewish Brigade had to leave the camp. But what difficulty cannot be overcome by people of idealistic devotion? A geography teacher in the elementary school, assisted by an able officer of the Brigade, proceeded to lay the foundation for a large secondary school.

In thé beginning they drafted educated laymen, converting them into teachers. It was an arduous job. They had to teach from memory, without books. But the teachers became creative, inspired by the indescribable enthusiasm and the immense eagerness of the pupils.

Within a short time a complete staff of able and qualified teachers emerged, and the curriculum ranged from Tanach and modern Hebrew literature to mathematics, English, chemistry, Latin, and so forth. A library was added to the school, as well as a health department with a full-time school doctor, a gymnasium and recreation hall.

Very properly the school was named The Jewish Brigade Hebrew Secondary School.

The canteen, where the pupils had their meals, was operated for both the elementary and the secondary schools, and in time the two institutions became integrated under a single pedagogical council.

The spirit of harmony and cooperation inside the camp was fostered by the Central Committee, which spared no effort in trying to meet the needs of all groups. Thus the Orthodox community was able to maintain their own religious education: a Talmud Torah, a Yeshiva, and two Beth Jacob girls' schools.

The partisan activities of the various movements in the camp brought color into every phase of camp life. They stimulated competition in sports, chess, and the like. They also provided outlets for talent in the arts. Boys and girls of the schools were active participants in the various movements, and, despite the arguments and rivalries, all united in a spirit of *Chalutziut,* which dominated Jewish life in Belsen.

Alongside the general, religious and educational institutions, a large ORT trade school was established in Belsen. Hundreds of pupils acquired professional skill in various trades under the guidance of competent instructors. "Torah" and "Derech Eretz" complemented each other in shaping the lives of young people and prepared them for Israel or productive lives elsewhere.

Thousands of men and women who are now useful citizens in many countries, all of them aware of their Jewish heritage, well-versed in Hebrew, and proud of their Jewishness, received their education at Belsen.

Belsen, which was once a symbol of Nazi monstrosity, became a symbol of Jewish spiritual revival, of the victory of the book over the sword.

From *Belsen,* op. cit., pp. 156-161.

THE TWO SCHOOLS IN POSTWAR LODZ

There are two Jewish schools in Lodz. One is a Yiddish school run by the Jewish Committee. The other is Hebrew and belongs to the Zionist movement.

Some 250 children are enrolled in the Yiddish school, about 150 in the other.

It was understood from the beginning that the Jewish Committee, which represents all Jewish parties, had worked out a curriculum satisfactory to all. This curriculum was to become official for all Jewish schools in Poland.

In the Committee school, Yiddish is the language of instruction, with Polish taught from the first grade on. All children, without exception, are taught Hebrew beginning with the third grade. The curriculum includes arithmetic, geography, history, and the natural sciences. English is taught in the upper grades. Children also receive lunch — two rolls each and a cup of coffee or cocoa.

I spent several hours in this school, visiting classrooms, talking to children and teachers. Where do these children come from? Sixty per cent of them have returned from Soviet Russia, thirty per cent from concentration camps and forest hideouts. The rest had been in hiding on the Aryan side, in Polish homes.

The majority, then, are repatriates. If they had not found sanctuary in Russia, there would indeed be few Jewish children left in Poland.

But not all Jewish children in Lodz go to the Yiddish or Hebrew school. There are some in Polish institutions. In fact, fifty-seven of the children here had already been going to Polish schools, but they were made to feel so unwelcome that they transferred to the Yiddish school.

The atmosphere here is warm and friendly. The children romp about and play. When it comes to lessons, however, they are quiet. In one class they are doing sums; in another they are reading a story; in a third a discussion is going on about foreign lands. Since I come from America, we all begin to talk about the Atlantic Ocean, about American cities, about the American people and about Jews in America. Next door they are learning a Hebrew poem by heart.

Each child has a story to tell. Each is both child and adult in one. Each has six years of war in his system.

The children gather in the assembly hall. I forget that there are only two hundred and fifty of them. When you are among them in the crowded hall and they all sing together, they seem to be so many more — they seem like a child nation, straining to live, to laugh, to sing. Sweetest of all are the little ones, tiny toddlers singing pretty, witty Jewish songs, like the one about the peacock that spoke Yiddish or the one about Joey who wore chopped liver on his nose. The children giggle for all they are worth.

The older children have their own repertoire. They know the ghetto songs. They sing of tattered Bible pages whose words soar away like pigeons. A favorite is the mordant satire by the ghetto poet Mordecai Gebirtig, written in 1942. In this song the Jews rejoice because the enemy has gobbled up so much of Europe that his belly, unable to hold more, is about to burst.

I look hard at the children — there is no harmony between their looks and voices. Eyes are bright with laughter, but their faces are as thin and wan as their clothes are shabby. They recite poems, familiar poems by famous Jewish writers — Manye Leib, Abraham Raizin, J.L. Peretz. They have no books, of course, they must learn everything by heart from scraps of paper.

They sing a song about a boy who was a "tradesman" in the ghetto, and the song is a mixture of bravado and melancholy:

O, my name is Israel
And I am running wild.
And O, my name is Israel,
I am the ghetto's child.
They've killed my friends.
They've killed my kin,
The ghetto's mine to whistle in.

I wonder; perhaps little Israel sits on a bench in this Yiddish school.

Leib Sheftel, president of the League for Labor Palestine, and a former teacher at the Hebrew high school in Vilna, takes me to the Hebrew school. Here, of course, the language of instruction is Hebrew. Children begin learning it from the first day. Education generally takes on a more national and Zionist character. In every class they spend two hours daily studying Hebrew, the Bible, the Prophets, Jewish history. Hebrew slogans decorate the walls.

"We have 150 children here now," the teachers tell me. "At one time we had 260, but 110 have gone to Germany, to the camps, to go on to Palestine from there."

All the children here understand and speak Hebrew. They ask questions and give answers in Hebrew. There are among them even some who have studied the Talmud. Where did they learn all this? How did they remember it all, in their partisan foxholes and concentration camps?

In the Yiddish school they studied and recited works by Yiddish poets; here they study the Hebrew poets — S. Shnayer, Chernichovsky, and Bialik. The teacher, a young woman in high boots, calls out a small, dark boy with big laughing eyes, and says to him, "Let's hear you sing 'To The Bird!' "

And I hear Bialik's best-loved poem sung in perfect Hebrew by a Polish-born boy no more than seven years old. The teacher tells me, "This lad was once a *marrano* — so was this one — and this little girl."

They call them *marranos* after the Spanish Jews of long ago, because during the years of war they pretended to be Christians. And now they are back in a Jewish school, reading out in Hebrew: "In the beginning God created the heaven and earth. . . ."

For countless generations Jewish children have been taught this in their schools. They sing out the words, instinctively perhaps, in the old familiar recitative.

Children with parents and orphaned children, children who were partisans and children back from Russia, together they are now rehearsing a new play for Purim — *The End of Haman and His Ten Sons*.

From *Ashes and Fire*, by Jacob Pat, published by International University Services Press, 1947, pp. 57-60.

A JEWISH BRIGADE AND THE CHILDREN

I saw the Palestinians doing more than rescue work. I saw a job of rehabilitation — the only real job of rehabilitation for the victims of Nazism that I saw being done anywhere in Europe — and I saw it being done without the backing of the great governments of the world, without UNRRA and without the Allied Military Government. I saw a work of reconstruction which they were doing on the little wild animals that were Jewish children from all over Europe. These little ones looked like wild animals. They had been so debased by the Hitlerian teachings against them that these children felt, indeed, that they were somehow inferior beings. They had been compelled to watch their grandfathers and the venerable old rabbis being forced to wash the lavatories with their prayer shawls and phylacteries. They had been forced to attend the slaughter of their kinsfolk, watch the Nazis bind their parents, sling them up by their feet, and slit their throats as they gloated, "This is how we kill kosher!"

What, then, could these children's minds conceive but that they were indeed on some lesser plane for having been born Jews. Their heads had grown deep into their shoulders. They went about constantly in an attitude of concealment, of being secretive. They carried heavy weapons about with them underneath their rags, heavy sticks, heavy stones, whatever they could find to protect themselves with. They ransacked the garbage pails of Europe. They hoarded rancid bits of food about their persons. And I saw these little boys and girls, these little wild animals, in the hands of the Palestinian soldiers, their little backs straightening, their heads going up; being put on a new path, not to the noose — which was inevitable if they had been permitted to continue in the way in which they had been going — but to pride and self-respect and dignity, and most important of all, on a path to the understanding of human responsibility which was such a beautiful characteristic of their new guardians. . . .

When our company came to Bari, I immediately set out to find the Jewish soldiers' club. I found Nahum, a Palestinian, and gave him Major A.'s message. "Would you like to see one of the children's farms we have established?" he asked me.

"Very much."

"There is one not far from Bari. Of course, we always have to take over a house at some distance from the military authorities."

We fixed a time for the next morning, and a small party started for the farm — two Jewish soldiers, two actors from my company that I had been permitted to invite, and myself. We left Bari traveling in a truck, and after a rather hard trip over a bombed-out road, through incredible wind and water, we finally arrived at a tumbledown little villa which was called by the Palestinians "Rishonim." As we got out of the truck, a small dog came at us, barking violently and behind him came two little boys about seven and eight, in rags; but the thing that distinguished them from the other Italian children I had seen was that they were in clean rags. I stooped down to pet the dog, and when he was quiet one of the little boys said to me, "Shalom."

I answered, "Shalom." And then I asked him, "Tell me, is this your little dog?"

He looked at me, very surprised, and began to laugh. "No, this isn't my little dog. He belongs to all of us."

This little creature who only yesterday had understood just one law, the law of self-preservation, already on the road to being a responsible, social human being! My eyes filled with tears of gratitude as these two little ones took my hands and led me into the house. In no time we were surrounded by the other children in the house — motherless, travel weary, pogrom weary, bomb weary, but with a new tranquillity forming for them even in that cold house and in their pieced-together but meticulously clean clothes. An aura of tragedy still hung about them, which had crept deep in their eyes, but there was also a wholesome, sweet spirit struggling to the surface despite their travail. Everything in the house had been created or restored by them with their own hands — their benches, their beds, their washing facilities, their food, their clothes.

It is impossible to conceive the hardships under which the Palestinians managed to bring some courage into this little group. Limited food, no heat, limited clothes! Children with bitter memories, children shaken to the foundations of their young souls, children who were given up as irredeemable by psychological experts who had come across Europe! A Palestinian soldier quartered in the neighborhood used to come out each day to teach them their studies, and a young Jewish army doctor went out every Sunday, his rest day, to nurse their sick little bodies.

The day we were there was not Sunday, but the doctor had driven all the way out to look at the throat of one of the little girls. I was taken on a tour of the house and farm by a charming thirteen-year-old Yugoslavian girl. She showed me everything with a half-shy manner, but her eyes danced brightly all the time. When we got to the room where the boys slept, she became somewhat embarrassed, because it wasn't quite neat enough for her taste, but she blushed very proudly when we inspected the girls' dormitory, because everything was neat and clean as a pin. She showed me the laundry, where they took turns doing the washing and the ironing, and finally the "peeng pawng" table, which stood in solitary splendor at one end of the laundry — on which a game served as a reward, no doubt, for the hardworking launderers and laundresses when they finished their day's task.

As we made our way back to the main room from which we had started, we passed a door which was locked. She tried the handle but couldn't make the door open and finally, unable to bring herself to pass this door completely, she stood up on her tiptoes and peeked in at the keyhole, which was rather high in this Italian door. As she gazed inside, a smile of pleasure crossed her face and she turned to me, saying, "Oh, you must take a peek in there and see what is in there!" I took a "peek" and I saw standing on the shelf behind this locked door — the only door of this children's farm which had to be locked — two little jars of preserves. It seems that on very, very special celebrations this door would be unlocked, the jars taken out and opened, and each child would be given a tiny taste of the precious sweet.

I found out somewhat later that my little guide had been a Yugoslavian partisan guerrilla; that she could shoot a gun straighter than many of our soldiers; that her mother, who had become very fearful of the child's growing up in the Yugoslavian woods amidst the horror and bloodshed, had stolen across the border, found the Palestinians and handed the little girl over to them, begging them to take care of her until they could get her to Palestine. The Palestinians had pleaded with the mother to stay. They had assured her that they would take care of her as well. But she had said, "No, I must go back. I have a debt to pay in the Yugoslavian woods for a husband and a mother, and I must go back." She went back and has not been heard from since.

I was greatly moved by the foster mother of the group. Her name is Rose Lustig. Rose Lustig is a German refugee woman who has lost all her own relatives in the Nazi cistern and who now is the only adult permanently living on this little farm, trying to take care of these little ones as best she can. Rose Lustig came up to me as I stood with some of the children and suddenly threw her arms about me. "I feel, somehow, that you are my sister. I feel so very close to you and my heart is warmed. I used to be afraid of Americans. I didn't know what they were like. Tell me, are they all like this? Are they all like you, or is it only you?"

I looked down into that worn face and the searching eyes. What could I say? I wanted to reassure her but found myself saying instead, "Don't expect too much. Don't expect too much from anyone. Just continue with the courageous work you are doing. Just continue being the fine, wonderful inspiration to these children that you are, and may you find your dream of a new life in Palestine, my sister. God bless you, Rose Lustig." I could not say any more without bursting into tears.

We started to depart after I had promised to write to them and send them photos, but the leavetaking was very difficult. The children didn't want us to go. Their eyes suddenly filled with tears. They had had enough of "good-byes" and every new one invariably would bring a well of torturous memories flooding to the surface. One of my companions tried to entertain them a little before we finally tore ourselves away, by telling them about the travels of his family — how his grandfather had come from Germany to New Zealand to settle, and how his father had gone from New Zealand to Australia, and how he had gone from Australia to the United States to live. One of the little boys looked up sadly and with the air of a wise old sage said, "It has taken your family three generations to do the traveling I have had to do in eight years."

All the way back to town, the faces of the children danced before my eyes. I was caught between a desire for tears and a frustrated desolation at not being able to help. I pondered the miracle of love I had just witnessed, and some understanding of the need of these children for Palestine began to come to me. What other country would be willing to make the sacrifices necessary to bring them back from the damned!

From *The Buried Are Screaming*, by Helen Waren, Beechhurst Press, 1948, pp. 31-36.

SOLDIERS ESTABLISH A HEBREW SCHOOL

The presence of Jewish units serving with the British Eighth Army restored the faith of the Italian Jewish population. Wherever the Jewish soldiers went, they looked for Jewish survivors and tried to help them. Money, food, and clothing were collected and distributed to the needy. They told the survivors about the settlement in Palestine and urged them to prepare for aliyah. *The Jewish soldiers felt that they had a double mission to perform — to fight the Nazi forces and to rescue the remnant of the Jewish people.*

As soon as they entered Rome, after its liberation on June 4, 1944, the soldiers sought out and collected stray Jewish children and established a school. One of these soldiers, Elimelech Cohen, himself a teacher, describes how by these efforts many children were saved and restored to a wholesome way of life.

With the liberation of Rome by the Allied armies, Jewish children were the first to be collected from the streets and placed in schools. Jewish soldiers from Eretz Yisrael liberated them from their hiding places, from the fear of death, and from searing humiliations. Most of them had been hidden in churches and monasteries, whose occupants in their great kindness had saved them either by ransom of money or ransom of soul. During that period when vagrant children were still running through the streets of the city, begging for a *carmella* (candy) or a cigarette, Jewish children were being gathered up by Jewish soldiers with brotherly compassion. They were brought together in the synagogue on Balboa Street, and the building soon gained famed throughout the city. The Jews knew and felt that there, in the upper chambers, Jewish life was springing forth in full daylight, that Jews were meeting their fellow Jews; free brothers from the Holy Land were meeting with brothers who had been miraculously rescued and who were yearning for redemption.

The number of children and youth grew from day to day. . . . The soldier from Eretz Yisrael was like a marvel in their eyes, a messenger from on high, a living symbol of the eternity of Israel.

The study of the Hebrew language, Hebrew songs and dances captured every Jewish heart. The snacks, the candy, and the chocolate also answered a vital need. The *Oneg Shabbat* gatherings were a joyous experience for all of them.

We started with 60 and we quickly reached 450 to 500 children between the ages of six and twelve. At first we were only six soldier-teachers who filled the daytime hours with Hebrew studies. The government schools were still closed. We were in full control of the environment. The children quickly became attached to the institution and the language. Soon the number of teachers rose to twenty-four, and an organized program of instruction was adopted, with two hours for Hebrew and two and a half for Italian.

At the beginning, children did not know their Hebrew names. With the opening of the school, a list of Hebrew names, Biblical and those used in Eretz Yisrael, was drawn up, and the gentile names became Judaized. "Cesare" was changed to "Israel," and Yitzhak (Isaac) quickly forgot that his name had been Eugenio. And if the parents objected, the children insisted and convinced them.

Kabbalat Shabbat (the ceremony welcoming the Sabbath) became an accepted activity every Friday. During the last period on that day, all the pupils assembled for a modest get-together. They recited and sang songs of the Sabbath and of the Land of Israel, and concluded with sweets and "goodies." Thus, the Sabbath became a day to which they looked forward with anticipation. The remnant Jews of Rome knew almost nothing about the Sabbath. They did not even know how to pray properly, nor did they understand the meaning of the prayers. Indeed, they attended the synagogue on Saturday, but at the conclusion of the prayers they went to business. Sunday was the day which they set aside for family visits, for walks and rest.

Our children were the ones who brought the sanctity of the Sabbath into the homes. They loved the Sabbath prayers and observed the Sabbath day. They lit the Sabbath candles and revived Jewish home life.

One of the difficulties at the beginning of our work was the lack of proper textbooks. The books which we had received from Israel were unsuitable for our children. We were confronted with an urgent need to produce books on the spot, and we created something out of nothing. . . .

The role of our soldiers in this activity was very substantial, whether personally or with money, or even more than that. During all the days of my work I had a feeling that I was fulfilling a lofty mission and that I must act with great fidelity and devotion in my task. When I covered the thin bodies of our children with clothes made from our soldiers' uniforms, a feeling of reverence came over me; I knew that the warmth of the clothing was accompanied by a lingering brotherly warmth. And when I distributed daily the chocolate which our soldiers had spared from their own rations, I felt that I was not only sweetening the children's bitter lives but that we were also promising them a sweetening of their future in the homeland. . . .

The joy of childhood was restored to the children. For many of them this was perhaps the first moment of joy in their lives, which had been filled with grief and oppression. They also introduced into their parents' home the revival of the hope for a free Jewish life. . . .

A class was established, consisting of twenty-five girls, ages fourteen to seventeen, whom I had gathered from the alleys and the noisy streets, where they were seeking cheap, easy sources of livelihood with the army. Most of them were from the poorer sections of the population (among them were some who had completed only one grade of public school). The meals that were provided for them, the clothing, and our friendly attitude drew them close to us. A program of studies in Hebrew and Italian was set for them in the morning hours, and vocational training in the afternoon. . . . The woolen garments of our soldiers were ripped and reknitted into gloves, socks, hats, and sweaters. These materials also made the school flag. . . .

The results of medical examinations revealed that one hundred boys and girls required convalescence. An empty palace which had been acquired by the Joint Distribution Committee and which was not being used was turned into a summer camp and a convalescent home. Every Friday we would receive ten additional children, who joined the ten who had been convalescing for a week. . . . All of them gained weight. . . . Many of them ate an egg for the first time in their lives. . . . In the playground, surrounded by shady trees, it was apparent by their games that they were resting sufficiently, eating well, and feeling happy. . . . In their happy, hearty laughter and in their childish mischief they seemed to be trying to recapture what they had been deprived of in their days of poverty and misery.

A.E.

From *Sefer Hahitnadvut* ("The Record of Military Volunteer Efforts of the Jews of Eretz Yisrael during World War II"), collected by Zeev Shefer, edited by Yitzhak Lamdon, published by Mosad Bialik, 1949, pp. 716-719.

18.

THE TRAUMA
AFTERWARD

In November 1979, the First International Conference of Children of Holocaust Survivors was held in New York City. It was held during the International Year of the Child, which was proclaimed by the United Nations Educational, Scientific, and Cultural Organization, and was scheduled to commemorate the Crystal Night atrocities (November 9–10, 1938). An analysis of the feelings of the children of survivors is presented below. The conference arose from the need of these children to meet with their peers and exchange experiences.

Reports of studies on the reactions of survivors' children were presented. In general, children of survivors who felt that they were "victims" suffered from anxieties and mistrust of outsiders and strangers, and were in greater need of staying close to their parents. Those who came of families who entertained a self-image as "fighters" manifested an attitude of courage and independence. The children strove to undo the Holocaust experience of their parents.

Survivors' children have been contributing articles to Martyrdom and Resistance, *published by the American Federation of Jewish Fighters, Camp Inmates, and Nazi Victims, which sponsored the conference, and other magazines.*

PAINFUL INHERITANCE

Helen Epstein, a child of survivors, studied and reported on the effects on the children born of parents who had experienced the Nazi horrors in the concentration camps. She is author of a bestseller, Children of the Holocaust, *published by Putnam.*

344

The Press Release from Stanford University puts it succinctly. "The trauma of the Nazi concentration camps," it reads, "is re-experienced in the lives of the children and even the grandchildren of camp survivors, according to Shamai Davidson, a visiting scholar.

"The effects of the systematic dehumanization are being transmitted from one generation to the next through severe disturbances in the parent-child relationship. These disturbances are currently being investigated in studies of children of survivors in Israel, Canada, and the U.S."

That is the story *Time* magazine reported under the headline "Legacy of Terror," attempting to make something complicated easy to assimilate. But in fact, nothing about this subject is easy to assimilate. There are no statistics. And no researcher in the field is even willing to guess how many children of survivors there are.

"There has been no extensive research done anywhere," says Davidson. "The subject is so complex, there are so many variables that it puts researchers off. It's difficult to find the non-clinical population because many parents don't want their children disturbed. Most people tend to deny a problem exists. They want to avoid confrontation with pain of this extremity and psychiatrists and psychoanalysts are no exception."

Just before the outbreak of World War II, there were over 8,861,000 Jews living in Europe. No one knows exactly how many survived. It is estimated that between four and five hundred thousand Jews spent the war years in labour camps, in the forests and the countryside. No more than 75,000 survived the concentration camps. Two of them were my parents.

Before I was five, I asked my mother: "Who put the number on your arm? Why? Did it hurt? Why don't I have grandparents? Why did the Germans kill them? Where are they buried? *Why* aren't they buried? Then where are they?"

My mother said that before the war, my father had a fiancée, two parents, and two brothers. All five were gassed to death in Auschwitz. Before the war, she herself had a mother, a father, and a husband. All three were shot dead by the German SS. Like most Czechoslovak Jews, she and my father had both been deported to the Terezin Ghetto, and then sent to a series of camps, including Auschwitz and Bergen-Belsen.

They met after the war and married as soon as they could assemble the requisite documents. Like most survivors, they had a child as soon as possible. I was born in Prague and named after my paternal grandmother, Helena, whom my father had adored. Seven months later, we immigrated to America, part of a massive, voluntary relocation of scattered survivors across the world.

Over 150,000 came to the U.S. and Canada. Some clustered in neighborhoods such as Crown Heights, Brooklyn, where a child like Irwin Blum could grow up thinking everybody's parents had been in a concentration camp. Others pushed on to Detroit, Toronto, San Francisco, or small towns like Asheville, North Carolina, where beauty queen Connie Adam remembers, "Not only were we different from the community but from the few other Jews in the community."

A few thousand survivors settled in Australia, as far away from Europe as possible. Several thousand emigrated to South America, where one girl was the classmate of several children of Nazis. The largest number, about 25,000, went to Israel, where memorials of the war were a part of their children's school field trips.

I became an American child. I watched the Mickey Mouse Club, played baseball, and memorized the score of every musical on Broadway. I seemed to be as well adjusted as any other little girl growing up on the upper West Side of New York. But when my mother took me to Carnegie Hall, I would often imagine a group of men in black coats bursting into the auditorium and shooting everybody dead.

Other times, I went to St. Patrick's Cathedral, crossed myself, and lit four candles for my grandparents. When I rode the subways at rush hour, I pretended the trains were going to Auschwitz.

Although these were important childhood rituals, it was not until I began interviewing other children of survivors that I found the reciprocity I needed to talk about them. While I was growing up, I tried to bury them. Although I saw it every day, I could not remember the four-digit tattoo on my mother's arm.

Violence and mutilation of any sort were very real to me. I knew that my mother's back had been irreparably damaged in concentration camp and that my father was possessed by a rage and sense of loss that took him away for hours at a time. I saw that our family was unlike any family on television or in the movies. It was certainly unlike any Jewish families I knew, or the ones I read about in the novels of Saul Bellow and Philip Roth.

There was no one to tell this to. My parents had a stake in my "normalcy"; any hint of disorder, I felt, would hurt them. My two brothers and I rarely discussed our family dynamics. My friends sensed a taboo and kept quiet. Most people appeared not to care. The war, which had partitioned our parents' lives into "Before" and "After," seemed not to have touched theirs.

In high school, we never got to World War II. In Sunday School and in books, grave voices evoked "the Six Million" and "the Holocaust" — abstract, antiseptic terms that had nothing to do with the messy, volatile emotions so palpable at home.

Other children of survivors I spoke with, whether they were raised in refugee communities in Israel or in non-Jewish neighborhoods in the U.S., recall the same sense of isolation.

Their response was to bury their feelings, just like the rest of the world. They studied hard, learned to play sports and instruments, entered the social and cultural life around them. "I never thought of myself as a child of survivors," many said.

Our parents had not yet become the subjects of books, films and doctoral dissertations; it was not difficult to ignore their difference. Besides, other things were happening. We grew up in the 1960s, when it was easy to be lost in a crowd of one's choice. We watched group after group — blacks, women, homosexuals, ethnics, single parents, students, even *block associations* — organize, brainstorm, and air vital issues. Some of us joined other groups, but we did not form our own. We surfaced singly, in such a variety of contexts that only someone working back from interviews could construct a chronology.

In 1971, the judges of the Miss America Pageant in Atlantic City were confronted by Connie Adam. In response to the application question, *What are interesting facts about yourself or your family which you would want publicized (anything you have done that is a bit different, hobbies, interests, etc.)?* the first Jewish Miss North Carolina had written, "I am a first-generation American. My parents, homeless and orphaned after surviving the Nazi concentration camps of World War II, came to America in quest of a new life."

In 1973, a group of Vietnam Veterans Against the War were driving to radio station WBAI in New York when one began to sing a German song. "I told him to shut up," recalls tax accountant Al Singerman. "I got very upset, and he wanted to know why, I said: 'What do you mean *why?*' I was sure I had told them my parents were in the camps. I mean, these were the only guys I trusted in the world."

In New York that year, six children of survivors published their feelings and questions in *Response,* a Manhattan-based quarterly with a circulation of 3,000. One year later, in a *Newsweek* cover story, designer Diane Von Furstenberg revealed that her mother "spent 14 months in a German concentration camp at the age of 19. When she got out, she weighed 44 pounds. I always think that somehow I am the answer to her."

While that issue was on the stands, a small notice began to appear in Boston's *The Real Paper,* in Cambridge bookstores, on university bulletin boards, and in kosher butcher shops: GROUP FORMING FOR CHILDREN OF HOLOCAUST SURVIVORS. CALL EVA.

"I saw that psychiatrists were beginning to extend the Survivor Syndrome to us, that severe pathology was being attributed to the second generation just as it had been to our parents," Eva Fogelman told me recently.

"I began to feel that this was all wrong. Sure we were affected. But not to the point where we're not functioning normally or where we have more psychological problems than the normal population."

She and Bella Savran, both psychotherapists, had been looking for a way to apply their skills to an area of personal concern. Last spring, they began to run "awareness groups" for children of survivors, similar to women's consciousness-raising groups or the rap groups organized by Vietnam Veterans. Their purpose was simply to air issues that had been kept secret for years.

Between us, the three of us have interviewed over seventy-five children of survivors.

Despite the diversity in age (eighteen to early thirties), family background, and occupation, they all described feelings of affinity to other children of survivors. "There's a tacit understanding between us," said one. "A completeness without conversation," said another.

Bella Savran found it incredible "hearing from other people's mouths the thoughts I had lived alone with for years."

The interviews I myself conducted were unlike any in my experience. Some people battled with the questions I posed. Some answered indifferently until one question hit a nerve. Some felt exhilarated. Others developed headaches and stomach pains. Often, I felt as if plasma were flowing between us.

"You have to share with the reader the inexplicable sense of turmoil it involves,'' said Mitchell Lerner, a twenty-two-year-old sociology student. ''You must somehow make your work more than storytelling, because storytelling doesn't allow dialogue. You must force your reader to achieve in himself a semblance of this chaos, to assemble his own tension in the place where he is the most private. Because you are making a private issue public.

''I always knew that my parents were in a concentration camp,'' said Mitchell. ''The fact that it wasn't talked about made me know it more. All I had to do was look at my mother's face, and I knew I'd better not ask her questions. I didn't want to make her cry. Even my sister didn't ask her questions. My father's stronger. She asked him.

''I could never remember what was said. I always had to ask dates over and over again. I always had to ask again how many brothers and sisters had died. I could never retain it. I always wanted to ask my father questions as a son. I never could. He would lapse into thoughtfulness, and for me the lapse was an answer. You know, the fact of the matter is I know nothing, even though I've heard it inside out.''

Memories crystallized for Mitchell as he talked. He recalled one incident very clearly. ''I was in grade ten. It was a break between classes, and this guy across the room looked over at me and said, 'Hey, Lerner, Hitler missed one.' I was shocked. I thought: What do I do? I didn't even know what I felt. He said it again, and I got up and walked out of the room.

''I began to cry, and my body began to shake. I went halfway down the hall and then I turned. I went back, tapped him on the shoulder, and struck him so hard in the mouth that he fell down on the floor. I was shaking. I felt terrific and terribly guilty.

''It forced me to think about everything I'd never thought about, all those things that were so unapproachable. I not only felt that I had avenged my father, but all the images of my uncles and grandparents. I could look at the pictures my father kept in his shoebox. I felt an angel had pushed my arm.''

Mitchell's ''angel'' is more than a metaphor for children of survivors, who frequently allude to ''lives'' they are living for in addition to their own. Like many other children, we were named after dead relatives. But our relatives were systematically murdered, and we often have no idea what our families owned or loved or even looked like. Our sole inheritance is the name we bear. Our parents enlarge it with ''name stories,'' beautiful or heroic tales of the person they loved. We invest it with magical significance.

''My Hebrew name is Serifka, which was my father's mother's name,'' said social worker Dina Rosenfeld. ''When I was young and my father took me to services. I used to say, 'My name is Serifka from Orhay.' I was never in Orhay in my life, but my grandmother lived there. This was my identification. My grandmother reincarnated.''

Doctoral candidate Robert Eli Rubenstein said, ''I'm very aware of being named after both my grandparents. It's a weak kind of substitute for having them, but it enables something to live on in me.''

Few of us remember the first time we were told ''name stories,'' just as few of us remember how we first found out about ''the War.''

''It seemed like my parents never talked to me except to say what the

Germans had done to them,'' said Al Singerman. ''I was told what the Germans did to my father's hands, his nails, his back. How my mother was struck on the head. I was able to listen for maybe ten minutes. Fifteen at most. Then I'd block my ears and yell 'I don't want to hear!' or I'd leave the room to make them stop. I'm thirty years old and I don't know my parents. They're like strangers to me.''

All the stories were underscored by hundreds of asides which our parents made every day. When they were provoked by our misbehavior, some of them shouted epithets like ''Idiots,'' ''Filth,'' or ''Swine'' — the same ones the Nazis had used against them.

One son remembers his mother screaming, ''Enemy of the Jews,'' when she lost her temper.

We all heard variations of: ''How can you behave like this to your parents? I wish I had my parents alive and here!'' or: ''Is this what I had to live for? I should have died there with the rest of them.''

The things children are told — no matter how disturbing — often make less of an impression than what they sense or observe.

We saw how insecure our parents were when they had dealings with officials, state troopers, judges, inspectors, policemen, parking attendants, even waiters in restaurants. Some of these ''authority'' figures were accorded a respect we found disproportionate; others inspired undue fear or anger. My father found it impossible to leave a gasoline station without having an argument with the attendant.

''When the Fire Department came to inspect the house wiring,'' said Al Singerman, ''I could not *believe* my aunt's behavior. She was practically groveling, she was so frightened. By two firemen!''

Researchers may not have penetrated the ''normal'' front our parents adopted, but we lived with their ''bad'' legs, arms, and backs, their recurrent illnesses, their anxieties about everything from food to the international political situation.

The paradox was that our parents were also the *toughest* people we encountered. They had learned new languages late in life, had changed professions, life-styles, and living quarters. They were awesomely competent at what they did; yet, unlike other parents we saw, their lives were centered on their children rather than careers.

''It's a family joke,'' said one daughter. ''We can't go into the next room without my father saying, 'Be careful.' It's become an automatic reflex with him.''

Other children of survivors speak of their parents living through them, succeeding through them, noting that each of their achievements was a victory against Hitler.

''A life that is not a 'given' but an unexpected 'gift,' '' wrote psychiatrist Vivian Rakoff about children of survivors in Montreal, ''may become not a life but a mission.''

Unlike many children with overprotective parents, our response was to protect them back.

''It's not as if they're the parents and we're the children,'' said Rochelle Kaplan. ''It changes all the time. I think a lot of other Canadian kids took their parents for granted. They were there to serve them mostly. We were trying always to shield each other from pain. We all worked hard at preserving the serenity. Terrible things had happened, so terrible they didn't even want to tell us what. Instead, they said all they wanted was for us to be happy and to see a beautiful new generation growing up. I felt it as a tremendous responsibility. I didn't know if I could do it.''

Although writers and filmmakers have developed elaborate theories of survival, our mothers and fathers were clearly at a loss to explain why they had lived while the rest of their families had died.

"We were strong and healthy,'' many told us. Others credited "God" or "luck.'' But as we grew older many of our parents began to say that they had survived the war in order to have us. Family was their first priority. They had few close friends and established a social life with their children.

Those survivors who were ill-suited to each other rarely divorced. They clung to their marriages because no one else was left, and when they did socialize, it was in tight, memory-bound groups.

"All they did was talk, talk, talk,'' recalled Connie Adam. "Other kids' parents went to cocktail parties, played cards, danced. The women got together by themselves; the men got together by themselves. My parents never did anything separately. And we children were usually included.''

Our parents did not mix well — not even with other Jews. They felt separated by experience, by different definitions and expectations of community. Many stayed away from organizations and synagogues. Many joined survivors' organizations. In either case, their children were left with no community of their own. We lived in a social vacuum, where the usual criteria of income, education or parental profession did not seem to apply.

When people asked us what our parents did, we also began to use the terms "Before'' and "After.'' We picked up our parents' attitudes toward authority, family, life and death, as well as their attitudes toward being Jews. Some of our parents took great pride in being Jews. Others displayed a confusing ambivalence. One son was not circumcised until the age of ten because his parents could not make up their minds whether or not to mark him as a Jew. One daughter passed as a Protestant until she went to college: that was what she saw her parents doing.

We noticed that our parents had an ambivalence about Americans as well. On the one hand, "they were the enemies of the Nazis, which made them our allies,'' said ski instructor Tom Epstein. "But,'' said one daughter, "my parents would always say: 'Americans? What do they know about life!' ''

Many parents said they were lifelong Democrats because Roosevelt had "ended the war.'' But the books they gave us to read contained contradictory information. Between 1941 and 1945, this country allowed an average of 5,000 Jews — about the population of an American high school — to immigrate each year.

We noticed all these things and absorbed them without any clarification. Many of us are just beginning to examine our responses today.

"I was frightened. I just really wanted to escape from the whole thing,'' said Rochelle Kaplan. "I come from a religious family and although I stayed observant, I didn't want to be conspicuously Jewish. I had very blond hair when I was young and when it started to turn dark I got very upset. At the time, I thought that was about being pretty, but I realize now that it was about being safe. I had this crazy idea that if people knew I was Jewish, I'd be one of the first to be taken away.''

Other children of survivors had nightmares that continued for years.

"It was always the same dream: a skeleton descending upon me in the darkness,'' said Al Singerman.

"I didn't dream about Hitler or Nazi Germany,'' said Eli Rubenstein. "I just dreamt about bad people coming to kill me and my relatives for no good reason.''

Many sons and some daughters had fantasies of revenge. "I loved watching Germans getting killed,'' was a phrase that recurred among those who became devotees of the war movies shown on television.

Yet most of us were instructed not to hate. As we became politically aware, we asked ourselves what we would have done as Germans in Germany, and felt guilty about not contributing to or working for a wide range of causes. We were also troubled by the question: would we, in our parents' place, have survived?

In the 1960s, while most of our contemporaries were busy throwing their parents' values out the window, we were trying to measure ourselves by their standards. We studied our parents; we *took on* their values.

"Most people I grew up with viewed their parents as part of a society they had to fit into,'' said one son. "My parents didn't come from this society. They came from a society that no longer exists. They were victims, not oppressors.''

The survival stories loomed large over our lives. They were a challenge, a test.

"If I was unhappy,'' wrote Toby Mostysser, "I would wonder whether I would have sustained the drive to stay alive through several years of the most abject misery. When I failed at something, whether it was at making friends or at finding a job, I wondered whether I would have had the ingenuity, the skill, the craft to have kept myself in food and shelter and out of the hands of the Germans, the Ukrainians, and the Poles.''

"I wanted to suffer,'' said Rochelle Kaplan, "because my parents and all our deceased relatives who were so brave and noble had suffered. I thought that, to be noble, I had to suffer too.''

Some of us did simple things. We scrimped on food, clothing or material possessions. We became involved in political demonstrations guaranteed to be herded by policemen. Some of us went to jail, some of us went to Germany to try to have the experience that separated us from our parents. A few of us actually managed to put ourselves in war situations, in border *kibbutzim* in Israel or, in at least one case, Vietnam.

"It was something I had to prove to myself,'' said Al Singerman, "that I too was a survivor. I *joined* the army! There was no doubt in my mind that my survival was going to be Vietnam.''

When my friends discovered I was writing about children of survivors, they asked why I persisted in such a "depressing'' avocation. I never had a ready answer, because I did not myself know why; all I knew was that it kept coming up, it was a part of me that never remained quiet for long. It turns out that most children of survivors feel more or less the same thing.

"I feel an obligation to tell the story of what happened," said Connie Adam. "People need to be reminded. They shouldn't be so naive and content to think it couldn't happen again. I think children of survivors appreciate that much more than the average person. Personally, I knew I didn't want to wait long to have children. I wanted my children to have grandparents. I feel very good about the fact that I have one baby and I'm expecting another one. I feel as if I'm paying my parents back for everything they've given me."

"I take life very seriously," said Eli Rubenstein. "I'm aware of evil in the world. I'm not complacent: I feel it requires an active struggle to prevent a revival of the sort of thing that led to the murder of my family. That brings out a certain activism in me that wouldn't be there otherwise."

"There was a whole civiilization wiped out, and only a few people remain from it," said Irwin Blum. "I feel an obligation to helping that culture survive. Whenever you allow anything to die you're continuing the Holocaust. But, if anything, it's the Germans who have to relate to that time. Our parents didn't commit genocide. There were people *in* the concentration camps, there were people who *ran* the concentration camps, there were people fighting the war, and there were people who went to the World Series in 1943. An entire era ended with the Holocaust and a new one began. Everyone has to relate to it."

From the *Jerusalem Post Magazine*, July 22, 1977, by Helen Epstein.

ADOPTION OR FOSTER HOME CARE?

Many were the legal cases involving relatives who wanted to adopt surviving children of families that had been exterminated, who had been raised by foster parents. Following is a typical case.

A year or two after World War II a seven-year-old boy arrived in Israel, together with a group of Youth Aliyah children. All his family had been exterminated in Poland. The boy had escaped miraculously, but the effects of his horrifying experiences left him with deep emotional scars. He was very tense and withdrawn, and whenever he saw a man in uniform with epaulets and military trappings he would tremble, lowering his eyes as if he wanted to disappear and flee. Because of his mental and emotional disorders, the Youth Aliyah medical staff thought it best to find a home for him where he would live with other boys of his age. They succeeded in finding such a family, and slowly the boy began to become accustomed to his new surroundings; his world began to expand, and life assumed new meaning and value.

Soon bonds of attachment formed between him and members of his new family. He began to show greater interest in his studies and won friends among his fellow pupils and teachers. It looked as if he were adapting quickly to his new environment, although he still suffered from recurring nightmares.

In the meantime it was discovered that he had a living relative — an aunt who was his mother's sister. She had emigrated to America several years before the war. As the war ended, she had instituted a worldwide search to learn whether anyone had remained alive in her family. At first the information that reached her was that all had been killed. However, one dim ray of light breached the darkness. Someone informed her that he had heard that a boy whose family name was similar to hers had been brought to Israel with a Youth Aliyah group. The aunt immediately communicated with the administration of the Youth Aliyah, and she was informed that indeed a boy who bore her family name had immigrated to Israel. After investigating, it became clear to her that the boy was her nephew.

The aunt, who was well-to-do and childless, decided to adopt him. She came to Israel and appeared one morning at the house of the foster parents. She opened her heart to them and pleaded that the boy be released to her. In order to prepare for any untoward eventualities, she had submitted a formal legal request to adopt the boy and take him to her home in America.

On the day the case came up in court, all who were concerned showed up: the aunt, the foster parents, a representative of the Youth Aliyah, representatives of American agencies, authorized attorneys for both sides, witnesses, and the boy. He was now thirteen years of age. During the time he had lived with his foster parents he had grown and developed beautifully. The judge was confronted with a difficult legal decision and with the knowledge that, whatever the outcome, one party would suffer.

The aunt, who was an imposing and capable woman, testified in a voice drenched with tears, concerning the heartrending tragedy of her large and distinguished family in Poland, all of whom had been destroyed. The boy was the only one left among the living. Fortunately she was in a position to provide for all his needs and take full care of him. Could the court justify separating them now that she had found him at long last?

The family in whose home the boy had been reared also had a strong case. They, too, presented forceful, valid arguments in their favor. They had received a frail, sick child. Now he was a grown and delightful lad. They and their children love him as if he were of their own flesh and blood. He had adjusted very satisfactorily and was a full member of the family. They were ready to adopt him legally. The boy's welfare should come first. Did not justice dictate that he should remain with them and not go off to a new land whose language and ways of life were foreign to him? He had suffered enough in his short life. Why expose him to new trials and tribulations?

The lawyers and the agency representatives argued the legal and procedural aspects of the case, whatever the decision might be.

Now came the boy's turn. He asserted that he was no longer a youngster. He had a mind of his own and felt freely justified in his stand. His arguments were simple and moving. The bloody experiences that he had lived through were still part of him. They had not yet been wiped out from his consciousness. Here in Israel he had already struck roots, and he feared any changes that he must inevitably confront in a new country. True, he was still young, but he was already fed up with wandering over the face of the earth and grappling with new challenges and life styles. No, he would not leave this land under any circum-stances. He would not reopen old wounds and begin a new life amidst new, strange conditions.

The judge found himself facing a difficult decision. No matter what the solution, he would cause pain and heartache to one of the parties concerned. Both parties truly loved the boy and were concerned for his health and welfare — so much so that the aunt and her husband expressed their readiness to liquidate their property in America and settle in Israel permanently.

The case ended finally with a compromise that satisfied both sides. They both signed an agreement stating, among other terms, that the boy would remain where he was. The aunt would rent an apartment near him. She would begin to study Hebrew, so as to learn to communicate with her nephew, and would be permitted to visit him frequently. Time and circumstances would determine what the future would hold for them.

Since the case was not been reopened later, it would appear that the arrange-ment was carried out satisfactorily by all concerned.

A.E.

From *Yaldei Emutzim* ("Adopted Children") by Israel Supreme Court Justice Shneur Z. Hissin, published by Masada Press, 1955, pp. 131-133. Reported by attorney Dr. R. Ruckenstein.

19.

EPILOGUE

When Simon Wiesenthal left Mauthausen Camp in 1945, he determined that we
must never forget. *He vowed to do everything he could to seek out the Nazi
murderers, wherever they might be hidden, and bring them to justice. He
proceeded to organize a comprehensive, up-to-date index of Nazi criminals. He
set up a documentation center to trace missing relatives. He succeeded in
molding world public opinion and influencing various governments to prose-
cute and punish the guilty. He strove with notable success to achieve the
establishment of central governmental agencies to collect and set up files of
those guilty as well as documentation centers of the victims, the living survivors, and so forth. Lately he has been active in abolishing statutes of
limitation which had been adopted in certain countries, specifying the year
after which it would not be possible to bring the murderers to trial. (Indeed,
recently West Germany has abolished its statute of limitation, which had
originally specified the year 1979.) He has worked tirelessly and closely with
various governments to achieve these ends. In short, he has succeeded in
arousing the world's awareness of the enormity of the crime and the duty of
mankind to punish the criminals, whoever and wherever they may be. In the
span of a few years, his lifework struck deep roots and attracted devoted
co-workers and worldwide attention. He especially achieved worldwide fame
for his work in tracing Adolf Eichmann, which finally led to Eichmann's
capture and death. He is doggedly determined to ferret out and bring to justice
Dr. Mengele, Martin Bormann, and other noted criminals. His base of operations in Vienna.*

355

His fascinating story is told with the cooperation of a well-known writer, Joseph Wechsberg, in his book, The Murderers Among Us, *from which the following epilogue is taken. The epilogue illustrates the efforts now being made to rewrite the history of the tragedy, by such individuals as A.R. Butz of Evanston, Illinois, who published an outrageous book,* The Hoax of the Twentieth Century, *as well as others in the East, who are issuing a series of tracts entitled* Did Six Million Really Die? The Truth at Last.

At half past nine one night in October 1958, a friend called me in great excitement in my apartment in Linz. Could I come at once to the Landestheater?

A performance of *The Diary of Anne Frank* had just been interrupted by anti-Semitic demonstrations. Groups of young people, most of them between fifteen and seventeen, had shouted, "Traitors! Toadies! Swindle!" Others booed and hissed. The lights went on. From the gallery the youthful demonstrators showered leaflets upon the people in the orchestra. People who picked them up read:

> This play is a fraud. Anne Frank never existed. The Jews have invented the whole story because they want to extort more restitution money. Don't believe a word of it! It's a fake!

The police were summoned and took down the names of several demonstrators, students at local high schools. Then the performance continued. When I arrived at the Landestheater the play had just ended, but there was still much excitement. Two police cars were parked in front of the theater, and groups of young people stood around discussing the incident. I listened to them. The consensus seemed to be that the demonstrators had been right. This whole Anne Frank business was a fraud. Just as well that somebody had the guts to show those Jews what they thought of them.

Many of these young people had not yet been born when Anne Frank went to her death. And now, here in Linz, where Hitler had gone to school and Eichmann had grown up, they were told to believe in lies and hatred, prejudice and nihilism.

The next morning I went to the police and looked at the names of the arrested youths. It wasn't easy — they had powerful friends, and their parents wanted to quash the whole thing. After all, it wasn't really serious, they said; just a few young people raising hell and having fun. I was told that the names of the students would be given to their schools for disciplinary action. No one was punished. The boys in Linz didn't matter, I thought, but something else did. A few weeks earlier, a Lübeck high-school teacher, *Studienrat* Lothar Stielau, had publicly declared that Anne Frank's diary was a forgery. He had been sued by the girl's father, and three experts had confirmed the authenticity of the diary. According to the *Frankfurter Allgemeine Zeitung,* the defendant had for "six hours haggled about the wording of a confession. . . . The youth of Germany should be protected from such an 'educator.' "

The disorders in Linz seemed more serious to me because they were symptomatic. These young rowdies were not guilty; but their parents and teachers were. The older people were trying to poison the minds of the young generation because they wanted to justify their own doubtful past. Many of them were trapped by their heritage of ignorance, hatred, and bigotry. They hadn't learned anything from history. My experiences during these past twenty years have convinced me that the people of Germany and Austria are divided into three groups. There are the guilty ones who have committed crimes against humanity, although sometimes these crimes cannot be proved. There are their accomplices — those who haven't committed crimes but knew about them and did nothing to prevent them. And there are the innocent people. I believe it is absolutely necessary to separate the innocent people from the others. The young generation is innocent. Many of the young people I know are willing to walk the long road toward tolerance and reconciliation. But only if a clean and clear accounting is given will it be possible for the youth of Germany and Austria to meet the young people on the other side of the road — those who remember, from personal experience or from the reports of their parents, the horrors of the past. No apology can silence the voices of eleven million dead. The young Germans who pray at the grave of Anne Frank have long understood this. Reconciliation is possible only on the basis of knowledge. They must know what really happened.

A few days after the demonstrations in Linz, I gave a lecture on neo-Nazism at the headquarters of the Vienna archdiocese. The discussion that followed lasted until two in the morning. A professor reported an incident that had happened to a friend, a priest who taught religion at the *Gymnasium* in Wels, not far from Linz. The priest had been talking about Nazi atrocities at Mauthausen. One of the students stood up.

"Father, it's no use talking about those things. We know that the gas chambers of Mauthausen served only for the disinfection of clothes."

The priest was shocked. "But you've seen the newsreels, the photographs. You saw the bodies."

"Made of papier-mâché," said the boy. "Nothing but clever propaganda to make the Nazis look guilty."

"Who said that?"

"Everybody knows it. My father could tell you a lot about these things."

The priest had reported the incident to the boy's school principal. An investigation was started, and a survey made in the region. More than fifty per cent of the students in that class had parents who had been active in the Nazi movement. Their fathers loved to tell their sons about the heroism and glory of their past — how they had joined the Nazi Party in Austria in the early 1930s (when it was illegal), had helped blow up trains and bridges, had printed and distributed illegal literature against the Dollfuss government. Later the fathers had become proud SS men. It is not easy for young people to grow up in such an environment and remain unaffected by it. Their fathers had been afraid, and quiet, during the early postwar years, but in the late 1950s they were once more talking nostalgically about the great past. The boys would listen excitedly. Their schoolteachers, many of them former Nazis, did nothing to challenge the glorious stories told by the students' fathers.

I read *The Diary of Anne Frank* several times. I read it as a member of the human race, whose dignity had been gravely hurt; as a Jew who had lost six million of his own people; as a man who had decided to live for the dead, who wanted punishment, not revenge; and as the father of a girl who was just as old as Anne Frank was when she wrote her diary. It was only the will of God that my girl was not born early enough to suffer the fate of Anne Frank. Yet Anne Frank had not suffered more than a million other children. Her book had appeared when people were becoming indifferent to the tragedy of the past, when many said that they didn't want to hear about it any more, that one must stop hating. The words of a child had torn down a wall of moral apathy. Her last scream had broken through a worldwide barrier of callousness. She was no longer an anonymous body in a mass grave. She had become everybody's child.

Two days after the incident at the Landestheater, I was with a friend in a coffee house in Linz. Everybody was talking about the incident. Could the boys be blamed for the sins of their elders? Certainly they were not responsible.

A group of *Gymnasium* students sat down at the next table. My friend called over a boy whose parents he knew well.

"Fritz, were you at the theater during the demonstrations?"

"Unfortunately not, but some boys in my class were there. Two were even arrested," Fritz said proudly.

"What do you think about it?" my friend said.

"Well — it's easy. There is no evidence that Anne Frank lived."

"But the diary?" I said.

"The diary may be a clever forgery. Certainly it doesn't prove that Anne Frank existed."

"She's buried in a mass grave in Bergen-Belsen."

He gave a shrug. "There is no proof."

Proof. One would have to produce proof — irrefutable proof that would convince these young skeptics. One would have to tear one single brick out of the edifice of lies that had been constructed; then the whole structure would collapse. But to find that one brick . . .

Something occurred to me. I said, "Young man, if we could prove to you that Anne Frank existed, would you except the diary as genuine?"

He looked at me. "How can you prove it?"

"Her father is alive."

"That proves nothing."

"Wait. Her father reported to the authorities that they were arrested by the Gestapo."

"Yes," the boy said impatiently. "We've heard all that."

"Suppose the Gestapo officer who actually arrested Anne Frank were found. Would *that* be accepted as proof?"

He seemed startled. The idea had never occurred to him.

"Yes," he said at last, reluctantly. "*If* the man himself admitted it."

It was simple: I had to find the man who had arrested Anne Frank fourteen years before. Tens of thousands of people had been taken away all over Europe by nameless little men, the anonymous handymen of death. Even in the concentration camp we didn't always know the names of our torturers. They were aware of the possible consequences and tried to camouflage their identity.

There was almost nothing to go on. The diary ended abruptly when Anne Frank had been taken away. Anne's father, Otto Frank, had owned the export firm of Kolen & Co. After the Nazi confiscation of all Jewish property in Holland, a Dutch employee of Kolen & Co., Paul Kraler, had taken the firm into trusteeship. He had helped the Franks hide in the attic of the building in Prinzengracht, where the firm had its offices.

In an appendix to the diary, Kraler recalled that after the arrest of the Franks he tried to intervene on their behalf at the Amsterdam Gestapo headquarters. He had spoken with the officer who had arrested the family, a Viennese SS man who, he said, was named Silvernagl. The intervention had not been successful. Kraler's report caused ironic comment among the Austrian Nazis. It was naturally well known that the name Silvernagl did not exist in Austria — further proof that the Anne Frank story was a fake.

I had very little to start out with. I knew that the SS man was Viennese or at least Austrian — many Austrians abroad call themselves Viennese. He must have been an SS man of low rank, since his job was to arrest people — SS *Schütze,* SS *Rottenführer* or, at the most, SS *Unterscharführer.*

That narrowed it down. The *v* in Silvernagl was probably Kraler's error; it could have been Silbernagel, a common name in Austria. Seven people named Silbernagel were listed in the Vienna telephone directory; almost a hundred more were in various city registers. The name was also well known in the provinces of Carinthia and Burgenland. If at least I knew the man's first name!

I continued to search. Among all the Silbernagels there must have been one who had held a low SS rank during the war and had served in Holland with the Gestapo. Names were investigated and eliminated. Rumors were sifted, facts checked. It was a long, tedious process, and I had to be extremely careful. If I implicated an innocent man, I might be sued for libel.

When the police want to find a motorist who has committed a crime, they can stop all cars and ask all the drivers for their licenses, and no one can protest. I couldn't do that. I found eight men named Silbernagel who had been Nazi Party members of SS men and were of the right age. One of them, a former *Obersturmführer* (a high rank, which automatically excluded him from my list), is now a prominent functionary in Burgenland. In any event, he had never been in Holland.

I asked a friend to contact private detective agencies and inquiry offices. He told each of them that he had been asked for a credit by a man named Silbernagel; always a different Silbernagel, to be sure. He said he wanted to check on the man's record during the Nazi era. We got much information, but none seemed to point to the man I was looking for. Once I asked a bank for the credit rating of a man named Silbernagel. Banks do a thorough job, but once again the result was negative. Two more Silbernagels were found to be former Nazis, but that was hardly a startling discovery. I came close to giving up the search, but then I remembered the arrogant faces of the boys in Linz. I wanted them to go to their fathers and tell them, "You lied, Anne Frank did exist. What other lies did you tell me?"

In 1963 I was invited to appear on the Dutch television network. In Amster-

dam, I went to the Anne Frank House, now a memorial, and I touched the walls
the girl had touched. I talked to the custodian of the house. He said he'd often wondered about the man who had taken the girl and her family away.
No one had any idea who it had been. He'd asked people and they had just
shrugged.

"Nineteen years is a long time," he said. "It seems hopeless."

"Nothing is ever hopeless," I said. "Just suppose that I found the SS man
who arrested her, and that he confessed that he had done it?"

The man gave me a long glance. "Then you would have written the missing
epilogue to Anne Frank's diary."

For a while I thought I should go and see Otto Frank, Anne's father. He *might*
remember the man who had come for them on the morning of August 4, 1944.
He *might* be able to describe him to me. Any lead would help. The SS man must
have changed in all these years — but there might be *something* to recognize
him by.

I did not contact Mr. Frank. I admit it was not only my reluctance at upsetting
this man who had suffered so much, at forcing him to search his memory once
again. Something else bothered me. Suppose Mr. Frank asked me *not* to do
anything about it? Could I comply with his request? I'd met other people who
had not wanted me to search for the people who had killed their fathers and
mothers and children. They said they couldn't bear it. "What the use?" they
asked. "You cannot bring back the dead. You can only make the survivors
suffer."

I was still wondering what to do when I read in the papers that Mr. Frank, at a
meeting in Germany, had spoken out in favor of forgiveness and reconciliation.
The German papers praised his magnanimity and tolerance. I respect Otto
Frank's point of view. He has revealed the ethics of a man who doesn't just
preach forgiveness but also practices it. But I am above all concerned with the
practical and legal aspects of the case. Time and again I saw how tolerance and
forgiveness were misunderstood by the Nazis. The fact that the father of Anne
Frank had pardoned the murderers of his child was cited as an important
argument in favor of ending the prosecution of all Nazi crimes. "What is good
enough for Otto Frank should be good enough for anyone," it was said. "If he
forgives, then all ought to forgive." Mr. Frank's conscience permits him to
forgive. My conscience forces me to bring the guilty ones to trial. Obviously we
operate on different ethical levels; we follow different paths. Somewhere our
paths meet, and we complete each other.

I remember a discussion I had after the war with a Catholic priest. He said,
"We must forgive them. They will come before the High Tribunal of God."

"Father," I said, "why is it that the very criminals who don't believe in God
always try to avoid human justice and prefer to await God's reckoning?"

He had no answer.

Presently friends in Holland told me that the SS man I was looking for might
not be named Silbernagel but Silbertaler. Several people called Silbertaler had
lived in Vienna before the war, but they were Jews and had disappeared. I found
three non-Jewish Silbertalers in Vienna and elsewhere in Austria, but none had
been active Nazis. I began to realize that it was highly improbable that I would

ever find the one historical witness I needed. I began to wonder whether this witness was still alive.

On my next visit to Amsterdam I happened to talk to two friends, both familiar with the case of Anne Frank. They were Ben A. Sijes of the Dutch Institute for War Documentation and a Mr. Taconis, a high-ranking Dutch police official. Many names were mentioned in the course of our conversation — SS leaders Wilhelm Harster, Alfons Werner, Willy Zoepf, Gertrud Slottke, and others who had worked for Eichmann. In our line of work, one criminal leads to another. There were new leads, new names I'd never heard of. As I got ready to leave, Taconis said he had some "travel literature" for me, and he smiled. He brought me a photostatic copy of the 1943 telephone directory of the Gestapo in Holland. There were about three hundred names in it.

"Read it on the plane," he said. "That will keep you awake."

"On the contrary. Looking through a telephone directory has a soporific effect on me. When I'm in a hotel room in a strange place, I usually look through the local directory. Always makes me sleepy."

The flight to Vienna lasted about two hours. I settled back in my seat and looked through the Gestapo directory. I was almost asleep when I turned to the page headed "IV, *Sonderkommando.*" Under "IV B 4, *Joden* [Jews]" I read:

Kempin
Buschmann
Sherf
Silberbauer

I was wide awake. Section IV B 4 had handled the roundup and transport of Jews to death camps. If anyone had tipped off the Gestapo about Jews hiding out somewhere in Holland, the report would inevitably reach Section IV B 4 in Amsterdam. All of a sudden the plane seemed to be very slow. I could hardly wait to get to Vienna. I knew that most officials of Section IV B 4 had been recruited from police forces in Germany and Austria, mostly among the *Kriminalpolizei* (detectives).

Back home, before I could take off my coat, I opened the Vienna telephone directory. My heart sank. There were almost a dozen people called Silberbauer. Probably there were many more in other Austrian city directories. If I had to investigate each of them, as I had the Silbernagels and Silbertalers before, years might go by. I had reached the stage where some deductive thinking was needed. I couldn't investigate everyone named Silberbauer. I decided I would look for a man of that name who had worked (or was still working) for the Vienna police. It was like solving an equation with many unknown factors with the help of one known factor. I had to start from a definite premise if I wanted to build a structure.

I called up *Polizeirat* Dr. Josef Wiesinger, head of Section IIc at the Ministry of the Interior, which deals with Nazi crimes. Wiesinger has often helped me with my investigations. I told him — rather boastfully, I'm afraid — that I found the Gestapo man who arrested Anne Frank.

"He's a Viennese policeman named Silberbauer," I said.

Wiesinger didn't call my bluff. "What's his first name?"

"I don't know his first name."

"There must be at least six men called Silberbauer on the Vienna police force," he said. "Which one do you want?"

"That should be easy to find. All you have to do is go through their service records. I want the man who was with Section IV B 4 in Amsterdam in August 1944."

"That was nineteen years ago," Wiesinger said skeptically.

"Your records go back that far, don't they?"

"All right," he said. "Submit a written request to my office."

On June 2, 1963, I mailed a detailed report. Several weeks went by. When I went to see Wiesinger in July about something else, I asked again about Silberbauer. He said the files of all policemen called Silberbauer were "still being examined." In September, when I was back from my vacation, I called him again. I was told that "so far nothing concrete had become known."

On October 15, Sijes and Taconis came from Amsterdam to discuss several war-crimes cases in Holland with me. We went to see Dr. Wiesinger. Once more I asked him about Silberbauer. My Dutch friends, I said, would be eager to get some news.

"Sorry," said Dr. Wiesinger. "We are not yet ready with this matter." I noticed a certain edge in his voice but wrote it off to impatience or overwork. I was wrong.

On the morning of November 11, *Volksstimme,* the official organ of Austria's Communist Party, came out with a sensational story. *Inspektor* Karl Silberbauer of the Vienna police force had been suspended "pending investigation and possible prosecution" for his role in the Anne Frank case. The Communists made the most of their scoop. Radio Moscow broadcast that the captor of Anne Frank had been unmasked "through the vigilance of Austria's resistance fighters and progressive elements." *Izvestia* later praised the detective work of the Austrian comrades.

I telephoned Dr. Wiesinger. He was embarrassed. "Naturally we would have preferred to have the story disclosed by you, and not by the Communists. How could we know that Silberbauer was going to talk? He was supposed to keep his mouth shut."

I decided not to keep mine shut either. I called a Dutch newspaper editor in Amsterdam and gave him the story. It made front-page news all over the world. I received more cables and letters than I had after Eichmann's capture. There were radio and TV interviews. Paul Kraler, now in Canada, told the world about how the Franks had lived up there in the attic. And in Switzerland, Mr. Frank said that he had always known that their Gestapo captor had been an SS man named Silberbauer.

Everybody was excited except the Austrian authorities, who said they didn't comprehend "what all the fuss was about," as one high-ranking official said to me. The journalists wanted to talk to Silberbauer, but the Minister of the Interior refused to release pictures of Silberbauer and tried to keep him incommunicado. I didn't go along with this. I gave Silberbauer's private address to a Dutch newspaperman. I thought the Dutch were entitled to at least one exclusive interview. When the Dutchman came to see Silberbauer, he found the police inspector (the second-lowest rank in the Austrian police) in a very angry mood. He said he'd been railroaded.

"Why pick on me after all these years? I only did my duty. We've just bought some new furniture, on installment, and now they suspended me. How am I going to pay for the furniture?"

"Don't you feel sorry about what you did?" the reporter asked.

"Sure I feel sorry. Sometimes I feel downright humiliated. Now each time I take a streetcar I have to buy a ticket, just like everyone else. I can no longer show my service pass."

"And what about Anne Frank? Have you read her diary?"

Silberbauer shrugged. "Bought the little book last week to see whether I'm in it. But I am not."

The reporter said, "Millions of people have read the diary before you. And you could have been the first who read it."

Silberbauer looked at him in surprise. "Say, that's true. I never thought of it. Maybe I should have picked it up from the floor."

If he had, no one would ever have heard of him — or of Anne Frank.

When Dr. Wiesinger had told me, on October 15, "We are not yet ready with this matter," he already knew that *Inspektor* Karl Silberbauer, attached to First District Police Headquarters, had admitted that he had been in charge of the Gestapo posse, that he had personally arrested Anne Frank and the other people in the attic in Amsterdam, on the morning of August 4, 1944. I asked Dr. Wiesinger why we had kept this information from me. He said he'd had "orders from above" to keep the matter a secret.

After the capitulation of Germany, Silberbauer had fled from the Netherlands and returned to Vienna. Since he had left the Vienna police force in 1943 to join the SS, he had to submit to "denazifiation" proceedings in 1952. He was cleared and returned to duty with the rank of inspector.

For a month after Silberbauer's confession, his superiors had done nothing. On October 4 he was suspended from service and was ordered not to mention a word about the whole matter, pending investigation. A month later, Silberbauer complained to a colleague that he'd had "some trouble because of that Anne Frank." The colleague, a member of the Communist Party of Austria — there are some Communists in Vienna's police force — reported the story to the Communist organization of former concentration-camp inmates. At a meeting on November 10, another man told the story. The following morning *Volksstimme* had its scoop.

The Austrian authorities found no evidence that Silberbauer was guility of the deportation of the Franks. A spokesman for the Interior Ministry said that the arrest of Anne Frank "did not warrant Silberbauer's arrest or prosecution as a war criminal." He had only obeyed orders. Disciplinary proceedings followed, because Silberbauer had concealed from the denazification board the fact that he had worked for the Jewish Affairs Section of the Gestapo in Holland.

Mr. Frank, asked to testify, said his captor had "only done his duty and acted correctly."

"The only thing I ask is not to have to see the man again," said Anne Frank's father.

A police review board exonerated Silberbauer of any official guilt. He is back on the Vienna police force, assigned to the *Erkennungamt* (Identification office).

Incidentally, Silberbauer had been working at police headquarters during all those years I'd been looking for him. It's a ten-minute walk from my office to headquarters. Probably we'd met in the street. And also, across from our Documentation Center there is a big textile store with a sign reading SILBER-BAUER. A second such store, also called SILBERBAUER, is next to the entrance to our building. Of course, Silberbauer doesn't matter at all. Compared to other names in my files, he is a nobody, a zero. But the figure before the zero was Anne Frank.

From *The Murderers Among Us: The Wiesenthal Memoirs,* edited by Joseph Wechsberg, New York: McGraw Hill, © 1967.

On October 29, 1979, the Jewish Telegraphic Association released the news of a landmark decision by the West German Supreme Court which stated that the unique fate of Jews give them a claim to regard and respect from all German citizens, that the Holocaust is part of the consciousness of Jews and it is a matter of their personal dignity to be perceived as the group who suffered persecution and to whom other citizens bear a moral responsibility.

The court said that respect for these feelings had to be regarded as a guarantee for the non-repetition of the past and an essential condition making it possible for Jews to live in Germany. Whoever denies the truth of past events denies to every Jew the respect to which he is entitled, the court declared.

It added that any attempt to justify, to gloss over, or to dispute the facts of the Holocaust shows contempt against every person identified with persecution. Finally, the court affirmed that the evidence of the facts of the Holocaust is overwhelming.

TEREZIN

That bit of filth in dirty walls,
And all around barbed wire.
And 300,000 souls who sleep,
Who once will wake
And once will see
Their own blood spilled.

I was once a little child,
Three years ago.
That child who longed for other worlds.
But now I am no more a child,
For I have learned to hate.
I am a grown-up person now,
I have known fear.

Bloody words and a dead day then,
That's something different from bogey men!

But anyway, I still believe I only sleep today,
That I'll wake up, a child again, and start to laugh and play.
I'll go back to childhood sweet like a briar rose,
Like a bell which wakes us from a dream,
Like a mother with an ailing child
Loves him with aching woman's love.
How tragic, then, is youth which lives
With enemies, with gallows ropes,
How tragic, then, for children on your lap
To say: this for the good, that for the bad.

Somewhere, far away out there, childhood sweetly sleeps,
Along that path among the trees,
There o'er that house,
Which was once pride and joy.
There my mother gave me birth into this world
So I could weep. . . .

— Hanul
Hochberg

Acknowledgments

Efforts have been made to obtain appropriate permissions to reprint the copyrighted materials included in this volume. Grateful acknowledgments are made to all those named below and in the pages that follow. If notified of errors and omissions, the editor and publisher will make necessary corrections in future editions.

"I Never Saw Another Butterfly" by Pavel Friedman, from *I Never Saw Another Butterfly*, edited by H. Volavkova. © 1964 McGraw-Hill Book Company. Used with permission.

"The Lament on the Slaughtered Jewish People" by Yitzhak Katzenelson, from *The Massacre of European Jewry*. Reprinted with permission of World Shomer Hatzair, Kibbutz Merhavian, Israel.

"How Their Little Hearts Must Have Trembled" by Kyril Sosnowsky. Reprinted from *The Tragedy of Children Under Nazi Rule*, 1962.

1. Prelude to Doom

"Don't Trust the Fox in the Green Meadow nor the Jew on His Oath;" "Letters by Teachers of German Public Schools;" "The Cuckoo and the Jew." All published by *Der Stürmer* in 1935 and quoted in *Conspiracy and Aggression: International Military Tribunal of Nazi War Criminals*, the United States Printing Office, 1946.

"Heil Hitler! 50 to 150 Times a Day," from *School for Barbarians* by Erika Mann, published by Modern Age Books, 1938, pp. 21–23.

"Skepticism and Participation" by Ilse McKee. Quoted in *Nazi Culture*, published by University Library, Grosset and Dunlap, 1966. Reprinted by permission.

"Neighbors in a Berlin Apartment House," from *Account Rendered: A Dossier on my Former Self* by Melita Maschmann. Trans. By Geoffrey Strachan (Abelard-Schuman). English language translation copyright © 1964 by Harper & Row, Publishers, Inc. Reprinted by permission of the publisher.

"Babi Yar," from *Babi Yar* by Anatoly Kuznetsov, trans. by Jacob Gurolsky. Copyright © 1966, 1967 by The Dial Press. Permission granted by The Dial Press.

"The Kristallnacht Riots and Pogroms," from *Crystal Night* by Rita Thalman and Emmanuel Feinermann. Reprinted by permission of the Holocaust Library, New York.

2. Jewish Children's Exodus

"Flight to England," from *We Came as Children* by Karen Gershon (London: Victor Gollancz Ltd., 1966). Reprinted by permission.

"Castles of Refuge in France," from *Out of the Fire* by Ernst Papanek with Edward Linn (New York: William Morrow, 1975). Reprinted by permission of The Sterling Lord Agency, Inc.

"First Youth Aliyah Group in Berlin," from a report by Franz and Ruth Ollendorf in *Let the Children Come* by Recha Freier (London: Weidenfeld and Nicolson, 1961). Reprinted by permission of Recha Freier.

"Henrietta Szold Welcomes First Youth Aliyah Group from Germany," from *Youth Aliyah Letters* by Henrietta Szold, Bulletin No. 2 (25 February 1934).

"Exiled Children Part from Their Doomed Parents at Camp Gurs, France, 1941," from *Contemporary Jewish Record* by Isaac Chomski (New York: American Jewish Committee). Reprinted with permission of the author.

3. Extirpating the Unborn Generation

"Mixed Marriages and Sterilization — A Cruel Hoax," from *Year of Fear* by Philip Mechanicus, trans. from the Dutch by Irene S. Gibbons. Reprinted by permission of Hawthorn Properties (Elsevier-Dutton Publishing Co., Inc.). Copyright © 1964 by Polak en Van Gennep, Amsterdam.

"Newborn Babies and Pregnant Mothers Put to Death, from "The Fate of Jeanette's Twins," from *I Was a Doctor in Auschwitz* by Giselle Perl (New York: International Universities Press, 1948). Reprinted by permission.

"Leo Baeck Prevents an Abortion." Reprinted with permission of Macmillan Publishing Co., Inc. from *Days of Sorrow and Pain: Leo Baeck and the Berlin Jews* by Leonard Baker. Copyright © 1978 by Leonard Baker.

4. Children in the Nazi Ghetto

"A Memorial to a Three-Year-Old" by Eliezer Yerushalmi, from *An Anthology of Holocaust Literature,* edited by J. Glatstein, I. Knox, and S. Margoshes (Philadelphia, PA: Jewish Publication Society of America, 1969). Trans by Adah Fogel. Reprinted by permission of the Jewish Publication Society of America.

"Families in the Bunkers," from *Bamachnot Lo Bachu (In the Camps They Did Not Weep)* by Dr. Aharon Peretz (Ramat Gan, Israel: Massada Press, 1960).

"Live Game," from *Bialy Orzel (The White Eagle),* trans. into Hebrew by Moshe Prager.

"We Will Not Hand Over the Children Alive," from *Reim Basa'ar (Comrades in the Storm)* by Fredka Mazia (Israel: Yad Vashem, 1964).

5. Spiritual Resistance

"School Life in the Vilna Ghetto: The First Year," from *Yerushalayim Shel d'Lita Bamri Uvashoah (The Jerusalem of Lithuania [Vilna] in Resistance and Destruction)* by Marck Dvorjecki. Published by the Israel Labor Party, 1951, pp. 215 – 22 (with deletions).

"An Underground Yeshiva in the Warsaw Ghetto" by Dr. Hillel Seidman, from *Warsaw Ghetto Diary.* Published by Central Association of Polish Jews in Argentina in cooperation with Federation of Polish Jews in America, Buenos Aires, 1947, pp. 221 – 26. Reprinted with permission of the author.

"Clandestine Hebrew High School in the Warsaw Ghetto," quoted in *Flame and Fury,* compiled by Yakov Shilhav, edited and trans. by Sara Feinstein (New York: Jewish Education Committee Press, 1962), pp. 28 – 30. Reprinted with permission.

"Self-Aid in the Ghetto" and "This Is Jewish Revenge." Reprinted with permission of Macmillan Publishing Co., Inc. from *Scroll of Agony: The Warsaw Diary of Chaim A. Kaplan, trans. and edited by Abraham I. Katsh.* Copyright © Abraham I. Katsh 1965.

"A Concert in Korczak's Orphanage," from *Warsaw Diary* by Michael Zylberberg (London: Vallentine, Mitchell & Co. Ltd.). Reprinted by permission of the publisher.

"Kiddush Ha-Shem by Son and Father," from *Zakhor (Remember)* by Eliezer Unger (Israel: Massada Press, 1946), pp. 151 – 53, 106.

"The Circumcision," from *Ani Maamin (I Believe)* (Israel: Mosad HaRav Kook, 1969), pp. 93*f*.

"In the Cemetery New Life Is Born," from *Pinkas Shavili* by Eliezer Yerushalmi (Israel: Masad Bialk and Yad Vashem, 1958), pp. 148 – 49.

6. Children's Diaries

Excerpts from *Anne Frank, The Diary of a Young Girl* by Anne Frank. Copyright 1952 by Otto H. Frank. Reprinted by permission of Doubleday & Company, Inc.

"Diary of Moshe Flinker: Thoughts of My People Never Leave My Mind," from *Diary of Moshe Flinker* (Israel: Yad Vashem, 1965), pp. 82– 84.

"Yitzhak Rudashevsky Records Aspects of Life in the Vilna Ghetto," from *Diary of a Boy from Vilna, Yitzhak Rudashevsky* (Israel: Hakibbutz Hameuchad and Ghetto Fighters House, 1973), pp. 51– 52. Trans. by Percy Matenko.

"Excerpts from the Diary of David Rubinovicz: The Rural Scene," from *Diary of David Rubinovicz* (Israel: Ghetto Fighters House and Hakibbutz Hameuchad, 1964), pp. 9, 23*f*, 29*f*, 69*f*.

"Eva Heyman's Diary: The Disintegration of Her Family," from *Diary of Eva Heyman* (Israel: Yad Vashem, 1974), trans. by Moshe M. Kohn, pp. 68– 78.

Extracts from Tamarah Lazerson's Diary: Discovering Zionism and Judaism," from *Tamarah's Diary* by Tamarah Lazerson (Israel: Ghetto Fighters House and Hakibbutz Hameuchad, 1966).

"Excerpts from Janina Heshele's Diary of Lvov," from *Hayeled Vehanoar BaShoa Ugvurah (Children and Youth in the Holocaust and Resistance)* (Israel: Kiryat Sefer, 1965), pp. 165– 76.

7. "What Happened to Me"—Children's Stories

"Haviva Dembinska: A Survivor of the Destruction of the Warsaw Ghetto," "Edmund Lubianker: A Survivor of Boryslaw, Near Lvov," from *Echad M'eer Ushnayim Mimishpachah (One of a City and Two of a Family)*, compiled by Benjamin Tench, Sifriat Poalim, 1947.

"A Boy Survives the Destruction of the Warsaw Ghetto," from *The Destruction and Rebellion of the Jews of Warsaw*, vol. II compiled and edited by Melech Neishtadt (Israel: General Workers Party of Eretz Yisrael, 1948), pp. 301– 6. Translated from the Yiddish.

"Five Years of Bitter Exile and Wanderings Through Siberia and African Jungles to Eretz Yisrael," "Hear, O Israel," "Written Down for the Sake of History," from *Rescued Children* by Bracha Habas. Published by Palestine Pioneer Library, n.d.

"Hiding in a Bunker, Passing as an Aryan: Manya's Unforgettable Story," from *Massacre of European Jewry*. Story by Lena Kichler; published by World Hashomer Haztair, 1963, pp. 166– 74.

8. Camps

"Deportation of Jewish Children from Paris to Drancy," from *Betrayal at the Vel d'Hiv* by Claude Lévy and Paul Tillard (New York: Hill & Wang, 1969), trans. by Inea Bushnag. Reprinted by permission of Georges Borchardt, Inc.

"What Happened to Four Thousand French Jewish Children," from *Mishpat Eichmann (Testimony at the Eichmann Trial)* by George Wellers (Israel: Yad Vashem, Israel Information Office, 1974), pp. 425– 46.

"Janusz Korczak Marches to Death with His Children," based on writings by Nahum Remba, Halina Pinconson, Anthony Shimansky and on works by Shimon Frost, *Jewish Education Magazine*, Winter 1963.

"Reception at Auschwitz," from pp. 49– 59 in *I Am Alive* by Kitty Hart (Abelard-Schuman). Copyright © 1961 by Kitty Hart. Reprinted by permission of Harper & Row, Publishers, Inc.

"Child Hell in Auschwitz," from *This Was Oswiecim, The Story of a Murder Camp* by Philip Friedman, trans. from the Yiddish by Joseph Leftwich (London: United Jewish Appeal, 1946).

"The Gas Chamber," from *Nazi Conspiracy and Aggression*, vol. VI, Office of United States Chief Counsel for Prosecution of Axis Criminality, U.S. Government Printing Office, 1946; vol. XI, pp. 1100– 3 (Document D251).

"A Deed of Savagery" by Leib Langfus, 1962, from *Aleph-Tav* Magazine, *Tel Aviv University Review*, Spring 1975.

"Dr. Mengele's Inhuman Experiments," from *Auschwitz, A Doctor's Eyewitness Account* by Dr. Miklos Nyiszli (New York: Fawcett Publications, 1960). Reprinted by permission.

"An Incomparable Atrocity: Story of a *Piepel*," from *Nerot Meukolim (Burnt Out Lights)* by Mordecai Shtrigler (Israel: Am Oved, 1946). Reprinted by permission.

"Changing *Piepels*," from *They Called Him Piepel* by K. Tzetnik (London: Blond, 1961), pp. 13– 29.

"Obliteration of the Corpses by the Death Brigade," from *The Death Brigade* by Leon Welles (New York: Holocaust Library, 1980). Reprinted by permission.

"Children's Identifications of Names Written in Blood," from *I Was a Doctor in Auschwitz* by Giselle Perl (New York: International Universities Press, 1948), pp. 48–52.

"Giving Birth in Auschwitz," from *I Was a Doctor in Auschwitz* by Giselle Perl (New York: International Universities Press, 1948), pp. 80–86.

"Halina Never Lost Hope," from *Hope Is the Last to Die* by Halina Birenbaum (Boston, MA: Twayne Publishers, 1967), pp. 136–41. Trans. from the Polish by David Welsch. Reprinted by permission of the author.

"Budee—The Camp the World Forgot" by Betty Steck. Copyright 1977, the JEWISH EXPONENT of Philadelphia. Reprinted with permission.

9. The Killer Squads

"The Kill," from *The Forest, My Friend* by Donia Rosen, published by Bergen-Belsen Memorial Press, trans. by Mordecai S. Chertoff, pp. 12–18.

"Portrait of a Nazi Killer of Children," from *The Eichmann Kommandos* by Michael A. Mussmano (Turbotville, PA: Macrae Smith, 1961), pp. 112–21.

10. Passing as Aryans

"Phimosis Is Not a Circumcision," from *A Bag Full of Marbles* by Joseph Joffo. Copyright © 1974 by Joseph Joffo. Reprinted by permission of Houghton Mifflin Company.

"Margo Bleaches Her Hair Blond to Survive," from *Bitter Herbs* by Marga Minco, trans. by Roy Edwards, © Oxford University Press 1960. Reprinted by permission of Oxford University Press.

"An Old Christian Woman Hides a Friend," from *The Forest, My Friend* by Donia Rosen. Quoted in *Flame and Fury,* compiled by Yaacov Shilhav, edited by Sara Feinstein, trans. by David Kuselewitz (New York: Jewish Education Committee Press, 1962).

"Horrors and Tragedy of a Winter in the Forest," from *Winter in the Forest* by Feiga Kammer, in *Anthology of Holocaust Literature,* op. cit., pp. 155–57. Trans. from the Yiddish by Moishe Spiegel.

"If Only I Could Be a Little Bug," from *Child of the Holocaust* by Jack Kuper (New York: The New American Library, 1980). Reprinted by permission.

11. Physical Resistance and Vitality

"A Boy Grows Up in Auschwitz," from *Anoshim V'Ofer (Men and Dust —Auschwitz and Birkenau)* by Yisrael Gutman and Leon Shlofsky.

"Determined to Live Through Auschwitz," from *Yaldut B'tzel Ha'arubah (Childhood in the Shadow of the Auschwitz Chimney)* by Zvi Goldberg. Special Edition, Israel, 1975, pp. 42–46.

"Sonderkommando in Birkenau" by Shaye Gertner, from *Anthology of Holocaust Literature,* op. cit., pp. 141–47.

"Blowing the Shofar in Auschwitz," from *Ani Maamin (I Believe)* by Rabbi Tzvi Hirsch Meislish (Israel: Mossad HaRav Kook), pp. 93*f*, p. 435. Quoted from "Responsa on Sanctification of God's Name" in *Shaar Machmadim,* 1964.

"A Sequence of Horrors in the Ghetto, Auschwitz, and Death March" by J.A. of Cracow. Copyright © 1978 by Isaiah Trunk. From the book *Jewish Responses to Nazi Persecution.* Reprinted with permission of Stein and Day Publishers.

"Gretel's Inscription," "The God Moment," "The Bread Crust," "An Imaginary Tune that Saved a Life," from *Hiyuniyut Yehdit Bashoah (Jewish Vitality During the Holocaust),* edited by Carmon A. and Oren I., Israel Office of Education and Culture, Dept. of Pedagogics, 1925, pp. 28*f*.

12. Family Camps in the Forests

"Motele, An Exemplar of the Child Partisan Movement," from *They Fought Back,* edited and trans. by Yuri Suhl (New York: Crown Publishers, 1975), pp. 262–67.

"David, A Partisan from the Editor's Home Town," from *Kiddush HaShem (Sanctification of God's Name)* by Sh. Niger (New York: Cyco Bicher Ferlag, 1948), pp. 646–48. Quoted from story by Jacob Pat in the *New York Jewish Daily Forward,* 19 June 1946.

"The Courage of a Ten-Year-Old Partisan" by Hananiah Kutin, trans. from the Hebrew from *One from a City and Two from a Family,* op. cit., pp. 224–28.

"Dr. Atlas's Forest Partisans," trans. from *Plugat Hadoctor Atlas (Dr. Atlas's Battalion),* by Shmuel Bernstein (Israel: Ghetto Fighters House and Hakibbutz Hameuchad, 1972), pp. 99*f*, 165*f*.

"Incidents in the Life of an Eleven-Year-Old Fighter," trans. from *Kiddush HaShem*, op. cit., pp. 650–53.

"Children Couriers in the Ghetto of Minsk," from *They Fought Back*, op. cit., pp. 241–45.

"Smuggling Arms for the Partisan Fighters," from *The Partisans: From the Valley of Death to Mount Zion* by Yitzhak Arad (New York: Holocaust Library, 1979). Used by permission.

"The Vow and the Charge," from *The Hundred Who Returned to Their Homeland* by Lena Kichler-Zilberman. Quoted in the *Guidelines to the Memorial Day of the Holocaust and Valor* (11 April 1972) (Israel: Office of Information and Education of the Israel Defense Forces).

13. Rescuers, Saviors and Righteous Gentiles

"A Discussion Pro and Con About the Rescuing of Jewish Children by Priests" by Emmanuel Ringelblum, from *Notes from the Warsaw Ghetto: The Journal of Emmanuel Ringelblum*, trans. by Jacob Sloan, copyright © 1958 Jacob Sloan. Reprinted by permission of McGraw Hill Book Company.

"Rescuing Children from the Ghetto in Soup Pots," from *Witness to Truth* by Nathan Shappel (New York: David McKay Co., 1974).

"How the French Saved Jewish Children," from *Menorah Journal* by Victor Bienstock, Spring 1945, pp. 93–97.

"The Little Dane: Blessed 'Mother' of Forty Children," from *Righteous Gentiles* by Aryah Bauminger (Israel Office of Education and Culture, 1967), pp. 33–38.

"The Affair of the Finaly Children" by Nicolas Baudy. Reprinted from *Commentary*, June 1953, by permission; all rights reserved.

"A Gift of Life from German Mothers," from *Children of Innocence*, op. cit., p. 31.

14. The Teheran Children

"Sands of Pahlevi," from *Red and White and the Aroma of Oranges: The Children of Teheran*, edited and trans. by BenZion Toma (Israel: World Zionist Organization, 1972), pp. 84–92.

"In Memoriam to the Children of Teheran" *(Yiskor Leyaldei Teheran)*, by Meir Ohad (Israel: Public Commission to Commemorate the Teheran Children, 1977), pp. 220–24.

"The Babies Who Wouldn't Cry," from an unpublished manuscript by Asher Lazar.

15. Palestine

"Memorandum to the Italian Foreign Minister from the Jerusalem Mufti," amin El Husseini.

"A Near Catastrophe at the Border of Austria and Italy," from *Heres U'Tkumah (Destruction and Revival)* by Moshe Weiszand (Israel: Hamenorah, 1970), p. 191*f*.

"Rescued from the S.S. Patria at the Haifa Port," from *Yeladim Mutzalim (Rescued Children)* by Bracha Habas, op. cit., pp. 63–73.

"Tel Aviv Children Battle the British," from article in *Commentary*, December 1945, by Meyer Leven.

"The Mute," from an unpublished manuscript by Asher Lazer.

16. Liberation

"Mama, May I Cry Now?" from *Testimony at the Eichmann Trial* by Abba Kovner, vol. I, p. 335, 1974.

"The March," from *World Over Magazine* by Helen Lazaros (New York: Board of Jewish Education of Greater New York), 7 April 1976.

"First Baby Born at Belsen Hails Liberation Day," from *I Was a Doctor in Auschwitz* by Giselle Perl, op. cit.

"The Children of Belsen," from *Belsen* by Hadassah Bimko-Rosensaft, published by *Irgun Sheerit Hapletah Mehaozor Habriti (Survivors of the Holocaust in the British Zone)*, 1957, Israel, pp. 98–105.

"Liberated After Living Through the Hell of Nine Camps," from an unpublished manuscript by Dr. Moshe Avital.

"We Shall Not Set Foot on Germany's Cursed Soil," from *Hameah Ligvulam (The Hundred Come Home)* by Lena Kichler Silberman (New York: Schocken, 1969), pp. 31–35.

"Thank You for Our Tears," from *Children of Innocence*, op. cit., pp. 20–22.

"A Reversal of Roles," from *Children of Innocence*, op. cit., pp. 20–22.

"Sweden Gladly Welcomes the Refugee Children," from *I'm Still Living* by Chava Kwinta (Toronto, Canada: Simon and Pierre Publishing Company, 1974), pp. 260–67. Reprinted with permission.

"The Postcard That Saved a Life," from *B'tzel Hashoah (In the Shadow of the Holocaust)* by Moshe Ishai (Israel: Ghetto Fighters House, 1973), pp. 161*ff.*

"A Mother and Her Daughters Are Reunited," from *Vehashemesh Zarchah (And the Sun Shone)* by Berta Federbar Saltz (New York: Holocaust Library, 1968). Reprinted by permission of the Holocaust Library.

"Stranger Than Fiction," from *Sridei Herev (Those Spared from the Sword)* by Ephraim Dekel (Israel: Israel Government Security Office, 1963), vol. I, pp. 107–8.

17. Rehabilitation

"Modern-Day Elijah in the Red Army," from *Mitofet el Tofet (From Inferno to Inferno)* by Leah Tzari and Tziviah Wildstein (Israel: Tarbut V'Hinuch, 1971), pp. 166–80.

"Ditta Cohen: A Story with a Dramatic Happy Ending," from *Yaldei Hashoah (Children of the Holocaust),* op. cit., pp. 81–86.

"The Cross," from *Imma, Hamutar Kvov Livkot (Mama, May I Cry Now?)* by Messiah Orlowitz-Rexnick (Israel: Moreshet-Sifriat Hapoalim, n.d.), pp. 258–76.

"The Miracle: Jewish Education Amid the Ruins of Belsen," from *Belsen,* op. cit., pp. 156–61.

"The Two Schools in Post-war Lodz," from *Ashes and Fire* by Jacob Pat (New York: International University Services Press, 1947), pp. 57–60.

"Palestinian Jewish Brigade Rehabilitates Victimized Children," from *The Buried Are Screaming* by Helen Waren (Beechurst, 1948), pp. 31–35.

"Jewish Soldiers Set Up a Hebrew School in Rome," from *Sefer Hahitnadvut (The Record of Military Volunteer Efforts of the Jews of Eretz Yisrael During World War II),* collected by Ze'ev Shefer, edited by Yitzhak Lamdom (Israel: Mosad Bialik, 1949), pp. 716–19.

18. The Trauma Afterward

"Painful Inheritance: Traumas and Tormenting Memories," from the *Jerusalem Post Magazine,* 22 July 1977, by Helen Epstein. Reprinted by permission.

"Adoption or Foster Home Care? A Case Before an Israeli Court," from *Yaldei Emutzim (Adopted Children)* by Shneur Z. Hissin (Israel: Massada Press, 1955), pp. 131–33. Reported by R. Ruckenstein.

19. Epilogue

"Rewriting History: The Case of Anne Frank," extracted from *The Murderers Among Us* by Simon Wiesenthal, McGraw-Hill and Bantam, 1967, by permission.

Index